Business Leadership

Joan V. Gallos

Editor

Foreword by Ronald A. Heifetz

—‏ఐ‏— Business Leadership

A Jossey-Bass Reader
(Second Edition)

John Wiley & Sons, Inc.

Published by Jossey-Bass
A Wiley Imprint
989 Market Street, San Francisco, CA 94103-1741—www.josseybass.com

Jossey-Bass books and products are available through most bookstores. To contact Jossey-Bass directly call our Customer Care Department within the U.S. at 800-956-7739, outside the U.S. at 317-572-3986, or fax 317-572-4002.

Jossey-Bass also publishes its books in a variety of electronic formats. Some content that appears in print may not be available in electronic books.

Credits are on page 595

Library of Congress Cataloging-in-Publication Data

Business leadership: a Jossey-Bass reader / Joan V. Gallos, editor.—2nd ed.
  p.   cm.— (The Jossey-Bass business & management series)
Includes bibliographical references and index.
  ISBN 978-0-7879-8819-7 (pbk.)
    1. Leadership. 2. Management. I. Gallos, Joan V.
HD57.7.B875 2008
658.4'092—dc22

                                                          2007019066

Printed in the United States of America
SECOND EDITION
PB Printing   10 9 8 7 6 5 4 3 2 1

The Jossey-Bass

Business & Management Series

For Christopher John Gallos Bolman and Bradley Garrison Bolman—Reach high, my sons, for stars lie hidden in your souls

Contents

⟿ Foreword

The demands of change have always challenged collective enterprise. People have faced new pressures and opportunities from the beginning of time, and many of our current ways of doing business are practices that have evolved in response to the adaptive challenges of their day. With change a constant in today's global business environment, adaptability remains critical for sustained success.

For nearly four million years our early ancestors lived in small bands that foraged for food. They developed ever increasing sophistication in the design of tools and strategies for hunting and movement; and their physical capacities grew through evolutionary change. About twelve thousand years ago people learned to domesticate plants and animals, and new abilities to store food allowed and required sustained settlements. Large numbers of people living together brought new needs for governing organizations and communities. These in turn were met by drawing on the small-group authority relationships that had worked so well before, now amended for greater complexity to fit the differing contexts of military command, civil governance, and commercial organizations.[1] Drawing on what anthropologists have identified as a capacity to internalize *the wisdom of elders,* our ancestors went on to form cultures with self-sustaining norms that required minimal reinforcement by authorities.[2]

This process of adaptation to new possibilities and challenges has continued over the course of written history, with growth and variation in the scope, structure, governance, strategy, and coordination of political and commercial enterprises. So has the evolution of our understandings of leadership.

Leadership is the process of mobilizing progress—fostering people's adaptive capacities to tackle tough problems and thrive.[3] The concept of *thriving* is drawn from evolutionary biology, in which a successful adaptation accomplishes three tasks. It preserves the accumulated wisdom of essential DNA; discards DNA that no longer serves current needs; and innovates to develop the organism's capacities to flourish in new ways and in more challenging environments.[4] Successful adaptations enable a living system to take the best from its history into the future. They are both conservative *and* progressive.

When we anchor the concept of leadership in the work of progress—in resolving contradictions within our cultural DNA or between our cultural DNA and the demands of our environment—we come to view authority and power as tools, rather than as ends in themselves. Neither authority nor power defines leadership, although both are central to its practice—and can, if misused, become significant constraints. Too many individuals in positions of power today do not exercise much leadership, and we need to understand more deeply how acquiring authority limits, not just enables, good leadership.

This volume reflects decades of work by multiple individuals to identify common principles of success and the leadership that helps to generate it. Looking through various lenses we have come to understand the workings of organizational adaptation in different ways, yet all appreciate how businesses and communities can thrive in new and challenging contexts. In my work across sectors and around the world, for example, I find that the logic of biological adaptation drawn from Darwin's theory of evolution provides insights into organizational and cultural adaptation. And I want to use six ideas as a suggestive set of properties to frame this wonderful collection of chapters. Let me begin with the links between leadership and change.

Leadership is about change, but not just any change. Many regressive and destructive actions generate change, but we would not consider them acts of leadership. Take, for example, the assassinations of Lincoln, Kennedy, King, Sadat, and Rabin. Or look at the daily murders and muggings that profoundly change lives in communities around the world. These are society's miscarriages. The change that we intuitively associate with leadership is enabling. Changing environments and new dreams demand new strategies and capacities and the leadership to mobilize them. As in evolution these new combinations and variations allow organizations to thrive under challenging circumstances rather than perish, regress, or contract. Our concepts of leadership, then, must wrestle with normative questions of value, purpose, and process. What does *thriving* mean for businesses operating in any particular context?

In biology, thriving means propagating. But in business, mission, objectives, and method are more complex. Thriving thus becomes a mix that includes short- and long-term shareholder value, quality of service, employee morale, and social and environmental impact. Adaptive success in a cultural rather than a Darwinian biological sense therefore requires business leadership that can orchestrate conflicting priorities among legitimate stakeholders in order to clarify the stakes. Moreover, priorities do not remain stable: they change as circumstances and contexts do. From this perspective, leadership operates within a dynamic tension where essential priorities and bottom lines are less clear than many initially imagine them to be.

Second, leadership is only partly about change. Most successful changes build on the past. They are rarely the result of a zero-based, ahistorical, start-over stance, except perhaps as a deliberate exercise in strategic rethinking. Most radical revolutions fail, and those that do succeed have more rather than less in common with the heritage that preceded them. The American Revolution, for example, created a political system and culture with deep roots in British and European cultures, systems, and thinking. In biological evolution most core processes are conserved, and although the DNA that changes may radically expand capacity, the actual amount of DNA that changes is very small. More than 98 percent of our current DNA, for example, is the same as that of a chimpanzee: it took less than a 2 percent DNA change to give humans dramatically greater capacity. The challenge for leadership, then, is to mobilize people to distinguish that which is essential from that which is expendable in their heritage and to innovate in ways that make efficient use of previous wisdom and know-how. Successful adaptations are always more conservative than progressive. Leadership consists of anchoring change in values, competencies, and strategic orientations that will endure.[5]

Third, innovation is an experimental activity, with more failure than success along the way. Evolutionary adaptation and "learning" accumulate and consolidate these successes over time. Sexual reproduction rapidly produces diversity, along with higher failure rates. As many as one-third of all pregnancies spontaneously abort, usually within the first weeks of conception, because the embryo's genetic variation is too radical to support life—too much critical DNA is missing. Similarly in business, Pfizer, for example, knows it must be willing to lose one billion dollars to find the next blockbuster cardiovascular drug. In such an environment, leadership needs an experimental mind-set to meet the adaptive pressures and opportunities of the marketplace. It must learn quickly from its actions and respond accordingly, rather than rely heavily on traditional planning and top-down decision making. In nature the tension between efficiency and creativity balances itself out. In the world of business those who lead may never find a perfect balance. They must learn to operate comfortably within the dynamic tension between efficiency and creativity and improvise as they go, buying time and resources along the way for the next sets of experiments and lessons to be generated.

Fourth, evolution is about diversity. It operates like a fund manager, diversifying nature's risk. Each example of conception is a variant—an experiment—with capacities somewhat different from the norm. By diversifying the gene pool, nature markedly increases the odds that some member of the population will have the capacity to survive in a changing ecosystem. In contrast, cloning, the original mode of reproduction, is extraordinarily efficient in generating high rates of propagation. It has, however, limited degrees of variation and is therefore far less likely to generate innovations for thriving in new environments.

As we can see, evolution does not operate by central planning. Its secret is variation, which in organizational terms could be called distributed intelligence.[6] No one could have predicted, for example, who would invent Post-it notes, but someone did. A key to effective leadership, then, is the know-how to shape a culture that values diverse views and rewards the practice of leadership with and without authority. If organizations rely on the genius of the few at the top, the odds of adaptive success go down. This is especially true for global businesses operating in many local microenvironments. All organizations need distributed leadership: people willing to initiate reflection and action, often against the grain and beyond their job description and formal authority, in order to develop the next relevant experiment and opportunity for growth.

Fifth, evolutionary adaptation significantly displaces and rearranges DNA. Similarly, cultural adaptation generates loss. Learning is often painful. One person's innovation can cause another person to feel incompetent, betrayed, or irrelevant. Not many people like to be displaced or rearranged. As students of leadership and change have long explored, adaptive pressures often generate a defensive reaction among people as they try to ameliorate the disruptions associated with their losses.[7] Leadership requires the diagnostic abilities to recognize those losses and the predictable defensive patterns of response that operate at the individual and systemic level. It also requires knowing how to counteract them.

Sixth, adaptive processes take time. Sometimes biological adaptations are quick, like bacterial resistance to penicillin. But generally, adaptations that generate significantly expanded capacities take thousands, or millions, of years. Intuitively, we know that experiments take time to show results. Although organizational and cultural adaptations seem lightning fast compared to most biological adaptive processes, they also need time in which people can consolidate new sets of norms and operations. Leadership requires persistence—and those who lead need to stay in the game, even while taking the heat along the way. Consider, for example, the story of Moses.

At the outset Moses thought that the two hardest parts of his job were persuading the Israelites to trust him and persuading Pharaoh to let his people go. After completing those jobs, getting to the Promised Land seemed pretty straightforward. After all, trade routes across the Sinai were well known and had been used for more than thirty thousand years. Moses did indeed accomplish his two initial goals, and within about eighteen months. But when he sent scouts to investigate the way ahead, they returned with reports not only of a fruitful land but also of cities with soldiers that looked like "giants." Hearing these reports the Israelites demanded that they return to Egypt, where they would be secure, even if that meant returning to slavery. Moses responded by falling on his face in despair. Getting to the Promised Land, he discovered, was an adaptive challenge beyond any expert solution he or a divine power could provide. The problem lay in the hearts, minds, and spirits of the people, as did the solution. Their cultural DNA had to change: they had to develop from a people enculturated to slavery into a self-governing society. Without that change, no solution could be found. When the people are the problem, the solution lies in them; and the reality is that people take time to learn new ways. Moses spent another thirty-eight years on the job—and even then, as we know, the job was not fully finished.[8]

My colleagues in this volume would all agree that leadership is essential for businesses of all kinds to tackle their tough challenges, innovate in order to thrive, and replace current structures and processes that no longer suffice. Mobilizing people to meet these tasks is at the heart of leadership. These efforts, over time, build an organization's adaptive capacity, enabling it to meet the ongoing stream of adaptive challenges posed by a world ever ready to offer new realities, opportunities, and pressures.

The authors in this volume draw on their study, teaching, and practice of leadership to identify common principles and contingencies that can guide practitioners toward leadership success. Our efforts here join a discussion on organizing and leading that goes back to the beginnings of written history—and oral traditions long before that. We stand on countless shoulders in undertaking this work to better understand adaptability and the leadership that generates it, and there is yet more work to be done in pushing the boundaries of our knowledge. I hope you enjoy this excellent volume and see it as an invitation to join us in exploring the frontiers of the leadership terrain.

November 2007

Ronald A. Heifetz
Cambridge, Massachusetts

⌐ᴠᴠᴠ⌐ Introduction and Acknowledgments

The call for leadership is strong: everyone seems to want more. A quick look at the front page of the daily newspaper confirms our collective yearning for leadership across sectors, institutions, and borders—more leaders, better leaders—to resolve the dilemmas and complexities of modern life. The assumption is that good leaders make a difference and that we are better off because of them. Test that yourself. Ask those around you: do we need more leadership around here? *Absolutely* is the likely reply.

Ask the same people *What is leadership?* and listen to their halting responses. I have asked this question of many would-be leaders. They are often surprised by their own inability to answer easily or confidently—and neither age, experience, nor career stage makes answering easier. Some are amused by the irony that they are investing their time, energy, and resources to learn how to do something that they cannot even define.

For some, leadership is synonymous with very good management. For others, it centers on persuasive abilities. Some see leadership as fostering a world of future possibilities, others as generating current business processes and decisions. Some understand leadership as a social phenomenon, whereas others are quick to equate it with a single heroic figure. Leadership is complex. All that we know confirms that. But if we do not understand at a basic level what leadership is (and is not), how can we prepare ourselves to lead well? And equally important, how will we know if we are leading effectively?

This volume explores the fundamentals of business leadership: what it is, how to do it, and what maximizes its success. Leadership is a social process, rooted in the values, behaviors, skills, knowledge, and ways of thinking of both leaders and followers. It is multidimensional in skill and orientation, and successful leaders need to understand people and organizations, tasks and processes, current context and past history, self and others. They need to attend to current realities while envisioning future possibilities. To do all this well, leaders need confidence and strategies for working competently across a wide range of diverse issues—from fostering the organizational clarity that comes from sound structures and policies to unleashing energy and creativity through bold visions, from creating learning organizations where workers mature and develop as everyday leaders to managing the conflict inevitable in a world of enduring differences. Leaders use mind, heart, and spirit in their work and require a helpful map to guide and direct their shuttling among multiple levels, processes, issues, and domains.

This volume was designed to help leaders develop and deepen their own map. It is intended to be a resource for both experienced business leaders and those aspiring to the role. Newcomers can read cover to cover and explore leadership's scope, purpose, methods, and possibilities. They will find everything they need to get started and grow in their leadership. Organizations need leadership at every level, and these chapters offer support for those with or without formal leadership positions at work. Experienced leaders will appreciate chapters that capture the best thinking on a range of topics—the complex nature of the work, essential skills and ways to enhance them, models for understanding the organizational terrain, ways to anticipate challenges and avoid pitfalls, and strategies to sustain oneself as a leader.

This book is intentionally inclusive in content—exploring the linkages among individual, organizational, and situational factors that contribute to leadership success. It celebrates the expanded understanding of leadership and leadership development that has evolved in response to the changing nature of organizations today, the global business environment, and advances in management theory. Leadership is a central force in the creation of healthy and effective organizations in an increasingly competitive and complex world. Taken together the chapters in this volume remind readers that leadership is more than tools and techniques. It is a values-based process that engages people in useful and significant ways to search for lasting solutions to today's—and tomorrow's—challenges.

ORGANIZATION OF THIS BOOK

In deciding what to include in this volume, I have kept one question in mind: what are the tools and insights that will help business leaders succeed as they set out to improve their organization's health and effectiveness? In everyday language, how can they make a real difference through their daily work? All the classic leadership ideas and strategies that help us answer that question are represented and updated in this volume. But readers will also find new contributions, created explicitly for this book, that expand our understandings in key areas and that stretch the ways we think about leadership and ourselves as leaders. There is little sense in producing a new book that tells the same old story.

This volume is divided into five parts. Each part is introduced by an *Editor's Interlude* that frames the issues to be examined, describes the rationale for the material included, and introduces each of the chapters in the section. As a whole this book flows from theory to practice: it begins with a set of ideas on how to understand the leadership process and moves to practical suggestions for ways to lead effectively and to sustain the efforts.

More specifically, Part One, "Framing the Issues: What Is Leadership?" explores the fundamental nature and elements of leadership. The chapters in this section offer opportunities to think systematically about leadership basics, applications, and competencies for success. The chapter authors distinguish leadership from other forms of influence, like authority, power, and dominance; identify necessary skills; and correct common myths about leading. The ability to lead well is clearly linked to one's capacity to decompose and demystify the process.

Part Two, "Becoming a Leader, Preparing for the Opportunities," examines the ongoing nature of leadership development and provides strategies and insights to prepare leaders for the opportunities ahead. Learning to lead well involves persistence, humility, and personal clarity. The authors in this section offer fundamental ways to accelerate the learning process.

The chapters in Part Three, "Understanding the Territory, Anticipating the Challenges," address essential ways to understand organizations and the larger context for leadership. Leadership is always contextual, and organizations in today's fast-paced, global world require leaders at all levels who understand the organizational lay of the land and how best to match their efforts and talents to the unique demands of each situation.

Part Four, "Making It Happen," contains the largest set of chapters in this volume. It begins with the basics of establishing credible footing as a leader and tackling the fundamentals of mission, vision, and strategy. It then provides sound advice for staying on track and identifying predictable forces that can derail leaders and their initiatives. Effective leadership can never be reduced to a simple checklist, but we can identify the basic tasks and issues that all leaders need to address and resolve.

Part Five, "Sustaining the Leader," explores ways for leaders to support themselves in order to sustain their leadership efforts. Strength of character and resolve matter. But so do strategies for surviving the inevitable attacks of angry opponents; for nourishing the soul; for building personal resilience; and for staying healthy, grounded, and hopeful.

ACKNOWLEDGMENTS

There are multiple people to thank, and it is hard to know where to begin. Many have contributed in different ways to this project. Let me start by thanking all the authors whose work is represented in this volume. They are the best thinkers on leadership today, and we all benefit from their wisdom and contributions. I trace the beginnings of my own interests in leadership to the seminal ideas of Warren Bennis, James MacGregor Burns, Edgar Schein, Lee Bolman, and Terrence Deal, and I feel honored to share their work with the readers of this volume.

Strong thanks goes next to Ronald Heifetz. His Foreword to this volume is a rich and provocative perspective on leadership and its role in facilitating adaptive change: a special gift from someone whose work reminds us that there are no easy answers to the question of how to lead well. Ron and I go back to my graduate school days, and I am pleased by this opportunity for us to work together again.

Special appreciation to Karen Ayas, Andre Delbecq, Loizos Heracleous, Claus Jacobs, Phil Mirvis, and Michael Sales who found time in their busy lives to write original chapters for this volume—some with short turnaround times—when I realized that their particular perspectives needed to be represented here.

The size of this volume should be some indication of all that it took to get this work to press. Kathe Sweeney, senior editor in the Business & Management and Public Administration Divisions at

Jossey-Bass, launched this project with her vision—the same creative sense of contribution that she brought to establishing the Jossey-Bass Reader series five years ago. She sustained it with her usual support, trust, and good cheer. Kathe is my writing muse and best supporter—and I appreciate that more than she knows. Jessie Mandle, my Jossey-Bass touchpoint, managed preproduction details with professionalism and warmth. And the Jossey-Bass production team was great. I particularly thank production editor Susan Geraghty who handled details with professionalism and class. And I again enjoyed working with Sheri Gilbert, who secured permissions and worked with impressive speed, accuracy, and grace.

Leadership is a lot easier to study than to provide, and I have special people to thank for that important lesson. University of Missouri-Kansas City (UMKC) chancellor emerita Eleanor Brantley Schwartz and former vice chancellor for academic affairs Marvin Querry enabled my return to university administration after a long hiatus; and former interim chancellor and president of the University of Missouri system Gordon Lamb and former provost Marjorie Smelstor provided other opportunities to serve, including appointments as special assistant to Gordon at UMKC and then as dean of the School of Education. Although filling many of these positions seemed akin to drinking water from a fire hose, the learning was invaluable—and I am a better person and professional because of it. I also appreciated the trust, support, and leadership lessons from these consummate professionals, whom I am honored today to call good friends.

On the local front I also have many people to thank. UMKC chancellor Guy Bailey does a strong job, keeping the ship afloat and sailing toward safe harbors. His ready support and encouragement of faculty are appreciated—and he even reads our books! Homer Erekson, dean of the Henry W. Bloch School of Business and Public Administration at UMKC, is a good colleague and a supportive dean; and I am pleased to include associate deans Lanny Solomon and Karyl Leggio on my list of valued colleagues and friends. Faculty members in the Bloch School's Department of Public Affairs—Robyne Turner, David Renz, Bob Herman, Arif Ahmed, and Nick Peroff—are impressive in their leadership to promote public service leadership and community development. I am in awe of their contributions and proud to be their colleague. They also graciously tolerated the ways in which this project consumed my time and focus. Special thanks to Samantha Silveira, administrative assistant in the Department of Public Affairs, for accepting the endless task of keeping me organized, informed, and almost on time.

Faculty members in the old Bloch Women Who Lunch Club add fun to a busy life. A tip of the hat to Doranne Hudson, Karyl Leggio, Marilyn Taylor, Nancy Day, Sidne Ward, Nancy Weatherholt, Robyne Turner, and Rita Cain for their collegiality. No one likes meetings, but I actually look forward to the Bloch School Marketing Steering Committee. I have learned about commitment and contribution from great professionals like Danny Baker, Christina Cutcliffe, Doranne Hudson, Maria Meyers, Victoria Prater, and Beverly Stewart. Every day leadership abounds at the Bloch School.

A bevy of talented Bloch School graduate students assisted me over the course of this project, and each deserves thanks. Erin Nelson, Ben Nemenoff, Jennifer Storz, and Abby Symonds got their share of opportunities to research databases and authors, carry library books, reformat files, and log time in front of the copying machine. Rebecca Williams tackled the complex task of tracking down authors, checking biographical facts, and confirming current addresses. We are in good hands if these students are examples of the public sector leaders of tomorrow.

Friends and close colleagues are wonderful, and I am blessed to have some of the greatest. Bob Marx and Joan Weiner were wonderful supports during this project, and our conversations always enrich me personally and professionally. Terry Deal deserves special mention for his inimitable magic and charm. TD is a character and a joy to talk with, whether we are bemoaning some ache or pain or chatting about a great new book. Three girl pals deserve special note. Sandy Renz, Beth Smith, and Amy Sales are there at a moment's notice for support and good cheer. Sandy's early morning delivery of fresh muffins and good humor as this project was winding to a close under trying circumstances was a real treat—and another example of her ongoing thoughtfulness. Beth is a model of activism, learning, love, and commitment. How I wish I could get her to write a book on her amazing life of contribution so as to glean her formula for leadership success! Amy welcomes me with open arms whenever I land on her doorstep, and our annual foray to the Berkshires each summer heals body and soul. And special thanks to Alan K. Duncan of the Mayo Clinic College of Medicine who reminded me of the power in compassionate leadership and who contributed in special ways to the spirit of this volume.

My family is the greatest, and the three boys on the home front deserve thanks beyond what can be written here. My sons, Brad and Chris Bolman, are talented young men who enrich my life. In addition, Brad lent his technology and file-organizing skills to the project, and his music, juggling stand-up comedy routines, and all around cheerfulness sustained the editor. Chris Bolman, hard-working young leader in the New York investment banking world and all-around chilled-out entertainer, contributed with comments on potential chapters as well as with his perspectives on what today's young business leaders need and use in their work. And Lee Bolman, my husband and closest colleague, has earned all the credit and appreciation offered here. He is cheerfully available 24/7 to his high-maintenance spouse. During this project he read drafts; repaired and replaced computers (again); cooked fabulous meals; and house-trained our new gorgeous yet impish young cockapoo, Douglas McGregor. Thank you, dear. As the years go by, I appreciate and love you more.

November 2007

Joan V. Gallos
Kansas City, Missouri

Teaching resources and curriculum materials to support the use of this volume in university classrooms and in executive education are available online from the publisher at the Wiley Higher Education site. They can be accessed directly via the following link:

http://he-cda.wiley.com/WileyCDA/HigherEdTitle/productCd-0787988197.html

Additional teaching supports are available at the editor's Web site: www.joangallos.com.

――ⵯⵯ― About the Editor

Joan V. Gallos is professor of leadership at the Henry W. Bloch School of Business and Public Administration at the University of Missouri-Kansas City, where she has also served as professor and dean of education, coordinator of university accreditation, special assistant to the chancellor for strategic planning, and director of the higher education graduate programs. Gallos holds a bachelor's degree cum laude in English from Princeton University, and master's and doctoral degrees from the Harvard Graduate School of Education. She has served as a Salzburg Seminar Fellow; as president of the Organizational Behavior Teaching Society; as editor of the *Journal of Management Education;* as a member of numerous editorial boards, including as a founding member of the *Academy of Management Learning and Education* journal; and as a member of regional and national advisory boards for such groups as the Organizational Behavior Teaching Society, the Forum for Early Childhood Organization and Leadership Development, the Kauffman and Danforth Foundations' Missouri Superintendents Leadership Forum, and the Mayor's Kansas City Collaborative for Academic Excellence. She has also served on the national steering committee for the New Models of Management Education project (a joint effort of the Graduate Management Admissions Council and the Association to Advance Collegiate Schools of Business); on the W. K. Kellogg Foundation College Age Youth Leadership Review Team; on the University of Missouri President's Advisory Council on Academic Leadership; and on civic, foundation, and nonprofit boards in greater Kansas City. Gallos has taught at the Radcliffe Seminars, the Harvard Graduate School of Education, the University of Massachusetts-Boston, and Babson College, as well as in executive programs at Harvard's Kennedy School of Government, the Harvard Graduate School of Education, the University of Missouri, Babson College, and the University of British Columbia. She has published on professional effectiveness, gender, and leadership education and is editor of *Organization Development: A Jossey-Bass Reader* (2006), coauthor of the books *Teaching Diversity: Listening to the Soul, Speaking from the Heart* (with V. Jean Ramsey and associates, Jossey-Bass, 1997) and *Reframing Academic Leadership* (with Lee G. Bolman, Jossey-Bass, forthcoming), and creator of a wide variety of published management education teaching materials. She received the Fritz Roethlisberger Memorial Award for the best article on management education in 1990 and was finalist for the same prize in 1994. In 1993, Gallos accepted the Radcliffe College Excellence in Teaching Award. In 2002 and 2003, she served as founding director of the Truman Center for the Healing Arts, based in Kansas City's public hospital, which received the 2004 Kansas City Business Committee for the Arts Partnership Award as the best partnership between a large organization and the arts.

PART ONE

Framing the Issues:
What Is Leadership?

The chapters in Part One offer answers to the basic question, *What is leadership?* They remind us that leadership is a complex social process, rooted in the values, skills, knowledge, and ways of thinking of both leaders and followers. Leadership always involves adaptive change, as Ronald Heifetz notes in the Foreword to this volume, and we think too simply when we equate leadership with the search for a simple answer to a current problem. Leaders help us understand our current reality and forge a brighter future from it. They see new opportunities, and manage a complex interactive process that supports individual and collective growth. In the process of this work, leaders face critical choices based on their reading of the circumstances, the individuals involved, and the possibilities that they see. And although there is widespread agreement that leadership is important and that effective leadership is vital, there is less clarity about what that really means or how that translates into effective action.

The word *leadership* has become an incantation, cautions John Gardner (1993), and its meaning has risen above common workplace usage. "There seems to be a feeling that if we invoke it often enough with sufficient ardor we can ease our sense of having lost our way, our sense of things unaccomplished, of duties unfulfilled" (p. 1). This kind of thinking clouds our perspectives toward everyday leaders and leadership—and makes it hard to understand how ordinary people can successfully wear the mantle. It also keeps us from looking below the surface—beyond leadership's aura—so that we fail to fully appreciate what leadership is and how it works.

The chapters in this section decompose leadership. They distinguish leadership from other forms of influence, like power, authority, and dominance; identify essential elements and skills; and correct common myths about leading. Together they offer the basis for a grounded framework and help us see that success requires

- A simple, not simplistic, definition of the leadership process
- Insight into one's purpose for leading
- Understanding of the organizational context in which one leads
- Appreciation for the unique challenges and opportunities inherent in each situation
- Clarity about what one brings to the leadership table

Savvy leaders develop their own conceptual framework about all this, a repertoire of skills to call upon, capacities for self-reflection and learning from experience, and a healthy respect for the difficulties and risks. The authors in this section provide rich opportunities to think more systematically about leadership basics, applications, and competencies for success.

Part One begins with a classic article from the *Harvard Business Review* by John P. Kotter, "What Leaders Really Do." This chapter explores the seminal distinction between leadership and management, identifying the two as complementary functions that contribute significantly and in their own ways to organizational effectiveness. Managers, says Kotter, bring order from chaos through planning, organizing, and controlling. Leaders, in contrast, help organizations cope with change and opportunity by focusing on vision, network building, and the relationships needed for a strong organizational future.

Good leadership is emotionally compelling. Effective leaders inspire and motivate, and those who know how to bring out the best in themselves and others help their organizations to thrive and grow. In fact, say Daniel Goleman, Richard Boyatzis, and Annie

McKee, the core of leadership lies in leaders' abilities to manage their own and others' emotional responses to each situation. The three authors explore the foundational role of emotional intelligence in leadership in Chapter Two, "Primal Leadership: The Hidden Power of Emotional Intelligence."

Leadership is about the ongoing process of building and sustaining a relationship between those who aspire to lead and those willing to follow. In Chapter Three, "The Five Practices of Exemplary Leadership," an excerpt from their best-selling book *The Leadership Challenge: How to Keep Getting Extraordinary Things Done in Organizations*, James M. Kouzes and Barry Z. Posner explore common patterns of action at the core of effective leadership. Authenticity, initiative, courage, and inspiration, as well as the abilities to frame engaging opportunities, foster collaboration, and empower others—qualities available to all no matter where they sit in the hierarchy—can enable groups of ordinary individuals to accomplish extraordinary things.

Leadership is multidimensional in skill and orientation. Successful leaders need to understand people and organizations, tasks and processes, self and others. They must attend to current realities while envisioning future possibilities, and need confidence and strategies for working competently across a wide range of diverse issues—from fostering the organizational clarity that comes from sound structures and policies to unleashing energy and creativity through bold visions, from creating learning organizations where workers mature and develop as everyday leaders to managing the conflict inevitable in a world of enduring differences. Leaders use mind, heart, and spirit in their work and require a map to guide and direct their shuttling among multiple organizational levels, processes, issues, and domains.

In Chapter Four, "Reframing Leadership," Lee G. Bolman and Terrence E. Deal propose four sets of common organizational issues or *frames*—structure, people, politics, and symbols—as a way to sort the myriad activities and concerns that compete for a leader's attention. Organizations are simultaneously sets of structural arrangements and practices, opportunities for human contribution, political arenas for negotiating differences, and creative outlets for individual passion and collective purpose. Successful leaders realize this, consciously balance their attention across all four sets of issues, and *reframe*—discipline themselves to deliberately view a situation or challenge from multiple perspectives.

Leadership is a human invention and process, and it is tempting to equate successful business leadership with a powerful CEO or charismatic senior executive. Although these individuals may indeed bring leadership to their organizations, James O'Toole reminds us in Chapter Five, "When Leadership Is an Organizational Trait," that overreliance on a single heroic figure distorts appreciation of leadership as an organizational function. High-performing companies, O'Toole has found, institutionalize the central tasks and responsibilities of leadership by incorporating them into their organizational cultures, systems, policies, and practices. In the process they avoid overreliance on one individual, compensate for weakness and leadership gaps at the top, and build organizational systems and structures of shared accountability that withstand the test of time, shifting markets, and succession plans.

CHAPTER ONE

What Leaders Really Do

John P. Kotter

eadership is different from management, but not for the reasons most people think. Leadership isn't mystical and mysterious. It has nothing to do with having "charisma" or other exotic personality traits. It is not the province of a chosen few. Nor is leadership necessarily better than management or a replacement for it. Rather, leadership and management are two distinctive and complementary systems of action. Each has its own function and characteristic activities. Both are necessary for success in an increasingly complex and volatile business environment.

Most U.S. corporations today are overmanaged and underled. They need to develop their capacity to exercise leadership. Successful corporations don't wait for leaders to come along. They actively seek out people with leadership potential and expose them to career experiences designed to develop that potential. Indeed, with careful selection, nurturing, and encouragement, dozens of people can play important leadership roles in a business organization.

But while improving their ability to lead, companies should remember that strong leadership with weak management is no better, and is sometimes actually worse, than the reverse. The real challenge is to combine strong leadership and strong management and use each to balance the other.

Of course, not everyone can be good at both leading and managing. Some people have the capacity to become excellent managers but not strong leaders. Others have great leadership potential but, for a variety of reasons, have great difficulty becoming strong managers. Smart companies value both kinds of people and work hard to make them a part of the team.

But when it comes to preparing people for executive jobs, such companies rightly ignore the recent literature that says people cannot manage *and* lead. They try to develop leader-managers. Once companies understand the fundamental difference between leadership and management, they can begin to groom their top people to provide both.

THE DIFFERENCE BETWEEN MANAGEMENT AND LEADERSHIP

Management is about coping with complexity. Its practices and procedures are largely a response to one of the most significant developments of the twentieth century: the emergence of large organizations. Without good management, complex enterprises tend to become chaotic in ways that threaten their very existence. Good management brings a degree of order and consistency to key dimensions like the quality and profitability of products.

Leadership, by contrast, is about coping with change. Part of the reason it has become so important in recent years is that the business world has become more competitive and more volatile. Faster technological change, greater international competition, the deregulation of markets, overcapacity in capital-intensive industries, an unstable oil cartel, raiders with junk bonds, and the changing demographics of the work force are among the many factors that have contributed to this shift. The net result is that doing what was done yesterday, or doing it 5% better, is no longer a formula for success. Major changes are more and more necessary to survive and compete effectively in this new environment. More change always demands more leadership.

Consider a simple military analogy: a peacetime army can usually survive with good administration and management up and down the hierarchy, coupled with good leadership concentrated at the very top. A wartime army, however, needs competent leadership at all levels. No one yet has figured out how to manage people effectively into battle; they must be led.

These different functions—coping with complexity and coping with change—shape the characteristic activities of management and leadership. Each system of action involves deciding what needs to be done, creating networks of people and relationships that can accomplish an agenda, and then trying to ensure that those people actually do the job. But each accomplishes these three tasks in different ways.

Companies manage complexity first by *planning and budgeting*—setting targets or goals for the future (typically for the next month or year), establishing detailed steps for achieving those targets, and then allocating resources to accomplish those plans. By contrast, leading an organization to constructive change begins by *setting a direction*—developing a vision of the future (often the distant future) along with strategies for producing the changes needed to achieve that vision.

Management develops the capacity to achieve its plan by *organizing and staffing*—creating an organizational structure and set of jobs for accomplishing plan requirements, staffing the jobs with qualified individuals, communicating the plan to those people, delegating responsibility for carrying out the plan, and devising systems to monitor implementation. The equivalent leadership activity, however, is *aligning people*. This means communicating the new direction to those who can create coalitions that understand the vision and are committed to its achievement.

Finally, management ensures plan accomplishment by *controlling and problem solving*—monitoring results versus the plan in some detail, both formally and informally, by means of reports, meetings, and other tools; identifying deviations; and then planning and organizing to solve the problems. But for leadership, achieving a vision requires *motivating and inspiring*—keeping people moving in the right direction, despite major obstacles to change, by appealing to basic but often untapped human needs, values, and emotions.

A closer examination of each of these activities will help clarify the skills leaders need.

Setting a Direction vs. Planning and Budgeting

Since the function of leadership is to produce change, setting the direction of that change is fundamental to leadership.

Setting direction is never the same as planning or even long-term planning, although people often confuse the two. Planning is a management process, deductive in nature and designed to produce orderly results, not change. Setting a direction is more inductive. Leaders gather a broad range of data and look for patterns, relationships, and linkages that help explain things. What's more, the direction-setting aspect of leadership does not produce plans; it creates vision and strategies. These describe a business, technology, or corporate culture in terms of what it should become over the long term and articulate a feasible way of achieving this goal.

Most discussions of vision have a tendency to degenerate into the mystical. The implication is that a vision is something mysterious that mere mortals, even talented ones, could never hope to have. But developing good business direction isn't magic. It is a tough, sometimes exhausting process of gathering and analyzing information. People who articulate such visions aren't magicians but broad-based strategic thinkers who are willing to take risks.

Nor do visions and strategies have to be brilliantly innovative; in fact, some of the best are not. Effective business visions regularly have an almost mundane quality, usually consisting of ideas that are already well known. The particular combination or patterning of the ideas may be new, but sometimes even that is not the case.

For example, when CEO Jan Carlzon articulated his vision to make Scandinavian Airlines System (SAS) the best airline in the world for the frequent business traveler, he was not saying anything that everyone in the airline industry didn't already know. Business travelers fly more consistently than other market segments and are generally willing to pay higher fares. Thus focusing on business customers offers an airline the possibility of high margins, steady business, and considerable growth. But in an industry known more for bureaucracy than vision, no company had ever put these simple ideas together and dedicated itself to implementing them. SAS did, and it worked.

What's crucial about a vision is not its originality but how well it serves the interests of important constituencies—customers, stockholders, employees—and how easily it can be translated into a realistic competitive strategy. Bad visions tend to ignore the legitimate needs and rights of important constituencies—favoring, say, employees over customers or stockholders. Or they are strategically unsound. When a company that has never been better than a weak competitor in an industry suddenly starts talking about becoming number one, that is a pipe dream, not a vision.

One of the most frequent mistakes that overmanaged and underled corporations make is to embrace "long-term planning" as a panacea for their lack of direction and inability to adapt to an increasingly competitive and dynamic business environment. But such an approach misinterprets the nature of direction setting and can never work.

Long-term planning is always time consuming. Whenever something unexpected happens, plans have to be redone. In a dynamic business environment, the unexpected often becomes the norm, and long-term planning can become an extraordinarily burdensome activity. This is why most successful corporations limit the time frame of their planning activities. Indeed, some even consider "long-term planning" a contradiction in terms.

In a company without direction, even short-term planning can become a black hole capable of absorbing an infinite amount of time and energy. With no vision and strategy to provide constraints around the planning process or to guide it, every eventuality deserves a plan. Under these circumstances, contingency planning can go on forever, draining time and attention from far more essential activities, yet without ever providing the clear sense of direction that a company desperately needs. After awhile, managers inevitably become cynical about all this, and the planning process can degenerate into a highly politicized game.

Planning works best not as a substitute for direction setting but as a complement to it. A competent planning process serves as a useful reality check on direction-setting activities. Likewise, a competent direction-setting process provides a focus in which planning can then be realistically carried out. It helps clarify what kind of planning is essential and what kind is irrelevant.

Aligning People vs. Organizing and Staffing

A central feature of modern organizations is interdependence, where no one has complete autonomy, where most employees are tied to many others by their work, technology, management systems, and hierarchy. These linkages present a special challenge when organizations attempt to change. Unless many individuals line up and move together in the same direction, people will tend to fall all over one another. To executives who are overeducated in management and undereducated in leadership, the idea of getting people moving in the same direction appears to be an organizational problem. What executives need to do, however, is not organize people but align them.

Managers "organize" to create human systems that can implement plans as precisely and efficiently as possible. Typically, this requires a number of potentially complex decisions. A company must choose a structure of jobs and reporting relationships, staff it with individuals suited to the jobs, provide training for those who need it, communicate plans to the work force, and decide how much authority to delegate and to whom. Economic incentives also need to be constructed to accomplish the plan, as well as systems to monitor its implementation. These organizational judgments are much like architectural decisions. It's a question of fit within a particular context.

Aligning is different. It is more of a communications challenge than a design problem. First, aligning invariably involves talking to many more individuals than organizing does. The target population can involve not only a manager's subordinates but also bosses, peers, staff in other parts of the organization, as well as suppliers, governmental officials, or even customers. Anyone who can help implement the vision and strategies or who can block implementation is relevant.

Trying to get people to comprehend a vision of an alternative future is also a communications challenge of a completely different magnitude from organizing them to fulfill a short-term plan. It's much like the difference between a football quarterback attempting to describe to his team the next two or three plays versus his trying to explain to them a totally new approach to the game to be used in the second half of the season.

Whether delivered with many words or a few carefully chosen symbols, such messages are not necessarily accepted just because they are understood. Another big challenge in leadership efforts is credibility—getting people to believe the message. Many things contribute to credibility: the track record of the person delivering the message, the content of the message itself, the communicator's reputation for integrity and trustworthiness, and the consistency between words and deeds.

Finally, aligning leads to empowerment in a way that organizing rarely does. One of the reasons some organizations have difficulty adjusting to rapid changes in markets or technology is that so many people in those companies feel relatively powerless. They have learned from experience that even if they correctly perceive important external changes and then initiate appropriate actions, they are vulnerable to someone higher up who does not like what they have done. Reprimands can take many different forms: "That's against policy" or "We can't afford it" or "Shut up and do as you're told."

Alignment helps overcome this problem by empowering people in at least two ways. First, when a clear sense of direction has been communicated throughout an organization, lower level employees can initiate actions without the same degree of vulnerability. As long as their behavior is consistent with the vision, superiors will have more difficulty reprimanding them. Second, because everyone is aiming at the same target, the probability is less that one person's initiative will be stalled when it comes into conflict with someone else's.

Motivating People vs. Controlling and Problem Solving

Since change is the function of leadership, being able to generate highly energized behavior is important for coping with the inevitable barriers to change. Just as direction setting identifies an appropriate path for movement and just as effective alignment gets people moving down that path, successful motivation ensures that they will have the energy to overcome obstacles.

According to the logic of management, control mechanisms compare system behavior with the plan and take action when a deviation is detected. In a well-managed factory, for example, this means the planning process establishes sensible quality targets, the organizing process builds an organization that can achieve those targets, and a control process makes sure that quality lapses are spotted immediately, not in 30 or 60 days, and corrected.

For some of the same reasons that control is so central to management, highly motivated or inspired behavior is almost irrelevant. Managerial processes must be as close as possible to fail-safe and risk-free. That means they cannot be dependent on the unusual or hard to obtain. The whole purpose of systems and structures is to help normal people who behave in normal ways to complete routine jobs successfully, day after day. It's not exciting or glamorous. But that's management.

Leadership is different. Achieving grand visions always requires an occasional burst of energy. Motivation and inspiration energize people, not by pushing them in the right direction as control mechanisms do but by satisfying basic human needs for achievement, a sense of belonging, recognition, self-esteem, a feeling of control over one's life, and the ability to live up to one's ideals. Such feelings touch us deeply and elicit a powerful response.

Good leaders motivate people in a variety of ways. First, they always articulate the organization's vision in a manner that stresses the values of the audience they are addressing. This makes the work important to those individuals. Leaders also regularly involve people in deciding how to achieve the organization's vision (or the part most relevant to a particular individual). This gives people a sense of control. Another important motivational technique is to support employee efforts to realize the vision by providing coaching, feedback, and role modeling, thereby helping people grow professionally and enhancing their self-esteem. Finally, good leaders recognize and reward success, which not only gives people a sense of accomplishment but also makes them feel like they belong to an organization that cares about them. When all this is done, the work itself becomes intrinsically motivating.

The more that change characterizes the business environment, the more leaders must motivate people to provide leadership as well. When this works, it tends to reproduce leadership across the entire organization, with people occupying multiple leadership roles throughout the hierarchy. This is highly valuable, because coping with change in any complex business demands initiatives from a multitude of people. Nothing less will work.

Of course, leadership from many sources does not necessarily converge. To the contrary, it can easily conflict. For multiple leadership roles to work together, people's actions must be carefully coordinated by mechanisms that differ from those coordinating traditional management roles.

Strong networks of informal relationships—the kind found in companies with healthy cultures—help coordinate leadership activities in much the same way that formal structure coordinates managerial activities. The key difference is that informal networks can deal with the greater demands for coordination associated with nonroutine activities and change. The multitude of communication channels and the trust among the individuals connected by those channels allow for an ongoing process of accommodation and adaptation. When conflicts rise among roles, those same relationships help resolve the conflicts. Perhaps most important, this process of dialogue and accommodation can produce visions that are linked and compatible instead of remote and competitive. All this requires a great deal more communication than is needed to coordinate managerial roles, but unlike formal structure, strong informal networks can handle it.

Of course, informal relations of some sort exist in all corporations. But too often these networks are either very weak—some people are well connected but most are not—or they are highly fragmented—a strong network exists inside the marketing group and inside R&D but not across the two departments. Such networks do not support multiple leadership initiatives well. In fact, extensive informal networks are so important that if they do not exist, creating them has to be the focus of activity early in a major leadership initiative.

CREATING A CULTURE OF LEADERSHIP

Despite the increasing importance of leadership to business success, the on-the-job experiences of most people actually seem to undermine the development of attributes needed for leadership. Nevertheless, some companies have consistently demonstrated an ability to develop people into outstanding leader-managers. Recruiting people with leadership potential is only the first step. Equally important is managing their career patterns. Individuals who are effective in large leadership roles often share a number of career experiences.

Perhaps the most typical and most important is significant challenge early in a career. Leaders almost always have had opportunities during their twenties and thirties to actually try to lead, to take a risk, and to learn from both triumphs and failures. Such learning seems essential in developing a wide range of leadership skills and perspectives. It also teaches people something about both the difficulty of leadership and its potential for producing change.

Later in their careers, something equally important happens that has to do with broadening. People who provide effective leadership in important jobs always have a chance, before they get into those jobs, to grow beyond the narrow base that characterizes most managerial careers. This is usually the result of lateral career moves or of early promotions to unusually broad job assignments. Sometimes other vehicles help, like special task-force assignments or a lengthy general management course. Whatever the path, the breadth of knowledge developed is helpful in all aspects of leadership. So is the network of relationships that is often acquired both inside and outside the company. When enough people get opportunities like this, the relationships that are built also create the strong informal networks needed to support multiple leadership initiatives.

Corporations that do a better-than-average job of developing leaders put an emphasis on creating challenging opportunities for relatively young employees. In many businesses, decentralization is the key. By definition, it pushes responsibility lower in an organization and in the process creates more challenging jobs at lower levels. Johnson & Johnson, 3M, Hewlett-Packard, General Electric, and many other well-known companies have used that approach quite successfully. Some of those same companies also create as many small units as possible so there are a lot of challenging lower level general management jobs available.

Sometimes these businesses develop additional challenging opportunities by stressing growth through new products or services. Over the years, 3M has had a policy that at least 25% of its revenue should come from products introduced within the last five years. That encourages small new ventures, which in turn offer hundreds of opportunities to test and stretch young people with leadership potential.

Such practices can, almost by themselves, prepare people for small- and medium-sized leadership jobs. But developing people for important leadership positions requires more work on the part of senior executives, often over a long period of time. That work begins with efforts to spot people with great leadership potential early in their careers and to identify what will be needed to stretch and develop them.

Again, there is nothing magic about this process. The methods successful companies use are surprisingly straightforward. They go out of their way to make young employees and people at lower levels in their organizations visible to senior management. Senior managers then judge for themselves who has potential and what the development needs of those people are. Executives also discuss their tentative conclusions among themselves to draw more accurate judgments.

Armed with a clear sense of who has considerable leadership potential and what skills they need to develop, executives in these companies then spend time planning for that development. Sometimes that is done as part of a formal succession planning or high-potential development process; often it is more informal. In either case, the key ingredient appears to be an intelligent assessment of what feasible development opportunities fit each candidate's needs.

To encourage managers to participate in these activities, well-led businesses tend to recognize and reward people who successfully develop leaders. This is rarely done as part of a formal compensation or bonus formula, simply because it is so difficult to measure such achievements with precision. But it does become a factor in decisions about promotion, especially at the most senior levels, and that seems to make a big difference. When told that future promotions will depend to some degree on their ability to nurture leaders, even people who say that leadership cannot be developed somehow find ways to do it.

Such strategies help create a corporate culture where people value strong leadership and strive to create it. Just as we need more people to provide leadership; in the complex organizations that dominate our world today, we also need more people to develop the cultures that will create that leadership. Institutionalizing a leadership-centered culture is the ultimate act of leadership.

John P. Kotter is the Konosuke Matsushita Professor of Leadership emeritus at Harvard Business School and the author of multiple, best-selling books on organizational leadership and change.

CHAPTER TWO

Primal Leadership
The Hidden Power of Emotional Intelligence

Daniel Goleman
Richard Boyatzis
Annie McKee

Great leaders move us. They ignite our passion and inspire the best in us. When we try to explain why they are so effective, we speak of strategy, vision, or powerful ideas. But the reality is much more primal: Great leadership works through the emotions.

No matter what leaders set out to do—whether it's creating strategy or mobilizing teams to action—their success depends on how they do it. Even if they get everything else just right, if leaders fail in this primal task of driving emotions in the right direction, nothing they do will work as well as it could or should.

Consider, for example, a pivotal moment in a news division at the BBC, the British media giant. The division had been set up as an experiment, and while its 200 or so journalists and editors felt they had given their best, management had decided the division would have to close.[1]

It didn't help that the executive sent to deliver the decision to the assembled staff started off with a glowing account of how well rival operations were doing, and that he had just returned from a wonderful trip to Cannes. The news itself was bad enough, but the brusque, even contentious manner of the executive incited something beyond the expected frustration. People became enraged—not just at the management decision, but also at the bearer of the news himself. The atmosphere became so threatening, in fact, that it looked as though the executive might have to call security to usher him safely from the room.

The next day, another executive visited the same staff. He took a very different approach. He spoke from his heart about the crucial importance of journalism to the vibrancy of a society, and of the calling that had drawn them all to the field in the first place. He reminded them that no one goes into journalism to get rich—as a profession its finances have always been marginal, with job security ebbing and flowing with larger economic tides. And he invoked the passion, even the dedication, the journalists had for the service they offered. Finally, he wished them all well in getting on with their careers. When this leader finished speaking, the staff cheered.

The difference between the leaders lay in the mood and tone with which they delivered their messages: One drove the group toward antagonism and hostility, the other toward optimism, even inspiration, in the face of difficulty. These two moments point to a hidden, but crucial, dimension in leadership—the emotional impact of what a leader says and does.

While most people recognize that a leader's mood—and how he or she impacts the mood of others—plays a significant role in any organization, emotions are often seen as too personal or unquantifiable to talk about in a meaningful way. But research in the field of emotion has yielded keen insights into not only how to measure the impact of a leader's emotions but also how the best leaders have found effective ways to understand and improve the way they handle their own and other people's emotions. Understanding the powerful role of emotions in the workplace sets the best leaders apart from the rest—not just in tangibles such as better business results and the retention of talent, but also in the all-important intangibles, such as higher morale, motivation, and commitment.

THE PRIMAL DIMENSION

This emotional task of the leader is *primal*—that is, first—in two senses: It is both the original and the most important act of leadership.

Leaders have always played a primordial emotional role. No doubt humankind's original leaders—whether tribal chieftains or shamanesses—earned their place in large part because their leader-ship was emotionally compelling. Throughout history and in cul-tures everywhere, the leader in any human group has been the one to whom others look for assurance and clarity when facing uncertainty or threat, or when there's a job to be done. The leader acts as the group's emotional guide.

In the modern organization, this primordial emotional task—though by now largely invisible—remains foremost among the many jobs of leadership: driving the collective emotions in a positive direc-tion and clearing the smog created by toxic emotions. This task applies to leadership everywhere, from the boardroom to the shop floor.

Quite simply, in any human group the leader has maximal power to sway everyone's emotions. If people's emotions are pushed toward the range of enthusiasm, performance can soar; if people are driven toward rancor and anxiety, they will be thrown off stride. This indicates another important aspect of primal leadership: Its effects extend beyond ensuring that a job is well done. Followers also look to a leader for supportive emotional connection—for empathy. All leadership includes this primal dimension, for better or for worse. When leaders drive emotions positively, as was the case with the sec-ond executive at the BBC, they bring out everyone's best. We call this effect *resonance.* When they drive emotions negatively, as with the first executive, leaders spawn *dissonance,* undermining the emotional foundations that let people shine. Whether an organization withers or flourishes depends to a remarkable extent on the leaders' effectiveness in this primal emotional dimension.

The key, of course, to making primal leadership work to everyone's advantage lies in the leadership competencies of *emotional intelli-gence:* how leaders handle themselves and their relationships. Leaders who maximize the benefits of primal leadership drive the emotions of those they lead in the right direction.

How does all of this work? Recent studies of the brain reveal the neurological mechanisms of primal leadership and make clear just why emotional intelligence abilities are so crucial.

THE OPEN LOOP

The reason a leader's manner—not just what he does, but how he does it—matters so much lies in the design of the human brain: what scientists have begun to call the *open-loop* nature of the limbic system, our emotional centers. A closed-loop system such as the circulatory system is self-regulating; what's happening in the circulatory system of others around us does not impact our own system. An open-loop system depends largely on external sources to manage itself.

In other words, we rely on connections with other people for our own emotional stability. The open-loop limbic system was a winning design in evolution, no doubt, because it allows people to come to one another's emotional rescue—enabling, for example, a mother to soothe her crying infant, or a lookout in a primate band to signal an instant alarm when he perceives a threat.

Scientists describe the open loop as "interpersonal limbic regulation," whereby one person transmits signals that can alter hormone levels, cardiovascular function, sleep rhythms, and even immune function inside the body of another.[2] That's how couples who are in love are able to trigger in one another's brains surges of oxytocin, which creates a pleasant, affectionate feeling. But in all aspects of social life, not just love relationships, our physiologies intermingle, our emotions automatically shifting into the register of the person we're with. The open-loop design of the limbic system means that other people can change our very physiology—and so our emotions.

Even though the open loop is so much a part of our lives, we usually don't notice the process itself. Scientists have captured this attunement of emotions in the laboratory by measuring the physiology—such as heart rate—of two people as they have a good conversation. As the conversation begins, their bodies each operate at different rhythms. But by the end of a simple fifteen-minute conversation, their physiological profiles look remarkably similar—a phenomenon called *mirroring*. This entrainment occurs strongly during the downward spiral of a conflict, when anger and hurt reverberate, but also goes on more subtly during pleasant interactions.[3]

In seventy work teams across diverse industries, for instance, members who sat in meetings together ended up sharing moods—either good or bad—within two hours.[4] Nurses, and even accountants, who monitored their moods over weeks or every few hours as they worked together showed emotions that tracked together—and the group's shared moods were largely independent of the hassles they shared.[5] Studies of professional sports teams reveal similar results: Quite apart from the ups and downs of a team's standing, its players tend to synchronize their moods over a period of days and weeks.[6]

CONTAGION AND LEADERSHIP

The continual interplay of limbic open loops among members of a group creates a kind of emotional soup, with everyone adding his or her own flavor to the mix. But it is the leader who adds the strongest seasoning. Why? Because of that enduring reality of business: Everyone watches the boss. People take their emotional cues from the top. Even when the boss isn't highly visible—for example, the CEO who works behind closed doors on an upper floor—his attitude affects the moods of his direct reports, and a domino effect ripples throughout the company's emotional climate.[7]

Careful observations of working groups in action revealed several ways the leader plays such a pivotal role in determining the shared emotions.[8] Leaders typically talked more than anyone else, and what they said was listened to more carefully. Leaders were also usually the first to speak out on a subject, and when others made comments, their remarks most often referred to what the leader had said than to anyone else's comments. Because the leaders' way of seeing things has special weight, leaders "manage meaning" for a group, offering a way to interpret, and so react emotionally to, a given situation.[9]

But the impact on emotions goes beyond what a leader says. In these studies, even when leaders were not talking, they were watched more carefully than anyone else in the group. When people raised a question for the group as a whole, they would keep their eyes on the leader to see his or her response. Indeed, group members generally see the leader's emotional reaction as the most valid response, and so model their own on it—particularly in an ambiguous situation, where various members react differently. In a sense, the leader sets the emotional standard.

Still, not all "official" leaders in a group are necessarily the emotional leaders. When the designated leader lacks credibility for some reason, people may turn for emotional guidance to someone else whom they trust and respect. This de facto leader then becomes the one who molds others' emotional reactions. For instance, a well-known jazz group that was named for its formal leader and founder actually took its emotional cues from a different musician. The founder continued to manage bookings and logistics, but when it came time to decide what tune the group would play next or how the sound system should be adjusted, all eyes turned to the dominant member—the emotional leader.[10]

HOW MOODS IMPACT RESULTS

Emotions are highly intense, fleeting, and sometimes disruptive to work; moods tend to be less intense, longer-lasting feelings that typically don't interfere with the job at hand. And an emotional episode usually leaves a corresponding lingering mood: a low-key, continual flow of feeling throughout the group.

Although emotions and moods may seem trivial from a business point of view, they have real consequences for getting work done. A leader's mild anxiety can act as a signal that something needs more attention and careful thought. In fact, a sober mood can help immensely when considering a risky situation—and too much optimism can lead to ignoring dangers.[11] A sudden flood of anger can rivet a leader's attention on an urgent problem—such as the revelation that a senior executive has engaged in sexual harassment—redirecting the leader's energies from the normal round of concerns toward finding a solution, such as improving the organization's efforts to eliminate harassment.[12]

While mild anxiety (such as over a looming deadline) can focus attention and energy, prolonged distress can sabotage a leader's relationships and can also hamper work performance by diminishing the brain's ability to process information and respond effectively. A good laugh or an upbeat mood, on the other hand, more often enhances the neural abilities crucial for doing good work.

Both good and bad moods tend to perpetuate themselves, in part because they skew perceptions and memories: When people feel upbeat, they see the positive light in a situation and recall the good things about it, and when they feel bad, they focus on the downside.[13] Beyond this perceptual skew, the stew of stress hormones secreted when a person is upset takes hours to become reabsorbed in the body and fade away. That's why a sour relationship with a boss can leave a person a captive of that distress, with a mind preoccupied and a body unable to calm itself: *He got me so upset during that meeting I couldn't go to sleep for hours last night.* As a result, we naturally prefer being with people who are emotionally positive, in part because they make us feel good.

EMOTIONAL HIJACKING

Negative emotions—especially chronic anger, anxiety, or a sense of futility—powerfully disrupt work, hijacking attention from the task at hand.[14] For instance, in a Yale study of moods and their contagion, the performance of groups making executive decisions about how best to allocate yearly bonuses was measurably boosted by positive feelings and was impaired by negative ones. Significantly, the group members themselves did not realize the influence of their own moods.[15]

For instance, of all the interactions at an international hotel chain that pitched employees into bad moods, the most frequent was talking to someone in management. Interactions with bosses led to bad feelings—frustration, disappointment, anger, sadness, disgust, or hurt—about nine out of ten times. These interactions were the cause of distress more often than customers, work pressure, company policies, or personal problems.[16] Not that leaders need to be overly "nice"; the emotional art of leadership includes pressing the reality of work demands without unduly upsetting people. One of the oldest laws in psychology holds that beyond a moderate level, increases in anxiety and worry erode mental abilities.

Distress not only erodes mental abilities, but also makes people less emotionally intelligent. People who are upset have trouble reading emotions accurately in other people—decreasing the most basic skill needed for empathy and, as a result, impairing their social skills.[17]

Another consideration is that the emotions people feel while they work, according to new findings on job satisfaction, reflect most directly the true quality of work life.[18] The percentage of time people feel positive emotions at work turns out to be one of the strongest predictors of satisfaction, and therefore, for instance, of how likely employees are to quit.[19] In this sense, leaders who spread bad moods are simply bad for business—and those who pass along good moods help drive a business's success.

GOOD MOODS, GOOD WORK

When people feel good, they work at their best. Feeling good lubricates mental efficiency, making people better at understanding information and using decision rules in complex judgments, as well as more flexible in their thinking.[20] Upbeat moods, research verifies, make people view others—or events—in a more positive light. That in turn helps people feel more optimistic about their ability to achieve a goal, enhances creativity and decision-making skills, and predisposes people to be helpful.[21] Insurance agents with a glass-is-half-full outlook, for instance, are far more able than their more pessimistic peers to persist despite rejections, and so they make more sales.[22] Moreover, research on humor at work reveals that a well-timed joke or playful laugher can stimulate creativity, open lines of communication, enhance a sense of connection and trust, and, of course, make work more fun.[23] Playful joking increases the likelihood of financial concessions during a negotiation. Small wonder that playfulness holds a prominent place in the tool kit of emotionally intelligent leaders.

Good moods prove especially important when it comes to teams: The ability of a leader to pitch a group into an enthusiastic, cooperative mood can determine its success. On the other hand, whenever emotional conflicts in a group bleed attention and energy from their shared tasks, a group's performance will suffer.

Consider the results of a study of sixty-two CEOs and their top management teams.[24] The CEOs represented some of the *Fortune 500*, as well as leading U.S. service companies (such as consulting and accounting firms), not-for-profit organizations, and government agencies. The CEOs and their management team members were assessed on how upbeat—energetic, enthusiastic, determined—they were. They were also asked how much conflict and tumult the top team experienced, that is, personality clashes, anger and friction in meetings, and emotional conflicts (in contrast to disagreement about ideas).

The study found that the more positive the overall moods of people in the top management team, the more cooperatively they worked together—and the better the company's business results. Put differently, the longer a company was run by a management team that did not get along, the poorer that company's market return.

The "group IQ," then—the sum total of every person's best talents contributed at full force—depends on the group's emotional intelligence, as shown in its harmony. A leader skilled in collaboration can keep cooperation high and thus ensure that the group's decisions will be worth the effort of meeting. Such leaders know how to balance the group's focus on the task at hand with its attention to the quality of members' relationships. They naturally create a friendly but effective climate that lifts everyone's spirits.

QUANTIFYING THE "FEEL" OF A COMPANY

Common wisdom, of course, holds that employees who feel upbeat will likely go the extra mile to please customers and therefore improve the bottom line. But there's actually a logarithm that predicts that relationship: For every 1 percent improvement in the service climate, there's a 2 percent increase in revenue.[25]

Benjamin Schneider, a professor at the University of Maryland, found in operations as diverse as bank branches, insurance company regional offices, credit card call centers, and hospitals that employees' ratings of service climate predicted customer satisfaction, which drove business results. Likewise, poor morale among frontline customer service reps at a given point in time predicts high turnover—and declining customer satisfaction—up to three years later. This low customer satisfaction, in turn, drives declining revenues.[26]

So what's the antidote? Besides the obvious relationships between climate and working conditions or salary, resonant leaders play a key role. In general, the more emotionally demanding the work, the more empathic and supportive the leader needs to be. Leaders drive the service climate and thus the predisposition of employees to satisfy customers. At an insurance company, for instance, Schneider found that effective leadership influenced service climate among agents to account for a 3 to 4 percent difference in insurance renewals—a seemingly small margin that made a big difference to the business.

Organizational consultants have long assumed a positive link of some kind between a business unit's human climate and its performance. But data connecting the two have been sparse—and so, in practice, leaders could more easily ignore their personal style and its effects on the people they led, focusing instead on "harder" business objectives. But now we have results from a range of industries that link leadership to climate and to business performance, making it possible to quantify the hard difference for business performance made by something as soft as the "feel" of a company.

For instance, at a global food and beverage company, positive climate readings predicted higher yearly earnings at major divisions. And in a study of nineteen insurance companies, the climate created by the CEOs among their direct reports predicted the business performance of the entire organization: In 75 percent of cases, climate alone accurately sorted companies into high versus low profits and growth.[27]

Climate in itself does not determine performance. The factors deciding which companies prove most fit in any given quarter are notoriously complex. But our analyses suggest that, overall, the climate—how people feel about working at a company—can account for 20 to 30 percent of business performance. Getting the best out of people pays off in hard results.

If climate drives business results, what drives climate? Roughly 50 to 70 percent of how employees perceive their organization's climate can be traced to the actions of one person: the leader. More than anyone else, the boss creates the conditions that directly determine people's ability to work well.[28]

In short, leaders' emotional states and actions do affect how the people they lead will feel and therefore perform. How well leaders manage their moods and affect everyone else's moods, then, becomes not just a private matter, but a factor in how well a business will do.[29]

And that gets us to how the brain drives primal leadership, for better or for worse.

—⟨≈⟩—

Daniel Goleman is codirector of the Consortium for Research on Emotional Intelligence in Organizations at Rutgers University and the best-selling author of multiple books on emotional and social intelligence. See also www.danielgoleman.info/blog.

—⟨≈⟩—

Richard Boyatzis is professor in the departments of organizational behavior, psychology, and cognitive science at Case Western Reserve University and in the department of human resources at ESADE. His research includes adult development, leadership, and emotional intelligence.

—⟨≈⟩—

Annie McKee is founder of the Teleos Leadership Institute, an international consulting firm providing services to senior leaders in the private sector and developing world. She teaches at the University of Pennsylvania's Graduate School of Education and the Wharton School's Aresty Institute of Executive Education.

CHAPTER THREE

The Five Practices of Exemplary Leadership

James M. Kouzes
Barry Z. Posner

Through our studies of personal-best leadership experiences, we've discovered that ordinary people who guide others along pioneering journeys follow rather similar paths. Though each case was unique in expression, each path was marked by common patterns of action. Leadership is not about personality; it's about practice. We've forged these common practices into a model and offer it here as guidance for leaders as they work to keep their own bearings and guide others toward peak achievements.

When getting extraordinary things done in organizations, leaders engage in these Five Practices of Exemplary Leadership:

- Model the Way.
- Inspire a Shared Vision.
- Challenge the Process.
- Enable Others to Act.
- Encourage the Heart.

These practices aren't the private property of the people we studied or of a few select shining stars. They're available to anyone, in any organization or situation, who accepts the leadership challenge. And they're not the accident of a special moment in history. They've stood the test of time, and our most recent research confirms that they're just as relevant today as they were when we first began our investigation over two decades ago—if not more so.

Model the Way

Titles are granted, but it's your behavior that wins you respect. As Gayle Hamilton, a director with Pacific Gas & Electric Company, told us, "I would never ask anyone to do anything I was unwilling to do first." This sentiment was shared across all the cases that we collected. Exemplary leaders know that if they want to gain commitment and achieve the highest standards, they must be models of the behavior they expect of others. Leaders model the way.

To effectively model the behavior they expect of others, leaders must first be clear about their guiding principles. Lindsay Levin says, "You have to open up your heart and let people know what you really think and believe. This means talking about your values." Alan Keith adds that one of the most significant leadership lessons he would pass along is, "You must lead from what you believe." Leaders must find their own voice, and then they must clearly and distinctively give voice to their values. As the personal-best stories illustrate, leaders are supposed to stand up for their beliefs, so they'd better have some beliefs to stand up for.

Eloquent speeches about common values, however, aren't nearly enough. Leaders' deeds are far more important than their words when determining how serious they really are about what they say. Words and deeds must be consistent. Exemplary leaders go first. They go first by setting the example through daily actions that demonstrate they are deeply committed to their beliefs. Toni-Ann Lueddecke, for example, believes that there are no unimportant tasks in an organization's efforts at excellence. She demonstrates this to her associates in her eight Gymboree Play & Music centers in New Jersey by her actions. As just one example, she sometimes scrubs floors in addition to teaching classes.

The personal-best projects we heard about in our research were all distinguished by relentless effort, steadfastness, competence, and attention to detail. We were also struck by how the actions leaders took to set an example were often simple things. Sure, leaders had operational and strategic plans. But the examples they gave were not about elaborate designs. They were about the power of spending time with someone, of working side by side with colleagues, of telling stories that made values come alive, of being highly visible during times of uncertainty, and of asking questions to get people to think about values and priorities. Modeling the way is essentially about earning the right and the respect to lead through direct individual involvement and action. People first follow the person, then the plan.

Inspire a Shared Vision

When people described to us their personal-best leadership experiences, they told of times when they imagined an exciting, highly attractive future for their organization. They had visions and dreams of what could be. They had absolute and total personal belief in those dreams, and they were confident in their abilities to make extraordinary things happen. Every organization, every social movement, begins with a dream. The dream or vision is the force that invents the future.

Leaders inspire a shared vision. They gaze across the horizon of time, imagining the attractive opportunities that are in store when they and their constituents arrive at a distant destination. Leaders have a desire to make something happen, to change the way things are, to create something that no one else has ever created before. In some ways, leaders live their lives backward. They see pictures in their mind's eye of what the results will look like even before they've started their project, much as an architect draws a blueprint or an engineer builds a model. Their clear image of the future pulls them forward. Yet visions seen only by leaders are insufficient to create an organized movement or a significant change in a company. A person with no constituents is not a leader, and people will not follow until they accept a vision as their own. Leaders cannot command commitment, only inspire it.

To enlist people in a vision, leaders must know their constituents and speak their language. People must believe that leaders understand their needs and have their interests at heart. Leadership is a dialogue, not a monologue. To enlist support, leaders must have intimate knowledge of people's dreams, hopes, aspirations, visions, and values.

Leaders breathe life into the hopes and dreams of others and enable them to see the exciting possibilities that the future holds. Leaders forge a unity of purpose by showing constituents how the dream is for the common good. Leaders ignite the flame of passion in others by expressing enthusiasm for the compelling vision of their group. Leaders communicate their passion through vivid language and an expressive style.

Whatever the venue, and without exception, the people in our study reported that they were incredibly enthusiastic about their personal-best projects. Their own enthusiasm was catching; it spread from leader to constituents. Their belief in and enthusiasm for the vision were the sparks that ignited the flame of inspiration.

Challenge the Process

Leaders venture out. None of the individuals in our study sat idly by waiting for fate to smile upon them. "Luck" or "being in the right place at the right time" may play a role in the specific opportunities leaders embrace, but those who lead others to greatness seek and accept challenge.

Every single personal-best leadership case we collected involved some kind of challenge. The challenge might have been an innovative new product, a cutting-edge service, a groundbreaking piece of legislation, an invigorating campaign to get adolescents to join an environmental program, a revolutionary turnaround of a bureaucratic military program, or the start-up of a new plant or business. Whatever the challenge, all the cases involved a change from the status quo. Not one person claimed to have achieved a personal best by keeping things the same. All leaders challenge the process.

Leaders are pioneers—people who are willing to step out into the unknown. They search for opportunities to innovate, grow, and improve. But leaders aren't the only creators or originators of new products, services, or processes. In fact, it's more likely that they're not: innovation comes more from listening than from telling. Product and service innovations tend to come from customers, clients, vendors, people in the labs, and people on the front lines; process innovations, from the people doing the work. Sometimes a dramatic external event thrusts an organization into a radically new condition.

The leader's primary contribution is in the recognition of good ideas, the support of those ideas, and the willingness to challenge the system to get new products, processes, services, and systems adopted. It might be more accurate, then, to say that leaders are early adopters of innovation.

Leaders know well that innovation and change all involve experimentation, risk, and failure. They proceed anyway. One way of dealing with the potential risks and failures of experimentation is to approach change through incremental steps and small wins. Little victories, when piled on top of each other, build confidence that even the biggest challenges can be met. In so doing, they strengthen commitment to the long-term future. Yet not everyone is equally comfortable with risk and uncertainty. Leaders also pay attention to the capacity of their constituents to take control of challenging situations and become fully committed to change. You can't exhort people to take risks if they don't also feel safe.

It would be ridiculous to assert that those who fail over and over again eventually succeed as leaders. Success in any endeavor isn't a process of simply buying enough lottery tickets. The key that unlocks the door to opportunity is learning. In his own study of exemplary leadership practices, Warren Bennis writes that "leaders learn by leading, and they learn best by leading in the face of obstacles. As weather shapes mountains, problems shape leaders. Difficult bosses, lack of vision and virtue in the executive suite, circumstances beyond their control, and their own mistakes have been the leaders' basic curriculum."[1] In other words, leaders are learners. They learn from their failures as well as their successes.

Enable Others to Act

Grand dreams don't become significant realities through the actions of a single person. Leadership is a team effort. After reviewing thousands of personal-best cases, we developed a simple test to detect whether someone is on the road to becoming a leader. That test is the frequency of the use of the word "we." In our interview with one leader, for instance, he used the word "we" nearly three times more often than the word "I" in explaining his personal-best leadership experience.

Exemplary leaders enable others to act. They foster collaboration and build trust. This sense of teamwork goes far beyond a few direct reports or close confidants. They engage all those who must make the project work—and in some way, all who must live with the results.

In today's "virtual" organization, cooperation can't be restricted to a small group of loyalists; it must include peers, managers, customers and clients, suppliers, citizens—all those who have a stake in the vision.

Leaders make it possible for others to do good work. They know that those who are expected to produce the results must feel a sense of personal power and ownership. Leaders understand that the command-and-control techniques of the Industrial Revolution no longer apply. Instead, leaders work to make people feel strong, capable, and committed. Leaders enable others to act not by hoarding the power they have but by giving it away. Exemplary leaders strengthen everyone's capacity to deliver on the promises they make. As a budget analyst for Catholic Healthcare West, Cindy Giordano would ask "What do you think?" and use the ensuing discussion to build up the capabilities of others (as well as educate and update her own information and perspective). She discovered that when people are trusted and have more discretion, more authority, and more information, they're much more likely to use their energies to produce extraordinary results.

Encourage the Heart

The climb to the top is arduous and long. People become exhausted, frustrated, and disenchanted. They're often tempted to give up. Leaders encourage the heart of their constituents to carry on. Genuine acts of caring uplift the spirits and draw people forward. Encouragement can come from dramatic gestures or simple actions. When Cary Turner was head of Pier 1 Imports' Stores Division, he once showed up in a wedding gown to promote the bridal registry. On another occasion, he promised store employees he'd parasail over Puget Sound and the Seattle waterfront if they met their sales targets. They kept their commitment; he kept his. As mayor of New York City, Rudy Giuliani wore different hats (literally) to acknowledge various groups of rescue workers as he toured ground zero after the World Trade Center towers were destroyed on September 11, 2001. But it doesn't take events or media coverage to let people know you appreciate their contributions. Terri Sarhatt, customer services manager at Applied Biosystems, looked after her employees so well that at least one reported that the time she spent with them was more valuable than the tangible rewards she was able to give out.

It's part of the leader's job to show appreciation for people's contributions and to create a culture of celebration. In the cases we collected, we saw thousands of examples of individual recognition and group celebration. We've heard and seen everything from handwritten thank-yous to marching bands and "This Is Your Life" ceremonies.

Recognition and celebration aren't about fun and games, though there is a lot of fun and there are a lot of games when people encourage the hearts of their constituents. Neither are they about pretentious ceremonies designed to create some phony sense of camaraderie. When people see a charlatan making noisy affectations, they turn away in disgust. Encouragement is curiously serious business. It's how leaders visibly and behaviorally link rewards with performance. When striving to raise quality, recover from disaster, start up a new service, or make dramatic change of any kind, leaders make sure people see the benefit of behavior that's aligned with cherished values. And leaders also know that celebrations and rituals, when done with authenticity and from the heart, build a strong sense of collective identity and community spirit that can carry a group through extraordinarily tough times.

LEADERSHIP IS A RELATIONSHIP

Leadership is an identifiable set of skills and practices that are available to all of us, not just a few charismatic men and women. The "great person"—woman or man—theory of leadership is just plain wrong. Or, we should say, the theory that there are only a few great men and women who can lead us to greatness is just plain wrong. We consider the women and men in our research to be great, and so do those with whom they worked. They are the everyday heroes of our world. It's because we have so many—not so few—leaders that we are able to get extraordinary things done on a regular basis, even in extraordinary times.

Our findings also challenge the myth that leadership is something that you find only at the highest levels of organizations and society. We found it everywhere. To us this is inspiring and should give everyone hope. Hope, because it means that no one needs to wait around to be saved by someone riding into town on a white horse. Hope, because there's a generation of leaders searching for the opportunities to make a difference. Hope, because right down the block or right down the hall there are people who will seize the opportunity to lead you to greatness. They're your neighbors, friends, and colleagues. And you are one of them, too.

There's still another crucial truth about leadership—more apparent to us this time around than it was before. It's something that we've known for a long time, but we've come to prize its value even more today. In talking to leaders and reading their cases, there was a very clear message that wove itself throughout every situation and every action: leadership is a relationship. Leadership is a relationship between those who aspire to lead and those who choose to follow.

Evidence abounds for this point of view. For instance, in examining the critical variables for success in the top three jobs in large organizations, Jodi Taylor and her colleagues at the Center for Creative Leadership found the number one success factor to be "relationships with subordinates."[2] We were intrigued to find that even in this nanosecond world of e-everything, opinion is consistent with the facts. In an on-line survey, respondents were asked to indicate, among other things, which would be more essential to business success in five years—social skills or skills in using the Internet. Seventy-two percent selected social skills; 28 percent, Internet skills.[3] Internet literati completing a poll on-line realize that it's not the web of technology that matters the most, it's the web of people.

Similar results were found in a study by Public Allies, an AmeriCorps organization dedicated to creating young leaders who can strengthen their communities. Public Allies sought the opinions of eighteen- to thirty-year-olds on the subject of leadership. Among the items was a question about the qualities that were important in a good leader. Topping the respondents' list is "Being able to see a situation from someone else's point of view." In second place, "Getting along well with other people."[4]

Success in leadership, success in business, and success in life has been, is now, and will continue to be a function of how well people work and play together. We're even more convinced of this today than we were twenty years ago. Success in leading will be wholly dependent upon the capacity to build and sustain those human relationships that enable people to get extraordinary things done on a regular basis.

THE TEN COMMITMENTS OF LEADERSHIP

Embedded in the Five Practices of Exemplary Leadership are behaviors that can serve as the basis for learning to lead. We call these the

Practice	Commitment
Model the Way	1. Find your voice by clarifying your personal values.
	2. Set the example by aligning actions with shared values.
Inspire a Shared Vision	3. Envision the future by imagining exciting and ennobling possibilities.
	4. Enlist others in a common vision by appealing to shared aspirations.
Challenge the Process	5. Search for opportunities by seeking innovative ways to change, grow, and improve.
	6. Experiment and take risks by constantly generating small wins and learning from mistakes.
Enable Others to Act	7. Foster collaboration by promoting cooperative goals and building trust.
	8. Strengthen others by sharing power and discretion.
Encourage the Heart	9. Recognize contributions by showing appreciation for individual excellence.
	10. Celebrate the values and victories by creating a spirit of community.

Exhibit 3.1.   The Five Practices and the Ten Commitments of Leadership.

Ten Commitments of Leadership (see Exhibit 3.1). These ten commitments serve as the guide for how leaders get extraordinary things done in organizations.

—◦◦◦—

James M. Kouzes is the Dean's Executive Professor of Leadership, Leavey School of Business, Santa Clara University; an award-winning professional speaker; and best-selling author of multiple books on leadership.

—◦◦◦—

Barry Z. Posner is dean and professor of leadership at the Leavey School of Business, Santa Clara University, and coauthor with Jim Kouzes of multiple books, leadership development instruments, videos, and empirical studies.

CHAPTER FOUR

Reframing Leadership

Lee G. Bolman
Terrence E. Deal

L eadership is universally offered as a panacea for social problems. A widely accepted canon holds that leadership is a very good thing that we need more of—at least, more of the right kind. Yet there is confusion about what leadership means and how much difference it can make. Sennett (1980, p. 197) writes, "Authority is not a thing; it is a search for solidity and security in the strength of others which will seem to be like a thing." The same is true of leadership. It is not a tangible thing. It exists only in relationships and in the imagination and perception of the engaged parties.

Leadership is distinct from authority, though authorities may be leaders. Authority and leadership are both built on voluntary obedience. If leaders lose legitimacy, they lose the capacity to lead. But many examples of obeying authority fall outside the domain of leadership. As Gardner (1989, p. 7) put it, "The meter maid has authority, but not necessarily leadership."

Leadership is also different from management, though the two are easily confused. One may be a leader without being a manager, and many managers could not "lead a squad of seven-year-olds to the ice-cream counter" (Gardner, 1989, p. 2). Bennis and Nanus (1985) offer the distinction that "managers do things right, and leaders do the right thing" (p. 21). Kotter (1988) sees management as primarily about structural nuts and bolts: planning, organizing, and controlling. But Gardner (1989) argues against contrasting leadership and management too sharply because leaders may "end up looking like a cross between Napoleon and the Pied Piper, and managers like unimaginative clods" (p. 3). He suggests several dimensions for distinguishing leadership from management. Leaders think long-term, look outside as well as inside, and influence constituents beyond their immediate formal jurisdiction. They emphasize vision and renewal and have the political skills to cope with the diverse needs of multiple constituencies.

In story and myth, leaders are often lonely heroes and itinerant warriors, wed only to their honor and cause (Bolman and Deal, 2006). But traditional notions of solitary, heroic leaders focus too much on individuals and too little on the stage where they play their parts. Leaders make things happen, but things also make leaders happen. We need only look at the transformation of Rudy Giuliani's image after September 11 to see that situation influences what leaders must do and what they can do. Giuliani found himself on-stage in an unplanned theater of horror, and he delivered the performance of his life. Another stage would have required, and permitted, different leadership. No single formula is possible or advisable for the great range of situations potential leaders encounter.

Heroic images of leadership convey the notion of a one-way process: leaders lead and followers follow. This blinds us to the reality of the relationship between leader and follower. Leaders are not independent actors; they both shape and are shaped by their constituents (Gardner, 1989; Simmel, 1950). Leaders often promote a new idea or initiative only after a large number of their constituents already favor it (Cleveland, 1985). Leadership, then, is not simply a matter of what a leader does but of what occurs in a relationship. Leaders' actions generate responses from others that in turn affect the leaders' capacity for taking further initiatives (Murphy, 1985).

It is common to equate leadership with position, but this relegates all those in the lowerarchy to the passive role of follower. It also reinforces the widespread tendency of senior executives to take on more responsibility than they can adequately discharge (Oshry, 1995; [also see Chapter Fourteen in this volume]). Administrators are leaders only to the extent that others grant them cooperation and follow their lead. Conversely, one can be a leader without a position of formal authority. Good organizations encourage leadership from many quarters (Kanter, 1983; Barnes and Kriger, 1986).

Leadership is thus a subtle, holistic process of mutual influence fusing thought, feeling, and action to produce cooperative effort in the service of purposes and values embraced by both the leader and the led.

REFRAMING LEADERSHIP

Dealing with people across challenging situations is a perennially perplexing aspect of leading. Executives are always looking for ideas to make the job easier. Too often, the search for simplicity overlooks important realities. Reframing—deliberately viewing a situation from multiple perspectives—offers a way to get beyond narrow and oversimplified views of leadership. Different perspectives or *frames* offer distinctive images of the leadership process. Depending on leader and circumstance, each frame can lead to compelling and constructive leadership, but none is right for all times and seasons. We have identified four frames: structural, human resource, political, and symbolic. For each, we examine skills and processes and propose rules of thumb for successful leadership practice.

Architect or Tyrant? Structural Leadership

Structural leadership evokes images of petty tyrants and rigid bureaucrats who never met a rule they didn't like. Little literature exists on structural leadership in comparison to the other frames. Some structural theorists have argued that leadership is neither important nor basic (Hall, 1987). But the effects of structural leadership can be powerful and enduring, even if the style is subtler and less obviously heroic.

One of the great architects in business history was Alfred P. Sloan, Jr., who became president of General Motors in 1923 and remained a dominant force in the company until his retirement in 1956. The structure and strategy he established made GM the world's largest corporation. He has been described as "the George Washington of the GM culture" (Lee, 1988, p. 42), even though his "genius was not in inspirational leadership but in organizational structures" (p. 43).

At the turn of the twentieth century, some thirty manufacturers produced automobiles in the United States. In 1899, they produced a grand total of about six hundred cars. Most of these small carmakers stumbled out of the starting gate, leaving two late entries, the Ford Motor Company (founded by Henry Ford in 1903) and GM (founded by William Durant in 1908) as front-runners to dominate the American auto industry. Henry Ford's single-minded determination to build an affordable car had Ford in a commanding lead when Sloan took over GM.

Under GM's founder, Billy Durant, the company's divisions operated as independent fiefdoms. Durant had built GM by buying everything in sight, thus forming a loose combination of previously independent firms. "GM did not have adequate knowledge or control of the individual operating divisions. It was management by crony, with the divisions operating on a horse-trading basis. The main thing to note here is that no one had the needed information or the needed control over the divisions. The divisions continued to spend lavishly, and their requests for additional funds were met" (Sloan, 1965, pp. 27–28).

Sloan recognized that GM needed a better structure. The dominant model of the time was a centralized, functional organization, but Sloan felt that such a structure would not work for GM. Instead, he created one of the world's first decentralized organizations. His basic principle was simple: centralize planning and resource allocation; decentralize operating decisions. Under Sloan's model, divisions focused on making and selling cars, while top management focused on long-range strategy and major funding decisions. Central staff made sure that top management had the information and control systems it needed to make strategic decisions.

The structure worked. By the late 1920s, GM had a more versatile organization with a broader product line than Ford. With Henry Ford still dominating his highly centralized company, Ford was poorly positioned to compete with GM's multiple divisions, each producing its own cars at different prices. GM's pioneering structure set the standard for others.

In the 1980s, GM found itself with another structural leader, Roger Smith, at the helm. The results were less satisfying. Like Sloan, Smith ascended to the top job at a difficult time. In 1980, his first year as GM's chief executive, all American automakers lost money. It was GM's first loss since 1921. Recognizing that the company had serious competitive problems, Smith relied on structure and technology to make it "the world's first 21st century corporation" (Lee, 1988, p. 16). He restructured vehicle operations and spent billions of dollars in a quest for paperless offices and robotized assembly plants. The changes were dramatic, but the results were dismal:

> No GM chairman has disrupted as many lives without commensurate rewards, has spent as much money without returns, or has alienated so many. . . . Few employees believe that [Smith] is in the least concerned with their well-being, and even fewer below executive row anticipate any measure of respect, or reward, for their contributions. No GM chief executive's motives have ever been as universally questioned or his decisions as thoroughly mistrusted [Lee, 1988, pp. 286–287].

Why did Smith stumble where Sloan succeeded? They were equally uncharismatic and neither had great sensitivity to human resource or symbolic issues. The answer comes down to how well each implemented the right structural form. Structural leaders succeed not because of inspiration but because they have the right design for the times and are able to get their structural changes implemented.

Effective structural leaders share several characteristics.

1. *Structural Leaders Do Their Homework:* Sloan was a brilliant engineer who had grown up in the auto industry. Before coming to GM, he was chief executive of an auto accessories company where he implemented a divisional structure. When GM bought his firm in 1916, Sloan became a vice president and board member. Working under Durant, he devoted much of his energy to studying GM's structural problems. He pioneered the development of more sophisticated internal information systems and better market research. He was an early convert to group decision making and created a committee structure to make major decisions. Roger Smith had spent his entire career with GM, but most of his jobs were in finance. Much of his vision involved changes in production technology, an area where he had little experience or expertise.

2. *Structural Leaders Rethink the Relationship of Structure, Strategy, and Environment:* Sloan's new structure was intimately tied to a strategy for reaching the automotive market. He foresaw a growing market, improvements in automobiles, and more

discriminating consumers. In the face of Henry Ford's stubborn attachment to the Model T, Sloan introduced the "price pyramid" (cars for every pocketbook) and the annual model change. Automotive technology in the 1920s was evolving almost as fast as electronics in the 1990s, and the annual model change soon became the industry norm.

Smith's vision was truncated, focused more on reducing costs than on selling cars. As he saw it, GM's primary competitive problem was high costs driven by high wages. He hoped to solve that by replacing workers with machines. He gave little support to efforts already under way to improve working conditions on the GM shop floor. Ironically, his two best investments—NUMMI and Saturn—succeeded precisely because of innovative approaches to managing people: "With only a fraction of the money invested in GM's heavily robotized plants, [the NUMMI plant at] Fremont is more efficient and produces better-quality cars than any plant in the GM system" (Hampton and Norman, 1987, p. 102).

3. *Structural Leaders Focus on Implementation:* Structural leaders often miscalculate difficulties of putting their design in place. They underestimate resistance, skimp on training, fail to build a political base, and misread cultural cues. As a result, they are thwarted by neglected human resource, political, and symbolic barriers. Sloan was no human resource specialist, but he intuitively saw the need to get understanding and acceptance of major decisions. He did that by asking for advice and by establishing committees and task forces to address major issues.

4. *Effective Structural Leaders Experiment, Evaluate, and Adapt:* Sloan tinkered constantly with GM's structure and strategy and encouraged others to do likewise. The Great Depression produced a drop of 72 percent in sales at GM between 1929 and 1932, but the company adapted adroitly to hard times. It increased its market share and made money every year. Sloan briefly centralized operations to survive the depression but decentralized once business began to recover. In the 1980s, Smith spent billions to modernize the corporation and cut costs, yet GM lost market share every year and continued to be the industry's highest-cost producer: "Much of the advanced technology that GM acquired at such high cost hindered rather than improved productivity. Runaway robots started welding doors shut at the new Detroit-Hamtramck Cadillac plant. Luckily for Ford and Chrysler, poverty prevented them from

indulging in the same orgy of spending on robots" ("On a Clear Day . . . ," 1989, p. 77).

Catalyst or Wimp? Human Resource Leadership

The tiny trickle of writing about structural leadership is swamped by a torrent of human resource literature. Human resource theorists typically advocate openness, mutuality, listening, coaching, participation, and empowerment. They view the leader as a facilitator and catalyst who motivates and empowers subordinates. The leader's power comes from talent, sensitivity, and service rather than position or force. Greenleaf (1973) argues that "The servant-leader makes sure that other people's highest priority needs are being served. The best test [of leadership] is: do those served grow as persons; do they, while being served, become healthier, wiser, freer, more autonomous, more likely themselves to become servants?" (p. 7).

Will managers who adhere to such images be respected leaders who make a difference? Or will they be seen as naïve and weak, carried along on the current of other people's energy? The leadership tightrope is real, and some hide behind participation and sensitivity as an excuse not to walk it. There are also many human resource leaders whose skill and artistry produce extraordinary results. These gifted leaders typically apply a consistent set of leadership principles:

1. *Human Resource Leaders Believe in People and Communicate Their Belief:* Human resource leaders are passionate about "productivity through people" (Peters and Waterman, 1982). They demonstrate this faith in their words and actions and often build it into a core philosophy or credo. Fred Smith, founder and CEO of Federal Express, sees "putting people first" as the cornerstone of his company's success: "We discovered a long time ago that customer satisfaction really begins with employee satisfaction. That belief is incorporated in our corporate philosophy statement: People—Service—Profit" (Waterman, 1994, p. 89).

2. *Human Resource Leaders Are Visible and Accessible:* Peters and Waterman (1982) popularized the notion of "management by wandering around"—the idea that managers need to get out of their offices and spend time with workers and customers. Pat Carrigan, the first woman plant manager at General Motors, modeled this technique in the course of turning around two GM plants, each with

a long history of union-management conflict (Kouzes and Posner, 1987). One worker commented that before Carrigan came, "I didn't know who the plant manager was. I wouldn't have recognized him if I saw him." When she left her first assignment after three years, the local union gave her a plaque. It concluded, "Be it resolved that Pat M. Carrigan, through the exhibiting of qualities as a people person, has played a vital role in the creation of a new way of life at the Lakewood plant. Therefore, be it resolved that the members of Local 34 will always warmly remember Pat M. Carrigan as one of us" (Kouzes and Posner, 1987, p. 36).

3. *Effective Human Resource Leaders Empower Others:* Human resource leaders often refer to their employees as "partners," "owners," or "associates." They make it clear that employees have a stake in the organization's success and a right to be involved in making decisions. In the 1980s, Jan Carlzon, CEO of Scandinavian Airlines System (SAS), built a turnaround effort intent on making the company "the best airline in the world for business travelers" (Carlzon, 1987, p. 46). To find out what the business traveler wanted, he turned to SAS's front-line service employees for ideas and suggestions. Focus groups generated hundreds of ideas and emphasized the importance of front-line autonomy to decide on the spot what passengers needed. Carlzon concluded that SAS's image to its customers was built out of a series of "moments of truth": fifteen-second encounters between employees and customers. "We cannot rely on rule books and instruction from distant corporate offices. We have to place responsibility for ideas, decisions, and actions with the people who are SAS during those 15 seconds. If they have to go up the organizational chain of command for a decision on an individual problem, then those 15 golden seconds will elapse without a response and we will have lost an opportunity to earn a loyal customer" (p. 66).

Advocate or Hustler? Political Leadership

Sometimes even in the private sector, leaders have to plunge into the political arena to move their company where it needs to go. Consider two chief executives in dissimilar eras: Lee Iacocca, chief executive of Chrysler when the company was near death in the late 1970s, and Carly Fiorina, CEO of Hewlett-Packard in 1999.

Iacocca's career had taken him to the presidency of Ford Motor Company. But on July 1, 1978, his boss, Henry Ford II, fired him, reportedly with the simple explanation, "I don't like you" (O'Toole,

1984, p. 231). Iacocca's unemployment was brief. Chrysler, desperate for new leadership, believed Iacocca was the answer.

Even though Iacocca had done his homework before accepting Chrysler's offer, things were worse than he expected. Chrysler was losing money so fast bankruptcy seemed inevitable. He concluded that the only way out was to persuade the U.S. government to guarantee loans. It was a tough sell; Congress, the media, and the American public were against the idea. Iacocca had to convince all of them that government intervention was in their best interest.

Like Iacocca, Fiorina came in to head a troubled giant. HP's problems were not as bad as Chrysler's; it was still profitable with more than $40 billion in annual revenue. But customer service was deteriorating, bureaucracy was stifling innovation, and HP seemed to be falling behind the technology curve. *BusinessWeek* described HP as part of "the clueless establishment" (Burrows and Elstrom, 1999, p. 76). Fiorina's arrival was big news. She was only the fifth CEO in HP's sixty-year history and the first to come from outside since Hewlett and Packard founded the company in a Palo Alto garage in 1938. She was also the first woman to head a company of HP's size in any industry. She brought strengths, including "a silver tongue and an iron will" (Burrows and Elstrom, 1999, p. 76). But she faced daunting challenges, especially after she set her sights on a merger with another, floundering, $40 billion company, Compaq. Her board supported her initiative, but the Hewlett and Packard heirs, who controlled more than 15 percent of HP's stock, didn't. Fiorina had to win a massive gunfight at the HP corral.

Ultimately, Iacocca got his guarantees and Fiorina got her merger by employing essential principles for political leaders.

1. *Political Leaders Clarify the Distinction Between What They Want and What They Can Get:* Political leaders are realists. They avoid letting all that they want cloud their judgment about what is possible. Iacocca translated Chrysler's survival into the realistic goal of getting enough help to make it through a couple of difficult years. He was careful to ask not for money but for loan guarantees, insisting that the guarantees would cost the taxpayers nothing. Once Fiorina knew she was in a nasty, public squabble, she zeroed in on one goal: getting enough votes to put the merger through.

2. *Political Leaders Assess the Distribution of Power and Interests:* Political leaders map the political terrain [see Chapter Twenty-Six in this volume] by thinking carefully about the key players, their

interests, and their power, asking: Whose support do I need? How do I go about getting it? Who are my opponents? How much power do they have? What can I do to reduce or overcome their opposition? Is this battle winnable? Iacocca needed the support of Chrysler's employees and unions, but he knew that they had little choice. The key players were Congress and the public. Congress would vote for the guarantees only if Iacocca's proposal had popular support. He concentrated his efforts there.

Fiorina knew she needed support from HP's board, analysts, and ultimately a majority of voting shares. She first went after her board's support, but ran into bad luck. Walter Hewlett, son of the HP cofounder, missed the meeting at which McKinsey consultants made the case for the merger. A month later, Hewlett voted reluctantly to approve the merger. But he had serious misgivings. The substantial layoffs touted as one of the merger's "synergies" amounted to abandoning the *HP Way* in Hewlett's mind. His doubts grew when HP's stock dropped some 40 percent after the merger announcement. A few weeks later, he announced that he would vote against the merger (Burrows, 2001). Fiorina now faced an uphill battle, with her job and her vision for HP both hanging on the outcome. Her only chance was to make a case persuasive enough to win the analysts and shareholders who were still on the fence.

3. *Political Leaders Build Linkage to Key Stakeholders:* Political leaders focus their attention on building relationships and networks. They recognize the value of personal contact and face-to-face conversations. Iacocca worked hard to build linkages with Congress, the media, and the public. He spent hours with members of Congress and testifying before congressional committees. After he met with thirty-one Italian American members of Congress, all but one voted for the loan guarantees. Said Iacocca, "Some were Republicans, some were Democrats, but in this case they voted the straight Italian ticket. We were desperate, and we had to play every angle" (Iacocca and Novak, 1984, p. 221).

Fiorina's primary target was institutional shareholders who held about 57 percent of the company's stock, and the analysts whose opinions mattered. Armed with a fifty-page document that laid out the strategic and financial rationale for the merger, Fiorina and Compaq CEO Michael Capellas hit the road, speaking to every analyst they could find. Fiorina focused on big picture, strategic issues, while Capellas backed her up on the nitty-gritty details of integrating the two firms. A particularly vital target was Institutional Shareholder Services, an advisory firm whose clients held more than a fifth of HP's stock. ISS's recommendation could easily make or break the deal. Though initially skeptical, ISS's lead analyst for the merger, Ram Kumar, said that the Fiorina/Capellas team's persuasiveness and command of detail won him over.

4. *Political Leaders Persuade First, Negotiate Second, and Coerce Only If Necessary:* Wise political leaders recognize that power is essential to their effectiveness; they also know to use it judiciously. William P. Kelly, an experienced public administrator, put it well: "Power is like the old Esso ad—a tiger in your tank. But you can't let the tiger out, you just let people hear him roar. You use power terribly sparingly because it has a short half-life. You let people know you have it and hope that you don't have to use it" (Ridout and Fenn, 1974, p. 10).

Sophisticated political leaders know that influence begins with an understanding of others' concerns and interests. What is important to them? How can I help them get what they want? Iacocca knew that he had to address the widespread belief that federal guarantees would throw millions of taxpayer dollars down a rat hole. He used advertising to respond directly to public concerns. He also spoke directly to congressional concerns. Chrysler prepared computer printouts showing how many jobs would be lost in every district if Chrysler went under.

Fiorina knew her biggest hurdle was the poor track record for big mergers. Walter Hewlett used Compaq's acquisition of fading giant Digital Equipment in 1998 as evidence that the deal would be a disaster. Fiorina developed a threefold argument based on competitive scale, cost savings, and management strength. She took the story on the road in countless meetings with analysts and institutional shareholders. HP buttressed the case with a blizzard of press releases, advertising, and direct mail.

As the battle intensified, Fiorina even resorted to the business equivalent of political attack ads. HP put out a press release designed to gently but firmly discredit Walter Hewlett as a semiclueless dilettante: "Walter Hewlett, an heir of HP co-founder Bill Hewlett, is a musician and academic who oversees the Hewlett family trust and foundation. While he serves on HP's board of directors, Walter has never worked at the company or been involved in its management" (Fried, 2002).

Iacocca and Fiorina won their respective battles. Chrysler pulled out of its tailspin, repaid its loans, ignited the minivan craze, and had many profitable years before it was acquired by German automaker Daimler Benz in 1998. Fiorina got her merger but lost her job because HP's profits kept falling short of her promises and board expectations. Her successor, Mark Hurd, however, has made the merger look good—and HP's profits and stock price have soared.

Prophet or Zealot? Symbolic Leadership

The symbolic frame represents a fourth turn of the leadership kaleidoscope. This lens sees an organization as both theater and temple. As theater, an organization creates a stage on which actors play their roles and hope to communicate the right impression to the right audience. As temple, an organization is a community of faith, bonded by shared beliefs, traditions, myths, rituals, and ceremonies. Symbolically, leaders lead through both their actions and words as they interpret and reinterpret experience, and they impart meaning and purpose to experience through phrases of beauty and passion.

Franklin D. Roosevelt reassured a nation in the midst of its deepest economic depression that "the only thing we have to fear is fear itself." Burns (1978) was mindful of leaders such as Roosevelt, Mohandas Gandhi, and Martin Luther King, Jr., when he drew a distinction between "transforming" and "transactional" leaders. Transactional leaders "approach their followers with an eye to trading one thing for another: jobs for votes, subsidies for campaign contributions" (1978, p. 4). Transforming leaders evoke their constituents' better nature and move them toward higher and more universal needs and purposes. They are visionaries whose leadership is inherently symbolic. Symbolic leaders follow a consistent set of practices and rules.

1. *They Lead by Example:* Symbolic leaders demonstrate their commitment and courage by plunging into the fray. Rudy Giuliani in the aftermath of September 11 is a dramatic case in point. Risking his own life, he moved immediately to the scene. When the first tower collapsed, he was caught for fifteen minutes in the rubble.

2. *They Use Symbols to Capture Attention:* When Diana Lam became principal of Mackey Middle School in Boston in 1985, she faced substantial challenges. Mackey had the usual urban school problems: decaying physical plant, poor discipline, racial tension, disgruntled teachers, and limited resources (Kaufer and Leader, 1987a). In such a situation, a symbolic leader does something visible

and dramatic to signal that change is coming. During the summer before assuming her duties, Lam wrote a personal letter to every teacher requesting an individual meeting. She met teachers wherever they wanted. She asked how they felt about the school and what changes they wanted. Then she recruited members of her family to repaint the school's front door and the most decrepit classrooms. "When school opened, students and staff members immediately saw that things were going to be different, if only symbolically. Perhaps even more important, staff members received a subtle challenge to make a contribution themselves" (Kaufer and Leader, 1987b, p. 3).

When Iacocca became president of Chrysler, one of his first steps was to announce that he was reducing his salary from $360,000 to $1 a year. "I did it for good, cold pragmatic reasons. I wanted our employees and our suppliers to be thinking: 'I can follow a guy who sets that kind of example'" (Iacocca and Novak, 1984, pp. 229–230).

3. *Symbolic Leaders Frame Experience:* In a world of uncertainty and ambiguity, a key function of symbolic leadership is plausible interpretations of experience. When Martin Luther King, Jr., spoke at the March on Washington in 1963, the opening line of his "I Have a Dream" speech was, "I am happy to join with you today in what will go down in history as the greatest demonstration for freedom in the history of our nation." He could have interpreted the event in a number of other ways: "We are here because progress has been slow, but we are not ready to quit"; "We are here because nothing else has worked"; "We are here because it's summer and a good day to be outside." Each version is technically as accurate as the next, but accuracy is not the issue. King's assertion was bold and inspiring; it told the audience that they were making history together.

4. *Symbolic Leaders Communicate a Vision:* One powerful way in which a leader interprets experience is by distilling and disseminating a vision—a persuasive and hopeful image of the future. Vision is particularly important in a time of crisis and uncertainty. When people are in pain, when they are confused and uncertain, or when they feel despair and hopelessness, they desperately seek meaning and hope.

Where does such vision come from? One view is that leaders create a vision and then persuade others to accept it (Bass, 1985; Bennis and Nanus, 1985). An alternative view is that leaders discover and articulate a vision that is already there in an unexpressed form (Cleveland, 1985). Kouzes and Posner (1987) put it well: "Corporate leaders know very well that what seeds the vision are those imperfectly formed images in the marketing department about what the customers really wanted and those inarticulate mumblings from the manufacturing folks about the poor product quality. . . . The best leaders are the best followers. They pay attention to those weak signals and quickly respond to changes in the corporate course" (p. 114).

Leadership is a two-way street, and no amount of charisma or rhetorical skill can sell a vision that reflects only the leader's values and needs. But leaders still play a critical role. They bring a unique, personal blend of poetry, passion, conviction, and courage to articulating a vision. They distill and shape the direction to be pursued. Most important, they choose which stories to tell to communicate the vision.

5. *Symbolic Leaders Tell Stories:* Symbolic leaders often embed their vision in a story about "us" and about "our" past, present, and future. Us could be the Sorbonne, Chrysler, or any other audience a leader hopes to reach. The past is usually a golden one, a time of noble purposes, and great deeds. The present is a time of trouble, challenge, or crisis—a critical moment to make fateful choices. The future is the dream: a vision of hope linked directly to greatness in the past.

This is just the kind of story that helped Ronald Reagan become president of the United States. Reagan's golden past was the frontier, a place of rugged, sturdy, self-reliant men and women who built a great nation and took care of themselves and their neighbors without the intervention of a monstrous national government. It was an America of small towns and volunteer fire departments. America had fallen into crisis, said Reagan, because "the liberals" had created a federal government that was levying oppressive taxes and eroding freedom through regulation and bureaucracy. Reagan offered a vision: a return to American greatness by "getting government off the backs of the American people" and restoring traditional American values of freedom and self-reliance. It got Reagan elected and worked again twenty years later in the election of a Reagan acolyte, George W. Bush.

The success of such stories is only partly related to their historical validity or empirical support. The central question is whether they are credible and persuasive to their audiences. A story, even a flawed story, will work if it taps persuasively into the experience, values, and aspirations of listeners. This reflects both the power and the danger of symbolic leadership. In the hands of a Gandhi or a King, the constructive power of stories is immense. Told by a Hitler, their destructive power is almost incalculable.

6. *Symbolic Leaders Respect and Use History:* Wise leaders attend to history and link their initiatives to the values, stories, and heroes of the past. Even as she unleashed massive changes at HP, Fiorina publicly told Bill and Dave stories and insisted on her fidelity to the *HP Way*.

SUMMARY

Though leadership is universally accepted as a cure for all organizational ills, it is also widely misunderstood. Many fail to recognize its relational and contextual nature and its distinction from power and position. Inadequate ideas about leadership produce oversimplified advice to managers. We need to *reframe* leadership to move beyond the impasse created by oversimplified models. Each of the four frames highlights significant possibilities for leadership, but each is incomplete in capturing a holistic picture of the work.

—⁓⁓—

Lee G. Bolman is the Marion Bloch Missouri Chair in Leadership at the University of Missouri-Kansas City and author of several best-selling books on leadership and organizations. For more information visit www.leebolman.com.

—⁓⁓—

Terrence E. Deal is professor emeritus at the Rossier School of Education at the University of Southern California and author of multiple, award-winning books on leadership, culture, and organizations.

CHAPTER FIVE

When Leadership Is an Organizational Trait

James O'Toole

I ncreasingly, the identities of corporations are mere reflections of the personalities of their leaders. Today, for example, a business magazine won't run a cover story about Ford Motor Company; instead, it will feature the company's CEO in a full-color spread. Indeed, recent research shows that the perceived image of a high-profile chief executive brings a premium to a company's stock. Investors thus join journalists in the personification of corporations, focusing on the characters, biographies, and alleged charisma of CEOs. As a result, American business organizations are portrayed as shadows of the "Great Men" who sit in the chief executive's chair. In the most extreme case, for all intents and purposes Warren Buffett *is* the Berkshire Hathaway corporation.

Academic theory follows practice. Over the last decade, the parsing of leadership styles has become *de rigueur* in American business schools, the subject of practical (and arcane) professorial research, as well as stacks of graduate dissertations. In continuing education seminars, in MBA classes, even at the undergraduate level, professors now teach students each to adopt the "right leadership style" for themselves—using "360 degree feedback" to make them aware of how they are perceived by others and to learn how to manage those perceptions. For those severely leadership-impaired, there is always that growth industry called executive coaching.

This focus on personality is peculiarly American, an outward manifestation perhaps of our collective unconscious in which the image of George Washington astride his powerful white steed is indelibly etched. Europeans have resisted such personification of leadership in recent times. Indeed after 1945, thanks to the likes of Hitler, Lenin, Stalin, Franco, and Mussolini, Europeans were more than happy to concede the whole field of leadership studies to Americans. If you don't count the scads of French books about Charles De Gaulle, Americans have owned leadership studies for most of the second half of the last century. During that time, we applied our theories not only to political leaders but to leaders of business corporations.

And, of course, we got it wrong. "We" meaning those of us in American business, academia, consulting, and journalism who discussed, studied, and wrote about leadership solely as an *individual* trait. While this obsession on a single personality is occasionally appropriate—particularly when the founding entrepreneur is still running a company—evidence offered here indicates that this perspective skews analysis away from organizational factors that are the more important drivers of performance. My colleagues and I came to this conclusion by accident. In early 1999, we began a research project on strategic leadership in conjunction with the World Economic Forum. For the previous decade, leadership sessions had been a good draw at the Forum's annual Davos conclave, but Forum members had grown tired of the thin gruel of CEO war stories, anecdotes, and homilies. We were charged with putting beef on the Davos leadership menu. We formed a research team to create a data base of hard information about the soft subject of leadership.

Working with Forum member corporations, we began our efforts with traditional premises about leaders—but were surprised to discover that the relative performance of large corporations could not be explained *adequately* by measures of the individuals who head them. We discovered that indeed most of the large global companies we studied operate under a traditional model of strong individual top leadership, and that the quality of that leadership bears on the overall performance of those companies. But we also noticed some companies we studied—and some business units within others—are characterized by a different leadership. Instead of leadership being a solo act—an aria sung by the CEO—it is a shared responsibility more like a chorus of diverse voices singing in unison.

Significantly, this characteristic is more than "cascading" leadership in which a strong leader at the top empowers others down the line. *Many of the key tasks and responsibilities of leadership are actually institutionalized in the systems, practices, and cultures of the organization.* What we observed is behavior that is not dependent on the personality or continuing support of whoever is the leader of the organization at any given time. In this different form of leadership—and without the presence of a high-profile leader or "superior" goading or exhorting them on—we observed that people at all levels in the organization:

- Act more like owners and entrepreneurs than employees or hired hands.
- Take the initiative to solve problems and act with a sense of urgency.
- Willingly accept accountability for meeting commitments and for living the values of the organization.
- Share a common philosophy and language of leadership that paradoxically includes tolerance for contrary views and a willingness to experiment.
- Create, maintain, and adhere to systems and procedures designed to measure and reward these distributed leadership behaviors.

Obviously, we did not invent this model of leadership nor do we believe that it is new. Doubtless, it has been around a long time and we, like others, missed it because we were blinded by the powerful light emanating from high-profile leaders. Thus we are not advocating a newly discovered "best way to lead." Instead, we call attention to a previously unnoticed—but equally viable—alternative to the traditional leadership model. Among other things, this discovery explains persistent contradictions to beliefs about leadership as solely an individual trait.

Why, for example, do some companies continually demonstrate the capacity to innovate, renew strategies and products, and outperform competition in their industries over the tenures of several, very different chief executives? Intel, for instance, has been a rip-roaring success under the leadership of Gordon Moore, Andrew Grove, and Craig Barrett. Why do some CEOs succeed in one organization only to turn in so-so performances in another? Consider George Fisher, a star at Motorola but less effective at Kodak. Conversely, why is it that some companies headed by singularly unimpressive CEOs rack up good performance records? Finally, why is it that academics are unable to quantify the relationship between CEO style on one hand and organizational performance on the other? In fact, they have found no objective correlation between those factors.

Moreover, history shows that businesses dependent on a single leader run a considerable risk. If that individual retires, leaves, or dies in office, the organization may well lose its capacity to succeed— witness the performance of General Motors after Alfred Sloan, ITT after Harold Geneen, Polaroid after Edwin Land, and Coca-Cola after Roberto Goizueta. Frequently, organizations learn the hard way that no one individual can save a company—and no individual, no matter how gifted, can be right all the time. As one CEO said, "None of us is as smart as all of us." Since leadership is, by definition, doing things through and with the efforts of others, it is obvious that there is little that a business leader, acting alone, can do to affect company performance (other than "look good" to investors).

In light of this, it should have been no surprise when our research revealed that *leadership is an institutional capacity, not solely an individual trait*, in many successful companies. In fact, many corporations whose names perennially appear on "most respected" lists have the highest institutionalized leadership capacities. Like individual IQs, these companies seemed to have collective LQs—leadership quotients—that can be measured, compared, and bolstered through direct efforts. Hence, we are now able to explain why companies like Intel, ABB, GE, BP, Ford, Nestlé, and Motorola continue to renew themselves year after year and over the tenures of different leaders. They have made conscious efforts to build their overall organizational leadership capacities. Instead of asking "What qualities do we need to develop in our leader?" these companies ask "What qualities do we need to develop in our organization?"

This kind of organizational leadership model has an additional plus. It allows companies to bypass the egos that are fairly common in executive suites and focus on identifying business-related activities as the source of ongoing leadership development. They stress improving the ability of leaders collectively to do their central tasks, rather than on trying to fix individuals. Again, it is not that individual leadership behaviors are unimportant, but that in some cases, it may be more effective to treat them as secondary to organizational issues. It is far easier for leaders to learn to do things differently in terms of business processes than it is for them to change who they are. In our experience, individual leaders often see more clearly (and with less threat) how and why they need to change when the reasons are business-related.

USING LEADERSHIP DATA AS AN OBJECTIVE FOCUS FOR CHANGE

In effect, our research uncovered an alternative model not only of leadership but of organizational change. By surveying the behavior of over three thousand leaders at all hierarchical levels and buttressing these observations with hundreds of interviews, we are creating an objective data bank about alternative ways leaders bring about strategic and organizational change. This data allowed our research team to pinpoint specific business systems and processes that leaders use as levers to bring about significant shifts in organizational behavior and improvements in business performance.

For example, at one large global high-tech company we surveyed leaders at five different levels to collect data on sixty items related to twelve categories of systems that leaders use to affect behavior:

- *Vision and Strategy:* Extent to which corporate strategy is reflected in goals and behaviors at all levels
- *Goal-Setting and Planning:* Extent to which challenging goals are used to drive performance
- *Capital Allocation:* Extent to which capital allocation decisions are objective and systematic
- *Group Measurement:* Extent to which actual performance is measured against established goals
- *Risk Management:* Extent to which the company measures and mitigates risk
- *Recruiting:* Extent to which the company taps the best talent available
- *Professional Development:* Extent to which employees are challenged and developed
- *Performance Appraisal:* Extent to which individual appraisals are used to improve performance
- *Compensation:* Extent to which financial incentives are used to drive desired behaviors

- *Organizational Structure:* Extent to which decision-making authority is delegated to lower levels
- *Communications:* Extent to which management communicates the big picture
- *Knowledge Transfer:* Extent to which necessary information is gathered, organized, and disseminated

In parallel interviews, we discovered that there were competing theories about why this company was not as profitable as its competitors. When we analyzed the survey data and fed the results data back to the top management team, they were able to compare the effectiveness of their systems to those of other companies. The data was unequivocal, and team members who had been in denial about some of the results—and divided about what was causing the rest—were then able to come to grips with their organizational problems and create an agenda for repairing the broken systems. They were also able, for example, to identify a "concrete layer" in their hierarchy where transmission of messages from top leadership was getting stuck on the way down the line.

The executives then began a change process by feeding the data back to the next two levels of the organization, building consensus about the roles and responsibilities of each level, clearly identifying what needed to be done and by whom. In the process, they asked us to prepare cases of how other companies dealt with similar problems. They discussed these in a series of four workshops over a two-month period, building a common language and approach to leadership. In sum, they were able to consciously raise their organizational LQ by addressing the systems that had the greatest impact on performance. The bottom line is that, by using those systemic levers, the executives became more effective change agents and leaders than they had been—even after having worked with organizational development experts in the past to alter their individual leadership styles.

BUILDING ORGANIZATIONAL COHERENCE AND AGILITY

In the highest-LQ organizations studied, leaders at all levels use ordinary systems like those involving goal setting, communications, capital allocations, and recruiting in a conscious way to create two prime attributes of long-term organizational success: coherence and agility. Coherence means that common behaviors are found throughout the organization and that they are directed toward the achievement of shared goals. Agility is the institutionalized ability to detect and cope successfully with changes in the external environment, especially when such changes are difficult to anticipate. Until recently, scholars had posited that companies with high levels of coherence were "built to last," and that the task of leadership was to get the right fit or alignment among key institutional systems and processes. We discovered that not all institutional coherence is good. For instance, bureaucratic alignment anchored in the habits of the past is deadly. Similarly, although agility has often been identified with corporate success, too much leads to chaos and wasting resources on duplicate efforts.

We found that organizations need to be coherent and agile at the same time. In fact, not only were the operating systems of high-LQ companies directed to those two ends, leaders viewed their prime task as creating both attributes. The highest-performing companies in our study actually align around agility: that is, their leaders rigorously measure and reward the seemingly loose entrepreneurial behaviors of market-responsiveness and risk taking. In essence, they create organizational coherence around shared business objectives while simultaneously encouraging the agility to meet discontinuous threats and opportunities.

A DISTINCTION WITH CONSEQUENCES

Does it make a real difference whether leadership is treated as an institutional capacity or individual trait? Yes. Fundamental premises drive behavior, and when leadership is thought of as an organizational trait there are profound organizational consequences upon which almost everything follows. For example, because ABB views leadership organizationally, its highly respected former CEO, Percy Barnevik, could retire at age fifty-four in full confidence that the company had the capacity to carry on successfully without him. Interestingly, this freed Barnevik to take on responsibilities for the Swedish Wallenberg family, ABB's largest shareholders, and enabled that company to make needed structural changes that had been closely identified with Barnevik's talents and tenure. Because Intel sees leadership as an organizational trait, the company did not miss a beat when CEO Andy Grove retired.

In fact, it was positioned to move on to a higher level with the capacity to take on new strategic challenges. How often is it that a company not only doesn't go into the tank when a respected CEO like Grove steps down, but actually renews itself with a fresh line of products and promising new areas of business? The successful hand-offs at ABB and Intel are not simply good succession planning. Rather, neither company is dependent on any one, two, or even half-dozen key leaders for its success. Observers will note that neither company talks much about individuals but instead focuses on building broad human capacity to manage the systems at the heart of their respective successes. That is what we found at our high-LQ companies.

THE ROLE OF ENABLING SYSTEMS

There is something palpably different about a company that emphasizes building enabling systems versus one that depends on a single personality at the top. Since the contributions of every leader are seen as important, there is concerted effort to define and measure leadership behavior down the line, place parallel emphasis on accountability at all levels for how the enabling systems are used, and make certain that the systems are used. But what do we mean by enabling systems? Here are four examples and how the high-LQ companies use them to institutionalize leadership:

Goal Setting and Planning. Some companies have religiously institutionalized the process of setting challenging goals to drive performance. Although great individual leaders can challenge and stretch followers, institutions can do the same through disciplined organizational processes. In several companies studied, there were formal mechanisms that ensured that leaders at all levels and at all times have a clear sense of how the organization is doing relative to its goals. Moreover, individual leaders are rewarded (and, yes, punished) based on rigorous measurement of performance against goals. While most organizations pay lip service to setting stretch goals and measuring things that are most important to the success of their business, we found few actually do it and stick with it, no ifs, ands, or buts—especially in the personality-based organizations where negative consequences for poor performers either didn't happen or were seen as a sign of not being the boss's favorites. In the most structured and disciplined of the processes observed, there is a high degree of involvement in goal setting, and highly participative processes of establishing performance metrics, thus ensuring an overall climate of organizational fairness—a climate previously associated only with the actions of an unusually trustworthy leader.

Risk Management. Perhaps the most surprising finding was the importance of risk management systems in creating leadership down the line. In some companies, this translated into formal processes that make certain that everyone understands the size and likelihood of the key risks facing the business. With this knowledge, leaders at all levels are able to take prudent risks, and they are enculturated to (and rewarded for) avoiding negative financial surprises. Because processes (not personalities) are paramount, capital allocation is seen as an objective process of pursuing business objectives, not pursuit of personal agendas. People are confident that objectively defensible projects will be funded and that the system behaves fairly when making capital allocation decisions.

Communications. There is a striking consensus among scholars and practitioners about the centrality of communications to the role of the leader. Significantly, we found examples of companies where this important task was viewed as the responsibility of every leader at every level. All leaders were also evaluated on how well they performed this task. In companies where leadership is institutionalized, leaders at all levels spend a significant amount of time communicating the big picture—the vision, strategy, mission, and purpose of the organization. At the operating level, they provide others ready access to information needed to do their work. We also found that those with the most relevant information have the greatest impact on decisions.

Recruiting. All companies recruit. But in high-LQ companies, recruiting is a prime task not of the HR department but of operating managers at all levels (including the CEO). These companies explicitly define selection criteria for new recruits that are closely related to overall corporate goals. Some, like sports teams, even recruit "the best talent available regardless of position" instead of looking to fill specific roles. Moreover, they include leadership criteria in their recruitment profiles, like interest in developing subordinates or ability to see leaders as teachers rather than bosses.

DIFFERENT IN COUNTLESS WAYS

What is striking from this study is that none of the companies stresses all twelve of the systems identified. Instead, each focuses on managing a few tightly. For example, one high-performing corporation keeps tight control of vision and communications, but leaves it to business units to make decisions relative to structure, recruitment, planning, and the rest. Significantly, we found no pattern in the choice of systems stressed, and no correlation between performance and systems emphasized. What seems important is a clear focus on any two or three key systems—the particular choices driven by the strategy, industry, or challenge faced by the company.

HIGH LQ: THE MORAL EQUIVALENT OF INDIVIDUAL LEADERSHIP

While having a Larry Ellison, Jack Welch, or Percy Barnevik at the helm is obviously desirable—and companies who have such talented leaders are indeed fortunate—such good fortune is rare. Companies with a high LQ, however, get many of the same benefits even if the top individual in the executive suite is not a superstar performer. More importantly, strong systems can make up for the morale-sapping effects of erratic, indecisive, weak, or egotistic leadership. It is here that students of organizational theory will recognize the link to what Max Weber was struggling with over a hundred years ago when he advocated bureaucracy over the alternative of his day: personality-driven, individual leadership. Weber may have solved the problems of capricious and politicized management with his solution of bureaucracy, but he introduced new ones in the immobility and rigidity that came to characterize not only his beloved Prussian civil service but, in time, the likes of General Motors, IBM, and AT&T. Now, after a century of struggling to choose between the Charybdis of arbitrary leadership and the Scylla of bureaucracy, high-LQ companies have a path to resolve the Weberian dilemma. These companies are not only coherent and agile, they are also no longer burdened with the vicissitudes of arbitrary individual leaders.

LESSONS FOR THE NEXT GENERATION OF LEADERS

A message that emerges loud and clear from our study is that CEOs don't need to know all the answers, and they don't have to do all the work of leadership by themselves. In fact, CEOs can create the systems under which others are encouraged to do many of the things that typically end up on the desk of a do-it-all top leader. We believe that it is easier to motivate and reward leaders down the line to take up the mantle of leadership than for a single CEO to try and provide detailed direction to hundreds, even thousands, of managers.

Our message to young leaders is not that the personality-driven model of leadership is headed for extinction, nor do we believe that it should be. Rather, we believe that more CEOs of large companies may be drawn to the organizational model of leadership for the simple reason that it is potentially more productive—and satisfying—to become a leader of leaders than risk trying to look like George Washington on a white horse. The bad news for those who like a *People* magazine approach to business journalism is there may be fewer "cover boy" CEO leaders in coming decades. The good news is that there may also be much more effective corporate leadership. As we have learned, leadership need not be just a solo act.

———

James O'Toole is research professor in the Center for Effective Organizations at the University of Southern California Graduate School of Business. He has authored fifteen books on corporate culture, ethics, and leadership. For more information see www.jamesotoole.com.

PART TWO

Becoming a Leader, Preparing for the Opportunities

How does one prepare for leadership? Effective leadership takes experience, reflection, practice, and wisdom acquired over time and circumstance. Learning to lead is a lifelong process. Human diversity, the infinite variety of leadership opportunities, and the social nature of leadership make it impossible to define any one learning path that guarantees the full range of competencies and understandings leaders need. Individual leaders bring their own skills, personalities, capacities, and limitations that add unique twists and turns to the learning journey. What prepares us best to seize the opportunity and lead? In the face of all this ambiguity, where do we begin?

An important first step is to accept that preparation for leadership is developmental. Like good wine, leadership skills and savvy mature over time and under appropriate conditions. Leaders expand their capacities through experiences and self-reflection—opportunities to consolidate strengths and identify areas for development. The accumulated wisdom enriches a leader's understanding of self, others, and the larger world. Persistence and a commitment to ongoing learning encourage leaders to embrace a holistic approach to readying themselves and to fully appreciate everyday actions and choices as precious opportunities to practice basic skills and develop leadership discipline. More important, a developmental perspective encourages the patience and self-forgiveness essential to the learning process. The authors in Part Two of this volume provide suggestions and strategies for individuals on the road to leadership success.

In Chapter Six, "The Seven Ages of the Leader," leadership sage Warren G. Bennis reminds us that Shakespeare got it right about life—and about leadership education. We all have a lifetime to mature fully into our role, and wisdom comes from embracing tasks and opportunities at different life stages. Leaders across the career-span take heed, suggests Bennis. Untested leaders—find a mentor and support system. Practicing neophytes—learn about the public face of leadership. Developing leaders and those rapidly rising to the top—respect the human side of enterprise. Acknowledged leaders—remember the full power and responsibility of the leadership mantle. Seasoned veterans—rein in your ego, share what you have learned, and recapture childlike joy in your efforts.

Knowing what to expect and how to learn from key experiences is important. Understanding the talents that you bring and that will sustain you in your leadership travels is equally vital. Required tasks that don't tap an individual's skills are drudgery; soul-renewing contributions that use the best of what an individual has to offer are a joy. In Chapter Seven, "The Traces of Talent," Marcus Buckingham and the late Donald O. Clifton provide strategies for leaders to reflect honestly on their true gifts. Monitoring one's spontaneous reactions, yearnings, areas of rapid learning, and satisfying choices reveals important clues, suggest the authors. High-level contributions require a clear sense of self and a good fit between the leader's talents and the demands of the situation.

Learning to lead is not about developing a textbook persona or fancy image. It is a process of understanding oneself—natural talents *and* flat sides—and knowing how to build a leadership approach that is consistent with one's character and abilities yet flexible enough to respond to the changing needs of the situation. In Chapter Eight, "Leadership Is Authenticity, Not Style," Harvard Business School professor and former head of Medtronic, Bill George, gives an honest account of what authenticity means for new and seasoned leaders. He talks openly about the pressures for performance, profits, and perfection that can challenge even the most values-centered leaders, and reminds all that effective leadership is really about service, caring, openness, empowering others, and contribution.

Authenticity is based in self-knowledge. It is also rooted in a strong sense of humility, hard work, personal courage, and realism. In Chapter Nine, "Level 5 Leadership: The Triumph of Humility and Fierce Resolve," Jim Collins draws on the extensive research that led to his best-selling book, *Good to Great: Why Some Companies Make the Leap . . . and Others Don't.* Collins confirms that strong top leadership is indeed essential for organizational greatness, but not the charismatic, flamboyant type celebrated in the popular business press or literature on heroic leadership. Great companies have leaders who, paradoxically, embrace personal humility and have strong professional will. Level 5 leaders take their companies to greatness with a simple set of leadership rules: know thyself, know the contribution you want to make, and get on with what you know you have to do.

The final three chapters in Part Two outline activities that build leadership discipline. They are the practices of the mind and heart that open leaders to creativity, innovation, and extraordinary contribution, and that prepare them for the challenges ahead. In Chapter Ten, "Thinking Gray and Free," Steven B. Sample, the successful, long-serving president of the University of Southern California, identifies two key requirements for leadership: intellectual independence and creativity. Sample believes that leaders can deepen their capacities for both with practice. He proposes two developmental activities for leaders: *thinking gray*—strategies to avoid natural inclinations for binary, right-wrong judgments in the face of complexity—and *thinking free*—ways to stretch individual and collective cognition beyond the tight constraints and fears that usually rule our thinking.

In Chapter Eleven, "Enhancing the Psycho-Spiritual Development of Leaders: Lessons from Leadership Journeys in Asia," Philip H. Mirvis and Karen Ayas illustrate a paradox in great leadership. Leadership is deeply personal, rooted in the mind and heart of the leader. At the same time, business leaders are most powerful when they acknowledge their shared humanity, connect strongly to others, and work to elevate the quality of life for their customers and communities. Mirvis and Ayas draw on their experiences with leading *learning journeys* for global leaders. They show how deep connections to indigenous people and persons in need, encounters with nature, opportunities for community service, and reflection on these experiences develop essential leadership understandings and practices.

Finally, in Chapter Twelve, Robert E. Quinn teaches leaders how to stay anchored in their convictions, true to core values, centered on the larger purpose of their contribution, and open to learning in "Moments of Greatness: Entering the Fundamental State of Leadership." Quinn's research found that, ironically, leaders who are most true to their authentic selves are also in a state markedly different from their usual state of being when they lead. These individuals enter what Quinn calls a *fundamental state of leadership,* and they attract others to their cause and purpose through a passionate focus on results, internal drive, commitment to others, and deep openness to information and the external world. Quinn provides simple questions individuals can use to get into the fundamental state of leadership and asserts that regular use of these questions prepares leaders for the opportunities ahead.

CHAPTER SIX

The Seven Ages of the Leader

Warren G. Bennis

My initial plunge into leadership came during World War II. I was a lieutenant in the infantry, 19 years old, and scared out of my wits. My orders were to assume command of a platoon on the front lines in Belgium. I arrived in the middle of the night, when most of the men were asleep. The platoon had taken up residence in a bombed out shell of a house. I was led into the kitchen by the platoon's runner, and he offered me a bench to sleep on. Instead, I put my sleeping bag on the floor, next to the rest of the men. Not that I slept. I lay awake all night, listening to the bombs explode. I was as green as can be and knew little about command—or the world, for that matter. When the others in the house began to stir, I heard one sergeant ask another, "Who's that?" "That's our new platoon leader," the man answered. And the sergeant said, "Good. We can use him."

Without realizing it, without having any idea what was the right thing to do, I had made a good first move. My entry had been low-key. I hadn't come in with my new commission blazing. In fact, I pretended to go to sleep on the floor. As a result, without drawing attention to myself, I learned something important about the men

I would be leading. I learned that they needed me—or, at least, they needed the person they would subsequently teach me to be. And teach me they did. Over the next few weeks in Belgium, my men, who had already seen combat, kept me alive. They also taught me how to lead, often by example. The sergeant who had greeted my arrival with approval became my lifeline, quite literally, teaching me such essential skills as how to ride through a war zone without getting blown up.

While few business leaders need worry about being blown up, my experience in Belgium was in many ways typical of first leadership experiences anywhere. I was coming into an existing organization where emotions ran high, relationships had been established, and the members of the organization harbored expectations of me that I was not yet fully aware of. My new followers were watching me, to see if and how I would measure up. Every new leader faces the misgivings, misperceptions, and the personal needs and agendas of those who are to be led. To underestimate the importance of your first moves is to invite disaster. The critical entry is one of a number of passages—each of which has an element of personal crisis—that every leader must go through at some point in the course of a career. Business school doesn't prepare you for these crises, and they can be utterly wrenching. But they offer powerful lessons as well.

Shakespeare, who seems to have learned more every time I read him, spoke of the seven ages of man. A leader's life has seven ages as well, and, in many ways, they parallel those Shakespeare describes in *As You Like It:* to paraphrase, infant, schoolboy, lover, soldier, general, statesman, and sage. One way to learn about leadership is to look at each of these developmental stages and consider the issues and crises that are typical.

I can't offer advice on how to avoid these crises because many are inevitable. Nor would I necessarily recommend that you avoid them, since dealing with the challenges of each stage prepares you for the next. But knowing what to expect can help the leader survive and, with luck, come through stronger and more confident. And so first to the leader on the verge—Shakespeare's infant, "mewling . . . in the nurse's arms."

THE INFANT EXECUTIVE

For the young man or woman on the brink of becoming a leader, the world that lies ahead is a mysterious, even frightening place. Few resort to mewling, but many wish they had the corporate equivalent of a nurse, someone to help them solve problems and ease the painful transition. Instead, the fortunate neophyte leader has a mentor, a concept that has its origins in Greek mythology. When Odysseus was about to go off to war, the goddess Athena created Mentor to watch over the hero's beloved son, Telemachus. The fact that Mentor had the attributes of both man and woman hints at the richness and complexity of the relationship, suggesting a deeper bond than that of teacher and student. In the real world, unfortunately, goddesses don't intervene and mentors seldom materialize on their own. While the popular view of mentors is that they seek out younger people to encourage and champion, in fact the reverse is more often true. The best mentors are usually recruited, and one mark of a future leader is the ability to identify, woo, and win the mentors who will change his or her life.

When Robert Thomas and I interviewed two generations of leaders for our book, *Geeks and Geezers,* we met a remarkable young real-estate and Internet entrepreneur, Michael Klein, who had recruited his first mentor when he was only four or five years old, as Robert and I wrote in our *Harvard Business Review* article, "Crucibles of Leadership" [see Chapter Thirty-Nine in this volume]. His guide was his grandfather, Max Klein, who was responsible for the paint-by-numbers craze that swept America in the 1950s and 1960s. The fad made Klein rich, but none of his children had the least interest in that business or any other. But little Michael did, and Max jumped at the chance to coach and counsel him, often in the course of long telephone conversations that continued until a few weeks before Max died. In effect, the older man served as a first-rate business school of one for his grandson, who became a multimillionaire while still in his teens.

It may feel strange to seek a mentor even before you have the job, but it's a good habit to develop early on. I was recruited as a mentor years ago while in the hospital for several weeks following a "coronary event." There, I had a remarkable nurse who seemed to anticipate my every need. We spent hours together, often talking late into the night. He told me of his ambition to become a doctor, although no one in his family in South Central Los Angeles had ever been to college. I was won over by his character and drive, as well as by the superb care he gave me. When he was ready to go to medical school, I did all I could to help, from putting him in touch with appropriate administrators to giving him a glowing recommendation. He had recruited me as skillfully as any executive headhunter and made me one of the first members of the team he needed to change his life. The message for the "infant executive"? Recruit a team to back you up; you may feel lonely in your first top job, but you won't be totally unsupported.

THE SCHOOLBOY, WITH SHINING FACE

The first leadership experience is an agonizing education. It's like parenting, in that nothing else in life fully prepares you to be responsible, to a greater or lesser degree, for other people's well-being. Worse, you have to learn how to do the job in public, subjected to unsettling scrutiny of your every word and act, a situation that's profoundly unnerving for all but that minority of people who truly crave the spotlight. Like it or not, as a new leader you are always onstage, and everything about you is fair game for comment, criticism, and interpretation (or misinterpretation). Your dress, spouse, table manners, diction, wit, friends, children, children's table manners—all will be inspected, dissected, and judged.

And nothing is more intense than the attention paid to your initial words and deeds, as any first-time presidential candidate can tell you. It's said of psychotherapy that the first ten minutes between doctor and patient are the most critical, and studies show that friendships formed by college students during orientation are the most enduring. Social psychologists have found that we base our judgments of people on extremely thin slices of behavior. We decide whether we are in sync or out of tune with another person in as little as two seconds.

So it is with leaders and organizations. Your first acts will win people over or they will turn people against you, sometimes permanently. And those initial acts may have a long-lasting effect on how the group performs. It is, therefore, almost always best for the novice to make a low-key entry. This buys you time to gather information and develop relationships wisely. It gives you an opportunity to learn the culture of the organization and benefit from the wisdom of those who are already there. A quiet entry allows the others in the group to demonstrate what they know. And it allows you to establish that you are open to the contributions of others. It shows them that you are a leader, not a dictator.

In retrospect, I realize that officer-candidate school had prepared me for my small triumph in that roofless house in Belgium. Even as the officers tried to cram all the survival skills we would need into four months of training, they told us again and again that the combat-seasoned men under our command would be our real teachers, at least at first. The same holds true in any organization. In the beginning, especially, your most talented, most seasoned, most decent followers will be the ones that keep you alive.

When Steve Sample became president of the University of Southern California in the early 1990s, he did a masterful job of easing in. He went to the campus incognito at least twice, and during one of those visits he attended a football game and spoke to faculty members and students who didn't know who he was. Those visits gave him a feel for the campus as it really was, not how the most assertive of his constituents wanted him to see it. And during his first six months, he did not make a single high-profile decision. He knew that the important things to be done could be deferred until the faculty, staff, and students were more comfortable with him and their relationships were more stable. Major changes in the first six months will inevitably be perceived as arbitrary, autocratic, and unfair, as much for their timing as for their content.

However, it is worth noting that, no matter what your first actions are, you can influence other people's image of you only to a limited extent. The people who will be working under your leadership will have formed an opinion about you by the time you walk into the office, even if they have never met you. They may love you, they may hate you, they may trust you or distrust you, but they've probably taken a stand, and their position may have very little to do with who you actually are. The leader often becomes a screen onto which followers project their own fantasies about power and relationships. To some degree, all leaders are created out of the needs, wants, fears, and longings of those who follow them. Events that predate your arrival will also shape followers' view of you. In an organization that's been through a crisis—several rounds of layoffs, say—people are liable to assume that you're there to clean house again and may respond with either open hostility or flattery in the hopes of keeping their jobs. Others may see you as their savior because of the bad leadership of your predecessor. Your first challenge is to try not to take your new followers' assessments too personally. The second—and far trickier—challenge is to embrace the fact that certain elements of their assessments may be accurate, even if they put you in an unflattering light.

THE LOVER, WITH A WOEFUL BALLAD

Shakespeare described man in his third age "sighing like furnace," something many leaders find themselves doing as they struggle with the tsunami of problems every organization presents. For the leader who has come up through the ranks, one of the toughest is how to relate to former peers who now report to you.

Shakespeare painted a compelling portrait of the problem in *Henry IV, Part II*. Before Prince Hal becomes Henry V, his relationship with the aging rogue Falstaff is that of student and fellow hell-raiser. For all Falstaff's excesses, he is often Hal's wise teacher, helping the future king see beyond the cloistered, narrow education traditionally afforded a prince to glimpse what his future subjects feel, think, and need. But when it comes time for Hal to assume his royal responsibilities, he rejects Falstaff, despite their having shared a sea of ale and the sound of "the chimes at midnight." Henry doesn't invite Falstaff to his coronation, and he pointedly tells the ribald knight, "I know thee not, old man."

Today's leaders would instantly recognize the young king's predicament. It's difficult to set boundaries and fine-tune your working relationships with former cronies. Most organizations, with the exception of the military, maintain the fiction that they are at least semi-democracies, however autocratic they are in fact. As a modern leader, you don't have the option of telling the person with whom you once shared a pod and lunchtime confidences that you know her not. But relationships inevitably change when a person is promoted from within the ranks. You may no longer be able to speak openly as you once did, and your friends may feel awkward around you or resent you. They may perceive you as lording your position over them when you're just behaving as a leader should.

I know of a young executive, let's call her Marjorie, who was recently promoted from middle management to head of the marketing department at a pharmaceutical company. One of three internal candidates for the job, she was close friends with the other two. Marjorie had already distinguished herself within the company, so it was no surprise that she got the promotion, even though she was the youngest and least experienced of the three. But the transition was much more difficult than she had anticipated. Her friends were envious. She would sometimes find herself in the awkward situation of attending an executive meeting at which one of her friends was criticized and then going straight to lunch with her. The new executive missed being able to share what she knew with her friends, and she missed their support. Her fellow executives had a more authoritarian style than she did, and some even advised her to drop her old friends, which she had no intention of doing. Her compromise was to try to divide her time between her new peers and her old. The transition was still hard, but she made a good early move: she had frank conversations with her friends, during which she asked them how they were feeling and assured them their friendships were important to her and would continue.

However tough it was for Marjorie, she had the advantage of knowing the organization and its players. The challenge for the newcomer is knowing who to listen to and who to trust. Leaders new to an organization are swamped with claims on their time and attention. Often, the person who makes the most noise is the neediest person in the group and the one you have to be most wary of, a lesson I learned more than 50 years ago from the renowned psychiatrist Wilfred Bion. At the time, Bion was doing pioneering work in the new practice of group psychotherapy. He warned his students: focusing your attention on the most clamorous of your followers will not only anger and alienate the healthier among them. It will distract you from working with the entire group on what actually matters, accomplishing a common mission.

Knowing *what* to pay attention to is just as important and just as difficult. In their efforts to effect change, leaders coming into new organizations are often thwarted by an unconscious conspiracy to preserve the status quo. Problem after problem will be dumped in your lap—plenty of new ones and a bulging archive of issues left unresolved by previous administrations—and responding to them all ensures that you will never have time to pursue your own agenda. When I arrived at the University of Cincinnati as president I was totally unprepared for the volume of issues that found their way to my desk, starting with the 150 pieces of mail I typically had to respond to each day. The cumulative effect of handling each of these small matters was to keep me from addressing what was truly important: articulating a vision for the university and persuading the rest of the community to embrace it as their own. It is at this stage that an inability to delegate effectively can be disastrous.

Newcomer or not, almost all leaders find themselves at some point in the position of having to ask others to leave the organization—firing them, to put it bluntly. This is always a painful task, if only because it usually devastates the person being let go and because the timing is never opportune. Facing you across the desk always seems to be the employee who's just delivered triplets or bought an expensive house. There's little available to guide leaders on how to do this awful business in a humane way; only remember that you have people's emotional lives in your hands in such circumstances as surely as any surgeon or lover does.

THE BEARDED SOLDIER

Over time, leaders grow comfortable with the role. This comfort brings confidence and conviction, but it also can snap the connection between leader and followers. Two things can happen as a result: leaders may forget the true impact of their words and actions, and they may assume that what they are hearing from followers is what needs to be heard.

While the first words and actions of leaders are the most closely attended to, the scrutiny never really ends. Followers continue to pay close attention to even the most offhand remark, and the more effective the leader is the more careful he or she must be, because followers may implement an idea that was little more than a passing thought. Forget this and you may find yourself in some less dramatic version of the situation King Henry II did when he muttered, of Thomas à Becket, "Will no one rid me of this meddlesome priest?" and four of his nobles promptly went out and murdered the cleric. Many modern-day Henrys have mused along the lines of, "We should be looking at our technology strategy," only to be confronted a few months later with thick PowerPoint presentations and a hefty consulting bill.

Followers don't tell leaders everything. I know of an executive I'll call Christine who had a close working relationship with the rest of her group. The department hummed along productively until the day one of her top performers, Joseph, showed up at her door, looking uncomfortable. He told her he'd been offered a job at another company and was planning to take it. The timing was terrible; the group was headed toward a major product launch. And Christine was stunned, because she and Joseph were friends and he had never expressed dissatisfaction with his position or the company. Why hadn't he told her he wanted a new opportunity? She would have created a job especially for him, and she told him as much. Unfortunately, it was too late. The fact is, however close Christine and Joseph were, she was still in charge, and few employees tell their bosses when they've talked to a headhunter. And because Christine and Joseph liked each other and had fun working together, she'd assumed he was satisfied.

A second challenge for leaders in their ascendancy is to nurture those people whose stars may shine as brightly as—or even brighter than—the leaders' own. In many ways, this is the real test of character for a leader. Many people cannot resist using a leadership position to thwart competition. I heard recently about an executive who had been well liked by his bosses and peers until he was promoted to head a division. Then those under him began to grumble about his management style, and it wasn't just sour grapes. His latest promotion had been a stretch, and he may have felt, for the first time in his career, vulnerable. Shortly thereafter, his employees began to notice that he was taking credit for their ideas and was badmouthing some of them behind their backs. When confronted about his behavior, he seemed genuinely surprised and protested that he was doing no such thing. Perhaps he was unconsciously trying to sabotage those under him to prop himself up. But those who reported to him began to leave, one by one. After a year, his reputation was such that nobody wanted to work with him, and he was asked to leave.

In contrast, authentic leaders are generous. They're human and may experience the occasional pang at watching someone accomplish something they cannot. But they are always willing—even anxious—to hire people who are better than they are, in part because they know that highly talented underlings can help them shine. Many of the greatest leaders of our times, including the Manhattan Project's Robert Oppenheimer, Xerox PARC's Bob Taylor, and even Walt Disney, had healthy enough egos to surround themselves with people who had the potential to steal their jobs.

THE GENERAL, FULL OF WISE SAWS

One of the greatest challenges a leader faces at the height of his or her career is not simply allowing people to speak the truth but actually being able to hear it. Once again, Shakespeare proves instructive. In *Julius Caesar,* that brilliant study of failed management, Caesar goes to the forum on the ides of March apparently unaware that he will die there. How could he not have known that something dreadful was going to happen on that inauspicious day? The soothsayer warns him to "beware the ides of March." There are signs of impending evil that any superstitious Roman would have been able to read, including an owl hooting during the day and a lion running through the streets. And then there is the awful dream that makes Calpurnia, Caesar's loving wife, beg him to stay home. She dreams that his statue gushed blood like a fountain with a hundred spouts. Shouldn't that have been clear enough for a military genius used to amassing and evaluating intelligence? If not, consider that Artemidorus, a teacher in Rome, actually writes down the names of the conspirators and tries three times to thrust the note of alarm into Caesar's hand, the last time seconds before Brutus and the gang fall upon him.

Caesar's deafness is caused as much by arrogance as anything else, and he is hardly the only leader to be so afflicted. Like many CEOs and other leaders, movie mogul Darryl F. Zanuck was notorious for his unwillingness to hear unpleasant truths. He was said to bark, "Don't say yes until I finish talking!" which no doubt stifled many a difference of opinion. A more current example can be seen in Howell Raines, the deposed executive editor of the *New York Times.* Among the many ways he blocked the flow of information upward was to limit the pool of people he championed and, thus, the number of people he listened to. Raines was notorious for having a small A-list of stars and a large B-list made up of everyone else. Even if Raines's division of the staff had been fair, which it certainly was not in the case of now-disgraced reporter Jayson Blair, the two-tier system was unwise and ultimately a career ender for Raines. He had so alienated the vast majority of people in the newsroom who knew what Blair was up to that they didn't even bother to warn him of the train wreck ahead, and he refused to believe the few who did speak up. The attitude of Raines and his managing editor, Gerald Boyd, was that their way was the only way. When a distinguished reporter dared to point out an error Boyd had made, Boyd literally handed him a coin and told him to call the *Los Angeles Times* about a job. The reporter promptly did, quitting the *New York Times* for the West Coast paper.

But the episode most clearly recalls Caesar's situation in that Raines seemed genuinely surprised when he was forced out in the summer of 2003. He had no doubt read Ken Auletta's lengthy profile of him that ran in the *New Yorker* in 2002, showing that Raines was widely perceived as arrogant. And he should have been a good enough newsman to be able to tell the difference between acceptance and angry silence on the part of those who worked for him. Arrogance kept Raines from building the alliances and coalitions that every leader needs. When Blair's journalistic crimes and misdemeanors came to light, there weren't enough people on the A-list to save Raines's professional life. Authentic leaders, by contrast, don't have what people in the Middle East called "tired ears." Their egos are not so fragile that they are unable to bear the truth, however harsh—not because they are saints but because it is the surest way to succeed and survive.

I've mentioned the wisdom of avoiding major change in the early months in a new position. At this stage, the challenge is different, because leaders further along in their careers are frequently brought in with a specific mandate to bring about change, and their actions have a direct and immediate impact on an organization's long-term fortunes. Hesitation can be disastrous. However, you still need to understand the mood and motivations of the people already in the company before taking action.

I wish I'd understood that when I arrived at the University of Cincinnati in 1971 with a mandate to transform the university from a local institution into a state one—a goal that was by no means widely shared among the faculty or, for that matter, the citizens of Cincinnati. One longtime university board member had warned me to keep a low profile until I had a better grasp of the conservative community and the people in it were more comfortable with me. I chose to ignore his wise counsel, believing that broad exposure of the university and, by extension, myself would benefit my cause. As a result, I accepted an invitation to host a weekly television show. Worse, the title of the show was *Bennis!* The exclamation point still makes me cringe. I might have been perceived as an arrogant outsider come to save the provinces under any circumstances, but *Bennis!* guaranteed that I would be viewed that way. That perception (all but indelible, as early perceptions tend to be) made it harder to realize my vision for the university.

The corporate world is filled with stories of leaders who failed to achieve greatness because they failed to understand the context they were working in or get the support of their underlings. Look at Durk

Jager, who lasted less than a year and a half at Procter & Gamble. Critics accused him of trying to change the company too much, too fast. But what Jager couldn't do was sell his vision of a transformed P&G to its staff and other stakeholders. His very able successor, A. G. Lafley, seemed at first to back off from Jager's commitment to "stretch and speed" but in fact Lafley has been able to bring about change every bit as radical as any Jager spoke of, including going outside the company for new ideas, a reversal of P&G's traditional "invented here" philosophy. How did Lafley manage? "I didn't attack," he told *BusinessWeek*. "I avoided saying P&G people are bad. . . . I preserved the core of the culture and pulled people where I wanted to go. I enrolled them in change. I didn't tell them."

THE STATESMAN, WITH SPECTACLES ON NOSE

Shakespeare's sixth age covers the years in which a leader's power begins to wane. But far from being the buffoon suggested by Shakespeare's description of a "lean and slippered pantaloon," the leader in this stage is often hard at work preparing to pass on his or her wisdom in the interest of the organization. The leader may also be called upon to play important interim roles, bolstered by the knowledge and perception that come with age and experience and without the sometimes distracting ambition that characterizes an early career.

One of the gratifying roles that people in late career can play is the leadership equivalent of a pinch hitter. When *New York Times* publisher Arthur Sulzberger, Jr., needed someone to stop the bleeding at the newspaper after the Blair debacle, he invited Howell Raines's predecessor, Joseph Lelyveld, to serve as interim editor. The widely respected journalist was an ideal choice, one who was immediately able to apply a career's worth of experience to the newspaper's crisis and whose tenure was unsullied by any desire to keep the job for the long term.

Consider, too, the head of a government agency who had chosen to retire from his leadership position because he had accomplished all his goals and was tired of the politics associated with his job. When an overseas office needed an interim leader, he was willing to step into the job and postpone retirement. He was able to perform an even better job than a younger person might have, not only because he brought a lifetime's worth of knowledge and experience but also because he didn't have to waste time engaging in the political machinations often needed to advance a career.

THE SAGE, SECOND CHILDISHNESS

As I've pointed out, mentoring has tremendous value to a young executive. The value accrues to the mentor as well. Mentoring is one of the great joys of a mature career, the professional equivalent of having grandchildren. It is at this time that the drive to prepare the next generation for leadership becomes a palpable ache. I wrote earlier of my relationship with the young nurse who had ambitions to become a doctor. Clearly, the young man benefited from our relationship, but so did I. I learned about the true nature of mentoring, about its inevitable reciprocity and the fact that finding and cementing a relationship with a mentor is not a form of fawning but the initiation of a valuable relationship for both individuals.

When you mentor, you know that what you have achieved will not be lost, that you are leaving a professional legacy for future generations. Just as my nurse clearly stood to benefit from our relationship, entrepreneur Michael Klein was indebted to his grandfather, Max. But imagine the joy Max must have felt at being able to share the wisdom he acquired over a lifetime as a creative businessman. The reciprocal benefits of such bonds are profound, amounting to much more than warm feelings on both sides. Mentoring isn't a simple exchange of information. Neuroscientist Robert Sapolsky lived among wild baboons and found that alliances between old and young monkeys were an effective strategy for survival. The older males that affiliated with younger males lived longer, healthier lives than their unallied peers. Whether monkey or human, individuals in a mentoring relationship exchange invaluable, often subtle information. The elder partner stays plugged into an ever-changing world, while the younger partner can observe what does and doesn't work as the elder partner negotiates the tricky terrain of aging.

When we compared older and younger leaders for *Geeks and Geezers,* we found that the ruling quality of leaders, adaptive capacity, is what allows true leaders to make the nimble decisions that bring success. Adaptive capacity is also what allows some people to transcend the setbacks and losses that come with age and to reinvent themselves again and again. Shakespeare called the final age of man "second childishness." But for those fortunate enough to keep their health, and even for those not as fortunate, age today is neither end nor oblivion. Rather, it is the joyous rediscovery of childhood at its best. It is waking up each morning ready to devour the world, full of hope and promise. It lacks nothing but the tawdrier forms of ambition that make less sense as each day passes.

———◈———

Warren G. Bennis is the University Professor and Distinguished Professor of Business Administration and founding chairman of the Leadership Institute at the University of Southern California, chair of the advisory board for the John F. Kennedy School of Government's Center for Public Leadership at Harvard, and author of more than thirty books on leadership.

CHAPTER SEVEN

The Traces of Talent

Marcus Buckingham
Donald O. Clifton

How can you identify your own talents? First, monitor your spontaneous, top-of-mind reactions to the situations you encounter. These top-of-mind reactions provide the best trace of your talents. They reveal the location of strong mental connections.

Kathie P., a senior manager for a computer software company, gave us a dramatic example. She was bound for her company's annual sales meeting in the Dominican Republic. Squeezing into her tiny seat she glanced around her to see who was sharing the puddle jumper. Spread out in the back row was Brad, the aggressive, opinionated, and impatient CEO. In front of him was Amy, a genius at the details of software design, the best in the company. Across from her was Martin, a gregarious, charming Brit who through his network of contacts had single-handedly turned around their flagging European operations. And then there was Gerry, the insipid head of marketing who as usual had angled his way into the seat next to Brad.

"The problems began right after takeoff," Kathie recalled. "We had just cleared the clouds when the alarm went off. I didn't even know planes had alarms, but suddenly it started braying like a donkey—eee-aww, eee-aww—filling the cabin with this terrible sound. The main lights went out, and the emergency lights started flashing red. As I felt the plane drop what seemed like a thousand feet in a second or two, I looked through the open cabin door and saw both pilots, necks flushed and stiff, turn to each other. I sensed immediately that neither of them had any idea what was going on.

"There was a moment of silence in the cabin—shock, I imagine—and then suddenly everyone started talking at once. Amy craned over and said, 'Kathie, can you see the dials? Can you see the dials?' Martin pulled out a tiny bottle of Smirnoff from his bag and jokingly cried out, 'At least give me one last drink!' Gerry started rocking back and forth, moaning, 'We are all going to die. We are all going to die.' Brad was immediately at the cockpit door. I still don't know how he squeezed out of those backseats, but there he was, screaming at the top of his lungs, 'What the hell do you think you guys are doing up here?'

"Me? What was I doing?" Kathie said. "Watching, I suppose, as always. The funny thing was, nothing was wrong with the plane at all. A faulty system had triggered the alarm, and then the pilots had just panicked and pushed the plane into a sharp descent."

Each of these reactions under extreme stress revealed dominant talents and to some extent helped explain each person's performance on the job. Kathie's keen observations of human nature undoubtedly contributed to her success as a manager. Amy's instinctive need for precision was the foundation for her genius at software design. Martin's ability to find the humor in every situation had presumably endeared him to his growing network of European clients. Brad's compulsion to take charge was the foundation for his leadership. Even Gerry's wailing was confirmation of his suspect backbone (this one is not a true talent since it is hard to see where and how it could be applied productively).

While this is a dramatic example of how people reveal themselves under stress, daily life offers thousands of less intense situations that also provoke revealing reactions.

Think of a recent party where you didn't know most of the guests. Who did you spend the majority of your time with, those you knew or those you didn't? If you were drawn to the strangers, you may be a natural extrovert, and your behavior may well reflect the theme that we call *woo,* defined as an innate need to *w*in *o*thers *o*ver. Conversely, if you actively sought out your closest friends and hung out with them all evening, resenting the intrusions of strangers, this is a good sign that *relator*—a natural desire to deepen existing relationships—is one of your leading themes.

Recall the last time that one of your employees told you he could not come to work because his child was sick. What was your first thought? If you immediately focused on the ill child, asking what was wrong and who was going to take care of her, this may be a clue that *empathy* is one of your strongest themes of talent. But if your mind instinctively jumped to the question of who would fill in for the missing employee, the theme *arranger*—the ability to juggle many variables at once—is probably a dominant talent.

Or how about the last time you had to make a decision when you did not have all the facts? If you relished the uncertainty, sure in your belief that any movement, even in the wrong direction, would lead to a clearer perspective, you are probably blessed with the theme *activator*, defined as a bias for action in the face of ambiguity. If you stopped short, delaying action until more facts became available, a strong *analytical* theme may well be the explanation. Each of these top-of-mind reactions implies distinct patterns of behavior and therefore offers clues to your talents.

While your spontaneous reactions provide the clearest trace of your talents, here are three more clues to keep in mind: *yearnings*, *rapid learning*, and *satisfactions*.

Yearnings reveal the presence of a talent, particularly when they are felt early in life. At ten years of age, the actors Matt Damon and Ben Affleck, already close friends, would find a quiet spot in the school cafeteria and hold meetings to discuss their latest acting "projects." At thirteen, Picasso was already enrolled in adult art school. At age five, the architect Frank Gehry made intricate models on the living room floor with wood scraps from his father's hardware store. And Mozart had written his first symphony by the time he turned twelve.

These are the eye-catching examples but the same holds true for each of us. Perhaps because of your genes or your early experiences, as a child you found yourself drawn to some activities and repelled by others. While your brother was chasing his friends around the backyard, you settled down to tinker with the sprinkler head, pulling it apart so that you could figure out how it worked. Your analytical mind was already making its presence known.

When your mother, as a surprise on your seventh birthday, took you to McDonald's instead of having a party at home as you had planned together, you burst into tears. Even at this tender age your disciplined mind resented surprises in your routine.

These childhood passions are caused by the various synaptic connections in your brain. The weaker connections manage little pull, and when well-intentioned mothers (or other terrible circumstances) force you down a particular path, it feels strange and makes you cry. By contrast, your strongest connections are irresistible. They exert a magnetic influence, drawing you back time and again. You feel their pull, and so you yearn.

Needless to say, social or financial pressures sometimes drown out these yearnings and prevent you from acting on them. The Booker Prize–winning novelist Penelope Fitzgerald, burdened by the demands of providing for her family without the help of her alcoholic husband, wasn't able to honor her urge to write until well into her fifties. Once released by their permanent separation, this urge proved as irresistible as a teenager's. Over the last twenty years of her life she published twelve novels, and before her recent death at eighty, she was widely considered at the top of her game, "the best of all British novelists," according to one of her peers.

Anna Mary Robertson Moses probably holds the record for stymieing a powerful talent. Born on a farm in upstate New York, she began sketching as a young child and was so intent on incorporating every nuance of her surroundings that she mixed the juice of berries and grapes to bring color to her drawings. But her ardent sketching was soon pushed aside by the demands of the farming life, and for sixty years she didn't paint at all. Finally, at the age of seventy-eight, she retired from farming, allowed herself the luxury of letting her talent loose, and, like Penelope Fitzgerald, was quickly borne aloft by its pent-up energy. By the time of her death twenty-three years later she had painted thousands of scenes remembered from her childhood, exhibited her pictures in fifteen one-woman shows, and became known around the world as the artist Grandma Moses.

Your yearnings may not prove quite as inexorable as those of Grandma Moses, but they will exert a consistent pull. They have to. Your yearnings reflect the physical reality that some of your mental connections are simply stronger than others. So no matter how repressive the external influences prove to be, these stronger connections will keep calling out to you, demanding to be heard. If you want to discover your talents, you should pay them heed.

Of course, you can occasionally be derailed by what one might call a "misyearning," such as yearning to be in public relations because of the imagined glamour of cocktail parties and receptions or aspiring to be a manager because of a need to control. (Obviously, the best way to diagnose a misyearning is to interview an incumbent in the role and learn what the day-to-day realities of the role are really like once the blush has left the rose.) These false signals aside, your yearnings are worth following as you strive to build your strengths.

Rapid learning offers another trace of talent. Sometimes a talent doesn't signal itself through yearning. For a myriad of reasons, although the talent exists within you, you don't hear its call. Instead, comparatively late in life, something sparks the talent, and it is the speed at which you learn a new skill that provides the telltale clue to the talent's presence and power.

Unlike Picasso, his precocious contemporary, Henri Matisse didn't feel any yearning toward painting. In fact, by the time he was twenty-one he had never even picked up a brush. He was a lawyer's clerk, and most of the time a sick and depressed lawyer's clerk. One afternoon while he was recuperating in bed after another bout of flu, his mother, in search of something—anything—to lighten his spirit, put a box of paints in his hands. Almost instantly both the direction and the trajectory of his life changed. He felt a surge of energy as though released from a dark prison and seeing the light for the first time. Feverishly studying a "how-to-paint" manual, Matisse filled his days with painting and drawing. Four years later, with no schooling but his own, he was accepted into the most prestigious art school in Paris and was studying under the master Gustave Moreau.

Frederick Law Olmsted needed a similar situation to spark his talent, but as with Matisse, once revealed, his talent launched him to levels of excellence in his field at an unprecedented pace. Olmsted, a restless man with little to show for his thirty years, discovered his life's calling (what today we call landscape architecture) when he visited England in 1850. There he was struck by, in his words, the "hedges, the English hedges, hawthorn hedges, all in blossom and the mild sun beaming through the watery atmosphere." A few years later, after returning to the United States and refining his ideas, he won the most extensive landscape design competition ever held: New York's Central Park. It was his first commission.

You may have had a similar experience. You start to learn a new skill—in the context of a new job, a new challenge, or a new environment—and immediately your brain seems to light up as if a whole bank of switches were suddenly flicked to "on." The steps of this skill fly down the newly opened connections at such speed that very soon the steps disappear. Your movements lose the distinctive jerkiness of the novice and instead assume the grace of the virtuoso. You leave your classmates behind. You read ahead and try things out before the curriculum says you should. You even become unpopular with your trainer as you challenge him with new questions and insights. But you don't really care because this new skill has come to you so naturally that you can't wait to put it into practice.

Of course, not everyone has experienced *eureka* moments that determined the direction of their lifelong career, but whether the skill is selling, presenting, architectural drafting, giving developmental feedback to an employee, preparing legal briefs, writing business plans, cleaning hotel rooms, editing newspaper articles, or booking guests on a morning TV show, if you learned it rapidly, you should look deeper. You will be able to identify the talent or talents that made that possible.

Satisfactions provide the last clue to talent. Your strongest synaptic connections are designed so that when you use them, it feels good. Thus, obviously, if it feels good when you perform an activity, chances are that you are using a talent.

This seems almost too simple, much like the advice that "if it feels good, do it." Clearly, it is not that simple. For various reasons—most of them having to do with our psychological history—nature has conspired to encourage a few of our more antisocial impulses. For example, have you ever caught yourself feeling good when someone else stumbles? Have you ever felt an impulse to put someone else down in public or even to shirk responsibility and blame someone else for your failings? Many people do, no matter how ignoble it seems. Each of these behaviors involves building one's good feelings on the back of someone else's bad feelings. These are not productive behaviors and should be avoided. Those tempted to use their talents to delight in other people's failure should perhaps reexamine their values.

You are better served by tuning your antenna toward identifying those positive activities that seem to bring you psychological strength and satisfaction. When we interviewed the excellent performers in our study, what was most striking was the sheer range of activities or outcomes that made people happy. Initially, when we asked people what aspect of their work they enjoyed the most, we heard a common refrain: Almost all of them liked their job when they met a challenge and then overcame it. However, when we probed a little deeper, the diversity—what they actually meant by "challenge"—emerged.

Some people derived satisfaction from seeing another person achieve the kind of infinitesimal improvement most of us would miss. Some loved bringing order to chaos. Some people reveled in playing the host at a major event. Some delighted in cleanliness, smiling to themselves as they vacuumed themselves out of a room. Some people were idea lovers. Some mistrusted ideas and instead thrilled to the analytical challenge of finding the "truth." Some people needed to match their own standards. Some, whether or not they had met their own standards, felt empty if they hadn't also outperformed their peers. For some people only learning was genuinely meaningful. For some people only helping others provided meaning. Some even got a kick out of rejection—apparently because it offered the chance to show just how persuasive they could be.

This list could legitimately become as long as the roll call of the entire human race. We are all woven so uniquely that each of us experiences slightly different satisfactions. What we are suggesting here is that you pay close attention to the situations that seem to bring you satisfaction. If you can identify them, you are well on your way to pinpointing your talents.

How can you identify your sources of satisfaction? Well, we need to tread carefully here. Telling someone how to know if she is genuinely enjoying something can be as vacuous as telling her how to know if she is in love. On some level, the only sage advice is "You either feel it or you don't."

We will take a risk however, and offer you this tip: When you are performing a particular activity, try to isolate the tense you are thinking in. If all you are thinking about is the present—"When will this be over?"—more than likely you are not using a talent. But if you find yourself thinking in the future, if you find yourself actually anticipating the activity—"When can I do this again?"—it is a pretty good sign that you are enjoying it and that one of your talents is in play.

Spontaneous reactions, yearnings, rapid learning, and satisfactions will all help you detect the traces of your talents. As you rush through your busy life, try to step back, quiet the wind whipping past your ears, and listen for these clues. They will help you zero in on your talents.

———·∞·———

Marcus Buckingham is an author, independent consultant, and a former Global Practice Leader for the Gallup Organization's Strength Management Practice. For more information visit www.MarcusBuckingham.com.

———·∞·———

The late Donald O. Clifton was the past chairman of the Gallup Organization and chair of the Gallup International Research and Education Center.

Leadership Is Authenticity, Not Style

Bill George

Not long ago I was meeting with a group of high-talent young executives at Medtronic. We were discussing career development when the leader of the group asked me to list the most important characteristics one has to have to be a leader in Medtronic. I said, "I can summarize it in a single word: authenticity."

After years of studying leaders and their traits, I believe that leadership begins and ends with authenticity. It's being yourself; being the person you were created to be. This is not what most of the literature on leadership says nor is it what the experts in corporate America teach. Instead, they develop lists of leadership characteristics one is supposed to emulate. They describe the styles of leaders and suggest that you adopt them.

This is the opposite of authenticity. It is about developing the image or persona of a leader. Unfortunately, the media, the business press, and even the movies glorify leaders with high-ego personalities. They focus on the style of leaders, not their character. In large measure, making heroes out of celebrity CEOs is at the heart of the crisis in corporate leadership.

THE AUTHENTIC LEADER

Authentic leaders genuinely desire to serve others through their leadership. They are more interested in empowering the people they lead to make a difference than they are in power, money, or prestige for themselves. They are as guided by qualities of the heart, by passion and compassion, as they are by qualities of the mind.

Authentic leaders are not born that way. Many people have natural leadership gifts, but they have to develop them fully to become outstanding leaders. Authentic leaders use their natural abilities, but they also recognize their shortcomings and work hard to overcome them. They lead with purpose, meaning, and values. They build enduring relationships with people. Others follow them because they know where they stand. They are consistent and self-disciplined. When their principles are tested, they refuse to compromise. Authentic leaders are dedicated to developing themselves because they know that becoming a leader takes a lifetime of personal growth.

BEING YOUR OWN PERSON

Leaders are all very different people. Any prospective leader who buys into the necessity of attempting to emulate all the characteristics of a leader is doomed to fail. I know because I tried it early in my career. It simply doesn't work.

The one essential quality a leader must have is to be your own person, authentic in every regard. The best leaders are autonomous and highly independent. Those who are too responsive to the desires of others are likely to be whipsawed by competing interests, too quick to deviate from their course or unwilling to make difficult decisions for fear of offending. My advice to the people I mentor is simply to be themselves.

Being your own person is most challenging when it feels like everyone is pressuring you to take one course and you are standing alone. In the first semester of business school we watched *The Loneliness of the Long Distance Runner*. Initially I did not relate to the film's message, as I had always surrounded myself with people to avoid being lonely. Learning to cope with the loneliness at the top is crucial so that you are not swayed by the pressure. Being able to stand alone against the majority is essential to being your own person.

Shortly after I joined Medtronic as president, I walked into a meeting where it quickly became evident that a group of my new colleagues had prearranged a strategy to settle a major patent dispute against Siemens on the basis of a royalty-free cross-license as a show of good faith. Intuitively, I knew the strategy was doomed to fail, so I stood alone against the entire group, refusing to go along. My position may not have made me popular with my new teammates, but it was the right thing to do. We later negotiated a settlement with Siemens for more than $400 million, at the time the second-largest patent settlement ever.

DEVELOPING YOUR UNIQUE LEADERSHIP STYLE

To become authentic, each of us has to develop our own leadership style, consistent with our personality and character. Unfortunately, the pressures of an organization push us to adhere to its normative style. But if we conform to a style that is not consistent with who we are, we will never become authentic leaders.

Contrary to what much of the literature says, your type of leadership style is not what matters. Great world leaders—George Washington, Abraham Lincoln, Winston Churchill, Franklin Roosevelt, Margaret Thatcher, Martin Luther King, Mother Teresa, John F. Kennedy—all had very different styles. Yet each of them was an entirely authentic human being. There is no way you could ever attempt to emulate any of them without looking foolish.

The same is true for business leaders. Compare three succeeding CEOs at General Electric: the statesmanship of Reginald Jones, the dynamism of Jack Welch, and the empowering style of Jeff Immelt. All of them are highly successful leaders with entirely different leadership styles. Yet the GE organization rallied around each of them, adapted to their styles, and flourished as a result. What counts is the authenticity of the leader, not the style.

Having said that, it is important that you develop a leadership style that works well for you and is consistent with your character and your personality. Over time you will have to hone your style to be effective in leading different types of people and to work in different types of environments. This is integral to your development as a leader.

To be effective in today's fast-moving, highly competitive environment, leaders also have to adapt their style to fit the immediate situation. There are times to be inspiring and motivating, and times to be tough about people decisions or financial decisions. There are times to delegate, and times to be deeply immersed in the details. There are times to communicate public messages, and times to have private conversations. The use of adaptive styles is not inauthentic and is very different from playing a succession of roles rather than being yourself. Good leaders are able to nuance their styles to the demands of the situation, and to know when and how to deploy different styles.

Let me share a personal example to illustrate this point. When I first joined Medtronic, I spent a lot of time learning the business and listening to customers. I also focused on inspiring employees to fulfill the Medtronic mission of restoring people to full health. At the same time, I saw many ways in which we needed to be more disciplined about decisions and spending, so I was very challenging in budget sessions and put strict controls on headcount additions. At first some people found this confusing. Eventually, they understood my reasons for adapting my style to the situation, and that I had to do so to be effective as their leader.

BEING AWARE OF YOUR WEAKNESSES

Being true to the person you were created to be means accepting your faults as well as using your strengths. Accepting your shadow side is an essential part of being authentic. The problem comes when people are so eager to win the approval of others that they try to cover their shortcomings and sacrifice their authenticity to gain the respect and admiration of their associates.

I too have struggled in getting comfortable with my weaknesses— my tendency to intimidate others with an overly challenging style, impatience, and occasional lack of tact. Only recently have I realized that my strengths and weaknesses are two sides of the same coin. By challenging others in business meetings, I am able to get quickly to the heart of the issues, but my approach unnerves and intimidates less confident people. My desire to get things done fast leads to superior results, but it exposes my impatience with people who move more slowly. Being direct with others gets the message across clearly but often lacks tact. Over time I have moderated my style and adapted my approach to make sure that people are engaged and empowered and that their voices are fully heard.

I have always been open to critical feedback, but also quite sensitive to it. For years I felt I had to be perfect, or at least appear that I was on top of everything. I tried to hide my weaknesses from others, fearing they would reject me if they knew who I really was. Eventually, I realized that they could see my weaknesses more clearly than I could. In attempting to cover things up, I was only fooling myself.

THE TEMPTATIONS OF LEADERSHIP

Congressman Amory Houghton, one of the most thoughtful members of the U.S. Congress, tells the story of his predecessor's advice as he was taking over as CEO of Corning Glass. "Think of your decisions being based on two concentric circles. In the outer circle are all the laws, regulations, and ethical standards with which the company must comply. In the inner circle are your core values. Just be darn sure that your decisions as CEO stay within your inner circle."

We are all painfully aware of corporate leaders that pushed beyond the outer circle and got caught, either by the law or by the financial failure of their companies. More worrisome are the leaders of companies who moved outside their inner circles and engaged in marginal practices, albeit legal ones. Examples include cutting back on long-term investments just to make the short-term numbers, bending compensation rules to pay executives in spite of marginal performance, using accounting tricks to meet the quarterly expectations of security analysts, shipping products of marginal quality, compromising security analysts by giving them a cut on investment banking deals, and booking revenues before the products are shipped in an effort to pump up revenue growth. The list goes on and on.

All of us who sit in the leader's chair feel the pressure to perform. As CEO, I felt it every day as problems mounted or sales lagged. I knew that the livelihood of tens of thousands of employees, the health of millions of patients, and the financial fortunes of millions of investors rested on my shoulders and those of our executive team. At the same time I was well aware of the penalties for not performing, even for a single quarter. No CEO wants to appear on CNBC to explain why his company missed the earnings projections, even by a penny.

Little by little, step by step, the pressures to succeed can pull us away from our core values, just as we are reinforced by our "success" in the market. Some people refer to this as "CEO-itis." The irony is that the more successful we are, the more tempted we are to take shortcuts to keep it going. And the rewards—compensation increases, stock option gains, the myriads of executive perquisites, positive stories in the media, admiring comments from our peers—all reinforce our actions and drive us to keep it going.

The test I used with our team at Medtronic is whether we would feel comfortable having the entire story appear on the front page of the *New York Times*. If we didn't, we went back to the drawing boards and reexamined our decision.

DIMENSIONS OF AUTHENTIC LEADERS

Let's examine the essential dimensions of all authentic leaders, the qualities that true leaders must develop. I have determined through many experiences in leading others that authentic leaders demonstrate these five qualities:

- Understanding their purpose
- Practicing solid values
- Leading with heart
- Establishing close and enduring relationships
- Demonstrating self-discipline

Acquiring the five dimensions of an authentic leader is not a sequential process; rather, leaders are developing them continuously throughout their lives.

Understanding Your Purpose

In Wonderland, Alice comes to a fork in the road where she sees a cat in a tree. Alice asks the cat which road to take. "That depends a good deal on where you want to get to," says the cat. "I don't much care where," says Alice. To which the cat replies, "Then it doesn't much matter which way you go."

To become a leader, it is essential that you first answer the question, "Leadership for what purpose?" If you lack purpose and direction in leading, why would anyone want to follow you?

Many people want to become leaders without giving much thought to their purpose. They are attracted to the power and prestige of leading an organization and the financial rewards that go with it. But without a real sense of purpose, leaders are at the mercy of their egos and are vulnerable to narcissistic impulses. There is no way you can adopt someone else's purpose and still be an authentic leader. You can study the purposes others pursue and you can work with them on common purposes, but in the end the purpose for your leadership must be uniquely yours.

To find your purpose, you must first understand yourself, your passions, and your underlying motivations. Then you must seek an environment that offers a fit between the organization's purpose and your own. Your search may take experiences in several organizations before you can find the one that is right for you.

The late Robert Greenleaf, a former AT&T executive, is well known for his concept of leaders as servants of the people. In *Servant Leadership,* he advocates service to others as the leader's primary purpose. If people feel you are genuinely interested in serving others, then they will be prepared not just to follow you but to dedicate themselves to the common cause.

One of the best examples of a leader with purpose was the late David Packard, co-founder of Hewlett-Packard. I met him in early 1969 when he was the new Deputy Secretary of Defense and I was the special assistant to the Secretary of Navy. Packard had taken a leave from H-P to serve his country. A big, powerful, yet modest man, he immediately impressed me with his openness, sincerity, and commitment to make a difference through his work.

He returned to H-P a few years later to build it into one of the great companies of its time through his dedication to the company's mission, known as "The H-P Way," and to excellence in R&D and customer service. He inspired H-P's employees to incredible levels of commitment. At his death he was one of the wealthiest people in the world, yet no one would ever have known it by his personal spending. Most of his money went into funding philanthropic projects. Dave Packard was a truly authentic leader, a role model for me and for many in my generation.

Then there's John Bogle, who for fifty years has been a man with a mission to transform the management of investors' funds. Bogle created the first no-load mutual fund in 1974 and founded Vanguard, the nation's leading purveyor of index funds. Bogle has not only been a pioneer in financial services, he has been the leading advocate of financial funds as stewards of their investors' money. His values and integrity stand in stark relief to those of others in the financial community who seek to use investment funds for their personal gain.

Practicing Solid Values

Leaders are defined by their values and their character. The values of the authentic leader are shaped by personal beliefs, developed through study, introspection, and consultation with others—and a lifetime of experience. These values define their holder's moral compass. Such leaders know the "true north" of their compass, the deep sense of the right thing to do. Without a moral compass, any leader can wind up like the executives who are facing possible prison sentences today because they lacked a sense of right and wrong.

While the development of fundamental values is crucial, integrity is the one value that is required in every authentic leader. Integrity is not just the absence of lying, but telling the whole truth, as painful as it may be. If you don't exercise complete integrity in your interactions, no one can trust you. If they cannot trust you, why would they ever follow you?

As Enron was collapsing in the fall of 2001, the *Boston Globe* published an article by a Harvard classmate of Enron CEO Jeff Skilling. The author described how Skilling would argue in class that the role of the business leader was to take advantage of loopholes in regulations and push beyond the laws wherever he could to make money. As Skilling saw the world, it was the job of the regulators to try and catch him. Sound familiar? Twenty-five years later, Skilling's philosophy caught up with him, as he led his company into bankruptcy.

One of my role models of values-centered leadership is Max De Pree, the former CEO of furniture maker Herman Miller. De Pree is a modest man guided by a deep concern for serving others; he is true to his values in every aspect of his life. His humanity and values can be seen through the exemplary way in which his company conducts itself. De Pree describes his philosophy of values-centered leadership in his classic book *Leadership Is an Art*. De Pree also subscribes to Greenleaf's ideas on servant leadership, and expands them by offering his own advice, "The leader's first job is to define reality. The last is to say thank you. In between the leader must become a servant and a debtor."

De Pree believes that a corporation should be "a community of people," all of whom have value and share in the fruits of their collective labor. De Pree practices what he preaches. While he was CEO, his salary was capped at twenty times that of an hourly worker. In his view tying the CEO's salary to that of the workers helps cement trust in leadership. Contrast that with today's CEOs, who are earning—on average—five hundred times their hourly workers' wage. As De Pree said recently, "When leaders indulge themselves with lavish perks and the trappings of power, they are damaging their standing as leaders."

Leading with Heart

Over the last several decades, businesses have evolved from maximizing the physical output of their workers to engaging the minds of their employees. To excel in the twenty-first century, great companies will go one step further by engaging the hearts of their employees through a sense of purpose. When employees believe their work has a deeper purpose, their results will vastly exceed those who use only their minds and their bodies. This will become the company's competitive advantage.

Sometimes we refer to people as being bighearted. What we really mean is that they are open and willing to share themselves fully with us, and are genuinely interested in us. Leaders who do that, like Sam Walton, founder of Wal-Mart, and Earl Bakken, founder of Medtronic, have the ability to ignite the souls of their employees to achieve greatness far beyond what anyone imagined possible.

One of the most bighearted leaders I know is Marilyn Nelson, chair and CEO of the Carlson Companies, the privately held hospitality and travel services giant. When she became CEO several years ago, she inherited a hard-nosed organization that was driven for growth but not known for empathy for its employees. Shortly after joining the company, Nelson had what she refers to as her "epiphany." She was meeting with the group of MBA students that had been studying the company's culture. When she asked the students for feedback, Nelson got a stony silence from the group. Finally, a young woman raised her hand and said, "We hear from employees that Carlson is a sweatshop that doesn't care."

That incident sent Nelson into high gear. She created a motivational program called "Carlson Cares." As the company was preparing for its launch, Nelson's staff told her they needed more time to change the culture before introducing the program. Nelson decided that she could not wait and decided to become the company's role model for caring and empathy. She immediately set out to change the environment, using her passion, motivational skills, and sincere interest in her employees and her customers. She took the lead on customer sales calls and interacted every day with employees in Carlson operations. Her positive energy has transformed the company's culture, built its customer relationships, accelerated its growth, and strengthened its bottom line.

Establishing Close and Enduring Relationships

As Krishnamurti says, "Relationship is the mirror in which we see ourselves as we are." The capacity to develop close and enduring relationships is one mark of a leader. Unfortunately, many leaders of major companies believe their job is to create the strategy, organization structure, and organizational processes and then just delegate the work to be done, remaining aloof from the people doing the work.

A detached style of leadership will not be successful in the twenty-first century. Today's employees demand more personal relationships with their leaders before they will give themselves fully to their jobs. They insist on having access to their leaders, knowing that it is in the openness and the depth of the relationship with the leader that trust and commitment are built. Bill Gates, Michael Dell, and Jack Welch have been so successful because they have connected directly with their employees and realized from them a deeper commitment to their work and greater loyalty to the company. Welch, in particular, is an interesting case because he was so challenging and hard on people. Yet it was those very challenges that let people know that he was interested in their success and concerned about their careers.

In *Eyewitness to Power,* David Gergen writes, "At the heart of leadership is the leader's relationship with followers. People will entrust their hopes and dreams to another person only if they think the other is a reliable vessel." Authentic leaders establish trusting relationships with people throughout the organization as well as in their personal lives. The rewards of these relationships, both tangible and intangible, are long lasting.

I always tried to establish close relationships with my colleagues, looking to them as a closely knit team whose collective knowledge and wisdom about the business vastly exceeds my own. Many corporate leaders fear these kinds of relationships. As another CEO said to me, "Bill, I don't want to get too close to my subordinates because someday I may have to terminate them." Actually, the real reason goes much deeper than that. Many leaders—men in particular—fear having their weaknesses and vulnerabilities exposed. So they create distance from employees and a sense of aloofness. Instead of being authentic, they are creating a persona for themselves.

Demonstrating Self-Discipline

Self-discipline is an essential quality of an authentic leader. Without it, you cannot gain the respect of your followers. It is easy to say that someone has good values but lacks the discipline to convert those values into consistent actions. This is a hollow excuse. None of us is perfect, of course, but authentic leaders must have the self-discipline to do everything they can to demonstrate their values through their actions. When we fall short, it is equally important to admit our mistakes.

Leaders are highly competitive people. They are driven to succeed in whatever they take on. Authentic leaders know that competing requires a consistently high level of self-discipline to be successful. Being very competitive is not a bad thing; in fact, it is an essential quality of successful leaders, but it needs to be channeled through purpose and discipline. Sometimes we mistake competitive people who generate near-term results by improving operational effectiveness for genuine leaders. Achieving operational effectiveness is an essential result for any leader, but it alone does not ensure authenticity or long-term success.

The most consistent leader I know is Art Collins, my successor as CEO of Medtronic. His self-discipline is evident every day and in every interaction. His subordinates never have to worry about what kind of mood Art is in, or where he stands on an important issue. Nor does he deviate in his behavior or vacillate in his decisions. He never lets his ego or emotions get in the way of taking the appropriate action. These qualities make working with Art easy and predictable, enabling Medtronic employees to do their jobs effectively.

Mother Teresa is a compelling example of an authentic leader. Many think of her as simply a nun who reached out to the poor, yet by 1990 she had created an organization of four thousand missionaries operating in a hundred countries. Her organization, Missionaries of Charity, began in Calcutta and spread to 450 centers around the world. Its mission was "to reach out to the destitute on the streets, offering wholehearted service to the poorest of the poor." Not only did she have a purpose, clear values, and a heart filled with compassion, she also created intimate relationships with people and exercised self-discipline, all the dimensions of an authentic leader. I doubt that any of us will ever be like Mother Teresa, but her life is indeed an inspiration.

—⟳—

Bill George is professor of management practice and the Henry B. Arthur Fellow of Ethics at the Harvard Business School and the former chairman and chief executive officer of Medtronic.

CHAPTER NINE

Level 5 Leadership
The Triumph of Humility and Fierce Resolve

Jim Collins

n 1971, a seemingly ordinary man named Darwin E. Smith became chief executive of Kimberly-Clark, a stodgy old paper company whose stock had fallen 36% behind the general market during the previous 20 years. Smith, the company's mild-mannered in-house lawyer, wasn't so sure the board had made the right choice—a feeling that was reinforced when a Kimberly-Clark director pulled him aside and reminded him that he lacked some of the qualifications for the position. But CEO he was, and CEO he remained for 20 years.

What a 20 years it was. In that period, Smith created a stunning transformation at Kimberly-Clark, turning it into the leading consumer paper products company in the world. Under his stewardship, the company beat its rivals Scott Paper and Procter & Gamble. And in doing so, Kimberly-Clark generated cumulative stock returns that were 4.1 times greater than those of the general market, outperforming venerable companies such as Hewlett-Packard, 3M, Coca-Cola, and General Electric.

Smith's turnaround of Kimberly-Clark is one the best examples in the twentieth century of a leader taking a company from merely good to truly great. And yet few people—even ardent students of business history—have heard of Darwin Smith. He probably would have liked it that way. Smith is a classic example of a Level 5 leader—an individual who blends extreme personal humility with intense professional will. According to our five-year research study, executives who possess this paradoxical combination of traits are catalysts for the statistically rare event of transforming a good company into a great one.

"Level 5" refers to the highest level in a hierarchy of executive capabilities that we identified during our research. Leaders at the other four levels can produce high degrees of success but not enough to elevate companies from mediocrity to sustained excellence. (For more details, see Exhibit 9.1, "The Level 5 Hierarchy.") And while Level 5 leadership is not the only requirement for transforming a good company into a great one—other factors include getting the right people

---

The Level 5 leader sits on top of a hierarchy of capabilities and is, according to our research, a necessary requirement for transforming an organization from good to great. But what lies beneath? Four other layers, each one appropriate in its own right but none with the power of Level 5. Individuals do not need to proceed sequentially through each level of the hierarchy to reach the top, but to be a full-fledged Level 5 requires the capabilities of all the lower levels, plus the special characteristics of Level 5.

Level 5
Executive
Builds enduring greatness through a paradoxical
combination of personal humility plus professional will.

Level 4
Effective Leader
Catalyzes commitment to and vigorous pursuit of a clear and
compelling vision; stimulates the group to high performance standards.

Level 3
Competent Manager
Organizes people and resources toward the effective
and efficient pursuit of predetermined objectives.

Level 2
Contributing Team Member
Contributes to the achievement of group objectives;
works effectively with others in a group setting.

Level 1
Highly Capable Individual
Makes productive contributions through talent,
knowledge, skills, and good work habits.

Exhibit 9.1.   The Level 5 Hierarchy.

on the bus (and the wrong people off the bus) and creating a culture of discipline—our research shows it to be essential. Good-to-great transformations don't happen without Level 5 leaders at the helm. They just don't.

NOT WHAT YOU WOULD EXPECT

Our discovery of Level 5 leadership is counterintuitive. Indeed, it is countercultural. People generally assume that transforming companies from good to great requires larger-than-life leaders—big personalities like Lee Iacocca, Al Dunlap, Jack Welch, and Stanley Gault, who make headlines and become celebrities.

Compared with those CEOs, Darwin Smith seems to have come from Mars. Shy, unpretentious, even awkward, Smith shunned attention. When a journalist asked him to describe his management style, Smith just stared back at the scribe from the other side of his thick black-rimmed glasses. He was dressed unfashionably, like a farm boy wearing his first J.C. Penney suit. Finally, after a long and uncomfortable silence, he said, "Eccentric." Needless to say, the *Wall Street Journal* did not publish a splashy feature on Darwin Smith.

But if you were to consider Smith soft or meek, you would be terribly mistaken. His lack of pretense was coupled with a fierce, even stoic, resolve toward life. Smith grew up on an Indiana farm and put himself through night school at Indiana University by working the day shift at International Harvester. One day, he lost a finger on the job. The story goes that he went to class that evening and returned to work the very next day. Eventually, this poor but determined Indiana farm boy earned admission to Harvard Law School.

He showed the same iron will when he was at the helm of Kimberly-Clark. Indeed, two months after Smith became CEO, doctors diagnosed him with nose and throat cancer and told him he had less than a year to live. He duly informed the board of his illness but said he had no plans to die anytime soon. Smith held to his demanding work schedule while commuting weekly from Wisconsin to Houston for radiation therapy. He lived 25 more years, 20 of them as CEO.

Smith's ferocious resolve was crucial to the rebuilding of Kimberly-Clark, especially when he made the most dramatic decision in the company's history: selling the mills. To explain: Shortly after he took over, Smith and his team had concluded that the company's traditional core business—coated paper—was doomed to mediocrity.

Its economics were bad and the competition weak. But, they reasoned, if Kimberly-Clark were thrust into the fire of the consumer paper products business, better economics and world-class competition like Procter & Gamble would force it to achieve greatness or perish.

And so, like the general who burned the boats upon landing on enemy soil, leaving his troops to succeed or die, Smith announced that Kimberly-Clark would sell its mills—even the namesake mill in Kimberly, Wisconsin. All proceeds would be thrown into the consumer business, with investments in brands like Huggies diapers and Kleenex tissues. The business media called the move stupid, and Wall Street analysts downgraded the stock. But Smith never wavered. Twenty-five years later, Kimberly-Clark owned Scott Paper and beat Procter & Gamble in six of eight product categories. In retirement, Smith reflected on his exceptional performance, saying simply, "I never stopped trying to become qualified for the job."

NOT WHAT WE EXPECTED, EITHER

We'll look in depth at Level 5 leadership, but first let's set an important context for our findings. We were not looking for Level 5 or anything like it. Our original question was, Can a good company become a great one and, if so, how? In fact, I gave the research teams explicit instructions to downplay the role of top executives in their analyses of this question so we wouldn't slip into the simplistic "credit the leader" or "blame the leader" thinking that is so common today.

But Level 5 found us. Over the course of the study, research teams kept saying, "We can't ignore the top executives even if we want to. There is something consistently unusual about them." I would push back, arguing, "The comparison companies also had leaders. So what's different here?" Back and forth the debate raged. Finally, as should always be the case, the data won. The executives at companies that went from good to great and sustained that performance for 15 years or more were all cut from the same cloth—one remarkably different from that which produced the executives at comparison companies in our study. It didn't matter whether the company was in crisis or steady state, consumer or industrial, offering services or products. It didn't matter when the transition took place or how big the company. The successful organizations all had a Level 5 leader at the time of transition.

Furthermore, the absence of Level 5 leadership showed up consistently across the comparison companies. The point: Level 5 is an empirical finding, not an ideological one. And that's important to note, given how much the Level 5 finding contradicts not only conventional wisdom but much of management theory to date. (For more about our findings on good-to-great transformations, see Exhibit 9.2, "Not by Level 5 Alone.")

Level 5 leadership is an essential factor for taking a company from good to great, but it's not the only one. Our research uncovered multiple factors that deliver companies to greatness. And it is the combined package—Level 5 plus these other drivers—that takes companies beyond unremarkable. There is a symbiotic relationship between Level 5 and the rest of our findings: Level 5 enables implementation of the other findings, and practicing the other findings may help you get to Level 5. We've already talked about who Level 5 leaders are; the rest of our findings describe what they do. Here is a brief look at some of the other key findings.

First Who
We expected that good-to-great leaders would start with the vision and strategy. Instead, they attended to people first, strategy second. They got the right people on the bus, moved the wrong people off, ushered the right people to the right seats—and then they figured out where to drive it.

Stockdale Paradox
This finding is named for Admiral James Stockdale, winner of the Medal of Honor, who survived seven years in a Vietcong POW camp by hanging on to two contradictory beliefs: His life couldn't be worse at the moment, and his life would someday be better than ever. Like Stockdale, people at the good-to-great companies confronted the most brutal facts of their current reality, yet simultaneously maintained absolute faith that they would prevail in the end. And they held both disciplines—faith and facts—at the same time, all the time.

Buildup-Breakthrough Flywheel
Good-to-great transformations do not happen overnight or in one big leap. Rather, the process resembles relentlessly pushing a giant, heavy flywheel in one direction. At first, pushing it gets the flywheel to turn once. With consistent effort, it goes two turns, then five, then ten, building increasing momentum until—bang!—the wheel hits its breakthrough point, and the momentum really kicks in. Our comparison companies never sustained the kind of breakthrough momentum that the good-to-great companies did; instead, they lurched back and forth with radical change programs, reactionary moves, and restructurings.

The Hedgehog Concept
In a famous essay, philosopher and scholar Isaiah Berlin described two approaches to thought and life using a simple parable: the fox knows a little about many things, but the hedgehog knows only one big thing very well. The fox is complex; the hedgehog simple. And the hedgehog wins. Our research shows that breakthroughs require a simple, hedgehog-like understanding of three intersecting circles: what a company can be the best in the world at, how its economics work best, and what best ignites the passions of its people. Breakthroughs happen when you get the hedgehog concept and become systematic and consistent with it, eliminating virtually anything that does not fit in the three circles.

Exhibit 9.2. Not by Level 5 Alone. (*continues*)

Technology Accelerators
The good-to-great companies had a paradoxical relationship with technology. On the one hand, they assiduously avoided jumping on new technology bandwagons. On the other hand, they were pioneers in the application of carefully selected technologies, making bold, farsighted investments in those that directly linked to their hedgehog concept. Like turbochargers, these technology accelerators create an explosion in flywheel momentum.

A Culture of Discipline
When you look across the good-to-great transformations, they consistently display three forms of discipline: disciplined people, disciplined thought, and disciplined action. When you have disciplined people, you don't need hierarchy. When you have disciplined thought, you don't need bureaucracy. When you have disciplined action, you don't need excessive controls. When you combine a culture of discipline with an ethic of entrepreneurship, you get the magical alchemy of great performance.

Exhibit 9.2.   Not by Level 5 Alone.

HUMILITY + WILL = LEVEL 5

Level 5 leaders are a study in duality: modest and willful, shy and fearless. To grasp this concept, consider Abraham Lincoln, who never let his ego get in the way of his ambition to create an enduring great nation. Author Henry Adams called him "a quiet, peaceful, shy figure." But those who thought Lincoln's understated manner signaled weakness in the man found themselves terribly mistaken—to the scale of 250,000 Confederate and 360,000 Union lives, including Lincoln's own.

It might be a stretch to compare the 11 Level 5 CEOs in our research to Lincoln, but they did display the same kind of duality. Take Colman M. Mockler, CEO of Gillette from 1975 to 1991. Mockler, who faced down three takeover attempts, was a reserved, gracious man with a gentle, almost patrician manner. Despite epic battles with raiders—he took on Ronald Perelman twice and the former Coniston Partners once—he never lost his shy, courteous style. At the height of crisis, he maintained a calm business-as-usual demeanor, dispensing first with ongoing business before turning to the takeover.

And yet, those who mistook Mockler's outward modesty as a sign of inner weakness were beaten in the end. In one proxy battle, Mockler and other senior executives called thousands of investors, one by one, to win their votes. Mockler simply would not give in. He chose to fight for the future greatness of Gillette even though he could have pocketed millions by flipping his stock.

Consider the consequences had Mockler capitulated. If a share flipper had accepted the full 44% price premium offered by Perelman and then invested those shares in the general market for ten years, he still would have come out 64% behind a shareholder who stayed with Mockler and Gillette. If Mockler had given up the fight, it's likely that none of us would be shaving with Sensor, Lady Sensor, or the Mach III—and hundreds of millions of people would have a more painful battle with daily stubble.

Sadly, Mockler never had the chance to enjoy the full fruits of his efforts. In January 1991, Gillette received an advance copy of *Forbes*. The cover featured an artist's rendition of the publicity-shy Mockler standing on a mountaintop, holding a giant razor above his head in a triumphant pose. Walking back to his office just minutes after seeing this public acknowledgment of his 16 years of struggle, Mockler crumpled to the floor and died of a massive heart attack.

Even if Mockler had known he would die in office, he could not have changed his approach. His placid persona hid an inner intensity, a dedication to making anything he touched the best—not just because of what he would get but because he couldn't imagine doing it any other way. Mockler could not give up the company to those who would destroy it, any more than Lincoln would risk losing the chance to build an enduring great nation.

A COMPELLING MODESTY

The Mockler story illustrates the modesty typical of Level 5 leaders. (For a summary of Level 5 traits, see Exhibit 9.3, "The Yin and Yang of Level 5.") Indeed, throughout our interviews with such executives, we were struck by the way they talked about themselves—or rather, didn't talk about themselves. They'd go on and on about the company and the contributions of other executives, but they would instinctively deflect discussion about their own role. When pressed to talk about themselves, they'd say things like, "I hope I'm not sounding like a big shot," or "I don't think I can take much credit for what happened. We were blessed with marvelous people." One Level 5 leader even asserted, "There are a lot of people in this company who could do my job better than I do."

By contrast, consider the courtship of personal celebrity by the comparison CEOs. Scott Paper, the comparison company to Kimberly-Clark, hired Al Dunlap as CEO—a man who would tell anyone who would listen (and many who would have preferred not to) about his accomplishments. After 19 months atop Scott Paper,

Personal Humility	Professional Will
Demonstrates a compelling modesty, shunning public adulation; never boastful.	Creates superb results, a clear catalyst in the transition from good to great.
Acts with quiet, calm determination; relies principally on inspired standards, not inspiring charisma, to motivate.	Demonstrates an unwavering resolve to do whatever must be done to produce the best long-term results, no matter how difficult.
Channels ambition into the company, not the self; sets up successors for even more greatness in the next generation.	Sets the standard of building an enduring great company; will settle for nothing less.
Looks in the mirror, not out the window, to apportion responsibility for poor results, never blaming other people, external factors, or bad luck.	Looks out the window, not in the mirror, to apportion credit for the success of the company—to other people, external factors, and good luck.

Exhibit 9.3.   The Yin and Yang of Level 5.

Dunlap said in *BusinessWeek*, "The Scott story will go down in the annals of American business history as one of the most successful, quickest turnarounds ever. It makes other turnarounds pale by comparison." He personally accrued $100 million for 603 days of work at Scott Paper—about $165,000 per day—largely by slashing the workforce, halving the R&D budget, and putting the company on growth steroids in preparation for sale. After selling off the company and pocketing his quick millions, Dunlap wrote an autobiography in which he boastfully dubbed himself "Rambo in pinstripes." It's hard to imagine Darwin Smith thinking, "Hey, that Rambo character reminds me of me," let alone stating it publicly.

Granted, the Scott Paper story is one of the more dramatic in our study, but it's not an isolated case. In more than two-thirds of the comparison companies, we noted the presence of a gargantuan ego that contributed to the demise or continued mediocrity of the company. We found this pattern particularly strong in the unsustained comparison companies—the companies that would show a shift in performance under a talented yet egocentric Level 4 leader, only to decline in later years.

Lee Iacocca, for example, saved Chrysler from the brink of catastrophe, performing one of the most celebrated (and deservedly so) turnarounds in U.S. business history. The automaker's stock rose 2.9 times higher than the general market about halfway through his tenure. But then Iacocca diverted his attention to transforming himself. He appeared regularly on talk shows like the *Today Show* and *Larry King Live,* starred in more than 80 commercials, entertained the idea of running for president of the United States, and promoted his autobiography, which sold 7 million copies worldwide. Iacocca's personal stock soared, but Chrysler's stock fell 31% below the market in the second half of his tenure.

And once Iacocca had accumulated all the fame and perks, he found it difficult to leave center stage. He postponed his retirement so many times that Chrysler's insiders began to joke that Iacocca stood for "I Am Chairman of Chrysler Corporation Always." When he finally retired, he demanded that the board continue to provide a private jet and stock options. Later, he joined forces with noted takeover artist Kirk Kerkorian to launch a hostile bid for Chrysler. (It failed.) Iacocca did make one final brilliant decision: He picked a modest yet determined man—perhaps even a Level 5—as his successor. Bob Eaton rescued Chrysler from its second near-death crisis in a decade and set the foundation for a more enduring corporate transition.

AN UNWAVERING RESOLVE

Besides extreme humility, Level 5 leaders also display tremendous professional will. When George Cain became CEO of Abbott Laboratories, it was a drowsy, family-controlled business sitting at the bottom quartile of the pharmaceutical industry, living off its cash cow, erythromycin. Cain was a typical Level 5 leader in his lack of pretense; he didn't have the kind of inspiring personality that would galvanize the company. But he had something much more powerful: inspired standards. He could not stand mediocrity in any form and was utterly intolerant of anyone who would accept the idea that good is good enough. For the next 14 years, he relentlessly imposed his will for greatness on Abbott Labs.

Among Cain's first tasks was to destroy one of the root causes of Abbott's middling performance: nepotism. By systematically rebuilding both the board and the executive team with the best people he could find, Cain made his statement. Family ties no longer mattered. If you couldn't become the best executive in the industry within your span of responsibility, you would lose your paycheck.

Such near-ruthless rebuilding might be expected from an outsider brought in to turn the company around, but Cain was an 18-year insider—and a part of the family, the son of a previous president. Holiday gatherings were probably tense for a few years in the Cain clan—"Sorry I had to fire you. Want another slice of turkey?"—but in the end, family members were pleased with the performance of their stock. Cain had set in motion a profitable growth machine. From its transition in 1974 to 2000, Abbott created shareholder returns that beat the market 4.5:1, outperforming industry superstars Merck and Pfizer by a factor of two.

Another good example of iron-willed Level 5 leadership comes from Charles R. "Cork" Walgreen III, who transformed dowdy Walgreens into a company that outperformed the stock market 16:1 from its transition in 1975 to 2000. After years of dialogue and debate within his executive team about what to do with Walgreens' food-service operations, this CEO sensed the team had finally reached a watershed: the company's brightest future lay in convenient drug-stores, not in food service. Dan Jorndt, who succeeded Walgreen in 1988, describes what happened next:

> Cork said at one of our planning committee meetings, "Okay, now I am going to draw the line in the sand. We are going to be out of the restaurant business completely in five years." At the time we had more than 500 restaurants. You could have heard a pin drop. He said, "I want to let everybody know the clock is ticking." Six months later we were at our next planning committee meeting and someone men-tioned just in passing that we had only five years to be out of the restaurant business. Cork was not a real vociferous fellow. He sort of tapped on the table and said, "Listen, you now have four and a half years. I said you had five years six months ago. Now you've got four and a half years." Well, that next day things really clicked into gear for winding down our restaurant business. Cork never wavered. He never doubted. He never second-guessed.

Like Darwin Smith selling the mills at Kimberly-Clark, Cork Walgreen required stoic resolve to make his decisions. Food service was not the largest part of the business, although it did add substan-tial profits to the bottom line. The real problem was more emotional than financial. Walgreens had, after all, invented the malted milk shake, and food service had been a long-standing family tradition dating back to Cork's grandfather. Not only that, some food-service outlets were even named after the CEO—for example, a restaurant chain named Corky's. But no matter; if Walgreen had to fly in the face of family tradition in order to refocus on the one arena in which

Walgreens could be the best in the world—convenient drugstores—and terminate everything else that would not produce great results, then Cork would do it. Quietly, doggedly, simply.

One final, yet compelling, note on our findings about Level 5: because Level 5 leaders have ambition not for themselves but for their companies, they routinely select superb successors. Level 5 leaders want to see their companies become even more successful in the next generation and are comfortable with the idea that most people won't even know that the roots of that success trace back to them. As one Level 5 CEO said, "I want to look from my porch, see the company as one of the great companies in the world someday, and be able to say, 'I used to work there.'" By contrast, Level 4 leaders often fail to set up the company for enduring success. After all, what better testament to your own personal greatness than that the place falls apart after you leave?

In more than three-quarters of the comparison companies, we found executives who set up their successors for failure, chose weak successors, or both. Consider the case of Rubbermaid, which grew from obscurity to become one of *Fortune*'s most admired companies and then, just as quickly, disintegrated into such sorry shape that it had to be acquired by Newell.

The architect of this remarkable story was a charismatic and brilliant leader named Stanley C. Gault, whose name became synonymous in the late 1980s with Rubbermaid's success. Across the 312 articles collected by our research team about the company, Gault comes through as a hard-driving, egocentric executive. In one article, he responds to the accusation of being a tyrant with the statement, "Yes, but I'm a sincere tyrant." In another, drawn directly from his own comments on leading change, the word "I" appears 44 times, while the word "we" appears 16 times. Of course, Gault had every reason to be proud of his executive success: Rubbermaid generated 40 consecutive quarters of earnings growth under his leadership—an impressive performance, to be sure, and one that deserves respect.

But Gault did not leave behind a company that would be great without him. His chosen successor lasted a year on the job and the next in line faced a management team so shallow that he had to temporarily shoulder four jobs while scrambling to identify a new number-two executive. Gault's successors struggled not only with a management void but also with strategic voids that would eventually bring the company to its knees.

Of course, you might say—as one *Fortune* article did—that the fact that Rubbermaid fell apart after Gault left proves his greatness as a leader. Gault was a tremendous Level 4 leader, perhaps one of the best in the last 50 years. But he was not at Level 5, and that is one crucial reason why Rubbermaid went from good to great for a brief, shining moment and then just as quickly went from great to irrelevant.

THE WINDOW AND THE MIRROR

As part of our research, we interviewed Alan L. Wurtzel, the Level 5 leader responsible for turning Circuit City from a ramshackle company on the edge of bankruptcy into one of America's most successful electronics retailers. In the 15 years after its transition date in 1982, Circuit City outperformed the market 18.5:1.

We asked Wurtzel to list the top five factors in his company's transformation, ranked by importance. His number one factor? Luck. "We were in a great industry, with the wind at our backs," he said. But wait a minute, we retorted, Silo—your comparison company—was in the same industry, with the same wind and bigger sails. The conversation went back and forth, with Wurtzel refusing to take much credit for the transition, preferring to attribute it largely to just being in the right place at the right time. Later, when we asked him to discuss the factors that would sustain a good-to-great transformation, he said, "The first thing that comes to mind is luck. I was lucky to find the right successor."

Luck. What an odd factor to talk about. Yet the Level 5 leaders we identified invoked it frequently. We asked an executive at steel company Nucor why it had such a remarkable track record for making good decisions. His response? "I guess we were just lucky." Joseph F. Cullman III, the Level 5 CEO of Philip Morris, flat out refused to take credit for his company's success, citing his good fortune to have great colleagues, successors, and predecessors, Even the book he wrote about his career—which he penned at the urging of his colleagues and which he never intended to distribute widely outside the company—had the unusual title *I'm a Lucky Guy*.

At first, we were puzzled by the Level 5 leaders' emphasis on good luck. After all, there is no evidence that the companies that had progressed from good to great were blessed with more good luck (or more bad luck, for that matter) than the comparison companies. But then we began to notice an interesting pattern in the executives at the comparison companies: They often blamed their situations on bad luck, bemoaning the difficulties of the environment they faced.

Compare Bethlehem Steel and Nucor, for example. Both steel companies operated with products that are hard to differentiate, and both faced a competitive challenge from cheap imported steel. Both companies paid significantly higher wages than most of their foreign competitors. And yet executives at the two companies held completely different views of the same environment.

Bethlehem Steel's CEO summed up the company's problems in 1983 by blaming the imports: "Our first, second, and third problems are imports." Meanwhile, Ken Iverson and his crew at Nucor saw the imports as a blessing: "Aren't we lucky; steel is heavy, and they have to ship it all the way across the ocean, giving us a huge advantage." Indeed, Iverson saw the first, second, and third problems facing the U.S. steel industry not in imports but in management. He even went so far as to speak out publicly against government protection against imports, telling a gathering of stunned steel executives in 1977 that the real problems facing the industry lay in the fact that management had failed to keep pace with technology.

The emphasis on luck turns out to be part of a broader pattern that we have come to call "the window and the mirror." Level 5 leaders, inherently humble, look out the window to apportion credit—even undue credit—to factors outside themselves. If they can't find a specific person or event to give credit to, they credit good luck. At the same time, they look in the mirror to assign responsibility, never citing bad luck or external factors when things go poorly. Conversely, the comparison executives frequently looked out the window for factors to blame but preened in the mirror to credit themselves when things went well.

The funny thing about the window-and-mirror concept is that it does not reflect reality. According to our research, the Level 5 leaders were responsible for their companies' transformations. But they would never admit that. We can't climb inside their heads and assess whether they deeply believed what they saw through the window and in the mirror. But it doesn't really matter, because they acted as if they believed it, and they acted with such consistency that it produced exceptional results.

BORN OR BRED?

Not long ago, I shared the Level 5 finding with a gathering of senior executives. A woman who had recently become chief executive of her company raised her hand. "I believe what you've told us about Level 5 leadership," she said, "but I'm disturbed because I know I'm not there yet, and maybe I never will be. Part of the reason I got this job is because of my strong ego. Are you telling me that I can't make my company great if I'm not Level 5?"

"Let me return to the data," I responded. "Of 1,435 companies that appeared on the *Fortune* 500 since 1965, only 11 made it into our study. In those 11, all of them had Level 5 leaders in key positions, including the CEO role, at the pivotal time of transition. Now, to reiterate, we're not saying that Level 5 is the only element required for the move from good to great, but it appears to be essential."

She sat there, quiet for a moment, and you could guess what many people in the room were thinking. Finally, she raised her hand again. "Can you learn to become Level 5?" I still do not know the answer to that question. Our research, frankly, did not delve into how Level 5 leaders come to be, nor did we attempt to explain or codify the nature of their emotional lives. We speculated on the unique psychology of Level 5 leaders. Were they "guilty" of displacement—shifting their own raw ambition onto something other than themselves? Were they sublimating their egos for dark and complex reasons rooted in childhood trauma? Who knows? And perhaps more important, do the psychological roots of Level 5 leadership matter any more than do the roots of charisma or intelligence? The question remains: Can Level 5 be developed?

My preliminary hypothesis is that there are two categories of people: those who don't have the Level 5 seed within them and those who do. The first category consists of people who could never in a million years bring themselves to subjugate their own needs to the greater ambition of something larger and more lasting than themselves. For those people, work will always be first and foremost about what they get—the fame, fortune, power, adulation, and so on. Work will never be about what they build, create, and contribute. The great irony is that the animus and personal ambition that often drives people to become a Level 4 leader stands at odds with the humility required to rise to Level 5.

When you combine that irony with the fact that boards of directors frequently operate under the false belief that a larger-than-life, egocentric leader is required to make a company great, you can quickly see why Level 5 leaders rarely appear at the top of our institutions. We keep putting people in positions of power who lack the seed to become a Level 5 leader, and that is one major reason why there are so few companies that make a sustained and verifiable shift from good to great.

The second category consists of people who could evolve to Level 5; the capability resides within them, perhaps buried, ignored, or simply nascent. Under the right circumstances—with self-reflection, a mentor, loving parents, a significant life experience, or other factors—the seed can begin to develop. Some of the Level 5 leaders in our study had significant life experiences that might have sparked development of the seed. Darwin Smith fully blossomed as a Level 5 after his near-death experience with cancer. Joe Cullman was profoundly affected by his World War II experiences, particularly the last-minute change of orders that took him off a doomed ship on which he surely would have died; he considered the next 60-odd years a great gift. A strong religious belief or conversion might also nurture the seed. Colman Mockler, for example, converted to evangelical Christianity while getting his MBA at Harvard, and later, according to the book *Cutting Edge* by Gordon McKibben, he became a prime mover in a group of Boston business executives that met frequently over breakfast to discuss the carryover of religious values to corporate life.

We would love to be able to give you a list of steps for getting to Level 5—other than contracting cancer, going through a religious conversion, or getting different parents—but we have no solid research data that would support a credible list. Our research exposed Level 5 as a key component inside the black box of what it takes to shift a company from good to great. Yet inside that black box is another—the inner development of a person to Level 5 leadership. We could speculate on what that inner box might hold, but it would mostly be just that: speculation.

In short, Level 5 is a very satisfying idea, a truthful idea, a powerful idea, and, to make the move from good to great, very likely an essential idea. But to provide "ten steps to Level 5 leadership" would trivialize the concept.

My best advice, based on the research, is to practice the other good-to-great-disciplines that we discovered. Since we found a tight symbiotic relationship between each of the other findings and Level 5, we suspect that conscientiously trying to lead using the other disciplines can help you move in the right direction. There is no guarantee that doing so will turn executives into full-fledged Level 5 leaders, but it gives them a tangible place to begin, especially if they have the seed within.

We cannot say for sure what percentage of people have the seed within, nor how many of those can nurture it enough to become Level 5. Even those of us on the research team who identified Level 5 do not know whether we will succeed in evolving to its heights. And yet all of us who worked on the finding have been inspired by the idea of trying to move toward Level 5. Darwin Smith, Colman Mockler, Alan Wurtzel, and all the other Level 5 leaders we learned about have become role models for us. Whether or not we make it to Level 5, it is worth trying. For like all basic truths about what is best in human beings, when we catch a glimpse of that truth, we know that our own lives and all that we touch will be the better for making the effort to get there.

—◊◊◊—

Jim Collins is a best-selling author, a student of enduring great companies and teacher to leaders throughout the corporate and social sectors, and a former faculty member at the Stanford University Graduate School of Business who now works from his management research laboratory in Boulder, Colorado.

CHAPTER TEN

Thinking Gray and Free

Steven B. Sample

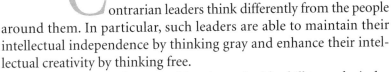ontrarian leaders think differently from the people around them. In particular, such leaders are able to maintain their intellectual independence by thinking gray and enhance their intellectual creativity by thinking free.

Conventional wisdom considers it a valuable skill to make judgments as quickly as possible, and conventional wisdom may well be right when it comes to managers. But contrarian wisdom argues that, for leaders, judgments as to the truth or falsity of information or the merits of new ideas should be arrived at as slowly and subtly as possible—and in many cases not at all.

One of the most rewarding aspects of teaching a class on leadership has been the opportunity to watch bright undergraduates learn to "think gray" while holding firmly to their core principles. Thinking gray is an extraordinarily uncommon characteristic which requires a good deal of effort to develop. But it is one of the most important skills which a leader can acquire.

Most people are binary and instant in their judgments; that is, they immediately categorize things as good or bad, true or false, black or white, friend or foe. A truly effective leader, however, needs to be able to see the shades of gray inherent in a situation in order to make wise decisions as to how to proceed.

The essence of thinking gray is this: don't form an opinion about an important matter until you've heard all the relevant facts and arguments, or until circumstances force you to form an opinion without recourse to all the facts (which happens occasionally, but much less frequently than one might imagine). F. Scott Fitzgerald once described something similar to thinking gray when he observed that the test of a first-rate mind is the ability to hold two opposing thoughts at the same time while still retaining the ability to function.

Generally the only time average people are instructed to think gray is when they are called to serve on a jury in a court of law (which may be one reason so many people regard jury duty as a colossal pain). Jurors are expected to suspend judgment until they have heard all the facts and arguments, and then and only then are they asked to reach a conclusion. I've never served on a jury myself, but talking with people who have and observing juries up close have convinced me that most jurors begin to make up their minds about a case before the trial even begins. And I suspect that most judges do as well.

After all, thinking gray is not a natural act, especially for people who see themselves as leaders. Our typical view of great leaders is that they are bold and decisive people who are strongly governed by their passions and prejudices. Who could imagine a Teddy Roosevelt or a Vince Lombardi thinking gray?

A black-and-white binary approach to thinking may in fact be a successful strategy for some leaders, especially if they must deal daily with fight-or-flight situations. But even many of the world's most noted military leaders were adroit at thinking gray on the battlefield. Napoleon, Washington, and Rommel all knew the value of suspending judgment about important matters, and especially about the validity of incoming intelligence, until the last possible moment.

There are three very real dangers to effective leadership associated with binary thinking. One is that leaders form opinions before it is necessary to do so, and in the process close their minds to facts and arguments that may subsequently come to their attention. The second danger is flip-flopping. Leaders hear something in favor of a proposition and decide on the spot that the proposition must be true. Later that same day they hear an argument against the proposition and decide that the proposition must be false. Many failed leaders have tended to believe the last thing they heard from the last person they talked to, thereby putting themselves and their followers through mental (and sometime physical) contortions which were both unnecessary and counterproductive.

The third danger relates to an observation by the German philosopher Friedrich Nietzsche to the effect that people tend to believe that which they sense is strongly believed by others. A well-developed ability to think gray is the best defense leaders can have against this kind of assault on their intellectual independence. Leaders may want to nurture a herd mentality among their followers, but they should never succumb to such thinking themselves.

Nietzsche's point was beautifully illustrated by an experiment fashioned by psychologist Solomon Asch a half-century ago and repeated by others many times since then. In the experiment, eight subjects, supposedly chosen at random, were brought together in a room and shown a series of cards on which were printed four vertical lines. Each subject was asked in turn to identify which one of the three lines on the right side of the card was the same length as the line on the left side of the card. The experiment was arranged so that seven of the eight "subjects" were in fact ringers who, with conviction and sincerity, would each identify the same one of the right-hand lines as being equal in length to the left-hand line, when in fact it was not. The one true subject in this experiment was then faced with either going along with the judgment of the group and declaring as true something he knew to be false, or taking a position which was at odds with the consensus opinion of his peers. Roughly three-quarters of the subjects went against their better judgment and joined in with the false consensus at least once.

As in so many other areas that are essential to effective leadership, the popular media are a major stumbling block to thinking gray. There is no such thing as an unbiased article in a newspaper or an objective sound bite on television news. On the contrary, reporters and editors are trained experts at getting you to believe what it is they have to say and to adopt their point of view. Indeed, à la Nietzsche, the media want you to believe that everyone else (or at least, every other important person) believes what it is they have to say. It is precisely this patina of believability and respectability that makes the popular media so attractive to us, especially when their messages comport with our own passions and prejudices. And it is precisely this same patina that stands in the way of our thinking gray.

The binary point of view already inherent in the popular media has become more pronounced, as straight coverage of politics has moved into a sports-section-like obsession with identifying winners and losers and successes and failures. A horse-race approach to political coverage, however, can rarely address adequately the complexities and nuances of developments in public policy.

Lest we go too far with this idea, let it be said that thinking gray—suspending our binary instincts—is really necessary for leaders for only the weightiest of issues. If they were to attempt to think gray about everything, their brains would become a jumbled mess. Decisions about clothes, food, popular music, and so forth are usually made in an off-the-cuff binary way, and that's perfectly fine.

However, these ordinary and routine types of decisions offer a wonderful chance to develop the discipline of thinking gray. One can use these situations as opportunities to practice suspending judgment. You don't have to decide right away whether you like a person you've just met, or whether you might eventually be able to appreciate a new food you've just tried, or whether you should see a particular movie you've recently heard about. Just for fun (or for practice) you can file away your first impressions about these and other relatively trivial matters, and reach conclusions with respect to them at a later date (or not at all). A great benefit of this exercise is that, when a truly important leadership issue surfaces, you will have had some practice in thinking gray.

Thinking gray is decidedly not the same thing as thinking skeptically. Skeptics initially place everything they hear or read in the "not true" box, with an implied willingness to move things to the "true" box if the accumulated evidence warrants such a transfer. There's often a hint of cynicism about the skeptic that can be very off-putting to followers. It's difficult for people to be inspired by a Doubting Thomas.

By contrast, the contrarian leader who can think gray doesn't place things he or she hears or reads in either the "not true" or the "true" box. These leaders are as open to enthusiastically embracing a new idea as they are to rejecting it. And they can truthfully compliment a lieutenant for having come up with a new idea or observation, without misleading the lieutenant as to whether they believe it to be good or true or useful.

A close cousin of thinking gray is what I like to call thinking free—free, that is, from all prior restraints. It's popular these days to talk about "thinking out of the box" or "brainstorming," but thinking free takes that process of inventiveness to the next level. The difference between thinking out of the box and thinking free can be understood when we imagine ourselves coming out of a heated swimming pool on a cool, brisk day. When we merely think out of the box, we stay in the cold just long enough to feel slightly uncomfortable, and then hastily retreat either back into the warm pool or indoors. But when we are truly thinking free, we stay out in the cold until we shiver and our teeth chatter. It's the ability to tolerate the cold long after it becomes unpleasant—to forcibly sustain our thinking free for more than a fleeting moment—that leads to the greatest innovations.

The key to thinking free is first to allow your mind to contemplate really outrageous ideas, and only subsequently apply the constraints of practicality, practicability, legality, cost, time, and ethics. As with thinking gray, thinking free is an unnatural act; not one person in a thousand can do it without enormous effort.

Here's a simple example. A leader brings a group of people together who share a common goal (e.g., keeping their company afloat in a brutally competitive market), but who have widely varying opinions as to how the goal might best be achieved. The leader asks each person in turn to propose an off-the-wall idea for achieving the goal, with the proviso that every other person in the group must respond with at least two reasons why the idea will work. The result is often surliness or sullen silence on the part of the participants. Most people are simply unable to force themselves to think positively for even a few minutes about an idea which they believe in their hearts is stupid, wrongheaded, immoral, impractical, or illegal.

Now please do not misunderstand me; I am not suggesting that leaders should pursue evil or illegal or ridiculous ideas. On the contrary, I have found that one's principles, passions, and prejudices always reassert control after a few minutes of thinking free. But during those few minutes, the leader or his or her associates just might come up with a truly original idea.

Congenital naysayers are among the greatest stumbling blocks to thinking free. Rather than imagining how a new idea might possibly work, they instinctively think of all the reasons why it won't. They sincerely believe they're doing everyone a favor by reducing the amount of time spent on bad or foolish ideas. But what they really do is undermine the creativity that can be harvested from thinking free. Most new inventions are merely novel combinations of devices or techniques that already exist. Thus, the key to successful invention often lies in getting one's brain to imagine new combinations of existing elements that solve a problem in a way no one has ever thought of before.

My favorite way to stimulate this kind of thinking free is to force myself to contemplate absolutely outrageous and impossible ways to address a particular problem. For example, in 1967 I was struggling to invent a new way to control a dishwasher, in order to replace the ubiquitous (and troublesome) clock-motor timer. At one point, I lay on the floor and forced myself to imagine hay bales, elephants, planets, ladybugs, sofas, microbes, newspapers, hydroelectric dams, French horns, electrons, and trees, each in turn and in various combinations controlling a dishwasher.

This exercise was, to say the least, extremely difficult and disconcerting, so much so that I could only do it for ten minutes at a time. But after a few such sessions I suddenly saw in my mind's eye an almost complete circuit diagram for a digital electronic control system for a home appliance. This system was unlike anything I or others had ever contemplated before. As a consequence my colleagues and I were able to establish a very strong patent position in this particular area of technology, and my invention was eventually employed in hundreds of millions of home appliances around the world.

As improbable as it might sound, this same approach to thinking free can lead to novel ways of addressing some of the competitive, political, legal, policy, and bureaucratic challenges one must confront as a leader. The key is to break free for just a few minutes from the incredibly tight constraints that rule our thinking almost all of the time, even when we dream or engage in so-called free association. Really thinking free is hard work, and it usually requires a good deal of effort and determination beyond simple daydreaming or mental freewheeling. It's tough to break out of the deep ruts in which our minds normally run. But the benefits that accrue to the leader from thinking free can be truly spectacular. Of course, microbes, hay bales and elephants never found their way into my application for a patent on a new way to control a home appliance. On the contrary, the solution to this problem involved a simple combination of standard electronic components—so simple, so nearly obvious, that I wondered why no one had ever thought of it before.

That's the way it is with so many innovations—they seem obvious once they've been discovered. But prior to that time, they are anything but obvious. For example, the benefits of universal adult suffrage seem obvious to twenty-first-century Americans, but it took millennia after the development of writing to discover and implement this idea (which was not fully adopted in England until 1928, when women were finally given the vote). The wheel-and-axle seems an obvious bit of technology to us today, but that was not discovered until thousands of years after the invention of the roller, and many human societies never discovered the wheel-and-axle on their own. The auto mall is an obvious way to increase the sales of new cars, but when I was a boy the Ford dealer in town wanted to be located as far away as possible from the Chevrolet dealer.

It's well known among engineers that the most important inventions in a particular field are often made by people who are new to that field—people who are too naïve to know all the reasons why something can't be done, and who are able to think more freely about seemingly intractable problems. The same is true of the leadership of institutions: fresh blood and outside perspectives can often turn an ailing organization around.

When my wife and I were interviewing in the early 1980s for the presidency of the State University of New York at Buffalo (SUNY-Buffalo, or the University at Buffalo, or UB for short), we saw a university with great underlying strengths and numerous superficial problems. Unfortunately, the problematic surface was all that was perceived by most of UB's constituencies at the time. Never in our lives had we encountered a university that was so down on itself or that was held in such low esteem by so many of its own faculty, students, administrators, townspeople, and alumni. The body politic of the university seemed to be bruised all over—whenever we touched it, no matter how gently, it seemed to quiver and shrink back a bit. For example, during the four months prior to my officially assuming the presidency in March of 1982, and during my first few months in office, I spoke directly with hundreds of UB's constituents. Almost invariably these conversations began with the other person saying something negative about the university. And during this same period I never met a single student who said that he or she was proud to be attending UB.

However, from my wife's and my perspective, the inner core, the infrastructure if you will, of the University at Buffalo was in exceedingly good health. We saw a university which had an excellent (albeit somewhat dispirited) faculty, competitive faculty salaries, good students who were willing to work hard, a loyal and supportive governing council, competent and dedicated staff, an active university foundation, a brand-new physical plant, mostly new scientific equipment, an outstanding library, and a long and distinguished academic history.

We also recognized that UB was in fact SUNY's flagship campus, although the vast majority of New Yorkers, and indeed most Buffalonians, would not have agreed with that statement in 1982. It seemed clear to us that, as the flagship public institution in a large and prosperous state, UB had a shot at becoming one of America's premier public universities.

There were of course formidable obstacles blocking UB's development. In addition to the spiritual malaise cited earlier, there loomed the fact that the city of Buffalo and its environs were mired in a deep recession, with unemployment rates running as high as 15 percent. Then too, the entire SUNY system was caught in the suffocating embrace of a huge state bureaucracy which was trying its best to micromanage everything at the university from coffee cups to student-contact hours.

And finally there was the fact that most New Yorkers seemed to view public higher education as being inherently inferior to private higher education. I recall how shocked I was when, early in my tenure at UB, I heard a trustee of the SUNY system say in public that "SUNY is the college of last resort." Good grief! I should have thought that every trustee would see the SUNY system as the college of first resort for all classes of New Yorkers, as is the case with the great public universities in other states.

Nonetheless, in spite of these difficulties and problems, my wife and I were convinced that UB's future was potentially very bright. Fortunately most members of the UB Council and a significant number of faculty and staff agreed. The next nine years more than justified Kathryn's and my seemingly unfounded optimism. By the end of that period UB had been elected to the prestigious Association of American Universities (only 61 of the more than 3,500 colleges and universities in America are members of the AAU; UB was the first public university in New York or New England to have been elected), sponsored research funding had tripled, applications for admission had doubled, we had completed or begun construction of more than two million square feet of new buildings at a cost of more than $400 million, UB was raising more private funds each year than all the other SUNY campuses combined, and *U.S. News and World Report* had named UB as one of the five most rapidly rising universities in the country.

Was it a miracle? No. Was the president a genius? No. It was just that my wife and I, coming from our experiences at the University of Nebraska, Purdue University, and the University of Illinois, were able to see UB and its surrounding community from a very different perspective. In other words, our thinking about UB was freer and less constrained than that of our colleagues and peers in western New York.

We often speak of the need for leaders to have vision. Creative imagination, which relates to the ability to think free, may in the end be every bit as important as vision. Many of us were tested on spatial relations in school, being asked to look at a number of pieces of a puzzle and imagine different ways in which those pieces might be combined. A similar act of imagination is a powerful tool for leaders.

Leaders have to be able to imagine different organizational combinations in their minds and see how they will play out. They have to be able to move people around in their minds and grasp how the people would respond to new situations. They have to be able to move resources and budgets around and be able to discern how those moves would affect the bottom line. They need to be able to look at complex human situations and sense how the outcome would be affected depending on the sequence in which they interact with various participants. If they cannot do these things using only their imagination—if they can only work with tangible, concrete data—they may well fail as leaders. It is too time-consuming, risky and expensive to conduct an actual experiment to test the feasibility of every new idea. Generally speaking, leaders must be able to accurately play out contingencies within the arena of their imagination.

But here's a bit of good news for would-be leaders who find it difficult to think free, and whose imaginations are, shall we say, a bit underdeveloped. It's not absolutely necessary that leaders themselves be a creative genius overflowing with original and inventive ideas in order to be effective. In many cases it's sufficient if leaders simply recognize and nurture thinking free among their followers, and then capitalize on the followers' creative ideas and imaginations. Indeed, many successful leaders would say it's more important that a leader's lieutenants be able to think free than it is for the leader to do so. (J. Robert Oppenheimer once said of his Manhattan Project team, "What we don't know we explain to each other.") Realistically, though, leaders whose own minds are stuck in a rut will find it very difficult to value imaginative thinking on the part of those around them.

One must always keep in mind that leadership is an art, not a science. Effective management may be a science (although I have my doubts), but effective leadership is purely an art. In this sense, leadership is more akin to music, painting, and poetry than it is to more routinized endeavors. When Franklin Roosevelt met Orson Welles, the president showed great deference to the media pioneer and actor, saying he wished he were as gifted a performing artist as Welles—to which Welles replied, "With all due respect, Mr. President, you are!"

All of the arts, when practiced at the highest levels of excellence, depend on a steady stream of fresh ideas and creative imagination. Make no mistake, Mozart was thinking free when he composed, even though his music may sound canonical today. As a former professional musician, I know that the best solos in jazz occur when the soloist frees his mind of prior constraints and makes up entirely new musical associations as he goes along. Can anyone view Picasso's paintings or Frank Gehry's buildings and not see flashes of unrestrained thought and imagination? And when I read Shakespeare I hear the cacophonous undertones of thinking free—his constant testing of unusual juxtapositions of words, his novel metaphors and similes, his making up of new words and stretching the meanings of old ones with impunity.

So it is with effective leadership. Leaders whose thinking is constrained within well-worn ruts, who are completely governed by their established passions and prejudices, who are incapable of thinking either gray or free, and who can't even appropriate the creative imagination and fresh ideas of those around them, are as anachronistic and ineffective as the dinosaur. They may by dint of circumstances remain in power, but their followers would almost certainly be better off without them.

—⟳⟳⟳—

Steven B. Sample is the tenth president and first holder of the Robert C. Packard President's Chair at the University of Southern California, member of the National Academy of Engineering for his contributions to consumer electronics and leadership in interdisciplinary research and education, and member of the American Academy of Arts and Sciences in recognition of his accomplishments as a university president.

CHAPTER ELEVEN

Enhancing the Psycho-Spiritual Development of Leaders
Lessons from Leadership Journeys in Asia

Philip H. Mirvis
Karen Ayas

> We started this journey knowing that it was about business, but instead we learned about humanity.

> I was able to get to know a great number of enlightened souls, but I also discovered myself.

hese are two reflections from Asian leaders of a multinational foods business who spent three days in ashrams, spiritual centers, micro-enterprises, and charities in India learning about community life. The business leaders tended to the needy, offered what help they could, and marveled at how much could be accomplished with so few resources. In a desert campsite for three days afterward, they shared and digested their experiences, and pondered the meaning and implications for their own leadership, their leadership group, and the business.

This chapter draws on the authors' firsthand observations and reflections from senior executives who participated in several of these leadership journeys to identify how deep connections to indigenous people and persons in need, meaningful encounters with nature, community service, and continuous reflection on these experiences made their ways into the executives' minds, hearts, and souls.

LEADERSHIP JOURNEYS

Annual journeys took the regional executives from this multi-national corporation—top country officials to marketers, supply chain managers, staff, and young leaders—to various locales within the company's business region. They traveled to Sarawak, Malaysia, to see devastated teak rainforests and meet the displaced Penan people; to Guilin, China, to meet villagers and understand their everyday needs; throughout India to study communal life and leadership; and to Sri Lanka to engage in service learning and provide tsunami relief. One intent was to open executives' eyes to economic, social, and environmental conditions in the region and thereby to inform their company's business strategies and social investments. A second was to expose the group members to new ways of being and working together in order to look afresh at their own organization and culture. A third, the subject of this chapter, was to stimulate their development as leaders.

The journeys were tribal experiences: leaders typically woke at dawn, dressed in local garb, exercised or meditated together, hiked from place to place, ate communally, swapped stories by the campfire, and slept alongside one another in tents. Daily experiences included meeting monks or a martial arts master, talking with local children or village elders, or simply reveling in the sounds and sights of nature. Considerable time was spent along the way in personal and collective reflection. The authors of this chapter helped to design, organize, and facilitate each of these journeys. Working with a team of researchers, they also prepared a *learning history* of each journey to document key insights for continued reflection (quotations used here come from those accounts).

The president of the Asian business, who authored and himself led the journeys, is interested in human development and believes spirituality is integral to leadership development. He drew from Stephen Covey's (2004) work, particularly the emphasis on development of the four intelligences—intellectual, physical, emotional, and spiritual.

Thus our journeys had multisensory activities and experiences that engaged the head, body, heart, and spirit. He also embraced M. Scott Peck's (1993) multidimensional consciousness—seeing it expand *to-and-from* the individual to the collective to a "force beyond ourselves." The journeys were, accordingly, multilevel experiences with solo, small-group, and communal moments. In addition, there were elements of discovery, contemplation, and serendipity along the way. The travel was to places of historical, cultural, or mystical significance, with the explicit intent of seeing the world and self afresh, and sharing the experience of being together with fellow travelers—not unlike a pilgrimage.

We recorded countless references to consciousness raising and personal transformation during these journeys. Many leaders, for example, talked of moments of self-discovery and of encountering their "true selves." They spoke of deeply connecting with the people they met and with one another. There was also talk of gaining insight into and being moved by the economic, social, and environmental conditions encountered. Finally, many leaders reported sensing a new mission on the journeys and concluded that they individually and collectively needed to find a "higher purpose" in their business lives. "Truly, this is a soul searching journey," said one leader upon reflection. "It is a journey of self-connecting, connecting with others, connecting with the universe, and certainly connecting with God."

PSYCHO-SPIRITUAL DIMENSIONS OF LEADERSHIP DEVELOPMENT

There is growing interest in developing the *whole* person and experimenting with holistic forms of leadership development—the case study here being one example (Mirvis, 1997, in press). The theorizing behind this references psychological phenomena, such as emotional intelligence, ego development, altruism, reciprocity, prosocial behavior, and the like. The long-standing but recently enriched literature on spirituality and leadership also speaks to these phenomena with complementary notions of spiritual intelligence, self-transcendence, unconditional love, generosity, service, and so on. In this chapter we combine these two frames of reference to consider some of the *psycho-spiritual* dimensions of leadership development: cultivating self-awareness, connecting to the other, forming into community, and discovering one's purpose. Let us look closely at each of these dimensions, drawing from the experiences of the journeys and reflections of the leaders on those experiences as they considered "Who am I?" "Who are you?" "Who are we?" and most important, "What is our purpose as business leaders?"

Cultivating Self-Awareness: *Who Am I?*

Most branches of psychology see self-knowledge as integral to human development and essential to being a healthy, functioning adult. Studies document how self-consciousness expands when people understand their familial roots and formative experiences, what moves and what puts them off, and also their highest hopes and deepest fears. Much of this fits into the rubric of *emotional intelligence* (EQ), which means, among other things, being in touch with one's makeup, proclivities, moods, and emotions, being able to recognize personal strengths and weaknesses, and understanding the impact one has on others (Goleman, 1995).

Not surprisingly, leadership development programs in many companies encourage employees to cultivate EQ through personality assessments, 360-degree feedback, coaching, and the like. These all have their place in personal development; however, we favor less structured, more timeless means to promote self-awareness among leaders. One approach involves personal reflection and storytelling about one's life experiences and lessons (Schön, 1983; Mirvis & Ayas, 2003).

Self-discovery and disclosure are a part of every leader's work in these Asian learning journeys. Most of the company's leaders in the region have written and shared their life stories with one another. "It's like a surgery of the soul. You begin to see the roots and patterns," says one young leader about this form of self-reflection, "and you understand what truly moves you." Biographical studies by psychologist Howard Gardner (1995) underscore this point by showing that formative experiences shape the beliefs and practices of leaders in almost every culture: they make up the leader's identity. The telling of identity stories, Gardner finds, builds deep connections between leaders and followers and, in particular, informs the identities of younger leaders.

During the China trip, after a hike into the mountains, the leaders wrote letters to "Mom and Dad" that surfaced heartfelt discussion about the emotional sides of leadership. Some ten or twelve leaders read their letters aloud, many striking the same themes:

> While writing to my parents I nearly choked with emotion as I real-
> ized how much I loved them. But I had never shared my feelings with
> them. I had always been taught that the open display of emotions was
> a sign of weakness. The credo of my clan is that "Men are born to face
> the challenges of this world. They do not cry. They lead. They are the
> pride of their family and must not fail." . . . Now I realize how much
> more I could have done if only I had sought the emotional support
> that I knew was there all along.

This kind of introspection is based on the psychodynamic notion that people reexperience their lives when they delve into the most emotionally charged aspects of their past (Freud, 1965). It helps to surface unexamined and repressed feelings about one's life course and to lift them up for fresh consideration. This form of self-discovery is integral to psychotherapy, where it strengthens the *observing ego* and helps people to gain a clearer self-picture (Klein, 1959). Reflections on Mom and Dad, although by no means akin to in-depth therapy, gave the leaders a chance to look into *who I am* with reference to parental influences.

There are, of course, other means in other traditions of knowing the self. Many of these Asian leaders, for example, turn to prayer, yoga, journaling, or meditation to explore their inner selves. In their various journeys together, they have been exposed to these disciplines as well as tai chi and deep breathing. This gives the lead-ers a taste of different forms of self-experience and, as a side ben-efit, allows them to see a variety of practices indigenous to their region.

An emphasis on *leading from within* seems to resonate with the Asian leaders, and these experiences help leaders locate their inner resources. The leaders meditated en masse each morning, and many felt a deep sense of knowing the self and tapping into their souls as they sat together in silence. One found harmony: "Silence sparks my emotions; it makes me surrender to my feelings and senses." Another found insight: "Silence is crucial for spiritualism. It is the only moment that you give your inner self the chance to talk to your outer self." Reflecting on their daily meditations, one said: "The time we spent learning about meditation was very worthwhile—I am remembering who I am and am determined to continue with the practice of meditation back home."

During the journeys there were also many occasions when encounters with the peoples of Asia lit up the leaders and stimulated deep reflections on the self. Listen to this self-examination by a young Indian:

> To be honest, when we went to communities and saw the devotion, dedication, and selfless service that they were providing, I was a little uncomfortable. Seeing how they're committed to training blind people, to building hospitals and training centers and all that, a feeling of guilt and discomfort arose: Am I doing something wrong that I'm not able to commit myself to such selfless service?

This is, in psychological parlance, the observing ego at work. But when inquiry turns to questions of one's place and purpose or, indeed, of the very meaning of life, the *transcendent ego* can also be activated (Peck, 1993). In such encounters, personal strivings and boundaries are surrendered, and the self opens and connects to the world of other beings and, in some cases, a higher power. Here is another Indian leader reflecting on his encounters:

> At the very outset let me admit that I feel humble and small because when I went to the Missionaries of Charity, I thought I was going to give and serve. I returned realizing how poor I am. I thought I had commitment but the sisters redefined this for me. I saw a courage that I have lacked—the courage to admit my weaknesses and seek help. I thought I was a loving and caring person. But the unconditional love to all and its manifestation in all the actions of the sisters made me wonder if my behavior towards my colleagues and even my family is indeed loving and caring or it is just a self-image I am carrying. This experience is another huge step in discovering the person that my mother raised, and I am grateful for this experience. Have I answered who am I? Not yet. But I am beginning to discover myself, and I am feeling at ease with myself with every layer I peel.

Russ Moxley (2000), among other scholars, asserts that this deep questioning and self-transcendence yields "spiritual power" that can be used to transform relationships with others.

Connecting to "Other": *Who Are You?*

Self-consciousness is essential to connecting to another, as only those who know themselves are able to understand the other and forge mutual ties. In turn, when trying to understand another person, people come to better understand themselves. George Herbert Mead (1934) terms this *role taking* or, more colloquially, putting your self in the place of others. This reciprocal role taking, over the life course, is central to socialization and the forming of identity; hence its relevance for developing the character of leaders.

Human relations training, common in organizational behavior curricula, stresses the importance of knowing the other as a key competency of leaders. Listening to and witnessing another's personal story is one means of cultivating this insight. Still, in the competitive business culture it is difficult to "lower the guard," as one leader put it, when sharing life stories with fellow executives. "The initial step of sharing personal information was difficult," he recalled. "But once you sense the value of truly connecting, building on it seemed relatively easy." "The important thing is to engage in the search and the inquiry into each other's cultures and mindsets, and into the relationship we have" said another. "To achieve this, one has to be open with oneself, understand one's own basic core values, and accept other people's differences 'as is.' This acceptance needs to be sincere and from the heart; without any prejudice, judgments and expectations."

This connecting to the other extends beyond the boundaries of the Asian leadership group. In the journey to China, for instance, leaders spent time "getting into the skin" of villagers. In the ancient hamlet of Xin Ping, the leaders worked alongside local people in their daily lives—sweeping streets, herding buffaloes, forming cement blocks, cooking noodles, and teaching. One commented:

> My experience "living" with the villagers was an eye opener. I was fortunate to be with a 72-year-old who had the energy of a 40-year-old woman. During her late 30s to early 40s she made sandals out of dried grass straw for Chinese soldiers. She narrated with enthusiasm how important these sandals were to protect the soldiers' feet while crossing marshlands and hiking mountains even during cold winter nights. Her simple understanding of the "big picture" and her role struck me . . . that no matter how small your role is . . . it is still part of the whole.

The leaders draw on a number of frameworks to enhance their consciousness of the self-and-other and gain a better understanding of who they are. They used, for example, various learning tools that helped them explore what is behind their perceptions and feelings (Argyris, 1982; Senge, 1990). On the journeys, leaders were asked to self-reflect whenever they connected with people along the way: *How am I reacting to this situation? To this person? What are my reactions telling me about my own assumptions about life and people?* Schein (2002) calls this "listening to ourselves."

At the same time, attention also turned to imagining: *What has this person's life been like? Why do they see things the way they do?* This is a different sort of self-listening in which the self makes inferences about what makes others tick and how they relate to their world. An Australian leader elaborated on the impact: "It's helping us develop empathy, to put yourself in the other person's shoes—your customer, your colleague, or one of your managers. You step outside of your own paradise and get a deep understanding that the way you do things is not the only way."

Recent interest in an *appreciative* style of leading (Cooperrider, 1990) has emphasized the positive potential of finding the goodness-in-the-other and improving the quality of human relationships. In seeing the sacredness of another, we also find it within ourselves.

In Sri Lanka this experience was palpable. The leaders spent several days cleaning up debris in schools and public buildings, helping local merchants to assess inventory and connect with suppliers, playing with children, and talking deeply with Sri Lankans, individually and in large gatherings. The report of a leader about his first encounter with a tsunami survivor illustrates the depth of the experience: "This man who had lost two of his family members told me how God has been kind to him—his neighbor had lost all of his five family members. He made me realize that there is such goodness in simple lives—where I have never bothered to look." Many had similar discoveries.

What did this soulful work teach the leaders? "We listened to the fears and hopes of the mothers, fathers, and children left behind in this beautiful but devastated country. We shed tears of pain, hope, and love," recalled one leader. "We shed even more tears when we realized that by simply sharing our spirit with them we made an incredible difference not only to their lives but also to our own. It continues to surprise me how care and service for others helps me discover my own love."

Forming into Community: *Who Are We?*

Naturally, such rich experiences of empathizing and connecting with the other, both emotionally and spiritually, made their way into the collective consciousness of the Asian leadership group. Forming the leaders into a work community engages what Peck (1987) calls a *group mind*—the ability of a collective to see both its constituent parts and the whole. His theories contend that this mindfulness develops organically through free-flowing conversation among a collection of people as they pay close attention to their own thoughts and feelings and to what is happening in the group overall.

The Asian leaders use a large-group discussion methodology, a variant of the dialogue process, to develop collective sensibilities (Isaacs, 1999). They sometimes talk in smaller, fifteen- to twenty-person groups, and sometimes as a full community of two hundred plus, all sitting in a circle, with everyone given the opportunity to speak, irrespective of rank or tenure. An expectation is set to speak openly and frankly, and to deal with the "difficult issues" that would otherwise be avoided or denied. There is also space for "process comments"—observations about how the collective is operating— and periodic moments of silence so that leaders can reflect quietly on what's been said and what they want to say next.

The process of getting to this collective mind, like all group development processes, is marked by conflict and paradoxes (Smith & Berg, 1987). The Asian leaders' first experiences with dialogue in China were difficult. One commented, "The first dialogue was very frustrating, despite my own pitiful efforts at involvement. In an Asian culture, it's not easy to speak out. The risk is very high to stand up and say something. It must be the right thing." "I was one of those who didn't stand up to talk," added another. "Why? Well, truthfully, I was scared. Nervous about standing up in front of 200 people to express how I feel. Not knowing if I could trust them." Then, she said, "It finally dawned on me that everything must come from the 'heart.' That is where it all begins."

To learn to dialogue among so many people across so many different cultures has taken time and patience. At the communal gathering in India, one year later, the Asian leaders, irrespective of nationality, spoke easily and naturally to the collective, built on each other's comments, challenged gracefully, and encouraged new voices to emerge. Said one, "It was great to see that words just poured out from everyone. We are starting to see the connections with each other."

What helped this mature? Time together, familiarity with one another, and a degree of psychological safety from past encounters all helped. The sharing of personal stories and in-the-moment thoughts and feelings also broke down barriers. "Whilst there are differences in our appearance, speech, and food," said one leader, "sharing innermost feelings and fears so openly bonded us emotionally." The leaders have also come to realize that intellect, wisdom, and virtues are not the heritage or characteristic of any particular nation or group of people. "We have different backgrounds," commented another leader. "I have to look into that deeply, open my mind up, and be big enough to accept each of you in my heart so we can have some sort of the same understanding and then become more united."

There are many psychodynamic models for bringing a group together. These typically involve "working through" group differences and conflicts by developing common understandings and norms. The model in the Asian leadership group has not been to work through differences by confronting them directly. Instead, the leadership body serves as a kind of container that holds differences and conflicts up for ongoing exploration. In the community-building tradition, such thoughtful, if sometimes heated, reflection on *who we are* yields a collective identity that at the same time preserves individuality and diversity in the community (Mirvis, 2002).

A true sense of community is born of inclusiveness and comes into being as a group transcends its members' differences. John Gardner (1995) terms this "wholeness incorporating diversity." In its more spiritualized conception, this feeling might be termed communion. Reflecting on this state, one leader commented:

> I feel very close to the Asia group. There was some weird sense of bonding that developed even though I didn't know more than half of the people. I really can't explain it but it was a sense of oneness or being together. It is strange because I felt this when we weren't even talking. It was a nice feeling. For the first time I experienced it outside my family. Maybe this is what we call community feeling.

Discovering Our Purpose: *Why Are We Here?*

These feelings of connection and communion focus on the internal characteristics of leaders and their community. What about their roles and responsibilities in the larger world? Reflecting on community work in India, one leader said, "Strong vibrant growing communities build around a relevant and compelling purpose." To answer the question, *What is our purpose as business leaders?* the Asian leaders made deep connections to the land and peoples of the region and learned from them. In principle, knowledge about economic, social, and environmental conditions can be gleaned from texts, talks, and conversations in any forum. But the experience of being there and seeing firsthand adds texture and arouses feelings and thus has greater potential to raise collective consciousness about conditions in the world (Wuthnow, 1991).

At a meeting in Sarawak, Malaysia, for instance, leaders' attention turned to the natural environment. There they encountered the terrible costs incurred in the clear-cutting of tropical rainforests. They heard a natural resources expert speak, and then to get physically involved and symbolically lend a hand, they cleaned a nearby beach of industrial flotsam and tourist trash. A trip upriver in hollowed-out wooden canoes took them to the village of the Penan people, where they met the village chief, medicine man, and tribe, and took a long walk with them through clear-cut forests. The experience led to earnest discussion of the benefits and the costs of economic growth in the region.

During the journey to China, attention turned to economics. A Pakistani noted meeting "villagers in rural China whose income was less then 125 USD per annum. Seventy percent of my country's 140 million population is similar to the family of the man I met today, while only 5 percent has a lifestyle similar to mine." He added, "I respect and value these villagers for who they are and what they deliver to all of us."

The journey to India added a social dimension to understandings of economics and of the world. Two reflections capture this powerfully:

> The contact with Indian communities really touched me as I saw voluntary work, devotion, sacrifice, purity, truth, belonging, affiliation, caring, working together in a responsible and dedicated fashion like a family. While family is so central to me in personal life, I feel that similar core thoughts need to be internalized and become a way of life in work life.

> Connecting with poverty in India reminds us that our company, as a member in Asia, has strong social responsibility. We need to build our

business success while taking on social responsibilities—to help to protect the environment, to relieve poverty . . . at the same time these actions will help our business grow.

The question of purpose was raised progressively over the journeys, becoming more and more profound. Time spent in Sarawak opened the leaders' eyes to the need to live with, rather than take from, the natural world. This in turn led to calls to incorporate criteria of environmental sustainability into the business's strategic and operating plans.

The journey to India opened new vistas on the question of purpose. One leader reported:

> We felt very small and humbled by all that the people were doing there. There was a feeling that they were actually contributing to society while we were doing things that were inconsequential. I raised this with the Maharaja and his answer was very clear. He said the community was working to empower the downtrodden whereas good businesses would eliminate the number of downtrodden. He therefore said that while they were working on curing the disease, we were working towards its eradication. He felt we were doing the more difficult and noble task.

The ongoing dialogues in India brought the leaders closer to the conclusion that organizations have to be driven by their missions rather than by numbers and processes. There was talk throughout of Jim Collins's (2001) findings on how companies moved from good to great.

In Sri Lanka, with the deeper realization of the interconnection of all things—or what Capra (1996) terms the *web of life*—a new sense of mission emerged for the Asian business. On a personal note, one leader stated, "I started getting the feeling that my work need not be confined to producing and selling as efficiently as possible but has a higher purpose of community service to the people of Asia." "This changes the paradigm of thinking that we are selling to consumers," said another one. "Instead we are serving our communities."

Over the course of these several journeys, an imperative emerged: the leaders had to put flesh onto their caring aspirations and translate them into a business mission to emphasize the healthy, nourishing aspects of food. Accordingly, these Asian leaders pledged to become responsible partners with the people of Asia and to address the health, vitality, and development of children and families through better food and beverages. They also pledged to be actively involved in communities and especially to understand and respond to the needs of the economically underprivileged and the children.

REFLECTIONS ON THE JOURNEYS

Does it go too far to speculate that the Asian leaders were connected to a new world that is *seeking to emerge*? Psychology today is filled with insights into and controversies over the relationship of mind and matter, the self, and the larger world in working life (Csikszentmihalyi, 2003). A provocative new study of one hundred fifty scientists and business leaders lends credence to the notion that we, as humans, can *presence* the future and be an active agent in its co-creation (Senge, Scharmer, Jaworski, & Flowers, 2004). But in the field of leadership and spirituality, this view of emergence is neither so controversial nor as provocative as it might otherwise seem. It follows from connecting deeply—at many levels of consciousness—to "the unseen order of things."

Encounters led the Asian leaders to see, feel, and embrace a common humanity with the people of Asia. But there was for many a deeper connection as well to a force or field larger than themselves. Some call this *karma* or *grace*. Other terms are *transcendence* or connecting to *universal consciousness*. Such larger-than-life themes were palpable on the recent journey to Sri Lanka, where leaders offered service to people and villages ravaged by the tsunami. During one memorable experience the leaders sat together with villagers who had "lost everything." One by one, village women told their stories, and the leaders bore witness to their trials and courage. A leader reflected on the impact: "We were all crying listening to their stories, but it brought them together, and it brought us together. We stood there with people we had met only one hour ago, hand in hand, in silence, tears pouring out our eyes in togetherness."

During personal reflections long into the night and on a solo journey to a quiet place, the leaders' sense of being a part of something larger than self was given voice. "For me, spirituality is about the interconnectedness between each and every one of us," reflected one leader. Another said: "We are all souls whether we are born in one religious family or another. This goes beyond body, birth, nationality, color, caste, religion, culture, etc. The original nature of soul is love, peace, happiness, mercy, tolerance, and patience. That's who we really are."

LESSONS ON LEADERSHIP JOURNEYS

While learning journeys of this scale might be beyond the means or interests of many business leaders, the lessons from them are relevant to every organization or school that wants to foster the psycho-spiritual development of its leaders and also to the teachers, trainers, and coaches who might assist them.

Nature as Teacher

The journeys took the leaders to different landscapes and natural environments. As countless sages and poets remind us, nature is a rich milieu for connecting deeply to the self and the cosmos. On these journeys the experience of connecting to nature produced a feeling of *deep ecology*. This psycho-spiritual philosophy is founded on the notion that all life's systems are interrelated and that anthropocentrism—human-centeredness—is a mistaken way of seeing things. Deep ecologists say that an ecocentric attitude is more consistent with the truth about the nature of life on earth. Arnie Naess, founder of the movement, contends that instead of identifying with our egos or immediate families, we can learn to identify with trees, animals, and plants, indeed the whole ecosphere.

The majestic mountains of Guilin, for example, led the leaders to reflect on their place in the cosmos. "This is not scenery," said one of their teachers, pointing to a lush valley. "This brings us food. It gives us air. It gives us water. It gives us light. When we die, we become this," as the sweep of his arm drew gazes to the magnificent setting in which the leaders were trekking. The impact of nature and the feeling of deep ecology were palpable for many. "One night in front of the campfire, I imagined that we were looked upon from a satellite. I saw a small campfire light in the middle of the earth. I felt how small we were and how small I was," commented one leader. "Great nature raises people," said another. "One can only reflect here with honesty and purity."

Integrating Experiences

The Asian journeys were multilayered, multisensory experiences that engaged the head, heart, body, and spirit. What seems crucial is to give leaders the time, space, and resources to integrate these manifold experiences and themselves. Obviously, personal journaling, reflection, and sense making help. Thoughtful questioning and structured introspection are also useful (Kriger, 2005; Hawley, 1993).

Sometimes lessons on integration come from surprising places. In China, for example, the leaders practiced tai chi with a master. When one leader asked, "How does a master do tai chi?" he told them that a master must be aware of himself, his opponent, the situation around him, and then forget it all when fighting. This opened up deep conversation among the leaders about how to integrate consciousness of the self, other, and the world when taking action. The fact that the teacher, nearly eighty and revered around the world, did not yet consider himself a true master, provoked new appreciation of discipline, persistence, and humility for the leaders.

Service Learning

Finally, all of the journeys involved community service. The aim of visiting Asia was not simply for benchmarking or learning about the region. It was to cultivate a deep feeling and profound respect for neighbors. As one leader put it, "Unconditional love is the way to cultivate connectivity, as it bridges different communities, different human beings." This is integral to what Erich Fromm (1956) calls the "art of loving." Psychologists posit that just as seeing the world through another's perspective helps people to grow beyond egocentrism, so empathizing with another is the antidote to human selfishness.

Community service teaches people about the world around them and about helping relationships. Many schools and some companies offer service learning programs. The journeys in Asia extended this to senior leaders and made it an important part of their development agenda (Ayas & Mirvis, 2005). While serving in communities, the leaders were asked to connect to the tacit rhythms of community life, be mindful of assumptions, be open to what they might experience, and thoughtfully reflect on the lessons for themselves and the business.

"I learned about the fundamental value of being human and of reaching out again and again," said one leader about her service experience in Sri Lanka. "Not only did I reach out to my Sri Lankan friends but much more to my colleagues." An expression of the depth of the lessons learned is captured by another leader:

> All human beings, no matter how desperate and hopeless, first and foremost need to feel that there are other human beings who care enough to give them their own time, money, and spirit. In all their hopelessness, they seek to believe that there is a possibility for a better world. To feel their own will to live and to feel their own soul again, they need to be in communion with others; they do not want to be left alone to suffer. When we started working on the building sites, most local people were bystanders, watching without any spark in their eyes and without the energy to give a helping hand in their own recovery. But when we started sharing stories and took the time to deeply share their pain, when we listened to their fears and hopes, we suddenly connected. And when we sang songs and danced with the children, we knew there was hope for a better future.

It is important to note that the Asian leaders do not regard these journeys as a retreat, a rejuvenating time away from their business lives. As is evident from their reflections, community service helps them see how to do their business and serve the world better. It helped reframe the socioeconomic mission of the business. As the company president said in reporting his lessons from service: "It's not business *and* the community, it's business *in* the community."

CULTIVATING A LEADERSHIP PHILOSOPHY

It is uncertain whether and how the leadership spirit developed through these journeys will be sustained in the Asian food corporation. No doubt the membership of the leadership team will change through personnel moves and turnover; and the team's constancy of purpose may also be challenged by competitive pressures, business conditions, and the sheer enormity of its newly discovered mission. There are many signs, however, that leaders throughout the region have embraced the spirit of the journeys. To further internalize such aspirations, many of these Asian leaders have developed and articulated their philosophies about leadership and conveyed it to their people through their *teacher-leader* role (Tichy, 2002). Many have led journeys with their own country teams, journeys involving self-reflection, community service, and the like.

Dorothy Marcic (1997) makes love the central organizing principle for what she sees as five key management virtues. These virtues are evident as these leaders apply insights from their connections to the peoples of Asia. Said one: "In the context of the larger things in the world, I feel I can do a more fulfilling job. Something bold that I will be proud of, something that has the humanity that I have valued."

—⟨⟩—

Philip H. Mirvis is an organizational psychologist whose research and private practice concerns large-scale organizational change and the character of the workforce and workplace; he is also the author of eight books and a senior research fellow at the Boston College School of Management, Center for Corporate Citizenship.

—⟨⟩—

Karen Ayas is a founding partner of the Ripples Group, specializing in large-scale organizational change and leadership development; teaches in the Rotterdam School of Management and at Babson College; is author of several books on change; and is currently coeditor of *Reflections,* published by the Society for Organizational Learning.

CHAPTER TWELVE

Moments of Greatness

Entering the Fundamental State of Leadership

Robert E. Quinn

As leaders, sometimes we're "on," and sometimes we're not. Why is that? What separates episodes of excellence from those of mere competence? In striving to tip the balance toward excellence, we try to identify great leaders' qualities and behaviors so we can develop them ourselves. Nearly all corporate training programs and books on leadership are grounded in the assumption that we should study the behaviors of those who have been successful and teach people to emulate them.

My colleagues and I have found that when leaders do their best work, they don't copy anyone. Instead, they draw on their own fundamental values and capabilities—operating in a frame of mind that is true to them yet, paradoxically, not their normal state of being. I call it the *fundamental state of leadership*. It's the way we lead when we encounter a crisis and finally choose to move forward. Think back to a time when you faced a significant life challenge: a promotion opportunity, the risk of professional failure, a serious illness, a divorce, the death of a loved one, or any other major jolt. Most likely, if you made decisions not to meet others' expectations but to suit what you instinctively understood to be right—in other words, if you were at your very best—you rose to the task because you were being tested.

Is it possible to enter the fundamental state of leadership without crisis? I've found that if we ask ourselves—and honestly answer—just four questions, we can make the shift at any time. It's a temporary state. Fatigue and external resistance pull us out of it. But each time we reach it, we return to our everyday selves a bit more capable, and we usually elevate the performance of the people around us as well. Over time, we all can become more effective leaders by deliberately choosing to enter the fundamental state of leadership rather than waiting for crisis to force us there.

DEFINING THE FUNDAMENTAL STATE

Even those who are widely admired for their seemingly easy and natural leadership skills—presidents, prime ministers, CEOs—do not usually function in the fundamental state of leadership. Most of the time, they are in their normal state—a healthy and even necessary condition under many circumstances, but not one that's conducive to coping with crisis. In the normal state, people tend to stay within their comfort zones and allow external forces to direct their behaviors and decisions. They lose moral influence and often rely on rational argument and the exercise of authority to bring about change. Others comply with what these leaders ask, out of fear, but the result is usually unimaginative and incremental—and largely reproduces what already exists.

To elevate the performance of others, we must elevate ourselves into the fundamental state of leadership. Getting there requires a shift along four dimensions.

First, we move from being comfort centered to being results centered. The former feels safe but eventually leads to a sense of languishing and meaninglessness. In his book *The Path of Least Resistance*, Robert Fritz carefully explains how asking a single question can move us from the normal, reactive state to a much more generative condition. That question is this: What result do I want to create? Giving an honest answer pushes us off nature's path of least resistance. It leads us from problem solving to purpose finding.

Second, we move from being externally directed to being more internally directed. That means that we stop merely complying with others' expectations and conforming to the current culture. To become more internally directed is to clarify our core values and increase our integrity, confidence, and authenticity. As we become more confident and more authentic, we behave differently. Others must make sense of our new behavior. Some will be attracted to it, and some will be offended by it. That's not prohibitive, though: When we are true to our values, we are willing to initiate such conflict.

Third, we become less self-focused and more focused on others. We put the needs of the organization as a whole above our own. Few among us would admit that personal needs trump the collective good, but the impulse to control relationships in a way that feeds our own interests is natural and normal. That said, self-focus over time leads to feelings of isolation. When we put the collective good first, others reward us with their trust and respect. We form tighter, more sensitive bonds. Empathy increases, and cohesion follows. We create an enriched sense of community, and that helps us transcend the conflicts that are a necessary element in high-performing organizations.

Fourth, we become more open to outside signals or stimuli, including those that require us to do things we are not comfortable doing. In the normal state, we pay attention to signals that we know to be relevant. If they suggest incremental adjustments, we respond. If, however, they call for more dramatic changes, we may adopt a posture of defensiveness and denial; this mode of self-protection and self-deception separates us from the ever-changing external world. We live according to an outdated, less valid, image of what is real. But in the fundamental state of leadership, we are more aware of what is unfolding, and we generate new images all the time. We are adaptive, credible, and unique. In this externally open state, no two people are alike.

These four qualities—being results centered, internally directed, other focused, and externally open—are at the heart of positive human influence, which is generative and attractive. A person without these four characteristics can also be highly influential, but his or her influence tends to be predicated on some form of control or force, which does not usually give rise to committed followers. By entering the fundamental state of leadership, we increase the likelihood of attracting others to an elevated level of community, a high-performance state that may continue even when we are not present.

PREPARING FOR THE FUNDAMENTAL STATE

Because people usually do not leave their comfort zones unless forced, many find it helpful to follow a process when they choose to enter the fundamental state of leadership. I teach a technique to executives and use it in my own work. It simply involves asking four awareness-raising questions designed to help us transcend our natural denial mechanisms. When people become aware of their hypocrisies, they are more likely to change. Those who are new to the "fundamental state" concept, however, need to take two preliminary steps before they can understand and employ it.

STEP 1: RECOGNIZE THAT YOU HAVE PREVIOUSLY ENTERED THE FUNDAMENTAL STATE OF LEADERSHIP. Every reader of this publication has reached, at one time or another, the fundamental state of leadership. We've all faced a great personal or professional challenge and spent time in the dark night of the soul. In successfully working through such episodes, we inevitably enter the fundamental state of leadership.

When I introduce people to this concept, I ask them to identify two demanding experiences from their past and ponder what happened in terms of intention, integrity, trust, and adaptability. At first, they resist the exercise because I am asking them to revisit times of great personal pain. But as they recount their experiences, they begin to see that they are also returning to moments of greatness. Our painful experiences often bring out our best selves. Recalling the lessons of such moments releases positive emotions and makes it easier to see what's possible in the present. In this exercise, I ask people to consider their behavior during these episodes in relation to the characteristics of the fundamental state of leadership.

Sometimes I also ask workshop participants to share their stories with one another. Naturally, they are reluctant to talk about such dark moments. To help people open up, I share my own moments of great challenge, the ones I would normally keep to myself. By exhibiting vulnerability, I'm able to win the group's trust and embolden other people to exercise the same courage. I recently ran a workshop with a cynical group of executives. After I broke the testimonial ice, one of the participants told us of a time when he had accepted a new job that required him to relocate his family. Just before he was to start, his new boss called in a panic, asking him to cut his vacation short and begin work immediately. The entire New England engineering team had quit; clients in the region had no support whatsoever. The executive started his job early, and his family had to navigate the move without his help. He described the next few months as "the worst and best experience" of his life.

Another executive shared that he'd found out he had cancer the same week he was promoted and relocated to Paris, not knowing how to speak French. His voice cracked as he recalled these stressful events. But then he told us about the good that came out of them—how he conquered both the disease and the job while also becoming a more authentic and influential leader.

Others came forward with their own stories, and I saw a great change in the group. The initial resistance and cynicism began to disappear, and participants started exploring the fundamental state of leadership in a serious way. They saw the power in the concept and recognized that hiding behind their pride or reputation would only get in the way of future progress. In recounting their experiences, they came to realize that they had become more purposive, authentic, compassionate, and responsive.

STEP 2: ANALYZE YOUR CURRENT STATE. When we're in the fundamental state, we take on various positive characteristics, such as clarity of vision, self-empowerment, empathy, and creative thinking. Most of us would like to say we display these characteristics at all times, but we do so only sporadically.

Comparing our normal performance with what we have done at our very best often creates a desire to elevate what we are doing now. Knowing we've operated at a higher level in the past instills confidence that we can do so again; it quells our fear of stepping into unknown and risky territory.

ASKING FOUR TRANSFORMATIVE QUESTIONS

Of course, understanding the fundamental state of leadership and recognizing its power are not the same as being there. Entering that state is where the real work comes in. To get started, we can ask ourselves four questions that correspond with the four qualities of the fundamental state.

To show how each of these qualities affects our behavior while we're in the fundamental state of leadership, I'll draw on stories from two executives. One is a company president; we'll call him John Jones. The other, Robert Yamamoto, is the executive director of the Los Angeles Junior Chamber of Commerce. Both once struggled with major challenges that changed the way they thought about their jobs and their lives.

I met John in an executive course I was teaching. He was a successful change leader who had turned around two companies in his corporation. Yet he was frustrated. He had been promised he'd become president of the largest company in the corporation as soon as the current president retired, which would happen in the near future. In the meantime, he had been told to bide his time with a company that everyone considered dead. His assignment was simply to oversee the funeral, yet he took it as a personal challenge to turn the company around. After he had been there nine months, however, there was little improvement, and the people were still not very engaged.

As for Robert, he had been getting what he considered to be acceptable (if not exceptional) results in his company. So when the new board president asked him to prepare a letter of resignation, Robert was stunned. He underwent a period of anguished introspection, during which he began to distrust others and question his own management skills and leadership ability. Concerned for his family and his future, he started to seek another job and wrote the requested letter. As you will see, however, even though things looked grim for both Robert and John, they were on the threshold of positive change.

Am I Results Centered?

Most of the time, we are comfort centered. We try to continue doing what we know how to do. We may think we are pursuing new outcomes, but if achieving them means leaving our comfort zones, we subtly—even unconsciously—find ways to avoid doing so. We typically advocate ambitious outcomes while designing our work for maximum administrative convenience, which allows us to avoid conflict but frequently ends up reproducing what already exists. Often, others collude with us to act out this deception. Being comfort centered is hypocritical, self-deceptive, and normal.

Clarifying the result we want to create requires us to reorganize our lives. Instead of moving away from a problem, we move toward a possibility that does not yet exist. We become more proactive, intentional, optimistic, invested, and persistent. We also tend to become more energized, and our impact on others becomes energizing.

Consider what happened with John. When I first spoke with him, he sketched out his strategy with little enthusiasm. Sensing that lack of passion, I asked him a question designed to test his commitment to the end he claimed he wanted to obtain:

> What if you told your people the truth? Suppose you told them that nobody really expects you to succeed, that you were assigned to be a caretaker for 18 months, and that you have been promised a plum job once your assignment is through. And then you tell them that you have chosen instead to give up that plum job and bet your career on the people present. Then, from your newly acquired stance of optimism for the company's prospects, you issue some challenges beyond your employees' normal capacity.

To my surprise, John responded that he was beginning to think along similar lines. He grabbed a napkin and rapidly sketched out a new strategy along with a plan for carrying it out, including reassignments for his staff. It was clear and compelling, and he was suddenly full of energy.

What happened here? John was the president of his company and therefore had authority. And he'd turned around two other companies—evidence that he had the knowledge and competencies of a change leader. Yet he was *failing* as a change leader. That's because he had slipped into his comfort zone. He was going through the motions, doing what had worked elsewhere. He was imitating a great leader—in this case, John himself. But imitation is not the way to enter the fundamental state of leadership. If I had accused John of not being committed to a real vision, he would have been incensed. He would have argued heatedly in denial of the truth. All I had to do, though, was nudge him in the right direction. As soon as he envisioned the result he wanted to create and committed himself to it, a new strategy emerged and he was reenergized.

Then there was Robert, who went to what he assumed would be his last board meeting and found that he had more support than he'd been led to believe. Shockingly, at the end of the meeting, he still had his job. Even so, this fortuitous turn brought on further soul-searching. Robert started to pay more attention to what he was doing; he began to see his tendency to be tactical and to gravitate toward routine tasks. He concluded that he was managing, not leading. He was playing a role and abdicating leadership to the board president—not because that person had the knowledge and vision to lead but because the position came with the statutory right to lead. "I suddenly decided to really lead my organization," Robert said. "It was as if a new person emerged. The decision was not about me. I needed to do it for the good of the organization."

In deciding to "really lead," Robert started identifying the strategic outcomes he wanted to create. As he did this, he found himself leaving his zone of comfort—behaving in new ways and generating new outcomes.

Am I Internally Directed?

In the normal state, we comply with social pressures in order to avoid conflict and remain connected with our coworkers. However, we end up feeling *less* connected because conflict avoidance results in political compromise. We begin to lose our uniqueness and our sense of integrity. The agenda gradually shifts from creating an external result to preserving political peace. As this problem intensifies, we begin to lose hope and energy.

This loss was readily apparent in the case of John. He was his corporation's shining star. But since he was at least partially focused on the future reward—the plum job—he was not fully focused on doing the hard work he needed to do at the moment. So he didn't ask enough of the people he was leading. To get more from them, John needed to be more internally directed.

Am I Other Focused?

It's hard to admit, but most of us, most of the time, put our own needs above those of the whole. Indeed, it is healthy to do so; it's a survival mechanism. But when the pursuit of our own interests controls our relationships, we erode others' trust in us. Although people may comply with our wishes, they no longer derive energy from their relationships with us. Over time we drive away the very social support we seek.

To become more focused on others is to commit to the collective good in relationships, groups, or organizations, even if it means incurring personal costs. When John made the shift into the fundamental state of leadership, he committed to an uncertain future for himself. He had been promised a coveted job. All he had to do was wait a few months. Still, he was unhappy, so he chose to turn down the opportunity in favor of a course that was truer to his leadership values. When he shifted gears, he sacrificed his personal security in favor of a greater good.

Remember Robert's words: "The decision was not about me. I needed to do it for the good of the organization." After entering the fundamental state of leadership, he proposed a new strategic direction to the board's president and said that if the board didn't like it, he would walk away with no regrets. He knew that the strategy would benefit the organization, regardless of how it would affect him personally. Robert put the good of the organization first. When a leader does this, people notice, and the leader gains respect and trust. Group members, in turn, become more likely to put the collective good first. When they do, tasks that previously seemed impossible become doable.

Am I Externally Open?

Being closed to external stimuli has the benefit of keeping us on task, but it also allows us to ignore signals that suggest a need for change. Such signals would force us to cede control and face risk, so denying them is self-protective, but it is also self-deceptive. John convinced himself he'd done all he could for his failing company when, deep down, he knew that he had the capacity to improve things. Robert was self-deceptive, too, until crisis and renewed opportunity caused him to open up and explore the fact that he was playing a role accorded him but not using his knowledge and emotional capacity to transcend that role and truly lead his people.

Asking ourselves whether we're externally open shifts our focus from controlling our environment to learning from it. It also helps us recognize the need for change. Two things happen as a result. First, we are forced to improvise in response to previously unrecognized cues—that is, to depart from established routines. And second, because trial-and-error survival requires an accurate picture of the results we're creating, we actively and genuinely seek honest feedback. Since people trust us more when we're in this state, they tend to offer more accurate feedback, understanding that we are likely to learn from the message rather than kill the messenger. A cycle of learning and empowerment is created, allowing us to see things that people normally cannot see and to formulate transformational strategies.

APPLYING THE FUNDAMENTAL PRINCIPLES

Just as I teach others about the fundamental state of leadership, I also try to apply the concept in my own life. I was a team leader on a project for the University of Michigan's Executive Education Center. Usually, the center runs weeklong courses that bring in 30 to 40 executives. It was proposed that we develop a new product, an integrated week of perspectives on leadership. C. K. Prahalad would begin with a strategic perspective, then Noel Tichy, Dave Ulrich, Karl Weick, and I would follow with our own presentations. The objective was to fill a 400-seat auditorium. Since each presenter had a reasonably large following in some domain of the executive world, we were confident we could fill the seats, so we scheduled the program for the month of July, when our facilities were typically underutilized.

In the early months of planning and organizing, everything went perfectly. A marketing consultant had said we could expect to secure half our enrollment three weeks prior to the event. When that time rolled around, slightly less than half of the target audience had signed up, so we thought all was well. But then a different consultant indicated that for our kind of event we would get few additional enrollments during the last three weeks. This stunning prediction meant that attendance would be half of what we expected and we would be lucky to break even.

As the team leader, I could envision the fallout. Our faculty members, accustomed to drawing a full house, would be offended by a half-empty room; the dean would want to know what went wrong; and the center's staff would probably point to the team leader as the problem. That night I spent several hours pacing the floor. I was filled with dread and shame. Finally I told myself that this kind of behavior was useless. I went to my desk and wrote down the four questions. As I considered them, I concluded that I was comfort centered, externally directed, self-focused, and internally closed.

So I asked myself, "What result do I want to create?" I wrote that I wanted the center to learn how to offer a new, world-class product that would be in demand over time. With that clarification came a freeing insight: because this was our first offering of the product, turning a large profit was not essential. That would be nice, of course, but we'd be happy to learn how to do such an event properly, break even, and lay the groundwork for making a profit in the future.

I then asked myself, "How can I become other focused?" At that moment, I was totally self-focused—I was worried about my reputation—and my first inclination was to be angry with the staff. But in shifting my focus to what they might be thinking that night, I realized they were most likely worried that I'd come to work in the morning ready to assign blame. Suddenly, I saw a need to both challenge and support them.

Finally, I thought about how I could become externally open. It would mean moving forward and learning something new, even if that made me uncomfortable. I needed to engage in an exploratory dialogue rather than preside as the expert in charge.

I immediately began making a list of marketing strategies, though I expected many of them would prove foolish since I knew nothing about marketing. The next day, I brought the staff together—and they, naturally, were guarded. I asked them what result we wanted to create. What happened next is a good example of how contagious the fundamental state of leadership can be.

We talked about strategies for increasing attendance, and after a while, I told the staff that I had some silly marketing ideas and was embarrassed to share them but was willing to do anything to help. They laughed at many of my naive thoughts about how to increase publicity and create pricing incentives. Yet my proposals also sparked serious discussion, and the group began to brainstorm its way into a collective strategy. Because I was externally open, there was space and time for everyone to lead. People came up with better ways of approaching media outlets and creating incentives. In that meeting, the group developed a shared sense of purpose, reality, identity, and contribution. They left feeling reasonable optimism and went forward as a committed team.

In the end, we did not get 400 participants, but we filled more than enough seats to have a successful event. We more than broke even, and we developed the skills we needed to run such an event better in the future. The program was a success because something transformational occurred among the staff. Yet the transformation did not originate in the meeting. It began the night before, when I asked myself the four questions and moved from the normal, reactive state to the fundamental state of leadership. And my entry into the fundamental state encouraged the staff to enter as well.

While the fundamental state proves useful in times of crisis, it can also help us cope with more mundane challenges. If I am going to have an important conversation, attend a key meeting, participate in a significant event, or teach a class, part of my preparation is to try to reach the fundamental state of leadership. Whether I am working with an individual, a group, or an organization, I ask the same four questions. They often lead to high-performance outcomes, and the repetition of high-performance outcomes can eventually create a high-performance culture.

INSPIRING OTHERS TO HIGH PERFORMANCE

When we enter the fundamental state of leadership, we immediately have new thoughts and engage in new behaviors. We can't remain in this state forever. It can last for hours, days, or sometimes months, but eventually we come back to our normal frame of mind. While the fundamental state is temporary, each time we are in it we learn more about people and our environment and increase the probability that we will be able to return to it. Moreover, we inspire those around us to higher levels of performance.

To this day, Robert marvels at the contrast between his organization's past and present. His transformation into a leader with positive energy and a willingness and ability to tackle challenges in new ways helped shape the L.A. Junior Chamber of Commerce into a high-functioning and creative enterprise. When I last spoke to Robert, here's what he had to say:

> I have a critical mass of individuals on both the staff and the board who are willing to look at our challenges in a new way and work on solutions together. At our meetings, new energy is present. What previously seemed unimaginable now seems to happen with ease.

Any CEO would be delighted to be able to say these things. But the truth is, it's not a typical situation. When Robert shifted into the fundamental state of leadership, his group (which started off in a normal state) came to life, infused with his renewed energy and vision. Even after he'd left the fundamental state, the group sustained a higher level of performance. It continues to flourish, without significant staff changes or restructuring.

All this didn't happen because Robert read a book or an article about the best practices of some great leader. It did not happen because he was imitating someone else. It happened because he was jolted out of his comfort zone and was forced to enter the fundamental state of leadership. He was driven to clarify the result he wanted to create, to act courageously from his core values, to surrender his self-interest to the collective good, and to open himself up to learning in real time. From Robert, and others like him, we can learn the value of challenging ourselves in this way—a painful process but one with great potential to make a positive impact on our own lives and on the people around us.

—◆◆◆—

Robert E. Quinn is the Margaret Elliott Tracy Collegiate Professor in Business Administration and professor of management and organizations at the University of Michigan. He has published articles and books on management and organizations, with a focus on leadership, vision, and change.

PART THREE

Understanding the Territory, Anticipating the Challenges

Leadership is always contextual. The unique demands of time, place, people, task, and organizational history affect the leadership path as well as the capacities needed to do the job well. Healing an ailing company requires savvy and strategies different from those needed to sustain progress in a well-functioning enterprise; heading a family-owned business has challenges that leading a public multinational doesn't, and vice versa; and the list goes on. To no one's surprise, research has found that leaders successful in one organization or situation are not always as effective in others. Context matters—and in today's fast-paced, competitive, global world, context matters more than ever. Leaders who understand how organizations work and possess strong diagnostic skills are more likely to match their efforts and talents to the demands of the situation. Leadership is hard work, and even experienced leaders are often surprised and tested by what they find.

The chapters in Part Three focus on the organizational world that today's business leaders serve: the predictable features in the organizational terrain, the shifts occurring in the business environment, and the opportunities and challenges that both present. What gives leaders a better handle on the leadership lay of the land?

The first two chapters in Part Three, "Mapping the Terrain," provide leaders with ideas and tools that help them decode and make sense of the complexities of organizational life. Organizations are subtle, complicated, and unpredictable, and effective leaders need to accurately read the circumstances in which they find themselves and make informed decisions.

Every leadership initiative is based on theories about how organizations work and what might make them better. Good theories—whether homegrown, borrowed from experts, or some combination of the two—guide leaders in their work. The reverse is also true: naive or distorted understandings send leaders blindly down the wrong path, squandering time, resources, and credibility along the way. In Chapter Thirteen, "Making Sense of Organizations: Leadership, Frames, and Everyday Theories of the Situation," Joan V. Gallos guides business leaders in becoming more discriminating consumers of the diverse models, frameworks, and advice that compete for their attention—and in applying their learnings effectively on the home front. Organizations are messy and complex, and leaders are expected to bring order from the chaos: ensure appropriate structural arrangements and policies to advance organizational goals, create and model strategies for motivating the workforce, foster the productive management of conflict and diversity, and support a healthy corporate culture. Multiframed thinking and skills in *reframing* are essential for a comprehensive yet manageable leadership strategy.

In Chapter Fourteen, "Leadership and the Power of Position: Understanding Structural Dynamics in Everyday Organizational Life," Michael J. Sales reminds business leaders that organizations are multifaceted social systems that take on a life of their own—and that system dynamics influence individual behavior more than leaders realizes. Those at the top see the organizational landscape differently from those down the hierarchy, and the differences are predictable and fateful. Managing social system–influenced behaviors enables leaders at any level to foster robust organizations open to learning, innovation, and change.

The next six chapters in Part Three, "Understanding Unique Features of the Challenge," address salient situational factors facing today's business leaders: globalization, technology, environmental concerns, and a diverse workforce. Change is constant for business leaders, and the most effective have strategies for scanning and staying attuned to the ever-shifting landscape. Taken together, these chapters also remind us why leadership is an art, not a one-size-fits-all science.

In Chapter Fifteen, "The Boundaryless Organization: Rising to the Challenges of Global Leadership," Ron Ashkenas, David Ulrich, Todd Jick, and Steve Kerr challenge common beliefs about leadership and organizations in the twenty-first century. Organizations have historically used role clarity, specialization, and control as the means to efficiency and equity. These legacies from century-old bureaucratic traditions are liabilities in a world where speed and the free movement of ideas, talent, decisions, and information across boundaries are essential for quality, innovation, and profit. The authors identify a leadership paradigm shift and offer fresh options for organizing in today's global world.

In a knowledge society, leadership effectiveness centers on valid information. Good business leaders foster a corporate culture where the organization learns from its experience, makes strong data-based decisions, and creates appropriate information systems to support its work. Leaders fool themselves, however, when they mistake collecting data for managing knowledge. In Chapter Sixteen, "Knowledge Management Involves Neither Knowledge nor Management," Marc S. Effron explores the myths and realities of knowledge management today and advocates that leaders take a critical role in shaping the ways their organizations can benefit fully from workers' intellectual capital. Posting information, sharing procedures, and building data archives achieve little of the intended knowledge management purpose. Knowledge comes from personal experience or through association with experienced others, counsels Effron. No database, however complete, provides that. True knowledge management requires people-centered strategies: increasing the opportunities for formal and informal face-to-face encounters, hiring individuals to screen data for quality and relevance, and installing reward systems that support knowledge sharing and organizational learning.

Real leadership is elevating and morally purposive, concludes Pulitzer Prize–winning historian James MacGregor Burns (1978; also see Chapter Twenty-Three in this volume). Leadership distinguishes itself from management by its creative vision for a bright future. Too many front-page examples of corporate greed and unethical behavior confirm what many have long suspected: public virtue has been largely replaced in the business world by an unrelenting focus on the bottom line (Bennis, 2003). The authors of Chapter Seventeen, "The Sustainability Sweet Spot: Where Profit Meets the Common Good," remind leaders that social responsibility need not be sacrificed for profits. In fact, good corporate citizenship and attention to the environment are powerful, often overlooked, business strategies for short- and long-term success. In an excerpt from *The Triple Bottom Line: How Today's Best-Run Companies Are Achieving Economic, Social and Environmental Success—and How You Can Too,* Andrew W. Savitz and Karl Weber illustrate ways to conduct business that mutually benefits all key stakeholders: employees, customers, business partners, local communities, and shareholders. Leaders hold the ultimate responsibility for identifying a company's sustainability sweet spot: the unique opportunity where the pursuits of profit and the larger common good blend seamlessly.

Mastering the leadership context means understanding one's followers. Effective leaders engage a broad constituency. In a world characterized by increasing workforce diversity, this translates into the need to appreciate human differences and develop skills for working productively with a wide range of people. Followers historically get short shrift in discussions of leadership and are too often portrayed as faceless and passive. A closer look reveals a host of unique individuals and organizational subgroups with important contributions to make—and the potential to make or break even the most skilled leader. The three final chapters in Part Three raise leaders' awareness of what the work world looks like through the eyes of different organizational citizens. Taken together, these chapters reinforce an essential truth: leaders, know thy people.

Geeks—the knowledge workers who create, maintain, and support information technology in organizations—are a special breed, cautions Paul Glen in Chapter Eighteen, "Leading Geeks: Technology and Leadership." They are "highly intelligent, usually introverted, extremely valuable, independent-minded, hard-to-find, difficult-to-keep" workers and key to innovation *and* efficiency. Leading geeks is different, according to Glen—traditional ways of thinking about power don't work, and traditional beliefs about roles and spans of control don't fit either. And now that technology permeates all functional areas of an organization, individuals at all levels need to know how to lead geeks.

Today's global world puts the importance of respecting and managing diversity on every leader's radar screen. Knowing how to do that well is a different matter. In Chapter Nineteen, "Leading in Black and White: Working Effectively Across the Racial Divide," Ancella B. Livers and Keith A. Caver draw on their work in the Center for Creative Leadership's African American Leadership program to explore common misunderstandings that can hinder interactions, communications, and leadership in today's diverse workplace. Experiences are often radically different for black and white colleagues in the same organization, and those differences influence workplace choices in powerful yet nondiscussable ways. Leaders who understand this are better prepared to create equitable and productive work environments for all.

Demographic characteristics and specialized job skills and cultures are two lenses for exploring the unique needs of followers. Career stage offers a third. Part Three closes with an exploration of work life for more than half of the current workforce—people in the middle years of their career. Chapter Twenty, "Managing Middlescence," taken from the popular *Harvard Business Review* article by Robert Morison, Tamara J. Erickson, and Ken Dychtwald, draws a stark portrait. The majority of mid-career employees in today's organizations are "burned-out, bottlenecked, and bored," and individuals and organizations both suffer as a result. Millions of talented workers are simply biding their time—on automatic pilot in jobs that no longer fulfill or challenge them—or planning their exits to greener pastures. The result: lost talent, institutional memory, and experience. There is hope, say the authors. Business leaders can learn to convert restless and stale performers into reinvigorated, productive, and recommitted midcareer employees.

CHAPTER THIRTEEN

Making Sense of Organizations

Leadership, Frames, and Everyday Theories of the Situation

Joan V. Gallos

In 1872, Aaron Montgomery Ward founded the first mail order business in America. He sent a simple, one-page flyer listing various bargains and products to farm families who, in the comfort of their homes, could look through the offerings, place an order, and receive purchased items by mail. Ward understood something important about the times: people in rural areas needed not be at the mercy of local merchants for the goods they needed. His insights launched a revolution, and his business boomed. Twenty years later Sears Roebuck entered the scene, and the race for dominance in the catalog market had begun.

Fast forward, to the 1920s. Robert Wood, the second in command then at Montgomery Ward, had a hobby of studying census data, and he saw the beginnings of a population shift from rural to urban and suburban areas (Lohr, 2006). To Wood, this suggested a radical change for Montgomery Ward from being a catalog retailer to a department store merchant near growing population centers. Wood's boss, CEO Theodore Merseles, rejected the notion, and Wood took his vision—and eventually himself—to Sears with disastrous consequences for Montgomery Ward. Wood's population prediction was right on target. Sears gained market shares by acting on it.

In 1945, Wood, by then chairman of Sears, did it again. He saw pent-up consumer demands from the war years fueling a post-war economic boom. He wanted Sears to benefit and began an aggressive, nationwide store-building campaign. Sears sales grew exponentially as a result. Where was Montgomery Ward during all this? Largely out of the game: its top leadership had a different theory of the post-war situation.

As Montgomery Ward CEO Sewell Avery saw it, depressions follow wars. Avery had studied history, and had charts in his office tracing commodity prices from the time of Napoleon (Sobel, 1999). The smart thing to do, Avery believed, was to keep Montgomery Ward's cash in the bank to weather the inevitable economic downturn. He refused to expand the company—and enjoyed thinking about his competitors spending themselves into bankruptcy. But the depression never came, and Montgomery Ward sat out one of the largest consumer spending sprees in modern history. As these stories illustrate, an organization's fate rests on the lenses its leaders bring to make sense of a situation. In his classic book *On Becoming a Leader,* Warren Bennis reinforces this simple truth. "When you understand," notes Bennis, "you know what to do" (2003, p. 55). Good sense making is at the heart of good leadership. Whether we call it executive wisdom, sound judgment, reflective practice (Schön, 1983), or learning from experience, the expectation is clear. Leadership involves the capacity to make sense of the ambiguities and challenges in organizational life and translate those understandings into appropriate choices and actions. Effective leaders avoid myopic or simplistic interpretations, build sound everyday theories that fit the situations in which they find themselves, and use those theories to facilitate the accomplishment of a larger good. The business lives of Monty Ward, Robert Wood, and Sewell Avery remind us that this is not always a simple and straightforward task.

A wealth of books and expert advice offers solutions to this challenge. Over the years leaders have been counseled to employ management by objectives, total quality management, reengineering, management by walking around, Six Sigma, quality of worklife programs, sociotechnical systems design, participative management, the search for excellence, the search for greatness, and the search for soul, to name only a few—and today's wisdom can quickly become yesterday's news. Sorting through the many models, studies, frameworks, and findings that compete for a leader's attention is not always easy. But we know that leaders serve their organizations best when they are both discriminating consumers of leadership theories *and* skilled translators of that learning into workable everyday strategies. Kurt Lewin, father of the applied social sciences, got it right—there's nothing so practical as a good theory.

Although this may sound academic to those who labor in the organizational trenches, good theories are pragmatic and grounded. They explain and predict. They serve as frameworks for making sense of the world, organizing diverse forms and sources of information, and taking informed action. Theories come in all shapes and sizes. They can be personal—tacit mental schemas that individuals develop over time from their unique life experiences, like Monty Ward's theories of rural marketing from his years of work as a traveling salesman. They can be research based—models that stem from experiments, formal explorations and analyses, and field studies of practice, like Robert Woods's beliefs about urban expansion from his study of census data. Whatever their origin, theories guide behavior, and leaders who can embrace and build good theories have a competitive advantage. A look at sense making offers insights into the challenges that those who do it face.

SENSE MAKING AND EVERYDAY THEORY BUILDING

The intricacies of sense making and its implications for action have been well developed in the organizational and information science literatures (see, for example, Argyris, 1982, 1985; Argyris, Putnam, & Smith, 1985; Argyris & Schön, 1978, 1982; Weick, 1985, 1993, 1995, 2007; Weick & Sutcliffe, 2001; Weick, Sutcliffe, & Obstfeld, 2005; Starbuck & Milliken, 1988). For our purpose here, the basics will do.

Sense making involves three fundamental steps: noticing something, deciding what to make of it, and determining what to do about it. Sense making is always incomplete and personal. Humans can attend to only a limited amount of the information and experiences available to them, and values, education, past experiences, cognitive capacities, physical abilities, and developmental limitations influence what each person sees and doesn't. Sense making is interpretive: when thrown into life's ongoing stream of experiences, unpredictable events, available information, and social encounters, people create unique explanations for themselves about what things mean. Contrast, for example, the distinctive beliefs about the post–World War II economy by the leaders of Sears and Montgomery Ward. Sense making is also action oriented.

People's personal interpretations contain prescriptions for how they and others should respond. The different leadership lenses at Sears and Montgomery Ward took the two companies down very different strategic paths.

It is important to recognize that the sense making process is not about finding truth with a capital "T"—although what each individual attends to and how he or she explains it might be closer to or farther from what others see. Sense making is a personal search for meaning, governed by criteria of plausibility and satisficing rather than accuracy. "We carve out order by leaving the disorderly parts out," concludes eminent psychologist, William James (2005), and a "good enough" explanation of the situation will stop the search for alternatives early in the hunt (March & Simon, 1958; Weick, 1995). Groopman (2000, 2007), for example, studied doctors' thinking and decision-making processes. His work reminds us how easily and non-consciously humans satisfice even in life-and-death situations. It also illustrates the costs. Multiple studies of autopsies, for example, have found that about 15 percent of all medical diagnoses are inaccurate. Inadequate medical knowledge, concludes Groopman, accounts for only 4 percent of doctors' mistakes. The vast majority are due to physician sense making errors: ignoring information and test results that contradict a fixed notion of the patient or an initial diagnosis.

Sense making and everyday theory building are close cousins. Together they reflect the deep human need for order, control, and meaning, and their relationship is intricately circular. People use their everyday theories to make sense of new experience, and over time their experience feeds back to reinforce or modify their theories. Theories influence what people see. That often means they won't see things that don't fit their preconceptions and won't revise their theories even when those theories no longer adequately explain and predict the world around them. Montgomery Ward CEO Sewell Avery clung tightly to his prediction of economic disaster in the face of clear and ample evidence to the contrary. He was sure the post-war boom was nothing but a bubble, and he accelerated his cash hoarding while profits soared at Sears (Sobel, 1999).

The process of sense making and everyday theory building is ongoing and largely tacit. Leaders are continuously registering some things, ignoring others, making interpretations, and determining what to do. This mostly occurs quickly, automatically, and outside of awareness. For that reason, everyday theories feel so obvious and real that they seem more like *Truth* and the way the world *really* is than the individual creations that they are. The tacit nature of the process can blind leaders to available alternatives and to gaps and inaccuracies in their framing (Argyris & Schön, 1982). It also means leaders feel little incentive to question their interpretations or retrace any of their steps from data selection through action. After the war, Avery fired any Montgomery Ward executive who suggested that the company should expand (Sobel, 1999).

Whether leaders think about it or not, they always have a choice for how they frame and interpret their organizational world—and their choices are fateful. A last-minute search for a stronger hanger to carry his suit to school for a debate tournament, for example, led my son to run up two flights of stairs, stub his toe, complain to his mother, and be late for his ride to school. His theory of the situation told him clothes hangers were upstairs—and not in the front-hall closet a few feet from where he started. On a more serious note the situation in Iraq would be markedly different today had U.S. personnel actually been "welcomed as liberators," the Bush administration's pre-war theory of the way the situation would develop.

In summary, leaders need good theories—whether homegrown, borrowed from others, or some combination of the two. Every leadership initiative is based on theories about how organizations work and what might make them better. How can leaders strengthen their theory building skills?

SORTING COMPLEXITY: LEVERAGING THE PLURALISM IN ORGANIZATIONAL THEORY

Modern organizations are complex beasts—and the changing nature of our fast-paced, technology-rich, competitive, global world only adds to their complexity. Successful collective action is no simple matter. Organizations are simultaneously finely tuned *machines* producing goods or services, extended *families* meeting human needs and employing individual talents for a larger good, political *jungles* teaming with enduring differences and competition for scarce resources, and *theaters* of worklife where organizational roles are played with drama and artistry. These images flow from the efforts of Bolman and Deal (1984, 2003, and Chapter Four in this volume) to synthesize and integrate the major traditions in organizational theory into four distinct areas: theories about organizational structure, people, political dynamics, and culture. Each of the four areas—Bolman and Deal call them *frames*—has its own view of the organizational landscape, rooted in distinct academic disciplines. Each also has its own points of focus, underlying assumptions, action logic, path to organizational effectiveness, and major advocates. Each frame captures an important slice of organizational reality, but alone is incomplete. Reliance on any one perspective can lead to mistaking a part of the field for the whole or to misinterpreting the root cause of events or challenges. Together, however, the four frames harness the pluralism in the organizational theory base, acknowledging its richness and complexity while organizing the major elements for easy access, recall, and application.

The *structural frame,* with its implicit image of an organization as a machine, views organizations as rational systems. It reinforces the importance of designing structural arrangements that align with an organization's goals, tasks, technology, strategy, and environment (see, for example, Galbraith, 2001; Hammer & Champy, 1993; Lawrence & Lorsch, 1986; Perrow, 1986). Differentiation of work roles and tasks provides clarity of purpose and contribution but also leads to the need for appropriate coordination and integration.

The *human resource frame* carries an image of an organization as a family. It captures well the symbiotic relationship between individuals and organizations: individuals need opportunities to express their talents and skills; organizations need human energy and contributions to fuel their efforts. When the fit is right, both benefit. Productivity is high when people feel motivated to bring their best to their work. The human resource frame has roots in the work of such seminal theorists as Chris Argyris (1962), Abraham Maslow (1954), and Douglas McGregor (1960). It also spawned the fields of organization development and change management (Gallos, 2006) and underpins many of the beliefs in the popular culture about good leading and organizing.

The *political frame* sees an organization as a jungle—an arena of enduring differences, scarce resources, power negotiations, and conflicts (for example, Cyert & March, 1963; Pfeffer, 1994; Smith, 1988). Diversity of values, beliefs, interests, behaviors, skills, and worldviews among workforce members is an unavoidable organizational reality. Such differences are often toxic but can also be a source of creativity and innovation when recognized and effectively managed (Thomas, 2006).

Finally, the theatrical image of the *symbolic frame* captures organizational life as an ongoing drama: individuals coming together to create context, culture, and meaning as they play their assigned roles and bring artistry and self-expression into their work (see, for example, Blustein, 2007; Cameron & Quinn, 1999; Cohen & March, 1974; Deal & Kennedy, 2000; Meyer & Rowan, 1983; Schein, 2004; Weick, 1995). Good theater fuels the moral imagination; it engages head and heart. Organizations that attend to the symbolic issues surrounding their own theater of work infuse everyday efforts with creativity, energy, and soul.

Table 13.1 outlines a four-frame approach to understanding organizations. It summarizes the assumptions and images that underpin each organizational perspective and also the frame-specific disciplinary roots, emphases, implicit action logics, and routes to organizational effectiveness.

The power of the four frames for organizational diagnosis rests in the fact that organizations are messy and complex. Organizations operate simultaneously on these four levels at all times and can require special attention to address problems in one area while the organization remains strong and functioning in others. Organizations need a solid architecture—rules, roles, policies, procedures, technologies, coordinating mechanisms, environmental linkages—that clearly channels resources and human talents into productive outcomes in support of organizational goals. At the same time, organizations must deal with the complexity of human nature by facilitating workplace relationships and training that motivate and foster high levels of both satisfaction and productivity. Enduring differences of all kinds play a central role in organizational life. They lead to misunderstandings, disagreements, ongoing needs to manage conflict, and differential levels of power and influence. Finally, every organization must build and sustain a culture that aligns with organizational purposes and values, inspires and gives meaning to individual efforts, and coordinates the diverse contributions of many.

Staying mindful of these four parallel sets of dynamics cultivates solid diagnostic habits for business leaders who need a comprehensive yet workable perspective on their ambiguous, ever-shifting organizational landscape. But such mindfulness is not easy. Human beings rely on limited cognitive perspectives to make sense of their world, readily fall back on habitual responses to problems and challenges, and remain blind to other options. Developmental limitations (Gallos, 1989, 2005) often collude to sustain an individual's beliefs that his or her way of thinking and seeing the world is "the only way"—when our only tool is a hammer, everything looks like a nail. Such natural human tendencies often keep leaders in their perceptual comfort

Frame	Image of Organization	Disciplinary Roots	Frame Emphasis	Underlying Assumptions	Action Logic	Path to Organizational Effectiveness
Structural	Machine	Sociology; industrial psychology; economics	Rationality; formal roles and relationships	1. Organizations exist to achieve established goals. 2. Specialization and division of labor increase efficiency and enhance performance. 3. Coordination and control ensure integration of individual and group efforts. 4. Organizations work best when rationality prevails. 5. Structure must align with organizational goals, tasks, technology, environment. 6. Problems result from structural deficiencies and are remedied by analysis and restructuring (Adapted from Bolman & Deal, 2003, p. 45.)	Rational analysis	Clear division of labor; creation of appropriate mechanisms to integrate individual, group, and unit efforts
Human resource	Family	Psychology; social psychology	The fit between individual and the organization	1. Organizations exist to serve human needs. 2. People and organizations both need each other. 3. When the fit between individual and organization is poor, one or both suffer: each exploits or is exploited. 4. When the fit between individual and organization is good, both benefit. (Adapted from Bolman & Deal, 2003, p. 115.)	Attending to people	Tailor the organization to meet individual needs; train the individual in relevant skills to meet organizational needs

Political	Jungle	Political science	Allocation of power and scare resources	1. Organizations are coalitions of diverse individuals and interest groups. 2. Differences endure among coalition members: values, beliefs, information, interests, behaviors, worldviews. 3. All important organizational decisions involve scarce resources: who gets what. 4. Scarce resources and enduring differences make conflict inevitable and power a key asset. (Adapted from Bolman & Deal, 2003, p. 186.)	Winning	Bargain; negotiate; build coalitions; set agendas; manage conflict
Symbolic	Theater	Social and cultural anthropology	Meaning; purpose; values	1. What is most important is not what happens but what it means to people. 2. Activity and meaning are loosely coupled: people interpret experiences differently. 3. People create symbols for conflict resolution, predictability, direction, hope. 4. Events and processes may be more important for what they express than what they produce. 5. Culture is the glue that holds organizations together through shared values and beliefs. (Adapted from Bolman & Deal, 2003, pp. 242–243.)	Building faith and shared meaning	Create common vision; devise relevant rituals, ceremonies, and symbols; manage meaning; infuse passion, creativity, and soul

Table 13.1. A Four-Frame Approach to Understanding Organizations.

zones and away from the very experiences that challenge them to break frame and embrace "more complicated" socioemotional, intellectual, and ethical reasoning (Weick, 1979). In essence, good diagnostic skills require leaders to employ multiple lenses to expand what they see. Leaders are more apt to use these lenses, however, when they have a framework that nudges them beyond their developmentally anchored propensities and into multiframe thinking.

To compound the issues, the ambiguity in organizational life leads to a host of possible explanations (and implicit solutions) for any problem. Take the simple case of two coworkers who engage regularly in verbal battles at work. A leader employing a human resource–based analysis of the situation, for example, might see a personality conflict between the two, clashing interpersonal styles, incompetence, or some personal problem for one or both of the employees. In this situation—as in most—if leaders set out to find a people-blaming explanation, they will. And once leaders determine that the problem requires people fixing, they will tackle it accordingly. When a group or organization falters, we look for someone to blame. If the team is losing, fire the coach. If the corporate strategy isn't meeting expectations, jettison the CEO. When relief efforts faltered in the wake of Hurricane Katrina's devastation of New Orleans, for example, much of the debate was about who to blame. The mayor of New Orleans? The governor of Louisiana? The director of FEMA? His boss, the director of Homeland Security? Or everyone's boss, the president? Heads predictably rolled, including that of Michael Brown, the FEMA director. Sometimes, changing horses is the best or even the only option, but too often it doesn't help because it solves the wrong problem.

If the underlying problems are really structural, changing people may not change anything. FEMA director Brown, after offering his own *mea culpa,* tried to tell Congress that there had been serious structural problems resulting from FEMA's poor integration into the Department of Homeland Security. FEMA had gone from being an independent agency with its own goals, priorities, and internal controls to being a stepchild in a new organizational home where, Brown said, people were more interested in terrorism than natural disasters. Brown was onto something important but was advised by Congress to focus more on his own "inadequacies." Brown is long gone, but the structural issues he identified remain. In their frame-based research across organizations, sectors, and nations, Bolman and Deal (2003) repeatedly found that the first and most common diagnosis of organizational inefficiency is interpersonal—blame people and explain everything that goes wrong as human error, folly, or treachery. Faulting individuals may be second nature to us all. But it blocks us from seeing structural weaknesses and other more subtle system dynamics (see, for example, Chapter Fourteen in this volume). The tendency to look first for the people problem should raise a red flag for leaders. Research on perception, sense making, and human development confirms that what we expect to see is exactly what we will see.

Looking beyond people and structure offers additional possibilities. In the Katrina case, effective relief efforts required cooperation among a number of different agencies and levels of government, each with its own interests and agendas. A political approach might have involved negotiations among the various players to arrive at a plan that all the key players could support.

A fourth diagnostic alternative is to use a symbolic lens to explore the cultural and dramatic elements. The agencies involved in Katrina's aftermath were unintentionally staging a drama titled *No Relief for the Suffering,* which played 24/7 on the television news and had "government incompetence fuels human tragedy" as its central plot. The damage was magnified by the widespread perception that poor African Americans were being neglected by their government. When government officials told reporters they were unaware of things that viewers had already seen on television, their credibility fell to near zero. Attention to the symbolic elements would have resulted in recognizing the criticality of conveying realistic messages of confidence, competence, and caring to both the victims and the American public. Contrast the handling of Katrina on the leadership stage to the calm, reassuring media presence of New York City mayor Rudy Giuliani in the days following the 9/11 attacks on the World Trade Center.

A FOUR-DIMENSIONAL DIAGNOSTIC MODEL: ISSUES, CHOICE POINTS, AND AREAS OF FOCUS

As the foregoing examples illustrate, each of the four frames offers a diagnostic lens on a distinct set of organizational dynamics. Each also points to a frame-consistent course of action for leaders. If the problem is structural, tweak the structure. If the problem is with the people, teach, train, coach, or counsel them or hire new people. Issues of power and politics imply the need to renegotiate, bargain, or share influence. Symbolic analyses focus on the meaning of organizational events to stakeholders inside and outside the organization and suggest ways to support the development of a healthy organizational culture and a hopeful future. Although any of the frames may account for what's happening in any given case, it is hard to know which one *really* does without first looking at them all. Any one frame may oversimplify a complex reality or send leaders blindly down the wrong path, squandering resources, time, and credibility along the way.

A comprehensive diagnostic picture is better launched with four questions: *What is going on structurally? What is happening from a human resource perspective? What is going on politically? What is happening on the symbolic front?* Taken alone, each question encourages consideration of an important slice of organizational life. Taken together, the four offer a systematic yet manageable examination of a full scope of organizational possibilities. Table 13.2 outlines key

Frame	Potential Issues and Areas to Investigate
Structural	Rules, regulations, goals, policies, roles, tasks, job designs, job descriptions, technology, business environment, chain of command, vertical and horizontal coordinating mechanisms, assessment and reward systems, standard operating procedures, authority spans and structures, spans of control, specialization and division of labor, information systems, formal feedback loops, boundary-scanning and management processes
Human resource	Needs, skills, relationships, norms, perceptions and attitudes, morale, motivation, training and development, interpersonal and group dynamics, supervision, teams, job satisfaction, participation and involvement, informal organization, support, respect for diversity, formal and informal leadership
Political	Key stakeholders, divergent interests, scarce resources, areas of uncertainty, individual and group agendas, sources and bases of power, power distributions, formal and informal resource allocation systems and processes, influence, conflict, competition, politicking, coalitions, formal and informal alliances and networks, interdependence, control of rewards and punishment, informal communication channels
Symbolic	Culture, rituals, ceremonies, stories, myths, symbols, metaphors, meaning, spirituality, values, vision, charisma, passions, commitment

Table 13.2.   Frame-Related Issues and Areas of Focus.

issues and concepts in each frame. It provides a checklist of sorts, identifying a range of possible frame-specific issues to investigate and potential areas of focus for data gathering, intervention, and change.

CENTRAL FRAME TENSIONS

Finally, each frame can also be understood as a unique set of central tensions that must be reconciled in making choices about organizational structure, HR concerns, ways to manage conflict, and culture. The tensions are universal and best thought of as endpoints on a series of continua, each with critical choice points that reflect trade-offs and the challenge of balancing competing forces. For example, the design of an appropriate system of rules, roles, procedures, and structural relationships to facilitate fulfillment of the organization's mission and purpose requires leaders to address four ongoing tensions:

- *Differentiation and integration:* how to divide up the tasks and work to be done and then coordinate the diverse efforts of individuals and groups
- *Centralization and decentralization:* how to allocate authority and decision making across the organization
- *Tight boundaries and openness to the environment:* how much to buffer and filter the flow of people and information in and out of the organization
- *Bureaucracy and entrepreneurism:* how to balance the requirement for consistency, predictability, and clarity with the need for autonomy, creativity, and flexibility

Working through these choices to achieve the right mix for any organization is hard and important work. But the aforementioned structural tensions are only one piece of the larger work to be done. Again, each frame has its own central tensions. A look within the symbolic frame, for example, identifies different yet equally significant concerns:

- *Innovation and respect for tradition:* how to foster newness and creativity while honoring the power and wisdom of the past
- *Individuality and shared vision:* how to "get the whole herd moving roughly west" without sacrificing the originality and unique contributions of talented individuals

- *Strong culture and permeable culture:* how to nurture shared values and norms while avoiding organizational repression and stagnation
- *Prose and poetry:* how to balance an organization's needs for accuracy, objectivity, and accountability with its requirement for beauty, inspiration, and soul

Table 13.3 summarizes the central tensions for each of the four frames.

In working with these four sets of competing forces, it is important to remember that there is value for organizations on both ends of each continuum. The challenge for any organization is to find the balance between or the combination of the two extremes that best fits its mission, purpose, values, and circumstances. All organizations need to divide up the work *and* integrate employee efforts. They need to foster the autonomy of individuals and units *and* the interdependence to accomplish common goals. They need to build on shared experience, skills, and values *and* use diversity to stay on the cutting edge. They need to stay grounded in reality *and* embrace innovation, artistry, and soul.

The challenge for leaders, then, is to stay cognizant of the full range of universal dilemmas and tensions and open to working with each. Leaders all have values or emotional preferences that favor one

Frame	Central Tensions
Structural	Differentiation and integration
	Centralization and decentralization
	Tight boundaries and openness to the environment
	Bureaucracy and entrepreneurism
Human resource	Autonomy and interdependence
	Employee participation and authority decision making
	Employee self-regulation and external controls
	Meeting individual needs and meeting organizational needs
Political	Authority-centered and partisan-centered
	Similarity and diversity
	Empowerment and control
	Individual and collective
Symbolic	Innovation and respect for tradition
	Individuality and shared vision
	Strong culture and permeable culture
	Prose and poetry

Table 13.3. Frame-Related Central Tensions.

end of a continuum or the other, and they may regularly push only in the direction of their personal comfort zones. Those personal biases, however, do organizations a disservice. We know, for example, that organizations require predictability, regularity, and consistency and that people are empowered and more productive with clarity of purpose, means, and contribution. On the one hand, rules, roles, policies, and standard operating procedures are a route to needed clarity. On the other hand, an overemphasis here can lead to rule-bound bureaucracies that stifle initiative and innovation, and a belief that restructuring is the solution for all ills.

Effective leadership is aided by an appreciation of all the options and choice points along the road to improved effectiveness. Attending simultaneously to the tensions in examining structure, people, politics, and symbols reminds leaders that there are multiple facets to organizing, each with its own contribution and promise. The four frames offer a map of the organizational terrain that aids leaders in knowing where they are, where they might go, and what they might gain or lose in choosing one direction or another. These frames also remind leaders that an important part of their job is reframing.

REFRAMING: USING AND TEACHING REFLECTION AND COGNITIVE ELASTICITY

In addition to using the four frames as a diagnostic device, leaders can also use them as a vehicle for *reframing*—deliberately examining a complex situation from multiple perspectives. Reframing is a skill that requires both knowledge about all four frames and practice in applying them, so as to make frame flipping second nature.

Schön and Rein (1994) identify important linkages among self-reflection, frames, and effective action. In the same way that a picture frame outlines and highlights an image chosen from a larger view, our personal frames delineate and bound our experience. But we don't realize this unless we can see our own thinking and recognize its limits. Otherwise we assume that what we see is what *is* and that anyone who sees things differently must be mistaken. The existence of nested layers of frames—individual, institutional, and cultural—compounds the problem. Individuals' personal frames develop out of experiences in families, organizations, and communities, which in turn have been influenced by a larger social and cultural milieu, and vice versa. These reciprocal influence loops reinforce and sustain each other. The authors believe that with practice individuals can learn to develop a *frame-critical rationality:* they can expand their personal capacities to see the impacts and limitations of their particular frame easily while engaged in interactions with others. This self-reflection in action—akin to the Buddhist tradition of *mindfulness* and recognition of the disparity between how the world appears to us and how it actually is (Dalai Lama, 2006)—is a crucial first step on the road to reframing.

Reframing, however, is a multistep process. Recognizing one's preferred frame or frames is important. But expanding frames of reference requires knowledge about alternative perspectives, appreciation of their potential contribution, and opportunities to practice looking at the same situation through multiple lenses. The multiframe model developed in this chapter supports that by offering an easy-to-remember template for expanding frame choices and understanding alternatives. It says to leaders, Study your own thinking and discover which of the four frames are least familiar or least palatable to you. Those are the ones you should learn more about. It also expands the role and contributions of a leader: leaders in essence become teachers who expand the framing capacities of their organizations and those who work in it.

By systematically and publicly exploring the structural, human resource, political, and symbolic components in any given situation, leaders assist their organization in identifying its dominant institutional frame—the shared assumptions and logic that tacitly drive organizational actions and underpin reward systems and strategies. Institutional frames often flow from organizational founders, become anchored in the organization's culture, and are tacitly passed along to newcomers socialized to see the institutional frame as *the* route to organizational success (Schein, 2004, and Chapter Twenty-Eight in this volume). Does your organization, for example, focus first on finding a structural response to new problems? Does it ignore the organization's culture and its consistency with corporate goals and strategy? Does it try to sweep conflict and political dynamics under the rug? Does it give inadequate attention to assessing and developing the competencies and self-reliance of key players?

Although all organizations function simultaneously as machines, families, jungles, and theaters, few are skilled in regularly monitoring and managing the ongoing tensions and needs in all four areas. Recognizing this and understanding the content and contribution of each frame enable organizations to expand their institutional lenses, identify areas and issues historically ignored, and better balance their attention across frames. Leadership development now includes a useful metacurriculum on reframing and cognitive elasticity, with top leaders modeling multiframe strategizing and the benefits of cross-frame discourse (Kuhn, 1996). As a result, organizations enhance their overall capacities for multiframed analysis and action while building new levels of organizational awareness and learning.

On an individual level, leaders can also serve as coaches to their staff members as they learn to expand and strengthen their own diagnostic and reframing skills. Reframing demands a tolerance for ambiguity, an appreciation of the social construction of reality, and skills in relative thinking—all developmentally sophisticated capacities (Gallos, 1989). Teaching the art and craft of reframing encourages individual growth and, when employed throughout the organization, can foster significant team and organization development as well (Torbert, 2006).

BEING A GENERALIST AND A SPECIALIST

This chapter begins with a promise to help leaders strengthen how they understand and work in their organizations. It ends with a caution and appreciation for the paradoxical nature of leadership. Leadership is too often confined to only one portion of a leader's work—providing vision, developing strategy, building a learning culture, making good use of workforce diversity. This is not surprising. Leadership is complex, and diverse skills and understandings are required to do it right. Simplifying leadership is a comforting albeit misleading way to wrap one's arms around a difficult job. Individuals often rise to leadership positions because of their specialized skills and strengths, and it is hard to think beyond what has worked so well before. In the language of this chapter, it is easy to see leadership as a single-frame process; however, there are risks in doing that in a multiframe world—and the organizational world is now more multiframed than ever (Bennis, 2003). The challenge for leaders is to become both frame generalists and specialists.

The advantages of specialization are that leaders can know more about a selected area, develop stronger skills in facilitating frame-related processes and diagnoses, and reflect their own values and talents. Using vertical and lateral coordination networks or implementing a company-wide Six Sigma program, for example, is dramatically different from fostering a culture that generates entrepreneurial spirit and drive. Implementing accountability systems based on complex metrics uses different leadership insights and strengths than supporting a multilevel, company-wide leadership development effort does. Given the limitations on a leader's time, talent, and energies, it is tempting for a leader to become a valued expert and resource in one set of frame understandings rather than in all of them.

Specialization, however, involves real risks. Leaders may find themselves challenged by issues outside their area of expertise. Specialization can also tighten frame blinders so that leaders just don't see problems and options beyond their own perspective. Consider the case of Robert L. Nardelli. After missing out in a three-way race to succeed Jack Welch at General Electric, Nardelli hired on as CEO of Home Depot. He replaced the founders who had built the wildly successful retailer on the foundation of an entrepreneurial, free-spirited "orange" culture in which managers ran their stores using "tribal knowledge," and customers counted on friendly, knowledgeable staff. Nardelli was a structural-frame leader who decided that Home Depot's future needed a heavy infusion of discipline, metrics, command and control, and lots of ex-military employees. Almost all the top execs and many of the front-line employees were replaced. For a while profits improved, but the stock languished, morale plummeted, and so did customer service. Where the founders had preached "make love to the customers," Nardelli cut staff, and by 2005 Home Depot came in dead last among American retailers in ratings of customer satisfaction. In 2006, Nardelli made news by running one of the shortest and most infuriating shareholder meetings in corporate history. It only took thirty minutes because he told the board to stay home, skipped the usual CEO speech, and answered no questions. His board pushed him out at the beginning of 2007, but gave him a $210 million severance package to cushion the blow.

Nardelli is only one of many examples demonstrating that leaders are at grave risk if they are not flexible, multiframe diagnosticians who can understand what's *really* happening and assess how well their talents and skills match current organizational needs. Competent leaders are specialists *and* generalists who need to embrace both sides of this core paradox.

This may seem like contradictory advice. Fletcher and Olwyler (1997) would disagree. Their work in understanding the role of paradox in optimal performance suggests the importance of simultaneously embracing two seemingly inconsistent paths without feeling the need to compromise on either. The most successful sprinters, for example, are simultaneously relaxed and tensed to meet the competition. Bill Gates is a genius in vision and in practicalities. Leaders are aided in their work when they successfully embrace the paradox of the specialist and the generalist, bring the benefits of both to their work, and model the power of flexible thinking by asking, What else might *really* be happening here?

—◁ΛΛ▷—

Joan V. Gallos is professor of leadership at the Henry W. Bloch School of Business and Public Administration at the University of Missouri-Kansas City and an award-winning author and management educator. For additional details visit www.joangallos.com.

CHAPTER FOURTEEN

Leadership and the Power of Position

Understanding Structural Dynamics in Everyday Organizational Life

Michael J. Sales

Kees Boeke's classic *Cosmic View: The Universe in 40 Jumps*,[1] illustrates an important truth: we are all embedded in multiple social systems, from the microworld of the family to the macrocosm of the universe. Although we prefer to see ourselves as unique individuals facing distinctive situations and choices, reality tells another story. We are actors operating in a predictable, everyday drama fashioned by the underlying structures and dynamics of organizational life. Our own system-influenced behaviors contribute to the drama's stability, but blindness to this reality keeps us clinging to the fantasy of autonomy. Effective leadership requires more of us: looking below the surface of everyday events, understanding the impact of system dynamics on individual behavior, and learning to leverage the power and possibility of organizational role and position. Only then can business leaders better monitor their

---

This chapter develops ideas originally published in "Understanding the Power of Position: A Diagnostic Model" by Michael J. Sales, a chapter in Joan V. Gallos (ed.), *Organization Development* (San Francisco: Jossey-Bass, 2006).

own responses and choices and facilitate interventions in which people and organizations seize their full possibilities and act with confidence and clarity.[2]

This chapter explores leadership and the power of position. It builds on the work of prominent systems theorist Barry Oshry, with whom I have worked for over twenty years.[3] Just as an iceberg stands on a hidden mountain, there is much beneath the surface of organizational events. This chapter lays bare the underlying crush that too often goes unseen—and that makes organizations predictably frustrating and seemingly wedded to suboptimal performance.[4] The chapter is divided into three sections. The first describes organizations on automatic pilot, where people operate reflexively and without awareness of the interaction between deep system structure and everyday events. The second discusses an alternative: *robust* organizations that actively prospect for opportunities and defend against threats. The third examines leadership strategies that can develop robust systems of vitality and beauty. The bottom line is that underlying system structures can be used to maintain the status quo or as a springboard for vibrant change.

ON AUTOMATIC PILOT: SEEING SYSTEMS AS THEY ARE

This exploration begins by stripping organizational complexity down to system essentials. There are four key positions that people occupy in all systems. They face predictable challenges in these positions and typically meet those challenges in predictable ways. The objective in this section is to describe and illustrate the basic structural characteristics of social systems so that leaders can see their own experiences in a new light.

A Four-Player Model

Organizational systems have four fundamental actors:

1. *Tops*, who have overall strategic responsibility for a system. Tops are usually referred to as *executives*. Every social system has its Tops: the CEO of the business, the parents in a family, the principal of a school, and so on. In business, Tops have significant spans of oversight. The greater the responsibility, the more Top they are.

2. *Bottoms,* who do the specific work of the organization, producing its goods and services. In many organizations, Bottoms receive hourly or piecework pay and perform tasks defined by others.

3. *Middles,* who stand between the Tops and the Bottoms and deliver information and resources developed in one part of the system to another part. On organizational charts Middles are the managers and supervisors.

4. *Environmental Players,* who need the organization's goods and services. They are often called *customers* and can be internal or external to the organization. Internal customers rely on the productivity of other parts of the organization to do their own work. Any stakeholders who interface with the organization in ways important to either party or to both—vendors, regulators, community organizations, institutions training the workforce— are also environmental players.

Every organizational subsystem also has its own Tops, Bottoms, Middles, and Environmental Players. An internal unit of an enterprise will have a Top who can be a Middle when the system is looked at through a wider-angle lens or a Bottom when the lens is pulled back further. For example, a department store cosmetics manager is a Top in relationship to counter clerks, a Middle in relationship to the director of merchandising, a customer to vendors, and a Bottom when decisions are made at the top to close or sell the store.

Players in Each Position Face Unique Challenges

The generic conditions faced by organizational players in their various system positions constitute challenges that define the architecture of the space. Imagine four similar rooms, each with a sign saying Top, Bottom, Middle, or Environmental Player. Anyone entering one of those rooms would breath the same air as those in another of the rooms, look at similar walls, and so on. But even though the nature of the space itself is constant, what people actually do in each of these rooms differs greatly.

Tops live in an "overloaded" space. They handle unpredictable, multiple sources of input. The more turbulent the environment, the greater the overload. Technological changes, globalization, disruptions in labor force or resource availability, and increased competition are all sources of turbulence that add to an executive's headaches.

Bottoms live in a "disregarded" space. They see things that are wrong with the organization and how it relates to the larger environment but feel powerless to do anything about them. Bottoms are frequently invisible to the Tops. The more Tops are overloaded, the greater their disregard for the Bottoms.

Middles live in a crunched, torn, and "disintegrated" space. Middles exist between Tops and Bottoms who want different or conflicting things from each other. Both want Middles to handle their issues, frequently without regard for the impact on Middles or others. Middles spend much of their energy running back and forth between their Tops and Bottoms. As a result they have little time for each other and are not an integrated group in the organization. In fact they often do not see other Middles as part of the same community. Middles are torn by their commitments, loyalties, and obligations to others. They are frequently seen by others as nice but incompetent and ineffectual, or as defensive, bureaucratic, and expendable. The more Tops and Bottoms spar, the greater the pressures on Middles.

Environmental Players live in a "neglected" space. In a world where Tops are overloaded, Bottoms are disregarded, and Middles are torn, who has attention for what is outside the institution? The more turbulent the organization's situation, the more Environmental Players find themselves put on hold (sometimes literally) while people inside the organization tend to something else.

People usually see themselves as inhabiting one organizational space but spaces can shift over time and circumstance. When the poorest of the poor lie awake at night solving the problem of how to feed their families, they are Tops.[5] When WorldCom's billionaire founder, Bernie Ebbers, got sent to prison for fraud, he became a Bottom. When a university dean is caught between the conflicting demands of her faculty and senior administration, she's a Middle despite her title as unit CEO.[6] Any time you are put on hold by a customer service representative, you fully experience being an Environmental Player!

Occupants of Each Space Face Their Own Kind of Stress

Players in each organizational space work to survive in the context of their worlds, and their system-influenced strategies make them distrustful of others.

Tops are wary of encounters and interactions that may increase their overload. They already have too much to do and too little time to do it. They limit their contact with others, even if they pay a price. Expert advice encouraging leaders to lead by wandering around makes sense, but it is not attractive to Tops who fear people wanting something that might add to their overload.

The case of Robert L. Nardelli, the fired CEO of Home Depot, can be viewed as an example. Some called Nardelli an "autocratic" leader, reliant on "command and control military style" managers who turned HD away from its customers and toward GE's "obsolete" and "mechanistic six sigma" process.[7] For many, Nardelli's performance at Home Depot's 2006 annual meeting sealed his fate: this CEO of the fourteenth largest U.S. corporation wrapped up an event affecting hundreds of thousands of shareholders within an hour, gave no speech, took no questions, and had none of his board show up.

On the face of it, this could seem a cut-and-dried case of an arrogant Top who simply "doesn't get it." But reframing the situation through a systemic lens offers an alternative view: here's a Top under pressure who delivered as promised, according to his board and a large number of impartial observers, but it is simply never enough. Nardelli came into "a very tough situation." The original HD entrepreneurs created a highly successful, high-growth business. "Nardelli was under intense pressure to continue that growth."[8]

And he did. In 2000, HD was doing about $40 billion in revenues. That grew to well over $80 billion during Nardelli's six-year tenure, with earnings per share increasing at a rate of over 20 percent a year. By employing almost 400,000 people—120,000 added during Nardelli's time at the helm—he could expect his claim that "we contributed significantly to the economic growth of the United States" to have credibility.[9] But, Home Depot's stock went down while its archrival Lowe's went up—reason enough for critics to berate Nardelli. Those pressures would make anyone wear an orange apron saying, "No Questions Means No Questions!"

Bottoms are regularly excluded from decisions about their own lives. Consider the hundreds of thousands of U.S. manufacturing layoffs and all the decisions to move activities off-shore in the last decade. Bottoms have every reason to be suspicious: others' actions too often upend their security. Bottoms frequently separate people into *us* and *them*—those who are like us and whom we can trust and those who are not like us and who are likely to do us harm.

Middles are beset with demands from above and below, from peers in other parts of their organization, and from Environmental Players such as customers. All of them want Middles to make the organization more responsive to their particular needs, regardless of the consequences for Middles and others. Middles find it hard to get Tops or Bottoms to listen to or act differently toward each other. Every interaction becomes a demand that Middles take care of something they don't feel competent to deal with or influential enough to affect. Every request becomes another chance for a Middle to look weak or bad.

Chronically neglected customers and other Environmental Players resist giving organizations the help they need to deal effectively with customer problems. Delays in delivery, quality missteps, muted responses to complaints, and so on, are often met by perturbed customers with annoyance and callousness, not empathy. These responses are understandable, but they generate and sustain antagonistic feedback loops that only accentuate customer dissatisfaction.

Again, these position-related dynamics exist in any hierarchy. Hierarchy is a permanent feature of virtually all human systems,[10] giving this four-player framework universal relevance.

Predictable Conditions Are Met with Predictable, Reflexive Responses

Typically, occupants of each system space greet their conditions with predictable responses. Oshry has observed thousands in a variety of laboratory conditions. And like others, such as Argyris and Schön, he has concluded that most people, most of the time, react in an instinctive way, especially under conditions of perceived stress.[11] Popular neuroscience has a term for this kind of reflexive response, the *amygdala hijack*, when neurochemicals bypass the executive center of the brain and instead flood the brain's emotional center. The result is the sudden onset of a highly emotional, fight-or-flight response.[12]

OCCUPANTS OF TOP SPACES TYPICALLY RESPOND TO TOP OVERLOAD BY REFLEXIVELY SUCKING IN RESPONSIBILITY TOWARD THEMSELVES AND AWAY FROM OTHERS. Once they've done that sucking in, they are burdened. George W. Bush's exclamation, "Being the president is a hard job!" in a 2004 presidential debate was a perfect example of a burdened Top talking. His lament is echoed by the findings of the Mayo Clinic's

Executive Health program: executive stress driven by work overload is the number one health concern for senior organizational leaders.[13]

A key feature of this Top automatic response is an assumption about responsibilities. The bigger the strategic importance, the more likely Tops are to conclude that they alone or with a small number of other Tops must address the problem. This intensifies their loneliness and burden.

MOST BOTTOMS AUTOMATICALLY RESPOND TO THEIR CHRONIC STATE OF DISREGARD BY BLAMING OTHERS AND HOLDING "THEM" RESPONSIBLE. Bottoms receive a lot of endorsement from other Bottoms and plenty of confirming evidence for their beliefs. Once Bottoms lock into blaming others, they experience their state as being oppressed: others are doing lousy things to them that they don't deserve. Consider the unsuccessful job applicant who blames his or her rejection on stereotypical thinking about ethnic groups, like Caucasians who blame affirmative action. When these chronic perceptions are held in the face of contradicting data, they represent a case of Bottom oppression.

MIDDLES TYPICALLY RESPOND BY "SLIDING" AND LOSING INDEPENDENCE OF THOUGHT AND ACTION. Middles live in a world of disagreement with people above and below. They also often stand between people inside and outside the organization, for example, between customers upset about service and the Bottom who delivered the service. Middles respond by making the conflicts of others their own. In doing so they lose their objectivity and increase the tearing they find in the Middle space. This space has the greatest prospect for burnout of any in the system.[14]

NEGLECTED ENVIRONMENTAL PLAYERS STAND BACK AND HOLD "IT" RESPONSIBLE FOR WHATEVER THEY ARE NOT GETTING. Customers want what they want when they want it and according to their specifications. They are dissatisfied with anything less. Because their stance rarely leads to changes in the delivery system, customers frequently feel righteous and screwed. The relationship of patrons to public transportation systems is a good example of customers standing back from a delivery system with which they could be intimately involved. A well-functioning public transportation system is a critical business concern. People need to get to and from work. But the general citizenry also needs to feel ownership. But because the decision-making processes are complex and extended in time, businesses and citizens tend to be poorly informed and disengaged. But that doesn't mean they don't loudly lament the poor functioning of buses, trains, trolleys, and the like, all of which have major implications for the efficient functioning of private industry.

Defensiveness Breeds Emotional Distance

To varying degrees, stress, blame, aggravation, and low levels of learning are prominent features of most organizations. When Tops are overloaded, Bottoms disregarded, Middles crunched and torn, and Environmental Players neglected, everyone is vulnerable to feeling uncared for. Such feelings are then manifested behaviorally and attitudinally in a variety of unhealthy ways. They eventually evolve into the intricate web of interpersonal feedback loops that Argyris and Schön call *automatically defensive learning systems*[15] that vary by one's system space. Bottoms tend to have greater awareness of the commonality of their condition. They are also more amenable to unity of action than Tops, Middles, or Environmental Players. Bottoms, for example, establish unions and other collective efforts to protect their rights and improve work conditions. *The greater the sense of Bottom vulnerability, the more intense the "negative" solidarity can be* when they organize against a common foe. Radical Islamists are an example of a people who feel very Bottom, to the point that they are willing to die in order to strike against perceived oppressors.

When Bottoms disagree their relations can quickly turn ugly, as they are primed to see the world in terms of right or wrong. Tension between poor U.S. citizens and illegal immigrants is a good example of both the solidarity within a Bottom group and the hostility toward perceived economic competitors. So are the commonplace office rumor mills, personalized attacks among coworkers, and occasional workforce violence[16] that can characterize life at the bottom.

Tops tend to be separated from each other by specialization of function. Specialization is a way of managing overload and complexity. However, hardening into one's own specialization can lead to disagreements over strategy, which Oshry calls *directional differentiation.*[17] Tops are highly attuned to the needs of their own arena. They are rarely as sensitive to other domains. Organizational culture is significantly determined by which Tops "win" the battle for strategic direction. Teaching hospitals, for example, may tilt research activities in the direction of MD faculty led by clinical chiefs rather than toward their PhD executives. In nonacademic health care research environments, the reverse could be true.

Because organizations are dominated by those who set the system's cultural tone, *Tops fight for relative status.* Tops will make strategic alliances with selected other Tops, often to the disadvantage of yet other Tops and in elaborate games of intrigue. Some Tops are absorbed with the trappings of power: the biggest office, the largest salary, the best-looking trophy spouse, the most impressive title, and so on. These alpha behaviors often indicate who gets the most attention, respect, and money—and who should be most feared.

Middles are more emotionally distant from each other than they are from the other sets of organizational actors. Middles spend their lives shuttling among Tops, Bottoms, and Environmental Players within the specialized silos that have been created for them and supported by the Tops. When Middles do not experience themselves as part of any group, however, they develop what Oshry calls an *"I" consciousness:*[18] what I know and care about is me and how I see the world. There is irony in this, as Middles share so many problems and issues. This lack of integration also makes Middles vulnerable to seeming ineffectual because many things "fall through the cracks" or "get bumped up" to Tops.

This disconnection among Middles can be manifested in minor matters. A customer, for example, asks a Bottom at a Barnes and Noble store to accept a large number of quarters as payment. The Bottom is not sure that quarters are an acceptable method of payment and asks a Middle running a particular operational function. The Middle responds with, "I am not in accounting and the accounting manager is away. You'll have to come back in later to talk to her." This is a Middle who does not see beyond the silo created by her position. "I" consciousness often translates into "it's not my job."

When organizations merge and Tops celebrate the savings from purging overlapping human resource pools, most of the time they are talking about eliminating Middles. Chronically and systemically separated from each other and locked in "I" consciousness, Middles have no way to defend each other nor a rationale for doing so. Anticipating all this can make them even more defensive in their relations with other organizational positions and with one another.

Finally, *a system's readily identifiable Environmental Players, such as customers and suppliers, may or may not join together,* depending on the situation specifics. Nongovernmental organizations, for example, might work closely with official environmental authorities to force a corporation to address a pollution matter. But when they do work together, the likelihood for significant tension between the organization and its critics adds to stress, emotional distance, and distrust.

Dominance Dynamics Create Additional Challenges

The constraints, stresses, and conditions of system dynamics have been thus far associated with the four system spaces (Tops, Middles, Bottom, and Environmental Players). Oshry adds dominance itself as an analytical lens.[19] *Dominants* are those with access to resources. They make and enforce the rules; they establish cultural norms. Dominants behave like cultural Tops even if they don't have the titles that makes their Top status official. They are distinguished from *Others*. Dominants influence a variety of cultural rules, such as how to dress; how to express oneself; and what constitutes good manners, appropriate beliefs, and commonly accepted values.

Dominant-Other issues and tensions are observable across arenas. Their impact can be seen in the intergroup dynamics of stable organizations.[20] The question of who dominates and who doesn't is always at play during organizational mergers and acquisitions. Dominance dynamics can be so frustrating that a number of law firms have opened successful "reverse merger" practices to put corporate players back in *status quo ante!*[21] The reality that many of the most menial, low-status jobs in America are held by non-English-speaking immigrants—many of whom are also not white—is another example of dominance dynamics in action.

Dominants and others have complicated but relatively well-defined relationships:

- *Dominants experience Others as strange.* In the view of Dominants, Others are off, wrong, inappropriate, and scary. In the extreme, Others can seem downright sinful, disgusting, primitive, and polluting. Leaders who value diversity should be aware of this dynamic.[22]

- *Dominants typically act to preserve their culture* in the face of perceived or actual threats. They stereotype, marginalize, ignore, suppress, trivialize, and exclude Others.

- *Dominants educate Others in order to shape them to become more "normal."* In the extreme, Dominants segregate, exile, enslave, and annihilate Others. Think Kathy Lee and sweatshops!

- *Others feel constrained, confused, oppressed, and angry in the context of a Dominant-controlled culture.* They frequently don't have any idea of how to act in a world where they are outsiders.

- *Others manifest a variety of behavioral responses to their condition.* Some adopt the norms and values of the Dominants and assimilate. Some resist, rebel, and complain. Others respond by performing their duties with apathy.

Dominant-Other Dynamics Are Another Form of Structurally Determined Reflex Responses

Like the reflex responses seen with Tops, Bottoms, Middles, and Environmental Players, the behaviors of Dominants and Others are largely unconscious and automatic in those who perform them. Those on the receiving end, however, are often very aware, especially if they don't like the behaviors. If asked, Dominants see themselves doing the "right" thing ("we've always done it this way"). And they have absolute clarity about what it takes to maintain their system power (for example, "immigrants threaten our way of life"). Others respond to constraints on their freedom with their own lack of consciousness, as if to say, "I had to. What else was I to do when they told me to shave my beard [go to the training program; stop bringing the *Gay Times* to lunch]?!"

Dominant-Other relations are self-reinforcing, like a dance that neither partner has the ability or will to stop. This makes stereotypes hard to alter. The permanence of white racism and assumptions of racial superiority are strong examples.[23] Further, when organizational Tops are also cultural Dominants, and Bottoms are Others, the prospects for transformative change are severely limited. Both sets of actors lock into their own views even as the need for transformation and the tension between the parties grow.

THE VISION: ROBUST HUMAN SYSTEMS

The dynamics discussed thus far show that organizations—and the people in them—are on automatic pilot more than they realize. People play their positions as Tops, Bottoms, Middles, or Environmental

Players unconsciously. Dominants and Others engage in predictable dances. No one sees choices or other options. These reflex responses increase stress and conflict throughout the system; reduce satisfaction and learning; and drain the fortitude, resilience, and intelligence needed to seize opportunities. Human systems on automatic are brittle: they resist the honest emotionality and disputation fundamental to good decision making.[24]

This section explores Oshry's alternative—*robust systems*. Robust systems weather adversity and seize the moment. How a system functions when people disagree is a good indicator of robustness. Rigid systems fear, defend, and suppress differences. Robust systems welcome, value, and use differences well.[25]

Recognize Basic System Elements

Leaders seeking to nurture robustness need to understand and actively manage four basic system elements:

1. *Differentiation* refers to how and how much a system elaborates differences, tolerates internal richness, and interacts with a complex environment. A great university or a mega-corporation like General Electric is intricately differentiated. Each tolerates and interacts with a variety of people and produces a range of products and offerings.

2. *Homogenization* refers to commonality: shared understanding of a topic, language, norms, relevant knowledge, and so on. Architects, for example, are exposed to a common curriculum and are literate in the same range of basic shapes, materials, and tools. People around the world recognize the most popular Beatles songs.

3. *Integration* refers to the power of shared mission, common purpose, and direction. Do people want the same objectives? Do they support each other? Do they exhibit natural teamwork? Do they help others play their roles better? Do they share information, identify group challenges, and so on? The answers manifest the state of integration.

4. *Individuation* is a system's willingness to accommodate the distinctiveness of its members. Is an organization like a Norwegian shoreline, with coves, crags, and crannies, or is it a golf green

with every blade of grass the same height? Does a system encourage personal expression or conformity? Individuation is associated with personal freedom. World-class universities like Berkeley, Oxford, and Harvard have high levels of individuation. People there "do their own thing." Characters and eccentrics abound, adding color to the system like light through a stained-glass window.

Balance the Elements

Usually without realizing it, individuals and systems choose to emphasize either differentiation or homogenization, integration or individuation. Their different choices create tensions and can complicate further the dynamics among the occupants of different system spaces locked in reflex and unconscious of the limitations of their point of view. The results for organizations are predictable.

DIFFERENTIATION WITHOUT HOMOGENIZATION LEADS TO TERRITORIALITY, SILOS, AND REDUNDANT RESOURCES. On the one hand, organizations that accentuate differentiation are likely to have finance departments, training programs, and hardware platforms for each distinct division. Conglomerates with a multiplicity of subcultures are often plagued by conflict between units with unique foci. On the other hand, homogenization without differentiation is *boring* and limits capacity for dealing with environmental variations. Think about an oil company that has never heard of alternative energy or a patriarchal textile firm with no interest in women's rights. In each case the system knows how to think and do as it currently does but has no capacity for the new or different.

A robust system has a yeasty give-and-take between differentiation and homogeneity: there are enough shared values, norms, and knowledge for each system agent to act as a *holon*,[26] a pixel that contains the totality of a system. At the same time, there is room and tolerance for a variety of behavior and endeavors. A good example of dynamic balance took place at 4:30 P.M. on September 11, 2001. The entire Congress of the United States stood on the steps of the Capitol, in a city that had been attacked seven hours earlier, and spontaneously sang "God Bless America." At that moment diverse voices blended, and knew and sang the same song.

INDEPENDENT PEOPLE COMMIT TO THE COMMON CAUSE WHEN INTEGRATION AND INDIVIDUATION ARE IN BALANCE. Integration without individuation suppresses entrepreneurial spirit and creativity. In the extreme, a Stalinistic regime is a logical outcome: everyone marching in formation but devoid of personality. In contrast, individuation without integration is chaos. People's actions are uncoordinated and self-focused, and the system's ability to achieve its mission is impaired. Pulitzer Prize–winning journalist Judith Miller's "running amok" at the *New York Times* is a prime example.[27]

Robust systems encourage both common focus and individuality. The *Apollo* space missions illustrate well how the astronauts related to their individual work, each other, and their common mission. The Boston Symphony Orchestra (BSO) is another example. The BSO is highly *differentiated*. It has many product lines and locations for its work, the two most prominent being Boston Symphony Hall and Tanglewood. The BSO sponsors tours, has links to schools and civic organizations, engages in recording activities, publishes music, plays many types of music, and so on. At the same time, music creates the BSO's *homogenization*. Everyone reads scores, is steeped in classical music, pays attention to the conductor, knows the history and worldwide reputation of the organization, and so on. The conductor, the musical scores, and the symphony traditions of quality and artistic expression *integrate* the organization. The BSO is one of the world's finest orchestras, and membership requires living up to established standards of excellence. At the same time, many of the musicians are individualists who could play almost anywhere—no one has to stay—but the diversity of opportunities, music, and activities makes the BSO an intriguing and exciting home for world-class musicians.

MOVING FROM REFLEXIVE TO ROBUST

There are five principles for transforming reflexive rigidity to robustness:

1. Strive for true partnership.

2. Take explicit leadership stands to guide behavior beyond the reflex of position.

3. Step into the fire of conflict.

4. Look for valuable enemies.

5. Don't stop thinking structurally or holistically about the system.

A Commitment to True Partnership
Makes a Real Difference

Partnership is at the heart of robust systems.[28] It involves commitment to others, a common mission, and a nuanced approach to differentiation, homogenization, integration, and individuation. Military operations like those depicted in the films *Band of Brothers* and *Saving Private Ryan* and the work of organizational cofounders like Bill Hewlett and Dave Packard in the early days of Hewlett-Packard are examples of what real partnerships look like.[29]

Leadership Stands Create Systemic Partnerships

Automatic system responses generate system vulnerability. Tops, Bottoms, Middles, and Environmental Players are set to not like each other and not get along well. Their prospects for productive partnerships are limited. Taking an explicit leadership stand from the vantage point of one's position, however, makes a difference—and Tops, Middles, and Bottoms each have their own leadership roles to play. A *stand* is the opposite of a reflex: you have to think about it and come to it on your own. A stand is a statement. Specific strategies, behaviors, and commitments flow from it. There are stands for each of the positions.

TOPS CREATE RESPONSIBILITY THROUGHOUT A SYSTEM. Tops can step back from the reflex response of sucking up work and responsibility and instead get everyone involved. This means sharing information so that others can see challenges and opportunities, developing more and different people to assume part of a Top's burden, or expanding people's involvement in important decision making. Sharing responsibility is not the same as avoiding it, and it is different from thinking no one else is willing or able to step up to the plate. A look at a Top leadership stand illustrates these differences.

Ron Newbower was vice president for research management at Massachusetts General Hospital, one of Harvard University's world-renowned teaching hospitals. His office oversaw technology transfer policies for the dissemination of medical technologies from the researcher's lab bench to the patient's bedside. Different interests were affected by the tech transfer policies, so these policies were often the subject of conflict and controversy. Rather than make important decisions in a vacuum, Newbower had prominent medical researchers at his institution visit centers around the United States to gather data on how others addressed tech transfer questions. The result was a deeper understanding of the hospital's dilemmas and options— and a good example of a Top who spread responsibility for strategic thinking and tactical policy throughout the organization.

BOTTOMS TAKE RESPONSIBILITY FOR THEMSELVES AND THE SYSTEM. Taking responsibility means stepping back from blaming others, especially higher-ups, and looking instead for opportunities to strengthen the organization, fix problems, and make a unique contribution by paying attention to something important that no one else attends to. A Bottom stand moves from complaining to taking on a project. Consider, for example, a young woman who joins the United Nations Secretariat as a low-level administrator. She has no training as a diplomat or manager, but she develops positive relationships with mentors, learns about the system, and works on project after project. Over time she becomes influential and a highly regarded senior director. This woman made the system's needs her own and ignored others who kept saying, "Why bother? Someone with your background is never going to move up."

MIDDLES MAINTAIN THEIR INDEPENDENCE OF THOUGHT AND ACTION. Oshry's work[30] suggests a number of leadership stands for Middles:

- Be the Top when you can: act as if power resides in the Middle.
- Be the Bottom when you have to: say no to the Top when you know something is wrong or won't work.
- Coach those with problems: help others work better rather than play repair person or make others' conflicts yours.
- Develop facilitation skills: bring people in conflict together to work through the issues.
- Integrate with peers: find structured activities that are antidotes to the dispersing nature of Middle space.

ENVIRONMENTAL PLAYERS MAKE THE ORGANIZATION'S DELIVERY SYSTEMS WORK FOR THEM. They step back from expecting the delivery system to take care of them and start seeing themselves as part of the solution. Ordinary citizens getting involved in government to change a law, policy, or unresponsive agency demonstrate this kind of leadrship stand.

Step into the Fire: Real Conflict Is Good for You!

Conflict is inevitable as people pursue their own objectives, values, and needs for power. The workings of human systems situate people differently in relationship to each other. Bottoms will be annoyed at Tops who try to create shared responsibility for organizational effectiveness: "I've got enough to do. Why should I worry about things that are your job?" Tops will resent Bottoms who want transparency and information: "Why are they trying to horn in on stuff they don't have the training to understand?" Middles will wonder what their job is: "If I'm not supposed to solve other people's problems, what *am* I supposed to do?" Others will be angry at Dominants for their blindness and wastefulness: "I have to clean your toilets because my kids are hungry, and you people are letting more food go to waste than we could ever eat!" Dominants will be angered by what they see as repeated requests from Others for special consideration: "You're always working the system to get what other people have worked hard their whole lives to achieve! Individualists will rebel against the judgment of the collective, integrationists at the eccentricities of a few. All of this is given; so accept conflict. Stand up for yourself in the fray, and expect others to do so as well.

Build Robustness by Valuing Enemies

As the Bob Nardelli story illustrates, once the attack is under way, system antagonists dehumanize each other. However, system productivity requires those who seem at odds to work together. Total victory in the face of opposition is attractive. Long-enduring stalemates are more common, and people have much to learn from their system enemies. Think about Newt Gingrich working with Hillary Clinton on national health care, John McCain talking with the men who shot down his jet in Vietnam, and Bill Gates saving archrival Apple with a $150 million loan and Steve Jobs letting him do it! Yitzhak Rabin once said, "You don't make peace with your friends." Rabin recognized the value in working with an enemy. Robust systems come from individuals' identifying others who scare or anger them, reaching out to understand these others, and looking for ways to work together.

Don't Stop Thinking About the System!

As this chapter illustrates, human behavior in organizations sits on top of deep structure. Awareness and choice are essential to break

---

- *Name the system you intend to influence.* Is it the entire organization? A subsystem? An indecisive leadership team? A Bottom group on strike? What are you attempting to influence?

- *Identify the key actors in the system.* Who are the Tops, Bottoms, Middles, and key Environmental Players?

- *Pick a particular issue for the system.* What specific dynamics need to be addressed within the chosen group (for example, burnout among the Tops, poorly functioning Middle communication processes, relations between Bottoms and Environmental Players)?

- *Map the system dynamics of the organization.* How do system dynamics and relationships among Tops, Middles, Bottoms, and Environmental Players affect the organization and the domain you are attempting to influence?

- *Develop data-based "incident reports" on each part of the organization.* Do the Tops, Bottoms, Middles, and Environmental Players appear to be dealing with predictable overload, disregard, crunch, and neglect? What strategy is each group using to address its condition?

- *Build an alliance with successes.* Are any of the players in the organization *not* using automatic, system-predicted strategies? If so, what are they doing that is different? How is that working for them? For the system as a whole? What would it take to ally with them? Could you encourage or support their leadership to take a stand?

- *Use the cultural lens.* If you're in a leadership position, you're probably a Dominant. What rules and norms are you following that Others disregard? If you're trying to lead change, you may be doing so from the position of an Other. How are you performing that role? Are you an assimilationist or a rebel?

- *Take a robustness pulse.* What is the balance between differentiation (the diversity in the system) and homogenization (the commonalities)? What are the dynamics between individuators (those who stand out as distinctive) and integrationists (those who support the overall purpose of the system)?

- *Develop an intervention strategy.* Where could you intervene and how? At the level of the automatic responses? By raising awareness of the need for balance and synergy among the core ingredients of robust systems?

- *Build a powerful network of support.* Who are (and who could be) your partners, allies, information sources, implementers, lieutenants, and valuable enemies? Why? How could each segment of the system act to add momentum to the change you want to set in motion? To block it? Do you have strong working relationships with the stakeholders whom you need for success? If not, what would facilitate those relationships?

Exhibit 14.1.   A Leader's Guide for System Change.

the dance of blind reflex—and are keys to organizational transformation and health. The humming sound of the social forces below the surface can be transformed into new music by the single action of one person. Concerted action by others can turn a simple tune into a symphony.

Every system needs and yearns for something to infuse it with vibrancy and life—make it more forceful, resilient, invigorated. Finding an organization's melody puts electricity in the air. Look at Jeffrey Immelt's *ecomagination* initiative for General Electric, and the positive energy galvanized by his announcement of a starting target for GE of $10 billion in ecologically related revenues. In one day Immelt put a stamp on the world's eleventh largest company very different from that of his predecessor, Jack Welch.[31] Immelt's leadership changed GE in the eyes of many. Exhibit 14.1 provides a guide to assist leaders in finding the right melody to release energy and creativity in their own organizations: seeing the power of positions and systems is a powerful place to start. What will happen to your leadership—to your life—as a result of doing so?

Michael J. Sales is a cofounder of Art of the Future, a strategic consulting firm in Waltham, Massachusetts, specializing in structural dynamics and organizational learning.

CHAPTER FIFTEEN

The Boundaryless Organization

Rising to the Challenges of Global Leadership

Ron Ashkenas
David Ulrich
Todd Jick
Steve Kerr

Twenty-first-century business is in the midst of a social and economic revolution, shifting from rigid to permeable structures and processes and creating something new: the *boundaryless organization.*

Consider these developments, once unimaginable:

- GlaxoSmithKline Pharmaceuticals has cut months out of the drug development process by replacing sequential clinical data collection, analysis, and regulatory reporting with cross-functional teams composed of statisticians, biometricians, clinical trials experts, data management experts, and others.

- General Electric managers routinely have fifteen to twenty direct reports. Often, there are no more than three or four layers of management between the CEO and frontline workers in a company of more than 300,000 people.

- Fidelity Investments, Charles Schwab, CSFB Direct, and Spear, Leads & Kellogg—brokerage competitors—have formed a joint venture to develop an electronic communications network for trading NASDAQ stocks online.

Business authors have described hundreds of similar innovations, declaring the rise of a "new organization" to which they have given many names: virtual organization, front/back organization, cluster organization, network organization, chaotic organization, ad hoc organization, horizontal organization, empowered organization, high-performing work team organization, process reengineered organization, and the list goes on.

Underlying the descriptions, however, is a deeper paradigm shift. The emergence of the boundaryless organization is the driving force and the constant is that these new organizations evoke different kinds of behavior. Specifically, behavior patterns conditioned by boundaries between levels, functions, and other constructs are replaced by patterns of free movement across those same boundaries. Rather than using boundaries to separate people, tasks, processes, and places, organizations are focusing on how to get through those boundaries—to move ideas, information, decisions, talent, rewards, and actions where they are most needed.

Our purpose in this chapter is to describe the boundaryless structures behind the new labels and lay out their underlying assumptions, the changes in behavior they generate, the results they can yield, and the leadership challenges and roles that the new structures pose. To do this, we delineate four types of boundaries that characterize most organizations:

- Vertical boundaries between levels and ranks of people
- Horizontal boundaries between functions and disciplines
- External boundaries between the organization and its suppliers, customers, and regulators
- Geographic boundaries between locations, cultures, and markets

BOUNDARYLESS BEHAVIOR: THE ART OF THE FLUID

Organizations have always had and will continue to have boundaries. People specialize in different tasks, and thus boundaries exist between functions. People have differing levels of authority and influence, so boundaries exist between bosses and subordinates. People inside a firm do different work than suppliers, customers, and other outsiders, so boundaries exist there as well. And people work in different places, under different conditions, and sometimes in different time zones and cultures, thus creating additional boundaries.

The underlying purpose of all these boundaries is to separate people, processes, and production in healthy and necessary ways. Boundaries keep things focused and distinct. Without them, organizations would be disorganized. People would not know what to do. There would be no differentiation of tasks, coordination of resources and skills, or sense of direction. In essence, the organization would cease to exist.

Given the necessity of boundaries, making a boundaryless organization does not require a free-for-all removal of all boundaries. Instead, we are talking about making boundaries more permeable, allowing greater fluidity of movement throughout the organization. The traditional notion of boundaries as fixed barriers or unyielding separators needs to be replaced by an organic, biological view of boundaries as permeable, flexible, moveable membranes in a living and adapting organism. In living organisms, membranes provide shape and definition. They have sufficient structural strength to prevent collapse into an amorphous mass, yet they are permeable. Food, oxygen, and chemical transmitters flow through them so that each part of the organism can contribute in its own way to the rest.

So it is with the boundaryless organization. Information, resources, ideas, and energy pass through its membranes quickly and easily so that the organization functions more effectively as a whole. Definition and distinctions still exist—there are still leaders with authority and accountability, people with special functional skills, distinctions between customers and suppliers, and work done in different places.

Like a living organism, the boundaryless organization also develops and grows, and the placement of boundaries may shift over time. The levels between top and bottom may decrease, functions merge to combine skills, or partnerships form between the firm and its customers or suppliers that change the boundaries of who does what.

Because the boundaryless organization is a living continuum, not a fixed state, the ongoing management challenge is to find the right balance and to determine how permeable to make boundaries and where to place them. But why should anyone make this effort? What is so important about becoming boundaryless?

A CHANGING PARADIGM FOR ORGANIZATIONAL SUCCESS

In recent years, almost all organizations have experimented with change aimed at creating more permeable boundaries. Whether it was called total quality, reengineering, reinvention, or business process innovation, many organizations have invested untold resources trying to make change happen.

The impetus behind many of these efforts has been the fall from grace or demise of some of the most highly regarded organizations in the world: IBM, Lloyd's of London, Eastern Air Lines, General Motors, Eastman Kodak, and others. Each experienced severe financial difficulties, crises in leadership, and major changes in direction. Nor is membership in this fallen-angels club limited to a handful of fields. The phenomenon crosses all lines from retail sales to automotive manufacturing, publishing to air travel, financial services to computers. It crosses geographic boundaries, with troubled giants found in North America, Europe, Asia, and Latin America. And the difficulties cannot be explained by lack of long-range strategy or intelligent planning. IBM, Kodak, and many of the others had and continue to have world-class planning functions and capabilities. The companies have not stumbled due to lack of technology or investment. In the past twenty years, for example, GM probably invested more in automation than any other company in the world. IBM's research investment was, for many years, far beyond the business norm.

Naturally, company-specific explanations can be offered. But such explanations miss the larger pattern. Each company slipped from invincible when it faced *a rate of change that exceeded its capability to respond*. When their worlds became highly unstable and turbulent, all lacked the flexibility and agility to act quickly. Most launched change efforts that share a common theme: to retool the organization to meet an entirely new set of criteria for success.

OUT WITH THE OLD—IN WITH THE NEW

For much of the twentieth century, four critical factors influenced organizational success.

- *Size.* The larger a company grew, the more it was able to attain production or service efficiencies, leverage its capital, and put pressure on customers and suppliers.

- *Role clarity.* To get work done efficiently in larger organizations, tasks were divided and subdivided, clear distinctions were made between manager and worker, and levels of authority were spelled out. In well-functioning organizations, everyone had a place, accepted it, and performed according to specifications.

- *Specialization.* As tasks were subdivided, specialties were created or encouraged to provide fine-grained levels of expertise. Thus finance, planning, human resources, information technology, inventory control, and many other tasks all became disciplines in their own right.

- *Control.* With all these specialized tasks and roles, most organizations needed to create controls to make sure the pieces performed as needed, coming together properly to provide whole products or services. Therefore, a major management function was to control the work of others to ensure that they were doing the right things, in the right order, at the right time.

Managers and organizational theorists focused on organizational structure as the primary vehicle for achieving effectiveness. They debated questions like:

- How many layers of management do we need?

- What signing authority will different levels have?

- What is the proper span of control?

- What is the best balance between centralization and decentralization?

- How do we describe and classify each job and set pay levels?

- How do we organize field locations and international operations?

Their goal was to create the organizational structure and attendant processes that would let a company maximize the four critical success factors. However, microprocessors, high-speed information processing and communications, and the global economy have conspired to radically shift the basis of competitive success. An exclusive focus on the old success factors of size, role clarity, specialization, and control has become a liability. Instead, the old need to be combined with a new and sometimes paradoxical set of success factors:

- *Speed.* Successful organizations today are increasingly characterized by speed in everything they do. They respond to customers more quickly, bring new products to market faster, and change strategies more rapidly than ever before. While size does not preclude speed, large organizations are like tankers. Their challenge is to act like a fast-moving small company while retaining access to the large company's broader resources.

- *Flexibility.* Organizations that move quickly are flexible. People do multiple jobs, constantly learn new skills, and willingly shift to different locations and assignments. Similarly, the organization pursues multiple paths and experiments. Role clarity can constrain flexibility—people locked into specific roles and responsibilities become unwilling to jump at a moment's notice and do whatever is needed.

- *Integration.* Organizations adept at shifting direction have processes that carry change into the institutional bloodstream, disseminating new initiatives quickly and mobilizing the right resources to make things happen. Instead of breaking tasks into pieces and assigning specialists to perform the pieces with precision, the organization creates mechanisms to pull together diverse activities as needed. The key to success is often the ability of those specialists to collaborate with others to create an integrated whole.

- *Innovation.* A world of rapid change makes innovation essential. Doing today's work in today's way becomes outdated quickly. So boundaryless organizations create innovative processes and environments that encourage and reward creativity, rather than stifle creative spirit with the systems of approvals and double-checks needed to preserve standard operating procedures and a focus on control.

In short, organizations designed to meet the old set of critical success factors alone are increasingly *incapable* of thriving or even surviving in the new world. Consider the contrast between retailers Sears and Wal-Mart.

THE GIANT AND THE UPSTART

Sears, for many years the world's largest retailer, succeeded with management based on structure and control. As the company grew, Sears leveraged its buying power through strong centralized functions. Almost all key decisions were made in its Chicago headquarters. The stores mirrored this control philosophy, allotting different levels of approval to various managerial levels, with all important decisions requiring travel far up the chain of command. The approach succeeded for years, as long as size, role clarity, specialization, and control were the drivers of competitiveness.[1]

Then, in the 1980s, the rules of the retail game changed. Consumers wanted lower prices, better service, and a constantly changing array of merchandise. In this environment, speed mattered more than size. Customers also wanted goods on the spot; they weren't willing to place orders and wait. At the same time, flexibility and integration proved able to drive out costs. Successful retailers gave people multiple jobs and designed integrated service functions. Innovation became critical to maintaining the edge in merchandise, service, and store layout.

In this new world, Sears began to slip. At first, management asked the traditional questions, looking to structure for answers and repeatedly restructuring, closing stores, and changing leaders. Nothing worked. It was not until Sears started trying to become a more "customer-focused company" and asked each store to find ways of identifying and serving customer needs that things began to turn around. Once it shifted focus, Sears was able to reduce corporate staff dramatically and move decision-making to stores and store managers. The new success factors compelled Sears to redesign itself.

In contrast, upstart Wal-Mart focused from its beginning on the new success factors. Founder Sam Walton's philosophy was to find out what customers wanted and provide it quickly and at lower cost than any competitor. This meant designing fast, flexible processes for gathering and using consumer and competitive intelligence. One such process is the weekly "quick market intelligence" (QMI) exercise at the heart of Wal-Mart's success.

QMI works like this: every Monday morning, two hundred or more Wal-Mart senior executives and managers leave Bentonville, Arkansas, to visit Wal-Mart stores and competitors in different regions of North America. For three and a half days, they talk to store managers, employees, and customers, learning about what is and is not selling. On Thursday evening, the fleet of Wal-Mart planes returns these executives to Wal-Mart headquarters. On Friday, in what they call the "huddle," they examine the quantitative data (computer-based reports of what is selling) and match the data with their field observations to make decisions about products and promotions. Each Saturday morning, a teleconference shares these ideas with over three thousand stores and gives everyone the game plan for the next week. The cycle time for ideas at Wal-Mart is measured in days, not weeks or months. Boundaries that would have led to committee meetings, task forces, and reporting up the chain of command in the old Sears have been replaced by executives who collect information from the source and act.

Even Wal-Mart store managers can move with speed, flexibility, and creativity. They can set up their own "corners" with merchandise they think will sell to local customers. If an idea works, it gets a larger test and sometimes expands nationwide. Similarly, managers can make pricing changes on the spot if they think a change is warranted or if a competitor has a lower price. They do not need to call Bentonville for permission.

Speed, flexibility, integration, and innovation have helped Wal-Mart to grow and thrive, even during downturns in the retail industry. Similar contrasts can be made between Microsoft and Digital Equipment (now part of Compaq) and between Southwest Airlines and TWA.

FOUR BOUNDARIES

In their quest to achieve the twenty-first-century success factors, organizations must confront and reshape four types of boundaries: vertical, horizontal, external, and geographic.

Vertical. Vertical boundaries represent layers within a company. They are the floors and ceilings that differentiate status, authority, and power: span of control, limits of authority, and the other manifestations of hierarchy. In a hierarchy, roles are clearly defined and more authority resides higher up in the organization than below. You can track the intensity of vertical bounding by the number of levels between the first-line supervisor and the senior executive and by the differences between levels. Hierarchical boundaries are defined by title, rank, and privilege.

In contrast, boundaryless organizations focus more on who has useful ideas than on rank and authority. Good ideas can come from anyone. These organizations make no attempt to dissolve all vertical boundaries—that would be chaos—but their permeable hierarchies give them faster and better decisions made by more committed individuals.

Horizontal. Horizontal boundaries exist between functions, product lines, or units. If vertical boundaries are floors and ceilings, horizontal boundaries are walls between rooms. Rigid boundaries between functions promote the development of local agendas that may well conflict with each other. Each functional area works to maximize its own goals, often to the exclusion of overall organizational goals.

Processes that permeate horizontal boundaries carry ideas, resources, information, and competence with them across functions so that customer needs are well met. Quality, reengineering, and high-performing work team initiatives often foster such processes. Once managers begin to move work quickly and effectively across functions or product lines, horizontal boundaries become subservient to the integrated, faster-moving business processes.

External. External boundaries are barriers between firms and the outside world—principally suppliers and customers but also government agencies, special interest groups, and communities. Traditional organizations draw clear lines between insiders and outsiders. Some of these barriers are legal, but many are psychological, stemming from varied senses of identity, strategic priorities, and cultures. These differences lead most organizations to some form of we-they relationship with external constituents.

While external boundaries provide positive identity for insiders ("I work for X!"), they also diffuse effectiveness. Often, customers could help a firm resolve internal problems—and have a keen interest in solutions. Similarly, suppliers want to see their customers succeed because successful customers buy more.

Geographic. Geographic or global boundaries exist when firms operate in different markets and countries. Often stemming from national pride, cultural differences, market peculiarities, or worldwide logistics, these boundaries may isolate innovative practices and good ideas, keeping a company from using the learning from a specific country and market to increase overall success.

With information technology, workforce mobility, and product standardization, global boundaries are quickly disappearing. Traditional work differences in Europe, Asia, and North America are being driven out by the need for more globally integrated products and services. At the same time, firms that succeed across global boundaries respect and value local differences as a source of innovation. Colgate Palmolive, for example, has worked to establish brand equities throughout the world. Its brand of toothpaste and tooth powder, for example, while adapted to local preferences for taste, color, and so on, has become global. Consumers in Europe, Australia, North America, and Asia can recognize the brand and find value in it. Creating global brand equities requires companies to think across global boundaries.

When vertical, horizontal, external, and geographic boundaries are traversable, the organization of the future begins to take shape. When rigid and impenetrable, they create the sluggish response, inflexibility, and slow innovation that cause premier companies to fall.

PERMEABILITY IN ACTION

To take a look at boundaryless behavior in action, consider GE Capital's private label credit card business, which is composed of two organizations, Card Services (CS) in the U.S. market, and Global Consumer Finance (GCF) outside the United States. Head-quartered in Stamford, Connecticut, the organizations provide private label credit card services to retail chains. GCF also provides consumer lending and banking products. CS and GCF customers include such retail chains as Macy's, Wal-Mart, Harrods, IKEA, and hundreds more.

In both revenue and human capital, CS and GCF are two of GE Capital's largest businesses, employing over twenty thousand people worldwide in a diverse range of functions and disciplines, including systems, telecommunications, customer service, marketing, finance, risk management, and product development. The businesses have state-of-the-art processing centers around the world, providing almost instantaneous customer service to retailers and millions of their cardholders.

Based on year 2000 data, GE Capital is the world's largest provider of private label credit cards. Assets total over $50 billion, and both CS and GCF are among the highest net income generators in the GE Company, growing at a double-digit rate each year. In addition, the company continues to expand aggressively, looking for major acquisitions in Europe, Latin America, and the Far East, while continuing to bring on major new customers in the United States.

In short, CS and GCF are enviable, successful businesses—financially sound, providing attractive rates of return, and satisfying their customers while also growing aggressively. And they're both boundaryless organizations. For example, when an associate in any of

GCF's thirty-one countries turns on a computer, a "GCF Workplace" screen appears—in one of twenty-five languages. Using this intranet, GCF associates can provide the same kinds of services, using the same measures and tools, with access to the same resources and knowledge banks, from almost anywhere in the world. And if managers or associates in different parts of GCF need to work together, they can take advantage of "Same Time," which allows them to hold meetings while sharing visuals and data in real time across the globe.

Customer service teams in the centers are responsible for credit card approvals, problem resolution, and accounts receivable for a portfolio of stores. In most cases, frontline associates in these teams have the authority and the tools to make decisions on the spot for customers, without having to check with supervisors or managers for approval.

From the standpoint of the credit card holder, these services seem to be provided by the retailer. CS and GCF thus function as invisible partners, responsible for managing the retailer's financial relationship with all credit card holders. In addition, a marketing group also works closely with each retailer to agree on the standards to apply to potential cardholders, the rates to charge, and the marketing programs and promotions to offer.

Seeing this level of success, few remember that in the early 1980s, GE was trying desperately to sell its credit card organization, then named Private Label. It had been in business for fifty years, yet its market share was a mere 3 percent. It was an old, tired business—a mediocre performer in a declining market—and its own strategic planners did not believe it had much of a future. They were convinced that private label credit cards would go the way of the dinosaurs, displaced by universal cards such as Visa, MasterCard, and American Express. "Why," they reasoned, "would consumers want to carry multiple credit cards when they could carry just one or two? And if that's the case, we don't have a business here!"

Private Label's outlook was bleak. Holding fast to his pledge to sell off businesses that could not become the number one or two performers in their industries, in 1982 GE's new chairman and CEO Jack Welch put it on the block. Fortunately for GE, potential buyers agreed that Private Label was a dying business. They stayed away. With little choice other than to make the best of it, GE Capital promoted Private Label insider David A. Ekedahl to run the business. His mission: keep it going as long as you can without losing money. Ekedahl did better than that.

Formulating External Boundaries

Private Label's transformation did not begin with a grand plan. In fact, as Ekedahl describes it, the objective was to keep the wolves at bay by adding new customers. However, Ekedahl and his managers first had to decide who the customers were and how to win their business. That analysis led to an important insight—the company needed to concentrate not just on the consumer (the end user of private label cards) but on the retailer as well.

By changing the long-standing external boundary that defined the customer, Ekedahl began a transformation that took Private Label light years forward. He realized that fast and flexible processing at a lower cost than could be provided by universal cards would be the critical success factor for retailers. If Private Label could get the retailers on board quickly, manage the volume of business efficiently, provide error-free processing, and manage customer databases, it would have tremendous retail leverage. And the information about customer buying patterns would then pay off even more in purchasing, promotions, and marketing decisions. But at this time, Private Label procedures for setting up a new retailer and working with an existing one were all incredibly cumbersome. To achieve fast and flexible processing, another boundary needed to be opened up.

Loosening Horizontal Boundaries

Dave Ekedahl's description of what happened next illustrates how key insights open up the path to the boundaryless organization.

> We had just signed up a new company to do their private label credit cards, and I wanted to go through the process of getting that client on board. I found that I had a lot of people in the room, but none of us had any idea what to do by ourselves. We needed dozens of other people. So I figured if this was what it took to get something done, I might as well organize around these kinds of processes. So we began to recreate our own organization around the major processes that needed to get done rather than just do it *ad hoc* all the time.

Making organizational structure mirror the way work actually got done, Ekedahl gradually transformed Private Label, leveling horizontal boundaries between systems and other business functions. The change was complex because the systems resources were all part of GE Capital, centralized and well defended by solid functional walls. No systems people were dedicated to Private Label; different resources were brought to bear whenever there was a particular need. Ekedahl was determined to change all this, but by no means was the transition smooth.

Early in 1989, Ekedahl tried to bridge the functions by sponsoring a joint conference with the central systems organization. At a rancorous concluding meeting, the systems people complained that they were not consulted soon enough in new customer conversions and were given unrealistic requirements and deadlines. Meanwhile, Ekedahl's marketing people accused the systems professionals of not delivering on their promises. Ekedahl found himself caught in the middle, wanting to create a cross-functional team yet forced to arbitrate between functions with walls too high for collaboration.

Ekedahl did not give up. First, he influenced the head of GE Capital's systems to dedicate a group of professionals to his business. Then he insisted that the systems and marketing people find new ways of working together, and he encouraged them to rethink their basic work processes. Although reluctant, the two groups eventually responded to Ekedahl's continuing pressure.

In 1990, Rich Nastasi, head of the systems group, began to work with the other business functions to cut the time required to bring a new retailer on board. A small cross-functional team mapped the typical process, which averaged eight weeks. Nastasi then brought together a group of systems, marketing, finance, and customer service people and challenged them to do the job in a matter of days, not weeks. To everyone's amazement, solutions began to emerge: earlier systems involvement in customer negotiations, standardized data collection procedures, ways of training customer personnel to help in the conversion, structured conversion procedures, and technical means of transferring electronic files more quickly.

Over the next few months, as the solutions were implemented, elapsed times dropped dramatically to less than a week for all but the largest new customers. Equally significant, the different functions put the solutions in place together. The walls were coming down. Less than a year later, Nastasi and his people were reporting directly to Ekedahl, as full-fledged members of the business team for what was now called Retailer Financial Services (RFS).

Flattening Vertical Boundaries

With RFS organized around key processes, a different organization took shape. Gradually, the company shifted from a centralized model where systems, credit, marketing, and customer service were all run out of Stamford to a hybrid model with both centralized and decentralized processes. The guiding idea was that processes to support specific customers should be managed in the field, close to those customers. Processes requiring consistency and control—financial reporting, credit scoring, systems processing, telecommunications—should be handled by the head office. Additional head office roles were to facilitate sharing of best practices, movement of key personnel, acquisition of new customers, and allocation of investment resources.

To shift processes to the field, RFS created "regional business centers." Retailer customers in each region looked to the centers for training in systems and procedures, development of mailing and promotional programs, management information, and the whole range of cardholder customer services, both through the mail and on the phone. The centers also managed credit risk—allowing a better balance between how much to market and how much risk to allow. The key, single focus of these centers was to help retailers become more successful.

Setting up regional centers, however, was expensive. Ekedahl was under pressure to reduce costs by increasing productivity. Although the business was willing to invest in automated dialers and on-line information systems, new technology did not improve productivity enough to pay for the added cost of the centers. This cost-cutting pressure led to a radically new organization. As Ekedahl explains:

> We originally came at it from a productivity point of view. We figured maybe we could save costs by not having so many management levels. So we asked a group of our associates how to do this. The exempt and the nonexempt people got together for a week and went way beyond what we had been expecting. They recommended that we organize around teams, with no managers whatsoever. I said, "what the heck, let's try it." So we did, starting with one business center in Danbury.

Setting up business centers without hierarchical boundaries was a fundamental revolution. And as in any revolution, there were casualties—managers who couldn't adjust, supervisors who couldn't find a place, and in particular, frontline associates who couldn't handle the increased accountability. For the first few years, several centers suffered high levels of associate turnover. It turned out to be hard to find employees able to function effectively as team players with no supervision and high responsibility. Despite careful screening and orientation, many still opted out after less than a year.

Eventually, through a dialogue helped along by a few outside experts in team processes, a pattern for success emerged. Teams were set up to serve all the needs of one large or several small retailers and the retailers' customers. All team members were cross-trained in all the skills needed for effective service, including handling billing problems and collections, changing credit lines, and changing customer data. The more senior or experienced people (in most cases, former supervisors) became roving trainers, documenters of procedures, and problem solvers.

The payoff from the first boundaryless business center was so great that Ekedahl and his team never seriously considered restoring the traditional vertical organization. Even with the turnover, productivity was still many times greater and overall costs far lower. And the customers loved the service they were now getting from a dedicated team that knew their business, consumers, and systems. They began to see the business teams as extensions of their own companies and not just service providers. Ekedahl decided that all new business centers should be set up in teams from the beginning. Thus when RFS bought the Macy's credit card and servicing portfolio in the early 1990s, the new business center established to handle the account was organized without managers from the start.

The Flexibility to Reinvent

By 1995, when Dave Ekedahl retired, RFS was considered a model of a successful, high-performance, boundaryless organization. But RFS was also facing a test of its capacity to survive—the retail industry was slowing down and RFS's largest customer, Montgomery Ward, was about to go under.

For years, Wards (as it was called) had an entire RFS division—based in Merriam, Kansas—dedicated to serving its cardholders. By 1998, Wards represented almost 40 percent of RFS's net income. So when Wards spiraled into decline during a nationwide credit squeeze, RFS's own profitability plummeted. To fix that, GE Capital asked

Edward Stewart, one of its executive vice presidents, to focus on restoring RFS to profitability. Stewart found that he had to reinvent the private label business, now called Card Services, all over again.

Obviously, Stewart's first step was to look for a solution to the problems with Wards. By exchanging debt for equity, Stewart helped GE Capital take a controlling interest in Wards and forced a series of moves—first taking the company into bankruptcy, and then bringing it out in a much-reduced form. Unfortunately, even the scaled-down Wards could not survive, and by the year 2000, the painful decision was made to close the doors and liquidate. Fortunately, a series of business plays mitigated the financial consequences of this decision. Stewart was able to strike a deal with Wal-Mart to take on its private label card business and, as part of the deal, flipped all the Wards cardholders to Wal-Mart. This dramatically reduced the level of credit write-offs, and maintained (and even added to) CS's volume. Stewart also engineered a trade of Bank One's private label business for GE Capital's bankcard business which also led to some much-needed financial gains. During this period, Stewart also "triaged the entire portfolio" with a more rigorous risk screen, which led to a reduction in nonperforming assets and a scaling down of the entire business.

These financial moves were not enough to restore CS to the needed levels of growth and profitability. In particular, the smaller (though better-performing) portfolio required costs to be reduced dramatically—but in ways that did not diminish customer service or destroy the vitality of the business.

Because CS was already a flexible, boundaryless organization, Stewart was able to take a page out of Ekedahl's book and refocus the organization once again around core processes—but this time to use new technologies as an enabler of productivity.

Throughout most of the 1990s, the old RFS had been a hybrid organization with some centralized functions along with regional units that each managed a separate P&L. At the end of the 1990s, Stewart consolidated all the units into one P&L. He built strong, centralized process organizations for customer service, marketing, and collections, and then closed 40 percent of the existing sites. Within this framework, Stewart asked each of his managers to use Six Sigma quality tools to achieve high levels of performance and service at much reduced costs. He then created a "digital dashboard" on the company intranet to track performance against agreed-upon standards. Down the side of this dashboard is a list of clients; across the top are the performance standards in areas such as computer up time, card authorization speed, call answering times, and so forth. The dashboard pulls data directly from the computer systems and telephone networks and displays it in real time—highlighting any metric that falls outside the variance standard. Functional managers can use it to track their processes. "Client leads" can use the same data to look at the performance for their customer. Associates themselves can look at their performance and see where they stand and where they need to improve.

To take this streamlining one step further, Stewart began to move whole processes to India, where they could be performed effectively at half the cost. Using telecommunications technology and Internet-based tools, by the beginning of 2001, over a thousand people in India were performing collections and customer service functions for clients in the United States. For the digitally enabled, boundaryless organization, location had become less relevant than customer-focused process efficiency. But the real payoff was a return to profitability and growth.

Crossing Geographic Boundaries

Until 1991, RFS was largely a U.S. business. With the 1991 acquisition of the credit card portfolio of Burton, a major U.K. retailer, Ekedahl and his team were thrust into global management. At first, the Burton organization was kept intact, reporting to Stamford as one more business center with only a minor exchange of ideas and systems technology. To people in Stamford, Burton was interesting but not critical. That soon changed.

Two factors propelled RFS into a global role. First, the traditional domestic market for growth was clearly full of uncertainties: retailers (such as Wards) were struggling and even going out of business, there was pressure to reduce credit card interest charges, and competitors were introducing new strategies such as co-branded cards. Second, Burton's processing capacity was underused. If RFS took on new portfolios in Europe, the Burton operations center could handle them with little incremental cost. By applying its world-class technology expertise, RFS could have a significant competitive advantage in Europe. So RFS began an acquisition binge in Europe. In less than two years, it had signed up dozens of new retail customers and purchased whole portfolios from banks and other financial institutions.

Suddenly, RFS had a major presence in Europe. The question was how to manage that. Given its strategic importance, should it be closely managed from Stamford? Or should it be managed locally from within Europe? Should its procedures and processes mirror the U.S. organization? Or should RFS Europe be allowed to develop its own way of doing things based on what worked in Europe and in each individual country? And how should European and U.S. personnel interact—as representatives of different divisions or as members of a synergistic team? And what would happen if RFS went on beyond Europe?

Early in 1993, Ekedahl appointed Dave Nissen, a seasoned RFS manager who had run both Private Label and the MasterCard program, to oversee the European expansion. Ekedahl hoped that putting someone who was familiar with U.S. operations in charge of the European acquisitions would combine the best thinking from the U.S. side with a deeper understanding of what worked in Europe. By the end of 1993, Ekedahl had appointed Nissen to head RFS International. Essentially, Nissen's charge was to create a European version of the RFS domestic operation—a series of regional business centers serving specific clients in their own languages, joined with a central processing facility (Burton) that achieved scale in operations. A small central staff, headquartered in Europe, would provide coordination, technical support, and best practices from both Europe and the United States. Nissen was also to search for acquisitions in other parts of the world.

Growing a business outside the United States, however, is not the same as building a domestic business, and RFS International was split off from RFS in 1994 to form an independent business called Global Consumer Finance. Freed from its U.S. parent, Nissen decided to shift the business model. He could not build enough scale in private label credit cards in any one country, so he diversified the business to include a range of consumer lending products such as personal loans, auto loans, and second mortgages. The myriad regulations meant that in many countries he needed to buy or open local banks to support these products.

With this model, Nissen was able to grow GCF rapidly, not only in Europe but in Asia as well. By encouraging cross-selling across a half-dozen key products, he built volume and scale in each country—and then applied the best process management and technology to make it efficient. But how do you manage across dozens of countries and languages—and thousands of branches—each of which has different regulations, cultures, and business quirks? Without a common framework, Nissen found that his own time was fragmented, and the business was becoming a "tower of Babel."

Nissen convened his senior management team at a hotel in Tarrytown, New York, in early 1999 to work on overcoming this geographic boundary. Together the team developed what came to be known as the "Tarrytown 21"—a set of twenty-one measures that each country in GCF would use to manage the business. As Nissen says, "We had lots of local CEOs running their businesses by gut. We needed to have all of them focusing on the same things. And if they are focusing on those measures, they will be successful. Then I can focus on acquisitions, sharing best practices, and hiring the best talent."

Since 1999, each GCF country manager has implemented the Tarrytown 21 which is now accessible through their intranet as "GCF Workplace." There is also a management rhythm for reviewing this data—all of which is displayed as variations on control charts—each month and quarter. Soon all of the data will be provided in real time through AIM, an automated information management system that will allow managers and associates to see how they did against the key measures every day. From its beginnings as an offshoot of RFS, GCF has grown into a business almost double the size of its parent—and poised to continue growing around the world.

GET READY FOR RESISTANCE

GE Capital's private label business journeyed successfully from a traditional structure to a boundaryless organization. But that journey took more than a decade. It was marked by pain, struggle, and doubt. And any organization that intends to become boundaryless must prepare itself for resistance, both from within and without.

Many find the thought of a boundaryless organization terrifying. After all, boundaries *are* organizations; they define what's in and what's out, who controls and who has status. Changing the nature of boundaries is akin to removing your own skin. People can feel threatened at an almost unconscious level.

Other threats are more consciously felt. For example, much has been written about middle managers' resistance to employee empowerment efforts. Such resistance is entirely rational. In most organizations, the core of the middle-management job has been to maintain the barriers between senior management strategy and workers' implementation of that strategy. When senior managers talk about empowerment, middle managers see their roles as boundary controllers vanishing. If employees can translate senior management strategy into decisions and interact directly with the top, what is left for middle managers to do? Some new roles open up for middle managers, but the ratio is not one-to-one. So the threat middle managers face is not only loss of power but actual loss of jobs.

Such threatened losses exist throughout organizations when barriers become more permeable. For example:

• Functional specialists may fear losing their technical edge if forced to spend time as generalists in cross-functional team activities.

• Individuals from different cultures may not want to team with one another or work for one another due to biases, stereotypes, and fears.

• Individuals from different cultures may have trouble communicating, due to different languages and world views.

• People at all levels may fear having to learn new rules of the game if traditional methods of advancement and career tracking change. Managers may fear embarrassment if information once typically hidden becomes shared with other levels.

• Former competitors within an organization or between organizations may find it difficult to learn how to collaborate.

In addition, two overriding psychological barriers block acceptance of the boundaryless organization. One function of boundaries is protection and a sense of security. If people could not only see through your walls but actually pass through them, your sense of security would vanish. Boundaries also give people a place to hide. In an organization with permeable boundaries, ineffective performance is highly visible, not just to a few but to many.

Given these threats to job, status, and security, it is no wonder that attempts to make boundaries more permeable trigger an organization's immune system. All kinds of resistance, overt and covert, begin to emerge.

Several years ago, for example, an executive decided that workers in a newly acquired plant should be reshaped into a "high performance/high involvement" workforce. Essentially, he wanted to create more permeable vertical and horizontal boundaries. He brought in a new plant manager who as a gesture of goodwill removed time cards.

Within days, forces of resistance went into play. Workers objected to the removal of time cards, pointing out that they could no longer use overtime to earn extra money. When the plant manager tried to convince them time clocks were removed because he "trusted them," they concluded that was camouflage for cutting pay. While this was going on, headquarters staff arrived to inventory machinery and tools in preparation for a plant expansion. Staff counting equipment fueled workers' mistrust. When the plant manager tried to postpone the inventory, he found himself in a power struggle with the corporate head of facilities. The battle escalated to the executive who had initiated the plant reshaping. Before he could resolve issues, the International Machinists Union instigated an organizing campaign that corporate HR decided to fight. Within months, the new plant manager was gone, the workforce was alienated, and relations between corporate manufacturing and engineering were strained. The immune system had done its work, surrounding and engulfing the foreign body of change.

MAKING IT HAPPEN

The shift to permeability is fraught with such threats, barriers, and resistance. Nonetheless, it is possible to identify and overcome predictable resistance and make the boundaryless organization a reality. Organizations can transform themselves. And thanks to pioneering organizations like GE Capital, the transformation no longer has to take a decade or be based on trial and error. Nor does it have to wait until external or environmental crises force the issue. There are lessons that have been learned to help accelerate the progress toward the boundaryless organization.

Creating the boundaryless organization is, at its heart, a leadership challenge. It is more than applying a series of tools and techniques, as the cases in this chapter have shown. The transformation of the traditional organization requires the transformation of traditional views of leadership. Leaders of a boundaryless organization differ from traditional managers. They spend their time differently; possess a different set of skills, beliefs, and attitudes; judge themselves differently; and view their careers in different ways. This shift also requires leaders—from the CEO to the first-line supervisors—to have the fire to make the transformation happen and work. Our intent in this chapter is to support organizational leaders as they chip away at their own boundaries—so that more organizations can experience the speed, excitement, and energy of the boundaryless world.

———⟊⟊⟊———

Ron Ashkenas is a managing partner of Robert H. Schaffer & Associates (Stamford, Connecticut) and the author of multiple books and articles on organizational change.

———⟊⟊⟊———

David Ulrich is professor of business at the University of Michigan and a partner at the consulting firm RBL Group. He has published over 100 articles and book chapters and twelve books.

———⟊⟊⟊———

Todd Jick is managing partner of the Center for Executive Development, the author of multiple books on management and change, and an educator and consultant in the arenas of human resource management and organizational behavior.

———⟊⟊⟊———

Steve Kerr is a senior adviser to Goldman Sachs and the author of five books and multiple articles on organizational behavior.

CHAPTER SIXTEEN

Knowledge Management Involves Neither Knowledge nor Management

Marc S. Effron

The death knell for knowledge management (KM) as a concept was sounded with a *Wall Street Journal* article chronicling McKinsey & Co.'s failure to manage its "knowledge" successfully. The article quotes from an internal McKinsey report that says despite having the requisite systems in place, "the ability of our consultants to tap into and effectively leverage our knowledge is poor. . . . Our knowledge base is mixed in quality and poorly structured. It takes much too long to find the right knowledge, and in many cases, the best existing knowledge is not identified and brought to the client."[1] If the world's most prestigious consulting firm could not successfully wrangle information, what hope was there for anyone else?

The failure at McKinsey was not its inability to categorize and retrieve the volumes of experience from its legions of Harvard-trained MBAs but rather the widely held Pollyanna-like belief that knowledge can actually be managed. Even though McKinsey had published numerous articles outlining the secrets to successful knowledge management,[2] it too missed the underlying truth. The sheer concept of knowledge management is fundamentally flawed—it involves neither knowledge nor management and therefore cannot be expected to succeed. Though KM seemed like a great idea, it's time that we relegate it to the dustbin of history and focus instead on helping organizations truly share the intellectual capital their workers possess.

Before you cite the example of Company X having improved productivity when workers in Singapore explained a new way to machine a widget to workers in Seattle, let's define some terms. The sharing of "best practices," a potentially dangerous sport of its own, doesn't constitute managing "knowledge," just sharing procedures. Similarly, training one group on a skill learned or improved by another group is exactly that, training, not KM. By putting my latest presentation on CEO succession into my firm's database, I have not managed any knowledge, merely posted information, making it accessible to a larger population.

To use a tired but in this case helpful device, the dictionary defines *knowledge* as "the fact or condition of knowing something with familiarity gained through experience or association."[3] This makes it impossible to acquire "knowledge" without either experiencing something yourself or interacting with someone else who has. What the cheerleaders define as KM is most frequently just information sharing, which certainly has its role but doesn't achieve the original intent of its proponents.

The fundamental, undeniable fact is that knowledge is intrinsic to human beings and is gained only by participating in an experience or having contextual understanding of that experience. The typical definition of KM as an information technology (IT)–based process run by chief knowledge officers to enable global sharing of best practices is nothing more than a string of threadbare consulting clichés. Knowledge exists only in people. However, all is not lost. The billions of dollars spent on consultants, IT systems, and training courses may still yield some small return if we're willing to take a very honest, even brutal look at the core truths about why KM doesn't work and how organizations must behave if they truly want shared knowledge.

WHY KNOWLEDGE MANAGEMENT DOESN'T WORK

It's not much of a challenge to think of a slew of clear reasons why KM is a failed concept and why organizations have not realized its lauded benefits despite the multiple billions of dollars being spent annually on the effort.[4] I can easily think of nine of them. These nine nails should keep the lid on the KM coffin so that the beast never again threatens corporate-kind.

1. There's No Accountability

If knowledge is adequately managed in an organization, who gets rewarded? If it's not, who gets penalized? Those questions define accountability but cannot be answered by those who promote KM. Although everyone wanted a piece of KM when it first emerged, no one ended up with clear accountability.

The early battle for accountability pitched human resources (HR) against IT as HR fought to claim KM as its own. Jack Fitz-Enz of the HR benchmarking Saratoga Institute, stated, "The open door for HR is that KM is not a technical issue. It is a human issue. This is HR's chance to be at the heart of the most important force in the 21st century—information."[5] Yet HR had then and still has today enough challenges managing other employee data. HR was not prepared to take accountability for the information residing in every employee's head. Likewise, IT's approach to classifying and storing data, albeit potentially very efficient, ignores the fundamental human aspect of actually transferring knowledge. In the end, no one has been accountable, so little has been accomplished.

2. There's No Quality Control

To paraphrase from George Orwell's *Animal Farm,* "All knowledge is equal, but some knowledge is more equal than other knowledge." As a veteran of knowledge database experiences at a Fortune 20 bank and a leading management consulting firm, I know that all too frequently these databases become nothing more than filing cabinets for every project that the professional staff completes, regardless of quality. Although we all do great work, some of that work is, by definition, our "best," and some is the firm's "best." Without a knowledgeable human to review and screen for quality every piece of information going into a database, you're asking the rest of the organization to fish for information in a polluted pond. Let's not even start with the question of who reviews all this information as it ages to ensure that it's still fresh and still represents the current best thinking in the organization.

3. It's Not Really Knowledge

As I stated earlier, knowledge cannot be stored in a database; only information can. In case you think that this is just a semantic argument, consider this: if I search a database for key success factors in implementing succession planning, I'll likely get a raft of reports and presentations on succession planning—information. It will be my responsibility to guess at the context and nuances that generated this information. However, if I ask Bob from down the hall, who has done twenty of these projects, I'm just about guaranteed to get something closer to knowledge, thanks to the context he can provide. Even the KM experts agree with this. According to George Bailey, PricewaterhouseCoopers's North American leader for innovation, "Everybody goes there [to the database] sometimes, but when they're looking for expertise, most people go down the hall."[6]

4. It's Push, Not Pull

Information gets into a database only if people put it there. It's difficult even for those with the best of intentions to remember to do this on a regular basis, and sometimes people don't have the best intentions. According to Robin Giang from the technology consulting firm International Data Corporation, "Knowledge is power, and to publish your knowledge is to relinquish it."[7] This long-acknowledged information-hoarding issue is still not adequately addressed at most companies. One highly intrusive way around this challenge is found in new "sifting" software that mines companies' e-mails to identify content expertise that isn't being shared. If I've sent ten e-mails on succession planning, I might be flagged as a knowledgeable source, whether accurate or not. Aside from the ethical questions that this technology raises, it leaves open the question "Are you getting better information or just more of it?"

5. There's No Incentive to Share

We're all team players who believe in the benefits of cooperation. We're all also very busy, and convincing busy professionals that sharing their information should be a priority must involve either a carrot or a stick. Most firms implementing KM made the false assumption that professionals would prioritize their time around stocking the database instead of pursuing the other dozen objectives that they would actually be rewarded for achieving. I know of no major corporation that measures and rewards employees' contributions to their "knowledge database."

6. The ROI Is Difficult to Prove

In a period of dramatic cutbacks in corporate discretionary spending, multimillion-dollar KM investments haven't proved their worth. Unlike customer relationship management software in which the financial benefits of improved customer relationships can be measured through traditional financial metrics like revenue per account, KM has no tangible measures of success. "Most of the benefit of [KM] is anecdotal," says Charles Lucier, Booz Allen's chief knowledge officer. "I can't prove it, but we do better work."[8] That level of proof might not be sufficient for today's CFOs.

7. There's Nothing for the CKO or CLO to Do

The hiring of a chief knowledge officer (CKO) or chief learning officer (CLO) in a company provides the other corporate executives with a greater sense of job security. They now know that they won't be the first person let go in the next round of layoffs. More than 25 percent of Fortune 500 companies had CKOs at the peak of the KM craze, but less than 20 percent of them have one today. A recent *Wall Street Journal* article chronicled the profession's challenge to define its worth to corporate America.[9] An industry consultant says that "CKOs are like a vitamin pill. They make you feel good, but in a bear market the only thing that really sells is painkillers."[10] The CKO or CLO position implies that it's possible (or desirable) for an individual or department to "manage" the knowledge of others. This is the same flaw that we saw in the beginning of the quality movement, when corporate quality departments arose to preach and teach continuous quality improvement. It wasn't until leaders like Larry Bossidy of AlliedSignal (now Honeywell) and Jack Welch of GE established Six Sigma as a way of doing business, not just a department, that many firms finally saw sustainable benefits from the exact same quality tools introduced years earlier.

8. It's Cultural

To overcome the barriers to sharing information, a company has to modify its corporate culture to overcome the natural aversion to doing this. Carla O'Dell, president of the American Productivity and

Quality Center, says that of the companies trying KM, fewer than 10 percent have succeeded in making it part of their culture.[11] Even companies with strong information-sharing systems fall into this trap.

At Ford Motor Company, the Best Practices Replication Process has delivered "billion-dollar benefits for the automaker."[12] However, this sophisticated system didn't allow Ford to spot the issues in the Firestone tires it placed on its Explorer SUVs. "Why did no one know about the [Firestone] tire problem? Two reasons. First, knowledge is best shared within communities. People with something in common talk more than strangers do. . . . Second, the more widely dispersed knowledge is, the more powerful the force required to share it."[13] Even the most sophisticated systems can't overcome the fundamental cultural behaviors in an organization.

9. It's a Fad

Not that all fads are bad, but it's important to recognize when that label rings true. KM as a concept rose and fell in lockstep with the dotcoms. It was fueled with the same excited type of "if we could just put information at people's fingertips!" naiveté. One great measure of when the KM bubble burst is the number of books published on the topic. According to the Knowledge Management Resource Center, that number fell from a high of fifty-seven in 2001 to a low of fifteen in 2002. That sound you hear is that last nail entering the KM coffin.

HOW KNOWLEDGE MANAGEMENT CAN WORK

Despite this dreary landscape, the potential remains to actually manage real knowledge in organizations and realize the financial benefits from doing so. What it takes to do this right, however, involves more than a new Web server and a fat consulting contract. It means paying attention to how people actually acquire knowledge and how they can most effectively transfer it to others.

The definition of *knowledge* stated earlier provides the key to how organizations can improve their capability in this area. Knowledge is gained through experience or association, something no database can give you but your experienced peers, superiors, and subordinates can. True knowledge management means acknowledging that increased person-to-person contact is the only sure way to improve the shared level of knowledge in an organization.

1. Realize Its Limitations

Although KM may marginally improve your firm's capabilities, it is highly unlikely that it will revolutionize your business. An example of this is the promising field of data mining in which large amounts of data are sliced and diced looking for heretofore unknown and potentially profitable correlations. As Michael Schrage of *Fortune* puts it, "Just because [you find that] single, left-handed, blond customers who drive Volvos purchase 1,450% more widgets on alternate Thursdays than their married, nonblond, right-handed, domestic-car-driving counterparts does not a marketing epiphany make."[14] Set realistic objectives for what you hope to achieve. Better to underpromise than to underdeliver.

2. Hold On to Your Best

One stated reason for developing KM is that the valuable knowledge stored in employees' heads could walk out the door tomorrow and never return. Since that's true, it seems like the most obvious solution is to retain that employee. You know which employees hold the most knowledge on key subjects. Make sure you use all the fundamental levers of employee engagement to keep them around: great developmental opportunities, a strong sense of purpose, and above-market compensation. To leverage their knowledge, set up interaction-based forums where they can share this knowledge with their peers and other interested parties. Tried and true venues, such as "lunch and learns" (or video "lunch and learns"), in which the expert presents the latest and greatest knowledge and discusses how this knowledge was gained, are likely more effective at sharing real knowledge than a search of the company's database.

3. Use Apprenticeships

It's difficult to argue that there is a more effective way to transfer knowledge than through an apprenticeship. You study, quietly observe, and practice your craft under the gaze of an expert until you've become skilled enough to actually do the job on your own.

Although this may seem more applicable to coppersmithing than corporations, the structure of work in most corporations provides plenty of opportunities for apprenticeship experiences. Staff junior people on projects, task forces, committees, and the other machinery of corporate life. Let them interact with the experts to gain knowledge from their more experienced colleagues and exposure to a broad range of experiences. Make them accountable to listen and learn and to participate where warranted. Provide them with clear objectives for what they're supposed to learn, give them the time to do it well, and measure whether the requisite knowledge has been acquired.

4. Anoint Experts and Set Expectations

Some people know more about certain things than others. Recognize that people like having a "go to" person, and hold your subject matter experts accountable to serving as this resource. Let everyone know who has expertise in certain areas (finally a good use for that database!), and include the responsibility to proactively share this information in the expert's performance measures. If the experts can convey their knowledge face to face, then actual knowledge, not just information, gets managed.

5. Rely on Human Interaction

You know all those company conferences and sales meetings you so efficiently moved to videoconferencing? It's time to start getting people back together, face to face, to actually share knowledge. The highly predictable answer you get from professionals evaluating nearly any conference or group get-together they have attended is that the unscheduled, interpersonal "networking" time was the most valuable. It's the interaction at venues like these that actually results in knowledge being shared.

6. Put Accountability Where It Belongs

Managing knowledge is a fundamental part of managing an organization, and accountability for it should rest with those in line management. Though HR or IT may install the computer system, line managers must be held accountable for getting quality information into the system. Line managers must also be held accountable to ensure that their team gets the experiences they need to acquire knowledge. In Hewitt Associates' "Top 20 Companies for Leaders" study, the use of development assignments to build capabilities differentiated the best firms from the also-rans.[15]

7. Sure, Have a Database

It's easier than paper for keeping track of information that supports knowledge. However, along with all the other conventions for storing and retrieving data, two key components must be in place for this database to be effective. First, you must have a live, knowledgeable human being screen every piece of information that goes into it to ensure that only the best work is accessible. While costly and bureaucratic, there's simply no substitute for this. Second, there must be incentives in place for sharing information. This means that you must have a method to track who is submitting information to the database for consideration and have a meaningful part of employees' annual incentive based on that sharing.

Is this a lot of effort? It probably is, but who ever said that trying to extract and categorize every piece of company information into a searchable database religiously serviced by your entire professional staff was going to be easy? Your challenge is to cut through the consultants' hype, take a hard look at the numbers, and realize that knowledge in an organization can only be derived from people.

—◦◦◦—

Marc S. Effron is vice president of talent management at Avon Products, Inc.

CHAPTER SEVENTEEN

The Sustainability Sweet Spot

Where Profit Meets the Common Good

Andrew W. Savitz
Karl Weber

> *It's up to us to use our platform to be a good citizen.*
> *Because not only is it a nice thing to do, it's a business*
> *imperative. . . . If this wasn't good for business,*
> *we probably wouldn't do it.*
> *—Jeffrey Immelt, CEO, General Electric [1]*

Business leaders with a superficial understanding of sustainability think of it as a distraction from their main purpose, a chore they hope can be discharged quickly and easily. "We're responsible corporate citizens, so let's write a check to the United Way or allow employees to volunteer for the local cleanup drive or food kitchen and get back to work."

This approach reveals a fundamental misunderstanding. Sustainability is *not* about philanthropy. There's nothing wrong with corporate charity, but the sustainable company conducts its business so that benefits flow naturally to all stakeholders, including employees, customers, business partners, the communities in which it operates, and, of course, shareholders.

It could be said that the truly sustainable company would have no need to write checks to charity or "give back" to the local community because the company's daily operations wouldn't deprive the community, but would enrich it. Sustainable companies find areas of mutual interest and ways to make "doing good" and "doing well" synonymous, thus avoiding the implied conflict between society and shareholders.

The vision of a company that renews society as it enriches its shareholders may seem remote, and for most companies it is. In this chapter, we propose a way to think about your company's current operations that might suggest an avenue for moving in that direction.

Think about sustainability as the common ground shared by your business interests (those of your financial stakeholders) and the interests of the public (your nonfinancial stakeholders). This common ground is what we call the sustainability sweet spot: the place where the pursuit of profit blends seamlessly with the pursuit of the common good. The best-run companies around the world are trying to identify and move into their sweet spots. And they are developing new ways of doing business in order to get there and stay there.

General Electric (GE) has long been considered an environmental scofflaw. It fought the U.S. Environmental Protection Agency (EPA) for years, trying in vain to avoid responsibility for polluting the Hudson and Housatonic Rivers with over one million pounds of toxic waste.[2] Jack Welch, GE's CEO and chairman, personally led the attack, which included arguing over settled science and challenging the entire federal hazardous waste cleanup program as unconstitutional, tactics widely considered irresponsible.

When Welch retired, many of the flattering reviews referred to GE's environmental record as Welch's one black eye. Now Jeffrey Immelt, his successor, appears to be plotting a new course—not because he and the company are born-again environmentalists, but because being pro-environment is smart business for GE.

In 2005 GE announced an initiative called Ecomagination. It is a powerful example of finding and working toward the sweet spot. It's "action that goes beyond compliance to benefit both society and the long term health of the enterprise," according to Ben Heineman, GE's senior vice president of law and public affairs.[3]

Ecomagination's main thrust is to create clean technology to help GE's customers reduce their environmental impacts, primarily carbon emissions. GE has announced it will double its annual investment in clean energy technologies to $1.5 billion by 2010 and will also double its revenues from eco-friendly products during the same time period.[4]

Addressing climate change presents GE with a huge business opportunity. GE's wind energy business has already quadrupled in revenues since it was acquired in 2002, and its fuel-efficient jet and locomotive engines and natural gas turbines are proving to be essential to customers needing additional ways to reduce their emissions.[5] GE has sold over $1 billion worth of wind and natural gas turbines to China since 2003.[6]

GE has found a significant overlap between its business interests and protecting the environment. And to expand the area of overlap, the company appears to be saying that the time has come for climate change regulations that will ultimately impose carbon restrictions on businesses in the United States.[7] GE is thus working to nudge the circle representing stakeholder concerns closer to the circle representing its business interests. The bigger the overlap, the better for GE.

GE's Ecomagination embodies the observation by Ian Davis, managing director of the management consulting firm of McKinsey & Company, that "large companies need to build social issues into strategy in a way that reflects their actual business importance."[8] GE has also spent large sums of money advertising Ecomagination, creating some suspicion that the campaign will be more hype than strategy—but that remains to be seen.

The overlap between winning increased market share and supporting healthier lifestyle habits is a sweet spot for PepsiCo. If the idea of healthy products sounds like a stretch for a company famous for its sugary sodas and salty snacks, think again. Having purchased Tropicana and Quaker Oats, PepsiCo has made the healthy-product sweet spot the fastest-growing segment of PepsiCo's North American product portfolio by far, with 2005 revenue growth about 2.5 times that of its traditional products. Social responsibility has thus helped PepsiCo earnings per share grow at a prodigious 13 percent in 2004 and to surpass Coca-Cola in market cap for the first time in history.[9]

PepsiCo is working toward other sweet spots too. Its business goal of cost reduction overlaps with a series of environmental improvements to reduce energy, waste, and packaging. Its goal of risk reduction overlaps with steps to address long-term water supply and quality concerns for communities in which its plants are located and for its crucial suppliers (such as farmers who supply corn for Frito-Lay brand chips). These responsible actions will benefit the environment and PepsiCo's neighbors and business partners even as they increase shareholder value and put the company's operations on a more sound, sustainable footing for decades to come.

The sweet spot embodies the literal meaning of "sustainability," making your company *viable for the long term* by managing according to principles that will strengthen rather than undermine the company's roots in the environment, the social fabric, and the economy. A business that occupies the sustainability sweet spot (or that strives to fit as much of its activities into that favored zone as possible) should have real long-term advantages over its rivals.

Imagine a company that historically earns its profits from a finite resource whose extraction and use degrades the environment—providing oil or coal, for example, which exist in limited supplies and generate harmful pollution. Such a business isn't sustainable in the long run; either the resources or the social tolerance for pollution on which it relies will eventually run out. Costs will rise as supplies dwindle and as social concerns translate into higher taxes, additional cleanup costs, and increased liability.

If it were possible for such a company to shift its business so as to eventually supply clean and renewable energy (such as wind or solar power) or conservation services while maintaining or even increasing revenues, that would be a responsible and profitable choice.

This is not a hypothetical case. British Petroleum (BP) adopted this long-term strategy when it rebranded itself "Beyond Petroleum" in 1998. BP has since reduced greenhouse gas emissions from its own production processes (saving an estimated $650 million thanks to improved efficiencies along the way) and has invested heavily in alternative energy sources, including solar power. BP is not yet sustainable by any means, but it is acting responsibly as it marches toward an ever larger sweet spot.

A MAP TO THE SWEET SPOT

Every action you take in business has two components: an impact on profits and an impact on the world. This can be represented by a four-celled matrix with two axes, which represent profitability and social benefit.

The northeast corner of the map is conceptually similar to the sweet spot, where stakeholders' interests and corporate interests overlap. Your goal is to get as much of your business activity into that quadrant as possible. You want every business decision to push you north and east. The value of the map emerges when you use it to plot the location of various businesses or activities in order to determine ways to move them in a northeasterly direction, or to generate ideas for quantum strategic change.

Suppose you own a business or manage part of one that is currently located in the northwest quadrant (profitable but not sustainable). Is it possible to devise ways of moving the business eastward (more sustainable) without moving south (less profitable)? DuPont has done so by moving from the chemical business toward the soy protein business without sacrificing revenues or profits. If you have a business in the southwest corner (neither profitable nor sustainable), can you find ways to base a turnaround on moving both north and east?

Your goal should be to develop strategies and change operations to move toward the northeast corner of the map. For example, an energy company that profits from burning dirty coal could devote its short-term research dollars toward clean-coal technology and its long-term effort toward a future in which most energy is derived from such renewable sources as solar, wind, hydroelectric, and geothermal power. Both initiatives embody migration toward the northeast corner of the map, where both profitability and social benefit are high.

Both small and large companies have changed their businesses to move further toward the northeast corner of the sustainability map.

Country Lanes is a tiny UK tour company that offers day trips and holiday travel, by bicycle or on foot.[10] Patrons must somehow find their way to the rendezvous point at which the tour begins. Country Lanes recently redesigned all its tours to begin at railway stations, with the result that 85 percent of its customers now use rail travel to get there. This has eliminated a million miles of automobile travel and 328 tonnes of carbon dioxide emissions per year. Business is up because customers now find it easier to get to the tours. Country Lanes also supports local business by encouraging its customers to spend money on snacks, drinks, and lunches from neighborhood pubs and shops.

When Toyota revealed its intention to create a new form of gasoline-electric car, one that would capture and use braking energy, the company was derided as an environmental do-gooder that would surely lose money. "We wondered if anyone would want one," admitted Takehisa Yaegashi, the senior Toyota engineer now known as the father of the hybrid.[11] Today Toyota can't manufacture the Prius fast enough to meet demand. The car is peppy, durable, and easy to drive, and gets up to 52 miles per gallon of gas in city driving. Waiting lists are sixteen months long in some parts of the United States and Japan. Over one hundred twenty thousand of the hybrids were shipped to the United States in 2005, more than doubling the previous year's figure, and hybrid versions of Toyota's Highlander and Lexus SUVs have entered the market.

Toyota now views hybrids as a central part of its strategy to become the number one car manufacturer in the world and break into the Big Three in the United States. The company recently announced that it will focus on selling one million hybrid vehicles a year worldwide (including six hundred thousand in the United States) by early in the next decade.[12]

Toyota made two bets at once: that both the price of gas and concern about air pollution would rise. Winning either bet might have made the car a success, but Toyota appears to have won both, making the Prius a worldwide phenomenon. The car is both good for Toyota's shareholders and good for the environment—a remarkable example of finding the sweet spot.

"PROVE IT!"

Many businesspeople find the simple logic behind the sweet spot compelling, but others require proof that sustainability creates financial benefits. They seek an assurance that's as good as gold—incontrovertible evidence that they can and will make more money practicing sustainable management than they will with good old-fashioned, short-term, profit-only thinking.

Let's start then with the testimony of those that help companies create gold. Goldman Sachs, Deutsche Bank, Credit Suisse, Banco do Brasil, and fifteen other multinational investment banks recently reported the following:

> [We] are convinced that in a more globalized, interconnected and competitive world the way that environmental, social and corporate governance issues are managed is part of companies' overall management quality needed to compete successfully. Companies that perform better with regard to these issues can increase shareholder value by, for example, properly managing risks, anticipating regulatory action, or accessing new markets, while at the same time contributing to the

sustainable development of societies in which they operate. Moreover, these issues can have a strong impact on reputation and brands, an increasingly important part of company value.[13]

Empirical evidence includes the share prices of companies listed in the Dow Jones Sustainability Index and the FTSE4Good Indexes, two listings of sustainability companies that have outperformed various market indexes. Companies that belong to the World Business Council for Sustainable Development outperformed their respective national stock exchanges by 15 to 25 percent over the past three years. From 1999 through 2003, the Winslow Green Index of one hundred "green-screened" companies increased in value by over 73 percent, whereas the members of the comparable benchmark Russell 2000 Index increased by less than 17 percent.[14]

"Companies pursuing growth in the triple bottom line tend to display superior stock market performance with favorable risk-return profiles," according to John Prestbo, president of Dow Jones Indexes. "Thus sustainability becomes a proxy for enlightened and disciplined management—which just happens to be the most important factor that investors do and should consider in deciding where to buy a stock."[15]

Exemplary environmental performance, long considered a proxy for good management, is now being touted by investment advisers as a measure of value—perhaps of hidden value, the savvy investor's favorite kind. UBS, the Swiss-based investment bank, recently opined, "Environmental performance indicators appear to be a possible indicator of strong operational performance. Strong environmental indicators in the presence of below-average profitability may signal an investment opportunity, in our view."[16]

It cannot be proved that sustainability is the reason behind the strong market performance of the companies that have embraced it, but when similar results continue year after year, the correlation implies causation. As Henry D. Thoreau, the American essayist and philosopher, famously remarked, "Some circumstantial evidence is very strong, as when you find a trout in the milk."

Those seeking the gold standard should recall that the cases for such strategic initiatives as Total Quality Management, Six Sigma, and reengineering were not proved before thousands of businesses invested billions of dollars in them. These concepts won widespread support because of case studies that illustrated their effectiveness, endorsements from well-known business leaders, their resonance with the zeitgeist of their times, and eventually (in some cases) because of financial results. The initial evidence supporting those programs was largely anecdotal, but, as Travis Engen, recently retired CEO of Alcan, once observed, the plural of *anecdote* is *data.*

Like most business strategies, sustainability is not a guarantee of financial success. It requires commitment, resources, and a change of direction, which entail costs and risks. The real question, as with all important business decisions, is this: Is sustainability a good bet for me and my company?

Sustainability is quickly becoming mainstream. Socially responsible initiatives, from the Prius to natural foods, from green buildings to eco-friendly clothes and cosmetics, from windpower to the beneficial reuse of industrial waste, have migrated from being considered heretical, to impractical, to visionary, and finally to common sense—usually as soon as they begin to turn a profit. Eventually they become part of business as usual, their controversial origins all but forgotten.

When Ralph Nader first began to argue that cars could be made much safer, he was dismissed by Detroit and most of the public as an agitator and a nutcase. Now all car companies strive for increased safety, and some, such as Volvo, have made it the centerpiece of their marketing.

Can a sustainable business strategy enhance profitability? Of course, but when it does, it usually travels on our mental maps from the space now labeled "sustainability" into the one more simply known as "good business."

THREE WAYS SUSTAINABILITY ENHANCES YOUR BUSINESS

Whether you find or even look for the sweet spot, the principles of sustainability can improve the management of your business in three fundamental ways—by helping you protect it, run it, and grow it.[17]

Protecting the Business

Protecting the business includes reducing risk of harm to customers, employees, and communities; identifying emerging risks and management failures early; limiting regulatory interventions; and retaining the explicit or implicit license to operate granted by government or by the community at large.

Biotechnology giant Monsanto made a concerted push into the field of bioengineering crops in the mid- to late 1990s. Monsanto's genetically modified (GM) seeds were supposed to offer farmers enormous competitive benefits—corn containing natural insecticides, and soybeans able to withstand potent weed killers. Monsanto had a powerful sweet spot proposition: that its pioneering efforts would give the company a leading position in a major new marketplace and provide a powerful new weapon in the battle against world hunger. "Monsanto is in a unique position to contribute to the global future," declared biodiversity advocate Peter Raven.[18]

But Monsanto executives failed to work with stakeholders in their development of the new genetically modified seeds initiative—a core principle of sustainable business. Monsanto dismissed early critics of GM products as anti-technology fanatics and failed to mount a concerted effort to educate consumers about the science behind genetic engineering.

Monsanto consequently found itself beset by a variety of attacks. A British scientist claimed that rats eating GM potatoes failed to grow properly, and a Cornell university study published in 1999 appeared to show that monarch butterfly caterpillars died after ingesting pollen from bioengineered corn. The accuracy of both claims was quickly challenged, but public fears about "Frankenfoods" now seemed to be bolstered by science.

Several European supermarket chains as well as American natural-food retailers announced that they would remove GM foods from their shelves, and major food companies, such as baby-food maker Gerber, vowed to keep their products free of GM ingredients. Embarrassingly, even the staff canteen at Monsanto's own UK headquarters announced it would ban GM food from its menu "in response to concern raised by our customers."[19]

Nonengineered soybeans began to sell at a premium over their modified counterparts—a sign that the market was rejecting GM foods. By the end of 2000, the stock market valued Monsanto's $5 billion-a-year agricultural business unit at less than zero, despite billions the company had invested in highly advanced science over the previous decade.[20]

Today the entire biotech industry is still struggling to win acceptance for bioengineered products in Europe and around the world—largely because of Monsanto's early failure to consider the demands of sustainability before launching this major business initiative.

Running the Business

Running the business includes reducing costs, improving productivity, eliminating needless waste, and obtaining access to capital at lower cost.

Eco-efficiency is a basic component of sustainability that applies to running your business. It means reducing the amount of resources used to produce goods and services, which increases a company's profitability while decreasing its environmental impact. The underlying theme is simple: pollution is waste, and waste is anathema because it means that your company is paying for something it didn't use. Given the clarity of this logic, it's amazing how few companies have diligently pursued eco-efficiency.

Consider the financial benefits from eco-efficiency enjoyed by STMicroelectronics (ST), the Swiss-based firm that is one of the world's largest manufacturers of semiconductors, with 2003 revenues of $7.2 billion and close to forty-six thousand employees worldwide. ST earmarks 2 percent of its annual capital investments for environmental improvements. The resulting efficiencies have trimmed the company's electricity use by 28 percent and its water use by 45 percent, with cost savings of $56 million in 2001, $100 million in 2002, and $133 million in 2003. Energy conservation projects pay for themselves within 2.5 years on average—an extraordinary return on investment. Former CEO and honorary chairman Pasquale Pistorio notes, "this proves the validity of the stance we have taken for years: ecology is free."[21]

Growing the Business

Growing the business includes opening new markets, launching new products and services, increasing the pace of innovation, improving customer satisfaction and loyalty, growing market share by attracting customers for whom sustainability is a personal or business value, forming new alliances with business partners and other stakeholders, and improving reputation and brand value.

Sustainability is a powerful engine of economic and business growth, driving innovation and new technologies. In 2004, $5.8 billion was spent on "green building" initiatives, the design and construction of eco-friendly, healthy, and efficient buildings.[22] Entire new businesses have been developed in support, including energy-saving home appliances, low-flow toilets, ultraefficient heating, solar heating and electricity, and superefficient cooling and insulation systems.

The sustainability mind-set is also helping companies think creatively about how to gain access to vast new markets that were once dismissed as unprofitable or even impossible. Significant businesses are being built at the "bottom of the pyramid," among the four billion people living on less than $2 per day, who collectively represent enormous untapped buying power. Companies that figure out how to sell goods and services to the poor will reap huge rewards in the decades to come and create new opportunity for those in need.

C. K. Prahalad, the business consultant who, along with Professor Stuart Hart, has studied opportunities at the bottom of the pyramid, explains how companies that respect the rights, needs, and interests of the poor can create new business models that in turn create economic opportunity for business and society.[23]

Prahalad cites Casas Bahia, a Brazilian retailer with sales of over $1.2 billion and over twenty thousand employees, which operates exclusively in the favelas, or shantytowns, where the poorest people of Brazil are found; Annapurna Salt, a Unilever brand that has captured a significant share of the market in India, Ghana, Kenya, Nigeria, and other African nations with small, low-priced packages of iodized salt specifically designed to help combat rampant iodine deficiency disorder among the poor; and Hindustan Lever Ltd., the largest soap producer in India, which has achieved sales of over $2.5 billion through innovative production, packaging, and marketing techniques that reach into many of the smallest and poorest villages in the subcontinent. This is pure sweet spot, creating profit while providing access to needed and affordable consumer goods, thereby stimulating economic growth and improving quality of life.

It takes ingenuity and creativity to find ways to reach customers at the bottom of the pyramid. But the effort is worthwhile, not just because of the sizeable profits to be earned in the short run but because of even greater long-term benefits to companies that win the patronage and loyalty of this huge group of consumers at the start of their march toward middle-class status—a transition that bottom-of-the-pyramid programs will help accelerate.

ADDITIONAL BUSINESS BENEFITS OF SUSTAINABILITY

So far we've focused on the hard side of the case for sustainability—the direct and measurable costs, primarily financial, of ignoring your stakeholders and their concerns, and the economic benefits that companies are enjoying by managing themselves or producing goods and services to assist others in the pursuit of the principles of sustainability. There's also a soft side, one that turns on opportunities and risks that may be harder to quantify: company reputation, employee satisfaction, customer goodwill, and the value of being considered a leader in your industry.

Wegmans, a privately held grocery chain with sales of $3.4 billion in 2004, was named the best company to work for in America by *Fortune* magazine.[24] The company offers higher-than-average wages, high-end training programs, college tuition assistance, and, perhaps most important, jobs designed to empower workers to make decisions to help customers. Wegmans commitment to these practices is expensive: the company spends 15 to 17 percent of sales on labor costs as opposed to the industry average of 12 percent. Wegmans has also spent over $54 million in tuition assistance over the past twenty years.

But employee satisfaction creates sizeable financial benefits for Wegmans. The company's costs related to turnover (for example, unemployment insurance, severance, training, lost productivity) are 6 percent of revenues compared to the industry average of 19 percent, which translates to a savings of approximately $300 million per year, far more than needed to cover the costs of the programs.

Moreover, the family-owned company is thriving in the face of competitive pressure from companies like Wal-Mart and Costco, and sees its employee retention programs as fundamental to its success. Wegmans margins are double those of America's four biggest grocery firms, and its sales per square foot are twice the industry average.

HARD CASES

Unfortunately, sustainability isn't always an easy win-win. Many situations arise, especially in the short term, where being sustainable imposes additional costs or redirects money away from shareholders and toward other stakeholders. Some of these situations are resolved as being in the long-term interest of shareholders, but others represent genuine, perhaps permanent conflicts of interest between shareholders and other stakeholders. These are the hard cases.

Many companies try to avoid those situations by seeking new sweet spot opportunities or concentrating on activities that will move them closer to the northeast corner of the Sustainability Map. But avoidance isn't always possible. The realities of the U.S. automobile industry, for example, include both consumer demand for gas-guzzlers and a cost structure that currently makes big cars more profitable than hybrids. It's impossible, not to mention highly unsustainable, for a company to act against its own financial interest. Demanding that the car companies or their executives do so is, to put it kindly, counterproductive.

There's a useful distinction between being *sustainable* and being *responsible*. The responsible action is for the automakers to meet the current demand for SUVs while working to alter consumer preferences and preparing to make hybrids profitable. Thus, when Bill Ford Jr. publicly describes the environmental downsides of SUVs and works to make the hybrid Ford Escape a winner in the marketplace, his behavior can be considered highly responsible even though his industry, company, and main products are not yet sustainable.

Similarly, we can't expect, nor do we want, the energy companies to give up on oil and gas production today because extracting and burning fossil fuels is unsustainable in the long term. But we can and should expect them to work hard to help society make the transition to renewable energy sources—as BP is doing, even while it maintains a high percentage of its current operations in oil and gas extraction.

Hardest of all is when there is *no* sustainable or responsible action to be taken. If, for example, genetically modified food is conclusively proved to be dangerous for consumers and bad for the planet (like leaded gasoline or asbestos-based insulation), the only responsible approach for companies in that business will be to close down their operations as fast as possible while trying to mitigate the adverse impacts of doing so. Any other choice would be socially irresponsible, making them the legitimate target of activists, responsible businesses, and society, while at the same time exposing their shareholders to ever-growing liability risks.

FINAL THOUGHTS

Sustainability enhances profitability for the vast majority of companies. It serves as a road map for doing business in an interdependent world. It offers new ways to protect your company from environmental, financial, and social risks; to run your company with greater efficiency and productivity; and to grow your company through the development of new products and services and the opening of new markets. It provides intangible benefits that include an improved corporate reputation, higher employee morale, and increased customer goodwill. Sustainability will set you and your organization on the path to long-term success.

―◁◌◌◌▷―

Andrew W. Savitz is president of Sustainable Business Solutions and a member of the steering committee of the Environmental and Natural Resources Program of the John F. Kennedy School of Government at Harvard.

―◁◌◌◌▷―

Karl Weber is a freelance writer who has coauthored several best-selling business books.

CHAPTER EIGHTEEN

Leading Geeks
Technology and Leadership

Paul Glen

I hope that you have begun this chapter with a head full of questions:

- What's different about leading geeks from leading anyone else?
- What can I do to better leverage my organization's investment in these expensive, valuable, and temperamental employees?
- What makes geeks so difficult to manage?

You might even have some skeptical thoughts like, leadership is leadership, isn't it? I welcome such questions because you're on your way to thinking about how the ideas and concepts in this chapter apply to you and your organization. The chapter sets out to explore fundamental questions and important concepts on leading geeks: who geeks are, why leading them is important, and how leadership of geeks differs from other types of leadership.

UNDERSTANDING GEEKS
Who Are Geeks?

Geeks are the knowledge workers who specialize in the creation, maintenance, or support of high technology. They have job titles like programmer, product manager, project manager, quality assurance engineer, system designer, system architect, program manager, technical writer, help desk technician, deployment specialist, trainer, network manager, Web designer, database administrator, desktop support technician, or telecommunications specialist. Some may even carry titles like chief information officer (CIO), chief knowledge officer (CKO), chief technical officer (CTO), development director, operations manager, and, on rare occasions, chief executive officer (CEO).

Thirty years ago, most geeks who found their way into the business world were part of the accounting department and kept out of sight in the basement, tending to a single massive computer secured behind locked doors in an air-conditioned room. They were rarely seen outside their isolated environment and were known only by the people who read the piles of reports generated on wide green-lined paper.

Today geeks are everywhere. They may still be clustered in one large department or scattered as members of functional departments like accounting, marketing, product development, or manufacturing. Everyone knows who they are. They are the people you go to when your desktop computer or laptop stops working. The people you call when you think you might have a virus infecting your system. They're the people you consult when you dream up a new way of helping your clients by putting previously unavailable information on a Web site. You call them when you realize that you could save labor and costs by adding only one field to a screen of a current application.

If your company's product is high tech, you'll find them in product development, research, engineering, distribution, manufacturing, and support. Whether or not you sell a high-tech product or service, you will usually find them in the information technology (IT) department and probably working with accounting, finance, marketing, sales, and customer service.

In short, geeks are the highly intelligent, usually introverted, extremely valuable, independent-minded, hard-to-find, difficult-to-keep technology workers who are essential to the future of your company.

Why Geeks Matter

Despite all the hype and hurry surrounding the new economy, a few simple truths shine through the fog:

- Over the past three decades, the pace of technological change has increased.
- Technological innovation remains one of the most important components of an organization's ability to compete in the marketplace.
- Geeks are the people who deliver technological innovation.

Geeks have become among the most important human resources within almost every organization. As the technology they supply and support has become indispensable to almost every function of a company, geeks themselves have become indispensable too.

As they have moved further into functional areas in organizations, more and more managers regularly come into contact with these unique and valuable employees. But they remain a mystery to most managers. Not only do geeks control strange, intricate, fragile, expensive, and indispensable systems, but as individuals they often prove hard to fathom. Corporate leaders, department managers, and functional managers who are perfectly capable of leading and managing in their area of specialty find geeks difficult to work with. Yet every leader, every sales manager, manufacturing manager, marketing specialist, accounting manager, customer service manager, purchasing manager, logistics manager, and human resource specialist must now be able to lead geeks. As each functional specialty within an organization becomes increasingly reliant on technology for its success, each person within those functional areas becomes reliant on his or her ability to interact with and lead geeks.

The Innovation Imperative

Whether or not you realize it, at this very moment, your organization is battling for its existence. All human institutions must constantly struggle to establish their relevance, attract attention, and mobilize resources to compete for survival.

In this constant competition, no organization can afford to become static. It may change and evolve at different rates, but ultimately, to stagnate is to invite competition or lose relevance. If the needs and demands of the market shift and an organization fails to follow, it will be marginalized. If competition moves in to fulfill the same needs of the same population with a more compelling offering, the original group must adjust to the new reality or risk losing relevance.

Successful organizations—ones that persist and maintain their relevance over long periods of time—meet that challenge with innovation. They continually strive to refine their value proposition. Occasionally, they may reinvent themselves completely, revisiting and redefining their overarching purpose, but usually innovation happens on a much smaller scale. They incrementally improve their products and services, raising value, lowering cost, or expanding markets. In this way, they constantly align with demands and meet competitive pressures.

Geeks and Innovation

So if organizations constantly need to renew their relevance, where do they turn for innovation? It would be tempting to answer "geeks," but that wouldn't be entirely true. The types of creativity and insight needed to reinvigorate an organization with innovative products, services, and processes can come from almost anywhere. But regardless of where ideas come from, increasingly you need geeks to implement them.

Ideas for new or enhanced products or services come from many places: customers, marketing, sales, manufacturing, product development, and product support. If the product is high tech, you need geeks to analyze the feasibility and design of new or enhanced products. But even if your product is more conventional, most new ideas include some information content within either the physical product or the production or distribution. Again, you need geeks.

Service and process innovations have become similarly information intensive and require geeks for implementation. Most innovations in services today are enabled by information technology. The interconnection of massive databases combined with the access to the Web has opened many new ways to service customers' information and transaction needs. Banking customers now expect to view all of their accounts in one place, at one time, with the click of a mouse in a Web browser or through personal financial management software like Quicken or Microsoft Money.

Geeks can also be a valuable source of ideas for innovation. Given their intimate knowledge of products and processes, they often find better ways to do things. They can be an integral part of the creative process of envisioning new products and services, as well as the processes and procedures to produce them.

To sum up, geeks are essential to innovation, and innovation is essential to the future of all enterprises. Without geeks in your enterprise, your future is in doubt. Simply having geeks, however, is not enough. They must be effectively integrated into the organization and focused on appropriate tasks. In other words, the future of your organization depends, along with other things, on your ability to lead geeks effectively.

WHY GEEK LEADERSHIP IS DIFFERENT

Why do we need a chapter devoted only to geeks when bookstore shelves are groaning under the weight of leadership tomes? In part because many of those make the point implicitly or explicitly that whom you are leading is essentially irrelevant and that effective leaders can lead anyone. But leading geeks is, in fact, different from leading others. There are three distinct reasons to look at geek leadership differently from more traditional approaches:

- Geeks are different from other people.
- Geek work is different from other work.
- Power is useless with geeks.

Geeks Are Different

Geeks are different from other people. If this comes as a shocking statement to you, you're either oblivious or unusually charitable. But let's face it: stereotypes exist for a reason, and although they can be cruel and insensitive, they often contain a kernel of truth. For geeks, it is certainly true.

Most writers on leadership, while acknowledging that leadership is a relationship between a leader and a group of followers, fail to acknowledge that the nature of the follower has anything to do with the nature of the relationship.

So the first thing you must accept if you want to lead geeks is that geeks are different. Then you must recognize how they are different from other employees. This is not about judging anybody, just appreciating differences. And then you have to adjust your leadership style to be productive with geeks. I'm not suggesting that you need to be disingenuous or phony. In fact, if you were, you would immediately set off any geek's hypocrisy detector. Still, you do need to adjust as you would in any relationship to the nature of others.

Geekwork Is Different

Not only are geeks different from other employees, but their work is quite different as well. Although it may not be obvious at first, the nature of geekwork imprints itself on the relationship between a leader and geeks just as much as the personality of geeks and leaders does.

When examining relationships in general, and work relationships in particular, we often underestimate the influence that the nature of the work imparts to both the organizational culture and individual relationships. The structure of day-to-day tasks imposes its own patterns of thinking on those who engage with them on an ongoing basis, and the assumptions induced by the work permeate the relationship among manager, leader, and follower. All are affected by the influence of the work. And in this case, geekwork imparts its own unique behavioral and cognitive patterns on the leadership relationship.

Power Is Useless with Geeks

The final reason that leading geeks is different from leading others is the diminished role that power plays in the relationship between leader and followers. Traditionally, leadership is conceptualized as a special form of power relationship where leaders have substantial influence over the behavior of followers and exercise that power for mutual benefit.

But here geekwork intervenes in the relationship and undermines power as a useful basis for the relationship between leader and geeks. While a manager may have substantial authority and power to control the behavior of geeks, behavior plays a much smaller role in the successful completion of geekwork than in other forms of work.

Geekwork is less about behavior and more about thought, ideas, and the application of creativity.

In more traditional forms of work, controlling employee behavior is the primary point of management. If the assembly worker responsible for attaching the wheel to the front of a car attaches that wheel to the car, then she has fulfilled her primary function: her behavior has delivered value. If a short-order cook at a restaurant accepts orders, cooks food, and hands it to the server, he has fulfilled his task. For geeks, it's different.

For geeks, behavior plays a much smaller part in the delivery of value. A programmer may sit at his desk all day and type keys on the keyboard quietly without bothering anyone else, but if he's typed a sonnet instead of a program, it's of no value to the organization. With geekwork, you are attempting to harness the creativity of individuals and groups in its purest form. And although behavior plays a role, it is substantially less important than in almost any other form of work.

Because power is about the regulation of behavior, it has very little effect on creativity. Traditional methods of exercising control have little positive effect on the inner state of mind of geeks. And so power itself becomes substantially less important a facet of the relationship between leaders and geeks. We must, therefore, rethink what it means to lead in the face of geekwork because most conceptions of leadership are intimately tied to notions of power.

WHAT IS GEEK LEADERSHIP?

Two models encapsulate what it takes to lead in light of the reduction in the role of power and the uniqueness of geeks and geekwork: the Context of Geek Leadership and the Content of Geek Leadership.

The Context of Geek Leadership

Leading effectively in this environment requires a picture of the lay of land: a conceptual model to help establish both new and familiar roadmarks about the relationships of geeks, leaders, geekwork, organizational culture, and the broader sociopolitical environment [see Figure 18.1].

A three-way relationship, which I call the tripartite relationship among geeks, leaders, and geekwork, lies at the center of this model. Ordinarily, leadership relationships are discussed only as having two

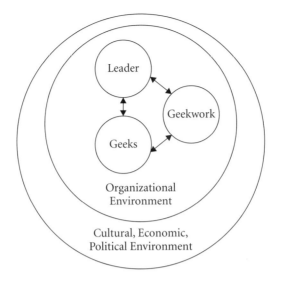

Figure 18.1.   The Context of Geek Leadership.

categories of parties: leaders and followers. But in the geek environment, the unique nature of geekwork—highly abstract, creative, and technical work—imposes so many demands on both geeks and leaders that you can think of it as a third party to the relationship. And remember, geeks as individuals and in groups are quite different from most other people, bringing to the workplace their own culture, values, and needs which must be accommodated.

The Content of Geek Leadership

The Content of Geek Leadership model describes the central roles, responsibilities, and tasks of someone who leads geeks. In contrast to the conventional model of hierarchical command and control, the leader of geeks plays a more enabling role, providing facilitation for projects and processes within the organization, representing geek needs to key external constituents and vice versa, nurturing motivation, and helping to manage ambiguity [see Figure 18.2]. Compare the Content of Geek Leadership with more conventional ideas about the responsibilities and tasks of leaders [as summarized in Figure 18.3]. Some of the tasks and responsibilities change relatively little, but others are radically different.

Both traditional and geek leaders, for example, furnish external representation almost identically. Both also seek to motivate their

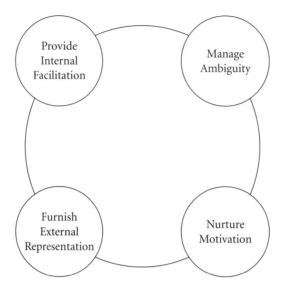

Figure 18.2.   The Context of Geek Leadership.

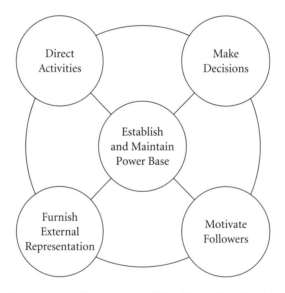

Figure 18.3.   The Context of Traditional Leadership.

followers, but here the methods are remarkably different. Conventional leaders focus on managing and directing the activities of followers rather than providing facilitation and making decisions rather than actively managing ambiguity.

Perhaps the most important difference is that traditional leaders concentrate on establishing and maintaining a power base to enforce decisions, direct activities, and motivate followers. For the geek leader, power is substantially less important for moving an organization forward. What is?

Harmonizing Content and Context

Geeks are best able to function at peak efficiency when everything makes sense. They become highly motivated and remarkably productive when they understand the mission, vision, and values of their overall organization; can clearly articulate their role within the organization and within specific projects; recognize technology's part in fulfilling the organization's goals; and feel that the values of the organization are consistently upheld by leaders and followers alike. Complete harmony is a rare and fragile state, but when the stars are aligned, political and emotional barriers to productivity fall for geeks.

A geek leader's goal and overall responsibility then is to build and maintain a state of harmonized content and context. The leader in essence creates and embodies a defining narrative that helps geeks make sense of the disparate facts in and surrounding their work. That is, they fulfill the essential human needs for meaning and purpose for those within their organizations who deliver technology. When these important human needs are fulfilled, geeks are free to focus on fulfilling an organization's technical needs.

SUMMARY: KEY IDEAS

- Geeks, as the creators and keepers of technology, are essential to every organization's ability to innovate and remain vibrant and viable.

- Because technology has permeated all functional areas of organizations, every manager must now know how to lead geeks.

- Many traditional approaches to leadership don't work when it comes to leading geeks for three key reasons: geeks are different from other people, geekwork is different from other work, and power is useless with geeks.

- Two simplifying models help clarify geek leadership: the Context of Geek Leadership describes the environment in which geek leadership takes place, and the Content of Geek Leadership describes the tasks and responsibilities of a geek leader.

- The ultimate goal of geek leadership is to harmonize the content and context in order to drive the productivity and creativity of geeks.

—◦◦◦—

Paul Glen helps technical organizations grow better leaders. He is a columnist for *Computerworld*, management consultant, and author of the award-winning book *Leading Geeks*, from which this chapter is excerpted.

CHAPTER NINETEEN

Leading in Black and White

Working Effectively Across the Racial Divide

Ancella B. Livers
Keith A. Caver

Many blacks in the workplace face a set of dynamics unique to being African American in a traditional white, male-dominated world. These differences, of which most white managers are unaware, can lead to miscues and distortions in communications and ultimately get in the way of effective performance and optimal productivity for organizations. This chapter sheds light on how leadership experiences for blacks are radically different from those of their white colleagues.

It begins with discussion of two omnipresent factors in the lives of black managers—the assumption of similarity and the effect of miasma—that influence how and why black managers take a different approach to the workplace. This chapter ends by outlining strategies we believe can help dispel blindness to difference.

THE ASSUMPTION OF SIMILARITY

The subject line of the e-mail says simply, "Working While Black." If you're an African American leader in corporate America, you've probably had this message forwarded to you. Its one-liners pointedly describe the black corporate experience.

- A coworker sees you and several black colleagues at a casual lunch. Back at the office she asks, "What was the meeting all about?"
- You tell your manager about a problem you are having and the response you get is, "You have got to be exaggerating! I find that hard to believe."
- You are told you are "rough around the edges" despite your completion of many professional development programs, and it is suggested you emulate the behavior of a person not of color.
- You are being recognized at a company banquet. As you approach the stage to receive your company's highest achievement award, your corporation's top executive exclaims, "Yo, homeboy, congratulations."
- After a coworker returns from a weekend in the sun, he runs to you on Monday morning and extending his arms to touch yours says, "Hey, I'm darker than you."
- You continually get more responsibility, but no authority.
- You have to perform at 250% to stay even.
- You have to document everything. You've learned the hard way.

The comments that have accompanied this e-mail—such as "Can I get a witness?" and "Amen!"—indicate that African Americans are having similar experiences in the workplace—and they aren't always pleasant. Regularly, often daily, African Americans are reminded through jokes, seemingly innocent statements, job assignments, and work relationships that they are different and, more important, that the difference is not a good one.

The irony is that the workplace often does not acknowledge these experiences. Although most workplaces do not tolerate blatant discrimination, the subtle signs suggest they remain inhospitable to blacks and other nontraditional leaders. By upholding an assumption that all people experience an equitable workplace—an assumption of similarity where there is a reality of difference—corporations create a fiction that many people accept as truth. It may be that the corporate workplace holds up this fiction of equality because it believes, misguidedly, that being "color-blind" will result in equal opportunity. It may also be that the workplace does not even consider the issue of color, whether to acknowledge or deny it.

Instead of leveling the playing field, the assumption of similarity where there is a reality of difference serves to marginalize blacks and other nontraditional leaders. By turning a blind eye to their unique, additional challenges in the workplace, corporations place blacks on unequal footing. By assuming that the playing field is level, non-black colleagues are able to dismiss charges of subtle discrimination. And minimizing the diverse experiences of people of color can lead to minimizing their contributions as well. People of color bring a different data set to certain corporate conversations because they have had different experiences both in and out of work. Corporate leaders who don't recognize or value those experiences are unlikely to tap into the knowledge and insight to be gained from them.

THE EFFECT OF MIASMA

Imagine going to work each day with the anticipation of running up against misperceptions, distortions, and sometimes completely fictional accounts of your behaviors from colleagues. "Maybe it will happen today and maybe it won't," the black manager might muse, for the possibility of misunderstanding is always lurking. This murky atmosphere of misperception and distortion in which black managers must work is a condition we call *miasma*. In simple terms, it operates like a low-lying cloud, surrounding those who have to bear extra burdens and exert extra energy in ways that are not directly related to the work itself. Black leaders respond to it with a certain wariness, a perceived self-defensive stance, and an expenditure of time and energy that is counterproductive or at the very least stifling.

There is an inverse relationship between miasma and the degree to which there is an acceptance of difference in organizations. When nontraditional leaders work with others or in organizations that have a low tolerance for individual or cultural differences, the resulting miasma they operate within becomes denser and potentially more difficult in which to maneuver. Increased miasma can lead to degraded communication, interpersonal interactions, and work performance as individuals become increasingly guarded, uncomfortable, and less participatory in their organizations. Conversely, in organizations with a higher degree of acceptance for differences, the miasma is less dense and more easily managed. In these instances, nontraditional leaders benefit from enhanced recognition, understanding, and valuing of their unique perspectives and potential contributions.

For African American managers, miasma gets more dense every time they experience communications laden with preconceptions, misconceptions, or lack of understanding. For example, a black leader might find herself in a situation where she thinks, "I'm being proactive, but he thinks I'm being aggressive." Black leaders in such cases experience a host of emotions, second-guess their reactions, and are fundamentally paralyzed when they could be moving forward. It is a drain on the individual and ultimately a drain on the organization.

Miasma is diaphanous, like a fog, difficult to grasp but ever present. The miasma surrounding any one person can be more or less dense depending on the individual situation and the people involved. Miasma is created by the introduction of difference into a situation and the responses to that difference. This action and reaction takes benign elements of difference, identity for example, and makes them flashpoints—areas that are rife for misinterpretation and misunderstanding. These elements and the cloud they create are miasma. The salient points of difference will vary for each nontraditional group, but the impact they have on the groups can be similar. If left unacknowledged and unmanaged, miasma can make individual and organizational relationships between nontraditional leaders and their more traditional counterparts more difficult and it can lessen organizational effectiveness. In our research on miasma, we found the six areas that are most salient for African Americans involve identity, responsibility, race and gender, networking, mentoring, and politically savvy.

An important goal for black leaders and managers is to discover how to work through miasma productively and not be impeded by it. The goal for organizations and for non-black colleagues who work within these organizations should be twofold: to understand the dynamic miasma creates for black leaders, and to determine how to reduce miasma to ensure that the organization is poised to best support and benefit from the efforts of all workers.

The effect of miasma is easier to see than the thing itself. In both our research at the Center for Creative Leadership (CCL) and our personal experiences, we have found that miasma has three major effects on African Americans:

- It reduces their trust in others.
- It fosters a belief that they must work twice as hard as others.
- It keeps them believing that they can never let down their guard.

These beliefs are unique and omnipresent burdens that many blacks carry. They create additional stress for black leaders working in traditionally white male workplaces. To navigate these real and perceived challenges requires the expenditure of an enormous amount of energy not usually required of whites.

ADDING IT ALL UP

Many of the African Americans we interviewed or surveyed have discussed the burden and stress they feel because they are black in corporate America. At each step, whether it is trust, responsibility, or feeling as if they have to work twice as hard, they explained the pressure these concerns add to their work life. "You constantly have to be conscious about things that other people don't have to worry about," said Rita Farax, an HR director at a national chemical company. For African Americans, the effects of this workplace stress are not additive but multiplicative. Black managers say they don't feel just a little more stress, they feel encompassed by it. "The stress associated with race can have a pervasive effect on all aspects of your life," says Darlene Winchester, a bank diversity manager.

The lesson that many blacks learn from work and other social experiences is that race always matters and it always matters all of the time. "In a very general way," says Deborah Raleigh, vice president of a national retail and food manufacturer, "it means that as a minority in a majority group, I will be different. Everything I do will be different. Even if I do the same things that everybody else does, it will be viewed as different because I'm different. And so I either live with that or get over it in order to survive."

Because they believe they are being treated and seen differently from many of their coworkers, black managers chafe against the rhetoric that denies their experience and tells them that all is equal. Consequently, when asked what their organizations could do differently, many said they want their companies to see them as human beings, full partners in an organization in which they too have a vested interest. Their wish, like others disenfranchised in the workplace, is that the corporate assumption of similarity would evolve into acceptance and valuing differences for everyone.

WHAT COLLEAGUES NEED TO KNOW

Many of the issues African Americans face in today's workplace are subtle. Consequently, people who are not black may not see them, and as a result, these people may choose to believe that difficulties don't exist. To blacks, others' inability to see race-related issues in the workplace is often perplexing, especially when whites and others have seemingly little difficulty identifying, understanding, and working through the subtle differences of many other work-related social and political issues. For example, recently a colleague was describing the effects of living in another culture. He talked about the inconveniences and irritations of living and working abroad, which although relatively minor, together added up to culture shock. He urged his colleagues to recognize that culture shock is real and that it has real effects on people—influencing how they do their work and live their lives. People listening to him nodded their heads knowingly; this was something invisible that they could now see. Yet when issues of difference are joined with assertions of potential inequality, blacks and other nontraditional leaders may find their concerns met with blank stares or surprise. The result leaves black leaders frustrated.

Just as African Americans have to deal with uncomfortable questions and truths about their own behaviors, responsibilities, and expectations in the workplace, other groups must also challenge themselves. Non-blacks have to ask themselves about their own responsibility in perpetuating attitudes, behaviors, and systems that benefit their own groups while quietly disempowering others. Non-blacks, and particularly whites, need to acknowledge their part in creating and maintaining the miasma within which many groups suffer. It affects the entire organization—human resources, retention rates, creativity, and the organization's competitive stance. Ultimately, it affects the bottom line.

This chapter ends by outlining strategies we believe can help dispel blindness to difference—the mind-set that contributes to miasma. Keep in mind that the following list is not exhaustive. It is intended to be a set of prompts on three sets of issues—self-development, education, and behavior—to stimulate your thinking about what will be appropriate and effective in your particular context, relationships, department, and organization.

SELF-DEVELOPMENT

Being comfortable with difference requires understanding oneself as well as those who are different from you. The following suggestions detail ways to explore your understanding of attitudes about difference and behaviors in response to it.

Understand that difference really does matter. It is important to recognize that when you are different from the majority, difference really matters, and it can affect virtually every aspect of your life. Helen Thompson, program manager for a national chemical company, sums up many blacks' experience when she says, "I don't think that there is a day that goes by that I'm not reminded that I'm black in this country." Another African American corporate manager recalls a similar insight she had when she first attended a black college. After her first month she noticed that because of the nearly all-black environment, she felt almost physically different, lighter somehow. "I finally realized that for the first time in my life, I wasn't dealing with race. I wasn't carrying it around with me, seeing it in others' eyes," she said. "It was wonderful, and I wondered if this is what it felt like to be white and not have to think of race every day, almost every moment." Being black, being different, is a pervasive experience. There is no getting away from it, and it has an effect on individuals internally—how they view and react to the world around them. Those who are different must also be constantly aware of how others respond to them, and must consider this going into almost every situation. Recognizing that this reality exists for your black colleagues can be your first step toward creating a better relationship with them, as you not only understand the strain their difference can bring but also accept them for who they are.

Be willing to broaden your outlook. In an increasingly diverse and global workplace, focusing solely on your own knowledge or experiences or those of a particular identity group (whether defined by race, economics, religion, gender, or some other factor) is limiting. The prevailing concept that the United States, and therefore each of its workplaces, is a vast melting pot is inaccurate. This country is more like a tossed salad, each ingredient distinct but contributing to the whole. When corporate citizens fail to recognize and appreciate the value of the difference that others bring with them into the work environment, they perpetuate the frustrations that black and other nontraditional executives experience as a result of having their uniqueness denied. And the valuable asset that this perspective of difference brings goes underutilized. In the new global economy, diversity is strength—a necessity.

Don't overassume similarities. Although it is important for groups to recognize their similarities, it is also important to honor and respect their differences. Making assumptions about similarities often means you may not truly be appreciating others or respecting individual differences. When people make unsubstantiated leaps to find commonalities, even their best intentions may go sadly awry. In your efforts to bridge the gulf of difference, you may, for example, assume a false similarity by adopting behaviors you believe are representative of a group. This might mean mimicking what you perceive to be another group's mannerisms as a way of "connecting" with them. In regard to your black colleagues, examples of this ill-conceived behavior are routinely greeting them or their family members by giving them "high fives" or using slang that is not part of your normal vocabulary. Such behaviors are annoying and almost always offensive.

On a related note, don't assume that because someone shares your gender, job title, or hometown that you and he are inherently alike. Unwarranted familiarity, for example, has adversely affected relationships between white women and women of color. Some white women believe they can speak for all women without regard for or in many cases understanding of the different experiences their sisters of color are having. Though it is true that many women's issues cut across racial, religious, and ethnic lines, to assume that the white female executive's reality is the only one that exists is to grossly underestimate and diminish the significance of the experience of executive women of color.

Keep issues in perspective. When talking to African Americans, it is important to appreciate the difference between individual concerns and matters of race. Be careful not to hold individual blacks responsible for national racial issues or assume that their personal perspective represents their group's—or that they even have an opinion on every racial issue. At some point almost every African American working in a corporate environment has been pinned to the wall by someone demanding an explanation for the behaviors of Jesse Jackson or Louis

Farrakhan or the random blacks seen on the news or at the local mall. Closer to home, whites regularly call on blacks to explain the behaviors, attitudes, and work performance of other African Americans in the organization. They probably don't know these people, and even if they do, they are not responsible for others' behaviors or accountable to you. In a similar vein, it is important to understand that when a black person champions an issue it is not necessarily a black issue. Be careful not to arbitrarily introduce race as an element in issues where it does not belong, or assume that race is an underlying theme in everything blacks discuss. Remember, what makes an issue racial is its content, not its messenger.

Don't expect blacks to fail. When it comes to race, it is critical to be honest with yourself about your assumptions and expectations. Don't assume that African Americans are underqualified, unwilling to excel, or going to fail. The truth is, some will fail and some will not, just like the members of any other racial, gender, or cultural group. Like others, African Americans will include some people who are sharp and some who are dull; there will be some who are prepared and some who are not. And when someone black does fail, that is never preordained by race.

Stretch your comfort zone. Recognize that if a cross-race relationship is going to grow, you and not the other person may have to be the one to change. Be willing to meet African Americans on their own terms and not just your own. If you are the leader, this may mean being open to assigning blacks to roles or responsibilities for which they have not been previously considered. You might also explore and challenge stereotypes and other assumptions you have about blacks and other nontraditional leaders. Then make a concerted effort, based on individual performance and contributions, to evaluate your direct reports equitably. If you are a peer or the direct report of an African American executive, you need to be willing to follow his or her lead in the same way you would any other executive, respecting both the person and his or her decisions. In either case, give blacks and others who are different the same consideration you are willing to extend to white males—the predominant group of leaders in the organization.

Keep mutual respect paramount. Treat people as you would like to be treated. This might seem a fairly simple rule, easy for all to follow and find value in. However, some blacks believe respect is hard to come by. Consider that in our survey, over half the respondents did not feel their identity as blacks was respected or appreciated in their organizations. This speaks volumes about the experiences of many of your black colleagues every day.

In seeking to contribute to a more equitable work environment for blacks and other nontraditional leaders, or even just to enhance relationships, you might, first, want to examine the degree and manner in which you mete out respect to others. You can do this by paying attention to how you communicate. Consider your language and others' verbal and nonverbal responses, and ask for feedback as appropriate. You might also show interest in others' lives, projects, and aspirations rather than assuming they are only interested in yours. Another way to show respect is to simply listen. Listen to blacks' ideas as well as their concerns, and genuinely share your opinions.

Respect is one of those fundamental benefits individuals automatically expect to be granted—although it can then be lost. Sometimes, particularly when there is rampant distrust, small cultural mannerisms can have significant meanings. Small things, such as whether you put your change on the counter or put it in the salesclerk's hand, suggest your level of respect. Whether you regularly talk directly with your black colleagues or tend to use intermediaries may reflect the degree of respect you have for them. Respect is not synonymous with liking someone. You are not expected to like every black person you meet, nor can you expect each one to like you; but each of you should be confident of receiving a certain level of respect that enables you to be productive and collaborative members of your organization.

EDUCATION

People often assume that because they work with other groups they also understand them. Unfortunately that assumption is erroneous more often than not. To understand other groups, you should educate yourself about them and you have to be willing to learn, even when the new information seems to be at odds with what you already know. To be truly educated you must also be willing to learn more about yourself than you may be comfortable with. Learning about groups and the individuals within a group are two different things. Both pursuits are important: the former to help develop closer relationships with African American colleagues, the latter to develop a more inclusive perspective of the changing dynamics of the workforce.

Learn about blacks and miasma. Read about, listen to, attend events with, and generally just get to know African Americans. Come at this discovery unbegrudgingly, with an open mind, and with your assumptions checked at the door. Take an inquiry approach that suggests that you are asking questions and gathering information with a willingness to learn. This does not necessarily mean that you should pepper your black colleagues with incessant questions. As you build close relationships with African Americans, you may find yourself getting into discussions about race. As you engage in these conversations, be aware of your assumptions so they don't impede your learning and communication processes. Joanna Gayle, vice president at a national financial institution, says she wants people to know her, not just what is on paper about her. Wilson Davis, lead technical specialist for a major tobacco company, adds that he wants people to understand his experience more completely: "They don't really know what it's like to be black, to grow up as a colored person, grow up to become Negro, and then evolve to be black. If they understood that better, we would have more harmony at work." In truth, learning, in-depth exploratory examination, is imperative if people are going to work more effectively with each other. But this learning is not likely to happen unless all parties involved trust each other enough to share. That comes with time and honest outreach.

Question your own perspectives. Check your own perspectives about race and roles. What are the assumptions behind your thoughts and behaviors? Do you assume, for instance, that because someone is African American she has an intimate knowledge of the cultures and customs of African nations? When you promote nontraditional leaders, do you bask in the pride of your accomplishment, as if you have done them a favor? Finally, do you habitually relegate African Americans and other nontraditional leaders to "acting" or "assistant" positions of authority rather than granting them the full responsibility and authority that you regularly bestow upon white males? Before you answer this last question, you should know that CCL research suggests that white males are indeed less likely than African Americans and white women to be given an acting or assistant role initially. Often people are unaware of the deeply ingrained beliefs that subtly guide their behaviors. Almost without conscious thought, these beliefs shape their decisions about who is fit for certain responsibilities. Most whites do not intentionally think "this person is an African American so she's not ready for this job." They just simply do not give her the job even though she is clearly qualified. That behavior, whether they intend it to be or not, whether it is conscious or not, is racism.

Seek feedback about your behaviors. Find trusted agents—nontraditionals among them—who can help you understand how your cross-racial, cross-gender, or cross-anything interactions are perceived. Ask them to give you feedback on how you come across in general or how you handled a particular situation. You can also use your trusted agents as sounding boards to help you determine the best course of action prior to dealing with particular issues or situations. Of course you need to have a relationship with this black person before you approach him or her for feedback. Remember that your trusted agents can speak only from their individual points of view. No one African American is the voice of black America. Each person, though, may be able to give you insights into how some African Americans might feel about your issue and why. However, be sensitive about whether you have established enough trust and intimacy with your trusted agents to have these conversations without putting them on the hot seat.

Be aware of your context. Familiarize yourself with the written and unwritten rules of your organization and consider what they mean for your African American colleagues. Who has access? Who has visibility? Who organizes formal and informal events? Who guides the corporate culture? By becoming better aware and understanding the context in which you and your black and other colleagues must work, you can gain insight into and appreciation for their perspectives and reactions. As you pay more attention to your context, also take pains to become aware of events that are happening beyond your specific area of responsibility.

BEHAVIOR

Self-awareness, education, and behavior are certainly important when we are discussing cross-race relations. Perhaps most important are the relationships between and among people. What can you do to create, enhance, or maintain a relationship?

Communicate openly and provide feedback. Remember that communication is best when it is two-way. So, listen to and seriously consider all perspectives, and share your insights with black managers in a way that is engaging, not condescending. Communicate openly with your African American colleagues. Be as honest with them as you are with other colleagues, and provide fair and objective feedback. If praise and encouragement are due, don't be stingy. If developmental feedback is called for, back it up with data and don't worry about accusations of racism. If you are being accused of racist behavior because of the feedback you are giving to another, you might, first, check your motivation for giving this person feedback, and assess the manner in which you do so. Would you, honestly, give the same feedback if the person looked more like you? Would you give it in the same way? If the answer to these questions is yes, you might then ask yourself if you have the data to support this feedback about the person's behavior and the impact it is having on the workplace. Finally, consider whether you are willing to help this person improve on the issues the feedback addresses. If you can comfortably answer yes to all these questions, you should give the person appropriate feedback, regardless of his or her protests of racism.

Don't limit interactions with black colleagues. We suggest you get to know your black colleagues better. You might start by going to their offices and chatting for a while about general business and perhaps even casual or personal matters, at a level where you both feel comfortable. As your interactions become more frequent and, we hope, increasingly unguarded, you might find that the subjects become more sensitive or personal. In this case continue to be open and to share. Listen to what these other people have to say about these various subjects without rushing to judgment, being defensive, or alienating them. Reflect your intent to foster a broader relationship and understanding with them, not just through your words but also through your actions.

African Americans have fewer opportunities to mentor or be mentored by others. Therefore another way of expanding your interactions with blacks is to take the leap, if you haven't done so already, and mentor someone you feel has promise. At the same time, be willing to be mentored by an African American leader. Black leaders can provide you with insights and skill development just as their more traditional counterparts can. By increasing your interactions with blacks and by making these interactions both formal and informal, you have a greater chance of enhancing your work effectiveness simply because you have a better knowledge of each other's styles and skill levels.

Allow for differences. Strive to accept African Americans in their entirety, without filtering their blackness or presupposing behaviors and setting expectations. This means that saying to someone, or even believing, "I don't see you as black; I just see you as a regular person" is not a compliment. Being black is not a characteristic that needs to be overlooked as if it were an unsightly blemish or a scar to diplomatically ignore. Blackness is an integral part of a person's being. It helps to shape the person's perspectives and typically helps define who the person is. Although blackness is not all an African American is, it is certainly a significant aspect and quality for that person. In the quest for a more inclusive and equitable organization, however, many leaders have gone too far in equating equality with sameness. Also contributing to this assumption of similarity may be people's discomfort with issues of difference in general and race in particular.

In a 1999 *HR Magazine* article, "If Diversity, Then Higher Profits?" Sherry Kuczynski explains that governmental regulatory policies and organizations focus on diversity initiatives that "strive to be color blind and gender blind and encourage people to see each other as 'just the same as everyone else.'" The problem, she says, "is that everyone is not the same." This reality of difference has got to be acknowledged. And more than that, the differences need to be appreciated and valued for their benefit to the organization.

Don't be afraid. Don't allow unfounded fear or discomfort to control your actions. When these emotions guide you, your well-intentioned behaviors can be viewed as awkward and may be subject to unflattering misinterpretations. For example, don't refrain from speaking to a black friend because she is with a group of other African Americans. Likewise, don't feel compelled to make a meaningless comment to blacks sitting together at a lunch table because of your unease in seeing them together. Instead be aware of when you are feeling uncomfortable, try to uncover and understand the source of your discomfort, and manage it.

Recognize and support "average" African Americans. Although some African American professionals achieve superstar status in organizations, it should come as no surprise that the majority of their black colleagues, like the majority of their white colleagues, are average, well-intentioned contributors to the company. Many of these "average" blacks believe they are being overlooked due to their race, because they see whites who are not extraordinarily talented move ahead faster and farther than they do. Although it may be true that the black superstars find both organizational opportunity and support to showcase their talents, not all black managers find the workplace as open, supportive, and accessible for upward mobility or recognition—not even to the extent of their average white colleagues. Nan Blunt, a manager for an executive development firm, told us that what gives her anxiety in the workplace is her concern about blacks who are just starting out or who are hard, average workers. "What happens if you just happen to be a black person who is just as good as other white people?" asked Blunt. If her concerns are well founded, it could mean that there is a storehouse of African Americans, and other nontraditional leaders, whose contributions may be undervalued and who themselves may be ignored, to the detriment of the organization's overall effectiveness.

To ensure that every member of the organization has an opportunity to excel, you may need to rethink some assumptions and review some of your behaviors. Examine the criteria you use for selecting those you will nurture or develop for the next level of responsibility. Consider how much time and energy you spend on those you consider average—are they being overlooked? Provide the same opportunities for all the average members of your organization, and support their efforts, regardless of their differences. For in doing so you enhance your organization's productivity by fully engaging its most valuable resource.

Demand and enforce equitable treatment. Every member of the organization has the right to be treated equitably. If you or others believe this is not happening, check your perceptions and document (when you can) the difference in treatment. If you are not a decision maker or policy enforcer, refer the matter to the appropriate individual or department. If after seeking help you do not believe the issue is being adequately addressed, go outside to an external agency for help or guidance. If you are in a position to do so as a leader, set policies that foster equitable corporate practices. In your own realm, encourage and enforce equitable practice in hiring, promotions, visibility, and job tasks and assignments.

Be a change agent. If you are a leader, especially if you are a traditional leader, use your status to become a change agent. Change is less threatening when it comes from within—changes in policy appear less radical when they come from a member of the mainstream. To be an effective change agent, you need to have established strong credibility. Remember, trust and accomplishments are requisites for garnering credibility, but don't be surprised if, as you work to produce change, your accomplishments increase and you receive greater trust from a more diverse group of colleagues. Being recognized as a visionary can strengthen your leadership role and influence.

———⟨ν/ν⟩———

Ancella B. Livers is group director of Global Open Enrollment programs at the Center for Creative Leadership in Greensboro, North Carolina, and the author of works on race in the workplace.

———⟨ν/ν⟩———

Keith A. Caver is the practice leader and manager of executive development for Development Dimensions International (DDI) in Bridgeville, Pennsylvania.

CHAPTER TWENTY

Managing Middlescence

Robert Morison
Tamara J. Erickson
Ken Dychtwald

B urned-out, bottlenecked, and bored. That's the current lot of millions of midcareer employees. In our research into employee attitudes and experiences, we heard many stories of midcareer restlessness, a phenomenon we call *middlescence*. There was the manager who was beginning to realize that he'd never become the company president, the senior executive who felt that she had sacrificed her life—and her spirit—for her job, and the technician who was bored stiff with his unchallenging assignments. Typical is the case of one productive and well-respected middle manager in his late forties. He was sandwiched between obligations at the office and at home, and his work group was demoralized after two rounds of downsizing. The company's structure had flattened, leaving fewer possibilities than ever for promotion, and he felt stalled. "This isn't how my life and career were supposed to play out," he told the employee counselor. "I don't know how much longer I can cope."

Like adolescence, middlescence can be a time of frustration, confusion, and alienation but also a time of self-discovery, new direction, and fresh beginnings. Today, millions of midcareer men and women are wrestling with middlescence—looking for ways to balance job responsibilities, family, and leisure while hoping to find new meaning in their work.

Midcareer employees—those between the ages of 35 and 54—make up more than half the workforce. One in four has managerial or supervisory responsibility. When in June 2004 we at Age Wave and the Concours Group conducted a survey with Harris Interactive of more than 7,700 U.S. workers, we found that people in this age bracket work longer hours than their older and younger counterparts, with 30% saying they put in 50 or more hours per week. Yet only 43% are passionate about their jobs, just 33% feel energized by their work, 36% say they feel that they are in dead-end jobs, and more than 40% report feelings of burnout.

Midcareer employees are the least likely to say that their workplace is congenial and fun or that it offers ample opportunity to try new things. As a group, they have the lowest satisfaction rates with their immediate managers and the least confidence in top executives. Only one in three agrees that top management displays integrity or commitment to employee development, and one in four often disagrees with the organization's policies on important employee matters. A fifth are seeking opportunities in other organizations, and a similar percentage are looking for a major career change. But 85% believe that career changes are very difficult these days. Family and financial pressures outside work make them conservative in their career choices, and many cannot afford moves that would involve cuts in pay or benefits. Other research has yielded similar findings: According to a 2005 Conference Board survey, the largest decline in job satisfaction over the past ten years occurred among workers between the ages of 35 and 44, and the second largest decline was among those aged 45 to 54. In short, far too many midcareer employees are working more, enjoying it less, and looking for alternatives.

THE PROBLEMS

Middlescent restlessness isn't new, but it plays out differently in different generations. It seems to be hitting today's midcareer workers harder than it hit their predecessors. Increased longevity, delayed (and multiple) marriages, and large numbers of two-career households have altered family patterns such that middlescents are often sandwiched at home between raising children and caring for aging parents precisely at the time when their job responsibilities are peaking.

Increased longevity also means that the average 50 year old today could be looking forward to 30 years or more of healthy, active life. That can be a blessing—time enough to learn new skills, start another career, build an entrepreneurial business, or shift priorities to give back to society. Or it can be a curse—for those without the financial resources to chart their own course, who instead face the prospect of having to work indefinitely at a job they don't really enjoy. Either way, it's a problem for their current employers.

Generationally, most of today's (and all of the older) midcareer employees are baby boomers, their values forged in the midst of the Vietnam War, Watergate, and the civil rights and women's rights movements. In middlescence many are asking themselves: Have I had the impact I expected to have? How can I make the next phase of my life as meaningful as possible? Earlier generations looked to their work for security and material success; the way to combat restlessness was usually to hunker down and focus on one's current job. Many of today's idealistic yet frustrated boomers have different goals—they'd be willing to trade some of their current success for greater significance in their lives and work, even if that means doing something altogether different.

Companies are ill-prepared to manage middlescence because it is so pervasive, largely invisible, and culturally uncharted. Many midcareer men and women may crave a fresh start but don't tell their bosses how they feel [see Exhibit 20.1, "Sources of Frustration"]. Employers view these people as solid corporate citizens, bank on their loyalty and commitment, and assume they're doing fine.

That neglect is bad for business: many companies risk losing some of their best people, who may opt for early retirement or seek more exciting work elsewhere. Firms are too often blindsided when valuable people up and quit. We met, for instance, with executives at an aerospace company that had recently lost a midcareer technical manager who wanted to grow but couldn't see any near term possibilities for advancement. His bosses knew this but did nothing, so the employee left to start his own consulting firm. In retrospect, the executives recognized that they could have easily found ways to make his job more interesting and challenging. As it is, they're hoping he'll eventually return.

Also bad for business are the many disaffected people who stay. Every day that an employee is less than fully engaged in his or her work, the company pays a price—a loss of energy and enthusiasm,

Career bottleneck
The baby boom generation is large, and too many people are competing for too few leadership positions in organizations that have been shedding layers of hierarchy. Next to job security, this is one of the biggest concerns of managers in their forties and fifties.

Work/life tension
Midcareer workers are sandwiched between commitments to children and parents, often at the same time that their work responsibilities are peaking.

Lengthening horizon
Those who are not accumulating sufficient wealth for retirement face the prospect of having to work many more years. Many of today's midcareer employees have been lavish spenders and sparse savers.

Skills obsolescence
Some struggle to adjust to new ways of working and managing in the information economy. Some hope that merely time or diligence will get them promoted into better and higher-paying jobs when what they most need is upgraded skills.

Disillusionment with employer
This includes insecurity and distrust following waves of downsizing, as well as resentment over the enormous compensation gaps between topmost executives and almost all other employees.

Burnout
People who have been career driven for 20 or more years are stretched and stressed, find their work unexciting or repetitive, and are running low on energy and the ability to cope.

Career disappointment
The roles employees play and the impact of their work fail to measure up to their youthful ideals and ambitions.

Exhibit 20.1.   Sources of Frustration.

a lack of innovation and focus. We have become convinced that the problem of burned-out, turned-off employees who stay is even more threatening to corporate productivity than the problem of turnover.

In the years ahead, both tangible talent shortages and growing disengagement from work will present unprecedented challenges to business productivity and growth. In our March 2004 HBR article, "It's Time to Retire Retirement," we wrote of strategies to combat the coming brain drain, as the vanguard of baby boomers approaches retirement age. But the solution to talent shortages doesn't lie in enticing just one generation of older workers to continue contributing; rather, companies need to make working past retirement (at least part-time) the norm from now on. That means making current work more enjoyable and enriching, because the way to retain your middlescents for the long haul is to reengage them today.

The best way to do so is to tap into their hunger for renewal and help them launch into new, more productive, more meaningful roles and careers. Millions of midcareer men and women would like nothing better than to convert their restlessness into fresh energy. They just need the occasion, and perhaps a little assistance, to unleash and channel all that potential energy. Chances are, you're already using some of the career revitalization techniques we'll recommend, but we'll wager you're focusing them mainly on your company's stars. It's time to apply them to the much broader, and too often neglected, constituency of midcareer employees.

SIX STRATEGIES FOR REVITALIZING CAREERS

You may not be able to offer everybody more money or a prestigious title, but you can give just about anybody a fresh challenge or a new start. As many of our examples show, the most successful careers are the ones that stay in motion.

You must, however, take two preliminary steps to prepare the ground. First, you need to *remove the barriers* to occupational mobility. Such barriers take many forms. Policies (formal or tacit) regarding required time in role between job changes may be too strict. Your organization may have a job-posting system but still fill most openings through under-the-table recruiting that bypasses official channels. Your company may be tacitly unwilling, or even unconsciously disinclined, to invest in extensive training for employees over a certain age. Managers may get away with blocking employees from new assignments, and policies forbidding such behavior may be enforced loosely, at best. And employees themselves may perceive role changes, career redirections, new training, lateral moves, and flexible work arrangements as signs of inadequacy or failure.

Second, be sure to *find the keepers*. If you can identify high potentials through your performance management system, then surely you can also identify the next tier down. You want to go beyond the stars (who are probably getting special attention already) to find the other valuable contributors—the B players, people who will probably never make it to the executive suite but whose skills and experience you need to retain. These are the people you'd like to see eventually moving into flex retirement, not full retirement. Once you've identified them, pay special attention not only to their potential, performance, and progress but also to any warning signs of middlescent disillusionment and stagnation.

To help you keep those keepers, we've identified six fundamental tools.

Fresh Assignments

A fresh assignment, often in a different geographical location or part of the organization, lets you take advantage of a person's existing skills, experience, and contacts while letting him or her develop new ones. The best assignments are often lateral moves that mix roughly equal parts old and new responsibilities.

During our interviews, for example, we met with Jeff Kimpan, a longtime HR executive at General Motors. He worked in Mexico during the mid-1980s, a period of explosive growth there. Then he joined the executive ranks, most recently running HR for worldwide manufacturing operations. In the spring of 2005, the HR director for the company's fast-growing China operation quit, and Jeff volunteered for the job. It was actually a step down in corporate status and scope, and his colleagues were shocked that he'd accept what seemed a less than lateral move. He acknowledges that he had to check his ego, but he was ready for a change, and he knew that he could apply what he'd learned 20 years earlier in Mexico. His children were grown, and he was excited about getting away from restructurings and downsizings to work in a growing business.

It isn't an easy job. The China operation hopes to double its sales in two years and redouble in four, so the unit was already facing shortages of experienced technical and professional people when Jeff arrived. But he's having fun. "I can't wait to get to work each day," he says. "I come home just as tired as I did in Detroit—it's just a better kind of tired. This place is like a lab: Solutions aren't known, and they have to be invented every day. You'd have to be dead not to have fun in this job."

Principal Financial Group routinely chooses empty nesters like Jeff for relocation, particularly those moves that would be difficult for employees with young and growing families. So does GE, which also taps experienced managers to integrate new acquisitions—an ideal way to offer an employee a change of scene and bring to bear a career's worth of organizational know-how. Diana Tyson, who has spent 22 years in organizational development with AT&T and now Lucent Technologies, recently left corporate headquarters for a year-long engagement in the fast-growing Asia-Pacific region. "After this experience, it would be a lot harder for another company to recruit me," she told us.

Marriott International's information resources group takes another innovative approach to the fresh assignment. Tenures there are long and turnover is low, which means high levels of competence but little potential for upward mobility. So senior managers have been offered opportunities to take on a second, lateral role, while off-loading some of their current responsibilities, as a way to introduce new challenges. For example, Patton Conner, the vice president of guest services systems, recently took on a second "day job" as the regional VP for information resources of Marriott Canada. George Hall, a veteran human resources manager, is now also managing application development for the HR function. His new peers around the table are his customers in his other role, which he says gives him terrific insights into how to solve their problems. The more-junior employees who report to people like Patton and George have a chance to take on greater responsibility, since their bosses now have more to do in other areas.

Dow Chemical is one of the best examples we've seen of a company that has truly removed the barriers to career revitalization. Executives there assume that careers will always be in motion and that employees of all ages should always be preparing for their next career within the company. Dow backs up that expectation with tools that help people plan their next roles. One such is a career opportunity map that helps people determine which skills to acquire and which jobs to seek out. Another is a global job-posting system that alerts people to opportunities in other areas. It's a flat organization, so this approach allows the company to offer new and different work, even if it can't offer everyone a promotion.

Hewlett-Packard's Cathy Lyons has had a half-dozen very different assignments within the company over the past 12 years, from running a manufacturing operation in Italy to managing the U.S. toner supplies business to her most recent assignment as chief marketing officer at corporate headquarters. She believes that three or four years is long enough to be in any one position. "When you've stopped learning, it's time to move on or step aside," she told us.

Career Changes

Middlescents often dream of—and in some cases end up pursuing—something fundamentally new. Yet jumping the corporate ship is risky, so an employer that can offer an attractive internal career change has a chance to retain valuable talent. An employee may develop a new specialty, assume an altogether different job, or sometimes return from a management track to an individual contributor role.

Before joining Prudential Financial's Prudential Relocation business, Jim Russo spent 13 years with a major competitor in a customer relations role that kept him on the road. Looking for less travel and more time with his young family, Jim joined Prudential Relocation's new Phoenix office in 2000 as director of service delivery, managing a team of 21. The move was good for work/life balance, but after a while Jim became disenchanted: "The job wasn't my strength or my passion. I didn't feel as motivated, I missed working directly with customers, and I felt I was just getting the job done." By all measures, he was doing a good job, but he knew the situation wasn't right.

Jim liked the company and networked with a variety of managers to learn what kinds of opportunities there might be. He landed a position in field sales, a role for which he had no direct experience but which seemed to play to his strengths. The results—for Jim and the company—were beyond excellent. As sales director for the West Coast, he went up against his former employer. "I'm competitive by nature, and the job really fit," he says. "It gave me new life, more passion, more confidence, and companywide recognition—I know I'm a more important part of the company, and that really matters." In his first year, Jim was one of the top two salespeople; in his second, he tripled his sales target. His advice to others: "You've got to have passion for the job to add value every day. If you find yourself just going through the motions, do something different—perhaps very different. We all have strengths; find yours and play to them."

Such career shifts should be a natural part of corporate life. Dave Nassef has had three distinct careers in his 30-plus years with Pitney Bowes. He started as a personnel manager in a factory and made a lateral move to marketing. When the company centralized HR, he was one of the few people with both manufacturing and marketing experience, and at 40 he was given HR responsibility for half the company. He's since changed careers within the firm twice—first to take on the newly created job of corporate ombudsman and problem solver and then to move into the policy sphere, representing Pitney Bowes in Washington in legislative matters relating to the mailing industry. Each time, Dave surprised everyone around him with his willingness—eagerness, even—to make a lateral move. Dave's philosophy: "You have to ask yourself whether you want to thrive in a company or merely survive. If you want to thrive, then be prepared to take the risk of making a career change."

Mentoring Colleagues

Putting experienced employees into mentoring, teaching, and other knowledge-sharing roles has the dual benefit of reengaging the mid-career worker and boosting the expertise and organizational know-how of less-experienced employees. For middlescents, serving as a mentor is a personally fulfilling way to share a lifetime of experience, give back to the organization, and make a fresh set of social connections in the workplace. Mentor relationships are often stereotyped as one-way transfers from old to young for the purposes of youthful personal development and career advancement. In fact, they should be viewed as a two-way pairing of knowledge to gain with knowledge to share.

That's how mentoring works at Intel, where the partner may outrank the mentor. The program began in a chip-making factory in New Mexico in 1997, when Intel was growing, and many of the factory's managers and technical experts were being transferred to new locations. New experts needed to be developed in a variety of fields. So the factory's top managers started matching partners with mentors who had the needed skills and knowledge. Today, a companywide employee database, which tracks skills attained and desired, helps match partners with mentors, who (thanks to the Internet) may be in another country. Both mentor and partner take a class to learn some guidelines—what to talk about, how to maximize the mutual benefit of their relationship—and then they set the details of that relationship in a contract that specifies goals and deadlines.

Mentoring is the best way to put the greatest number of midcareer workers into knowledge-sharing roles. But there are other ways. It's common practice for experienced and expert employees to develop and deliver training programs. They can also teach and guide colleagues through internal-consulting roles, participate in business performance reviews, and lead business improvement projects. Many midcareer workers are happy to take charge of change initiatives, which are especially appealing as a way to assist colleagues, improve results, and serve the higher mission of the enterprise.

Fresh Training

Corporate training today is disproportionately aimed at the young (especially new employees who need to learn the basics) and at the high potentials. The tacit assumptions are that midcareer people have been trained already, and what little additional training they might need they get on the job. These assumptions are, at best, only partly true.

Many of today's midcareer workers are well educated and have retained their love of learning. They know that increasing their skills will raise their chances for personal and professional advancement. However, many find themselves too busy for extensive education and training; personal development time comes at the sacrifice of other responsibilities, both on the job and off. And some people, especially those who have reached positions of authority, stop seeking development opportunities because they hesitate to take risks or don't want to admit that they have things to learn.

Meanwhile, too many organizations foster a silent conspiracy against education: They cut the training and development budget first in lean times. They stand silent when managers discourage employees from seeking training on the grounds that it will interfere with getting the work done. And they fail to require managers to set career development plans for all their employees. As a result, many midcareer workers are overdue for a serious infusion of training—which can include refresher courses, in-depth education to develop new skills, and brief introductions to new ideas or areas of business that expand their perspectives and trigger their interest in learning more.

Fresh training is, of course, often integral to career changes as well as to employee retention. Lincoln Electric's Leopard Program, for instance, was designed explicitly to enable employees to "change their spots." When patterns of demand for steel fabrication products changed, the company trained dozens of factory and clerical staff volunteers to become assistant salespeople. In some Japanese manufacturers, assembly-line workers regularly train to become product service technicians. After years on the line, such employees literally know the products inside and out, and probably want a change of work. And the U.K.'s National Health Service is responding to chronic nursing shortages by training aides to become nurses—a shift to a very different career path.

Sabbaticals

One of the best ways to rejuvenate, personally and professionally, is simply to get away from the routine of the job for a significant amount of time. A common feature of academic employment relationships, sabbaticals remain rare and underused in the business world. In 2001, Hewitt Associates surveyed more than 500 organizations in the United States and found that just 5% offered sabbaticals, either paid or unpaid. Yet a survey the same year by Principal Financial Group found that more than 50% of employees say they long for a sabbatical but feel they can't take one because of financial concerns or employer discouragement. Employers' reluctance centers on cost and, for key employees, potential disruption to business operations. Employees' reluctance comes from fear that taking a leave will somehow mark them as less committed than those who don't interrupt their work. One manager in the media industry said that her company had made an apparently generous offer of an eight-week paid sabbatical every few years. But, she added, she knew of not a single person who had taken advantage of the benefit. It was universally assumed that when you returned, you'd find your desk out in the hall. You might not be fired, exactly, but the general opinion was that you'd be displaced. This perception is unfortunate because people tend to return from sabbaticals more committed than ever. They've had a chance to recharge, to do something different, and they're appreciative of their companies for giving them the opportunity.

There are organizations that get it—that know that the cost of replacing a middlescent worker in need of a break may far outweigh the cost of the paid time off. Intel employees are eligible for an eight-week sabbatical, with full pay, after every seven years of full-time service. Silicon Graphics' regular full-time employees in the United States and Canada can take six weeks paid time off after four years. Adobe Systems offers three paid weeks off after every five years of service. Arrow Electronics offers up to ten weeks after seven years.

Hallmark Cards uses sabbaticals not only to get people out of the routine of work but also to place them into enlightening settings with the goal of recharging their artistic talent. They might spend time at the company's innovation center; go on "creative research travel" to museums, conferences, inspiring locales, or places where they can study customers and social trends; or simply spend time at the company's 172-acre farm. Most Hallmark sabbaticals are brief, but senior creative staff can also be honored with a sabbatical award of six months away from work to pursue an area of artistic exploration.

Wells Fargo's Volunteer Leave program, more than 20 years in operation, offers employees with at least five years' service and a qualifying performance rating the opportunity to work in a community service setting of their choosing for up to four months in a calendar year while receiving full pay and benefits. The work they do is often inspiring: People have used the time to volunteer at a camp for cancer victims; to represent Mothers Against Drunk Driving, traveling across the country to speak with high school students; and to work in Armenia to help women develop small businesses. This last was so successful that the project was adopted by the United Nations, and the participant was allowed to extend her leave to assist the UN in setting it up. For its part, the company reaps benefits on several fronts, including good publicity both within the corporation and out in the communities where participants are serving. The most important benefit, of course, is a returning employee who is highly energized and recommitted to the organization.

Expanding Leadership Development

Many of the executives we spoke with in our research cited shortages in their leadership succession pipelines. On the face of it, this is surprising because, in terms of raw numbers, there are plenty of midcareer workers eager to move up the ladder and fill senior management slots. But corporate restructuring and flattening organizations have eroded the old career paths, and people can't accumulate the needed set of leadership skills on the job. The situation is sadly ironic—midcareer managers are frustrated by the lack of promotion opportunities, and corporate executives are concerned with a lack of candidates with the right experience. The solution is to widen access to leadership development programs to both rejuvenate midcareer managers and refill the leadership pipeline.

Participation in leadership development programs is a form of recognition of an employee's value and potential, and workers graduate from them with a renewed commitment to the organization's goals.

But in many companies, it's difficult for people not already recognized as high potentials to get in line for these opportunities. We strongly recommend admitting late bloomers, making it easier for midcareer employees to take advantage of these programs.

Independence Blue Cross has put one-third of its top 600 people, most of them midcareer employees, through a leadership program focused on individual development and learning by doing. It includes a weeklong session at the Wharton School, individual coaching and career development planning, and work on an important business project. The insurer is now thinking about creating a graduate course for people who have already been through the program. The company is also trying to maintain career momentum after the program through a broader-based approach to succession planning and by finding its graduates new assignments that enable them to move around the business more.

The fast track should have both off- and on-ramps. A communications company shared the story of one individual who dropped off and then rejoined his company's fast track. A 12-year veteran, he had come up through finance, been deemed a high potential, and then plateaued and started to look elsewhere. Top managers at first figured, "Oh well, he wasn't CFO material anyway." But later they took a look at people who had dropped out of the high-potential program to find out why. This employee had stalled in his career because he hadn't found work that really excited him. After further assessment, he became procurement director for a product line, where his innate skills and enthusiasm as a negotiator, financial analyst, and savvy gambler paid off. In his first year, he saved the company $20 million doing work he loves.

REKINDLE NOW

We're not talking about rescuing a few stragglers at the corporation's fringe; we're talking about tens of millions of capable midcareer employees who are frustrated in their desire to do something new and exciting, who are stymied in their wish to contribute to the organization's success in different ways. What's stopping companies from tapping into all that potential? Perhaps it's the assumption that careers belong to employees—that people are ultimately responsible for developing their own skills, for marketing themselves, and for charting their own paths. This is true; the responsibility for career moves belongs primarily to the individual, and most employees would agree. But the fact is, organizations create the conditions under which career initiatives flourish or fade. It's in the enlightened self-interest of the organization to remove the institutional barriers to individual fulfillment and ambition, to pay the attention and devote the resources needed to keep new possibilities open and revitalize careers. This isn't paternalism—or a return to employment practices of yesterday. It's good management.

Over the next ten years, workforce demographics will turn against employers. If your organization wants to control its fate (and costs) when the boomer retirement wave and associated brain drain hit with full force, start today to systematically retain—and recruit—people with the skills and capabilities you will want to keep on hand for the long run. Recognize that many of your midcareer employees are in middlescence: For personal and professional reasons, they're getting restless. Don't just assume they'll stay, and then hope for the best. Reengage them by energizing their careers now. [See Exhibit 20.2, "Avoiding Midcareer Crisis," for questions to guide the process.]

To understand and encourage career rejuvenation for your organization's midcareer workers, answer these ten questions:

1. Who are your keepers? Besides those on the leadership track, who has the skills, experiences, attitude, and adaptability you need most for the long term?

2. How many of your midcareer employees need to rejuvenate some of their skills or careers?

3. Are you employing any methods to rejuvenate midcareer workers? Which work best?

4. How freely does experience, knowledge, and talent flow in your company? Can employees move around the organization? What's clogging the arteries?

5. How consistently do you make each job assignment work not only for overall business performance but also for individual employee growth?

6. Do you tap people for fresh assignments when their personal circumstances change (for example, when their children grow up and leave home)?

7. Do you encourage employees to change careers within your organization?

8. Do you offer sabbaticals?

9. How often do you hire midcareer people, including workforce reentrants?

10. Do you know which jobs are particularly suited to midcareer candidates? For which jobs do you avoid hiring or assigning them? What implicit biases are holding you back?

Exhibit 20.2.   Avoiding Midcareer Crisis.

The techniques we've recommended are not exclusively for mid-career workers, of course, but they will have the greatest impact on this cohort. They should prove neither expensive nor difficult to practice, and the payback—renewed commitment and productivity on the one hand, reduced replacement cost on the other—hits right away. The actions we recommend are largely a matter of paying closer attention to the often silent majority—the midcareer employees who form the heart and backbone of your workforce.

—⟪⟫—

Robert Morison is executive vice president and director of research at the Concours Group, a professional service firm supporting senior executives.

—⟪⟫—

Tamara J. Erickson is a McKinsey Award–winning author and expert on enhancing workforce productivity. She is president of the Concours Institute, the research and development arm of the Concours Group.

—⟪⟫—

Ken Dychtwald is the founder, president, and CEO of Age Wave, a think tank and consulting firm, and author of multiple books on aging-related issues.

Making It Happen

Everything to this point in the volume sets the stage for issues explored in Part Four: making leadership happen. The next fourteen chapters provide advice on how leaders can get started on the right foot, keep their efforts on track, and avoid predictable pitfalls. Leadership is intentional social action. It involves establishing strong relationships with others to forge a shared purpose and direction. The collaborative nature of leadership makes great things possible. It also adds to the complexity. It is not easy to get the whole herd moving roughly west, and effective leadership can never be accomplished with a simple checklist. Yet there are basic tasks that all leaders need to recognize and resolve. Where do leaders begin? What can guide their efforts?

The first five chapters in Part Four focus on the basics: how to establish credible footing as a leader and tackle the fundamentals of mission, vision, and strategy. As the old adage goes, beginnings are everything. They are periods of excitement and possibility for both leaders and followers, and a leader's ability to quickly get on top of the situation, establish relationships with important stakeholders, and build momentum is key. In Chapter Twenty-One, "The First Ninety Days of

Leadership," Michael Watkins provides the blueprint for a smooth start. Actions taken in the first three months on the job, concludes Watkins, can largely determine a leader's long-term success or failure.

Making things happen in organizations requires two fundamentals: a clear mission and coordinated efforts in support of it. In Chapter Twenty-Two, "What Is Our Mission?" the late Peter F. Drucker explores the linkages between good leadership and a good mission statement. A leader's primary responsibility, according to Drucker, is to ensure that people at all levels of the organization know its mission—the organization's ultimate reason for being. They must also understand it, support it, convey it simply to others, and live it.

Mission and vision are tightly linked. Once an organization knows the contribution it wants to make, it needs a way to see what successful accomplishment of that mission would bring. Chapters Twenty-Three and Twenty-Four tackle the importance of crafting an effective organizational vision. In Chapter Twenty-Three, "The Power and Creativity of a Transforming Vision," Pulitzer Prize–winning presidential biographer James MacGregor Burns explores the larger purposes of vision. A creative vision is more than one leader's personal dream. It is a powerful vehicle for engaging others, and the right vision can transform the course of history in positive and growth-filled ways. Creative visions require leaders who know how to frame shared values and possibilities in ways that elevate the aspirations of others and provide hope for a brighter future. The ultimate test, however, is the leader's ability to deliver: mobilize ongoing support, engage others in collaborative action, and accomplish the real-world change as promised. How does a leader do that?

In Chapter Twenty-Four, "Finding the Right Vision," Burt Nanus gets down to the nitty-gritty. He explores the essential properties and sources of a strong corporate vision, the steps for successfully crafting or revising one, and common vision misconceptions. A catchy restatement of organizational purpose or mission is often mistaken for a vision, but nothing could be further from the truth. A vision is an inspirational act of shared faith—a mental model of a better future that evolves over time in response to the organization's ability to enact it. Good visions set high standards: they are ambitious, engaging, and clarifying.

Strategy flows from mission and vision. It is an organization's long-term action plan for accomplishing its goals. The future of every organization hinges on its ability to forge a creative and workable strategy and to build company-wide commitment to it. In Chapter Twenty-Five, "Developing Strategy: The Serious Business of Play," Loizos Heracleous and Claus D. Jacobs suggest a *playful* approach to strategy development that elevates creativity, strengthens organizational culture, and fosters important leadership and team development.

With credibility, shared commitment, mission, vision, and strategy in place, business leaders are off and running. How do they stay on course? The next six chapters in Part Four suggest critical areas and issues for their attention.

People need each other to get things done. However, enduring differences and scarce resources make interdependence and collaboration difficult. Astute leaders, according to Lee G. Bolman and Terrence E. Deal, are constructive organizational politicians who know how to navigate in a world of chronic scarcity and diversity. In Chapter Twenty-Six, "The Leader as Politician: Navigating the Political Terrain," Bolman and Deal teach business leaders to develop a workable leadership agenda, build solid bases of support, and manage relationships with both allies and opponents.

Conflict is inevitable—and generative—in an inherently political world. Leaders who understand that embrace conflict as a productive opportunity for creative problem solving and "wise trade-offs" among competing organizational objectives. In Chapter Twenty-Seven, "Want Collaboration? Accept—and Actively Manage—Conflict," Jeff Weiss and Jonathan Hughes explore the natural temptation to avoid conflict, and provide strategies leaders can use to manage conflict better.

Effective leaders create and change culture, says Edgar H. Schein in Chapter Twenty-Eight, "Creating and Managing a Learning Culture: The Essence of Leadership." Managers, in contrast, work within it. Influencing corporate culture—the unique set of shared values, norms, beliefs, and actions that characterize an organization's approach to its work—is not easy. Nonetheless, Schein argues, it is the only unique thing of real importance that leaders do. In this chapter, Schein, a founding father of organizational culture studies, examines the leader's unique role in fostering a culture that facilitates learning and change.

All business leaders need to know something about managing change. They live in a world where businesses regularly face new or more challenging markets, technologies, information, environmental forces, and competitors—and where change is essential to staying alive. Chapter Twenty-Nine, "Leading Change: Why Transformation Efforts Fail," by John P. Kotter, identifies eight common mistakes in leading change and provides tested strategies to avoid them.

Effective business leaders need the big picture—the ability to see the organization as a whole, understand the contributions of individual units and departments, and act for the larger good. When they do, they assume the role of *enterprise leaders* and enable their organization to bring its full resources to its customers and services. In Chapter Thirty, "Leading at the Enterprise Level," Douglas A. Ready explores the role and function of enterprise leaders, their challenges, and organizational strategies for developing this new breed of business leader.

"Leadership without the discipline of execution is incomplete and ineffective," assert Larry Bossidy, Ram Charan, and Charles Burck in Chapter Thirty-One, "Execution: The Gap Nobody Knows." Companies are quick to blame their failures on poor strategies. More often than not, these strategies are fine. They are simply not well executed—and the authors of this chapter advise business leaders on how to change that fact. Effective leaders embrace execution as an essential responsibility. They also know that it is their job to foster more disciplined and integrated approaches to strategy development, and to embed systematic attention to implementation and accountability into the corporate culture.

The final three chapters in Part Four offer words of warning. As this volume demonstrates, leadership is complex, highly differentiated work that can challenge any leader to the core. And the life of a business leader is filled with stress: long hours, unrealistic deadlines, conflicting expectations, pressures, unanticipated problems, and overload. Temptations abound for quick fixes and shortcuts, and sheer overload contributes to poor choices and wrong turns that can derail leaders, careers, and organizations. Those forewarned about the darker side of what they might find are better able to avoid the pitfalls—or at least recognize early when they are stepping too close to the edge.

Business organizations are human enterprises, populated by individuals who respond with a range of emotions to the challenges, disruptions, pressures, and demands found every day at work. But when the emotional cards are dealt too quickly, widely, or often—as they are during nonstop change, reorganization, massive turnovers, budget crunches, or downsizing, or when working with an abusive boss—workplace pain accumulates. During times like these, organizations can be helped by compassionate insiders who take it upon themselves to ease the overload, help others work through their pain, and keep people focused in positive ways on the work at hand. These unsung heroes, claim the late Peter J. Frost and Sandra Robinson in Chapter Thirty-Two, "The Leader as Toxin Handler: Organizational Hero and Casualty," deserve praise and support. They keep the ship afloat but pay a personal price for their skills in wedding empathy with organizational problem solving. Leaders at all levels of the organization are natural magnets for these kinds of toxic situations, and they may find themselves unexpectedly in the toxin handler role. Frost and Robinson offer strategies for staying personally healthy and professionally productive.

In Chapter Thirty-Three, Barbara Kellerman examines "Bad Leadership—and Ways to Avoid It." She offers a typology of seven kinds of bad leadership, illustrating a range of ineffectiveness from simple incompetence to demonstrated evil. Leaders who know how they might go astray are better prepared to avoid the traps—or to avoid sitting complaisantly when those around them are snared.

In the Broadway musical *Wicked*, Glinda, the Good Witch of the West in the famous Land of Oz, sings, "There are bridges you cross you didn't know you crossed until you've crossed." It is easy to get caught up in the pressures and technical demands of work. And even the best leaders can find themselves drifting down a slippery slope, unsure of how they got there and where it all will end. To avoid this, business leaders need to understand the ethical implications of their choices. They face a dual ethical responsibility at work. They must be clear about the values that anchor them and they must foster a culture where ethical standards are clear and frequently discussed. In Chapter Thirty-Four, "Good or Not Bad: Standards and Ethics in Managing Change," Kim S. Cameron provides a provocative starting point for reflecting on ethical standards, the meaning of virtuous contribution, and the ethical responsibilities of leadership. Beware, advises Cameron: avoiding harm is not the same as doing good!

CHAPTER TWENTY-ONE

The First Ninety Days of Leadership

Michael Watkins

T he president of the United States gets 100 days to prove himself; you get 90. The actions you take during your first three months in a new job will largely determine whether you succeed or fail. Transitions are periods of opportunity, a chance to start afresh and make needed changes in an organization. They are also periods of acute vulnerability because you lack established working relationships and a detailed understanding of your new role. If you fail to build momentum during your transition, you will face an uphill battle from that point forward.

The stakes are obviously high. Failure in a new assignment can spell the end of a promising career. But making a successful transition is about more than just avoiding failure. Some leaders do derail (and when they do, their problems can almost always be traced to vicious cycles that developed in the first few months on the job). But for every leader who fails outright, there are many others who survive but do not realize their full potential. As a result, they lose opportunities to advance in their careers, and they endanger the health of their organizations.

This chapter is as much about *transition acceleration* as it is about failure prevention. It provides a blueprint for condensing the time it will take you to get on top of the job, regardless of your level in your organization. If you succeed in this, you will free up time to concentrate on fixing problems and exploiting opportunities in your new organization. After all, your goal should be to arrive as rapidly as possible at the breakeven point, where you are a net contributor of value to your new organization, not a net consumer. Every minute you save by being systematic about accelerating your transition is a minute you gain to build the business.

Given the stakes, it is surprising how little guidance is available to new leaders about how to transition more effectively and efficiently into new roles. There are plenty of books and articles on leadership, but few directly address transitions at all.[1] Also, excellent resources on managing organizational change exist, but most implicitly assume the change agent is already settled in the organization, with the necessary knowledge and relationships in place to plan, build support for, and carry out transformation initiatives.

The reality is that the process of leading change often occurs in tandem with a leader's transition into a new role. This chapter is intended to fill a gap in the leadership literature. It offers a blueprint for addressing the linked challenges of personal transition and organizational transformation that confront leaders in their first few months in a new job.

FUNDAMENTAL PROPOSITIONS

From observing new leaders and experimenting with methods of accelerating transitions, I have strong beliefs about the challenges of transitions and what it takes to succeed in meeting them. Five propositions form the foundation of my approach to transition acceleration.

The first proposition is that *the root causes of transition failure always lie in a pernicious interaction between the situation, with its opportunities and pitfalls, and the individual, with his or her strengths and vulnerabilities.* Failure is never just about the flaws of the new leader. Indeed, the failed leaders whom I studied had all achieved significant successes in the past. Nor is it ever just about a no-win situation in which not even a superhuman leader could have carried the day. The business situations facing leaders who derail are no tougher than those in which others succeed brilliantly. Transition failures happen when new leaders either misunderstand the essential demands of the situation or lack the skill and flexibility to adapt to them.

The second proposition is that *there are systematic methods that leaders can employ to both lessen the likelihood of failure and reach the breakeven point faster.* Early in my efforts to develop a framework for accelerating transitions at all levels, an experienced manager told me, "You can't do that." When I asked why, he said, "Because every transition is unique." This is true, of course. It is also misleading. Sure, every transition is unique if you look at its details. But viewed from a higher vantage point, we can discern types of transitions that share common features, including common traps. Consider, for example, making a transition from functional vice president to general manager. Every leader who makes this leap encounters similar challenges, such as the need to let go of reliance on functional expertise. (The transition from frontline supervisor to manager of managers represents a similar challenge at a lower level.[2]) The specific business situations that confront transitioning leaders also vary. But specific types of transition situations, such as start-ups and turnarounds, share certain features and imperatives. Further, there are fundamental principles—for example, securing early wins—that underpin success in transitions at all levels, whether one is a new supervisor or a new CEO. The key, then, is to *match your strategy to the situation.* This is a core theme to which we will return.

The third proposition is that *the overriding goal in a transition is to build momentum by creating virtuous cycles that build credibility and by avoiding getting caught in vicious cycles that damage credibility.* Leadership is about leverage. The new leader is, after all, just one person. To be successful, she will have to mobilize the energy of many others in her organization. Her vision, her expertise, her drive can serve as a seed crystal in the new organization, one that will grow exponentially into new and more productive patterns of behavior. Too often, however, the new leader behaves more like a virus: Her early actions alienate potential supporters, undermine her credibility, and stimulate defensive reactions. As a vicious cycle takes hold, the organization's immune system gets activated and the new leader is attacked by clumps of killer cells, encapsulated, and finally expelled.

The fourth proposition is that *transitions are a crucible for leadership development and should be managed accordingly.* Precisely because they strengthen diagnostic skills, demand growth and adaptation, and test personal stamina, transitions are an indispensable development experience for every company's high-potential leaders.

My fifth and final proposition is that *adoption of a standard framework for accelerating transitions can yield big returns for organizations.* Each year over half a million managers enter new positions in *Fortune* 500 companies alone.[3] Given the frequency with which people take on new jobs, and the impact of each transition on others in the organization, it helps a lot if everyone—bosses, direct reports, and peers—speaks the same "transition language." Why shouldn't every person who is getting to know a new boss employ a shared set of guidelines to build that critical relationship? Also, adopting standard approaches to learning about a new organization, securing early wins, and building coalitions translates into speedier organizational adjustments to the unavoidable stream of personnel shifts and environmental changes. Adopting a rational framework for transition acceleration translates into real bottom-line impact.

SUCCESS STRATEGIES FOR NEW LEADERS

Why is so little good advice available about accelerating transitions? In part, the answer is because there are many different kinds of transitions; thus, it is not enough to come up with general rules or one-size-fits-all advice. Consider the following pairs of transition situations. How do the definitions of success and the imperatives for making effective transitions differ in these cases?

- Promotion to a more senior role in marketing versus moving from marketing to a position as general manager of a business unit

- Moving to a new position within your existing organization versus moving to a new company

- Moving from a staff position to line management versus moving from line to staff

- Taking over a group facing very serious problems versus taking over a group widely and accurately viewed as very successful

The point? The challenges of transition acceleration vary depending on situational factors. It matters a great deal whether you are making a key career "passage" in terms of level in the organization, whether you are an insider or an outsider, whether you have formal authority, and whether you are taking over a successful or troubled group.[4] Thus, it is essential that you match your strategy to the situation you face. Practical advice has to be tailored to the situation, the level of the new leader, his or her experience with the organization, and the condition of the business.

To illustrate the power of a systematic approach to transition acceleration, consider the challenge a new leader faces in diagnosing his new organization's business situation. How does he characterize the challenges and opportunities? How does he reach consensus with his new boss and direct reports about what actions need to be taken? Without a conceptual framework to guide diagnosis and planning, this turns out to be a lot of work. It is also easy to blunder into dangerous misunderstandings with bosses or direct reports about what needs doing. Even if the new leader achieves the necessary shared understanding, he is likely to have consumed significant time and energy in the process and might have missed some important opportunities and failed to identify some ticking time bombs.

Now suppose instead that the new leader is counseled to figure out early on whether his new job is a *start-up, turnaround, realignment,* or *sustaining-success* situation. Suppose too that he has clear descriptions of the challenges and opportunities typical of each of these situations and actionable guidelines for establishing priorities in each one. What changes?

This diagnostic tool, called the STARS model (for Start-up, Turnaround, Realignment, and Sustaining success), powerfully accelerates the new leader's diagnosis of his new organization and his development of effective action plans. It also helps the new leader to more rapidly reach a shared understanding of the situation with other key players, including his boss and direct reports. Whether he is taking over an entire organization or managing a group or a short-term project, he can use this tool to accelerate his transition.

So take heart. There are structural similarities in challenges and opportunities, and corresponding guidelines—must do's and don't do's—for different types of transitional situations. The key is to engage in careful diagnosis, adapt some general principles to the demands of the situation, and create a 90-day acceleration plan for yourself. The conceptual backbone of that road map is ten key transition challenges:

1. *Promote yourself.* This doesn't mean hiring your own publicist. It means making the mental break from your old job and preparing to take charge in the new one. Perhaps the biggest pitfall you face is assuming that what has made you successful to this point in your career will continue to do so. The dangers of sticking with what you know, working extremely hard at doing it, and failing miserably are very real.

2. *Accelerate your learning.* You need to climb the learning curve as fast as you can in your new organization. This means understanding its markets, products, technologies, systems, and structures, as well as its culture and politics. Getting acquainted with a new organization can feel like drinking from a fire hose. You have to be systematic and focused about deciding what you need to learn and how you will learn it most efficiently.

3. *Match strategy to situation.* There are no universal rules for success in transitions. You need to diagnose the business situation accurately and clarify its challenges and opportunities. Start-ups, for instance—of a new product, process, plant, or a completely new business—share challenges quite different from those you would face while turning around a product, process, or plant in serious trouble. A clear diagnosis of the situation is an essential prerequisite for developing your action plan.

4. *Secure early wins.* Early wins build your credibility and create momentum. They create virtuous cycles that leverage the energy you are putting into the organization to create a pervasive sense that good things are happening. In the first few weeks, you need to identify opportunities to build personal credibility. In the first 90 days, you need to identify ways to create value, improve business results, and get to the breakeven point more rapidly.

5. *Negotiate success.* Because no other single relationship is more important, you need to figure out how to build a productive working relationship with your new boss and manage his or her expectations. This means carefully planning for a series of critical conversations about the situation, shared expectations,

leadership styles and strengths, resources, and your personal development. Crucially, it means developing and gaining consensus on your 90-day plan.

6. *Achieve alignment.* The higher you rise in an organization, the more you have to play the role of organizational architect. This means figuring out whether the organization's strategy is sound, bringing its structure into alignment with its strategy, and developing the systems and skill bases necessary to realize strategic intent.

7. *Build your team.* If you are inheriting a team, you will need to evaluate its members and perhaps restructure it to better meet the demands of the situation. Your willingness to make tough early personnel calls and your capacity to select the right people for the right positions are among the most important drivers of success during your transition. You will need to be both systematic and strategic in approaching the team-building challenge.

8. *Create coalitions.* Your success will depend on your ability to influence people outside your direct line of control. Supportive alliances, both internal and external, will be necessary to achieve your goals. You should therefore start right away to identify those whose support is essential for your success, and to figure out how to line them up on your side.

9. *Keep your balance.* In the personal and professional tumult of a transition, you will have to work hard to maintain your equilibrium and preserve your ability to make good judgments. The risks of losing perspective, getting isolated, and making bad calls are ever present during transitions. There is much you can do to accelerate your personal transition and to gain more control over your work environment. The right advice-and-counsel network is an indispensable resource.

10. *Expedite everyone.* Finally, you need to help everyone in your organization—direct reports, bosses, and peers—accelerate their own transitions. The quicker you can get your new direct reports up to speed, the more you will help your own performance. Beyond that, the benefits to the organization of systematically accelerating everyone's transitions are potentially vast.

If you succeed in meeting these core challenges, you will have a successful transition. Failure to surmount any one of them, however, is enough to cause potentially crippling problems.

Michael Watkins is professor of practice in organizational behavior at INSEAD in Fontainebleau, France, where he teaches leadership and negotiation in INSEAD's Advanced Management Program, and founder of Genesis Advisers, a transition acceleration consultancy.

What Is Our Mission?

Peter F. Drucker

~*~ Each institution exists to make a distinctive difference in the lives of individuals and in society. Making this difference is the mission—the organization's purpose and very reason for being. Each of more than one million nonprofit organizations in the United States may have a very different mission, for example, but changing lives is always the starting point and ending point. A mission cannot be impersonal; it has to have deep meaning, be something you believe in—something you know is right. A fundamental responsibility of leadership is to make sure that everybody knows the mission, understands it, and lives it.

Many years ago, I sat down with the administrators of a major hospital to think through the mission of the emergency room. As do most hospital administrators, they began by saying, "Our mission is health care." And that's the wrong definition. The hospital does not take care of health; the hospital takes care of illness. It took us a long time to come up with the very simple and (most people thought) too-obvious statement that the emergency room was there to give assurance to the afflicted. To do that well, you had to know what really went on. And, to the surprise of the physicians and nurses, the function of a good emergency room in their community was to tell eight out of ten people there was nothing wrong that a good night's sleep wouldn't fix. "You've been shaken up." Or "the baby has the flu. All right, it's got convulsions, but there is nothing seriously wrong with the child." The doctors and nurses gave assurance.

We worked it out, but it sounded awfully obvious. Yet translating the mission into action meant that everybody who came in was seen by a qualified person in less than a minute. The first objective was to see everybody, almost immediately—because that is the only way to give assurance.

IT SHOULD FIT ON A T-SHIRT

The effective mission statement is short and sharply focused. It should fit on a T-shirt. The mission says why you do what you do, not the means by which you do it. The mission is broad, even eternal, yet directs you to do the right things now and into the future so that everyone in the organization can say, "What I am doing contributes to the goal." So it must be clear, and it must inspire. Every board member, volunteer, and staff person should be able to see the mission and say, "Yes. This is something I want to be remembered for."

To have an effective mission, you have to work out an exacting match of your opportunities, competence, and commitment. Every good mission statement reflects all three. You look first at the outside environment. The organization that starts from the inside and then tries to find places to put its resources is going to fritter itself away. Above all, it will focus on yesterday. Demographics change. Needs change. You must search out the accomplished facts—things that have already happened—that present challenges and opportunities for the organization. Leadership has no choice but to anticipate the future and attempt to mold it, bearing in mind that whoever is content to rise with the tide will also fall with it. It is not given to mortals to do any of these things well, but, lacking divine guidance, you must still assess where your opportunity lies.

Look at the state of the art, at changing conditions, at competition, the funding environment, at gaps to be filled. The hospital isn't going to sell shoes, and it's not going into education on a big scale. It's going to take care of the sick. But the specific aim may change. Things that are of primary importance now may become secondary or totally irrelevant very soon. With the limited resources you have—and I don't just mean people and money but also competence—where can you dig in and make a difference? Where can you set a new standard of performance? What really inspires your commitment?

WHY DOES THE ORGANIZATION EXIST?

Defining the mission is difficult, painful, and risky. But it alone enables you to set goals and objectives and go to work. Unless the mission is explicitly expressed, clearly understood, and supported by every member of the organization, the enterprise is at the mercy of events. Decision makers throughout will decide and act on the basis of different, incompatible, and conflicting ideas. They will pull in opposing directions without even being aware of their divergence, and your performance is what suffers. Common vision, understanding, and unity of direction and effort of the entire organization depend on defining the mission and what the mission should be.

MAKE PRINCIPLED DECISIONS

One cautionary note: Never subordinate the mission in order to get money. If there are opportunities that threaten the integrity of the organization, you must say no. Otherwise, you sell your soul. I sat in on a discussion at a museum that had been offered a donation of important art on conditions that no self-respecting museum could possibly accept. Yet a few board members said, "Let's take the donation. We can change the conditions down the road." "No, that's unconscionable!" others responded, and the board fought over the issue. They finally agreed they would lose too much by compromising basic principles to please a donor. The board forfeited some very nice pieces of sculpture, but core values had to come first.

Consider this wonderful sentence from a sermon by that great poet and religious philosopher of the seventeenth century, John Donne: "Never start with tomorrow to reach eternity. Eternity is not being reached by small steps." We start with the long range and then feed back and say, "What do we do today?" The ultimate test is not the beauty of the mission statement. The ultimate test is your performance.

—◈—

The late Peter F. Drucker was professor of social science and management at Claremont Graduate University, a best-selling author, and consultant to the world's leading corporations and nonprofit organizations.

CHAPTER TWENTY-THREE

The Power and Creativity of a Transforming Vision

James MacGregor Burns

If you're teaching a class in leadership and want to fire up a lively discussion, just pose this old chestnut of a question: "Was Adolf Hitler a leader?"[1] The last time I tried this, in an honors class, a woman student vehemently answered, "YES." Evil though he was, she declared, he mirrored the hopes and hates of the German people, he won elections, and he fulfilled his promises by changing Germany along the lines his followers wanted—so how could he not be called a leader? She had the class all but convinced and almost had me, too. Almost.

It was not, of course, that she was in any way pro-Hitler, who stands as perhaps the most universally detested man in all of human history. The problem is confusion not about Hitler but about the essence of leadership. Is leadership a neutral thing, a mechanical process or power potential available equally to a Hitler and a Gandhi? Or should it be defined as a *good* thing? According to Joanne Ciulla, a leading authority on the ethics of leadership, the "question of what constitutes a good leader lies at the heart of the public debate on leadership."[2]

I see three types of standards or norms as they relate to leadership. *Virtue* refers to the "old-fashioned" norms of conduct—habits of action—such as chastity, sobriety, cleanliness, honesty in personal relationships, self-control. These normally develop early in life, especially in the home, under, as child psychologist Robert Coles has insisted, exemplary parental leadership.[3] Children learn the rules and sometimes take them quite strictly, turning them back on parents with the cry, "but it's not *fair!*" and so provide a little leadership themselves. *Ethics* reflect modes of more formal and transactional conduct—integrity, promise keeping, trustworthiness, reciprocity, accountability—supremely expressed in the golden rule. In leadership terms, as leadership scholar Joseph C. Rost has written, ethics are the criteria for "the ways leaders and followers interact as they attempt to influence one another and other people."[4] By transforming *values,* I mean such lofty public principles as order, liberty, equality (including brotherhood and sisterhood), justice, the pursuit of happiness.

Politicians all too often offer vivid examples of the distinctions among virtues, ethics, and public values. Franklin Roosevelt as a young man transgressed the virtue of marital fidelity and later as president violated a cardinal ethical value when he lied to the country about the extent to which the American navy was aiding British ships against Nazi submarines, at a time when the United States was supposed to be neutral. Bill Clinton was roundly criticized for his unvirtuous conduct with a young White House intern. Still, he was found more gravely at fault—and was impeached—for lying about it. In this case the American public seemed to understand the difference between virtue and ethics.

Did FDR's and Clinton's lapses in virtue trump their transforming values? Many say that leaders' failings in virtue and ethics send wrong messages and can even influence people's behavior. Others argue that these messages are superficial and ephemeral, that the real test of presidents' values lies in their degree of success as leaders, in their realization of public values, in the good they did for the country. FDR led in the transformation of American government and society. Could Clinton rightly claim that his own leadership was successful enough—produced changes that benefitted the people—to neutralize his failings? We can wait for historians with longer perspectives to deal with that question.

So *was* Hitler a leader, even a transforming leader? Certainly he "transformed" Germany! But by what standards could his rulership be measured? Clearly he would not be described as virtuous or ethical except by Nazi standards. His own "higher" vision was to restore order in the increasingly turbulent Germany of the early 1930s and then create a "Greater Germany" that would dominate Europe if not the world. In fact he left his country in defeat and devastation, so he was a terrible failure measured even by his own standards. If we test him instead by

Enlightenment values of liberty and equality, he was a fanatical enemy of both. Nor did Hitler achieve another of what I call transforming values, one that perhaps embodies the others: he failed—utterly—to create for the people of Germany lasting, meaningful opportunities for the pursuit of happiness. My answer, then, to the question I put to my students: Hitler ruled the German people, but he did not lead them.

Transforming leaders define public values that embrace the supreme and enduring principles of a people. These values are the shaping ideas behind constitutions and laws and their interpretation. They are the essence of declarations of independence, revolutionary proclamations, momentous statements by leaders that go to the core meaning of events, that define what is at stake, such as the Gettysburg Address. Such values are not ordinarily part of the daily discourse of the citizenry. But at testing times when people confront the possibilities—and threat—of great change, powerful foundational values are evoked. They are the inspiration and guide to people who pursue and seek to shape change, and they are the standards by which the realization of the highest intentions is measured. Transforming values lie at the heart of transforming leadership, determining whether leadership indeed can be transforming.

THE TRANSFORMING VISION

On the face of it, nothing is more mysterious than the sources of creative ideas, unless it is the linkage between those ideas and the process of leadership. In that process, creativity appears as a response to frustrated wants and needs. But if frustration is the spur, its resolution takes many forms. The potential for creativity may be crushed from the start because of despotic parents, powerful pressures for conformity and harmony, religious or ideological fervor that bars independent thinking. Or creative thinking may be nurtured among sympathetic friends and colleagues who, however, weaken or flatten out its force and novelty, whether because of constraints on their own vision or in order to win wider acceptance of new ideas.

Creativity also breaks through restraints, most transformationally, perhaps, in those bursts of inspiration so contrary to conventional thinking that they seem to come from nowhere. Such innovative uncommon sense transcends routine problem solving to address the deep human needs and crises from which it emerges.

Crisis is the prime source of transforming creativity, as when familiar meanings become exhausted or debased or inadequate to account for severe changes or threats of change. Or meanings may have become the preserve of a subgroup or elite who wield them to exclude alternatives that might challenge their dominance. In conditions of what political scientist Peter C. Sederberg has called "explanatory collapse,"[5] real, growing wants are ignored or delegitimated, defined out of existence. Values such as liberty and equality are proclaimed while people are neither free nor equal. Forms of justice cloak arbitrary power. Creative leadership in the American Revolution, for example, was spurred by the yawning divide between the professed values of the ruling British—representation in government, say—and their actual treatment of the colonials.

Transformational creativity can flourish amid such tensions. Innovative political theorists, wrote political scientist Sheldon Wolin, were motivated "by a profound belief that the world had become deranged," affording "an opportunity for a theory to reorder" it.[6] Conventional restraints are loosened as new explanations are sought. The unthinkable becomes thinkable, perhaps even imperative.

Sensitivity to deep conflict between accepted meanings and actualities—and frustration at the inability to reconcile the two—is creativity's precondition. Cognitive dissonance, as social psychologist Leon Festinger found, is a "motivating state"[7] for change. It produces a powerful need to reduce or to eliminate doubt, perplexity, contradiction, incongruity, and other conceptual conflicts through a search for new explanations. Or, as the Czech playwright and, later, president Václav Havel described his struggles as a dissident against a regime of topsy-turvy values, "The deeper the experience of an absence of meaning—in other words, of absurdity—the more energetically meaning is sought."[8]

As the creative mind breaks down the "institutionalization of hypocrisy," sociologist Kenneth Keniston wrote in a study of the American New Left and hippies, "the universal gap between principle and practice appears in all of its nakedness."[9] This recognition is only a beginning. Creative leadership is more than a critique. The "decomposition" of old meanings opens "new spaces and new prospects for action"[10] where the creative mind can roam to find fresh and vital answers to basic questions amid complexity, conflict, and change. The creative insight is, in short, transforming. It might raise a fundamental challenge to an existing paradigm or system, calling for its overthrow and replacement, or it might call for a deep restructuring, or the inclusion of significant excluded elements, or perhaps a revitalization, a new birth of "founding principles."

So the spark of creative leadership is both destructive and constructive, through a process that analysts of collective action call "framing work." The frame refers to a value-laden "condensation" of the meanings and assumptions that underlie our sense both of society and of our own place in it. A frame is what we take for granted as we interpret the way things are, as though it were God-given or natural or at least beyond our own making—until we are given strong reason to question it. Creative leadership, then, "re-frames" meanings to close the gap between ideas and actualities.

Creative leadership re-frames values above all, as the highest-order and most potentially transformational "condensations" of our sense of the world and ourselves. Its critique of the gap between wants or values and actualities involves moral judgment, while its remedy—its vision of what might be—is grounded in the fulfillment of a moral purpose, in bringing values to life, and its achievement is measured, finally, by the same standards it has used to condemn the old regime: fulfillment of the principles it professes.

Re-framing means the transformation of values. Thomas Rochon has outlined three ways of values-change: "value conversion," where the "new valuations" of what is important, just, or legitimate "contradict and replace the old"; "value connection," meaning the creation of a "conceptual link between phenomena previously thought to be unconnected"; and "value creation," as with the emergence of "conservation" as a new value during Theodore Roosevelt's presidency.[11] Social movement scholar Sidney Tarrow points out that new meanings are not "fabricated out of whole cloth," but blend "inherited and invented fibers" to create a new frame.[12] But all transforming values, new or old, are deeply and freshly dyed in fundamental human wants.

The *philosophes* of the Enlightenment gave new meaning to "equality," at once condemning the institutional inequalities of the ancient régime and opening vast new possibilities for change. The French revolutionaries elevated "fraternity" to the status of a supreme value, thus transforming the meaning of community and nation. "Happiness" apart, perhaps, the American revolutionaries did not innovate values so much as they revitalized those that were their inheritance, infusing with fresh power the transforming civic values the British had tarnished and overturned.

For creativity to become leadership, however, conceptual transformation is not enough. As scientists must go beyond "revolutions on paper" and put their ideas to the test in a struggle to win acceptance by their peers, all the more so must creative leadership. Leadership is a social phenomenon, and leaders are "intimately tied to other people and the effects of their actions on them."[13] According to Wolin, the groundbreaking political theorists were motivated by "the ideal of an order subject to human control and one that could be transfigured through a combination of thought and action."[14] They intended "not simply to alter the way men look at the world, but to alter the world."[15] Plato, Machiavelli, Hobbes, Marx—all considered their new ideas to be guides to healing their sick societies. They meant to *lead*.

So the ultimate test of creative leadership lies not only in having a new idea but in bringing it to life, accomplishing the real-world change it promises. To do so, the would-be leader must reach out to others for help. But would-be followers will respond only if the new frame articulated by creative leadership speaks directly to them, to their underlying wants, discontents, and hopes. They, too, as Sederberg noted, must "experience something of an explanatory collapse."[16] They, too, must know the "aha!" moment of realization, grasp the urgency of the need for change, see its possibility, and envision its direction. They are transformed in a way closely parallel to the earlier experience of the emergent leader. But transforming leadership mobilizes only those who are, if latently, ready to be mobilized, and then only if the frame is true to their wants.

The "truth" of a transforming frame is in its potency, its ability to strike a deep chord. A resonant frame can liberate a person from the isolation of frustrated, unacknowledged wants, into the realm of new and shared meanings, to become a "reflective participant"[17] in what creativity scholar Robert Paul Weiner described as a collective effort to shape and reshape those meanings "as they grow and change through the interaction of the participants and in the crucible of theory and praxis."[18]

At their best, creative thought and action engender, for leaders and followers together, the conviction that the reality of their situation is not, in the words of the great Brazilian educator and theorist of liberation Paulo Freire, "a closed world from which there is no exit," but "a limiting situation which they can transform,"[19] a mobilizing and empowering faith in the collaborative struggle for real change.

—◦◦◦—

James MacGregor Burns, professor emeritus at Williams College, is the Pulitzer Prize–winning presidential biographer, a pioneer in the study of leadership, and senior scholar at the James MacGregor Burns Academy of Leadership at the University of Maryland.

CHAPTER TWENTY-FOUR

Finding the Right Vision

Burt Nanus

> *Do not worry about holding high position; worry*
> *rather about playing your proper role.*
>
> *—Confucius*

When I was serving as director of the University of Southern California's Center for Futures Research, I was visited by a senior executive of a fast-growing food manufacturing company. He was concerned about the future of his company. "Are your sales or profits declining?" I asked. "On the contrary," he replied, "they've never been better." "Do you have a problem with marketing or product obsolescence?" I suggested. "No, our product position just seems to be getting stronger each year." "Well, then, are you worried about keeping your technological edge or finding good workers or meeting a challenge from foreign competition?" I wondered. "Not at all," he said, "we're the best in our industry."

"Look here," I finally said with some exasperation, "just what is it that's bothering you?" "Well," he explained, "that's just it. Everything is going so well that I'm getting uneasy. Maybe we've just been lucky until now. Maybe I'm missing something. Or maybe there's something just over the horizon that will clobber us. Besides, when things were tough, I was so busy managing crises that I never had time to think about the future. I used to believe that if everything's going well, leave it alone, or as the old adage says, 'If it ain't broke, don't fix it.' Now I know that's wrong. The best time to try something new, to take risks, to move off in a different direction is in good times, not bad. Isn't that what leadership is all about—fixing things that aren't broken?"

Of course, he was right on the mark. The cause of my visitor's concern soon became clear. As a leader, he sensed he might have to provide a new direction for his organization. The old vision, the one originally provided by the founder of the company, had been spectacularly correct and brought the firm to its current high level of success. But the world was changing, and my visitor wondered whether the original vision would still provide the right direction over the next decade. He was concerned, properly so, with the question "what's next, and why?" He was starting the search for a new vision.

His concern was anything but frivolous. Progress in organizations, like all human progress, is driven by the idealism and optimism captured in a persuasive and appealing vision of the future. In fact, Margaret Mead, the great anthropologist, found this to be a universal human trait, as true for primitive tribes, nomads, and subsistence farmers as for the most industrialized communities in the world. In her own eloquent words: "From comparative materials, it seems quite clear that the utopias men live by are of vital importance in such mundane matters as whether they will struggle to preserve the identity of their society, their class, their religion, or their vocation; whether they will plant trees which take two lifetimes to mature; whether they will take thought to stop the forests from being depleted, the good soil from being washed into the sea, or the gene pool from becoming exposed to too much radiation" (Mead, 1971, p. 44).

But not just any vision will do. Strong leaders want to find that special vision that will shift their organizations into overdrive, that will speed things up in the right direction while conserving energy and power. To be effective, to truly inspire and motivate excellence and achievement in organizations, leaders must find the right vision from among the many good and bad possibilities always available. The purpose of this chapter is to provide some guidance in making that choice.

PROPERTIES OF A GOOD VISION

If your childhood was like mine, you dreaded the inevitable question from well-meaning friends and relatives: "and what do you want to be when you grow up?" How in the world were we supposed to know?

When I was small, I didn't even know what the possibilities were. Once I saw a firefighter on a big red truck and immediately that was what I wanted to be. The next week I'd want to be the cowboy I'd seen in a movie or a favorite teacher or a shortstop for the New York Yankees. As I grew older, the images proliferated. I thought about being a lawyer like my Uncle Leon, an astronaut, an architect, the governor of a state, a mathematician, or maybe president of a big company. The trouble was, I hadn't the slightest idea what people really did in those jobs, and I knew there were many other careers I hadn't even heard of.

Images are like that. They explode inside your head and can dazzle and overwhelm you with a collage of apparently limitless possibilities. But of course, most of us never seriously take any steps to become an astronaut or a professional athlete. Most of the images that appear in our brains are recognized as unrealistic, unattainable, uninformed, or undesirable. They soon lose their power to feed our fantasies or motivate our behaviors. They are not the right visions, the ones that we expect to make a difference in our lives.

So what are we looking for in a vision? To start with, we need to acknowledge that a vision is a mental model of a future state of a process, a group, or an organization. As such, it deals with a world that exists only in the imagination, a world built upon plausible speculations, fabricated from what we hope are reasonable assumptions about the future, and heavily influenced by our own judgments of what is possible and worthwhile. A vision portrays a fictitious world that cannot be observed or verified in advance and that, in fact, may never become reality. It is a world whose very existence requires an act of faith.

Does this seem too flimsy a fabric upon which to weave our tapestry of intentions? Would you, like many leaders, rather make decisions solely on the basis of history? Consider, then, that history itself is much like a vision—only facing backward. In its own way, history is also a mental model of questionable accuracy and frequent reformulation. After all, the events and people described by the historian no longer exist, and some, like King Arthur and Robin Hood, may never have existed. The mental construct we call history is nearly always based on secondary sources that are woefully fragmented and incomplete. The historian examines a mass of incomplete raw material, selects from among the supposed "facts" those that fit a particular interpretation of events, adds a healthy dose of speculation about all the things that may have happened for which no evidence exists, and tries to weave together a story that purports to tell not just what happened but also why it happened and what resulted.

If you still want to think of history as "reality" you have only to think of any recent public event now fading into history—say, the Kennedy assassination, the Watergate break-in, or the Iran-Contra affair. Despite the minute scrutiny of thousands of distinguished scholars, journalists, and jurists and hundreds of thousands of pages of testimony and interpretation, there are still large domains of uncertainty about exactly what happened in these events, why they occurred, and what their long-range consequences may be. And these were sensational, widely covered, intensely scrutinized events! What about the many developments that are not even noticed today, much less recorded, that will become part of the "factual" record only in retrospect, perhaps a hundred years from now, when historians try to reconstruct what happened in the late twentieth century as we have tried to understand the fall of Rome?

So it is clear that history, like vision, is also a mental model. For all its pretensions to reality, history is heavily conjectural, full of judgments and values, and frequently reflects the historian's desire to influence today's policies. And, as we've just discussed, even our knowledge of the present is necessarily incomplete.

Thus, we may well wonder whether these mental constructs—"history" and "current events"—are really that much more substantial bases on which to act than a plausible vision of the future. From the perspective of leadership, they are not, for compared with history or current events, a vision is a mental construct that we have within our power to transform into reality. In fact, a vision is the only form of mental model that people and organizations can bring into being through their commitment and actions, and therein lies its usefulness and its power.

A second property of all visions is that they are idealistic, what Margaret Mead called utopian. A vision has no power to inspire or energize people and no ability to set a new standard or attract commitment unless it offers a view of the future that is clearly and demonstrably better for the organization, for the people in the organization, and/or for the society within which the organization operates. Often the vision is something entirely new—not a variation on existing activities, not a copy of what some other organization is doing—but something genuinely new, an innovative departure that clearly represents progress and is a step forward. The vision, in short, must be manifestly desirable, a bold and worthy challenge for those who accept it.

So any vision is a mental model of a desirable or idealistic future for the organization. But beyond that, what about the better visions, those that have the ability to renew or transform an organization? Consider Toyota's dream of producing a vehicle—later called the Lexus—engineered to go beyond the existing standards of high-performance luxury automobiles. Or consider Walt Disney's vision, as he described it, for a new kind of amusement park:

> The idea of Disneyland is a simple one. It will be a place for people to find happiness and knowledge. It will be a place for parents and children to spend pleasant times in one another's company: a place for teachers and pupils to discover greater ways of understanding and education. Here the older generation can recapture the nostalgia of days gone by, and the younger generation can savor the challenge of the future. Here will be the wonders of Nature and Man for all to see and understand. Disneyland will be based upon and dedicated to the ideals, the dreams and hard facts that have created America. And it will be uniquely equipped to dramatize these dreams and facts and send them forth as a source of courage and inspiration to all the world.
>
> Disneyland will be something of a fair, an exhibition, a playground, a community center, a museum of living acts, and a showplace of beauty and magic. It will be filled with the accomplishments, the joys and hopes of the world we live in. And it will remind us and show us how to make those wonders part of our own lives [Thomas, 1976, pp. 246–247].

Powerful and transforming visions like these tend to have special properties:

- They are *appropriate for the organization and for the times.* They fit in terms of the organization's history, culture, and values, are consistent with the organization's present situation, and provide a realistic and informed assessment of what is attainable in the future. This is not to suggest that the organization will not be changed by the vision. It almost certainly will be, perhaps quite radically. But if the vision is not appropriate for the organization, the time, cost, and pain of transformation may be so great as to make implementation of the vision all but impossible. In this case, a totally new organization might be a better choice, as IBM found when it decided to enter the personal computer business.

- They *set standards of excellence and reflect high ideals.* They depict the organization as a responsible community with a sense of integrity that strengthens and uplifts everyone in it.

- They *clarify purpose and direction.* They are persuasive and credible in defining what the organization wants to make happen and, therefore, what are legitimate aspirations for people in the organization. They provide agendas that create focus and hold out hope and promise of a better tomorrow.

- They *inspire enthusiasm and encourage commitment.* They widen the leader's support base by reflecting the needs and aspirations of many stakeholders, transcending differences in race, age, gender, and other demographic characteristics, and drawing stakeholders into a community of concerns about the future of the organization.

- They are *well articulated and easily understood.* They are unambiguous enough to serve as a guide to strategy and action and to be internalized by those whose efforts are needed to turn the vision into reality.

- They *reflect the uniqueness of the organization,* its distinctive competence, what it stands for, and what it is able to achieve.

- They are *ambitious.* They represent undisputed progress and expand the organization's horizons. Often, they call for sacrifice and emotional investment by followers, which are forthcoming because of the inherent attractiveness of the vision.

Visions that have these properties challenge and inspire people in the organization and help align their energies in a common direction. They prevent people from being overwhelmed by immediate problems because they help distinguish what is truly important from what is merely interesting. In a sense, these visions program the mind to selectively pay attention to the things that really matter.

Such visions also play a key role in designing the future by serving as the front end of a strategy formulation process. When Toyota articulated its Lexus vision—that is, to produce a new line of cars that exceeded the then-existing standards of high-performance luxury automobiles—it still needed a strategy for attaining the vision. The vision provided the direction, but the strategy provided the frame-work for getting there. Among other things, the strategy undoubtedly included objectives relating to the intended technical quality and per-formance of the car, some marketing and production goals, a refor-mulation of supplier and distribution arrangements, and carefully drawn financial projections.

A good strategy may be indispensable in coordinating manage-ment decisions and preparing for contingencies, but a strategy has cohesion and legitimacy only in the context of a clearly articulated and widely shared vision of the future. A strategy is only as good as the vision that guides it, which is why purpose and intentions tend to be more powerful than plans in directing organizational behavior. As Yogi Berra is reported to have said, "If you don't know where you're going, you might end up someplace else."

WHAT VISION IS NOT

You might conclude from the preceding section that a vision is some sort of magic elixir that cures all organizational ills. This is unfortu-nately not the case. For every Lexus, there may be a score of Edsels. No matter how well formulated, a vision can fail if it is inappropriate or if it is poorly communicated or implemented. Sometimes visions fail because they were overly ambitious or unrealistic from the start. Sometimes they are overtaken by events and become obsolete before they can be realized.

For a balanced view of what vision can and cannot accomplish, we must be clear on what vision is not:

- While a vision is about the future, it is *not a prophecy* (although after the fact it may seem so). If I say my vision is to become a great writer, I certainly am not predicting that I will become one, no matter how much my vision may shape my style of writing or my approach to a subject. Although there have been visions so powerful that those who first offered them seem in retrospect to be prophets—for example, Mahatma Gandhi's vision of an independent India or Henry Ford's vision of a car in every garage—these visions had power not because they were prophecies but because of the way they captured the imagina-tion of others, mobilized resources, and reshaped the reality of their times.

- A vision is *not a mission.* To state that an organization has a mission is to state its purpose, not its direction. For example, the mission of a farmer hasn't changed in thousands of years: it is to grow food and bring it to market at a price that pays for all the costs of production and provides an acceptable standard of living (or profit) for the farmer. However, one particular farmer might have a vision of passing on to his children a farm with twice the acreage he currently has, while another may dream about opening a canning operation on her property, and a third may aim to be a pioneer in growing organic vegetables.

- A vision is *not factual.* It doesn't exist and may never be realized as originally imagined. It deals not with reality but with possible and desirable futures. It is full of speculation, assumptions, and value judgments. In organizations that depend heavily on the decision-making model of fact gathering, performance measurement, and verification, vision may seem to be an anachronism. But the absence of a factual basis for vision does not necessarily imply a lack of information or substance. Visions should be the well-informed results of systematic processes that ensure some degree of comprehensiveness and confidence.

- A vision *cannot be true or false.* It can be evaluated only relative to other possible directions for the organization. That is, it can be seen as better or worse, more or less rational, safer or riskier, more or less appropriate, or even just good enough.

- A vision is *not static,* enunciated once for all time. The unraveling of the Soviet Union is eloquent testimony to the dangers of staying with a vision—in this case, the Marxist-Leninist ideal—long after it has proven wrong and counterproductive. Rather, vision formulation should be seen as a dynamic process, an integral part of the ongoing task of visionary leadership. Part of the genius of the American system is an electoral process that forces the testing and redevelopment of a vision for the future of the nation every four years.

- A vision is *not a constraint on actions,* except for those inconsistent with the vision. Instead, it is designed to unleash and then orient the energies of the organization in a common direction, to open up opportunities rather than to restrict them, and to serve as a catalyst for the changes needed to ensure the long-term success of the venture.

Thus far, we have been discussing what vision is, what it is not, and how to tell the difference between good and bad visions. But where does a vision come from? Is it simply a dream born mysteriously in the mind of a leader, a rare stroke of genius, or can it be the result of a considered and systematic process?

WHERE VISION COMES FROM

My wife and I like to travel. Every so often, we'll come to a building or a town square that quite literally stops us in our tracks. It might be a cathedral, an unusual house, or maybe a particularly beautiful park or public monument. As we gaze at the arresting sight, I always wonder, "How in the world did the architect or artist think of that?" After all, where there is now what seems such a perfectly natural and obvious part of the landscape was at one time just an empty lot full of weeds.

Every remarkable artistic achievement starts as nothing more than a dream, usually of one individual, and not infrequently contested and ridiculed by friends and colleagues. Such a dream is a vision not much different from one a leader develops for an organization, for leadership itself is also an art form. Visionary leaders, like artists, are astute and perhaps idiosyncratic observers and interpreters of the real world. Leaders, like artists, try to rearrange the materials at their disposal—that is, the people, processes, and structures of an organization—to create a new and more powerful order that will succeed and endure over time. And the best visionary leaders, like the best artists, are always seeking to communicate directly and viscerally a vision of the world that will resonate with the deepest meanings of people and cause them to embrace it as worthwhile and elevating.

Denise Shekerjian, in an excellent study of forty winners of the MacArthur "genius grants," concluded that the great ideas of these artists, scientists, and social movers and shakers were born of a combination of instinct and judgment. She says: "What intuition provides is an inkling, an itch, a yearning, a mist of possibilities. What judgment provides is structure, assessment, form, purpose. Blend them together—and in the example of Robert Coles [Pulitzer Prize–winning author and child psychiatrist], season this marriage with a strong dose of moral imagination—and you will begin to recognize the tiny, pert buds of opportunity that, if pursued, may well lead to a dramatic flowering of the most creative work of your career" (1990, p. 170).

So where does a leader's vision come from? Vision is composed of one part foresight, one part insight, plenty of imagination and judgment, and often, a healthy dose of chutzpah. It occurs to a well-informed open mind, a mind prepared by a lifetime of learning and experience, one sharply attuned to emerging trends and developments in the world outside of the organization. Creativity certainly plays an important part, but it is a creativity deeply rooted in the reality of the organization and its possibilities.

We mustn't pretend that vision is always the result of an orderly process. It often entails a messy, introspective process difficult to explain even by the person who conceives the vision. Vision formation is not a task for those who shun complexity or who are uncomfortable with ambiguity. Still, there are some basic elements that are part of all attempts to formulate vision. Specifically, they are information, values, frameworks, and insight.

While vision is in a very real sense a dream, it is a special kind of dream built upon information and knowledge. The art of developing an effective vision starts with asking the right questions—and asking lots of them.

Values are the principles or standards that help people decide what is worthwhile or desirable. They are abstract ideas that embody notions of what truly matters, or should matter, in the performance of an organization and in the ways an organization satisfies its responsibilities to its constituencies—workers, customers, investors, and the rest of society.

Your values as a leader guide your selection of a vision in a variety of ways. Values influence the questions you ask about possible directions. They guide the choice of information you seek to answer the questions and how the information is evaluated. They determine which possible visions you consider, what criteria you use to select among them, and what measures of success you use to judge whether your organization is moving toward its vision.

Information and values are the raw materials within a structure or framework that allows you to see the big picture. One important part of that framework is your mental model of how your organization and its industry or peer group operates. Another part is a set of scenarios that captures your understanding of how the outside world may change in the future and what implications those changes may have for your organization.

It all comes together as a result of synthesis or insight. Sometimes a powerful intuition and drive in the hands of a strong leader are all that is needed. For example, the growth and shape of Southern California is often attributed to Harry Chandler and the Chandler family, who controlled the *Los Angeles Times* and were major landowners in the area. Chandler sensed what would work, decided what would be the best developmental path for Los Angeles and the region, and then simply made it happen. As Halberstam describes it: "They are Chandlers; their bustling prosperous region exists to an uncommon degree because they envisioned it that way. They did not so much foster the growth of Southern California as, more simply, invent it. . . . The city is horizontal instead of vertical because they were rich in land, and horizontal was good for them, good for real estate. There is a port because they dreamed of a port. . . .[Harry Chandler] was a dreamer, and he was always dreaming of the future of Los Angeles, of growth and profit; the commercial future of Los Angeles, tied as it was to the commercial future of Harry Chandler" (1979, p. 136).

Even here, however, one detects a considerable amount of calculation at work, the fruit of analysis and contemplation (if not blatant self-interest) rather than intuition or insight all alone. Intuition is a creative process still somewhat mysterious and poorly understood. However, intuition rarely stands alone and can be assisted by several structured methods.

Finally, the vision must be successfully implemented. As Warren Bennis and I said in an earlier work: "In the end, the leader may be the one who articulates the vision and gives it legitimacy, who expresses the vision in captivating rhetoric that fires the imagination and emotions of followers, who—through the vision—empowers others to make the decisions that get things done. But if the organization is to be successful, the image must grow out of the needs of the entire organization and must be 'claimed' or 'owned' by all the important actors" (1985, p. 109).

There are few things sadder for an organization than an exciting vision that is poorly implemented. Remington Rand, for example, entered the computer business more than forty years ago because it saw the revolutionary potential for such devices. For a short time, it virtually owned the world computer market, but it was a classic case of a great vision poorly implemented. Many years passed before Remington Rand's executives fully accepted the new machine and committed the company to the technical support, marketing, service, and other functions necessary to make computers truly useful for customers. And by the time they did, IBM, which saw the vision much later than Remington Rand but implemented it much better, had obtained an unassailable market advantage.

GETTING STARTED

Let's assume you are setting out to develop a new vision for your organization. Where do you start?

- Learn everything you can about your organization, similar organizations, and your industry. There is no substitute for being well informed on the strengths and vulnerabilities of your own group and on the challenges and opportunities in its environment.

- Bring your major constituencies (for example, customers, investors, the local community, the board of directors, unions, suppliers, and so on) into the visioning process, at first simply through informal conversations and later by soliciting formal suggestions. At a minimum, make sure you completely understand their expectations and needs and the dependence of your organization on their support.

- Keep a playful open mind as you explore the options for a new vision. The correct sense of direction for your organization may be obvious, but don't bet on it! After all, everybody in the industry may be moving in a certain direction, but that doesn't mean it is right for your organization. Indeed, that in itself may be sufficient reason to set off down another path.

- There is no need—and certainly no expectation—that your final choice of vision be your own original idea. Often some of the best ideas for new directions float up from the depths of the organization, but only if they are sought and welcomed when they arrive. Encourage inputs from all your colleagues and subordinates, involve them in the visioning process, and let them know how much you appreciate them all the way through.

- If you are new to the organization, don't disparage the previous leadership or its vision. Everyone knows that you'll be doing some things differently, and they will expect some changes in direction. Instead, show that you understand and appreciate the existing vision, praise your predecessors for bringing the organization to its current stage, and promise to move on, retaining the best of the past but taking full benefit of expected opportunities in the future.

Ultimately, no matter how much help you receive, no matter if the vision was first developed by others and merely adopted and embraced by you, your success as a visionary leader will be measured by the effectiveness of your vision in moving the organization forward. That is what leaders are paid for and, more important, why they are respected and followed.

—◦◦◦—

Burt Nanus is professor of management emeritus at the University of Southern California and author of multiple books on leadership and management.

CHAPTER TWENTY-FIVE

Developing Strategy
The Serious Business of Play

Loizos Heracleous
Claus D. Jacobs

> *You can discover more about a person in an*
> *hour of play than in a year of conversation.*
>
> *—Plato*

Strategy development in organizations is serious business. The origin of the term *strategy* in the work of ancient Greek army generals, or *strategoi*, underlies the traditional view of strategy as comprehensive analysis and planning that is rational, analytical, objective, and top down. With this prevailing emphasis on left-brain activity and ways of thinking, the lack of systematic development or widespread use of emergent, right-brain ways of approaching strategy development and strategic leadership should come as no surprise. Leaders in search of such creative ways to foster innovative thinking and strategizing within their organizations have too often been left to luck, coincidence, or their own devices. What options are available to support their efforts?

This chapter examines the important role of play in creative strategizing and leadership effectiveness. We begin by exploring the

---

This chapter develops ideas originally presented in L. Heracleous and C. D. Jacobs, "The Serious Business of Play," *MIT Sloan Management Review*, Fall 2005, pp. 19–20.

links between play and effective strategy and describe how current art- and humanities-based approaches to leadership development and a play-based strategizing activity can bridge false dichotomies in management thinking that limit creativity. Then we compare strategizing through serious play and traditional approaches and discuss the organizational benefits of learning to play with serious intent. We concludes with advice on ways to play seriously in conducting organizational planning and with a discussion of the important role of leadership in this process.

LINKING PLAY, LEADERSHIP DEVELOPMENT, AND STRATEGIZING

Developmental psychology and anthropology have long known that play enhances critical cognitive and interpretive skills and engenders a sense of emotional fulfillment at every stage of human development (Sutton-Smith, 1997; Winnicott, 1971). Play is also inherently group or community oriented and as such contributes in important ways to the development of shared language, identity, and social practices among those involved (Huizinga, 1950). Play provides a safe environment conducive to surfacing, debating, and diffusing assumptions, values, and ideas—its potency and energy deriving from the imaginative, fresh, and experimental issues that surface and from the context of the play itself. In light of what research tells us about play's multiple benefits, organizational strategists' neglect of play as something irrelevant, messy, ambiguous, or subjective seems ironically nonrational.

However, engaging senior managers in play activities to develop shared views of company mission and vision, speculate about competitors, act out different scenarios for an industry's future, or even spark or test novel strategic directions is unthinkable in many management circles. What would enlighten these organizations and strategic leaders to understand the value of what we like to call *playing with serious intent* (Jacobs & Heracleous, 2005, 2006)? How can such play be orchestrated with maximum impact?

One set of management education experiences sheds light on the positive power and possibilities of play for increasing workplace effectiveness. In recent years, organizations as diverse as Unilever, McGraw-Hill, and the Boston Consulting Group have employed arts- and humanities-based executive development programs that use jazz improvisation, art appreciation, theater, poetry, and other creative modes to foster imagination, critical self-awareness, flexible thinking, collaboration, and improved presentation skills (Seifter & Buswick, 2005; Mirvis & Gunning, 2006).

At Oxford University, for example, the Strategic Leadership Program, which is designed to further leadership development for those in top organizational positions, takes its participants through several creative sessions of self-discovery. In one, senior leaders are asked to visit the Ashmolean Museum and select an object that they particularly like. This is followed by a plenary session during which the leaders are shown with their chosen objects in large photographs and asked to engage each other in discussion of why their chosen objects spoke to them and what this says about them as individuals and as organizational leaders. In another session, leaders are asked to select a poem that speaks personally to them, prepare and recite it to the group, and then engage with others in joint sense making about the impact and meaning of the poem for them.

These arts- and humanities-based techniques share a similar approach of drawing on an artifact—a piece of art or a poem in the Oxford program. In other instances, toy construction materials, such as Lego blocks, Play-Doh, magnets, or simple wooden bricks, might be used to the same ends. These activities use what psychologists call a *projective technique,* that is, they capitalize on the human capacity to experience the world at levels deeper than simple cognition through engaging with objects and then externalizing and examining the experience. Long used in psychotherapy, projective techniques aim at bypassing the conscious, linear, rational self to draw on subconscious, prereflexive thoughts, emotions, assumptions, and perspectives that, once surfaced, can be shared and debated.

These activities also share similar principles that are important for our discussion here. They offer an important vehicle for a kind of reflection and learning that bridges several false dualities permeating management thinking: the dichotomies between play and work; art and business; mind and body; reason and emotion; structure and ambiguity. As they engage in these activities, leaders are helped to appreciate the limits arising from holding tight to these dualities and the benefits arising from seeing connections rather than differences. They see existing issues and challenges in a new light: the letting go and shifting gears in these playful activities enables leaders to access parts and levels of their experiences, their brains, and their consciousness that they do not ordinarily use. More important, the leaders are offered a model that they can bring back to their workplaces for strengthening key competencies for effective strategic leadership: opening up options, using new lenses to see things differently, tapping into imagination and inventiveness, and fostering meaningful individual and organization development.

An example of how this model has been applied successfully to strategy development shows its possibilities. Senior management teams from multinational companies were asked to use a variety of three-dimensional materials to develop shared representations of their organizational world. Team members were asked individually and then collectively to build representations of their company, its competitive landscape including key stakeholders, and the perceived relations among these elements (Buergi, Jacobs, & Roos, 2005). The results were complex and imaginative, and the development process involved energetic and intellectually demanding debate.

The representations became, in essence, *embodied metaphors* of the different organizations, which could then be explored, compared, and decoded by the participants. They offered the same access to new ways of seeing that the senior leaders at Oxford experienced when examining their leadership through engagement with art from the Ashmolean. We use the term *embodied metaphors* to capture two distinctive features. First, there is newness in the direct relationship between the participants and their constructions. The resulting representations are not existing metaphors from individual participants' cognitive repertoires but shared creations constructed through an iterative, interactive, team process over a period of time. The creations then hold, or *embody*, the beliefs and understandings of the collective. And second, the constructions are not verbal metaphors or one-dimensional representations like maps or matrices. They are tangible entities extending into three-dimensional space and can be touched, moved, and examined from various angles—affording, for example, an interesting metaphoric look at the underbelly of an organization. They are ripe with interpretive meaning for individuals and for the collective team. The meanings build and manifest themselves during both the construction and discussion phases of the activity, as the dynamic nature of play allows the executives to express more ideas and emotions in their creations than they may initially be aware of themselves.

Such sessions effectively combine strategizing with the highly dialogical and imagery-rich process of playful sense making. In our experience, participants find the sessions demanding, involving, energizing, insightful, and enjoyable. We have observed strong individual and shared motivation during the activity, as well as bonding among managers whose relationships may have been less than close beforehand. We have also seen increased organizational capacities for employing valuable insights from the experience, even when the outcomes are emotionally, politically, or cognitively challenging. Even though the process of strategizing is lighthearted and playful, the outcomes and consequences are serious and relevant.

COMPARING SERIOUS PLAYING AND TRADITIONAL STRATEGIZING

Playing with serious intent is more complex than simpler idea-generating techniques, such as brainstorming. It is a structured method of thoughtful reflection and interaction with lasting consequences. The images and metaphors that participants develop remain part of the organization's strategic conversations long after the play has ended. However, this kind of playing with serious intent is not a substitute for conventional strategizing. It is a complement. Serious play is to traditional strategizing as strategic thinking is to strategic planning. Strategic thinking is free-wheeling, innovative, and divergent; traditional strategizing is analytical, convergent, and conventional. Strategic thinking discovers imaginative strategies and envisions novel futures; strategic planning operationalizes strategic directions and supports the strategic thinking process (Heracleous, 1998). Both processes are essential for competitive success and can be used in different sequences. Creative play sessions, for example, can begin the strategic visioning process and develop generative thought that will then be sorted and operationalized through more convergent and analytical planning processes. Alternatively, serious play sessions can follow strategic planning activities, serving as a means of surfacing and stimulating open discussion and debate about the meaning and interpretation of various strategic decisions.

In 2003, for example, the CEO of a Swiss-based, private banking group planned to launch a major, go-to-market strategic initiative (Jacobs & Heracleous, 2006). The initiative was labeled "I know my banker" and aimed to provide a more distinctive, customer-focused, private banking service drawing on the creative use of traditional banking processes and supports. To kick off the initiative the CEO invited department heads and their direct reports to a one-day retreat where participants would explore the new strategic concept and its consequences through the creation of representational models of the organization after the change. The hoped-for retreat outcomes were to create shared understanding of the new initiative and to achieve clarity about new actions needed to implement it.

The serious play activity enabled the participants to engage safely in intense debates and discussions on a range of important issues: who the customers for the new service should be; how to actually encourage customers to get to know their bankers better; what the initiative might mean for the group's definitions of the banker's role; whether the initiative was a technical systems effort, a customer relationship marketing activity, a data-mining approach, a new method for building client trust, or some combination of these; and more. The embodied metaphors built were a potent way to surface and explore the issues and the differences in group members' assumptions about these issues.

For example, one construction presented the bank as a complicated machine bigger than the client's space and the banker-client relationship as one in which the bank worked to match its offerings to clients' demands—a rather technocratic, mechanistic, transactional interpretation of "I know my banker." This contrasted with another model that portrayed the initiative as a series of progressively closer banker-client relationships and deeper mutual understandings—an anthropocentric, developmental, relationship-oriented undertaking. These major differences surfaced easily and in a nonthreatening manner as participants compared the models, and had a significant impact on subsequent bank actions. The CEO saw the lack of shared understanding. He requested that the head of marketing postpone the initiative launch and redesign the "I know my banker" program—this time using a more inclusive process and close collaboration with the department heads as well as some of the workshop attendees. A few months later the redesigned initiative was introduced more smoothly than would have been possible before the serious play retreat. Table 25.1 summarizes the characteristics of traditional strategizing techniques and strategizing through serious play.

Traditional Strategizing	Strategizing Through Serious Play
Approach is planned, deductive, analytical, top down.	Approach is emergent, inductive, based on narrative, group oriented.
Analysis process aims to reduce complexity, sanitize, normalize.	Construction process aims to highlight richness, interrelationships and interactions, expansivity.
Strategist is detached, objective, distant.	Strategist is attached, engaged, personally and often emotionally involved.
Output is plans, charts, figures, conventional statements.	Output is 3-D constructions; embodied metaphors; unique, visible, and memorable artifacts and meanings.

Table 25. 1.   Characteristics of Strategizing Approaches.

BENEFITS OF PLAYING WITH SERIOUS INTENT

Serious play produces five central strategic benefits for a company. First, play produces *insights and potential shifts in managers' mind-sets* that are difficult to gain through other, more conventional meetings and sessions. For example, the senior strategist team of a company we'll call TelCo, a leading European mobile phone service provider recently acquired by a major competitor, gathered to review the company's strategy through serious play. The team's shared construction portrayed the organization as a flotilla of ships moving toward a lighthouse that represented the brand. Each ship represented a specific country's operations. When constructing the organization's environment, one participant suggested that an overlooked, powerful competitor from another part of the world might be "coming in from left field." She placed a large, bulky model of the competitor on a bookshelf behind the table to illustrate that even though the competitor was not in TelCo's current landscape, it was ominously present and eyeing TelCo's market. The sheer size of the competitor's model, its location and looming posture, sparked a debate that helped the strategists acknowledge their previous blind spots. They also considered potential responses and actual scenarios for dealing with the potential competitor, doing so with an urgency and focus that would have been difficult to muster without the power of the visuals before them. Creating concrete representations of inherently ambiguous strategic issues is a potent way to focus and mobilize timely, action-oriented responses.

In the same workshop, participants zeroed in on their brand as needing to be addressed. The physical representation of the brand as a lighthouse looming over the landscape led to realization that rather than guiding or driving the company, the brand might in fact be a barrier to swiftly maneuvering in the right direction. This led to the playful but richly symbolic gesture of moving the lighthouse from the front of the table to the back, behind the flotilla of ships— and examining how team members felt about this. In addition to encouraging a discussion of the brand and its effects, this exploration led the team to reconsider the design and focus of an upcoming, large-scale executive training and development program that had originally been designed around the organization's conception of its brand.

Serious play sessions like these expand individual diagnostic and planning skills in the short and long term. Repeated play sessions enable participants to become more proficient in exploring out-of-the-box alternatives and seeing multiple points of view. The result is higher levels of executive flexibility and organizational adaptability. Once a concrete representation is developed and examined—as opposed to an abstract idea discussed—individuals also seem to find it easier to face personal or organizational blind spots. Over time, mind-sets shift and developmental growth occurs.

Second, play provides a safe context in which senior teams can *surface and discuss contentious or critical management issues.* For example, the senior team of a leading food product packaging company was divided on whether after-sales activities were of strategic relevance or a mere *hygiene factor* that could be outsourced to third parties. Team members engaged in serious play, constructing models of their organization and its environment, including key competitors and clients. The company was portrayed as a large, solid, inflexible castle and the competitors were portrayed as moveable, adaptive pirates' nests in the sea surrounding the castle. The senior team examined the construction by looking at the situation from the customers' perspectives. Team members suddenly appreciated the strategic relevance of after-sales activities for customer satisfaction and retention and subsequently explored potential alliances to help the company provide world-wide, high-quality after-sales service.

Third, play *surfaces issues that have been seen as politically sensitive or undiscussable.* For example, constructed models can reveal how the CEO and the senior managers are viewed by others in the organization. We have found that these constructions often show the CEO positioned higher than or physically detached from the representation of the organization itself. These CEOs often wear symbols of power like a crown or sword—sometimes they even hold a whip or look away from the organization—and are depicted leading the way. Although activity participants may not be immediately able to explain the reasons they represented their CEO in a certain way, the reality of the embodied metaphor invites a safe, yet important inquiry into CEO and senior manager behavior and how these executives are viewed by the rest of the organization. Sometimes leaders are irritated by the way they are depicted. Most are surprised and recognize that playful exploration of their image, role, and behavior can prompt a much richer and more honest discussion than *360-degree feedback* and other evaluation techniques can. An unexpected or contradictory representation of the CEO offers group members a context for shared sense making. This feedback is also grist for the leader's personal growth and leadership development.

Fourth, group-oriented, interactive play develops and draws on rich imagery, metaphors, and stories, not just facts, figures, and statistics. This in turn enables organizational members to *develop a memorable shared language* for future work together. Individuals report that their insights and the embodied metaphors from the sessions continue to inform their thinking, improve their organizational strategizing, and break down walls of interfunctional or interdivisional separation. When members of the strategy department of a leading global cell phone production company gathered to review their strategizing processes and practices, they constructed a model of their organization as a set of loosely connected physical structures clustered around a central tower. A porous, dotted line represented the brand as the integrative force of the firm. The core of the construction was surrounded by a set of gates representing portals to future issues that the organization would need to address—issues that ranged from adversarial concerns like hostile acquisitions by competitors to potentially beneficial organizational options like strategic alliances. The dominant, unifying metaphor of gates to the future enriched the strategists' awareness that there were several potential futures and gave them a shared language for discussing their options, choices, and plans.

Fifth, playing seriously *enhances the involvement and ownership of organizational participants* and contributes to team building. For example, the European members of the senior management group of a leading U.S.-based software company gathered to encourage a common identity and foster lateral collaboration in their recently formed and highly diverse management team. They constructed an urban landscape with diverse structures that could connect to each other only through "antennae relationships" with the managing director or other centrally located senior individuals. The representation highlighted the difficulty of achieving a common identity and collaboration among the different country operations under the current conditions. It also focused team members on exploring why the difficulty existed and working together to determine appropriate actions. Participants were energized by their recognition of the challenge before them. When the group was exploring how the company was perceived by competitors and customers, one participant became so excited that he climbed on the table to add a feature to the model.

HOW TO PLAY SERIOUSLY AND THE ROLE OF LEADERSHIP IN PLAY

A prime function of leadership is strategic visioning and opening organizational options for the future. How then can a company best play seriously to achieve these ends? And what is the role of leadership in fostering productive play? Playing seriously may not always be the most appropriate choice for an organization's stage of strategizing: it manifests differences and creative tensions and lends itself best to times where novelty, difference, and ambiguity are appreciated and productive. Leaders need to understand their organization's strategic stage and needs, the purpose of their use of serious play, and their reasons for involving others. Serious play is more appropriate in the early stages of strategy development and in critical reviews of implemented strategy, for example, than it is in the stages of operational planning and in performance reviews.

Paradoxically, playing with serious intent cannot be spontaneous. It must be organized, supported with adequate resources, and simultaneously flexible to allow creative "foolishness" to emerge at the same time that a serious focus on delivering useful insights on real strategic issues is maintained. This points to prerequisites for organizational leaders: they must do their homework and know what the organization's significant strategic challenges are, commit to exploring these challenges fully, and allocate the necessary time and resources. Rushed play sessions lose their effectiveness: functional and goal-constrained thinking takes over.

A skilled facilitator helps to ensure the healthy and productive generation, debate, and integration of ideas. Such a facilitator is aware of specific play dynamics, can ensure a group-created embodied metaphor and genuinely interactive process, and can probe for the hidden meanings in the group's representations. Why, for example, does a group choose to portray a 3G license as a tiger and an elephant tied around the organization's symbolic neck? Why is the CEO of the acquiring company holding a machine gun and accompanied by black-hat-wearing accountants? Why are the organization's strategic planning processes portrayed as disoriented animals in search of direction? Why are the interconnections among the corporate divisions portrayed as broken? What should the organization do to address the issues and challenges identified? And so on.

Playing with serious intent is holistic and encompasses elements of strategic issue identification and scenario development. It is crucial for the success of a play intervention to capture all the issues, questions, potential answers, doubts, scenarios, and stories surfaced by the technique and to translate them into a format and record that makes them accessible and useful in other subsequent and more formal stages of strategy development.

Leaders face a special challenge in serious play. They need to muster and demonstrate emotional maturity and gracefully accept the feedback and implied critiques of their own and their organization's shortcomings and strategic misalignments. At the same time, leaders need to demonstrate that they take the play seriously and to enhance their own acceptance, ownership, and commitment to the outcomes by playfully participating in the process with others. Leaders who do this are also cautioned to relinquish control and behave as open and equal members of the construction team. Any defensive or dominating behavior on their part may cause the group to produce "politically correct" representations and a meaningless exercise. Leaders gain the most from the process when they come prepared to share their own stories and metaphors, recognize the power of involving participants not usually part of strategy-developing teams in the process, allow freewheeling discussion and respectfully listen to explorations of controversial or contentious issues, and appreciate the added benefit of learning about the mind-sets of subordinates who are crucial for company success.

Taking play seriously means taking the outcomes seriously too. There is plenty of hard work that needs to happen after the play sessions to translate the insights and directions into workable processes and actions. It is the leader's overall responsibility to ensure that this important work is done and that the organization is prepared to address even controversial outcomes in a respectful, productive, and developmental manner. Playing seriously is an enjoyable way for organizations to differentiate themselves from their competitors and overcome strategic obstacles. It may not be as simple as it first sounds, but playing with serious intent is worth every bit of the investment.

—⌇⌇⌇—

Loizos Heracleous is professor of strategy at Warwick Business School in the United Kingdom and an associate fellow at Templeton College and at the Said Business School, Oxford University.

—⌇⌇⌇—

Claus D. Jacobs is senior research fellow in strategy and organization at the Institute of Management at the University of St. Gallen, a visiting associate scholar of Templeton College, Oxford, and a fellow of the Daimler Benz Foundation.

CHAPTER TWENTY-SIX

The Leader as Politician
Navigating the Political Terrain

Lee G. Bolman
Terrence E. Deal

The space shuttle *Challenger* disaster teaches a chilling lesson about how political pressures distort momentous decisions. Similarly, the implosion of firms such as Enron and WorldCom shows how the unfettered pursuit of self-interest by powerful executives can bring even a giant corporation to its knees. Many believe that the antidote is to free leadership from politics. But this is unrealistic. Enduring differences lead to multiple interpretations of what is important, and even what is true. Scarce resources require tough decisions about who gets what. Interdependence means that people cannot ignore one another; they need each other's assistance, support, and resources. Under such conditions, efforts to eliminate politics drive differences under the rug or into the closet. There they fester into counterproductive, unmanageable forms. In a world of chronic scarcity, diversity, and conflict, the astute leader is a constructive politician who exercises four key skills: agenda setting, mapping the political terrain, networking and forming coalitions, and bargaining and negotiating.

AGENDA SETTING

Structurally, an agenda outlines a goal and a scheduled series of activities. Politically, agendas are statements of interests and scenarios. In reflecting on his experience as a university president, Warren Bennis (1989) arrived at a deceptively simple observation: "It struck me that I was most effective when I knew what I wanted" (p. 20). Kanter's study of internal entrepreneurs in American corporations (1983), Kotter's analysis of effective corporate leaders (1988), and Smith's examination of effective U.S. presidents (1988) all reached a similar conclusion: the first step in effective leadership is setting an agenda.

The effective leader creates an "agenda for change" with two major elements: a *vision* balancing the long-term interests of key parties and a *strategy for achieving the vision*, recognizing competing internal and external forces (Kotter, 1988). The agenda must impart direction while addressing the concerns of major stakeholders. Kanter (1983) and Pfeffer (1992) underscore the close relationship between gathering information and developing a vision. Pfeffer's list of key political attributes includes "sensitivity"—knowing how others think and what they care about so that your agenda responds to their concerns. Kanter (1983) adds: "While gathering information, entrepreneurs can also be 'planting seeds'—leaving the kernel of an idea behind and letting it germinate and blossom so that it begins to float around the system from many sources other than the innovator" (p. 218). A vision without a strategy remains an illusion. A strategy has to recognize major forces working for and against the agenda.

Agendas never come neatly packaged. The bigger the job, the more difficult it is to wade through clamoring issues to find order amid chaos. Contrary to Woody Allen's dictum, success requires more than just showing up. High office, even if the incumbent enjoys great personal popularity, is no guarantee. Ronald Reagan was remarkably successful in his first year as president following a classic strategy for winning the agenda game: "First impressions are critical. In the agenda game, a swift beginning is crucial for a new president to establish himself as leader—to show the nation that he will make a difference in people's lives. The first one hundred days are the vital test; in those weeks, the political community and the public measure a new president—to see whether he is active, dominant, sure, purposeful" (Smith, 1988, p. 334).

Reagan began with a vision but without a strategy. He was not gifted as a manager or a strategist, despite extraordinary ability to portray complex issues in broad, symbolic brushstrokes. Reagan's staff painstakingly studied the first hundred days of four predecessors. They concluded that it was essential to move with speed and focus. Pushing competing issues aside, they focused on two: cutting taxes and reducing the federal budget. They also discovered a secret weapon in David Stockman, the only person in the Reagan White House who really understood the federal budget process. According to Smith, "Stockman got a jump on everyone else for two reasons: he had an agenda and a legislative blueprint already prepared, and he understood the real levers of power. Two terms as a Michigan congressman plus a network of key Republican and Democratic connections had taught Stockman how to play the power game" (p. 351). Reagan and his advisers had the vision; Stockman brought strategic direction.

MAPPING THE POLITICAL TERRAIN

It seems foolhardy to plunge into a minefield without knowing where explosives are buried, yet leaders unwittingly do it all the time. They launch a new initiative with little or no effort to scout the political turf. A simple way to develop a political map for any situation is to create a two-dimensional diagram mapping the key stakeholders (who are the players in the game), power (how much clout each player is likely to exercise), and interests (what each player wants). A political map that shows little serious opposition suggests a quick and easy win. A map that paints a very different picture of the political terrain—more intense resistance and more powerful opponents—forecasts a stormy process imbued with protracted conflict. Though less comforting, the map that identifies the potential resistance and opponents has an important message: success requires substantial effort to realign the existing field of political forces. The third and fourth key skills of the leader as politician, discussed in the next two sections, include strategies for doing just that.

NETWORKING AND BUILDING COALITIONS

The *Challenger* disaster occurred despite recognition of the O-ring problem by engineers at both Morton Thiokol and NASA. For a long time, they tried to get their superiors' attention, mostly through memos. Six months before the accident, Roger Boisjoly, an engineer at Morton Thiokol, wrote: "The result [of an O-ring failure] would be a catastrophe of the highest order—loss of human life" (Bell and Esch, 1987, p. 45). Two months later, another Thiokol engineer wrote a memo that opened, "HELP! The seal task force is constantly being delayed by every possible means" (p. 45). The memo detailed resistance from other departments in Thiokol. A memo to the boss is sometimes effective, but it is just as often a sign of political innocence. Kotter (1985) suggests four basic steps for exercising political influence:

1. Identify relevant relationships (figure out who needs to be led).

2. Assess who might resist, why, and how strongly (figure out where the leadership challenges will be).

3. Develop, wherever possible, relationships with potential opponents to facilitate communication, education, or negotiation.

4. If step three fails, carefully select and implement either more subtle or more forceful methods.

These steps underscore the importance of developing a sufficient power base. Moving up the ladder confers authority but also incurs increasing dependence, because success depends on the cooperation of many others (Kotter, 1985, 1988). People rarely give their best efforts and fullest cooperation simply because they were ordered to do so. They accept directions when they perceive the people in authority as credible, competent, and sensible.

The first task in building networks and coalitions is to figure out whose help you need. The second is to develop relationships so people will be there when you need them. Middle managers seeking to promote change typically begin by getting their boss on board (Kanter, 1983). They then move to "preselling" or "making cheerleaders": "Peers, managers of related functions, stakeholders in the issue, potential collaborators, and sometimes even customers would be approached individually, in one-on-one meetings that gave people a chance to influence the project and [gave] the innovator the maximum opportunity to sell it. Seeing them alone and on their territory was important: the rule was to act as if each person were *the* most important one for the project's success" (p. 223).

Once you cultivate cheerleaders, you can move to "horse trading": promising rewards in exchange for resources and support. This builds a resource base that helps in getting the necessary approvals and mandates from higher management (Kanter, 1983). Kanter found that the usual route to success in "securing blessings" is to identify critical senior managers and to develop a polished, formal presentation to sway their support. The best presentations respond to both substantive and political concerns. Senior managers typically care about two questions: Is it a good idea? How will my constituents react? Once innovators obtain higher management's blessing, they can formalize the coalition with their boss and make specific plans for pursuing the project (Kanter, 1983).

The basic point is simple: as a leader, you need friends and allies to get things done. To get their support, you need to cultivate relationships. Hard-core rationalists and incurable romantics sometimes react with horror to such a scenario. Why should you have to play political games to get something accepted if it's the right thing to do? Like it or not, political dynamics are inevitable under conditions most leaders face every day: ambiguity, diversity, and scarcity.

Ignoring or misreading those dynamics is costly. Smith (1988) reports a case in point. Thomas Wyman, board chairman of the CBS television network, went to Washington in 1983 to lobby U.S. Attorney General Edwin Meese. A White House emergency forced Meese to miss the meeting, and Wyman was sent to the office of Craig Fuller, one of Meese's top advisers:

> "I know something about this issue," Fuller suggested. "Perhaps you'd like to discuss it with me."
>
> "No, I'd rather wait and talk to Meese," Wyman said.
>
> For nearly an hour, Wyman sat leafing through magazines in Fuller's office, making no effort to talk to Fuller who kept working at his desk just a few feet away.
>
> Finally, Meese burst into Fuller's office, full of apologies that he wouldn't have time for substantive talk. "Did you talk to Fuller?" he asked.
>
> Wyman shook his head.
>
> "You should have," Meese said. "He's very important on this issue. He knows it better than any of the rest of us. He's writing a memo for the president on the pros and cons. You could have given him your side of the argument" [Smith, 1988, pp. xviii–xix].

Wyman missed an important opportunity because he failed to test his assumptions about who actually had power.

BARGAINING AND NEGOTIATION

We often associate bargaining with commercial, legal, and labor relations settings. From a political perspective, bargaining is central to all decision making. The horse trading Kanter describes as part of coalition building is just one of many examples. Negotiation is needed whenever two or more parties with some interests in common and others in conflict need to reach agreement. Labor and management may agree that a firm should make money and offer good jobs to its employees but disagree on how to balance pay and profitability. Engineers and top managers at Morton Thiokol had a common interest in the success of the shuttle program. They differed sharply on how to balance technical and political trade-offs.

One of the best-known win-win approaches to negotiation was developed by Fisher and Ury (1981) in *Getting to Yes*. They argue that people too often engage in "positional bargaining": they stake out positions and then reluctantly make concessions to reach agreement. Fisher and Ury contend that positional bargaining is inefficient and misses opportunities to create an agreement beneficial to both parties. They propose an alternative: "principled bargaining," built around four strategies.

The first strategy is to *separate the people from the problem*. The stress and tension of negotiations can easily escalate into anger and personal attack. Because every negotiation involves both substance and relationship, the wise negotiator will "deal with the people as human beings and with the problem on its merits."

The second rule of thumb is to *focus on interests, not positions*. If you get locked into a particular position, you might overlook other ways to achieve the goal. An example is the 1978 Camp David treaty. Israel and Egypt were at an impasse over where to draw the boundary between the two countries. Israel wanted to keep part of the Sinai, while Egypt wanted all of it back. Resolution became possible only when they looked at each other's underlying interests. Israel was concerned about security: no Egyptian tanks on the border. Egypt was concerned about sovereignty: the Sinai had been part of Egypt from the time of the Pharaohs. The parties agreed to give all of the Sinai back to Egypt while demilitarizing large parts of it (Fisher and Ury, 1981).

Fisher and Ury's third recommendation is to *invent options for mutual gain*, looking for new possibilities that bring advantages to both sides. Parties often lock onto the first alternative that comes to mind and stop searching. Efforts to generate more options increase the chance of a better decision.

Fisher and Ury's fourth strategy is to *insist on objective criteria*— standards of fairness for both substance and procedure. When a school board and a teachers' union are at loggerheads over the size of a pay increase, they can look for independent standards, such as the rate of inflation or the terms of settlement used in other districts.

Fisher and Ury devote most of their attention to creating value— finding better solutions for both parties. They downplay the question of claiming value. Yet there are many examples in which shrewd value-claimers have done very well. In 1980, Bill Gates offered to license an operating system to IBM about forty-eight hours before he had actually obtained the rights. Meanwhile, Microsoft neglected to mention to QDOS's owner, Tim Paterson of Seattle Computer, that they were buying his operating system to resell it to IBM. Microsoft gave IBM a great price: only $30,000 more than the $50,000 they'd paid for it. But they were smart enough to retain the rights to license it to anyone else. At the time, IBM was an elephant and Microsoft was a flea. Almost no one except Gates saw the possibility that people would want an IBM computer made by anyone but IBM. But the new PC was so successful, IBM couldn't make enough of them. Within a year, Microsoft had licensed MS-DOS to fifty companies, and the number kept growing (Mendelson and Korin, n.d.). Onlookers who wondered why Microsoft was so aggressive and unyielding in battling the Justice Department's antitrust suit twenty years later might not have known that Gates had been a dogged value claimer for a long time.

Value claiming gives us another picture of the bargaining process:

1. Bargaining is a mixed-motive game. Both parties want an agreement but have differing interests and preferences. (IBM and Microsoft both wanted an operating system deal. But the IBM negotiators probably thought they were stealing candy from babies by buying it royalty-free for a measly $80,000. Meanwhile, Gates was already dreaming about millions of computers running his code.)

2. Bargaining is a process of interdependent decisions. What each party does affects the other. Each player wants to be able to predict what the other will do while limiting the other's ability to reciprocate. (IBM was racing to bring its PC to market; a key challenge was making sure IBM had an operating system to go with it.)

3. The more player A can control player B's level of uncertainty, the more powerful A is. (Microsoft was an intermediary between Seattle Computer and IBM but kept each in the dark about the other.)

4. Bargaining involves judicious use of *threats* rather than sanctions. Players may threaten to use force, go on strike, or break off negotiations. In most cases, they much prefer not to bear the costs of carrying out the threat.

5. Making a threat credible is crucial. It is effective only if your opponent believes it. A noncredible threat weakens your bargaining position and confuses the process.

6. Calculation of the appropriate level of threat is also critical. If I underthreaten, I may weaken my own position. If I overthreaten, you may not believe me, may break off the negotiations, or may escalate your own threats.

Creating value and claiming value are both intrinsic to the bargaining process. How does a leader decide how to balance the two? At least two questions are important: "How much opportunity is there for a win-win solution?" and "Will I have to work with these people again?" If an agreement can make everyone better off, it makes sense to emphasize creating value. If you expect to work with the same people in the future, it is risky to use value-claiming tactics that leave anger and mistrust in their wake. Leaders who get a reputation for being manipulative and self-interested have a hard time building networks and coalitions they need for future success.

Axelrod (1980) found that a strategy of conditional openness works best when negotiators need to work together over time. This strategy starts with open and collaborative behavior and maintains the approach if the other responds in kind. If the other party becomes adversarial, however, the negotiator responds in kind and remains adversarial until the opponent makes a collaborative move. It is, in effect, a friendly and forgiving version of tit for tat—do unto others as they do unto you. Axelrod's research revealed that this conditional openness strategy worked better than even the most fiendishly diabolical adversarial strategy.

A final consideration in balancing collaborative and adversarial tactics is ethics. Bargainers often deliberately misrepresent their positions—even though lying is almost universally condemned as unethical (Bok, 1978). This leads to a profoundly difficult question for the leader as politician: What actions are ethical and just?

MORALITY AND POLITICS

Block (1987), Burns (1978), and Lax and Sebenius (1986) explore ethical issues in bargaining and organizational politics. Block's view assumes that individuals empower themselves through understanding: "The process of organizational politics as we know it works against people taking responsibility. We empower ourselves by discovering a positive way of being political. The line between positive and negative politics is a tightrope we have to walk" (Block, 1987, p. xiii).

Block argues that bureaucratic cycles often leave individuals feeling vulnerable, powerless, and helpless. If we confer too much power to the organization or others, we fear that the power will be used against us. Consequently, we develop manipulative strategies to protect ourselves. To escape the dilemma, managers need to support organizational structures, policies, and procedures that promote empowerment. They must also empower themselves.

Block urges managers to begin by building an "image of greatness"—a vision of what their department can contribute that is meaningful and worthwhile. Then they need to build support for their vision by negotiating agreement and trust. Block suggests dealing differently with friends than with opponents. Adversaries, he says, are simultaneously the most difficult and most interesting people to deal with. It is usually ineffective to pressure them; a better strategy is to "let go of them." He offers four steps for letting go: (1) tell them your vision, (2) state your best understanding of their position, (3) identify your contribution to the problem, and (4) tell them what you plan to do, without making demands.

Such a strategy might work for conflict originating in a misunderstanding of one's self-interest. But in a situation of scarce resources and durable differences, bringing politics into the open may backfire. It can make conflict more obvious and overt but offer little hope of resolution. Block argues that "war games in organizations lose their power when brought into the light of day" (1987, p. 148), but the political frame questions that assumption.

Burns's conception of positive politics (1978) draws on examples as diverse and complex as Franklin Roosevelt and Adolf Hitler, Gandhi and Mao, Woodrow Wilson and Joan of Arc. He sees conflict and power as central to leadership. Searching for firm moral footing in a world of cultural and ethical diversity, Burns turned to the motivation theory of Maslow (1954) and the ethical theory of Kohlberg (1973). From Maslow he borrowed the idea of the hierarchy of motives. Moral leaders, he argued, appeal to a higher level on the needs hierarchy.

From Kohlberg he adopted the idea of stages of moral reasoning. At the lowest, "preconventional" level, moral judgment is based primarily on perceived consequences: an action is right if you are rewarded and wrong if you are punished. In the intermediate or "conventional" level, the emphasis is on conforming to authority and established rules. At the highest, "postconventional" level, ethical judgment rests on general principles: the greatest good for the greatest number, or universal and comprehensive moral principles.

Maslow and Kohlberg offered a foundation on which Burns (1978) constructed a positive view of politics:

> If leaders are to be effective in helping to mobilize and elevate their constituencies, leaders must be whole persons, persons with full functioning capacities for thinking and feeling. The problem for them as educators, as leaders, is not to promote narrow, egocentric self-actualization, but to extend awareness of human needs and the means of gratifying them, to improve the larger social situation for which educators or leaders have responsibility and over which they have power. What does all this mean for the teaching of leadership as opposed to manipulation? "Teachers"—in whatever guise—treat students neither coercively nor instrumentally but as joint seekers of truth and of mutual actualization. They help students define moral values not by imposing their own moralities on them but by positing situations that pose moral choices and then encouraging conflict and debate. They seek to help students rise to higher stages of moral reasoning and hence to higher levels of principled judgment [pp. 448–449].

In Burns's view, positive politics evolve when individuals choose actions appealing to higher motives and higher stages of moral judgment. Lax and Sebenius (1986), regarding ethical issues as inescapable, present a set of questions to help leaders decide what is ethical:

1. Are you following rules that are mutually understood and accepted? (In poker, for example, everyone understands that bluffing is part of the game.)

2. Are you comfortable discussing and defending your action?
(Would you want your colleagues and friends to be aware of it?
Your spouse, children, or parents? Would you be comfortable if
it were on the front page of your local newspaper?)

3. Would you want someone to do it to you? To a member of your
family?

4. Would you want everyone to act that way? Would the resulting
society be desirable? (If you were designing an organization,
would you want people to act that way? Would you teach your
children to do it?)

5. Are there alternatives that rest on firmer ethical ground?

Although these questions do not yield a comprehensive ethical
framework, they embody four important principles of moral judgment. These are instrumental values—guidelines not about the right
thing to do but about the right way of doing things. They do not
guarantee right action, but they substantially reduce ethical risks. As
evidence, we note that these values are regularly ignored wherever we
find an organizational scandal.

1. *Mutuality.* Are all parties to a relationship operating under the
same understanding about the rules of the game? Enron's Ken
Lay was talking up the company's stock to analysts and employees even as he and others were selling shares. In the period when
WorldCom illegitimately improved its profits by booking some
of its operating expenses as capital investments, it made major
competitors look bad and generated considerable puzzlement.
Top executives at both AT&T and Sprint felt the heat from analysts and shareholders and wondered, *What are we doing wrong?
Why can't we get the results they're getting?*

2. *Generality.* Does a specific action follow a principle of moral
conduct applicable to all comparable situations? When World-
Com violated a basic accounting principle to inflate its results,
it was secretly breaking the rules, which does *not* amount to following a broadly applicable rule of conduct.

3. *Openness.* Are we willing to make our thinking and decisions public and confrontable? It was Justice Oliver Wendell
Holmes who observed many years ago that "sunlight is the best

disinfectant." Keeping others in the dark was a consistent theme in the corporate ethics scandals of 2001–02. Enron's books were almost impenetrable, and the company was hostile to anyone who asked questions, such as *Fortune* reporter Bethany McLean. Enron's techniques for manipulating the California energy crisis had to be secret to work. One device involved creating the appearance of congestion in the California power grid, and then getting paid by the state for "moving energy to relieve congestion without actually moving any energy or relieving any congestion" (Oppel, 2002, p. A1).

4. *Caring.* Does this action show care for the legitimate interests of others? Enron's effort to protect its share price by locking in employees so they couldn't sell Enron shares in retirement accounts as the market plunged is only one of many examples of putting the interests of senior executives ahead of everyone else's.

The scandals of the early 2000s were not unprecedented; such a wave is a predictable feature of the trough that follows every business boom. The 1990s, for example, gave us Ivan Boesky and the savings and loan crisis. There was another wave of corporate scandals back in the 1970s, and in the 1930s the president of the New York Stock Exchange literally went to jail in his three-piece suit (Labaton, 2002). There will always be temptation whenever gargantuan egos and large sums of money are at stake. Top managers too rarely think or talk about the moral dimension of management and leadership. Porter (1989) notes the dearth of such conversation: "In a seminar with seventeen executives from nine corporations, we learned how the privatization of moral discourse in our society has created a deep sense of moral loneliness and moral illiteracy; how the absence of a common language prevents people from talking about and reading the moral issues they face. We learned how the isolation of individuals—the taboo against talking about spiritual matters in the public sphere—robs people of courage, of the strength of heart to do what deep down they believe to be right" (p. 2).

If we choose to banish moral discourse and leave leaders to face ethical issues alone, we invite dreary and brutish political dynamics. In a pluralistic secular world, an organization cannot impose a narrow ethical framework on employees. But it can and should take a moral stance. It can make its values clear, hold employees accountable, and validate the need for dialogue about ethical choices. Positive politics, absent an ethical framework and a moral dialogue, is no more likely to occur than farming without sunlight or water.

SUMMARY

The question is not whether organizations are political but rather what kind of politics they will have. Political dynamics can be sordid and destructive. But politics can also be the vehicle for achieving noble purpose. Organizational change and effectiveness depend on leaders' political skills. Constructive politicians recognize and understand political realities. They know how to fashion an agenda, map the political terrain, create a network of support, and negotiate with both allies and adversaries. In the process, they encounter a practical and ethical dilemma: when to adopt an open, collaborative strategy or when to choose a tougher, more adversarial approach. They have to consider the potential for collaboration, the importance of long-term relationships, and most important their own values and ethical principles.

—◦◦◦—

Lee G. Bolman is the Marion Bloch Missouri Chair in Leadership at the University of Missouri-Kansas City and author of several best-selling books on leadership and organizations. For more information visit www.leebolman.com.

—◦◦◦—

Terrence E. Deal is professor emeritus at the Rossier School of Education at the University of Southern California and author of multiple, award-winning books on leadership, culture, and organizations.

CHAPTER TWENTY-SEVEN

Want Collaboration?

Accept—and Actively Manage—Conflict

Jeff Weiss
Jonathan Hughes

The challenge is a long-standing one for senior managers: How do you get people in your organization to work together across internal boundaries? But the question has taken on urgency in today's global and fast-changing business environment. To service multinational accounts, you increasingly need seamless collaboration across geographic boundaries. To improve customer satisfaction, you increasingly need collaboration among functions ranging from R&D to distribution. To offer solutions tailored to customers' needs, you increasingly need collaboration between product and service groups.

Meanwhile, as competitive pressures continually force companies to find ways to do more with less, few managers have the luxury of relying on their own dedicated staffs to accomplish their objectives. Instead, most must work with and through people across the organization, many of whom have different priorities, incentives, and ways of doing things.

Getting collaboration right promises tremendous benefits: a unified face to customers, faster internal decision making, reduced costs through shared resources, and the development of more innovative products. But despite the billions of dollars spent on initiatives to improve collaboration, few companies are happy with the results. Time and again we have seen management teams employ the same few strategies to boost internal cooperation—strategies often based on seemingly sensible but ultimately misguided assumptions. They restructure their organizations and reengineer their business processes. They create cross-unit incentives. They offer teamwork training. While such initiatives yield the occasional success story, most have only limited impact in dismantling organizational silos and fostering collaboration—and many are total failures.

So what's the problem? Most companies respond to the challenge of improving collaboration in entirely the wrong way. They focus on the symptoms ("Sales and delivery do not work together as closely as they should") rather than on the root cause of failures in cooperation: conflict. The fact is, you can't improve collaboration until you've addressed the issue of conflict.

This can come as a surprise to even the most experienced executives, who generally don't fully appreciate the inevitability of conflict in complex organizations. And even if they do recognize this, many mistakenly assume that efforts to increase collaboration will significantly reduce that conflict, when in fact some of these efforts—for example, restructuring initiatives—actually produce more of it.

Executives underestimate not only the inevitability of conflict but also—and this is key—its importance to the organization. The disagreements sparked by differences in perspective, competencies, access to information, and strategic focus within a company actually generate much of the value that can come from collaboration across organizational boundaries. Clashes between parties are the crucibles in which creative solutions are developed and wise trade-offs among competing objectives are made. So instead of trying simply to reduce disagreements, senior executives need to embrace conflict and, just as important, institutionalize mechanisms for managing it.

There are a number of straightforward ways that executives can help their people—and their organizations—constructively manage conflict. These can be divided into two main areas: strategies for managing disagreements at the point of conflict and strategies for managing conflict upon escalation up the management chain. These methods can help a company move through the conflict that is a necessary precursor to truly effective collaboration and, more important, extract the value that often lies latent in intra-organizational differences. When companies are able to do both, conflict is transformed from a major liability into a significant asset.

STRATEGIES FOR MANAGING DISAGREEMENTS AT THE POINT OF CONFLICT

Conflict management works best when the parties involved in a disagreement are equipped to manage it themselves. The aim is to get people to resolve issues on their own through a process that improves—or at least does not damage—their relationships. The following strategies help produce decisions that are better informed and more likely to be implemented.

DEVISE AND IMPLEMENT A COMMON METHOD FOR RESOLVING CONFLICT. Consider for a moment the hypothetical Matrix Corporation, a composite of many organizations we've worked with, whose challenges will likely be familiar to managers. Over the past few years, salespeople from nearly a dozen of Matrix's product and service groups have been called on to design and sell integrated solutions to their customers. For any given sale, five or more lead salespeople and their teams have to agree on issues of resource allocation, solution design, pricing, and sales strategy. Not surprisingly, the teams are finding this difficult. Who should contribute the most resources to a particular customer's offering? Who should reduce the scope of their participation or discount their pricing to meet a customer's budget? Who should defer when disagreements arise about account strategy? Who should manage key relationships within the customer account? Indeed, given these thorny questions, Matrix is finding that a single large sale typically generates far more conflict inside the company than it does with the customer. The resulting wasted time and damaged relationships among sales teams are making it increasingly difficult to close sales.

Most companies face similar sorts of problems. And, like Matrix, they leave employees to find their own ways of resolving them. But without a structured method for dealing with these issues, people get bogged down not only in what the right result should be but also in how to arrive at it. Often, they will avoid or work around conflict, thereby forgoing important opportunities to collaborate. And when people do decide to confront their differences, they usually default to the approach they know best: debating about who's right and who's wrong or haggling over small concessions. Among the negative consequences of such approaches are suboptimal, "split-the-difference" resolutions—if not outright deadlock.

Establishing a companywide process for resolving disagreements can alter this familiar scenario. There is an array of conflict resolution methods a company can use. But to be effective, they should offer a clear, step-by-step process for parties to follow. They should also be made an integral part of existing business activities—account planning, sourcing, R&D budgeting, and the like. If conflict resolution is set up as a separate, exception-based process—a kind of organizational appeals court—it will likely wither away once initial managerial enthusiasm wanes.

At Intel, new employees learn a common method and language for decision making and conflict resolution. The company puts them through training in which they learn to use a variety of tools for handling discord. Not only does the training show that top management sees disagreements as an inevitable aspect of doing business, it also provides a common framework that expedites conflict resolution. Little time is wasted in figuring out the best way to handle a disagreement or trading accusations about "not being a team player"; guided by this clearly defined process, people can devote their time and energy to exploring and constructively evaluating a variety of options for how to move forward. Intel's systematic method for working through differences has helped sustain some of the company's hallmark qualities: innovation, operational efficiency, and the ability to make and implement hard decisions in the face of complex strategic choices.

PROVIDE PEOPLE WITH CRITERIA FOR MAKING TRADE-OFFS. At our hypothetical Matrix Corporation, senior managers overseeing cross-unit sales teams often admonish those teams to "do what's right for the customer." Unfortunately, this exhortation isn't much help when conflict arises. Given Matrix's ability to offer numerous combinations of products and services, company managers—each with different training and experience and access to different information, not to mention different unit priorities—have, not surprisingly, different opinions about how best to meet customers' needs. Similar clashes in perspective result when exasperated senior managers tell squabbling team members to set aside their differences and "put Matrix's interests first." That's because it isn't always clear what's best for the company given the complex interplay among Matrix's objectives for revenue, profitability, market share, and long-term growth.

Even when companies equip people with a common method for resolving conflict, employees often will still need to make zero-sum trade-offs between competing priorities. That task is made much easier and less contentious when top management can clearly articulate the criteria for making such choices. Obviously, it's not easy to reduce a company's strategy to clearly defined trade-offs, but it's worth trying.

At Blue Cross and Blue Shield of Florida, the strategic decision to rely more and more on alliances with other organizations has significantly increased the potential for disagreement in an organization long accustomed to developing capabilities in-house. Decisions about whether to build new capabilities, buy them outright, or gain access to them through alliances are natural flashpoints for conflict among internal groups. The health insurer might have tried to minimize such conflict through a structural solution, giving a particular group the authority to make decisions concerning whether, for instance, to develop a new claims-processing system in-house, to do so jointly with an alliance partner, or to license or acquire an existing system from a third party. Instead, the company established a set of criteria designed to help various groups within the organization—for example, the enterprise alliance group, IT, and marketing—to collectively make such decisions.

The criteria are embodied in a spreadsheet-type tool that guides people in assessing the trade-offs involved—say, between speed in getting a new process up and running versus ensuring its seamless integration with existing ones—when deciding whether to build, buy, or ally. People no longer debate back and forth across a table, advocating their preferred outcomes. Instead, they sit around the table and together apply a common set of trade-off criteria to the decision at hand. The resulting insights into the pros and cons of each approach enable more effective execution, no matter which path is chosen.

USE THE ESCALATION OF CONFLICT AS AN OPPORTUNITY FOR COACHING. Managers at Matrix spend much of their time playing the organizational equivalent of hot potato. Even people who are new to the company learn within weeks that the best thing to do with cross-unit conflict is to toss it up the management chain. Immediate supervisors take a quick pass at resolving the dispute but, being busy themselves, usually pass it up to their supervisors. Those supervisors do the same, and before long the problem lands in the lap of a senior-level manager, who then spends much of his time resolving disagreements. Clearly, this isn't ideal. Because the senior managers are a number of steps removed from the source of the controversy, they rarely have a good understanding of the situation. Furthermore, the more time they spend resolving internal clashes, the less time they spend engaged in the business, and the more isolated they are from the very information they need to resolve the disputes dumped in their laps. Meanwhile, Matrix employees get so little opportunity to learn about how to deal with conflict that it becomes not only expedient but almost necessary for them to quickly bump conflict up the management chain.

While Matrix's story may sound extreme, we can hardly count the number of companies we've seen that operate this way. And even in the best of situations—for example, where a companywide conflict-management process is in place and where trade-off criteria are well understood—there is still a natural tendency for people to let their bosses sort out disputes. Senior managers contribute to this tendency by quickly resolving the problems presented to them. While this may be the fastest and easiest way to fix the problems, it encourages people to punt issues upstairs at the first sign of difficulty. Instead, managers should treat escalations as opportunities to help employees become better at resolving conflict.

At KLA-Tencor, a major manufacturer of semiconductor production equipment, a materials executive in each division oversees a number of buyers who procure the materials and component parts for machines that the division makes. When negotiating a companywide contract with a supplier, a buyer often must work with the company commodity manager, as well as with buyers from other divisions who deal with the same supplier. There is often conflict, for example, over the delivery terms for components supplied to two or more divisions under the contract. In such cases, the commodity manager and the division materials executive will push the division buyer to consider the needs of the other divisions, alternatives that might best address the collective needs of the different divisions, and the standards to be applied in assessing the trade-offs between alternatives. The aim is to help the buyer see solutions that haven't yet been considered and to resolve the conflict with the buyer in the other division.

Initially, this approach required more time from managers than if they had simply made the decisions themselves. But it has paid off in fewer disputes that senior managers need to resolve, speedier contract negotiation, and improved contract terms both for the company as a whole and for multiple divisions. For example, the buyers from three KLA-Tencor product divisions recently locked horns over a global contract with a key supplier. At issue was the trade-off between two variables: one, the supplier's level of liability for materials it needs to purchase in order to fulfill orders and, two, the flexibility granted the KLA-Tencor divisions in modifying the size of the orders and their required lead times. Each division demanded a different balance between these two factors, and the buyers took the conflict to their managers, wondering if they should try to negotiate each of the different trade-offs into the contract or pick among them. After being coached to consider how each division's business model shaped its preference—and using this understanding to jointly brainstorm alternatives—the buyers and commodity manager arrived at a creative solution that worked for everyone: They would request a clause in the contract that allowed them to increase and decrease flexibility in order volume and lead time, with corresponding changes in supplier liability, as required by changing market conditions.

STRATEGIES FOR MANAGING CONFLICT UPON ESCALATION

Equipped with common conflict resolution methods and trade-off criteria, and supported by systematic coaching, people are better able to resolve conflict on their own. But certain complex disputes will inevitably need to be decided by superiors. Consequently, managers must ensure that, upon escalation, conflict is resolved constructively and efficiently—and in ways that model desired behaviors.

ESTABLISH AND ENFORCE A REQUIREMENT OF JOINT ESCALATION. Let's again consider the situation at Matrix. In a typical conflict, three salespeople from different divisions become involved in a dispute over pricing. Frustrated, one of them decides to hand the problem up to his boss, explaining the situation in a short voice-mail message. The message offers little more than bare acknowledgment of the other salespeoples' viewpoints. The manager then determines, on the basis of what he knows about the situation, the solution to the problem. The salesperson, armed with his boss's decision, returns to his counterparts and shares with them the verdict—which, given the process, is simply a stronger version of the solution the salesperson had put forward in the first place. But wait! The other two salespeople have also gone to their managers and carried back stronger versions of their solutions. At this point, each salesperson is locked into what is now "my manager's view" of the right pricing scheme. The problem, already thorny, has become even more intractable.

The best way to avoid this kind of debilitating deadlock is for people to present a disagreement jointly to their boss or bosses. This will reduce or even eliminate the suspicion, surprises, and damaged personal relationships ordinarily associated with unilateral escalation. It will also guarantee that the ultimate decision maker has access to a wide array of perspectives on the conflict, its causes, and the various ways it might be resolved. Furthermore, companies that require people to share responsibility for the escalation of a conflict often see a decrease in the number of problems that are pushed up the management chain. Joint escalation helps create the kind of accountability that is lacking when people know they can provide their side of an issue to their own manager and blame others when things don't work out.

A few years ago, after a merger that resulted in a much larger and more complex organization, senior managers at the Canadian telecommunications company Telus found themselves virtually paralyzed by a daily barrage of unilateral escalations. Just determining who was dealing with what and who should be talking to whom took up huge amounts of senior management's time. So the company made joint escalation a central tenet of its new organization-wide protocols for conflict resolution—a requirement given teeth by managers' refusal to respond to unilateral escalation. When a conflict occurred among managers in different departments concerning, say, the allocation of resources among the departments, the managers were required to jointly describe the problem, what had been done so far to resolve it, and its possible solutions. Then they had to send a joint write-up of the situation to each of their bosses and stand ready to appear together and answer questions when those bosses met to work through a solution. In many cases, the requirement of systematically documenting the conflict and efforts to resolve it—because it forced people to make such efforts—led to a problem being resolved on the spot, without having to be kicked upstairs. Within weeks, this process resulted in the resolution of hundreds of issues that had been stalled for months in the newly merged organization.

ENSURE THAT MANAGERS RESOLVE ESCALATED CONFLICTS DIRECTLY WITH THEIR COUNTERPARTS. Let's return to the three salespeople at Matrix who took their dispute over pricing to their respective bosses and then met again, only to find themselves further from agreement than before. So what did they do at that point? They sent the problem back to their bosses. These three bosses, each of whom thought he'd already resolved the issue, decided the easiest thing to do would be to escalate it themselves. In the end, the decision was made unilaterally by the senior manager with the most organizational clout. This result bred resentment back down the management chain. A sense of "we'll win next time" took hold, ensuring that future conflict would be even more difficult to resolve.

It's not unusual to see managers react to escalations from their employees by simply passing conflicts up their own functional or divisional chains until they reach a senior executive involved with all the affected functions or divisions. Besides providing a poor example for others in the organization, this can be disastrous for a company that needs to move quickly. To avoid wasting time, a manager somewhere along the chain might try to resolve the problem swiftly and decisively by herself. But this, too, has its costs. In a complex organization, where many issues have significant implications for numerous parts of the business, unilateral responses to unilateral escalations are a recipe for inefficiency, bad decisions, and ill feelings.

The solution to these problems is a commitment by managers—a commitment codified in a formal policy—to deal with escalated conflict directly with their counterparts. Of course, doing this can feel cumbersome, especially when an issue is time-sensitive. But resolving the problem early on is ultimately more efficient than trying to sort it out later, after a decision becomes known because it has negatively affected some part of the business.

In the 1990s, IBM's sales and delivery organization became increasingly complex as the company reintegrated previously independent divisions and reorganized itself to provide customers with full solutions of bundled products and services. Senior executives soon recognized that managers were not dealing with escalated conflicts and that relationships among them were strained because they failed to consult and coordinate around cross-unit issues. This led to the creation of a forum called the Market Growth Workshop (a name carefully chosen to send a message throughout the company that getting cross-unit conflict resolved was critical to meeting customer needs and, in turn, growing market share). These monthly conference calls brought together managers, salespeople, and frontline product specialists from across the company to discuss and resolve cross-unit conflicts that were hindering important sales—for example, the difficulty salespeople faced in getting needed technical resources from overstretched product groups.

The Market Growth Workshops weren't successful right away. In the beginning, busy senior managers, reluctant to spend time on issues that often hadn't been carefully thought through, began sending their subordinates to the meetings—which made it even more difficult to resolve the problems discussed. So the company developed a simple preparation template that forced people to document and analyze disputes before the conference calls. Senior managers, realizing the problems created by their absence, recommitted themselves to attending the meetings. Over time, as complex conflicts were resolved during these sessions and significant sales were closed, attendees began to see these meetings as an opportunity to be involved in the resolution of high-stakes, high-visibility issues.

MAKE THE PROCESS FOR ESCALATED CONFLICT RESOLUTION TRANSPARENT. When a sales conflict is resolved by a Matrix senior manager, the word comes down the management chain in the form of an action item: Put together an offering with this particular mix of products and services at these prices. The only elaboration may be an admonishment to "get the sales team together, work up a proposal, and get back to the customer as quickly as possible." The problem is solved, at least for the time being. But the salespeople—unless they have been able to divine themes from the patterns of decisions made over time—are left with little guidance on how to resolve similar issues in the future. They may justifiably wonder: How was the decision made? Based on what kinds of assumptions? With what kinds of trade-offs? How might the reasoning change if the situation were different?

In most companies, once managers have resolved a conflict, they announce the decision and move on. The resolution process and rationale behind the decision are left inside a managerial black box. While it's rarely helpful for managers to share all the gory details of their deliberations around contentious issues, failing to take the time to explain how a decision was reached and the factors that went into it squanders a major opportunity. A frank discussion of the trade-offs involved in decisions would provide guidance to people trying to resolve conflicts in the future and would help nip in the bud the kind of speculation—who won and who lost, which managers or units have the most power—that breeds mistrust, sparks turf battles, and otherwise impedes cross-organizational collaboration. In general, clear communication about the resolution of the conflict can increase people's willingness and ability to implement decisions.

During the past two years, IBM's Market Growth Workshops have evolved into a more structured approach to managing escalated conflict, known as Cross-Team Workouts. Designed to make conflict resolution more transparent, the workouts are weekly meetings of people across the organization who work together on sales and delivery issues for specific accounts. The meetings provide a public forum for resolving conflicts over account strategy, solution configuration, pricing, and delivery. Those issues that cannot be resolved at the local level are escalated to regional workout sessions attended by managers from product groups, services, sales, and finance. Attendees then communicate and explain meeting resolutions to their reports. Issues that cannot be resolved at the regional level are escalated to an even higher-level workout meeting attended by cross-unit executives from a larger geographic region—like the Americas or Asia Pacific—and chaired by the general manager of the region presenting the issue. The most complex and strategic issues reach this global forum. The overlapping attendance at these sessions—in which the managers who chair one level of meeting attend sessions at the next level up, thereby observing the decision-making process at that stage—further enhances the transparency of the system among different levels of the company. IBM has further formalized the process for the direct resolution of conflicts between services and product sales on large accounts by designating a managing director in sales and a global relationship partner in IBM global services as the ultimate point of resolution for escalated conflicts. By explicitly making the resolution of complex conflicts part of the job descriptions for both managing director and global relationship partner—and by making that clear to others in the organization—IBM has reduced ambiguity, increased transparency, and increased the efficiency with which conflicts are resolved.

TAPPING THE LEARNING LATENT IN CONFLICT

The six strategies we have discussed constitute a framework for effectively managing organizational discord, one that integrates conflict resolution into day-to-day decision-making processes, thereby removing a critical barrier to cross-organizational collaboration. But the strategies also hint at something else: that conflict can be more than a necessary antecedent to collaboration.

Most companies view conflict as an unnecessary nuisance—but that view is unfortunate. When a company begins to see conflict as a valuable resource that should be managed and exploited, it is likely to gain insight into problems that senior managers may not have known existed. Because internal friction is often caused by unaddressed strains within an organization or between an organization and its environment, setting up methods to track conflict and examine its causes can provide an interesting new perspective on a variety of issues. In the case of Matrix, taking the time to aggregate the experiences of individual salespeople involved in recurring disputes would likely lead to better approaches to setting prices, establishing incentives for salespeople, and monitoring the company's quality control process.

At Johnson & Johnson, an organization that has a highly decentralized structure, conflict is recognized as a positive aspect of cross-company collaboration. For example, a small internal group charged with facilitating sourcing collaboration among J&J's independent operating companies—particularly their outsourcing of clinical research services—actively works to extract lessons from conflicts. The group tracks and analyzes disagreements about issues such as what to outsource, whether and how to shift spending among suppliers, and what supplier capabilities to invest in. It hosts a council, comprising representatives from the various operating companies, that meets regularly to discuss these differences and explore their strategic implications. As a result, trends in clinical research outsourcing are spotted and information about them is disseminated throughout J&J more quickly. The operating companies benefit from insights about new offshoring opportunities, technologies, and ways of structuring collaboration with suppliers. And J&J, which can now piece together an accurate and global view of its suppliers, is better able to partner with them. Furthermore, the company realizes more value from its relationship with suppliers—yet another example of how the effective management of conflict can ultimately lead to fruitful collaboration.

J&J's approach is unusual but not unique. The benefits it offers provide further evidence that conflict—so often viewed as a liability to be avoided whenever possible—can be valuable to a company that knows how to manage it.

———

Jeff Weiss is a founding partner of Vantage Partners, where he consults on complex negotiations and alliance management; a member of the faculties of the Tuck School of Business and the U.S. Military Academy at West Point; and author of research studies and articles on conflict management, negotiation, and partner management.

———

Jonathan Hughes is a partner at Vantage Partners, where he heads the Sourcing and Supplier Management Practice; author of numerous articles on negotiation, collaboration, and relationship management; and a founder and vice president of development for Vantage Technologies (recently merged with Janeeva Inc.).

CHAPTER TWENTY-EIGHT

Creating and Managing a Learning Culture

The Essence of Leadership

Edgar H. Schein

It can be argued that the only thing of real importance that leaders do is create and manage culture, that the unique talent of leaders is their ability to understand and work with culture, and that it is an ultimate act of leadership to destroy culture when it is viewed as dysfunctional. What distinguishes leadership from management or administration is that leaders create and change culture, while managers and administrators act within it. By defining leadership in this manner, I am not implying that culture is easy to create or change, or that formal leaders are the only determiners of culture. However, if the group's survival is threatened because elements of its culture have become maladapted, it is ultimately the function of leadership at all levels of the organization to recognize and do something about it. In this sense, leadership and culture are conceptually intertwined.

There is much speculation nowadays about the direction in which the world is heading and what all of this means. Globalism, knowledge-based organizations, the information age, the biotech age, the loosening of organizational boundaries, and so on all have one theme in common—we basically do not know what the world of tomorrow will be like, except that it will be *different,* more *complex,* more *fast-paced,* and more *culturally diverse* (Hesselbein, Goldsmith, & Somerville, 1999; Global Business Network, 2002; Schwartz, 2003; Michael, 1985, 1991). This means that *organizations and their leaders will have to become perpetual learners.* When we pose the issue of perpetual learning in the context of cultural analysis, we confront a paradox. Culture is a stabilizer, a conservative force, a way of making things meaningful and predictable. Management consultants and theorists have asserted that "strong" cultures are desirable as a basis for effective and lasting performance. But strong cultures are by definition stable and hard to change. If the world is becoming more turbulent, requiring more flexibility and learning, does this not imply that strong cultures will increasingly become a liability? Or is it possible to imagine a culture that, by its very nature, is learning oriented, adaptive, and flexible? To translate that question into leadership terms, what is the direction in which the leaders of today should be pushing cultural evolution? What leadership characteristics and skills are needed to perceive the organizational needs of tomorrow and implement the changes needed to survive?

WHAT MIGHT A LEARNING CULTURE LOOK LIKE

A first attempt to describe the characteristics of a learning culture leads to identifying the following ten key issues.

1. A PROACTIVITY ASSUMPTION. A learning culture would assume that the appropriate way for humans to behave is to be proactive problem solvers and learners. The learning leader must also portray confidence that active problem solving leads to learning, thereby setting an appropriate example for others in the organization. It will be more important to be committed to the learning *process* than to any particular solution. In the face of greater complexity, the leader's dependence on others to generate solutions will increase, and we have overwhelming evidence that new solutions are more likely to be adopted if the members of the organization have been involved in generating them.

2. A COMMITMENT TO LEARNING TO LEARN. A learning culture must have a "learning gene" in its organizational DNA: members must hold the shared assumption that learning is a good thing and something

worth investing in, and that learning to learn is itself a skill to be mastered. Learning must include not only learning about changes in the external environment but also learning about internal relationships and how well the organization is adapted to the external changes. One key to learning is to get feedback and to take the time to reflect, analyze, and assimilate its implications. Another key is the ability to generate new responses, try new ways of doing things, and obtain feedback on the results of the new behaviors. This takes time, energy, and resources. A learning culture must value reflection and experimentation, and give its members the time and resources to do it.

3. A POSITIVE ASSUMPTION ABOUT HUMAN NATURE. Learning leaders must have faith in people and believe that ultimately human nature is good—and, in any case, malleable—and that people will learn if provided with the resources and necessary psychological safety. Learning implies a desire for survival and improvement. If leaders start with assumptions that people are basically lazy and passive, that people have no concern for organizations or causes above and beyond themselves, they will inevitably create organizations that will become self-fulfilling prophecies. Such leaders will train their employees to be lazy, self-protective, and self-seeking, and they will then cite those characteristics as proof of their original assumptions about human nature. One might wonder why Douglas McGregor's (1960) insight into this problem in terms of Theory X (cynical mistrust of people) and Theory Y (idealistic trust of people) still has not taken hold.

4. AN ASSUMPTION THAT THE ENVIRONMENT CAN BE DOMINATED. A learning culture must contain the shared assumption that the environment is to some degree manageable. A passive organization that assumes that it must accept its niche will have more difficulty learning as the environment becomes more turbulent. Adaptation to a slowly changing environment is also a viable learning process, but the way that the world is changing will make that less and less possible.

5. A COMMITMENT TO TRUTH THROUGH PRAGMATISM AND INQUIRY. A learning culture must contain the shared assumption that solutions to problems derive from a deep belief in inquiry and a pragmatic search for truth. What must be avoided is the automatic assumption that wisdom and truth reside in any one source or method. As the problems we encounter change, so too will our learning methods. For some purposes we will rely on normal science; for others, we will have to find truth in experienced practitioners; for still others, we will have to collectively experiment and live with errors until better solutions are found. Knowledge and skill will be found in many forms, and what I call a *clinical research process*—in which helpers and clients work things out together—will become more and more important. One might say that in the learning organization, we will have to *learn how to learn*. The toughest problem for learning leaders will be to come to terms with their own lack of expertise and wisdom. The learning task in learning cultures becomes a shared responsibility.

6. AN ORIENTATION TOWARD THE FUTURE. There is an optimal time orientation for learning, somewhere between the very far future and the near future. One must think far enough ahead to be able to assess the systemic consequences of different courses of action, but also think in terms of the near future to assess whether or not one's solutions are working. A similar argument can be made about assumptions about optimal units of time—should we think primarily in terms of minutes, hours, days, months, quarters, years, decades? This will, of course, depend on the task and the kind of learning that is going on, but the optimal assumption is that one should pick medium-length time units for assessment: enough time to test whether a proposed solution is working but not so much time that one persists with a proposed solution that is clearly not. For any given task, the learning leader will have to make an instant diagnosis of what an optimal time orientation and a medium length of time is, and that will vary from situation to situation. As the world becomes more complex, we will be less and less able to rely on standard time units such as quarters or years.

7. A COMMITMENT TO FULL AND OPEN TASK RELEVANT COMMUNICATION. A learning culture must be built on the assumption that communication and information are central to organizational well-being and must therefore create a multi-channel communication system that allows everyone to connect to everyone else. This does not mean that all channels will be used or that any given channel will be used for all things. What it means is that anyone must be able to communicate with anyone else in the organization and that everyone assumes that telling the truth as best one can is positive and desirable. This principle of openness does not suspend all the cultural rules pertaining to face or adopt a definition of openness equivalent to "letting it all hang out"—there is ample evidence that such behavior can create severe problems across hierarchical boundaries and in intercultural settings. It means, rather, that one must become sensitive to *task-relevant information* and be as open as possible in sharing that. One of the important roles for the learning leader will be to specify, in terms of any given task, what the minimum communication system must be and what kind of information is critical to effective problem solving and learning.

8. A COMMITMENT TO DIVERSITY. The more turbulent the environment, the more likely it is that the more diverse organizations will have the resources and capacities to cope with unpredicted events. Therefore, the learning leader should stimulate diversity and promulgate the assumption that diversity is desirable at the individual and subgroup levels. Such diversity will inevitably create subcultures, but those subcultures will eventually be a necessary resource for learning and innovation. For diversity to be a resource, however, the subcultures must be connected and must learn to value each other enough to learn something of each other's culture and language. A central task for the learning leader, then, is to ensure good cross-cultural communication and understanding throughout the organization. Laissez-faire leadership does not work, because it is in the nature of subgroups and subcultures to protect their own interests. Optimizing diversity requires higher-order coordination mechanisms and mutual understanding.

9. A COMMITMENT TO SYSTEMIC THINKING. As the world becomes more complex and interdependent, the ability to think systemically, analyze fields of forces and understand their joint causal effects on each other, and abandon simple linear causal logic in favor of complex mental models will become more critical to learning. There are many variations of systemic thinking, such as "systems thinking" as promulgated by Senge (1990) and Sterman (2000), systemic thinking in biology, systemic thinking in family therapy, and so on. The learning leader must believe that the world is intrinsically complex, nonlinear, and interconnected, and that most phenomena are multiply caused.

10. A COMMITMENT TO CULTURAL ANALYSIS FOR UNDERSTANDING AND IMPROVING THE WORLD. Finally, a learning culture must understand the concept of culture and the learning leader must be willing and able to work with culture [Schein, 2004].

THE EVOLVING ROLE OF A LEARNING LEADER

The role of the learning leader changes in different stages of organizational evolution. In launching and growing an organization, leaders externalize their own assumptions and embed them gradually and consistently in the mission, goals, structures, and working procedures of the group. Whether we call these basic assumptions the guiding beliefs, the theories-in-use, the mental models, the basic principles, or the guiding visions on which founders operate, there is little question that they become major elements of the emerging culture of the organization.

In a rapidly changing world, the learning leader-founder must not only have vision, but also be able both to impose it and to evolve it as external circumstances change. Inasmuch as the new members of an organization arrive with prior organizational and cultural experiences, a common set of assumptions can be forged only by clear and consistent messages as the group encounters and survives its own crises. The culture creation leader therefore needs persistence and patience: to be simultaneously clear and strong in articulating a vision and open to change if that very vision becomes maladaptive.

Once an organization develops a substantial history of its own, however, its culture becomes more of a cause than an effect. The culture now influences the strategy, the structure, the procedures, and the ways in which the group members will relate to each other. Culture becomes a powerful influence on members' perceiving, thinking, and feeling, and these predispositions, along with situational factors, will influence the members' behavior. Because it serves an important anxiety-reducing function, culture at this stage of organizational evolution will be clung to even if it becomes dysfunctional. Leaders at this stage need, above all, the insight and skill to help the organizational culture evolve into whatever will be most effective for the organization's future.

In the mature organization, if it has developed a strong unifying culture, that culture now defines even what is to be thought of as leadership, what is heroic or sinful behavior, and how authority and power are to be allocated and managed. Thus, what leadership has created now either blindly perpetuates itself or creates new definitions of leadership, which may not even include the kinds of entrepreneurial assumptions that started the organization in the first place. The first problem of the mature and possibly declining organization, then, is to find a process to empower a potential leader who may have enough insight and influence to overcome some of the constraining cultural assumptions. Conceived of in this way, leadership is the capacity to surmount the very organizational culture that the leader him- or herself helped to create: to be able to perceive and think about ways of doing things that are different from what the current organizational assumptions imply.

To fulfill this role adequately, learning leaders must be well connected to those parts of the organization that are themselves well connected to the external environment—the sales organization, purchasing, marketing, public relations, legal, finance, and R&D. Learning leaders must also be able to listen to disconfirming information coming from these sources and to assess the implications for the future of the organization. Only when they truly understand what is happening and what will be required in the way of organizational change can they begin to take action in starting a learning process. Much has been said of the need for vision in leaders, but too little has been said of their need to listen, to absorb, to search the environment for trends, and to build the organization's capacity to learn.

BECOMING A LEARNING LEADER

A learning culture assumes that the world is intrinsically a complex field of interconnected forces in which multiple causations are more likely than linear or simple causes. The fundamental function of learning-oriented leadership in a turbulent world, then, is to promote these kinds of assumptions. Leaders themselves, however, must first hold such assumptions, become learners themselves, and then learn to recognize and systematically reward behavior based on those assumptions in others.

An analysis of organizational culture makes it clear that leadership is intertwined with culture formation, evolution, transformation, and destruction. Culture is created in the first instance by the actions of leaders; culture is also embedded and strengthened by leaders. When culture becomes dysfunctional, leadership is needed to help the group unlearn some of its cultural assumptions and learn new assumptions. Such transformations sometimes require what amounts to conscious and deliberate destruction of cultural elements, which in turn requires the ability to surmount one's own taken-for-granted assumptions, see what is needed, and enable the group to evolve toward acceptance of new cultural assumptions. Without this leadership, groups would not be able to adapt to changing environmental conditions. What, then, is really needed to be a leader in this sense?

It seems clear that the leader of the future must be a perpetual learner. This will require:

1. New levels of perception and insight into the realities of the world and into him- or herself

2. Extraordinary levels of motivation to go through the inevitable pain of learning and change, especially in a world with looser boundaries in which one's own loyalties become more and more difficult to define

3. The emotional strength to manage one's own and others' anxiety as learning and change become more and more a way of life

4. New skills in analyzing and changing cultural assumptions

5. The willingness and ability to involve others and elicit their participation

Learning and change cannot be imposed on people. Their involvement and participation are needed in diagnosing what is going on, in figuring out what to do, and in actually bringing about learning and change. The more turbulent, ambiguous, and out of control the world becomes, the more the learning process must be shared by all members of the social unit doing the learning.

In the end, we must give organizational culture its due. Can we recognize—as individual members of organizations and occupations, as managers, as teachers and researchers, and sometimes as leaders—how deeply our own perceptions, thoughts, and feelings are culturally determined? Ultimately, we cannot achieve the cultural humility that is required to live in a turbulent and culturally diverse world unless we can see cultural assumptions within ourselves. In the end, cultural understanding and cultural learning starts with self-insight.

———

Edgar H. Schein is Sloan Fellows Professor of Management emeritus at the MIT Sloan School of Management. He has authored fourteen books on organizational culture and management.

CHAPTER TWENTY-NINE

Leading Change

Why Transformation Efforts Fail

John P. Kotter

Over the past decade, I have watched more than 100 companies try to remake themselves into significantly better competitors. They have included large organizations (Ford) and small ones (Landmark Communications), companies based in the United States (General Motors) and elsewhere (British Airways), corporations that were on their knees (Eastern Air Lines), and companies that were earning good money (Bristol-Myers Squibb). These efforts have gone under many banners: total quality management, reengineering, right sizing, restructuring, cultural change, and turnaround. But, in almost every case, the basic goal has been the same: to make fundamental changes in how business is conducted in order to help cope with a new, more challenging market environment.

A few of these corporate change efforts have been very successful. A few have been utter failures. Most fall somewhere in between, with a distinct tilt toward the lower end of the scale. The lessons that can be drawn are interesting and will probably be relevant to even more organizations in the increasingly competitive business environment of the coming decade.

The most general lesson to be learned from the more successful cases is that the change process goes through a series of phases that, in total, usually require a considerable length of time. Skipping steps creates only the illusion of speed and never produces a satisfying result. A second very general lesson is that critical mistakes in any of the phases can have a devastating impact, slowing momentum and negating hard-won gains. Perhaps because we have relatively little experience in renewing organizations, even very capable people often make at least one big error.

ERROR #1: NOT ESTABLISHING A GREAT ENOUGH SENSE OF URGENCY

Most successful change efforts begin when some individuals or some groups start to look hard at a company's competitive situation, market position, technological trends, and financial performance. They focus on the potential revenue drop when an important patent expires, the five-year trend in declining margins in a core business, or an emerging market that everyone seems to be ignoring. They then find ways to communicate this information broadly and dramatically, especially with respect to crises, potential crises, or great opportunities that are very timely. This first step is essential because just getting a transformation program started requires the aggressive cooperation of many individuals. Without motivation, people won't help and the effort goes nowhere.

Compared with other steps in the change process, phase one can sound easy. It is not. Well over 50% of the companies I have watched fail in this first phase. What are the reasons for that failure? Sometimes executives underestimate how hard it can be to drive people out of their comfort zones. Sometimes they grossly overestimate how successful they have already been in increasing urgency. Sometimes they lack patience: "Enough with the preliminaries; let's get on with it." In many cases, executives become paralyzed by the downside possibilities. They worry that employees with seniority will become defensive, that morale will drop, that events will spin out of control, that short-term business results will be jeopardized, that the stock will sink, and that they will be blamed for creating a crisis.

A paralyzed senior management often comes from having too many managers and not enough leaders. Management's mandate is to minimize risk and to keep the current system operating. Change, by definition, requires creating a new system, which in turn always demands leadership. Phase one in a renewal process typically goes nowhere until enough real leaders are promoted or hired into senior-level jobs.

Transformations often begin, and begin well, when an organization has a new head who is a good leader and who sees the need for a major change. If the renewal target is the entire company, the CEO is key. If change is needed in a division, the division general manager is key. When these individuals are not new leaders, great leaders, or change champions, phase one can be a huge challenge.

Bad business results are both a blessing and a curse in the first phase. On the positive side, losing money does catch people's attention. But it also gives less maneuvering room. With good business results, the opposite is true: convincing people of the need for change is much harder, but you have more resources to help make changes.

But whether the starting point is good performance or bad, in the more successful cases I have witnessed, an individual or a group always facilitates a frank discussion of potentially unpleasant facts: about new competition, shrinking margins, decreasing market share, flat earnings, a lack of revenue growth, or other relevant indices of a declining competitive position. Because there seems to be an almost universal human tendency to shoot the bearer of bad news, especially if the head of the organization is not a change champion, executives in these companies often rely on outsiders to bring unwanted information. Wall Street analysts, customers, and consultants can all be helpful in this regard. The purpose of all this activity, in the words of one former CEO of a large European company, is "to make the status quo seem more dangerous than launching into the unknown."

In a few of the most successful cases, a group has manufactured a crisis. One CEO deliberately engineered the largest accounting loss in the company's history, creating huge pressures from Wall Street in the process. One division president commissioned first-ever customer-satisfaction surveys, knowing full well that the results would be terrible. He then made these findings public. On the surface, such moves can look unduly risky. But there is also risk in playing it too safe: when the urgency rate is not pumped up enough, the transformation process cannot succeed and the long-term future of the organization is put in jeopardy.

When is the urgency rate high enough? From what I have seen, the answer is when about 75% of a company's management is honestly convinced that business-as-usual is totally unacceptable. Anything less can produce very serious problems later on in the process.

ERROR #2: NOT CREATING A POWERFUL ENOUGH GUIDING COALITION

Major renewal programs often start with just one or two people. In cases of successful transformation efforts, the leadership coalition grows and grows over time. But whenever some minimum mass is not achieved early in the effort, nothing much worthwhile happens.

It is often said that major change is impossible unless the head of the organization is an active supporter. What I am talking about goes far beyond that. In successful transformations, the chairman or president or division general manager, plus another 5 or 15 or 50 people, come together and develop a shared commitment to excellent performance through renewal. In my experience, this group never includes all of the company's most senior executives because some people just won't buy in, at least not at first. But in the most successful cases, the coalition is always pretty powerful—in terms of titles, information and expertise, reputations and relationships.

In both small and large organizations, a successful guiding team may consist of only three to five people during the first year of a renewal effort. But in big companies, the coalition needs to grow to the 20 to 50 range before much progress can be made in phase three and beyond. Senior managers always form the core of the group. But sometimes you find board members, a representative from a key customer, or even a powerful union leader.

Because the guiding coalition includes members who are not part of senior management, it tends to operate outside of the normal hierarchy by definition. This can be awkward, but it is clearly necessary. If the existing hierarchy were working well, there would be no need for a major transformation. But since the current system is not working, reform generally demands activity outside of formal boundaries, expectations, and protocol.

A high sense of urgency within the managerial ranks helps enormously in putting a guiding coalition together. But more is usually required. Someone needs to get these people together, help them develop a shared assessment of their company's problems and opportunities, and create a minimum level of trust and communication. Off-site retreats, for two or three days, are one popular vehicle for accomplishing this task. I have seen many groups of 5 to 35 executives attend a series of these retreats over a period of months.

Companies that fail in phase two usually underestimate the difficulties of producing change and thus the importance of a powerful guiding coalition. Sometimes they have no history of teamwork at the top and therefore undervalue the importance of this type of coalition. Sometimes they expect the team to be led by a staff executive from human resources, quality, or strategic planning instead of a key line manager. No matter how capable or dedicated the staff head, groups without strong line leadership never achieve the power that is required.

Efforts that don't have a powerful enough guiding coalition can make apparent progress for a while. But, sooner or later, the opposition gathers itself together and stops the change.

ERROR #3: LACKING A VISION

In every successful transformation effort that I have seen, the guiding coalition develops a picture of the future that is relatively easy to communicate and appeals to customers, stockholders, and employees. A vision always goes beyond the numbers that are typically found in five-year plans. A vision says something that helps clarify the direction in which an organization needs to move. Sometimes the first draft comes mostly from a single individual. It is usually a bit blurry, at least initially. But after the coalition works at it for 3 or 5 or even 12 months, something much better emerges through their tough analytical thinking and a little dreaming. Eventually, a strategy for achieving that vision is also developed.

In one midsize European company, the first pass at a vision contained two-thirds of the basic ideas that were in the final product. The concept of global reach was in the initial version from the beginning. So was the idea of becoming preeminent in certain businesses. But one central idea in the final version—getting out of low value-added activities—came only after a series of discussions over a period of several months.

Without a sensible vision, a transformation effort can easily dissolve into a list of confusing and incompatible projects that can take the organization in the wrong direction or nowhere at all. Without a sound vision, the reengineering project in the accounting department, the new 360-degree performance appraisal from the human resources department, the plant's quality program, the cultural change project in the sales force will not add up in a meaningful way.

In failed transformations, you often find plenty of plans and directives and programs, but no vision. In one case, a company gave out four-inch-thick notebooks describing its change effort. In mind-numbing detail, the books spelled out procedures, goals, methods, and deadlines. But nowhere was there a clear and compelling statement of where all this was leading. Not surprisingly, most of the employees with whom I talked were either confused or alienated. The big, thick books did not rally them together or inspire change. In fact, they probably had just the opposite effect.

In a few of the less successful cases that I have seen, management had a sense of direction, but it was too complicated or blurry to be useful. Recently, I asked an executive in a midsize company to describe his vision and received in return a barely comprehensible 30-minute lecture. Buried in his answer were the basic elements of a sound vision. But they were buried—deeply.

A useful rule of thumb: if you can't communicate the vision to someone in five minutes or less and get a reaction that signifies both understanding and interest, you are not yet done with this phase of the transformation process.

ERROR #4: UNDERCOMMUNICATING THE VISION BY A FACTOR OF TEN

I've seen three patterns with respect to communication, all very common. In the first, a group actually does develop a pretty good transformation vision and then proceeds to communicate it by holding a single meeting or sending out a single communication. Having used about .0001% of the yearly intracompany communication, the group is startled that few people seem to understand the new approach. In the second pattern, the head of the organization spends a considerable amount of time making speeches to employee groups, but most people still don't get it (not surprising, since vision captures only .0005% of the total yearly communication). In the third pattern, much more effort goes into newsletters and speeches, but some very visible senior executives still behave in ways that are antithetical to the vision. The net result is that cynicism among the troops goes up, while belief in the communication goes down.

Transformation is impossible unless hundreds or thousands of people are willing to help, often to the point of making short-term sacrifices. Employees will not make sacrifices, even if they are unhappy with the status quo, unless they believe that useful change is possible. Without credible communication, and a lot of it, the hearts and minds of the troops are never captured.

This fourth phase is particularly challenging if the short-term sacrifices include job losses. Gaining understanding and support is tough when downsizing is a part of the vision. For this reason, successful visions usually include new growth possibilities and the commitment to treat fairly anyone who is laid off.

Executives who communicate well incorporate messages into their hour-by-hour activities. In a routine discussion about a business problem, they talk about how proposed solutions fit (or don't fit) into the bigger picture. In a regular performance appraisal, they talk about how the employee's behavior helps or undermines the vision. In a review of a division's quarterly performance, they talk not only about the numbers but also about how the division's executives are contributing to the transformation. In a routine Q&A with employees at a company facility, they tie their answers back to renewal goals.

In more successful transformation efforts, executives use all existing communication channels to broadcast the vision. They turn boring and unread company newsletters into lively articles about the vision. They take ritualistic and tedious quarterly management meetings and turn them into exciting discussions of the transformation. They throw out much of the company's generic management education and replace it with courses that focus on business problems and the new vision. The guiding principle is simple: use every possible channel, especially those that are being wasted on nonessential information.

Perhaps even more important, most of the executives I have known in successful cases of major change learn to "walk the talk." They consciously attempt to become a living symbol of the new corporate culture. This is often not easy. A 60-year-old plant manager who has spent precious little time over 40 years thinking about customers will not suddenly behave in a customer-oriented way. But I have witnessed just such a person change, and change a great deal. In that case, a high level of urgency helped. The fact that the man was a part of the guiding coalition and the vision-creation team also helped. So did all the communication, which kept reminding him of the desired behavior, and all the feedback from his peers and subordinates, which helped him see when he was not engaging in that behavior.

Communication comes in both words and deeds, and the latter are often the most powerful form. Nothing undermines change more than behavior by important individuals that is inconsistent with their words.

ERROR #5: NOT REMOVING OBSTACLES TO THE NEW VISION

Successful transformations begin to involve large numbers of people as the process progresses. Employees are emboldened to try new approaches, to develop new ideas, and to provide leadership. The only constraint is that the actions fit within the broad parameters of the overall vision. The more people involved, the better the outcome.

To some degree, a guiding coalition empowers others to take action simply by successfully communicating the new direction. But communication is never sufficient by itself. Renewal also requires the removal of obstacles. Too often, an employee understands the new vision and wants to help make it happen. But an elephant appears to be blocking the path. In some cases, the elephant is in the person's head, and the challenge is to convince the individual that no external obstacle exists. But in most cases, the blockers are very real.

Sometimes the obstacle is the organizational structure: narrow job categories can seriously undermine efforts to increase productivity or make it very difficult even to think about customers. Sometimes compensation or performance-appraisal systems make people choose between the new vision and their own self-interest. Perhaps worst of all are bosses who refuse to change and who make demands that are inconsistent with the overall effort.

One company began its transformation process with much publicity and actually made good progress through the fourth phase. Then the change effort ground to a halt because the officer in charge of the company's largest division was allowed to undermine most of the new initiatives. He paid lip service to the process but did not change his behavior or encourage his managers to change. He did not reward the unconventional ideas called for in the vision. He allowed human resource systems to remain intact even when they were clearly inconsistent with the new ideals. I think the officer's motives were complex. To some degree, he did not believe the company needed major change. To some degree, he felt personally threatened by all the change. To some degree, he was afraid that he could not produce both change and the expected operating profit. But despite the fact that they backed the renewal effort, the other officers did virtually nothing to stop the one blocker. Again, the reasons were complex. The company had no history of confronting problems like this. Some people were afraid of the officer. The CEO was concerned that he might lose a talented executive. The net result was disastrous. Lower level managers concluded that senior management had lied to them about their commitment to renewal, cynicism grew, and the whole effort collapsed.

In the first half of a transformation, no organization has the momentum, power, or time to get rid of all obstacles. But the big ones must be confronted and removed. If the blocker is a person, it is important that he or she be treated fairly and in a way that is consistent with the new vision. But action is essential, both to empower others and to maintain the credibility of the change effort as a whole.

ERROR #6: NOT SYSTEMATICALLY PLANNING FOR AND CREATING SHORT-TERM WINS

Real transformation takes time, and a renewal effort risks losing momentum if there are no short-term goals to meet and celebrate. Most people won't go on the long march unless they see compelling evidence within 12 to 24 months that the journey is producing expected results. Without short-term wins, too many people give up or actively join the ranks of those people who have been resisting change.

One to two years into a successful transformation effort, you find quality beginning to go up on certain indices or the decline in net income stopping. You find some successful new product introductions or an upward shift in market share. You find an impressive productivity improvement or a statistically higher customer-satisfaction rating. But whatever the case, the win is unambiguous. The result is not just a judgment call that can be discounted by those opposing change.

Creating short-term wins is different from hoping for short-term wins. The latter is passive, the former active. In a successful transformation, managers actively look for ways to obtain clear performance improvements, establish goals in the yearly planning system, achieve the objectives, and reward the people involved with recognition, promotions, and even money. For example, the guiding coalition at a U.S. manufacturing company produced a highly visible and successful new product introduction about 20 months after the start of its renewal effort. The new product was selected about six months into the effort because it met multiple criteria: it could be designed and launched in a relatively short period; it could be handled by a small team of people who were devoted to the new vision; it had upside potential; and the new product-development team could operate outside the established departmental structure without practical problems. Little was left to chance, and the win boosted the credibility of the renewal process.

Managers often complain about being forced to produce short-term wins, but I've found that pressure can be a useful element in a change effort. When it becomes clear to people that major change will take a long time, urgency levels can drop. Commitments to produce short-term wins help keep the urgency level up and force detailed analytical thinking that can clarify or revise visions.

ERROR #7: DECLARING VICTORY TOO SOON

After a few years of hard work, managers may be tempted to declare victory with the first clear performance improvement. While celebrating a win is fine, declaring the war won can be catastrophic. Until changes sink deeply into a company's culture, a process that can take five to ten years, new approaches are fragile and subject to regression.

In the recent past, I have watched a dozen change efforts operate under the reengineering theme. In all but two cases, victory was declared and the expensive consultants were paid and thanked when the first major project was completed after two to three years. Within two more years, the useful changes that had been introduced slowly disappeared. In two of the ten cases, it's hard to find any trace of the reengineering work today.

Over the past 20 years, I've seen the same sort of thing happen to huge quality projects, organizational development efforts, and more. Typically, the problems start early in the process: the urgency level is not intense enough, the guiding coalition is not powerful enough, and the vision is not clear enough. But it is the premature victory celebration that kills momentum. And then the powerful forces associated with tradition take over.

Ironically, it is often a combination of change initiators and change resistors that creates the premature victory celebration. In their enthusiasm over a clear sign of progress, the initiators go overboard. They are then joined by resistors, who are quick to spot any opportunity to stop change. After the celebration is over, the resistors point to the victory as a sign that the war has been won and the troops should be sent home. Weary troops allow themselves to be convinced that they won. Once home, the foot soldiers are reluctant to climb back on the ships. Soon thereafter, change comes to a halt, and tradition creeps back in.

Instead of declaring victory, leaders of successful efforts use the credibility afforded by short-term wins to tackle even bigger problems. They go after systems and structures that are not consistent with the transformation vision and have not been confronted before. They pay great attention to who is promoted, who is hired, and how people are developed. They include new reengineering projects that are even bigger in scope than the initial ones. They understand that renewal efforts take not months but years. In fact, in one of the most successful transformations that I have ever seen, we quantified the amount of change that occurred each year over a seven-year period. On a scale of one (low) to ten (high), year one received a two, year two a four, year three a three, year four a seven, year five an eight, year six a four, and year seven a two. The peak came in year five, fully 36 months after the first set of visible wins.

ERROR #8: NOT ANCHORING CHANGES IN THE CORPORATION'S CULTURE

In the final analysis, change sticks when it becomes "the way we do things around here," when it seeps into the bloodstream of the corporate body. Until new behaviors are rooted in social norms and shared values, they are subject to degradation as soon as the pressure for change is removed.

Two factors are particularly important in institutionalizing change in corporate culture. The first is a conscious attempt to show people how the new approaches, behaviors, and attitudes have helped improve performance. When people are left on their own to make the connections, they sometimes create very inaccurate links. For example, because results improved while charismatic Harry was boss, the troops link his mostly idiosyncratic style with those results instead of seeing how their own improved customer service and productivity were instrumental. Helping people see the right connections requires communication. Indeed, one company was relentless, and it paid off enormously. Time was spent at every major management meeting to discuss why performance was increasing. The company newspaper ran article after article showing how changes had boosted earnings.

The second factor is taking sufficient time to make sure that the next generation of top management really does personify the new approach. If the requirements for promotion don't change, renewal rarely lasts. One bad succession decision at the top of an organization can undermine a decade of hard work. Poor succession decisions are possible when boards of directors are not an integral part of the renewal effort. In at least three instances I have seen, the champion for change was the retiring executive, and although his successor was not a resistor, he was not a change champion. Because the boards did not understand the transformations in any detail, they could not see that their choices were not good fits. The retiring executive in one case tried unsuccessfully to talk his board into a less seasoned candidate who better personified the transformation. In the other two cases, the CEOs did not resist the boards' choices, because they felt the transformation could not be undone by their successors. They were wrong. Within two years, signs of renewal began to disappear at both companies.

There are still more mistakes that people make, but these eight are the big ones. I realize that in a short article everything is made to sound a bit too simplistic. In reality, even successful change efforts are messy and full of surprises. But just as a relatively simple vision is needed to guide people through a major change, so a vision of the change process can reduce the error rate. And fewer errors can spell the difference between success and failure.

———✦✦✦———

John P. Kotter is the Konosuke Matsushita Professor of Leadership emeritus at Harvard Business School and the author of multiple, best-selling books on organizational leadership and change.

CHAPTER THIRTY

Leading at the Enterprise Level

Douglas A. Ready

F or the past couple of decades, companies have focused on creating strong leaders of business units and influential heads of functions—men and women responsible for achieving results in one corner of an organization. But they have not paid as much attention to a more important challenge: developing leaders who see the enterprise as a whole and act for its greater good. And that perspective has become increasingly necessary as companies seek to provide not just products but broad-based customer solutions.

It is easy to understand why companies emphasized the development of strong unit and functional leaders. Since the 1980s, the dominant view has been that effective organizations are highly decentralized and therefore, in theory, able to respond more quickly to customers. As business units became increasingly autonomous, the leaders who reaped the most praise and attention were bold, independent business builders. The challenge for those in the corporate center was to manage, not to lead, and to be as hands-off as possible in their dealings with those running the businesses or the regions.

But left unchecked, such autonomy can produce an organizational culture defined by a take-it-or-leave-it, product-push mentality. The demise of companies that were icons of their industries, such as Digital Equipment Corp. or Polaroid Corp., is evidence of this danger. These companies were once technology leaders with great products, but the spirit of autonomy that they fostered eventually led to the creation of product silos overseen by powerful leaders. Customers had a choice: They could buy the products on offer or go elsewhere. When other companies began to offer better technologies, the two giants' products were no longer competitive, and customers fled.

Today, even cutting-edge products are not enough to ensure customer loyalty. Customers are stepping up demands for integrated solutions to their problems. While companies have developed new strategies for meeting those demands, many have yet to change their thinking about what constitutes effective leadership in this environment. Decentralization itself is not the issue. The main point is that solutions strategies cannot be implemented by leaders who have a product-push silo mentality. Until companies recognize this fact, they will be frustrated in their efforts to deliver integrated customer solutions by a gap between their strategies and their capabilities.

It is imperative, then, for companies to be able to identify and develop enterprise leaders—people who can deliver differentiated value by bringing the total resources of their companies to their customers. In order to link strategy to leadership development, they must be able to answer three questions: What are the key elements of the enterprise leader's job? Why is learning to lead at the enterprise level such a difficult challenge? And what can companies do to identify and develop enterprise leaders?

THE ENTERPRISE LEADER'S JOB

On a simple level, an enterprise leader is anyone accountable for the economic and social welfare of the total enterprise, across divisions, businesses, functions and locations. An enterprise leader might run a business unit or oversee a major function but will make decisions with the entire corporation in mind. In other words, "enterprise leader" is not a job title—the term represents a way of thinking and behaving. Effective enterprise leaders excel at four tasks that may be difficult to quantify but are essential to any company's ability to compete.

First, enterprise leaders focus organizational attention on the customer, setting priorities and driving out distractions. Second, they build multiple organizational capabilities simultaneously, especially in the areas of strategic competence and organizational character. Third, they reconcile the tensions—between growth and stability, for example—which are embedded in any organization. Finally, they create alignment by building consistency between an organization's statements of purpose, its processes, and the skills and behaviors required of its people. These four broad tasks encapsulate some of the hardest work that a manager will ever attempt. A closer look at each aspect reveals the challenges facing the enterprise leader.

Focusing Organizational Attention

Massive complexity is a fact of life today, but successful enterprise leaders don't ignore it or run from it. Instead, they search it out and reduce it so that others in the organization can focus on the firm's customers.

At PricewaterhouseCoopers, enterprise leaders brought order to chaos in order to successfully complete the merger that created the world's largest professional services firm. In the late 1990s, when Price Waterhouse merged with Coopers & Lybrand, the newly combined company had 165,000 employees and conducted business in more than 120 countries. Demand for the new firm's services required the company to hire 1,000 professionals per week, on average, in order to keep up. But there was a downside, as within six months clients began complaining to senior executives that PwC's client knowledge was slipping. The firm's people were operating without the strategic purpose and cultural compass that they needed to be effective.

PwC's top 10 executives (the Global Leadership Team) then met with the top 50 senior managers at the next tier to reduce the complexity brought on by so much opportunity. The group's mantra for the next year was "ruthless prioritization." PwC's then-CEO, James Shiro, was advocating an integration strategy to the firm's partners, but employees at the grass roots didn't know what "integration" meant for them or what they were expected to do to bring it about. Absent a clear explanation, a generic term like integration could be taken to mean "slow, bureaucratic decision making."

The new team of senior leaders focused PwC's businesses on areas in which they could add value that would differentiate the firm from others in the industry. Given PwC's emphasis on client service, the team made small but important changes to the strategy: PwC would commit to becoming "intelligently integrated," meaning it would integrate only if and when doing so would provide more value to its clients. The team also worked to repair the organization's cultural compass. Although the two companies had well-articulated values before the merger, PwC's senior leaders created a compelling new set of core values that would serve as a code of employee conduct for the merged firm. They rallied the entire organization behind the new direction. Clients stopped grumbling about the lack of focus and client knowledge, and PwC, despite the slumping economy, emerged as the market force envisioned by its leaders when they negotiated the merger.

Building Capabilities

Companies can be thought of as what they do—as seen in their strategic vision and the way they execute it—and as who they are, as revealed by their organization's code of conduct and cultural norms. The "doing" aspects of the enterprise leader's job can be thought of as building strategic competence, while the "being" aspects are a matter of building organizational character. Leaders with an enterprise perspective understand the importance of building strategic competence and organizational character simultaneously.

Consider how the enterprise leadership team at Continental AG in Hanover, Germany, identified and built new organizational capabilities when the company embarked on a large-scale strategic and cultural transformation.

In the mid-1990s, Continental was the world's fourth-largest tire manufacturer. It was an OEM supplier to many prestigious auto manufacturers and had a vibrant replacement business throughout Europe. But in a fiercely competitive market known for its tight margins, it was only modestly profitable. And the company's newly appointed CEO, Hubertus von Grünberg, knew that globalization would disrupt regional players such as Continental. He and his enterprise leadership team of 50 decided that the company must transform itself from a European tire manufacturer into something much more complex: a tier-one supplier of high-technology integrated wheel, brake and chassis systems to the global automobile industry. Cross-border strategic alliances and acquisitions would be the key to the accomplishment of this objective.

The obstacles to success were large. Continental had not grown through partnerships or acquisitions, and thus its leadership lacked both the mind-set and skills to carry out the new strategic direction. Recognizing this reality, von Grünberg decided to embark on a massive team-building and capability-building effort. In conflict with his personal style (and level of comfort), he engaged his enterprise leadership team in open dialogue on the challenges facing the company. This was not as simple as it may sound: The monthly meetings were at first very tense—the executives had to learn to trust von Grünberg, and the future direction of the company was at stake. Over time, as it became clear that no one would be punished for being honest, the tension abated and the group's members came to trust one another.

The leadership group also worked intensively on practical matters, learning how to execute cross-border partnerships and acquisitions, to work across cultural boundaries and to lead cross-border project teams. The company brought in some new executives who had such capabilities and dismissed others who demonstrated that they were unwilling or unable to change.

Within two years, Continental had achieved what it set out to do. After making several critical acquisitions from ITT Automotive and undertaking a series of successful cross-border joint ventures in Indonesia and Eastern Europe, Continental continued to make high-quality tires but was also well positioned to provide systems to the world's automakers. A central ingredient of the transformation's success was the willingness and capacity of Continental's leaders to subordinate the narrower interests of unit and functional leaders and focus attention on doing what was right for the company as a whole and its customers.

Reconciling Tensions

It is all too common for a company's top executives to play up the importance of managing innovation and growth in order to remain competitive. Yet often in that same firm, the environment feels anything but innovative and the focus of attention is on cost containment, not growth. Does that mean the company's top team is deliberately deceptive or disingenuous? No, but the problem reveals one of the enterprise leader's most difficult jobs: dealing with the inherent ambiguities that stem from the notion of building strategic competence and organizational character simultaneously.

A couple of years ago, a large manufacturer with a well-developed culture of paternalism and a belief in lifetime employment for its employees spotted an acquisition opportunity—a perfect fit for its growth strategy. The economic benefits of the deal, however, would bear fruit only if the company shed 10,000 jobs soon after the deal was struck. There was no chance to grow organically after the acquisition to salvage those jobs. The analysts eyeing the deal, well aware of the paternalistic nature of the acquiring firm, signaled their uneasiness with the transaction in the absence of major cost cutting beforehand. Even though the manufacturer was healthy and growing, its top management team decided the deal was critical to its future. The company then cut 5,000 of its own employees in order to win the analysts' approval of the purchase, guarding against a serious erosion of its stock price.

This example highlights the built-in tensions that top executives must wrestle with. In developing strategic capabilities, they have to balance their need to develop a vision of tomorrow with the importance of making decisions that will satisfy customers today. In managing organizational character, they need to build strong cohesive cultures while being prepared to lead dramatic change and reinvention. For the manufacturer, the success of its long-term strategy depended in part on a short-term path of cost cutting and job reductions—a move that was in direct conflict with the company's longstanding organizational culture. Although the company's leaders went ahead with the reduction in head count, they eliminated as many jobs as possible through attrition and created outplacement centers for laid-off employees.

Creating Alignment

One can find useful examinations of different aspects of the leader's role in a variety of books and articles. Some stress how important it is for those at the top to provide their organizations with purpose; others emphasize the need for leaders to form culture or to stimulate innovation or growth. But problems arise if companies treat such topics as stand-alone issues rather than as interlocking components of a system. Effective enterprise leaders are skilled at simultaneously managing five processes in order to create organizational alignment. This systems view of the enterprise leader's role in creating organizational alignment can be thought of as managing the five M's: meaning, mind-set, mobilization, measurement and mechanisms for renewal.

In 2002, Canada's RBC Financial Group had to realign the organization when it added a major new initiative to its shortlist of strategic priorities. Having learned through research that its customers felt it was too focused on products, RBC planned to transform itself into a firm that provided integrated solutions for all its clients' financial needs. CEO Gordon Nixon referred to the initiative as "implementing cross-platform leverage." He convened RBC's Group Council, made up of the company's top 125 leaders, and asked for their help in creating the organizational alignment needed to turn the new strategy into a reality.

The enterprise leaders first had to acknowledge that there was no shared sense of meaning in the company about the cross-platform strategic initiative. There was no passion for the term and little understanding of what cross-platform leverage would look and feel like if it were operational throughout RBC. The enterprise leadership team met this challenge by shaping a collective definition of what cross-platform leverage would mean for every business and in every function in the company. Next, the team conducted an audit of the company's culture and mind-set and articulated the behavioral changes that would be needed, first by the team itself and then across the entire organization, to implement the new strategy. The company would have to abandon the strong unit-oriented culture that had been the norm at RBC for decades. The profile of an effective executive at RBC would have to change from that of the strong individual performer to one who mobilized resources across boundaries.

The enterprise leaders also examined which resources they would need to mobilize so that RBC could excel at the new strategy. Processes and IT systems that didn't support integration had to be replaced with knowledge-sharing processes that facilitated the improvement of client knowledge. The team also took a close look at metrics and incentives. Rewards that had been focused on individual and unit performance were replaced by those that focused on enterprise performance and improvements in client satisfaction. Finally, the team identified mechanisms for renewal—committing to meet every few months, for example, to review progress—which would help RBC avoid complacency.

In less than one year, RBC's enterprise leadership team reshaped the company's strategy, changed relationships across divisions and revamped its performance and talent management processes. It successfully brought about the organizational alignment that was needed to change RBC's capabilities, culture, and institutional mind-set to focus on delivering integrated customer solutions.

AN UNNATURAL ACT

Having considered the key elements of the enterprise leader's job, companies then need to ask why developing such leaders is so difficult. Indeed, there are three major obstacles built in to many organizations that make developing enterprise leadership virtually an unnatural act.

The first obstacle can be found in organizational culture, which often favors unit over enterprise leadership.

It takes leadership from the top to break the mold of cultural norms. One of the first things Sam Palmisano did as IBM Corp.'s new chairman and CEO was to change the name of IBM's Enterprise Leadership Group to the Enterprise Leadership Team. While that may sound trivial, this seemingly minor change sent a clear message that IBM's culture of celebrating individual contributors and rewarding hero-leaders was coming to an end and would be replaced by a strong emphasis on teamwork.

A second obstacle to developing leaders with an enterprise perspective is the emphasis on specialized expertise in many companies. Several major consulting firms contend that the identification, articulation and development of competencies should be the cornerstone of a company's leadership development efforts. This view is so prevalent that it would be difficult to find a handful of major companies whose leadership initiatives do not have competency frameworks as their foundation. And such frameworks have much to recommend in them. The logic of competencies is linear, illustrating how company strategy is linked to certain organizational capability requirements, which are connected to a set of skills and leadership behaviors that need to be developed in order to execute the strategy.

Yet while competency frameworks provide anchors for understanding leadership development requirements, they have tended to focus on individual rather than team development. The focus on individual development can prevent people from taking the broader view and seeing the company as an interconnected whole, with challenges that cannot be met by expertise in one area or success in one unit. Moreover, an excessive reliance on competencies tends to drive individuals to strengthen their particular expertise rather than to stretch themselves for new challenges, such as making the transition from unit to enterprise leadership.

The third obstacle is that contrary to strategic goals, reward systems—like many organizational cultures—often favor the accomplishments of individual units at the expense of corporate success. Imagine a company in which the CEO and top team have articulated an integration-based strategy that will require company leaders to think and act across boundaries and on behalf of the entire enterprise. Now imagine that the company's reward system offers leaders incentives for achieving unit success, even when they fail to behave as enterprise leaders. Which will win out in the end—a theoretical statement about integration or a powerful incentive system that rewards unit performance?

OVERCOMING THE OBSTACLES

Fortunately, companies are not helpless in the face of these impediments to enterprise leadership development. The approach to this issue taken by PwC, Continental, BP, RBC and IBM holds lessons for other organizations. These companies, which differ by industry, size and strategic intent, have at least one thing in common: They focus attention on three ways of grooming individuals to be enterprise leaders.

THEY CREATE CULTURES IN WHICH LEADERS ARE HELD ACCOUNTABLE FOR HAVING AN ENTERPRISE PERSPECTIVE. Top-team commitment is critically important to the development of leaders with an enterprise orientation. CEOs and top executive teams must not only believe in the importance of developing enterprise leaders, they must also do whatever it takes to create a culture of accountability—one that ensures that emerging leaders possess a cross-boundary enterprise perspective.

To create that culture, top executives must develop a well-thought-out point of view on the importance and role of enterprise leadership in the company. The IBM Leadership Framework is a prime example. Accountability-based cultures reward individuals for results, so it is important for companies to make clear that they expect all leaders in the organization to develop future enterprise leaders. This policy should also include consequences for those who fail to cultivate such leaders.

THEY CREATE OPPORTUNITIES FOR NEXT-GENERATION ENTERPRISE LEADERS TO EMERGE. Top executives must reinforce the culture of accountability by giving potential leaders the chance to develop an enterprise view. While that may seem obvious, this critically important step is often avoided on one pretext or another. At RBC, however, division leaders engaged in a widespread cross-fertilization of talent to show they supported the company's strategy. They made key jobs available to high-potential senior executives in order to develop their enterprisewide perspectives.

THEY INSTALL HR PROCESSES THAT SUPPORT THE COMPANY'S LEADERSHIP DEVELOPMENT PHILOSOPHIES. Companies that effectively develop enterprise leaders create process infrastructures that support their leadership frameworks and leadership development activities. Such infrastructures combat the "cream will rise to the top" philosophy, in which leaders simply emerge because of their innate talent. They minimize the risk that the pool of enterprise leaders will be too small for lack of enough cream.

These companies differentiate between the skills and behaviors of unit and enterprise leaders. They have talent-tracking processes that spot "high potentials" as quickly as possible. They provide multiple opportunities for those people to receive feedback early in their careers, enabling them to develop as unit or enterprise leaders. And they have career and performance management processes that don't punish individuals for taking risks. This is important because companies often use the criterion of repeated success as a screen in determining who is, and who isn't, a high-potential leader, making it risky for individuals to take on roles that might lead to their derailment.

BRIDGING THE STRATEGY-CAPABILITIES GAP

Many companies are populated with senior executives who are graduates of the leader-as-hero school of leadership. But as customers step up their demands for solutions, those companies will need to change their views on what constitutes effective leadership. Increasingly, tomorrow's senior executives will need to lead with an enterprise perspective. It will take time to develop these leaders and even more time for them to learn how to come together in teams.

Companies that fail to develop leaders who can work effectively across unit, functional and geographic boundaries will be unable to close the strategy-capabilities gap. But those that work on identifying and developing their next generation of enterprise leaders will be well prepared to deliver on the promise of providing innovative solutions for their customers.

—◦◦◦—

Douglas A. Ready founded and leads ICEDR, the global learning network in global talent development. He is also visiting professor at the London Business School and a consultant on organizational and leadership resources and HR development practices.

CHAPTER THIRTY-ONE

Execution

The Gap Nobody Knows

Larry Bossidy
Ram Charan
with Charles Burck

he CEO was sitting in his office late one evening, looking tired and drained. He was trying to explain to a visitor why his great strategic initiative had failed, but he couldn't figure out what had gone wrong.

"I'm so frustrated," he said. "I got the group together a year ago, people from all the divisions. We had two off-site meetings, did benchmarking, got the metrics. McKinsey helped us. Everybody agreed with the plan. It was a good one, and the market was good.

"This was the brightest team in the industry, no question about it. I assigned stretch goals. I empowered them—gave them the freedom to do what they needed to do. Everybody knew what had to be done. Our incentive system is clear, so they knew what the rewards and penalties would be. We worked together with high energy. How could we fail?

"Yet the year has come to an end, and we missed the goals. They let me down; they didn't deliver the results. I have lowered earnings estimates four times in the past nine months. We've lost our credibility with the Street. I have probably lost my credibility with the board. I don't know what to do, and I don't know where the bottom is. Frankly, I think the board may fire me."

Several weeks later the board did indeed fire him.

This story—it's a true one—is the archetypal story of the gap that nobody knows. It's symptomatic of the biggest problem facing corporations today. We hear lots of similar stories when we talk to business leaders. They're played out almost daily in the press, when it reports on companies that should be succeeding but aren't: Aetna, AT&T, British Airways, Campbell Soup, Compaq, Gillette, Hewlett-Packard, Kodak, Lucent Technologies, Motorola, Xerox, and many others.

These are good companies. They have smart CEOs and talented people, they have inspiring visions, and they bring in the best consultants. Yet they, and many other companies as well, regularly fail to produce promised results. Then when they announce the shortfall, investors dump their stocks and enormous market value is obliterated. Managers and employees are demoralized. And increasingly, boards are forced to dump the CEOs.

The leaders of all the companies listed above were highly regarded when they were appointed—they seemed to have all of the right qualifications. But they all lost their jobs because they didn't deliver what they said they would. In the year 2000 alone, forty CEOs of the top two hundred companies on *Fortune*'s 500 list were removed—not retired but fired or made to resign. When 20 percent of the most powerful business leaders in America lose their jobs, something is clearly wrong.

In such cases it's not just the CEO who suffers—so do the employees, alliance partners, shareholders, and even customers. And it's not just the CEO whose shortcomings create the problem, though of course he or she is ultimately responsible.

What is the problem? Is it a rough business environment? Yes. Whether the economy is strong or weak, competition is fiercer than ever. Change comes faster than ever. Investors—who were passive when today's senior leaders started their careers—have turned unforgiving. But this factor by itself doesn't explain the near-epidemic of shortfalls and failures. Despite this, there are companies that deliver on their commitments year in and year out—companies such as GE, Wal-Mart, Emerson, Southwest Airlines, and Colgate-Palmolive.

When companies fail to deliver on their promises, the most frequent explanation is that the CEO's strategy was wrong. But the strategy by itself is not often the cause. Strategies most often fail because they aren't executed well. Things that are supposed to happen don't happen. Either the organizations aren't capable of making them happen, or the leaders of the business misjudge the challenges their companies face in the business environment, or both.

Former Compaq CEO Eckhard Pfeiffer had an ambitious strategy, and he almost pulled it off. Before any of his competitors, he saw that the so-called Wintel architecture—the combination of the Windows operating system and Intel's constant innovation—would serve for everything from a palm-held to a linked network of servers capable of competing with mainframes.

Mirroring IBM, Pfeiffer broadened his base to serve all the computing needs of enterprise customers. He bought Tandem, the high-speed, failsafe mainframe manufacturer, and Digital Equipment Corporation (DEC) to give Compaq serious entry into the services segment. Pfeiffer moved at breakneck speed on his bold strategic vision, transforming Compaq from a failing niche builder of high-priced office PCs to the second-biggest computer company (after IBM) in just six years. By 1998 it was poised to dominate the industry.

But the strategy looks like a pipe dream today. Integrating the acquisitions and delivering on the promises required better execution than Compaq was able to achieve. More fundamentally, neither Pfeiffer nor his successor, Michael Capellas, pursued the kind of execution necessary to make money as PCs became more and more of a commodity business.

Michael Dell understood that kind of execution. His direct-sales and build-to-order approach was not just a marketing tactic to bypass retailers; it was the core of his business strategy. Execution is the reason Dell passed Compaq in market value years ago, despite Compaq's vastly greater size and scope, and it's the reason Dell passed Compaq in 2001 as the world's biggest maker of PCs. As of November 2001, Dell was shooting to double its market share, from approximately 20 to 40 percent.

Any company that sells direct has certain advantages: control over pricing, no retail markups, and a sales force dedicated to its own products. But that wasn't Dell's secret. After all, Gateway sells direct too, but it has fared no better than Dell's other rivals. Dell's insight was that building to order, executing superbly, and keeping a sharp eye on costs would give him an unbeatable advantage.

In conventional batch production manufacturing, a business sets its production volume based on the demand that is forecast for the coming months. If it has outsourced component manufacturing and just does the assembling, like a computer maker, it tells the component suppliers what volumes to expect and negotiates the prices. If sales fall short of projections, everybody gets stuck with unsold inventory. If sales are higher, they scramble inefficiently to meet demand.

Building to order, by contrast, means producing a unit after the customer's order is transmitted to the factory. Component suppliers, who also build to order, get the information when Dell's customers place their orders. They deliver the parts to Dell, which immediately places them into production, and shippers cart away the machines within hours after they're boxed. The system squeezes time out of the entire cycle from order to delivery—Dell can deliver a computer within a week or less from the time an order is placed. This system minimizes inventories at both ends of the pipeline, incoming and outgoing.

Build-to-order improves inventory turnover, which increases asset velocity, one of the most underappreciated components of making money. Velocity is the ratio of sales dollars to net assets deployed in the business, which in the most common definition includes plant and equipment, inventories, and accounts receivable minus accounts payable. Higher velocity improves productivity and reduces working capital. It also improves cash flow, the life blood of any business, and can help improve margins as well as revenue and market share.

Inventory turns are especially important for makers of PCs, since inventories account for the largest portion of their net assets. When sales fall below forecast, companies with traditional batch manufacturing, like Compaq, are stuck with unsold inventory. What's more, computer components such as microprocessors are particularly prone to obsolescence because performance advances so rapidly, often accompanied by falling prices. When these PC makers have to write off the excess or obsolete inventory, their profit margins can shrink to the vanishing point.

Dell turns its inventory over eighty times a year, compared with about ten to twenty times for its rivals, and its working capital is negative. As a result, it generates an enormous amount of cash. In the fourth quarter of fiscal 2002, with revenues of $8.1 billion and an operating margin of 7.4 percent, Dell had cash flow of $1 billion from operations. Its return on invested capital for fiscal 2001 was 355 percent—an incredible rate for a company with its sales volume. Its high velocity also allows it to give customers the latest technological improvements ahead of other makers, and to take advantage of falling component costs—either to improve margins or to cut prices.

These are the reasons Dell's strategy became deadly for its competitors once PC growth slowed. Dell capitalized on their misery and cut prices in a bid for market share, increasing the distance between it and the rest of the industry. Because of its high velocity, Dell could show high return on capital and positive cash flow, even with margins depressed. Its competition couldn't.

The system works only because Dell executes meticulously at every stage. The electronic linkages among suppliers and manufacturing create a seamless extended enterprise. A manufacturing executive we know who worked at Dell for a time calls its system "the best manufacturing operation I've ever seen."

The chronic underperformers we've mentioned so far have lots of company. Countless others are less than they could be because of poor execution. The gap between promises and results is widespread and clear. The gap nobody knows is the gap between what a company's leaders want to achieve and the ability of their organization to achieve it.

Everybody talks about change. In recent years, a small industry of changemeisters has preached revolution, reinvention, quantum change, breakthrough thinking, audacious goals, learning organizations, and the like. We're not necessarily debunking this stuff. But unless you translate big thoughts into concrete steps for action, they're pointless. Without execution, the breakthrough thinking breaks down, learning adds no value, people don't meet their stretch goals, and the revolution stops dead in its tracks. What you get is change for the worse, because failure drains the energy from your organization. Repeated failure destroys it.

These days we're hearing a more practical phrase on the lips of business leaders. They're talking about taking their organizations to the "next level," which brings the rhetoric down to earth. GE CEO Jeff Immelt, for example, is asking his people how they can use technology to differentiate their way to the next level and command better prices, margins, and revenue growth.

This is an execution approach to change. It's reality-based—people can envision and discuss specific things they need to do. It recognizes that meaningful change comes only with execution.

No company can deliver on its commitments or adapt well to change unless all leaders practice the discipline of execution at all levels. Execution has to be a part of a company's strategy and its goals. It is the missing link between aspirations and results. As such, it is a major—indeed, *the* major—job of a business leader. If you don't know how to execute, the whole of your effort as a leader will always be less than the sum of its parts.

EXECUTION COMES OF AGE

Business leaders are beginning to make the connection between execution and results. After Compaq's board fired Pfeiffer, chairman and founder Ben Rosen took pains to say that the company's strategy was fine. The change, he said, would be "in execution. . . . Our plans are to speed up decision-making and make the company more efficient." When Lucent's board dismissed CEO Richard McGinn in October 2000, his replacement, Henry Schacht, explained: "Our issues are ones of execution and focus."

But for all the talk about execution, hardly anybody knows what it is. When we're teaching about execution, we first ask people to define it. They think they know how, and they usually start out well enough. "It's about getting things done," they'll say. "It's about running the company, versus conceiving and planning. It's making our goals." Then we ask them how to get things done, and the dialogue goes rapidly downhill. Whether they're students or senior executives, it is soon clear—to them as well as to us—that they don't have the foggiest idea of what it means to execute.

To understand execution, you have to keep three key points in mind:

- Execution is a discipline, and integral to strategy.
- Execution is the major job of the business leader.
- Execution must be a core element of an organization's culture.

Execution Is a Discipline

People think of execution as the tactical side of business. That's the first big mistake. Tactics are central to execution, but execution is not tactics. Execution is fundamental to strategy and has to shape it. No worthwhile strategy can be planned without taking into account the organization's ability to execute it. If you're talking about the smaller specifics of getting things done, call the process implementation, or sweating the details, or whatever you want to. But don't confuse execution with tactics.

Execution is a systematic process of rigorously discussing hows and whats, questioning, tenaciously following through, and ensuring accountability. It includes making assumptions about the business environment, assessing the organization's capabilities, linking strategy to operations and the people who are going to implement the strategy, synchronizing those people and their various disciplines, and linking rewards to outcomes. It also includes mechanisms for changing assumptions as the environment changes and upgrading the company's capabilities to meet the challenges of an ambitious strategy.

In its most fundamental sense, execution is a systematic way of exposing reality and acting on it. Most companies don't face reality very well. As we shall see, that's the basic reason they can't execute. Much has been written about Jack Welch's style of management—especially his toughness and bluntness, which some people call ruthlessness. We would argue that the core of his management legacy is that he forced realism into all of GE's management processes, making it a model of an execution culture.

The heart of execution lies in the three core processes: the people process, the strategy process, and the operations process. Businesses that execute, as we shall see, prosecute them with rigor, intensity, and depth. Which people will do the job, and how will they be judged and held accountable? What human, technical, production, and financial resources are needed to execute the strategy? Will the organization have the ones it needs two years out, when the strategy goes to the next level? Does the strategy deliver the earnings required for success? Can it be broken down into doable initiatives? People engaged in the processes argue these questions, search out reality, and reach specific and practical conclusions. Everybody agrees about their responsibilities for getting things done, and everybody commits to those responsibilities.

The processes are also tightly linked with one another, not compartmentalized among staffs. Strategy takes account of people and operational realities. People are chosen and promoted in light of strategic and operational plans. Operations are linked to strategic goals and human capacities. Most important, the leader of the business and his or her leadership team are deeply engaged in all three. *They* are the owners of the processes—not the strategic planners or the human resources (HR) or finance staffs.

Execution Is the Job of the Business Leader

Lots of business leaders like to think that the top dog is exempt from the details of actually running things. It's a pleasant way to view leadership: you stand on the mountaintop, thinking strategically and attempting to inspire your people with visions, while managers do the grunt work. This way of thinking is a fallacy, one that creates immense damage.

An organization can execute only if the leader's heart and soul are immersed in the company. Leading is more than thinking big, or schmoozing with investors and lawmakers, although those are part of the job. The leader has to be engaged personally and deeply in the business. Execution requires a comprehensive understanding of a business, its people, and its environment. The leader is the only person in a position to achieve that understanding. And only the leader can make execution happen, through his or her deep personal involvement in the substance and even the details of execution.

The leader must be in charge of getting things done by running the three core processes—picking other leaders, setting the strategic direction, and conducting operations. These actions are the substance of execution, and leaders cannot delegate them regardless of the size of the organization. Only a leader can ask the tough questions that everyone needs to answer, then manage the process of debating the information and making the right trade-offs.

Only the leader who's intimately engaged in the business can know enough to have the comprehensive view and ask the tough incisive questions. And only the leader can set the tone of the dialogue in the organization. Dialogue is the core of culture and the basic unit of work. How people talk to each other absolutely determines how well the organization will function. Is the dialogue stilted, politicized, fragmented, and butt-covering? Or is it candid and reality-based, raising the right questions, debating them, and finding realistic solutions? If it's the former— as it is in all too many companies—reality will never come to the surface. If it is to be the latter, the leader has to be on the playing field with his management team, practicing it consistently and forcefully.

Specifically, the leader has to run the three core processes and has to run them with intensity and rigor. Here's how this chapter's first author, Larry Bossidy, ensures that these processes are effectively carried out.

> When I appoint a new business manager, I call her into the office to discuss three issues. First, she is to behave with the highest integrity. This is an issue where there are no second chances—breach the rule, and you're out. Second, she must know that the customer comes first. And finally I say, "You've got to understand the three processes, for people, strategy, and operations, and you've got to manage these three processes. The more intensity and focus you put on them, the better you make this place. If you don't understand that, you've got no chance of succeeding here."

> Companies that do these processes in depth fare dramatically better than those that just *think* they do. When things are running well, I spend 20 percent of my time on the people process. When I'm rebuilding an organization, it's 40 percent. I'm not talking about doing formal interviews or selecting staff; I mean really getting to know people. When I go out to visit a plant, I'll sit down for the first half hour with the manager. We'll have a discussion about the capability of his people, looking at who is performing well and who needs help. I'll go to a meeting of the whole staff and listen to what they have to say. Then I'll sit down after the meeting and talk about my impressions of the people and write a letter confirming the agreements made at the meeting. And I'll assess people's performance not just at our formal reviews but two or three times a year.

Leaders often bristle when we say they have to run the three core processes themselves. "You're telling me to micromanage my people, and I don't do that," is a common response. Or, "It's not my style. I'm a hands-off leader. I delegate, I empower."

We agree completely that micromanaging is a big mistake. It diminishes people's self-confidence, saps their initiative, and stifles their ability to think for themselves. It's also a recipe for screwing things up—micromanagers rarely know as much about what needs to be done as the people they're harassing, the ones who actually do it.

But there's an enormous difference between leading an organization and presiding over it. The leader who boasts of her hands-off style or puts her faith in empowerment is not dealing with the issues of the day. She is not confronting the people responsible for poor performance, or searching for problems to solve and then making sure they get solved. She is presiding, and she's only doing half her job.

Leading for execution is not about micromanaging, or being "hands-on," or disempowering people. Rather, it's about active involvement—doing the things leaders should be doing in the first place. As you read on, you'll see how leaders who excel at execution immerse themselves in the substance of execution and even some of the key details. They use their knowledge of the business to constantly probe and question. They bring weaknesses to light and rally their people to correct them.

The leader who executes assembles an architecture of execution. He puts in place a culture and processes for executing, promoting people who get things done more quickly and giving them greater rewards. His personal involvement in that architecture is to assign the tasks and then follow up. This means making sure that people understand the priorities, which are based on his comprehensive understanding of the business, and asking incisive questions. The leader who executes often does not even have to tell people what to do; she asks questions so they can figure out what they need to do. In this way she coaches them, passing on her experience as a leader and educating them to think in ways they never thought before. Far from stifling people, this kind of leadership helps them expand their own capabilities for leading.

Jack Welch, Sam Walton, and Herb Kelleher of Southwest Airlines were powerful presences in their organizations. Just about everybody knew them, knew what they stood for, and knew what they expected of their people. Was it because of their forceful personalities? Yes, but a forceful personality doesn't mean anything by itself. "Chainsaw Al" Dunlap, the celebrated and outspoken champion of savage cost-cutting, had a forceful personality—and he wrecked the companies he was supposedly turning around.

Are leaders like Jack, Sam, and Herb good communicators? Again, yes, but. Communication can be mere boilerplate, or it can mean something. What counts is the substance of the communication and the nature of the person doing the communicating—including his or her ability to listen as well as to talk.

Maybe such people are good leaders because they practice "management by walking around." We've all read the stories about Herb or Sam popping up on the front lines to chat with baggage handlers or stockroom clerks. Sure, walking around is useful and important—but only if the leader doing the walking knows what to say and what to listen for.

Leaders of this ilk are powerful and influential presences because they *are* their businesses. They are intimately and intensely involved with their people and operations. They connect because they know the realities and talk about them. They're knowledgeable about the details. They're excited about what they're doing. They're passionate about getting results. This is not "inspiration" through exhortation or speechmaking. These leaders energize everyone by the example they set.

In his last year as GE's CEO, Jack Welch—as he had done for twenty years in the job—spent a week of ten-hour days reviewing the operating plans of the company's various units. He was intimately involved in the back-and-forth dialogue. Even at the end of his career, Jack wasn't presiding. He was leading by being actively involved.

Execution Has to Be in the Culture

It should be clear by now that execution isn't a program you graft onto your organization. A leader who says, "Okay, now we're going to execute for a change," is merely launching another fad of the month, with no staying power. Just as the leader has to be personally involved in execution, so must everyone else in the organization understand and practice the discipline.

Execution has to be embedded in the reward systems and in the norms of behavior that everyone practices. Indeed, focusing on execution is not only an essential part of a business's culture, it is the one sure way to create meaningful cultural change.

One way to get a handle on execution is to think of it as akin to the Six Sigma processes for continual improvement. People practicing this methodology look for deviations from desired tolerances. When they find them, they move quickly to correct the problem. They use the processes to constantly raise the bar, improving quality and throughput. They use them collaboratively across units to improve how processes work across the organization. It's a relentless pursuit of reality, coupled with processes for constant improvement. And it's a huge change in behavior—a change, really, in culture.

Leaders who execute look for deviations from desired managerial tolerances—the gap between the desired and actual outcome in everything from profit margins to the selection of people for promotion. Then they move to close the gap and raise the bar still higher across the whole organization. Like Six Sigma, the discipline of execution doesn't work unless people are schooled in it and practice it constantly; it doesn't work if only a few people in the system practice it. Execution has to be part of an organization's culture, driving the behavior of all leaders at all levels.

Execution should begin with the senior leaders, but if you are not a senior leader, you can still practice it in your own organization. You build and demonstrate your own skills. The results will advance your career—and they may just persuade others in the business to do the same.

WHY PEOPLE DON'T GET IT

If execution is so important, why is it so neglected? The real problem is that *execution* just doesn't sound very sexy. It's the stuff a leader delegates. Do great CEOs and Nobel Prize winners achieve their glory through execution? Well, yes, in fact, and therein lies the grand fallacy.

The common view of intellectual challenge is only half true. What most people miss today is that intellectual challenge also includes the rigorous and tenacious work of developing and proving the ideas. Perhaps it's the result of the TV generation's upbringing, believing a mythology in which ideas develop instantly into full-blown outcomes.

There are different kinds of intellectual challenges. Conceiving a grand idea or broad picture is usually intuitive. Shaping the broad picture into a set of executable actions is analytical, and it's a huge intellectual, emotional, and creative challenge.

Nobel Prize winners succeed because they execute the details of a proof that other people can replicate, verify, or do something with. They test and discover patterns, connections, and linkages that nobody saw before. It took Albert Einstein more than a decade to develop the detailed proof explaining the theory of relativity. That was the execution—the details of proof in mathematical calculations. The theorem would not have been valid without the proof. Einstein could not have delegated this execution. It was an intellectual challenge that nobody else could meet.

The intellectual challenge of execution is in getting to the heart of an issue through persistent and constructive probing. Let's say a manager in the X division plans an 8 percent sales increase in the coming year, even though the market is flat. In their budget reviews, most leaders would accept the number without debate or discussion. But in an execution company's operating review, the leader will want to know if the goal is realistic. "Fine," she'll ask the manager, "but where will the increase come from? What products will generate the growth? Who will buy them, and what pitch are we going to develop for those customers? What will our competitor's reaction be? What will our milestones be?" If a milestone hasn't been reached at the end of the first quarter, it's a yellow light: something's not going as planned, and something will need to be changed.

If the leader has doubts about the organization's capacity to execute, she may drill down even further. "Are the right people in charge of getting it done," she may ask, "and is their accountability clear? Whose collaboration will be required, and how will they be motivated to collaborate? Will the reward system motivate them to a common objective?" In other words, the leader doesn't just sign off on a plan. She wants an explanation, and she will drill down until the answers are clear. Her leadership skills are such that everyone present is engaged in the dialogue, bringing everyone's viewpoint out into the open and assessing the degree and nature of buy-in. It's not simply an opportunity for her managers to learn from her and she from them; it's a way to diffuse the knowledge to everyone in the plan.

Suppose the issue is how to increase productivity. Other questions will be asked: "We have five programs in the budget, and you say we're going to save at least a couple million dollars on each one. What are the programs? Where is the money going to be saved? What's the timeline? How much is it going to cost us to achieve it? And who is responsible for it all?"

Organizations don't execute unless the right people, individually and collectively, focus on the right details at the right time. For you as a leader, moving from the concept to the critical details is a long journey. You have to review a wide array of facts and ideas, the permutations and combinations of which can approach infinity. You have to discuss what risks to take, and where. You have to thread through these details, selecting those that count. You have to assign them to the people who matter, and make sure which key ones must synchronize their work.

Such decision making requires knowledge of the business and the external environment. It requires the ability to make fine judgments about people—their capabilities, their reliability, their strengths, and their weaknesses. It requires intense focus and incisive thinking.

It requires superb skills in conducting candid, realistic dialogue. This work is as intellectually challenging as any we know of.

Leadership without the discipline of execution is incomplete and ineffective. Without the ability to execute, all other attributes of leadership become hollow.

——◦◦◦——

Larry Bossidy is the retired chairman and CEO of Honeywell International, and the former chairman and CEO of AlliedSignal and COO of General Electric Credit.

——◦◦◦——

Ram Charan is an adviser to CEOs and senior executives in companies ranging from start-ups to the *Fortune* 500 and a best-selling author on leadership, innovation, execution, and global strategy.

——◦◦◦——

Charles Burck, a former editor for *Fortune* magazine, is a writer and editor who focuses on business leadership issues.

CHAPTER THIRTY-TWO

The Leader as Toxin Handler

Organizational Hero and Casualty

Peter J. Frost
Sandra Robinson

A s a senior project manager at a public utility company, Michael had thrived in his job for nearly a decade. His team of 24 engineers worked quickly and effectively together and was often the source of creative ideas that helped the rest of the organization. All that changed, however, when the utility's board brought in a hard-charging CEO and made Michael one of his direct reports. "He walked all over people," Michael recalls. "He made fun of them; he intimidated them. He criticized work for no reason, and he changed his plans daily. Another project manager was hospitalized with ulcers and took early retirement. People throughout the organization felt scared and betrayed. Everyone was running around and whispering, and the copy machine was going nonstop with resumes. No one was working. People could barely function."

Rather than watch the organization come to a standstill, Michael stepped between the new CEO and his colleagues. He allowed people to vent their frustrations to him behind closed doors and even cry or shout. At meetings, when the CEO picked on coworkers, Michael stood up for them—and often ended up taking verbal beatings.

He also played the role of the CEO's front man, translating his seemingly irrational directives so that people could put them into action. "He's not such a bad guy," was Michael's common refrain. "Underneath it all, he wants the best for the company."

Michael kept at it for three years, until the board fired the CEO. By then, however, Michael was considering leaving not just the company but his profession. "I didn't know if I could take the heat in a large organization anymore," he says. "In the end, I stayed with the company, but I took a year off from being a manager and just worked with the team. I had to recharge."

Take the heat—that's how Michael describes his role of absorbing and softening the emotional pain of his organization. It was a critical role, too. After the bad-tempered CEO was gone, members of Michael's team told the board that they had kept at their work largely because of Michael's soothing words, compassionate listening, and protection.

Michael is what we call a *toxin handler*, a manager who voluntarily shoulders the sadness, frustration, bitterness, and anger that are endemic to organizational life. Although toxin handlers may be found at every level in organizations, many work near the top—they run the marketing or new-product development department, for instance, or oversee several cross-functional teams. Virtually all of them carry a full load of "regular" work, and do so very well. In fact, it is often their superior performance that affords them the job security to play the role of toxin handler in the first place.

Toxin handlers are not new. They are probably as old as organizations, for organizations have always generated distress, just as they have always generated feelings of joy and fulfillment. Strong emotions are part of life; they are part of business. And yet there has never been a systematic study of the role that toxin handlers play in business organizations. For the past two years, they have been at the center of our research: we have interviewed and observed about 70 executives who are either toxin handlers themselves or have managed people in the role. Our goal has been to understand what toxin handlers do, why they do it, and how organizations can support them.

Research on topics such as organizational pain is sometimes derided for being soft or unrealistic or even for being "politically correct." "Those people," the criticism goes, "don't understand how real organizations work. Companies can't be bothered with making everyone feel warm and fuzzy. There's a bottom line to worry about."

But our study did not start with an assumption that organizations, per se, are responsible for their employees' personal happiness. Rather, we were motivated to study toxin handlers because of their strategic importance in today's business environment.

In our current market-based and knowledge-driven world, success is a function of great ideas, which, of course, spring from intelligent, energized, and emotionally involved people. But great ideas dry up when people are hurting or when they are focused on organizational dysfunction. It is toxin handlers who frequently step in and absorb others' pain so that high-quality work continues to get done. For that reason alone, understanding toxin handlers is essential: to miss their contribution, or to underestimate it, is to neglect a powerful source of organizational effectiveness.

The contribution of toxin handlers merits attention for another critical reason. Organizations must recognize the toxin handlers in their midst so that their important work can be supported before a crisis strikes. Because although toxin handlers save organizations from self-destructing, they often pay a steep price—professionally, psychologically, and sometimes physically. Some toxin handlers experience burnout; others suffer from far worse, such as ulcers and heart attacks.

WHAT TOXIN HANDLERS DO

To illustrate the varied tasks toxin handlers take on, consider Alexandra, a vice president at a large financial institution in New York. Technically speaking, Alexandra was responsible for commercial and small-business accounts, but in reality she spent at least half of her time counseling coworkers. For instance, she frequently played peacemaker between the bank's large administrative staff and its constant stream of new M.B.A.'s.

"They always came in acting like they owned the world. Let's just say they tended to be pretty arrogant and heavy-handed with the secretaries and clerical workers," Alexandra recalls. "They offended them so much that they couldn't concentrate on their work. So first I had to explain to the staff that these young professionals were really good people inside, just seriously lacking in interpersonal skills. Then I had to pull the new M.B.A.'s into my office and help them understand that being a boss didn't mean bossing people around. And I had to do that without getting their backs up, otherwise they would have panicked, and that would have killed productivity. It was incredibly delicate stuff.

"I also spent hours on end talking other managers through their fears and insecurities around our possible merger with another bank," Alexandra says. "It was in the newspaper regularly, and people would come running to my office. Everyone was terrified they were going to get fired. One by one, I would calm everybody down so they could get back to their real jobs."

In general, then, toxin handlers alleviate organizational pain in five ways:

They listen empathetically. When staff members burst into his office on fire with anger and frustration, Michael, the project manager in our first example, almost always pointed them toward a chair while he closed the door. At that point, he would let them cool down without interruption. "I didn't say much," Michael recalls. "But I would look them in the eye and do a lot of nodding." Toxin handlers are experts at such nonjudgmental, compassionate listening.

They suggest solutions. Toxin handlers don't just listen, however, they also solve problems. Alexandra actively counseled staff members on how to speak with M.B.A.'s to avoid confrontations, and she similarly schooled M.B.A.'s in office etiquette. She often advised secretaries, for instance, to meet with the M.B.A.'s early in their tenures to lay out explicit ground rules for communication.

They work behind the scenes to prevent pain. When toxin handlers see a surefire case of organizational pain on the horizon, they typically leap into action to douse it. Consider the case of a talented employee who had lost her self-confidence working for a difficult boss and was bound to be transferred, against her wishes, to another department. Working without the knowledge of the unhappy employee, a toxin handler in the organization negotiated for weeks to move the woman to a department known for its upbeat boss and interesting work. The toxin handler commented later, "The whole thing had to be done very tactfully and with political sensitivity, including getting buy-in from the HR department, or the woman would have been labeled a whiner and a loser, and I would have been accused by her boss of meddling. In the end, everyone won." The woman, interestingly, never learned the story behind her transfer.

They carry the confidences of others. Toxin handlers can be like priests. In hearing and keeping secrets well, they allow their coworkers to walk away less troubled. Alexandra let her colleagues off-load their fears about the bank's merger onto her, and they returned to their jobs renewed. Similarly, Alan, a human resources manager at an insurance company, frequently listened to anguished colleagues who were preparing to fire someone.

They reframe difficult messages. Like Michael, who occasionally served as the abusive CEO's front man, toxin handlers act as diplomats and organizational translators. Alexandra heard staff members screaming about obnoxious new M.B.A.'s, but she delivered the message in language they could accept. "A company is like a small town," she often began, "where a bad reputation is hard to lose."

Another toxin handler was told by his boss, "Tell those idiots out there to get their act together and finish the job by Friday or else they're all doomed." The manager pulled his staff together and put the directive as such: "The boss needs us to complete this task by Friday, so let's put our heads together and see what we need to do to meet this deadline." By taking the sting out, the toxin handler allowed his staff to focus on the challenge of the directive without seeing it as an attack on their capabilities. The pain was managed, and the job got done.

FILLING A NEED

Toxin handlers are not new, but our research strongly suggests that two trends in recent years have intensified the need for them. Foremost among them is the growing prevalence of change initiatives. Pursuing the mantra that nonstop change is not just good, it's downright essential, many executives have spent the past decade reengineering, restructuring, and reinventing their organizations. In many cases, such transformations have created enormous shareholder value. Invariably, they have also caused confusion, fear, and anguish among employees.

Downsizing is the other trend that has increased the need for toxin handlers. Whenever a company lays off employees, the people left behind feel a backwash of guilt and fear. As the question "Who will be next?" swirls around the organization, toxin handlers step in to soothe nerves and redirect people's energies back to work.

Although change and downsizing have increased in recent years, some types of organizational pain have always been—and will always be—with us. For instance, every organization experiences bursts of incidental distress: a beloved manager dies in a plane crash, a major division faces an unexpected broadside from an upstart competitor, or senior managers simply do something unwise.

By contrast, some organizational pain is chronic: the organizations themselves are toxic, systematically generating distress through policies and practices. The most common of these are unreasonable stretch goals or performance targets, but toxicity is also created by unrelenting internal competition—toxic organizations love "horse races." Moreover, organizations that are chronically toxic are usually characterized by cultures of blame and dishonesty. No one takes responsibility for mistakes. In fact, people work assiduously to cover them up.

The final reason that toxin handlers exist is because the business world has toxic bosses. People like the CEO in our first story create organizational pain through insensitivity or vindictive behavior. Other toxic bosses cause pain because they are unwilling to take on the responsibilities of leadership, leaving subordinates hanging, confused, or paralyzed—or all three. Still others are toxic because of their extraordinarily high need for control, looking over the shoulders of people who have a job to do. Finally, some toxic bosses are unethical, creating conditions that compromise their colleagues and subordinates.

Toxic bosses very often work in tandem with a toxin handler. That's not surprising, since toxic bosses without handlers can be found out and then may face censure or even be fired. (It is worth noting that many toxic bosses are highly adept at managing their own bosses.) In one case we studied, a toxic boss had brought his chief lieutenant—his toxin handler—with him from one job to another for 15 years. The toxin handler routinely filtered the toxic boss's anger and prevented chaos. After meetings filled with belligerent tirades, for instance, the toxin handler would walk from office to office, explaining the boss's "real" opinions and assuring people he was not as angry as he seemed. And so the organizations they worked for continued to function.

THE TOLL OF TOXIN HANDLING

Managing organizational pain is vital to the health of the enterprise—but at great cost to the health of the toxin handlers themselves. The negative repercussions of toxin handling are particularly high when the role is played for too long or when there is no letup in the stream of emotional problems to which they are exposed, as is the case in companies with chronic toxicity.

The most common toll of toxin handling—whatever its cause—is burnout, both psychological and professional. Remember that Michael, the project manager described at the opening of this chapter, took a year off from project management to recover. But toxin handling can also take a physical toll. Most professional pain managers—be they counselors or psychiatrists—have been trained to recognize the physical warning signs of too much stress, such as stiff necks, nausea, and headaches. But toxin handlers are amateurs. Unlike workers at a real radioactive site, they do not have clothing, equipment, or procedures to protect them. They toil in danger zones completely exposed.

Dave Marsing is a case in point. In 1990, Marsing was assigned to turn around one of Intel's microprocessor fabrication plants near Albuquerque, New Mexico. The situation he inherited was dire: the plant's yield rates were bad and getting worse. The company's senior managers were pressing very hard for a quick solution to the problem. Employees were in pain, too, saying unrealistic pressure from above had them anxious and frustrated. "I was trying to be a human bridge between all the parts of the company and cope with all the emotions," Marsing recalls. "On the outside, I was soothing everybody, and work was getting back on track. But on the inside, I was in turmoil. I couldn't sleep, couldn't eat." Two months after Marsing arrived on the job, he suffered a near-fatal heart attack. He was 36 years old. (Currently the vice president of Intel's technology and manufacturing group and general manager of assembly and test manufacturing, Marsing says, "The heart attack was the result of a hereditary condition that got pushed over the edge from the stress.")

Savannah is another toxin handler who became physically ill after playing the role for several months. Savannah led a team assigned to implement a new program that based promotion on performance rather than seniority. Resistance was enormous, but in this case, the program went through. In the process, however, Savannah's team was brutalized by many members of the organization. "It was a case of 'kill the messenger,'" Savannah says.

As a toxin handler, Savannah worked hard to protect her team from the worst of the attacks. A senior manager who opposed the new policy, for instance, sent a scathing and personally insulting letter to one team member. Savannah intercepted it and sent back a memo that instructed him to send all future correspondence directly to her. Another senior manager who was opposed to the policy tried to punish Savannah's team by moving it to smaller, less attractive office space. Savannah deflected the move, and her team stayed put, but, she recalls, "I was as stressed as I ever have been in my life. At work, I would be strong for my team, but at home, I cried a lot. I slept away from my husband, although I didn't actually sleep very much, and often felt terribly depressed. The worst, though, were the panic attacks, which would come on so suddenly. My heart would pound, and I would lose my breath."

Dave Marsing and Savannah are not unusual. Many managers in our research told us of bouts of depression, severe heart palpitations, chronic sleeplessness, and cases of pneumonia.

These anecdotal cases are consistent with scientific evidence of a strong link between stress and illness. That link was first documented in the 1950s by Dr. Hans Selye, the renowned Canadian medical researcher who found that overwhelming stress leads to a breakdown of the protective mechanisms in the body—in other words, that stress compromises the body's immune system. In 1993, Bruce McEwen and Eliot Stellar reviewed two decades of research on the connection between stress and disease. Their analysis, published in the *Archives of Internal Medicine*, concluded that stress can compromise the immune system so severely that it raises blood pressure, weakens resistance to viral infections, increases the risk of heart attacks, and hastens the spread of cancer. Incidentally, the report says, stress puts intense pressure on the biological areas most susceptible to attack. Thus, if Harry's cardiovascular system is prone to weakness, his response to stress might be a heart attack. If Carmen's intestinal system is her weak spot, then stress for her may show up in chronic stomach ailments.

A study published in the *Journal of Advancement in Medicine* in 1995 demonstrated just how long the effects of stress can last. Researchers asked groups of healthy volunteers to focus on two emotions: either anger or compassion. Measures were then taken of a key immune system antibody, secretory immunoglobulin A—called IgA—which helps the body resist invading bacteria and viruses.

The researchers found that when the volunteers spent just five minutes remembering an experience that made them feel angry or frustrated, their IgA levels increased briefly then dropped substantially and stayed low for five hours. When volunteers focused on feelings of care and compassion, IgA levels rose and remained at a high level for six hours. What this study suggests is that simply remembering an emotion can have a strong impact on a person's health. Consider the implications for toxin handlers. When they go home and remember the events of their day, they certainly experience a drop in their IgA levels that lasts for hours, since the act of remembering surely lasts longer than five minutes at a time.

In addition to having an effect on the toxin handlers' immune systems, the stress triggered by negative emotions can influence neural pathways in the brain. As people think repeatedly about what makes them angry, stronger and stronger circuits are built in their brains. That increases the level of emotional distress until a neural architecture is built that supports those feelings. They become easier pathways to activate and run. They become our hot buttons.

Thus, the situation for toxin handlers—who shoulder the stress of others in addition to their own—would seem to be all the more dangerous. "Caregivers are human, too," says Dr. Michael Myers, a psychiatrist and clinical professor at the University of British Columbia. "As a specialist in physician health, I treat many physicians each year for clinical depression. Those in administrative medicine tell me how hard it is to cope with the problems of their staff doctors and other health professionals. The administrators have lost their ability to keep their armor in place."

HANDLING TOXIN HANDLERS

The toll of managing organizational pain cannot be ignored: either organizations should better support toxin handlers in their role or they should make them unnecessary in the first place through practices that systematically manage and diffuse organizational pain. Our focus here will be on support because our years of experience studying organizational behavior, in addition to the prevalence of toxin handlers in our research, suggests that toxin handlers will be with us as long as organizations give rise to strong emotions. In other words, forever.

Acknowledge the Dynamic

The first step in supporting toxin handlers is for executives to acknowledge, simply, that toxin handlers exist and that they play a critical role. Of course, in reality, there is nothing simple about such a public admission. A culture of toughness infuses many organizations, and a high value is often placed on technical competence. Emotional competence is irrelevant; it doesn't show up on the bottom line, or so the thinking goes.

One other aspect of corporate life makes organizational pain a difficult, even dangerous, topic to bring to the table. Middle and senior managers are usually expected to tough it out during hard times. As one manager in our study recalls, "After a particularly bitter strike that churned up a lot of agony and anger, the company provided counseling for the workers. There was nothing for any managers. We were expected to suck in our emotions, stay quiet, and cope alone." Indeed, managers at the company felt, perhaps rightly, that to talk about their feelings would have hurt their careers.

And yet, despite the strong corporate ethic not to discuss organizational pain—let alone thank toxin handlers—we think that when executives do so, the effects are likely to be immediate and positive. Take the case of a team leader at a media company who had played the toxin-handling role during a brutal six-month merger process in which many employees lost their jobs. The team leader had managed to hit all of her financial goals during the upheaval, and she expected that would be the main focus of her performance review. It was. But if her boss had also focused on how the woman saved the emotional health of the merger's survivors, we are confident that her response would have been relief and pride, and perhaps renewed energy.

Raising consciousness about the toxin handler role requires that a forum be established in the company to talk about the topic. It needs, for instance, to get onto the agenda of management meetings or retreats, and it needs a champion to ensure that it gets sufficient time and attention in these settings. Of course, it is unrealistic to expect that toxin handling and its consequences will be discussed openly when its source is a toxic boss. The toxic boss needs to learn about the dynamic in a more neutral setting, such as a conference of senior managers from several organizations. (This could only happen in the best-case scenario, however, because toxic bosses often lack a high enough degree of self-awareness to apply the discussion to themselves.)

Ultimately, a critical ingredient of any successful consciousness-raising about toxin handling is the recognition that effective pain management can—and does—contribute to the bottom line. No company can afford to let talented employees burn out. Nor can it afford to have a reputation as an unfriendly or unhappy place to work. Many good people simply won't join. It is essential, then, to make the business case for recognizing the work of toxin handlers. Otherwise, that role will stay in the closet, where most people are comfortable with it.

Arrange for Toxin Handlers to Share Their Experiences

Executives can minimize the toll on toxin handlers by bringing them together or by arranging for them to meet periodically with professionals who are trained to help them decompress and rejuvenate. Of course, this presumes that toxin handlers know who they are or can be readily identified. Thus the process of raising consciousness can be a very important precondition to setting up the necessary support for toxin handlers.

It is possible for handlers themselves to take the lead in making this happen. Executives shouldn't count on support groups forming on their own, however, especially since most toxin handlers pride themselves on a high tolerance for personal pain. As one CEO in our study notes, "These folks don't know when to ask for help; they're too busy giving it. And it would kill them to let others down by breaking down themselves." Better, then, to suggest that the organization's toxin handlers meet with one another, and even arrange such meetings. And better yet to bring in experts who can guide toxin handlers through conversations that allow them to see, understand, and appreciate the pressures of what they do. Experts can also help toxin handlers tell if they are dangerously close to burning out or presenting worrisome physical symptoms.

That's what happened to one manager in our study who had been a toxin handler for two years during a company restructuring. The manager tells us, "It took a therapist to help me to recognize that I was taking it into my gut. I was ignoring all the signs my body was sending me. I was taking things very personally. The therapist allowed me to hear myself in denial."

Finally, a professional can help some toxin handlers learn how to say no. One manager in our research tells us, "I learned that it was possible to say 'no' with options." Until that point, the manager had had a lot of trouble turning away people who needed to vent their emotions and, as a result, he was drowning under the workload of his real job and his toxic-handling role. "I learned that 'no' doesn't mean 'I don't care,' and it doesn't mean 'not ever.' It can mean, 'No, I can't do this, but I could do this.' Or, 'No, I can't help you now, but how about tomorrow?' Or, 'No, I can't help you, but let me find someone who can.'" That insight, the manager says, made work manageable again.

Reassign the Toxin Handler to a Safe Zone

Even when other actions, such as counseling, can help toxin handlers deal with stress, it also makes sense to move them out of the stressful situation. These moves need not be long term. One company, for instance, sent a toxin handler who was showing signs of burnout to a two-week conference in Florida. The conference was work related—there were at least three hours of meetings a day—but also included heavy doses of rest and relaxation. It was, in essence, a bit of a forced vacation. There needs to be a high level of trust, openness, and cultural support in the organization for this solution to work. Otherwise, there is a distinct risk that toxin handlers will feel threatened by such an assignment and think they have done something wrong and that their career is in jeopardy.

Research conducted in 1995 confirms the healing power of taking breaks. Andre Delbecq of the Leavey School of Business at Santa Clara University and Frank Friedlander of the Fielding Institute in Santa Barbara, California, studied the habits and routines of 166 business leaders in the computer and health care industries who were known to be happy, healthy, and well balanced. All of the participants in the study worked in companies undergoing rapid change, and inasmuch, managed considerable organizational pain. The researchers found that while the leaders' habits and routines varied widely, they frequently took short (two- to five-day) vacations, typically with their families. "The breaks allowed the leaders to step back, regain a fresh perspective on themselves and their situations," Delbecq observed, "Each time, they returned to work like new people."

In extreme cases of organizational distress, however, a short break is not enough to restore a toxin handler, and organizations should consider reassigning them to parts of the company that are less in the throes of emotional distress. Naturally, most toxin handlers will resist. They value what they do and understand its importance to the organization's well-being. Thus, it is important that the decision to relocate toxin handlers be thoroughly discussed with them. But when executives sense that a manager is overloaded by the role, they must act despite the toxin handler's objections. Later, when the spell is broken, the toxin handlers may come to see the wisdom of such an intervention and may even appreciate the spirit in which it was done.

Model "Healthy" Toxin Handling

If managing organizational pain is an open topic, then managers can feel comfortable demonstrating how to do it right. Following his heart attack, Dave Marsing made it a point to show other managers how to stay calm at work, even under intense pressure. "I try, to the greatest extent possible, to maintain a level of calmness in the face of frantic issues," he says. "I try to be as objective as possible in discussions, and if I'm in a face-to-face meeting with someone who has a short fuse, I'll sit right next to that person to make sure the fuse is never lit. I do that by being calm, even overly calm. When things get heated, I even change my voice. I will consciously take a deeper breath, or two deep breaths, in front of everybody to get them to calm down a little bit and talk about the specifics, about solutions."

Marsing also encourages his staff to keep their work and personal lives in balance. "When I coach the people who report to me, who manage very large sites around the company, I tell them how important it is to spend more time with their families, to spend more time exercising, to get some help to assist them to work through administrative things, rather than putting in extraordinarily long, tense days." Indeed, Marsing believes that teaching toxin handlers how to stay healthy in what is inherently an unhealthy role is one of his most important jobs as an executive.

MAKING TOXIN HANDLERS OBSOLETE

Can an organization systematically manage the emotional pain that it generates—making toxin handlers entirely unnecessary? It's unlikely, but our research has found several practices that remove from individuals the burden of alleviating emotional pain. Consider the practice of public grieving. In some organizations, executives create opportunities for employees to participate in rituals that, frankly, resemble funerals. For instance, when a Canadian company was acquired and folded into a former competitor from France, managers from the acquired business invited employees to a church-like ceremony where the company was eulogized by executives and hourly workers alike. Afterward, people went outside and, one by one, threw their old business cards into a coffin-shaped hole in the ground, which was then covered by dirt as a dirge played on a bagpipe. The event may sound ridiculous, but it did serve a healing purpose. Employees said later that they had buried their old company and were ready to embrace the new one.

The effectiveness of public grieving perhaps explains why Stanley Harris of Lawrence Technological University in Southfield, Michigan, and Robert Sutton of Stanford University's Department of Industrial Engineering, who studied dying organizations in the United States in the 1980s, were struck by "the prevalence of parties, picnics, and other social occasions during the final phases of organizational death. People had the opportunity to express sadness, anger, grief, perhaps in some cases even relief, during these ritualized ceremonies. Often people cried."

Another way companies can systematically manage organizational pain is to outsource the task. For instance, companies often hire consultants to steer or galvanize change initiatives. Some of these change experts are—by dint of experience—capable toxin handlers. If the toxin-handling role is explicitly given to them, then it won't as easily fall to in-house managers.

They can often be more objective than insiders, and they can also provide more pointed feedback than managers who have to face their colleagues daily. One caveat, however: for external consultants to be effective toxin handlers, they must be trusted and credible. One Australian manager who attempted to hire external consultants to deal with a toxic situation in his company quickly found resistance because employees felt the outsiders didn't understand the painful situation well enough to help resolve it. "People in pain won't go to outsiders unless they believe the consultants really know how things are in the company," he says.

Finally, companies can systematically manage organizational pain by providing employees with stress training. Such training could decrease the demand for toxin handlers—people would be able to deal with their emotions on their own—and also help toxic handlers understand how to help themselves. Several stress-training programs exist. For example, one used by both Motorola and Hewlett-Packard during strategic change projects was developed by HeartMath in Boulder Creek, California. The program uses several techniques, such as Freeze-Frame, which teaches employees to recognize a stressful feeling, then freeze it—that is, take a time-out and breathe more slowly and deeply. Freeze-Frame concludes with steps based on the biomedical notion of improving balance in the autonomic nervous system, brain, and heart that help employees handle stress differently from their usual reflex reaction. Instead of impulsively jumping in to take over another person's pain, for example, employees are taught to catch their breath, collect their thoughts, connect with their emotions, and then ask the other person to analyze his or her own unhappiness. Returning a problem to its sender may seem like a minor change, but for toxin handlers, it is a radical departure from standard operating procedure.

Programs like those offered by HeartMath come at a price. But they may well be worth the costs saved through greater retention and productivity.

IN GOOD COMPANY

When we began our research on managing emotional pain, we expected resistance—even denial—from senior executives. We did find some. But more often, we found executives who were aware that their organizations spawned anger, sadness, fear, and confusion as a matter of course. And we found scores of people who managed those feelings as toxin handlers or watched with gratitude and concern as others did. In many cases, our interviews about toxin handling were highly charged. Some cried as they recalled its demands; others felt anger. A few spoke of remorse.

Mainly, our research unearthed feelings of relief. Executives and middle managers alike indicated that this was the first time they had been able to talk about organizational pain. We are sure that it is neither possible, nor even desirable, to remove all pain in organizations. Emotional pain comes not only from downsizing, bad bosses, and change. It also accompanies the commitment and passion of individuals striving for excellence. Nevertheless, managing the pain of others, whatever its source, is hard work. It needs to be given the attention and support it deserves for everyone's benefit—the health of employees is a key element in the long-term competitiveness of companies and of our society. People who have felt alone in managing organizational pain, or in caring for people who do, should know that they are in good company.

—⟨∿⟩—

The late Peter J. Frost was the Edgar F. Kaiser Professor of Organizational Behavior at the University of British Columbia's Sauder School of Business, a widely published author, and the first executive director of the Organizational Behavior Teaching Society.

—⟨∿⟩—

Sandra Robinson is professor of organizational behavior and human resource management at the University of British Columbia's Sauder School of Business.

CHAPTER THIRTY-THREE

Bad Leadership–and Ways to Avoid It

Barbara Kellerman

After looking at hundreds of contemporary cases involving bad leaders and bad followers in the private, public, and nonprofit sectors, and in domains both domestic and international, I found that bad leadership falls into seven groups:

- Incompetent
- Rigid
- Intemperate
- Callous
- Corrupt
- Insular
- Evil

To posit a typology is to invite argument. No less an expert than Max Weber, the German sociologist whose three types of authority— rational-legal, traditional, and charismatic—continue to influence leadership scholars some eighty years after his death, was wary of his critics. "The fact that none of these three ideal types . . . is usually to be found in historical cases in 'pure' form, is naturally not a valid objection to attempting their conceptual formulation in the sharpest possible form," Weber wrote. "Analysis in terms of sociological types has, after all . . . certain advantages which should not be minimized."[1]

Let me echo Weber's defense and provide a few cautionary notes:

- These types are no "purer" than any other types.
- The range is wide. Some leaders and followers are very bad; others are less bad. Moreover, in some cases the consequences of bad leadership are major, in others minor.
- Opinions change. When Harry Truman left office in 1953, his approval rating was a dismal 32 percent. But in 2000, historians rated him among the greatest of American presidents, just behind Lincoln, Franklin Roosevelt, Washington, and Theodore Roosevelt.[2]
- Views differ. Was Thomas Krens, controversial director of New York's Guggenheim Museum, "an egomaniac who squandered the museum's resources on a quest to expand his empire"? Or was he instead a "brilliant, misunderstood radical who inherited an institution with a relatively small endowment and stagnant program and wanted to try something more daring than mounting the umpteenth Picasso show"?[3]
- As it is used here, the word *type* does not mean personality type, nor do I intend to suggest that to be rigid, for example, is a personal trait in evidence at every turn. Rather, *rigid* refers to a set of behaviors in which leaders and followers mutually engage and that result in bad leadership.

Nevertheless, dividing the universe of bad leadership into seven types gives us, as Weber says, certain advantages. First, the ability to distinguish among the ways of being bad orders an untidy world, where the idea of bad leadership is as confusing as it is ubiquitous. Second, the seven types serve a practical purpose. They make it easier to detect inflection points—points at which an intervention might have stopped bad leadership or at least cut it short. Finally, the types make meaning of being bad. They enable us to know better and more clearly what bad leadership consists of.

Before I describe the seven types, two additional notes. First, the first three types of bad leadership tend to be bad as in ineffective, and the last four as in unethical. I set up a continuum in which the first type of bad leadership, incompetence, is far less onerous than the last type of bad leadership, evil. But of course the lines blur: Sometimes leaders and followers are ineffective and unethical. For this reason I simply describe the seven types of bad leadership in sequence. Second, although bad followers are as integral to bad leadership as are bad leaders, in the following section the brief examples allude only to the leader.

INCOMPETENT

Bernadine Healy served effectively as dean of the Ohio State University Medical School and as the first woman director of the National Institutes of Health. But during her brief tenure (1999–2001) as head of the American Red Cross, Healy lost her touch. She was a driven professional, determined rapidly to change the deeply ingrained Red Cross culture, with which she was unfamiliar. In short order, members of the staff, as well as the fifty-member Red Cross board, decided that Healy was too assertive, too critical, and too pitiless. Once she compounded her errors by presiding over a debacle involving donations accumulated in the wake of the attack on the World Trade Center, she was dismissed. In short, whatever Healy's previous successes, and for whatever reasons, as leader of the Red Cross she was incompetent.[4]

Incompetent Leadership—the leader and at least some followers lack the will or skill (or both) to sustain effective action. With regard to at least one important leadership challenge, they do not create positive change.

Incompetent leaders are not necessarily incompetent in every aspect. Moreover, there are many ways of being incompetent. Some leaders lack practical, academic, or emotional intelligence.[5] Others are careless, dense, distracted, slothful, or sloppy, or they are easily undone by uncertainty and stress, unable effectively to communicate, educate, or delegate, and so on. Note also that the impact of incompetent leadership is highly variable. Sometimes, as in the case of pilot error, it leads to disaster. At other times it amounts to mere bungling.[6]

RIGID

As soon as he took office, Thabo Mbeki, who succeeded Nelson Mandela as president of South Africa in 1999, took issue with the West and its approach to AIDS. Mbeki maintained that HIV did not cause AIDS, that leading AIDS drugs were useless and even toxic, and that poverty and violence were at the root of his country's rapidly growing problem with the lethal disease.

As a result of his hostility to the West and his notoriously unyielding quest for an African remedy, Mbeki continued to withhold from HIV-positive pregnant women the antiretroviral drugs that would have cut in half the transmission of the disease to their babies.[7]

Rigid Leadership—the leader and at least some followers are stiff and unyielding. Although they may be competent, they are unable or unwilling to adapt to new ideas, new information, or changing times.

Mbeki can be described by Barbara Tuchman's phrase "woodenheaded"—a leader who consistently refuses to be "deflected by the facts."[8] Rigid leaders can be successful up to a point. But if they refuse to change with the changing wind, the result will be bad leadership.

INTEMPERATE

Russian President Boris Yeltsin, an alcoholic, was often intoxicated in private and in public, much to the embarrassment of his government and the Russian people. In 1999, to take only one example, Yeltsin was too drunk to get off a plane to greet the visiting prime minister of Ireland, who was left cooling his heels on the tarmac.[9] Alcoholism is a disease. But Yeltsin's failure to treat his problem affected his capacity to serve as Russia's head of state.

Intemperate Leadership—the leader lacks self-control and is aided and abetted by followers who are unwilling or unable effectively to intervene.

In their book *Leadership on the Line*, Ronald Heifetz and Marty Linsky cautioned leaders to control their impulses: "We all have hungers that are expressions of our normal human needs. But sometimes those hungers disrupt our capacity to act wisely or purposefully."[10] Because we live in a time when all top leaders are grist for the media mill, the risk of such disruption is far greater than it was in the past.

CALLOUS

Most Americans who have interest in such matters know the story of Martha Stewart. She has become rich and famous by figuring out that homemaking—cooking, gardening, entertaining, cleaning, indeed every conceivable domestic chore—could reflect artistry as well as drudgery.

But even before her indictment on charges stemming from insider trading, Stewart had acquired a bad reputation. Although she is a brilliantly accomplished and hard-working businesswoman, nearly from the start of her career she has been rumored to be unpleasant and unkind, particularly to employees. How many of these personal attacks are the consequence of Stewart's being a woman in a man's world is difficult to say. Most observers would agree that the rules for women at the top of the corporate hierarchy are different from the rules for men. Most would likely also agree that if Stewart is not exactly a monster or a sociopath, she can be mean. Described variously as a harridan, an uncaring mother, and nasty to those in her employ, Stewart has made bad manners part of her legend: "Neighbors and acquaintances said she was aloof, inconsiderate, and selfish. Employees said she was 'hot-tempered and unreasonable and left them little time to cultivate a garden of their own.' It was as if she created a vision that none around her could live in."[11]

Callous Leadership—the leader and at least some followers are uncaring or unkind. Ignored or discounted are the needs, wants, and wishes of most members of the group or organization, especially subordinates.

CORRUPT

In 1983, Michigan mall developer A. Alfred Taubman bought Sotheby's, the legendary auction house known, along with Christie's, for having cornered the market on the sale of fine art, jewelry, and furniture. Because the auction business had become increasingly competitive, by the mid-1990s Taubman and his Christie's counterpart, Sir Anthony Tennant, were illegally conspiring to raise commission rates.

A few years later the scheme was discovered, and in 2001 Taubman was found guilty of price-fixing, sentenced to a year and a day in prison, and ordered to pay a $7.5 million fine. In addition, Sotheby's and Christie's were ordered to settle class action suits with more than one hundred thousand customers for $512 million.[12]

Taubman did not act alone. For her part in the price-fixing scheme, Sotheby CEO Diana (Dede) Brooks was sentenced to six months of home detention, three years of probation, and one thousand hours of community service. Brooks, a Yale-educated former Citibank executive whose tenure at Sotheby's had been viewed as highly successful, was spared a more severe sentence only because she cooperated with government investigators to provide evidence against Taubman.

Corrupt Leadership—the leader and at least some followers lie, cheat, or steal. To a degree that exceeds the norm, they put self-interest ahead of the public interest.

Corrupt leaders are usually motivated by power or greed—by the desire, in any case, to acquire more of a scarce resource. For example, to make more money, corrupt leaders take bribes, sell favors, evade taxes, exaggerate corporate earnings, engage in insider trading, cook the books, defraud governments and businesses, and in other ways cut corners, bend rules, and break the law.

INSULAR

When the streets of Monrovia began to run with blood, Liberians begged President George W. Bush to intervene, to stop the conflict by sending troops. At first he dithered, siding for a time with those who said, in effect, "Our hands are too full to rescue a distant people determined to murder one another."[13]

Those who chose to differ, Secretary of State Colin Powell among them, argued for intervention on the grounds of national interest and because they considered it the right thing to do. "Liberia is not just another African country," one interventionist argued. "It is an American creation, founded by former slaves 150 years ago, reflecting our image and legacy."[14]

In terms of American foreign policy this might be considered yet another debate between isolationists and interventionists. But as far as the quality of leadership is concerned, the debate over whether or not to intervene in Liberia reflected the tension between those who believe that leaders are responsible only to their own constituencies and those who consider that they have a broader mandate—one that includes trying to stop large numbers of men, women, and children from being hacked to death, even in a distant land.

Insular Leadership—the leader and at least some followers minimize or disregard the health and welfare of "the other"—that is, those outside the group or organization for which they are directly responsible.

EVIL

In 1991, Foday Sankoh, an itinerant photographer and army corporal with a primary school education, gathered a group of guerillas and started a civil war in Sierra Leone. Sankoh was known for his extraordinary charisma. But his followers, many of them poor boys from the countryside, were notorious above all for their brutality. They killed, raped, and spread terror across the small West African nation by chopping off the hands, arms, and legs of innocent civilians—men, women, and children alike. Sankoh was unperturbed. In fact, when some of his close associates spoke out against the flagrant abuses and violations of human rights, they were summarily executed.[15] In 2000, Sankoh was captured by British troops operating under the auspices of the United Nations; later he was turned over to the Special Court for Sierra Leone. The seventeen-count indictment charged him with crimes against humanity, including murder, rape, and extermination. Foday Sankoh died in custody in July 2003.

Evil Leadership—the leader and at least some followers commit atrocities. They use pain as an instrument of power. The harm done to men, women, and children is severe rather than slight. The harm can be physical, psychological, or both.

Evil leaders are not necessarily sadistic. But some experts argue that our notion of evil should include the intent not only to terrorize but also to prolong suffering. They believe that all evildoers derive some sort of satisfaction from hurting others.[16]

THE HEART OF DARKNESS: SEEING IT, AVOIDING IT

Making meaning of being bad is difficult. Problems of objectivity and subjectivity inevitably muddy the water. In all but the most egregious cases, opinions will differ about who deserves to be called a bad leader and why. Notwithstanding, we know three important things:

1. Sometimes leaders, and followers, make a difference.

2. Sometimes this difference is significant.

3. Sometimes the outcome is bad.[17]

It is my hope and intention that by discussing and distinguishing among the primary forms of bad leadership, we might ourselves avoid becoming entangled, both as bad leaders and as bad followers. We cannot stop or slow bad leadership by sticking our heads in the sand. Amnesia, wishful thinking, the lies we tell as individuals and organizations, and all the other mind games we play to deny or distort reality get us nowhere. Avoidance inures us to the costs and casualties of bad leadership, and that is why it festers, virtually unabated.

This is where followers come in. *Bad leadership will not, cannot, be stopped or slowed unless followers take responsibility for rewarding the good leaders and penalizing the bad ones.* Therefore, this chapter concludes with suggestions for both leaders and followers.

LEADERS: SELF-HELP

The following corrections suggest how leaders can strengthen their personal capacities to be at once effective and ethical.

Limit your tenure. When leaders remain in positions of power for too long, they tend to acquire bad habits. They are increasingly prone to become complacent and grandiose, to overreach, to deny reality, and to lose their moral bearings.

Share power. When power is centralized, it is likely to be misused, and that puts a premium on delegation and collaboration.

Don't believe your own hype. For leaders to buy their own publicity is the kiss of death.

Get real and stay real. Virtually every bad leader named in this chapter lost touch with reality to some degree.

Compensate for your weaknesses. When he came into office Bill Clinton knew that his strength was domestic policy and his weakness was foreign policy. So, for example, when Rwanda became a crisis, he should have made it a point to surround himself with experts on Africa.

Stay balanced. More than a few bad leaders were famous workaholics, far more dedicated to their jobs than they were to family and friends. This is a danger.

Remember the mission. This matters, especially when the group or organization is dedicated to public service.

Stay healthy. Marion Barry, the former mayor of Washington, D.C., is an example of a leader whose physical and mental health was impaired throughout most of his time in public office. He should have sought help.

Develop a personal support system. All of us should have aides, associates, friends, or family members who will save us from ourselves.

Be creative. The past should never determine the future nor narrow the available options.

Know and control your appetites. These include the hunger for power, money, success, and sex.

Be reflective. Virtually every one of the great writers on leadership— Plato, Aristotle, Lao Tzu, Confucius, Buddha—emphasizes the importance of self-knowledge, self-control, and good habits.

FOLLOWERS: WORKING WITH OTHERS

The following corrections suggest how followers can work with each other, and with their leaders, to get the best work done in the best possible way.

Find allies. The easiest way for the powerless to become powerful is to find other like-minded people with whom to work. There is strength in numbers.

Develop your own sources of information. Relying on people in positions of authority for correct and complete information is not smart. The interests of leaders and followers do not necessarily coincide.

Take collective action. Collective action can be taken on a modest scale, such as getting a small group together to talk to the boss or getting residents of an apartment building to withhold the rent until heat is restored. Or it can be taken on a much larger scale. Since the mid-1980s, people power has made a difference in the Philippines, in the former Soviet Union and in Eastern Europe, and even in China.

Be a watchdog. More striking than anything else about the spate of corporate scandals at Enron, WorldCom, and the New York Stock Exchange, among others, is the degree to which boards abdicated their responsibility to exercise oversight, to mind the store. What's most curious about all this is that on paper, CEOs are responsible to their boards. But as we have seen repeatedly, board members who were suppose to exercise oversight did not and in fact went along with whatever the CEO was doing.

Hold leaders to account. I suggest that leaders establish a system of checks and balances. Followers have this responsibility as well. Stakeholders of all kinds should secure transparency, open discussions, and meaningful participation. And they should seek to effect institutional changes that will make leaders more responsible and accountable.

———✴———

Barbara Kellerman is the James MacGregor Burns Lecturer in Public Leadership at Harvard University's Kennedy School of Government, former executive director of the Kennedy School's Center for Public Leadership, and author of multiple books and articles on leadership.

CHAPTER THIRTY-FOUR

Good or Not Bad

Standards and Ethics in Managing Change

Kim S. Cameron

～ MANAGING CHANGE REQUIRES FIXED POINTS

The technology currently exists to put the equivalent of a full-size computer in a wristwatch, or to inject the equivalent of a laptop computer into the bloodstream. The newest computers are relying on etchings onto molecules instead of silicone wafers. The mapping of the human genome is probably the greatest source for change, for not only can a banana now be changed into an agent to inoculate people against malaria, but the potential to develop new human organs and to regulate physiological processes in ways previously unimagined promises to dramatically alter population life styles. Over 100 animals have been patented to date, and 4 million new patent applications related to bioengineering are filed each year (Enriquez, 2000). Almost no one dares predict the changes that will occur in the next 10 years. Moreover, not only is change ubiquitous and unpredictable, but almost everyone also assumes that its velocity will increase exponentially (Quinn, 2004; Weick & Sutcliffe, 2001).

Unfortunately, when everything is changing, change becomes impossible to manage. Without a stable, unchanging reference point, direction and progress are indeterminate. Airplane piloting offers an instructive metaphor. Without a stable, unchanging referent such as land or the horizon, it is impossible to steer a plane. Pilots with no visual or instrumentation contact with a fixed point are unable to navigate. Consider the last flight of John Kennedy, Jr., who began to fly up the New England coast at dusk. He lost sight of land and, when it grew dark, the horizon line as well. The result was disorientation, and he flew his plane into the ocean, likely without even knowing he was headed toward the water. He was unable to manage the continuously changing position of his airplane without a standard that remained unchanged.

The same disorientation afflicts individuals and organizations in situations where there are no unchanging referents. When nothing is stable—no clear fixed points or undisputed guiding principles exist—people are left with nothing by which to steer. It becomes impossible to tell up from down or progress from regress. When nothing is stable—that is, an absence of fixed points, dependable principles, or stable benchmarks—people tend to make up their own rules (Weick, 1993). They make sense of the ambiguity and chaos they experience by deciding for themselves what is real and what is appropriate—based on criteria such as personal past experience, immediate payoff, expediency, or personal reward (March, 1994).

In the ethical arena, it has become clear recently that in high-pressure, high-velocity environments, some individuals in the energy-trading, telecommunications, financial services, and accounting industries simply made up their own rules. They ended up cheating, lying, waffling, or claiming naiveté, not only because it was to their economic advantage, but also because they had created their own rationale for what was acceptable. They operated in rapidly evolving, complex, and high-pressure environments where rules and conditions changed constantly. Although their actions are now judged to be unethical and harmful to others, within the rationale they had created for themselves, those actions made perfect sense at the time (Mitchell, 2001).

As an example, Maurice (Hank) Greenberg, an icon in the insurance industry and CEO and chairman of America's largest insurance company, American International Group, was forced to resign recently because he personally orchestrated a complex transaction that regulators now believe unfairly elevated the value of AIG's stock. In a transaction with Warren Buffett's General Reinsurance 5 years earlier, Greenberg indicated that he was merely trying to "shore-up AIG's reserves," but he operated in a way that was deceptive and crossed the ethical line. Unremitting and escalating demands for financial growth, changing financial practices, and fluid accounting principles created a condition where Greenberg felt justified in his complicated maneuvering (Valdmanis, 2005). He merely defined reality in a way that provided an advantage to AIG. Widely publicized examples from Enron, Freddy Mac, Tyco, Global Crossing, Texaco, Arthur Andersen, WorldCom, and other firms replicate this pattern. Leaders created rationales meant to create a legitimate advantage, even while violating ethical standards.

Such conditions illustrate why ethics, standards, rules, and social responsibility have become so important in governing organizational and managerial behavior. Ethical reforms have led to, among other things, the Sarbanes-Oxley legislation—widely considered to be an enormous cost and productivity drain on U.S. companies because of its requirements for documentation and oversight—and an emphasis on corporate social responsibility which has motivated organizations to address troublesome issues in the environment (e.g., pollution, poverty, health care, environmental sustainability); redress existing problems (e.g., cleaning up waterways); or work to prevent harm (e.g., filtering smokestacks). In other words, rules and standards meant to guide what is right and wrong, appropriate and inappropriate, legal and illegal have escalated in the interest of identifying fixed points. Consequently, they are receiving more and more attention in the curricula of schools of business.

ETHICS AS AN INSUFFICIENT FIXED POINT

The problem is standards that avoid harm are not the same as standards that lead to doing good. For example, Bradley, Brief, and Smith-Crowe (2005) differentiated between organizations that are "good" versus those that are "not bad." To date, the dominant (although not exclusive) emphasis in the ethics literature has been on avoiding harm, fulfilling contracts, and obeying the law (Handelsman, Knapp, & Gottlieb, 2002; Paine, 2003). That is, in practice, ethics are understood and implemented as duties

(Rawls, 1971). They are usually specifications designed to avoid injury or prevent damage (Orlikowski, 2000). Ghoshal (2005: 77) went so far as to argue that the dominant management theories are based on harm-avoiding assumptions at best and an amoral ideology at worst. Current management ideology, he argued, "is essentially grounded in a set of pessimistic assumptions about both individuals and institutions—a 'gloomy vision' (Hirschman, 1970) that views the primary purpose of social theory as one of solving the 'negative problem' of restricting the social costs arising from human imperfections." In other words, ethical regulations (and even management theory) are accused of focusing, by and large, on the duties and obligations of individuals and organizations to avoid harm.

Unfortunately, rules and standards that initially appear to guide ethical obligations and socially responsible action may actually lead to the reverse. For example, unions often "work to rule"—doing only what is specified in contracts and rules—as a substitute for going on strike. This pattern of behavior quickly destroys normal organizational functioning. Similarly, following the letter of the law in accounting practices, environmental pollution standards, or performance appraisal systems often leads to the opposite of the intended outcome—in particular, recalcitrance, rigidity, resistance, and rebellion (Cameron, 1998). Moreover, specifying ways to prevent injurious outcomes is subject to change as conditions change—as in the cases of rules governing civil rights, death, marriage, and financial reporting. Hence, ethics may not serve as an adequate fixed point and may not always identify universalistic standards. Rules meant to specify duty to avoid harm may be inadequate standards because they change and do not always lead to desirable outcomes (Caza, Barker, & Cameron, 2004).

Put more succinctly, avoiding the bad is not the same as pursuing the good, and a central argument here is that ethical standards must be supplemented with another standard referred to as a virtuousness standard. The value of distinguishing these two conditions is apparent if we consider a continuum in which three points are identified—a condition of negative deviance on the left, a normal or expected condition in the center, and a positively deviant or highly desirable condition on the right. This continuum illustrates the difference between ethics—traditionally defined as an absence of harm—and virtuousness—the perpetuation of goodness (see Cameron, 2003).

To understand the continuum, think first of the human body. The large majority of medical research, and almost all of a physician's time, is spent on the gap between the left point on the continuum (illness) and the middle point (health), which represents an absence of illness or injury. Relatively little scientific attention is given to the gap between physiological health (middle point) and vitality or wellness (right-hand point). Mayne (1999), for example, found that studies of the relationship between negative phenomena and health outnumbered studies of the relation between positive phenomena and health by 11 to 1. More than 90% of National Institutes of Health–funded research focuses on how to close the gap between a state of illness and a state where illness is absent.

The same is true of psychology. Seligman (2002) reported that more than 99% of published psychological research in the last 50 years has focused on the gap between the left and middle points on the continuum—overcoming depression, anxiety, stress, or emotional difficulties. Relatively little attention has been paid to the gap between a condition of psychological or emotional health and a state of vitality, flourishing, or "flow" (Csikszentmihalyi, 1990). Most of what is known about human physiology and psychology, in other words, relates to avoiding or overcoming illness and harm—similar to the emphasis in the ethics literature. Unethical behavior produces harm, violates principles, and does damage. Ethical behavior usually refers to an absence of harm—behaving consistently, being trustworthy, not damaging others, addressing or redressing societal problems, fulfilling one's duty (Ghoshal, 2005; Caza, Barker, & Cameron, 2004). However, the right side of the continuum refers to conditions that extend beyond the avoidance of harm or the maintenance of the current system. Terms such as honor, goodness, benevolence, and ennoblement describe a condition of virtuousness.

VIRTUOUSNESS AS A SUPPLEMENTAL FIXED POINT

Virtuousness in this sense is what individuals aspire to be when they are at their very best. The word is derived from the Greek *arete*, which means excellence. It refers to that which represents the highest of the human condition. States of virtuousness represent conditions of flourishing and vitality (Lipman-Blumen, & Leavitt, 1999), meaningful purpose (Becker, 1992), ennoblement (Eisenberg, 1990), personal flourishing (Weiner, 1993), and that which leads to health, happiness, transcendent meaning, and resilience in suffering (Myers, 2000; Ryff & Singer, 1998). It is the basis of "moral muscle," willpower, and stamina in the face of challenge (Baumeister & Exline, 1999; Emmons, 1999; Seligman, 1999).

Unfortunately, the concept of virtuousness is often relegated to theology, philosophy, or mere naiveté. Fineman (2006) argued, for example, that virtuousness is culturally restrictive and narrowminded. Its relevance in the world of work or in the management curriculum is often viewed with skepticism or distain. A 17-year analysis of the language appearing in the *Wall Street Journal*, for example, revealed increasing usage of competitive and aggressive language in reference to business (e.g., compete, battle, defeat) but almost no linkage between business and terms such as virtue, compassion, and integrity (Margolis & Walsh, 2003). Moreover, practicing managers frequently reflect the attitude that virtuous concepts are irrelevant in the high-velocity, resource constrained, and turbulent battleground of business. "Virtuousness may be fine as a discussion topic at a late night coffee bar, but it's too soft and syrupy to be taken seriously in my world of competitive positioning, customer demands, and shareholder performance pressure" (personal communication from a corporate CEO). One result is almost total negligence of such topics in the business school classroom.

On the other hand—and this is the crucial point—virtuousness can, and should, serve as a fixed point to guide individual and organizational behavior in times of ambiguity, turbulence, and high-velocity change. This is because virtuousness represents what people aspire to be at their best, and those aspirations are universal and unchanging in essentially all societies, cultures, and religions (see Peterson & Seligman, 2004; Kidder, 1994). Contrary to Fineman's (2006) claims, virtuousness is not culturally constricted and applicable only to North America. It represents Aristotle's "goods of first intent," which have long been claimed to be characteristics of the best of the human condition. Without virtuousness as a supplement to ethics, in other words, no unchanging fixed point exists with which to manage change. Moreover, when virtuousness is demonstrated, positive individual and organizational outcomes accrue.

One part of the research agenda emerging in the field of positive organizational scholarship is an investigation of the role of virtuousness in individual and organizational performance. An irony associated with virtuousness is that, by definition, virtuousness is inherently desirable. No payback or reward is required for virtuousness to be universally treasured. On the other hand, without a business case being made for virtuousness—i.e., evidence of its relevance to organizational performance—it is usually ignored as a standard to guide individual or organizational action.

Hence, a series of studies were conducted in which virtuousness was assessed in various kinds of organizations. In one, Cameron, Bright, and Caza (2004) examined recently downsized organizations in a variety of industries, all of which were facing environments characterized by high degrees of change. The research assessed members' ratings of numerous organizationally facilitated virtues such as compassion, integrity, forgiveness, trust, and optimism (concepts included on lists of universally valued virtues, e.g., Peterson & Seligman, 2004). Empirical results revealed that virtuous organizations significantly outperformed less virtuous organizations on a series of outcome measures, including profitability, productivity, innovation, quality, customer retention, and employee loyalty. In another study of the U.S. airline industry after the tragedy of September 11th, the airline companies demonstrating virtuousness universally outperformed other airlines—that is, they lost less money, their stock price recovered faster and to a greater extent, and passenger miles remained higher (Gittell, Cameron, & Lim, 2006). Studies of health care, military, and governmental organizations show that organizations facing financial exigency and layoffs encountered fewer of the problems associated with downsizing and performed better than organizations in parallel situations that did not demonstrate the same virtuous orientation (Cameron, 1998; Cameron, Kim, & Whetten, 1987; Cameron & Lavine, 2006). In other words, in conditions of high-velocity, turbulent, and complex environments, virtuous firms made more money than less virtuous firms. Virtuous firms recovered from downsizing and retained customers and employees to a greater extent than nonvirtuous firms. And virtuous firms were more creative and innovative than nonvirtuous firms (Cameron, 2003).

The implication of these research findings highlights the importance of a virtuous fixed point in addition to an ethical fixed point in managing change. That is, in order to cope effectively and perform successfully in turbulent conditions, individuals and organizations must certainly avoid doing harm—that is, they must adhere to ethical rules—but they must also act virtuously—that is, they must foster virtuousness and the best of the human condition. Virtuousness is associated with positive outcomes, not just the absence of negative outcomes. Virtuousness produces positive energy in systems, enables growth and vitality in people, builds social capital, and enhances the probability of extraordinary performance (see Cameron, Dutton, & Quinn, 2003). Virtuousness pays dividends. Doing good helps organizations to do well (Cameron, Bright, & Caza, 2004). In conditions of turbulent change, virtuousness serves as an essential fixed point—a benchmark for making sense of ambiguity—as well as a source of resilience, protecting the system against harm.

Virtuousness has this kind of impact because of two core attributes. It produces an amplifying effect, and it produces a buffering effect. The amplifying effect refers to the self-perpetuating nature of virtuousness. Specifically, virtuousness is contagious. People are inherently attracted to virtuous acts, so that when they observe them, they are inspired by them (Sandage & Hill, 2001). They are elevated by virtuousness, so it tends to be reproduced (Fredrickson, 2003). In organizations, this amplifying effect spreads and expands and, eventually, becomes part of the structure and culture of the firm (Cameron & Caza, 2002). At the individual level, when people work in a virtuous environment, they tend to be more physically and mentally healthy (Ryff & Singer, 1998; Weiner, 1993). Virtuous individuals tend to make better decisions (Staw & Barsade, 1993) and to be more creative (George, 1998). At the interpersonal level, virtuousness is associated with affiliative feelings (Haidt, 2000), fosters high-quality connections (Dutton, 2003), and leads to the formation of social capital (Bolino, Turnley, & Bloodgood, 2002). At the organizational level, it produces positive emotionality, meaningfulness, and mutual reinforcement in the organization (Dutton & Heaphy, 2003; Gittell, 2003; Fredrickson, 2001; Cohen & Prusak, 2001). The amplifying nature of virtuousness, in other words, causes it to replicate itself and to improve organizational performance over time.

The buffering effect of virtuousness refers to its capacity to protect individuals and organizations against dysfunction, harm, or illness at both the individual and organizational levels of analysis. Seligman and Csikszentmihalyi (2000) reported that virtues such as courage, optimism, faith, integrity, forgiveness, and compassion all have been found to protect against psychological distress, addiction, and dysfunctional behavior. Learned optimism, for example, prevents depression and anxiety in children and adults, roughly halving their incidence (Seligman, 1991). Similarly, virtuousness buffers individuals from the negative consequences of personal trauma (Seligman, Schulman, DeRubeis, & Hollon, 1999), and the cardiovascular, emotional, and intellectual systems in individuals recover significantly more rapidly and completely when they experience virtuous behaviors (Fredrickson, Mancuso, Branigan, & Tugade, 2000). Individuals who experience virtuousness suffer less psychological distress and engage in fewer destructive behaviors in response to adverse events (Seligman & Csikszentmihalyi, 2000).

At the organizational level, virtuousness also serves a buffering function by contributing to the speed and effectiveness of recovery from setbacks (Dutton, Frost, Worline, Lilius, & Kanov, 2002; Wildavsky, 1991). Downsizing, for example, is an organizational change that almost universally produces undesirable organizational outcomes and ambiguous conditions (Cameron, 1994). Its presence produces at least 12 recurring problem behaviors that lead to poor performance (Cameron, 1998). Virtuousness buffers the organization from such effects by protecting feelings of solidarity (Masten, Hubbard, Gest, Tellegen, Garmezy, & Ramirez, 1999), preserving social capital, enhancing collective efficacy, and clarifying purposefulness and vision (Sutcliffe & Vogus, 2003; Masten et al., 1999; Weick, Sutcliffe, & Obstfeld, 1999). Virtuousness also enhances relational coordination (Gittell, 2001, 2002) and helps create resilience that allows the organization to recover quickly (Gittell, Cameron, & Lim, 2006).

Recent research in positive organizational scholarship has begun to highlight the role played by virtuousness in enhancing and enabling spectacular performance in organizations. In an environment characterized above all by escalating turbulence and high-velocity change, a hallmark of high-performing systems is not only the demonstration of ethical behavior—the absence of harm—but also the demonstration of virtuousness—producing and enabling goodness. Ethics and virtues can both serve as essential fixed points in a sea of chaotic change and uncertainty. Because ethical standards may be unstable, however, they must be supplemented by virtuous standards—universal aspirations that focus on the best of the human condition. Whereas ethics receives by far the most attention in management classes, textbooks, scholarly literature, and managerial practice (Ghoshal, 2005), more focus on virtuousness in organizational dynamics is needed to enable self-reinforcing positive outcomes. The topic of virtuousness in the management classroom is a needed addition to the management curriculum.

—◠◠◠—

Kim S. Cameron is professor of management and organizations in the Ross School of Business and professor of higher education in the School of Education at the University of Michigan. He has published multiple books on organizations and is currently studying the effects of positive practices and virtuousness on organizational performance.

PART FIVE

Sustaining the Leader

In "The Secret Sharer," novelist Joseph Conrad offers a powerful portrait of leadership development from the inside out. Readers are privy to the inner struggles of a young sea captain seeking to understand the meaning of leadership and what he must do to rise to the challenge. The young captain has technical know-how: training from a top seafaring academy and solid experience as first mate on comparable vessels. At the helm for the first time, however, he is surprised by what he finds—and finds out about himself. Leadership is a lot harder and less glamorous than he expected: followers must be earned, the pace of the work is swift and steady, decisions are often made in the face of ambiguity, and mistakes can be costly to the leader and the entire enterprise. And leadership is lonely work. It engages mind, heart, body, and soul—and even the most prepared are never fully certain they will succeed until tested.

Conrad's story, however, is hopeful—and a reminder that leaders need to strengthen and support themselves in order to serve others and their organizations well. The young sea captain faces his vulnerabilities head on, and develops strategies to sustain himself in his darkest hours. He embraces self-reflection, accepts his limitations, and digs deep into his moral core for inner strength. He builds skills as a reflective practitioner (Schön, 1995) and learns by examining his impact on those around him. He also finds a confidant—a controversial stranger that he has let on board—to support his growth. By the story's end, the captain feels finally ready to take the helm— self-aware, open to learning, confident, and humble.

What can business leaders do to strengthen their character, resilience, and resolve? What gives them strength in the face of challenge? How can they best sustain themselves, their efforts, and their ongoing development in the face of inevitable twists and turns in the leadership journey? The chapters in Part Five answer those questions.

Leadership has its dangers. As Conrad's young sea captain discovered, a leader's choices are fateful for the leader and for others, and personal needs can cloud professional judgment. Followers' mixed feelings about the boss add risk to the equation. Followers want powerful leaders who can deliver, yet fear those who may challenge their comfortable status quo. In such a world, leaders are always vulnerable, and they need tactics to protect themselves from their own and others' efforts to undermine their initiatives. Ronald A. Heifetz and Marty Linsky provide these strategies in Chapter Thirty-Five, "A Survival Guide for Leaders."

Leadership is service to a larger good, and the creativity and persistence necessary for success are fueled by clarity of purpose and pride in one's contribution. Corporate scandals, greed, and emphasis on bottom-line profits mirror a spiritual crisis in the business sector. They also raise important questions about whether successful corporate careers require sacrificing personal integrity or a focus on a larger social good. No, counsels David Batstone, in Chapter Thirty-Six, "Preserving Integrity, Profitability, and Soul." Leaders sustain their own morale and creativity—and serve their companies best—when they honor a common sense of justice and fairness and help their organizations to do so as well. "Corporate workers are looking for a new vision," says Batstone, "a path to save the corporate soul—and just maybe their own."

"Leadership learning" seems counterintuitive, note David L. Dotlich, James L. Noel, and Norman Walker in Chapter Thirty-Seven, "Learning for Leadership: Failure as a Second Chance." The careers of successful leaders often reveal a series of what the authors call leadership *passages*— tests like those faced by Conrad's young sea captain, which demonstrate whether the leader has the right stuff. Passages offer important opportunities for leaders to strengthen themselves and expand their understanding of the larger world. The young sea captain built confidence and inner strength by reflecting on his experiences—and what leaders do when they recognize a gap between their current skills and the demands of the situation makes all the difference. Even failure becomes a blessing when it provides a critical opportunity to learn.

Conrad's young captain reminds leaders that inner spiritual growth matters. Leadership always seems simpler from the outside. Internal struggles, conflicting passions, and doubts of the soul are all par for the course. Leadership is gritty and emotionally charged, and the spiritual disciplines offer a grounded base from which to approach the work. Spiritual maturity is at the heart of effective business leadership, says Andre L. Delbecq, in Chapter Thirty-Eight, "Nourishing the Soul of the Leader: Inner Growth Matters." It involves finding one's life calling, leveraging personal passions for a larger social good, bringing a moral compass to decision making, and using spiritual disciplines like prayer and meditation to sustain a leader's health and healthy openness to new opportunities and to others.

A moral grounding and clear sense of purpose sustain leadership. So does resilience, say Warren G. Bennis and Robert J. Thomas in Chapter Thirty-Nine, "Resilience and the Crucibles of Leadership." All leaders face trials and uncertainty in their efforts to make a difference. Bennis and Thomas call these leadership "crucibles"—experiences that force leaders to grapple with their current reality, question themselves, determine what really matters, and emerge stronger and more committed from the adversity. Resilience is more than survival. It involves growth: learning the importance of perseverance and emerging from trying circumstances with hope.

This volume began by discussing the differences between leadership and good management. It ends by reinforcing one primary difference. Leaders foster hope. In Chapter Forty, "Choose Hope: On Creating a Hopeful Future," Andrew Razeghi clarifies that hope is more than wishful thinking. Hope takes courage: strong faith, solid thinking, creativity, willful action, and persistence in the face of the unknown. The common call for more leadership, better leadership, is often in reality a plea for a hopeful leader, one who can help those who are lost find their way. Choose hope, advises Razeghi. Nothing motivates followers—or sustains leaders—like the recognition of a bright and better world.

CHAPTER THIRTY-FIVE

A Survival Guide for Leaders

Ronald A. Heifetz
Marty Linsky

T hink of the top executives in recent years who, after periods of considerable success, have crashed and burned. Or think of individuals in less prominent positions, perhaps people spearheading significant change initiatives in their organizations, who have suddenly found themselves out of a job. Think about yourself. In exercising leadership, have you ever been removed or pushed aside?

Let's face it, to lead is to live dangerously. While leadership is often depicted as an exciting and glamorous endeavor, one in which you inspire others to follow you through good times and bad, such a portrayal ignores leadership's dark side: the inevitable attempts to take you out of the game.

Those attempts are sometimes justified. People in top positions must often pay the price for flawed strategy or bad decisions. But frequently, something more is at work. We're not talking here about conventional office politics; we're talking about the high-stake risks you face whenever you try to lead an organization through difficult but necessary change. The risks during such times are especially high because change that truly transforms an organization—be it a multibillion-dollar company or a ten-person sales team—demands that people give up things they hold dear: daily habits, loyalties, ways of thinking. In return for these sacrifices, they may be offered nothing more than the possibility of a better future.

We refer to this kind of wrenching organizational transformation as "adaptive change," something very different from the "technical change" that occupies people in positions of authority on a regular basis. Technical problems, while often challenging, can be solved by applying existing know-how and the organization's current problem-solving processes. Adaptive problems resist these kinds of solutions because they require individuals throughout the organization to alter their ways; as the people themselves are the problem, the solution lies with them. Responding to an adaptive challenge with a technical fix may have short-term appeal. But to make real progress, sooner or later those who lead must ask themselves and the people in the organization to face a set of deeper issues and to accept a solution that may require turning part or all of the organization upside down.

It is at this point that danger lurks. And most people who lead in such a situation—swept up in the action, championing a cause they believe in—are caught unawares. Over and over again, we have seen courageous souls blissfully ignorant of an approaching threat until it was too late to respond.

The hazard can take numerous forms. You may be attacked directly in an attempt to shift the debate to your character and style and avoid discussion of your initiative. You may be marginalized, forced into the position of becoming so identified with one issue that your broad authority is undermined. You may be seduced by your supporters and, fearful of losing their approval and affection, fail to demand they make the sacrifices needed for the initiative to succeed. You may be diverted from your goal by people overwhelming you with the day-to-day details of carrying it out, keeping you busy and preoccupied.

Each one of these thwarting tactics—whether done consciously or not—grows out of people's aversion to the organizational disequilibrium created by your initiative. By attempting to undercut you, people strive to restore order, maintain what is familiar to them, and protect themselves from the pains of adaptive change. They want to be comfortable again, and you're in the way.

So how do you protect yourself? Over a combined 50 years of teaching and consulting, we have asked ourselves that question time and again—usually while watching top-notch and well-intentioned folks get taken out of the game. On occasion, the question has become painfully personal; we as individuals have been knocked off course or out of the action more than once in our own leadership efforts. So we are offering what we hope are some pragmatic answers that grow out of these observations and experiences. We should note that while our advice clearly applies to senior executives, it also applies to people trying to lead change initiatives from positions of little or no formal organizational authority.

This "survival guide" has two main parts. The first looks outward, offering tactical advice about relating to your organization and the people in it. It is designed to protect you from those trying to push you aside. The second looks inward, focusing on your own human needs and vulnerabilities. It is designed to keep you from bringing yourself down.

A HOSTILE ENVIRONMENT

Leading major organizational change often involves radically reconfiguring a complex network of people, tasks, and institutions that have achieved a kind of modus vivendi, no matter how dysfunctional it appears to you. When the status quo is upset, people feel a sense of profound loss and dashed expectations. They may go through a period of feeling incompetent or disloyal. It's no wonder they resist the change or try to eliminate its visible agent. We offer here a number of techniques—relatively straightforward in concept but difficult to execute—for minimizing these external threats.

Operate in and Above the Fray

The ability to maintain perspective in the midst of action is critical to lowering resistance. Any military officer knows the importance of maintaining the capacity for reflection, especially in the "fog of war." Great athletes must simultaneously play the game and observe it as a whole. We call this skill "getting off the dance floor and going to the balcony," an image that captures the mental activity of stepping back from the action and asking, "What's really going on here?"

Leadership is an improvisational art. You may be guided by an overarching vision, clear values, and a strategic plan, but what you actually do from moment to moment cannot be scripted. You must respond as events unfold. To use our metaphor, you have to move back and forth from the balcony to the dance floor, over and over again throughout the days, weeks, months, and years. While today's plan may make sense now, tomorrow you'll discover the unanticipated effects of today's actions and have to adjust accordingly. Sustaining good leadership, then, requires first and foremost the capacity to see what is happening to you and your initiative as it is happening and to understand how today's turns in the road will affect tomorrow's plans.

But taking a balcony perspective is extremely tough to do when you're fiercely engaged down below, being pushed and pulled by the events and people around you—and doing some pushing and pulling of your own. Even if you are able to break away, the practice of stepping back and seeing the big picture is complicated by several factors. For example, when you get some distance, you still must accurately interpret what you see and hear. This is easier said than done. In an attempt to avoid difficult change, people will naturally, even unconsciously, defend their habits and ways of thinking. As you seek input from a broad range of people, you'll constantly need to be aware of these hidden agendas. You'll also need to observe your own actions; seeing yourself objectively as you look down from the balcony is perhaps the hardest task of all.

Fortunately, you can learn to be both an observer and a participant at the same time. When you are sitting in a meeting, practice by watching what is happening while it is happening—even as you are part of what is happening. Observe the relationships and see how people's attention to one another can vary: supporting, thwarting, or listening. Watch people's body language. When you make a point, resist the instinct to stay perched on the edge of your seat, ready to defend what you said. A technique as simple as pushing your chair a few inches away from the table after you speak may provide the literal as well as metaphorical distance you need to become an observer.

Court the Uncommitted

It's tempting to go it alone when leading a change initiative. There's no one to dilute your ideas or share the glory, and it's often just plain exciting. It's also foolish. You need to recruit partners, people who can help protect you from attacks and who can point out potentially fatal flaws in your strategy or initiative. Moreover, you are far less vulnerable when you are out on the point with a bunch of folks rather than alone. You also need to keep the opposition close. Knowing what your opponents are thinking can help you challenge them more effectively and thwart their attempts to upset your agenda—or allow you to borrow ideas that will improve your initiative. Have coffee once a week with the person most dedicated to seeing you fall.

But while relationships with allies and opponents are essential, the people who will determine your success are often those in the middle, the uncommitted who nonetheless are wary of your plans. They have no substantive stake in your initiative, but they do have a stake in the comfort, stability, and security of the status quo. They've seen change agents come and go, and they know that your initiative will disrupt their lives and make their futures uncertain. You want to be sure that this general uneasiness doesn't evolve into a move to push you aside.

These people will need to see that your intentions are serious—for example, that you are willing to let go of those who can't make the changes your initiative requires. But people must also see that you understand the loss you are asking them to accept. You need to name the loss, be it a change in time-honored work routines or an overhaul of the company's core values, and explicitly acknowledge the resulting pain. You might do this through a series of simple statements, but it often requires something more tangible and public—recall Franklin Roosevelt's radio "fireside chats" during the Great Depression—to convince people that you truly understand.

Beyond a willingness to accept casualties and acknowledge people's losses, two very personal types of action can defuse potential resistance to you and your initiatives. The first is practicing what you preach. In 1972, Gene Patterson took over as editor of the *St. Petersburg Times*. His mandate was to take the respected regional newspaper to a higher level, enhancing its reputation for fine writing while becoming a fearless and hard-hitting news source. This would require major changes not only in the way the community viewed the newspaper but also in the way *Times* reporters thought about themselves and their roles. Because prominent organizations and individuals would no longer be spared warranted criticism, reporters would sometimes be angrily rebuked by the subjects of articles.

Several years after Patterson arrived, he attended a party at the home of the paper's foreign editor. Driving home, he pulled up to a red light and scraped the car next to him. The police officer called to the scene charged Patterson with driving under the influence. Patterson phoned Bob Haiman, a veteran *Times* newsman who had just been appointed executive editor, and insisted that a story on his arrest be run. As Haiman recalls, he tried to talk Patterson out of it, arguing that DUI arrests that didn't involve injuries were rarely reported, even when prominent figures were involved. Patterson was adamant, however, and insisted that the story appear on page one.

Patterson, still viewed as somewhat of an outsider at the paper, knew that if he wanted his employees to follow the highest journalistic standards, he would have to display those standards, even when it hurt. Few leaders are called upon to disgrace themselves on the front page of a newspaper. But adopting the behavior you expect from others—whether it be taking a pay cut in tough times or spending a day working next to employees on a reconfigured production line—can be crucial in getting buy-in from people who might try to undermine your initiative.

The second thing you can do to neutralize potential opposition is to acknowledge your own responsibility for whatever problems the organization currently faces. If you have been with the company for some time, whether in a position of senior authority or not, you've likely contributed in some way to the current mess. Even if you are new, you need to identify areas of your own behavior that could stifle the change you hope to make.

In our teaching, training, and consulting, we often ask people to write or talk about a leadership challenge they currently face. Over the years, we have read and heard literally thousands of such challenges. Typically, in the first version of the story, the author is nowhere to be found. The underlying message: "If only other people would shape up, I could make progress here." But by too readily pointing your finger at others, you risk making yourself a target. Remember, you are asking people to move to a place where they are frightened to go. If at the same time you're blaming them for having to go there, they will undoubtedly turn against you.

In the early 1990s, Leslie Wexner, founder and CEO of the Limited, realized the need for major changes at the company, including a significant reduction in the workforce. But his consultant told him that something else had to change: long-standing habits that were at the heart of his self-image. In particular, he had to stop treating the company as if it were his family. The indulgent father had to become the chief personnel officer, putting the right people in the right jobs and holding them accountable for their work. "I was an athlete trained to be a baseball player," Wexner recalled during a recent speech at Harvard's Kennedy School. "And one day, someone tapped me on the shoulder and said, 'Football.' And I said, 'No, I'm a baseball player.' And he said, 'Football.' And I said, 'I don't know how to play football. I'm not 6' 4", and I don't weigh 300 pounds.' But if no one values baseball anymore, the baseball player will be out of business. So I looked into the mirror and said, 'Schlemiel, nobody wants to watch baseball. Make the transformation to football.'" His personal makeover—shedding the role of forgiving father to those widely viewed as not holding their own—helped sway other employees to back a corporate makeover. And his willingness to change helped protect him from attack during the company's long—and generally successful—turnaround period.

Cook the Conflict

Managing conflict is one of the greatest challenges a leader of organizational change faces. The conflict may involve resistance to change, or it may involve clashing viewpoints about how the change should be carried out. Often, it will be latent rather than palpable. That's because most organizations are allergic to conflict, seeing it primarily as a source of danger, which it certainly can be. But conflict is a necessary part of the change process and, if handled properly, can serve as the engine of progress.

Thus, a key imperative for a leader trying to achieve significant change is to manage people's passionate differences in a way that diminishes their destructive potential and constructively harnesses their energy. Two techniques can help you achieve this. First, create a secure place where the conflicts can freely bubble up. Second, control the temperature to ensure that the conflict doesn't boil over—and burn you in the process.

The vessel in which a conflict is simmered—in which clashing points of view mix, lose some of their sharpness, and ideally blend into consensus—will look and feel quite different in different contexts. It may be a protected physical space, perhaps an off-site location where an outside facilitator helps a group work through its differences. It may be a clear set of rules and processes that give minority voices confidence that they will be heard without having to disrupt the proceedings to gain attention. It may be the shared language and history of an organization that binds people together through trying times. Whatever its form, it is a place or a means to contain the roiling forces unleashed by the threat of major change.

But a vessel can withstand only so much strain before it blows. A huge challenge you face as a leader is keeping your employees' stress at a productive level. The success of the change effort—as well as your own authority and even survival—requires you to monitor your organization's tolerance for heat and then regulate the temperature accordingly.

You first need to raise the heat enough that people sit up, pay attention, and deal with the real threats and challenges facing them. After all, without some distress, there's no incentive to change. You can constructively raise the temperature by focusing people's attention on the hard issues, by forcing them to take responsibility for tackling and solving those issues, and by bringing conflicts occurring behind closed doors out into the open.

But you have to lower the temperature when necessary to reduce what can be counterproductive turmoil. You can turn down the heat by slowing the pace of change or by tackling some relatively straightforward technical aspect of the problem, thereby reducing people's anxiety levels and allowing them to get warmed up for bigger challenges. You can provide structure to the problem-solving process, creating work groups with specific assignments, setting time parameters, establishing rules for decision making, and outlining reporting relationships. You can use humor or find an excuse for a break or a party to temporarily ease tensions. You can speak to people's fears and, more critically, to their hopes for a more promising future. By showing people how the future might look, you come to embody hope rather than fear, and you reduce the likelihood of becoming a lightning rod for the conflict.

The aim of both these tactics is to keep the heat high enough to motivate people but low enough to prevent a disastrous explosion— what we call a "productive range of distress." Remember, though, that most employees will reflexively want you to turn down the heat; their complaints may in fact indicate that the environment is just right for hard work to get done.

We've already mentioned a classic example of managing the distress of fundamental change: Franklin Roosevelt during the first few years of his presidency. When he took office in 1933, the chaos, tension, and anxiety brought on by the Depression ran extremely high. Demagogues stoked class, ethnic, and racial conflict that threatened to tear the nation apart. Individuals feared an uncertain future. So Roosevelt first did what he could to reduce the sense of disorder to a tolerable level. He took decisive and authoritative action—he pushed an extraordinary number of bills through Congress during his fabled first 100 days—and thereby gave Americans a sense of direction and safety, reassuring them that they were in capable hands. In his fireside chats, he spoke to people's anxiety and anger and laid out a positive vision for the future that made the stress of the current crisis bearable and seem a worthwhile price to pay for progress.

But he knew the problems facing the nation couldn't be solved from the White House. He needed to mobilize citizens and get them to dream up, try out, fight over, and ultimately own the sometimes painful solutions that would transform the country and move it forward. To do that, he needed to maintain a certain level of fermentation and distress. So, for example, he orchestrated conflicts over public priorities and programs among the large cast of creative people he brought into the government. By giving the same assignment to two different administrators and refusing to clearly define their roles, he got them to generate new and competing ideas. Roosevelt displayed both the acuity to recognize when the tension in the nation had risen too high and the emotional strength to take the heat and permit considerable anxiety to persist.

Place the Work Where It Belongs

Because major change requires people across an entire organization to adapt, you as a leader need to resist the reflex reaction of providing people with the answers. Instead, force yourself to transfer, as Roosevelt did, much of the work and problem solving to others. If you don't, real and sustainable change won't occur. In addition, it's risky on a personal level to continue to hold on to the work that should be done by others.

As a successful executive, you have gained credibility and authority by demonstrating your capacity to solve other people's problems. This ability can be a virtue, until you find yourself faced with a situation in which you cannot deliver solutions. When this happens, all of your habits, pride, and sense of competence get thrown out of kilter because you must mobilize the work of others rather than find the way yourself. By trying to solve an adaptive challenge for people, at best you will reconfigure it as a technical problem and create some short-term relief. But the issue will not have gone away.

In the 1994 National Basketball Association Eastern Conference semifinals, the Chicago Bulls lost to the New York Knicks in the first two games of the best-of-seven series. Chicago was out to prove that it was more than just a one-man team, that it could win without Michael Jordan, who had retired at the end of the previous season.

In the third game, the score was tied at 102 with less than two seconds left. Chicago had the ball and a time-out to plan a final shot. Coach Phil Jackson called for Scottie Pippen, the Bulls' star since Jordan had retired, to make the inbound pass to Toni Kukoc for the final shot. As play was about to resume, Jackson noticed Pippen sitting at the far end of the bench. Jackson asked him whether he was in or out. "I'm out," said Pippen, miffed that he was not tapped to take the final shot. With only four players on the floor, Jackson quickly called another time-out and substituted an excellent passer, the reserve Pete Myers, for Pippen. Myers tossed a perfect pass to Kukoc, who spun around and sank a miraculous shot to win the game.

The Bulls made their way back to the locker room, their euphoria deflated by Pippen's extraordinary act of insubordination. Jackson recalls that as he entered a silent room, he was uncertain about what to do. Should he punish Pippen? Make him apologize? Pretend the whole thing never happened? All eyes were on him. The coach looked around, meeting the gaze of each player, and said, "What happened has hurt us. Now you have to work this out."

Jackson knew that if he took action to resolve the immediate crisis, he would have made Pippen's behavior a matter between coach and player. But he understood that a deeper issue was at the heart of the incident: Who were the Chicago Bulls without Michael Jordan? It wasn't about who was going to succeed Jordan, because no one was; it was about whether the players could jell as a team where no one person dominated and every player was willing to do whatever it took to help. The issue rested with the players, not him, and only they could resolve it. It did not matter what they decided at that moment; what mattered was that they, not Jackson, did the deciding. What followed was a discussion led by an emotional Bill Cartwright, a team veteran. According to Jackson, the conversation brought the team closer together. The Bulls took the series to a seventh game before succumbing to the Knicks.

Jackson gave the work of addressing both the Pippen and the Jordan issues back to the team for another reason: If he had taken ownership of the problem, he would have become the issue, at least for the moment. In his case, his position as coach probably wouldn't have been threatened. But in other situations, taking responsibility for resolving a conflict within the organization poses risks. You are likely to find yourself resented by the faction that you decide against and held responsible by nearly everyone for the turmoil your decision generates. In the eyes of many, the only way to neutralize the threat is to get rid of you.

Despite that risk, most executives can't resist the temptation to solve fundamental organizational problems by themselves. People expect you to get right in there and fix things, to take a stand and resolve the problem. After all, that is what top managers are paid to do. When you fulfill those expectations, people will call you admirable and courageous—even a "leader"—and that is flattering. But challenging your employees' expectations requires greater courage and leadership.

THE DANGERS WITHIN

We have described leadership tactics you can use to interact with the people around you, particularly those who might undermine your initiatives. Those can help advance your initiatives and, just as important, ensure that you remain in a position where you can bring them to fruition. But from our observations and painful personal experiences, we know that one of the surest ways for an organization to bring you down is simply to let you precipitate your own demise.

In the heat of leadership, with the adrenaline pumping, it is easy to convince yourself that you are not subject to the normal human frailties that can defeat ordinary mortals. You begin to act as if you are indestructible. But the intellectual, physical, and emotional challenges of leadership are fierce. So, in addition to getting on the balcony, you need to regularly step into the inner chamber of your being and assess the tolls those challenges are taking. If you don't, your seemingly indestructible self can self-destruct. This, by the way, is an ideal outcome for your foes—and even friends who oppose your initiative—because no one has to feel responsible for your downfall.

Manage Your Hungers

We all have hungers, expressions of our normal human needs. But sometimes those hungers disrupt our capacity to act wisely or purposefully. Whether inherited or products of our upbringing, some of these hungers may be so strong that they render us constantly vulnerable.

More typically, a stressful situation or setting can exaggerate a normal level of need, amplifying our desires and overwhelming our usual self-discipline. Two of the most common and dangerous hungers are the desire for control and the desire for importance.

Everyone wants to have some measure of control over his or her life. Yet some people's need for control is disproportionately high. They might have grown up in a household that was either tightly structured or unusually chaotic; in either case, the situation drove them to become masters at taming chaos not only in their own lives but also in their organizations.

That need for control can be a source of vulnerability. Initially, of course, the ability to turn disorder into order may be seen as an attribute. In an organization facing turmoil, you may seem like a god-send if you are able (and desperately want) to step in and take charge. By lowering the distress to a tolerable level, you keep the kettle from boiling over.

But in your desire for order, you can mistake the means for the end. Rather than ensuring that the distress level in an organization remains high enough to mobilize progress on the issues, you focus on maintaining order as an end in itself. Forcing people to make the difficult trade-offs required by fundamental change threatens a return to the disorder you loathe. Your ability to bring the situation under control also suits the people in the organization, who naturally prefer calm to chaos. Unfortunately, this desire for control makes you vulnerable to, and an agent of, the organization's wish to avoid working through contentious issues. While this may ensure your survival in the short term, ultimately you may find yourself accused, justifiably, of failing to deal with the tough challenges when there was still time to do so.

Most people also have some need to feel important and affirmed by others. The danger here is that you will let this affirmation give you an inflated view of yourself and your cause. A grandiose sense of self-importance often leads to self-deception. In particular, you tend to forget the creative role that doubt—which reveals parts of reality that you wouldn't otherwise see—plays in getting your organization to improve. The absence of doubt leads you to see only that which confirms your own competence, which will virtually guarantee disastrous missteps.

Another harmful side effect of an inflated sense of self-importance is that you will encourage people in the organization to become dependent on you. The higher the level of distress, the greater their hopes and expectations that you will provide deliverance. This relieves them of any responsibility for moving the organization forward. But their dependence can be detrimental not only to the group but to you personally. Dependence can quickly turn to contempt as your constituents discover your human shortcomings.

Two well-known stories from the computer industry illustrate the perils of dependency—and how to avoid them. Ken Olsen, the founder of Digital Equipment Corporation, built the company into a 120,000-person operation that, at its peak, was the chief rival of IBM. A generous man, he treated his employees extraordinarily well and experimented with personnel policies designed to increase the creativity, teamwork, and satisfaction of his workforce. This, in tandem with the company's success over the years, led the company's top management to turn to him as the sole decision maker on all key issues. His decision to shun the personal computer market because of his belief that few people would ever want to own a PC, which seemed reasonable at the time, is generally viewed as the beginning of the end for the company. But that isn't the point; everyone in business makes bad decisions. The point is, Olsen had fostered such an atmosphere of dependence that his decisions were rarely challenged by colleagues—at least not until it was too late.

Contrast that decision with Bill Gates's decision some years later to keep Microsoft out of the Internet business. It didn't take long for him to reverse his stand and launch a corporate overhaul that had Microsoft's delivery of Internet services as its centerpiece. After watching the rapidly changing computer industry and listening carefully to colleagues, Gates changed his mind with no permanent damage to his sense of pride and an enhanced reputation due to his nimble change of course.

Anchor Yourself

To survive the turbulent seas of a change initiative, you need to find ways to steady and stabilize yourself. First, you must establish a safe harbor where each day you can reflect on the previous day's journey, repair the psychological damage you have incurred, renew your stores of emotional resources, and recalibrate your moral compass. Your haven might be a physical place, such as the kitchen table of a friend's house, or a regular routine, such as a daily walk through the neighborhood. Whatever the sanctuary, you need to use and protect it. Unfortunately, seeking such respite is often seen as a luxury, making it one of the first things to go when life gets stressful and you become pressed for time.

Second, you need a confidant, someone you can talk to about what's in your heart and on your mind without fear of being judged or betrayed. Once the undigested mess is on the table, you can begin to separate, with your confidant's honest input, what is worthwhile from what is simply venting. The confidant, typically not a coworker, can also pump you up when you're down and pull you back to earth when you start taking praise too seriously. But don't confuse confidants with allies: Instead of supporting your current initiative, a confidant simply supports you. A common mistake is to seek a confidant among trusted allies, whose personal loyalty may evaporate when a new issue more important to them than you begins to emerge and take center stage.

Perhaps most important, you need to distinguish between your personal self, which can serve as an anchor in stormy weather, and your professional role, which never will. It is easy to mix up the two. And other people only increase the confusion: Colleagues, subordinates, and even bosses often act as if the role you play is the real you. But that is not the case, no matter how much of yourself—your passions, your values, your talents—you genuinely and laudably pour into your professional role. Ask anyone who has experienced the rude awakening that comes when they leave a position of authority and suddenly find that their phone calls aren't returned as quickly as they used to be.

That harsh lesson holds another important truth that is easily forgotten: When people attack someone in a position of authority, more often than not they are attacking the role, not the person. Even when attacks on you are highly personal, you need to read them primarily as reactions to how you, in your role, are affecting people's lives. Understanding the criticism for what it is prevents it from undermining your stability and sense of self-worth. And that's important because when you feel the sting of an attack, you are likely to become defensive and lash out at your critics, which can precipitate your downfall.

We hasten to add that criticism may contain legitimate points about how you are performing your role. For example, you may have been tactless in raising an issue with your organization, or you may have turned the heat up too quickly on a change initiative. But, at its heart, the criticism is usually about the issue, not you. Through the guise of attacking you personally, people often are simply trying to neutralize the threat they perceive in your point of view. Does anyone ever attack you when you hand out big checks or deliver good news? People attack your personality, style, or judgment when they don't like the message.

When you take "personal" attacks personally, you unwittingly conspire in one of the common ways you can be taken out of action—you make yourself the issue. Contrast the manner in which presidential candidates Gary Hart and Bill Clinton handled charges of philandering. Hart angrily counterattacked, criticizing the scruples of the reporters who had shadowed him. This defensive personal response kept the focus on his behavior. Clinton, on national television, essentially admitted he had strayed, acknowledging his piece of the mess. His strategic handling of the situation allowed him to return the campaign's focus to policy issues. Though both attacks were extremely personal, only Clinton understood that they were basically attacks on positions he represented and the role he was seeking to play.

Do not underestimate the difficulty of distinguishing self from role and responding coolly to what feels like a personal attack—particularly when the criticism comes, as it will, from people you care about. But disciplining yourself to do so can provide you with an anchor that will keep you from running aground and give you the stability to remain calm, focused, and persistent in engaging people with the tough issues.

WHY LEAD?

We have failed if this "survival manual" for avoiding the perils of leadership causes you to become cynical or to shun the challenges of leadership altogether. We haven't touched on the thrill of inspiring people to come up with creative solutions that can transform an organization for the better. We hope we have shown that the essence of leadership lies in the capacity to deliver disturbing news and raise difficult questions in a way that moves people to take up the message rather than kill the messenger. But we haven't talked about the reasons that someone might want to take these risks.

Of course, many people who strive for high-authority positions are attracted to power. But in the end, that isn't enough to make the high stakes of the game worthwhile. We would argue that, when they look deep within themselves, people grapple with the challenges of leadership in order to make a positive difference in the lives of others.

When corporate presidents and vice presidents reach their late fifties, they often look back on careers devoted to winning in the marketplace. They may have succeeded remarkably, yet some people have difficulty making sense of their lives in light of what they have given up. For too many, their accomplishments seem empty. They question whether they should have been more aggressive in questioning corporate purposes or creating more ambitious visions for their companies.

Our underlying assumption in this chapter is that you can lead and stay alive—not just register a pulse, but really be alive. But the classic protective devices of a person in authority tend to insulate them from those qualities that foster an acute experience of living. Cynicism, often dressed up as realism, undermines creativity and daring. Arrogance, often posing as authoritative knowledge, snuffs out curiosity and the eagerness to question. Callousness, sometimes portrayed as the thick skin of experience, shuts out compassion for others.

The hard truth is that it is not possible to know the rewards and joys of leadership without experiencing the pain as well. But staying in the game and bearing that pain is worth it, not only for the positive changes you can make in the lives of others but also for the meaning it gives your own.

—–≈—–

Ronald A. Heifetz is the King Hussein bin Talal Lecturer in Public Leadership and cofounder of the Center for Public Leadership at Harvard's John F. Kennedy School of Government, partner in the consulting firm Cambridge Leadership Associates, and author of multiple works on leadership.

—–≈—–

Marty Linsky is cofounder of Cambridge Leadership Associates, a leadership development consulting firm; adjunct lecturer in public policy at Harvard's John F. Kennedy School of Government; and former chief secretary/counselor to Massachusetts governor William Weld and assistant minority leader of the Massachusetts House of Representatives.

CHAPTER THIRTY-SIX

Preserving Integrity, Profitability, and Soul

David Batstone

─∞∞─ Think about how much of our lives we spend at work," the executive of a New York publishing house said wistfully to me. "Then consider how ambivalent—and perhaps a bit ashamed— most of us feel about the corporations who employ us."

He is not alone. Corporate workers from the mailroom to the highest executive office express dissatisfaction with their work. They feel crushed by widespread greed, selfishness, and quest for profit at any cost. Apart from their homes, people spend more time on the job than anywhere else. With that kind of personal stake, they want to be part of something that matters and contribute to a greater good.

Sadly, those aspirations often go unmet. Trust in our financial and commercial institutions is eroding. Truth be told, the corporate crisis is as much spiritual as it is financial. Yes, fortunes are won or lost on the ability to anticipate trends and create products that meet those demands. But capitalizing on innovation is not enough today. A company's success also hinges on whether, in the eyes of its employees and the public, it honors a common sense of justice.

"Whatever company I work for in the future, I'll never again trust at face value what top executives say." A deep sense of betrayal marks these words spoken by a Global Crossing vice president who was laid off just weeks before the broadband telecommunications company filed for federal bankruptcy protection amid questions about its accounting. Along with thousands of other Global Crossing employees, she did not receive severance pay. "When top executives laid us off, they must have known they were going to file for bankruptcy and that they'd never have to pay us severance," she says, adding that some senior officials left the company with generous exit packages. "Maybe what they did was legal, but it feels unethical, especially when you look at how they treated themselves."[1]

Workers are six times more likely to stay in their jobs when they believe that their company acts with integrity, according to Walker Information, a research company that measures employee satisfaction and loyalty at the workplace. But when workers mistrust their bosses' decisions and feel ashamed of their firm's behavior, four out of five workers feel trapped at work and say they are likely to leave their jobs soon.[2]

To thrive, corporations need to take account of this crucial shift in social values. Dispirited workers do not perform well; low morale saps the passion and creativity that otherwise would be unleashed on behalf of a company's mission. Corporate workers are looking for a new vision, a path to save the corporate soul—and just maybe their own.

SOUL SEARCHING

What is it about the corporation that can make joining it feel as if we're making a bargain with Mephisto for our soul?

Nearly fifty years ago, my father launched his professional career in the corporate world, joining General Electric in a management training program. He then made a horizontal move to Union Carbide and finally fled the corporate world altogether a few years later to start a family-owned retail business. My dad could not point to any specific conflict he had with the corporation, and, now in retirement, he wrestles with the *what-ifs* had he stayed and patiently climbed his way up the corporate ladder. At the time, however, my dad deplored the feeling that he was just another number in an impersonal organization, a cog in the machine.

In his 1956 classic, *The Organization Man*, William Whyte gave ample evidence that my father did not face his spiritual struggle alone. Whyte showed that the growth of large organizations, while leading to vast economic and political changes, was having an equally dramatic impact on the individuals who worked inside them. Their collision with the corporate structure stripped workers of a sense of uniqueness and forced them to make decisions not of their own choosing. These observations led Whyte to a radical conclusion: "We do need to know how to cooperate with The Organization but, more than ever, so do we need to know how to resist it."[3]

That legacy is still deeply rooted in our popular consciousness. Recall the number of movies you have seen that feature heroic characters who fight against the greed of a corporate giant to save their community. Hollywood has made an icon of the underdog fighting incredible odds to do the Right Thing.

Is it really meaningful, then, to talk of a corporate soul? After all, the corporation was created in part to protect individuals from being held personally responsible for the actions of a public entity. It also offers a more efficient structure for aggregating capital that yields the potential for higher profits. None of these objectives depends on promoting the dignity and worth of individuals or their communities. The corporation's harshest critics in fact depict it as a cold, calculating machine.

In this chapter, I argue that a corporation has the potential to act with soul when it puts its resources at the service of the people it employs and the public it serves. That journey begins once a company seeks to align its mission with the values of its workers. It is unrealistic to expect that all of the workers' values will match those of the company, of course. But when that alignment moves closer together, the morale of the company is transformed.

Precisely for that reason, senior managers need to step back occasionally from the tyranny of the urgent and ask their own people, "Why is it that you want to work here?" If workers cannot get inspired about the company, they will not communicate a compelling message to customers. A vital corporation helps its people to think, plan, and express their dignity in the way they carry out their daily tasks on behalf of the enterprise. In other words, it tends to its soul. Read Tom Higa's story, which follows, and I think you will agree.

HOW MUCH IS ENOUGH?

Tom Higa operated his Chevron gas station on a corner block in San Francisco for over twenty-five years.[4] It was the old-fashioned kind of shop where the attendant would wash the windows and kick the tires. Tom began working at the gas station as an attendant in 1964. After eight years of hard work, he took over as owner and picked up the station lease with Chevron.

Tom is exceptionally popular in his community. He hired locally over the years and provided a high quality of service to his customers. In turn, Tom owes a great debt to his neighbors. They saved his business.

Back in 1989, Chevron gave Tom the shocking news that it would not renew his station lease. The underground storage tanks on the property were in need of replacement at a cost of about $150,000. Oil company officials told him that the station was outdated and no longer matched the image of what a Chevron station should look like.[5]

Tom didn't see it coming. He had consistently met or surpassed the gas sales Chevron had set for his station; in fact, his operation was returning a healthy 12 percent profit margin on average. "I wasn't going to become a millionaire, but I earned enough to keep my family secure and deliver a good return to the corporation. I don't know what profit level it would take to satisfy Chevron," wondered Tom.[6]

The financial analysts back at Chevron headquarters indeed had crunched the numbers and concluded they could do better. By closing Tom's business, demolishing the station, and building a commercial building on the site, the property could return at least a 15 percent profit margin. Chevron corporate saw it as a clear-cut business decision to maximize profits.

Tom went into a panic. What other livelihood could a man nearing fifty with two young children and a lifelong career at a gas station pursue? Chevron officials suggested he might enter a computer-training course. To Tom, the idea was absurd; such a career detour did not match his skill set or his interests. He knew what he had a passion for, and that was running a gas station.

The neighbors were upset as well. They wanted a service station in the community, not another commercial building. "The whole neighborhood loves this place," remarked one of Tom's long-time customers. "They're honest and friendly and trustworthy, and they give real good service. Isn't that the kind of image a company wants?"[7]

The neighbors leaped into action. They sent hundreds of letters and a long list of signatures on a petition to Chevron urging the corporation to reconsider. Copies also were sent to San Francisco's city hall, and they landed on the desk of Mayor Art Agnos.

Agnos backed a thriving private sector in his city, but he also took seriously his responsibility to protect the interests of citizens.[8] He placed a call to Chevron's corporate headquarters, and within days, one of its senior managers paid a visit to his office.

The mayor asked the Chevron manager whether the neighborhood had presented an accurate picture of Tom Higa's business. Did Tom really hit his numbers for gas sales quarter after quarter? Yes, the manager confirmed, but then went on to review the business case for Agnos, emphasizing how the corporation could raise its profit margin with the execution of its plan.

Agnos searched for a compromise. How about delaying the plan for another eight to ten years until Tom was closer to retirement age? No, the manager responded; the company was determined to move forward now.

His stubborn and callous attitude angered Agnos. The mayor informed him that Chevron's plans to develop the property might not go as smoothly as the company had projected. In fact, he threatened him on the spot with a stringent environmental impact procedure that in all likelihood would lead to delays and substantial unforeseen costs.

A pitched political struggle ensued in San Francisco. The details will not be fully recounted here, but suffice it to note that Agnos and the city council went ahead with the environmental impact legislation, Chevron's plans to repurpose the property were thwarted, and Tom Higa's Chevron went on to operate at a healthy profit for another decade.

There's an added behind-the-scenes piece to this drama that underscores the values at stake. While he was mayor, Agnos held a quarterly luncheon with the chief executive officers (CEOs) of the major corporations with headquarters in San Francisco. The atmosphere turned chilly shortly after the mayor's showdown with Chevron. Agnos recalls entering the dining room to an awkward silence. Moments after all were seated to begin lunch, the CEO of one of California's major banks raised his voice so that all gathered could hear: "Arthur, you realize that we're pretty upset at you over this environmental legislation."

Agnos paused a second before replying, "Okay, I guess that's understandable, but let me give you my perspective. Here's a man with a family to support, owner of his own franchise for sixteen years, and the business is thriving. Then a wealthy corporation announces it's going to shut him down. He's always made money for the company, yet some green analyst in headquarters figures on paper the company can make a few percentage points more. So let me ask you something: How much is enough?"

All conversation and movement came to a stop. Agnos, it seems, had uttered an unpardonable blasphemy. The bank executive came back with emotion: "Arthur, the very fact that you can ask that question terrifies me."

Agnos let another agonizing half-minute pass, each player waiting for the next move in this awkward chess game. He then drove home his point: "So, guys, I ask you again: How much is enough? Since no one has responded, I guess the answer is that there's never enough, no matter what the cost."

Agnos had raised the relevant question: How does a business calculate the cost of personal livelihood and community vitality? For the financial analysts at Chevron, at least, the Right Thing to do lies plainly in front of us in the numbers.

But raw numbers can tell many tales. In this instance, the effort to close Tom's business may have ended up being more costly than Chevron had anticipated. It could not quantify the financial impact of a tarnished company reputation once the saga was dragged through the media. Nor could it calculate the strategic impact on other Chevron franchises once word spread that reaching, and even surpassing, targets for gas sales would not protect them from foreclosure. Finally, it could not put a financial figure on the low morale of Chevron employees at corporate headquarters, who surely felt something less than pride in their company's efforts. In short, a strong business case can be made that Chevron's decision to close down Tom Higa's service station was costly indeed.

FINDING COMMON GROUND

The vast majority of corporate executives would say, at least in their more candid moments, that their firm's public responsibility begins and ends with their shareholders. "What is enough?" you ask. "More than last quarter" is what they answer. That is the measure by which they are hired, compensated, and fired. It is also the plumb line that the stock market uses to reward or punish their companies.

Over the past two decades, public markets have tended to be unrealistic about the growth curve of individual enterprises. Even the best-run companies are subject to the rise and fall of economic cycles, but one bad quarterly earnings report these days and a company's stock gets hammered on the trading floor. This quarterly vision practically forces senior managers to look for short-cuts that will inflate short term results at the expense of long-term sustainability.

For that reason, the burden for reinventing corporate behavior extends beyond the executive office. It is vital for other stakeholders who participate in the business web to reevaluate the ways they work, invest, partner, supply, and consume.

The problems at Enron, for instance, cannot be isolated to a small group of executives who looked to enrich themselves. When the going was good and Enron was reporting mind-blowing profits, few people cared that they could not make heads or tails of the company's financial statements. The desire to believe the illusion led lots of eyes to gloss over the obvious signs of chicanery. Once Enron started to stumble and report losses, the emperor's clothes fell off with startling quickness.

Given this landscape, I try to be very practical about what it takes to change corporate behavior. We are in dire need of senior management who have the vision and courage to make good choices when the payoff may not be immediately apparent on the balance sheet. But in most cases, they will need to be convinced that doing the Right Thing will have a positive effect on their firms' bottom line, or at least will not add to the cost of doing business.

I realize that "doing the Right Thing" may seem quite subjective as a standard for corporate behavior. Business leaders rarely talk about the values that shape the character of a corporation and make an impact on its financial performance. But they do exist. There are eight principles that I consider the most crucial for corporate performance:

- *Principle One:* The directors and executives of a company will align their personal interests with the fate of stakeholders and act in a responsible way to ensure the viability of the enterprise.

- *Principle Two:* A company's business operations will be transparent to shareholders, employees, and the public, and its executives will stand by the integrity of their decisions.

- *Principle Three:* A company will think of itself as part of a community as well as a market.

- *Principle Four:* A company will represent its products honestly to customers and honor their dignity up to and beyond a transaction.

- *Principle Five:* The worker will be treated as a valuable team member, not just a hired hand.
- *Principle Six:* The environment will be treated as a silent stakeholder, a party to which the company is wholly accountable.
- *Principle Seven:* A company will strive for balance, diversity, and equality in its relationships with workers, customers, and suppliers.
- *Principle Eight:* A company will pursue international trade and production based on respect for the rights of workers and citizens of trade partner nations.

Companies that incorporate these eight principles into their operations do not put themselves at a competitive disadvantage. In fact, substantial evidence indicates that principled companies excel financially over the long haul. Towers Perrin, the management consulting firm, took a close look at twenty-five companies that enjoy a strong reputation for public integrity and are rated year in and year out as desirable places to work. That model group includes well-known corporations like Southwest Airlines, Johnson & Johnson, Applied Materials, and Procter & Gamble. Towers Perrin analyzed the market performance of these principled companies over a fifteen-year period and then compared their returns to those generated by public companies at large. The results: the principled companies delivered a total shareholder return of 43 percent, while the shareholder return of Standard & Poor's 500 performed at less than half that figure: 19 percent.[9]

A snapshot of Johnson & Johnson may offer a clue to why principled companies excel. In its corporate credo, Johnson & Johnson lists the stakeholders that its employees are asked to honor with their business decisions: first, customers; second, coworkers; third, management; fourth, the communities where the company operates; and fifth, shareholders. Lest we think that Johnson & Johnson is a philanthropic endeavor, the company credo also declares the obvious: "Business must make a sound profit." But the company does pledge that profit will not eclipse its other priorities.

In 1982, the Johnson & Johnson credo was put to the test when a major disaster hit. Eight people died from ingesting cyanide-laced Tylenol capsules. Johnson & Johnson executives made a decision immediately to recall 31 million bottles of Tylenol from store shelves even before the cause for the crisis could be determined. The company also promptly redesigned product containers and introduced tamper-proof packaging. Although Johnson & Johnson turned out to be blameless, the crisis ended up costing the company $240 million and cut its profits on $5 billion in revenues that year almost in half. But its decisive action ended up saving the Tylenol brand and generating a wave of goodwill from its customers.[10]

The Johnson & Johnson experience underscores why corporations would be foolish to sacrifice their credibility at the altar of earnings reports. Long-term market value does not rise or fall independent of a company's social impact. And like it or not, every action a corporation takes may be interpreted as a statement about what it stands for.

ACCOUNTING FOR THE GOOD

If we had to settle on one philosophy that rules business operations today, it seems to be captured by this mantra: If you can't measure it, you can't account for it. That's precisely the reason that many efforts to translate principles into corporate practices languish at the point of execution. Most senior managers today feel an escalating pressure to conform to higher standards of integrity. But if they cannot understand how to identify and measure their outcomes, they are likely to consider principles a matter of image, not substance. We know, however, that a company's capacity to integrate the eight principles presented in this chapter determines its overall business performance. The Towers Perrin study cited indicates the potential impact on shareholder return over an extended period. There are also three other prime areas where we see business principles impacting success—and which become another way to assess the impact of principles on corporate performance:

- A principled company will fortify its reputation.
- A principled company will be more likely to avoid costly lawsuits.
- A principled company will manage its business network more effectively.

Reputation: The Guardian of Your Brand

A brand is the visual, emotional, and cultural image that we associate with a company or a product. While the daily grind of business is about sales, brand building looks to create a bond and loyalty that lasts. Over time, customers develop a personal affinity with a brand; once they feel betrayed, their fury lashes out as it would toward a fallen politician or movie star.

Reputation is not the same as a brand. We attribute character to people, and we do the same thing to companies. Reputation is the perceived character a company holds in the public eye. A company's reputation in large part depends on its ability to meet the expectations of a broad range of stakeholders.

A lot of companies have a strong brand but lack a well-established reputation. Sony and Pepsi-Cola, for instance, can boast solid brands, but neither really has much of a reputation. When we think of Volvo, on the other hand, we think safety, which is an example of a reputation holding up a brand.

Reputation serves as the guardian of the company brand. A company can take years to build a brand yet destroy it overnight with a soiled reputation. Arthur Andersen is a prime example of a firm that took a short-cut marked by dollar signs and undercut a brand that had been carefully cultivated over nine decades.

In today's business climate, reputation has become as important as brand. For starters, it is a key asset for attracting employees. A Cone/Roper study finds that corporate reputation is the second most important factor for people choosing an employer. Remarkably, job candidates rate reputation more highly than starting salary or fringe benefits.[11] People put a high premium on working for a firm that can be trusted.

Customers and investors also are highly influenced by a firm's reputation. Nearly four out of five Americans say they at least consider reputation when buying a company's product, and 36 percent call it an "important" factor in their purchasing decision, according to a survey conducted by Hill and Knowlton. The same study shows that more than 70 percent of investors consider reputation in their decisions even if that choice means lowering their financial returns.[12] Now here's the bad news: consumers give very few companies high marks for reputation. Less than 2 percent of Americans surveyed look at U.S. companies as "excellent corporate citizens," and more than half rate corporations as "below average" in social responsibility.[13]

Going After Carrots and Avoiding Sticks

While some business leaders like to pin the spate of corporate scandals on a few rotten apples in the barrel, the American public believes they reflect more fundamental problems with the way corporations do business. In a Washington Post/ABC News poll, roughly three of four people viewed the malfeasance of WorldCom, Enron, and Global Crossing as "a sign of broader problems with the way many companies report their financial condition." Fewer than one in four believe that these scandals are "pretty much isolated incidents."[14]

The public thirsts for justice in the business world. If corporations are unwilling to take the steps necessary to amend their behavior, citizens will turn to the courts and legislators to set the standards. Historically, the levels of public trust in American business determine how much citizens look to their government to regulate business.

To date, the punitive stick has focused on a practice that the corporate world euphemistically calls aggressive accounting, and in many cases is nothing more than cooking the books. In April 2002, the Securities and Exchange Commission (SEC) levied a fine of $10 million on the Xerox Corporation, at the time the largest penalty ever given a public company in connection with financial reporting violations. As part of the settlement with the SEC, Xerox was forced to restate its earnings for a five-year period.[15] In levying such a stiff penalty, the SEC was sending a clear message to corporate America: if we can go after an established, well-respected player like Xerox, any company can be exposed and punished.

A business professor at the University of Pittsburgh, Jeff Frooman, measured the stock market's reaction to incidences of corporate misconduct. He took a close look at twenty-seven separate incidents when a corporation was slapped with punitive measures, such as regulatory fines, environmental lawsuits, and product recalls. The pattern he found should be a strong caveat to all who are responsible for corporate governance: offending companies suffered significant losses in shareholder wealth that in most cases they never recovered.[16]

Delivering on Trust Across the Network

The modern corporation does not live as an island unto itself. It swims within a sea of network-based enterprises that extend from manufacturing to distribution to marketing. As a result, many of a company's key relationship assets—the people whom it must trust to succeed—are located outside the corporate structure. Despite that fact, a firm is held accountable for every action that takes place in its name across the network enterprise. That fact alone should raise real concerns about the effectiveness of conventional structures of governance.

The operation of a business has a new level of transparency today. Because network-based enterprises are so heavily information driven, just about every policy, administrative action, investment, or transaction eventually reaches the public domain. Over the Internet, hundreds of millions of people have at their fingertips an effective tool for getting access to and sharing information. The higher the profile of a brand, the greater is the scrutiny of its activities.

Executives at Boise, the giant timber company, can attest to the daunting challenge this level of transparency creates. Over the past decade, Boise has faced intense pressure from consumers and distributors to end the harvesting of old-growth trees. At the prompting of environmentalists, a diverse group of customers including Kinko's, L. L. Bean, Patagonia, and the University of Notre Dame started boycotting the company's paper products. Explaining his company's decision to cancel its contract with Boise, John Sterling of the clothing company Patagonia, said, "There will always be companies that don't care where their lumber and paper come from, but as their customers become more sophisticated about environmental issues, they're going to have to pay closer attention to the practices of suppliers that sell them wood products."[17]

The consumer boycott and erosion to its brand forced Boise to reevaluate all its supplier relationships, and in March 2002, it announced that it would drastically reduce old-growth logging. An official for the timber industry, disappointed that Boise caved in to public pressure, complained, "It's blackmail any way you slice it. As more and more retailers fall victim to this extortion campaign, it could definitely have an impact on the industry."[18]

What this timber industry official fails to understand is that we have entered a new era. Network enterprises cannot ignore the values of their customers and partners. The savvy corporation will not treat public scrutiny as blackmail, but instead will see it as an opportunity to strengthen its reputation with customers. Because environmentalists are holding the business enterprise accountable for its impact on the earth, most large corporations are putting protocols and standards in place to address their concerns. Absent standards of accountability, a firm risks a reputation breakdown anywhere in its network.

Change can begin anywhere in the corporation. A good number of the corporate innovators do not hold an executive title. To make a major impact on the organization, however, an initiative eventually will need to gain the enthusiastic backing of leaders at the executive and board levels. They have the means to introduce new practices across the company and the responsibility to govern their execution. The importance of leading and governing with integrity is integral to success.

CLOSING THOUGHTS: FROM SUCCESS TO SIGNIFICANCE

I wrote this chapter for people who work in corporations. Many friends and colleagues tell me they feel trapped. Although corporations often offer them the best platform and set of rewards to develop their career, they wonder whether they are selling out—their life priorities, integrity, promises they make to themselves and others. Lots of us are too cynical to believe it can be otherwise, but it can be. In fact, evidence indicates that a business will thrive once it aligns itself with the values that drive its customers and workers. To get there, the people inside a company need to ask themselves, again and again, one question: *What are we in business for?*

I keep coming back to a message that Russell Ackoff gave his students at the Wharton School: "Profit is a means, not an end." That hit home for me most powerfully when I was CEO of a start-up company in the late 1990s. At the time, new technologies were forcing corporations to rethink the way they ran their business operations. The blur of innovation made it difficult to separate the real from the hype. My company saw an opportunity; become the trusted adviser matching business needs with working technology. I'll spare you the rest.

Back then, I spared no words or effort on behalf of my company. Anyone who has passed through fire and storm to launch a business will never forget the experience. I worked with my executive team eighty or ninety hours a week to write a business plan (and rewrite it daily, or so it seemed) and to develop financial projections, sales strategies, technology platforms, and operational protocols. All the while, we were also out courting potential customers and investors, making the rounds to blue-chip venture capitalists and corporate fund managers, looking for the best partners to fuel our enterprise.

After nine months and few victories, it looked as if our ship was coming in. We were introduced to Michael Milken, who was busy stitching together a group of companies under one canopy named Knowledge Universe (KU). Our company fit well into KU's strategic plan, and our services were complementary to some of the assets Michael already had acquired. Over a series of meetings, we negotiated the details of our business relationship. Michael wanted KU to be the sole investor in our company, and he pledged tens of millions of dollars as long as we met a schedule of performance benchmarks. In exchange, KU would acquire a huge slice of our company.

Although Michael's legacy will forever be linked to junk bonds, corporate raiders, and a prison sentence, he dealt with our team in good faith and earned my respect. He is a tough-as-nails negotiator and possesses the most brilliant financial mind I have ever encountered.

As we were closing in on a deal with KU, I decided to jump off the spinning carousel to clear my head. I took my family to Lake Tahoe for a few days of hiking and boating. Midway through the holiday, Michael called. We went over a few final details, and then he put to me his final test: "David, I trust you realize that once we make this deal, this company will be your life."

I swallowed hard, told him I completely understood, and the call ended with a few pleasantries. In fact, his words thudded on top of me like a ton of bricks. The impact was immediate and served as a catalyst for a spiritual awakening. It was not as if I was doing anything that violated my moral compass. I can imagine any number of people who, being in the same position, could accept the investment, and it would be the best possible decision for them. But I was forced to confront my motivation—my purpose for being in this business. Down deep I knew the reason: I was hawking widgets, pieces of technology. I had no passion, none at all, to help corporations solve their operational dilemmas and become more efficient. To be completely honest, I was in it for the money.

This will be your life. Once off the telephone and returning to my family in the cabin, I put together a mental inventory of the things that I deeply valued. I saw four small children who had not seen much of their dad for the previous year. I thought of my love for university teaching, passion for writing, and the profound meaning I gained promoting human development in poverty-stricken countries. What was the price tag I could put on all that? *Priceless,* my inner voice replied.

I returned home several days later with the clarity I was looking for. I would resign. Most difficult of all was sharing the decision with my executive team. Meeting with them was the second test of my conviction, because I knew they would try to talk me out of it. I don't blame them for trying. We were finally on the cusp of our reward. My pulling out meant disaster. Michael was investing in our management team as much as our business. Although I felt terrible for letting them down, I knew that I could not go forward. We floated the option of accepting KU's investment and then six to twelve months down the road finding a new CEO. But I rejected that idea out of hand. I was sure of Michael's intention and playing that game would be nothing short of betrayal.

The next day, I contacted Michael and explained my decision to step down as CEO. He was surprised at first, but our conversation soon turned philosophical. He shared that he too believed in using one's talents to make a meaningful contribution to the world and made note of his own philanthropic work. Creating financial wealth enabled him to do those things, he added, implying I was making a false choice between significance and financial success. What I said in reply—and believe firmly to this day—is that living with soul transcends the matter of money. One cannot give enough money away to heal a broken spirit. Nor, for that matter, does turning one's back on money ensure the slightest degree of enlightenment. The person who lives his or her life in pursuit of success—be that measured by wealth, fame, or social status—will be sorely disenchanted with the pot at the end of the rainbow. Success alone cannot satisfy our deepest longings for significance.

At this moment, the corporate world sorely needs leaders—not people with titles, but true leaders at every level of the corporation— to live with soul. I am inclined to believe that for most people, it is not a new path but a truth about themselves that awaits discovery. Once they start living out of that discovery, they will inspire everyone who surrounds them. No greater tribute could we receive from a coworker than hearing: *You, my friend, are the soul of this place.*

———

David Batstone is a professor of ethics at the University of San Francisco, where he has served as the National Endowment for the Humanities Chair for his work in technology and ethics; a founding editor of *Business 2.0*; and senior editor of *Motto* magazine.

CHAPTER THIRTY-SEVEN

Learning for Leadership

Failure as a Second Chance

David L. Dotlich

James L. Noel

Norman Walker

> *Adversity has the effect of eliciting talents which in prosperous circumstances would have lain dormant.*
>
> *—Horace*

One of us met recently with the new CEO of a large company who was profiling his team of direct reports. As the CEO talked with us, he focused on the skills and background of each direct report. Impressed with the diversity of the group, we asked, "Is there anything that everyone on your team has in common?"

He nodded. "At one point or another, each one of us has been fired."

The CEO said this proudly. To him, being fired was a badge of merit. His direct reports had been through tough times and learned from their experience. Because they had once been terminated, members of his team had grown personally and professionally. Difficult, unpredictable events had forced them to turn inward, address their flaws, and seek to understand how they may have contributed to their own dismissal. Termination had tested their resiliency—a trait crucial to leadership in competitive businesses. They were survivors.

These experiences are also *passages* because, as the word indicates, they take you from one place to another; you see the world and yourself differently after you've gone through the events and emotional states

Joining a company

Moving into a leadership role

Accepting the stretch assignment

Assuming responsibility for a business

Dealing with significant failure for which you are responsible

Coping with a bad boss and competitive peers

Losing your job or being passed over for promotion

Being part of an acquisition or merger

Living in a different country or culture

Finding a meaningful balance between work and family

Letting go of ambition

Facing personal upheaval

Losing faith in a system

Exhibit 37.1. Thirteen Common Passages.

that define each passage. [See Exhibit 37.1 for a list of the thirteen passages that senior leaders mention most often and describe as particularly compelling or intense.] What you may not experience, however, is permission to discuss these experiences openly and share your insights with others because many companies today prefer to avoid addressing either these passages or their significance. You may have been encouraged to "keep going" and, as a result, denied yourself the richness, significance, and growth inherent in significant life and leadership events, even when painful. So although you may have shielded yourself from the pain and self-doubt that comes with the journey, you didn't get to reap the true leadership development benefits. As "bad" as a passage may sound, it is not the event itself that hurts a career but how you react to it. It is how you handle working for a bad boss, being fired, or being acquired that determines whether the impact is positive or negative and whether you become a stronger leader or remain the same. Failure gives you a second chance to learn.

Failure of any kind tells you something about yourself. It grabs your attention and, if you can remain non-defensive, suggests that perhaps you don't know something you need to know. Unfortunately, many people don't capitalize on this second chance to learn. In working with many large global companies, we can say unequivocally that organizations aren't fond of failure. Most large companies don't give leaders the time to reflect on the experience or the permission to admit their vulnerabilities. In the wake of business failure, mistake, error, or disappointment, many leaders deny (to themselves and others) their own role. CEOs account for disappointing earnings by blaming "unexpected circumstances." Senior executives cite consumer behavior, currency fluctuation, pricing, unruly competitors, or some other external event as a logical explanation for negative outcomes. Few leaders ever say, "I screwed up."

If you aspire to obtain a top leadership position, however, you can't continually scapegoat and deny your failures. Through coaching many successful, accomplished leaders, we have observed that personal accountability differentiates learners from laggards. Acknowledging and expressing the negative feelings that accompany failure opens the door to change.

We use the SARA (Shock, Anger, Rejection, Acceptance) model to describe the four emotional reactions leaders experience in encountering situations or outcomes they don't like:

1. *Shock:* You acknowledge your surprise that you messed up, others don't like you, or you failed to meet your own or others' expectations.

2. *Anger:* You are furious that things didn't go according to plan.

3. *Rejection:* You blame someone or something for events and reject the information or your role in creating the outcome.

4. *Acceptance:* You accept your vulnerability and acknowledge that failure and your feelings are part of being human.

Dealing with these feelings can be difficult if you're left to your own devices. Appreciating them as important passages can help you deal with them effectively and facilitate learning.

WAYS TO CREATE A NEW IDENTITY

In one sense, "leadership learning" is counterintuitive. In *The Leadership Pipeline*, Jim Noel, along with coauthors Ram Charan and Steve Drotter, suggests that executives make "turns" in the pipeline—from individual contributor to manager, for instance—based on their success in their previous job. Each turn requires new skills, values, and use of time, as well as significant adaptation to a new role. The individual contributor's skill as a salesperson earned him a promotion to sales manager, but the skills required for a managerial position are different from those of an individual contributor. Nonetheless, he still relies on the salesperson skills that brought him success in the past. This is perfectly natural, but it will prevent him from learning and growing as a manager. His instinct will be to rely on what he knows and to avoid tasks that require what he doesn't know.

People often go through passages relying on behaviors and attitudes that served them well in the past. Passages, though, challenge your self-definition ("I'm always successful" or "I'm usually in control"). Undertaking a stretch assignment, living abroad, mourning the death of a loved one, or dealing with a bad boss all communicate to people that "you're not in Kansas anymore." It's difficult to ignore the signs that life has changed and that you need to change with it. Of course, some people do ignore the signs. But each passage presents a new opportunity to learn and grow, and if you see it as such, you can dramatically improve your leadership effectiveness.

Learning from a passage, however, isn't possible unless you let go of your past assumptions. In other words, you must admit that some of the very attributes, qualities, attitudes, and skills that made you successful in the past won't necessarily make you successful in the future and that your old knowledge may no longer be applicable. Such an admission makes you vulnerable; you feel exposed as a novice after enjoying your role as an experienced pro. This is a tough psychological transition, especially because you may not even be aware the transition is taking place. In coaching senior executives who encounter a significant passage, we encourage them to admit their vulnerability as the precursor to learning.

Typically, you're so caught up in the excitement of a passage or the complex issues it raises that learning from it is the last thing on your mind. For instance, you've just been given the task of turning a business around—a business that's critical to the company's future. Weighed down with high expectations and excited about proving yourself, you feel you need to be the expert right from the start, that you must hit the ground running. As a result, you plunge into the assignment, focused only on getting it done rather than stepping back and figuring out what you really need to know to do the assignment effectively and how you can maximize your first months in the new role. Companies such as Dell and Johnson & Johnson are beginning to intervene at this point and help leaders with this passage through transition coaching, but usually companies don't do that. Leaders may receive advice from bosses or mentors, but the advice is usually technical in nature, confined to achieving the task set before them. It's only when things don't go well that they begin to receive the feedback they really need.

To maximize learning in each passage, be willing to give up your identity. For instance, this could mean no longer defining yourself as a star, a winner, or super-achiever. The process of evolving one's identity is often unconscious and subtle and occurs over a period of time. But it is central to the process of learning. It may mean no longer wrapping your identity around your spouse (if you go through a divorce) or your home or neighbors (when you move to another state or country). Only letting go of the old identity makes it possible to forge a new one—as a manager, a single person, or a resident of a foreign country. To forge this identity, you'll need to acquire new skills and beliefs, and this acquisition is central to the learning process.

EXAMPLE OF ADVERSITY AS A SPUR TO LEARNING

Andrew was a technological wizard—a brilliant guy who did well as an MIS executive at a *Fortune* 100 company and someone we encountered in a recent leadership development program. In certain ways, Andrew was the prototypical high-tech leader. He loved nothing better than spending time immersing himself in software design, emerging from behind his computer screen only to bounce ideas off other technically savvy colleagues. As sharp as he was, Andrew didn't establish any strong relationships at work. It wasn't that he was antisocial; he just was so goal-oriented that he didn't feel compelled to have lengthy conversations about anything but work. As a result, people often felt that Andrew used them—milked them for knowledge and then ignored them on more personal matters.

One unbelievable day, Andrew was in a severe auto accident that left him partially paralyzed. For the next six months, lucky to be alive, he recuperated and worked on his physical rehabilitation. At first, Andrew was depressed. He had worked nonstop since graduating from college, and his partial paralysis and rehabilitation prevented him from returning to work. Even worse, he couldn't work on the computer because both his wrists had been broken, and nerve damage made it difficult for him to type. It was a terribly frustrating time, and Andrew was filled with self-doubt and pity.

Gradually, he emerged from his funk. As part of the rehab process, he met other people with various injuries and began communicating with them on an emotional level; they talked about their fears and their hopes for the future. He joined a support group that served not only as a clearinghouse of information for people with severe injuries but paved the way for friendships with a variety of people outside the high-tech world. After Andrew regained most of his wrist function and returned to work, he found himself much more willing to talk with and listen to others. Though he still loved designing software, he was much more willing to help others when they were having problems with their designs. Before his accident, Andrew was never considered a candidate for team manager, despite his technical skills. After his return to work, however, he was promoted to this position because he had learned to relate to people in ways that fostered their development. Andrew's organization considered emotional intelligence a critical leadership skill, and when he clearly had acquired it, it made him a prime candidate for managing the team.

Andrew was forced to learn because of the adversity he unexpectedly encountered. He took advantage of the learning available in his passage. Through reflection and conversations, he learned a lot about himself, helping him create a new, more effective identity.

THE VALUE OF FAILURE

In the broadest sense of the term, Andrew failed when he experienced partial paralysis. Specifically, his body failed, and at that time all his skills and knowledge were inadequate to deal with what he was going through. Andrew could have chosen to become stuck in his failure, and for many leaders whose careers do not unfold according to their own plans and prescriptions, remaining stuck is an unfortunate outcome. Andrew could have remained bitter about the bad luck that caused him to be at the wrong place at the wrong time. Instead, he opened himself up to new people and possibilities. His failure was a catalyst for change and growth.

Most people who move through life experiencing one success after another are shallow. In fact, as professional coaches we can often quickly distinguish between senior executives who have encountered and overcome failure and those who have continually ascended the corporate hierarchy with no detours or unplanned stops. Without a failure or two along the way, leaders never have to move out of their comfort zones, adjust their identities, or develop their capacity for compassion. This isn't to say that failure is fun or should be sought. Failing hurts. Too much of it can damage your career or, more important, your life.

Failure, though, can also deepen you. It gives you a sense of your own fallibility and forces you to reassess your point of view. As Andrew discovered, increased empathy is a common byproduct of failure. You can gain key relationship-building skills that you'd never acquire if your life were failure-free.

To understand how failure helps you learn, try the following exercise:

1. Identify something significant you failed at in your personal or professional life. It can be anything from a marriage to a job. Be specific about the failure. Summarize the failure in a sentence, and be sure to use the word *fail*, for example:

   I was one of three candidates for the general manager position at my company, but I *failed* to be selected.

   I *failed* as a father to my teenaged son because I pushed him too hard and hurt the relationship.

2. Describe how you felt about the failure immediately after it occurred. Did you blame others for the failure? Did you act like the world had come to an end? Did you question your ability or intelligence?

3. Now move forward in time. Using hindsight, list any positive outcomes from the failure. Include any positives in the following categories:

   • Skills you acquired

   • Lessons you learned

   • Relationships you established

4. Identify how the failure may have changed you as a person. Specify traits or attitudes that you developed as a result of the failure. Do a before-and-after portrait of yourself, and note whether the "after" portrait represents a wiser, more mature person.

Most people recognize the value of failure only months or years later. Senior executives are often comfortable publicly discussing their failures that happened two years ago but not two days ago. Our goal is help you to recognize the value of failure in "real time," so that when you're going through a passage, you can capitalize on its ability to help you learn and grow as a leader.

———⤳~~⤵———

David L. Dotlich is a former executive vice president of Honeywell International, author of multiple books on leadership, and managing partner of CDR International, a unit of Mercer Delta Consulting.

———⤳~~⤵———

James L. Noel, a principal of CDR International, is the former director of executive education for General Electric's Crotonville.

———⤳~~⤵———

Norman Walker, until recently worldwide head of human resources for Novartis, has also served as the top human resource officer for Grand Met, Kraft Foods, and Ford Motor Company.

CHAPTER THIRTY-EIGHT

Nourishing the Soul of the Leader

Inner Growth Matters

Andre L. Delbecq

—◦◦◦— This chapter posits that spiritual maturity informs organizational leadership in important ways. It is written to provoke reflection on the questions of how and why that is so.

Early in my academic career, speaking of God, transcendence, or spirituality in the context of work was out of bounds. Psychology and sociology were the mother disciplines of leadership. For many, even ethics was a doubtful overlay of philosophy. It is not surprising then that when the workplace spirituality movement emerged in the latter half of the twentieth century, it did so within the world of practice—outside the university and even largely outside mainstream churches, temples, and synagogues.[1] The majority of leaders in corporate America today believe that inner spiritual growth matters,[2] and those I work with attest that without development of a spiritual inner self, leadership goes astray. The continuing leadership scandals in religious, governmental, not-for-profit, and private sector organizations bear witness to their concern. And exploration of the spiritual dimensions of leadership is now seen as a legitimate, enriching perspective within the academy and by the professional and business press.[3]

The moral character of leadership matters. We understand that intuitively. In 1999, Melvin McKnight, professor of management at Northern Arizona University, taught me to begin leadership teaching with a phenomenological exercise: ask participants to describe a leader who was a destructive force in their careers. Then ask them to describe a leader who was a positive force. Compare the two lists, and it is easy to compose a proxy measure of spiritual intelligence. A sense of what is spiritual seems deeply embedded in human consciousness.[4]

Amram and Dryer have formulated an emergent conceptualization of spiritual intelligence. This intelligence involves[5]

- Experiencing meaning through a call for service
- Using modes of knowing and states of consciousness beyond linear thought (prayer, meditation, silence, intuition, and so forth)
- Aligning with essence, the sacred, divine, or universal life force
- Sensing and seeking the wholeness, unity, and interconnection among all things
- Living consciously with intention and mindful presence
- Being openly curious and accepting of reality (including the negative or shadow sides of life)
- Appreciating positives: faith, hope, gratitude, and optimism
- Nurturing relationships with respect, empathy, and compassion toward self and other
- Displaying responsible freedom from conditioning, attachments, and fears
- Acting with integrity to a clear code of values
- Possessing humble receptivity and openness

Others will judge the validity of this list in terms of their own spiritual traditions, but for me, spirituality is both a *worldview* and a *path*.[6] The worldview may be (in)formed by one of the great religious or wisdom traditions; may be an eclectic mixture of spiritual insights; may be theistic, transcendent, or nontheistic. It is, however, always intertwined with a person's life history, experiences, upbringing, personality, and sense of self. This worldview becomes the inner compass that informs action. The path is the set of disciplines (prayer, meditation, reflection, worship, ascetic practice, and the like) that over time frees the individual from the tyranny of the false self—the shadow side—so that fear, anxiety, greed, and hubris no longer dominate behavior and choice.

In the interest of full disclosure, my worldview is informed by Roman Catholic traditions, and my ideas have been influenced by that lens and my life history. At the same time, I am not an official spokesperson for my tradition, nor am I an interreligious scholar. I offer one person's perspective on the essential links between spirituality and leadership effectiveness. I write with humility as someone who sees these links through *his* spiritual lenses informed by *his* tradition and *his* study of other traditions. (To save us all from tedious repetition, I refrain from using "I believe" or "from my perspective" throughout this chapter.)

SPIRITUALLY INSPIRED LEADERSHIP: THE GOOD COMPANY

In 2004, a group at Santa Clara University set out to explore how spiritual intelligence and maturity play out in organizational leadership. We conducted a Delphi survey and subsequently gathered senior executives, theologians, and management scholars. We posed a question: What is your description of an organization that manifests elements of spirituality? A number of characteristics emerged:

1. Accomplishes its central purpose through leadership motivated by a strong sense of calling

2. Is driven by a deep sense of mission

3. Embraces subsidiarity

4. Is an organizational community sensitive to human dignity

5. Is committed to a stewardship of resources that understands efficiency and effectiveness as spiritual values, not simple market imperatives

6. Is attentive to the common good, justice, and the needs of the poor.

Looking into these descriptors allows us to see the powerful interplay among spiritually inspired leadership, good organizational leadership, and organizational effectiveness.

Accomplishes Its Central Purpose Through Leadership Motivated by a Strong Sense of Calling

Mission, vision, and purpose are brought to life by the sense of *calling* that organizational leaders possess. It is easy to infer a leader's calling when looking back through history. Think of Abraham Lincoln, Martin Luther King Jr., Nelson Mandela, Henry Ford, or David Packard. The unfolding of a calling in daily life is much more mysterious. Parker Palmer tackles this as a central theme in his wise book, *Let Your Life Speak: Listening for the Voice of Vocation.*[7] He proposes that we cannot design or intend our vocation. Rather we must listen for and surrender to our calling.

Commonsense wisdom tells us that our calling should be the intersection between our gifts and society's needs. That advice is empty unless understood within the complex unfolding of a life journey. Only then do we see the mysterious nature of calling. Winston Churchill as failed secretary of the Navy could not have envisioned himself someday holding the destiny of Great Britain in his hands during the Battle of Britain. Gandhi as a failed London attorney could not have foreseen himself as the liberating leader of a free India. Eisenhower as an administrative staff officer learning what we now call supply chain logistics—hardly the glamorous side of a military career!—probably did not foresee himself becoming the supreme allied commander during World War II. Early in her public life, Eleanor Roosevelt, who perceived herself as an unattractive woman in a dysfunctional marriage, painfully shy, and in despair from her move to Washington, could not have envisioned herself one day being introduced as the most admired woman in the world when named the first secretary general of the United Nations. Martin Luther King Jr. as a minister in a small Southern Baptist church could not have conceived of himself as the father of a civil rights movement. As Henry Ford struggled with auto assembly in his small company, he probably did not focus on initiating a manufacturing revolution. And David Packard in his garage was not thinking of himself as the creator of one of the most important companies in Silicon Valley.

As these biographical examples illustrate, a complex developmental journey of *becoming* precedes the *doing* that we label a leader's calling. Howard Gardner has documented this journey.[8] It includes long periods of preparation, skills development, watchful waiting, setbacks, failures, and delayed gratification. In spiritual language, dark nights and openness to the mystery of suffering are the stuff of character and skills development prior to the actions that history remembers.[9] These developmental periods prepare leaders to know themselves, compassionately identify with an unmet human need, and initiate the efforts that become their leadership legacy. Their combination of personal integration, authenticity, human concern, and actions inspires others to join them in the search for complex solutions.

There are challenges, however, as a leader's call begins to clarify itself. Leaders must stay aware and focused. Rabbi Zalman Schachter-Shalomi reminds leaders:

> Avoid the tragedy that follows if you silence your inner voice in deference to the litany of outsider voices. . . . Just as you get graded incompletes in college for starting but not finishing courses, you also receive incompletes from life itself, which is the metaschool in which we are all enrolled.[10]

Growing confidence in one's calling also raises the dangers of hubris—overconfidence, overreliance on self, and illusions of creating the perfect solution. Dag Hammarskjöld reminds us of the temptations when he differentiates individuals who seek to "be" (powerful, successful, rich, in control, publicly acclaimed) from individuals who seek to "do" (serve a larger cause on behalf of others). Choose your own label for the doers: higher level of functioning, psychic integration, or spiritual maturity. However we describe them, these leaders navigate the perils and heed the advice in the great Hindu scripture, *Bhagavad Gita:* "Those who are motivated only by the fruits of ambition are miserable, for they are constantly anxious about the results of what they do."[11]

These leaders resist the notion that worldly success is the longed-for fruit of great leadership. They find ways to balance the courage required to lead change with humility, and they accept that the results of their work might not be immediate.[12] Indeed, the hero's journey, as illustrated by the lives of Abraham Lincoln and Martin Luther King Jr., testifies that leaders often never see their dreams brought to fruition.

The bottom line for business leaders is that the authenticity of a leader's calling motivates others to action. The great spiritual traditions outline an archetypal leadership journey in which leaders become personally deeper and more integrated over time. This work is sustained by what the organizational literature sees as the pillars of transformational change: clear vision, the ability to engage and enlist others, and risk taking.[13] Courage allows leaders to persist in the face of inevitable setbacks, detours, and failures, as does the realization that their leadership journey can end long before they enjoy the full fruits of success. The great spiritual traditions say that leadership requires an integrated self:[14] the leader's "conversion" from a false self trapped in fear, greed, and distortion to a true self steeped in compassion and integrity. Followers support and are touched by visions that address important human needs.

Is Driven by a Deep Sense of Mission

The tight linkage between an integrated leader's calling and an organization driven by a deep sense of mission is best illustrated through stories. Let me begin with a CEO who heads a major retail clothing chain. He grew up in a poor Irish family. He remembers delivering newspapers to lovely suburban homes and being embarrassed by his scruffy clothing. He did not attend an elite college—I am not sure he even finished college. He went to work in retailing because it did not require fancy educational credentials, and worked his way up the corporate ladder. As CEO he articulated a compelling organizational mission rooted in his own life experience: make clothing of good quality and style at a price affordable to modest-income families, hire individuals of promise with modest educational credentials and provide rewarding career paths and gain sharing normally only available to those with advantaged educational backgrounds, and treat all customers with dignity and respect. Of course he was a shrewd businessman, understood supply chain logistics, and structured a profitable enterprise. But the power of a vision infused by his authenticity, the integrity of his beliefs, and his meta-values of respect for the human condition and dignity for those in poverty attracted others to the corporate mission and created a unique company culture. The calling that flowed from and through his life experience was translated into a larger organizational purpose and meaning. And I know of few senior executives who were as beloved by employees at every level of the organization as this man.

Shifting to a different industry, I think of a brilliant CEO and pioneer in computer information databases. Educated at a leading scientific university, enthralled with computers, and possessing an incisive scientific mind, he foresaw the ability of the computer to sift information for scientific endeavors. Before the Internet was available outside scientific circles, he developed a commitment to equalize access to scientific information worldwide, for researchers from Nairobi to Peoria. He intuited a world where geography would be no barrier to knowledge, and saw the computer's ability to facilitate the search for heuristics hidden in large databases. His mental acuity, intellectual curiosity, and respect for information sharing led to his sense of being called to form a pioneering company to further this mission. He enjoyed the technological challenges but found his managerial competences challenged by the project, especially as the company grew. Admitting this demonstrated great humility for someone technically brilliant but less tutored in managerial matters.

In both these cases the leader's sense of calling emerged out of his life journey and experiences and penetrated an organization's mission. This is not automatic: Collins and Porras, for example, found that a leader's charisma does not always translate into an enduring organization.[15] How the leader's calling and passions can best be institutionalized into a lasting organizational culture is beyond the scope of this chapter. The point here is that leaders always inform the meanings embedded in the dominant organizational culture. Selection, training, rewards, sanctions, and socialization processes reinforce that culture, but there is an important initial energy that flows between the leader's understanding of an organization's ultimate purpose and the culture that emerges. An organizational purpose that is integral to a leader's life story and values—that flows from both head and heart—and is infused with human service beyond a leader's private, opportunistic agenda has powerful credibility and seeds for a compelling organizational culture. The opportunity to create this is there for us all.

My regular commute on the difficult freeway from Alameda to Santa Clara, California, gives me ample time to meditate during rush hours, and I have come to envision my fellow travelers as a liturgical parade:

- The biotech executive on his way to the Oakland airport, traveling to seek financial support for his firm's work to remediate Type II diabetes, is like a Franciscan mendicant on behalf of the sick—*I was sick and you healed me.*

- The educational administrator on her way to a curriculum meeting at Cal State to advocate for courses serving those for whom English is not a first language speaks for newcomers who could otherwise be lost—*I was a stranger and you welcomed me.*

- The owner of Fred's Wrench House, an auto repair shop, keeps commuter cars going for those of modest economic means who would otherwise lack transportation from affordable housing to their places of employment—*I was poor and you supported me.*

My freeway, like all organizations, is filled with everyday leaders whose work has spiritual meaning. People can talk about their organizations in purely business terms, but their ultimate purposes transcend simple business stories. Their true mission conveys a larger human meaning: the provision of opportunities, products, and services that matter to humankind. There is power in that realization.

Embraces Subsidiarity

I speak of the distribution of organizational power, influence, and decision making with the word *subsidiarity*, taken from the social justice literature.[16] The term captures the involvement of and openness to others, the norm that decision making should include individuals affected by the decision, and beliefs that authority should involve the levels of the organization that have hands-on knowledge and responsibility.[17]

The organizational literature discusses how involving relevant stakeholders increases the quality of decisions, the probability that subtle elements of a problem will be identified, shared ownership, cooperation, and ease of implementation. We know from research that this is true. We also know that better than half the strategic decisions made fail because of a leader's human weaknesses: the anxiety, impatience, need for control, and hubris that lead to shortcutting information gathering or the inability to accept nonconfirming information.[18] I have written elsewhere on the relationship between the spiritual discipline of discernment and strategic decision failure,[19] and here reaffirm the relationship between leaders' self-integration and their ability to actualize principles of subsidiarity.

Spiritual integration involves learning self-love, differentiating it from narcissism, and developing capacities to fully love and embrace others.[20] This process of purgation, illumination, and unification is a cycle that repeats itself through life. Purgation rids the self of flaws like greed, ambition, and lust for power. Illumination opens the mind to the laws of spiritual functioning, sees virtue as an expression of the true nature of human dignity, and acknowledges the will to embrace goodness. Unification is a sense of oneness with the divine, others, and all of creation.[21] All the spiritual traditions speak in their own ways to the importance of this cycle as the route to higher levels of spiritual functioning.[22] But it is one thing to know of appropriate behaviors and another to act accordingly under great pressures. The critical question for leaders is how does this necessary integration occur?

Prayer, meditation, ascetic practices, self-reflection and mindfulness, worship, and gratitude are one path. They draw attention away from the self, diminish the messages of the ego, and place the mystery of spirit and the needs of others in the foreground.[23] In the traditions of Abraham (Judaism, Christianity, Islam), our progress is a divine gift, which these disciplines prepare us to accept.[24]

Regardless of spiritual tradition the managers and executives that I work with are clear that they have two challenges on their leadership journeys: *becoming* and *doing*. They understand that leaders on a spiritual path wrestle with the dark sides of the contemporary business world:[25] work and work structures that deny human dignity, inequity in distribution of income, hubris and greed, destructive consequences from globalization and hypercompetition, environmental degradation, ethical violations, and more. In response, they act. I know of executives serving on compensation committees to modify excessive executive pay and ensure fair wages for the lowest echelons of the workforce; two leaders heading teams creating "green" corporate architecture; a chemical firm CEO who champions efforts to convert all the firm's products to earth-friendly and sustainable formulations. I've seen executives undertake difficult negotiations to ensure health care, education, and just wages for workers when manufacturing is outsourced offshore; I know of numerous challenges to the system by accounting and financial executives to disclose unethical financial dealings; and I could go on. These leaders found the spiritual courage to confront aspects of business contradictory to their deeply held values. Their courage parallels their engagement in the cycle of spiritual growth.

In the Christian tradition the outcomes associated with progress through the cycles of the spiritual journey are wisdom, understanding, counsel, fortitude, knowledge, and fear of the Lord.[26] Managers who have studied with me composed their own list of changes achieved through meditation and spiritual disciplines:

- Improved capacities to listen—less need to dominate
- More patience with others—less judgmental and self-asserting
- Greater adaptability—less desire to control events and others
- Greater focus—less distraction and anxiety
- Greater ability to devote self to service through work—less frustration with burdens and irritants at work
- More hopefulness and joyfulness even in times of difficulty—less cynicism and pessimism
- Greater overall serenity and trust
- More confidence in using personal competencies—deeper knowledge of self-limitations, more trust that things will work out
- Persistence and diligence—less withdrawal and self-occupation when under stress

Their list is congruent with extensive current research, especially on the benefits of meditation.[27]

An individual honed through spiritual disciplines and grace can be present to others in a more open manner than before and can more calmly face conflict and unresolved tensions. The inner spiritual journey, therefore, enables leaders to remain faithful to the difficult requirements of subsidiarity: the deep involvement of others and self-forbearance in building consensus, negotiating conflicts, and engaging in ethical and moral judgments. Subsidiarity requires periods of reflection to evolve the necessary intuitive and nonlinear thinking processes, the patience for searching more fully and avoiding premature closure, and the humility to remain open to nonconfirming evidence and unanticipated experiences. "Being the change you wish to lead" is difficult, and not territory for the spiritually immature. Impatient, compulsive, and power-driven leaders shortcut the process—even as organizational changes resulting in less hierarchy, more loose-coupling, increasingly fluid boundaries, and faster change increase the need for leadership maturity. The rewards are great for leaders who travel the spiritual journey: abilities to better facilitate strategic decision making—what the executives that I work with see as the central task of leadership—and health benefits such as better immune responses, quicker physical recovery, lower blood pressure, and enhanced ability to endure pain.[28]

Is an Organizational Community Sensitive to Human Dignity

Integrated leaders create communities that foster human dignity. Meaningful work experiences are best found in organizations that encompass a noble purpose, are led by individuals who infuse the ethos of the organization with their own greater sense of calling, and have cultures that endorse participatory decision processes. Meaningful work is motivating and satisfying; having one's gifts and contributions integrated into decision processes is self-affirming. When the organization's culture also offers opportunities for growth and career advancement and provides appropriate compensation and rewards, all seems right. Yet even then, modern organizational life contains seeds of dissatisfaction for its leaders.

In my last five years of work with technology leaders, I have asked them to identify their greatest sources of organizational stress and dissatisfaction. They consistently name two: (1) overload and a resulting imbalance between attention given to work and time spent with family and (2) expectations for human perfection. Their concerns are echoed by primary care physicians at the American College of Physician Executives who tell me that stress is the gravest health threat in North America and that they frequently see stress as the prelude to severe mental and physical health problems among working professionals.

OVERLOAD AND WORK-FAMILY IMBALANCE. To be sure, the duties of leadership are complex and numerous. Days are filled with intense and never-ending challenges.[29] Answering one's calling means accepting additional burdens. Strategic decision making requires enabling significant stakeholder involvement, negotiating conflict, and managing difficult trade-offs and resources. There are frequent, unscheduled meetings and interactions on emergent problems, requiring active listening, facilitation, and rapid tactical problem solving. There are symbolic events where the leader has to be energized, upbeat, hopeful, and steady in the face of numerous pressures, and there are work requirements that touch the darker sides of organizational life, such as conveying bad news or dealing with bad performance or malevolent behavior.[30] The tasks are made more difficult by the strong personalities attracted to work in high-performing organizations. In short, there is little external respite for leaders.

When the *outer* environment is complex, it becomes critical that the *inner* remain centered and balanced. The Sufi poet Rumi speaks of that need this way:[31]

> You have scattered your awareness in all directions and your vanities are not worth a bit of cabbage.
>
> The root of every thorn draws the water of your attention toward itself.
>
> How will the water of your attention reach the fruit?
>
> Cut through the evil roots, cut them away.
>
> Direct the bounty of God to spirit and to insight, not the knotted and broken world outside [Rumi-Mathnawi, V, 1084–1086].

The leadership challenge is to find ways to be present to the complexities yet retain inner calmness and *presence*.[32] Leaders I have worked with who are successful in this often turn to the spiritual disciplines for inward centering amid outward complexity.[33] Their practices often include beginning the day with a form of meditation—zazen, Transcendental Meditation, Christian centering prayer, heyschia, the Jesus prayer, Kabbalah meditation, or Vedanta— to abandon focus on their own thoughts and emotions.[34] It was a surprise to find action-oriented leaders drawn to forms of meditation that surrender into the "cloud of unknowing."[35] Yet their reasoning makes perfect sense: they seek simple refreshment in resting in the mystery of spirit and releasing preferences, worries, plans, and compulsive thoughts. By beginning their day with such a discipline, they enter it centered and in touch with inner peace.

During the unfolding actions of the day or before a meeting, phone call, or public event, these same individuals often practice some form of mindfulness. They center through a short spiritual pause and take up their next challenge fully present and back in touch with inner peace. They are conscious not to allow an activity just completed or some future task to inappropriately intrude on the "now."

As they leave work, these leaders engage in a review of the day similar to the *examen* of Ignatius of Loyola, founder of the Jesuits[36]—although few if any know this specific tradition. The leaders mentally reflect on the day's events, express gratitude for blessings received, and notice where darkness in self or others has emerged during the day's struggles. They resolve to do better if they have erred, and commend the day to God's mercy, the 10,000 things, karma, or however they understand mystery. They use behaviors that parallel those of burn unit nurses and oncology physicians who do not take the trials of the day home. Note in this process, however, that the leaders do not suppress emotions, intuitions, or ideation. They engage in a reflective process that enables them to return to family for rest and rehabilitation. Although they may work long hours, home is sanctuary. These leaders also preserve as much of their weekends as possible for family, and many take the honoring of the Sabbath seriously within their own traditions.

Executives in a study on family-work tensions often admitted that it took a while for them to learn the importance of such practices.[37] Burnout often precipitated turning to spiritual disciplines to regain life balance. The leaders were clear that the issue was less about time management than about the management of energy and inner self. Executives in my seminars confirm that. Without use of spiritual disciplines, external pressures, ambition, fear, materialism, greed, and other expressions of darkness came to dominate, just as the poet Rumi warned.

HUMAN IMPERFECTION. It is motivating to work for an organization that aims to meet high standards of performance and benchmarks of excellence. But there is danger when such aspirations slip into institutional hubris, and the organization sets unattainable standards, or the institution shifts its culture from high aspiration to punishment for not attaining unrealistic goals. Seeking perfection seems part of a North American idolatry centered on celebrity worship, youth, beauty, and material success.[38]

Spiritually mature leaders accept and are present to the truth of their own limitations and the limitations of others. They can, to put it in metaphoric terms, describe the oversensitive soprano or the always depressed baritone without judgment and produce a strong opera despite the human imperfections of the performers. Indeed, they can see in others the gifts that offset any weaknesses. One CEO, for example, expressed appreciation for a CFO whom others found troublesomely conservative. The CEO appreciated the CFO's detailed attention to exploring the financial impact of decisions as an important check on the exuberance of an entrepreneurial management team.

Mature leaders also acknowledge their personal limitations by self-limiting their tenure in office.[39] They understand that the gifts of a management team exceed those of any leader, appreciate the need for different leadership at different stages of company growth, recognize when their essential contributions have been made and institutionalized, and willingly make space for a successor possessing different gifts.[40] These leaders understand that the human condition is imperfect and see a key part of their contribution as filling in for the flat sides of others on their team.

Jean Vanier, a theologian and founder of L'Arche communities for handicapped adults, has expressed the spiritual perspective that applies here in these moving words:[41]

> If we are accepted with our limitations as well as our abilities, community gradually becomes a place of liberation. We shouldn't seek the ideal community. It is a question of loving those whom God has set beside us today. . . . It is with them that we are called to create.

The managerial literature on high-performing teams contains little about human imperfection. It tells us that team composition can facilitate achievement; however, the undertone is idealistic, perfectionist, and intolerant. Spiritual traditions speak of imperfection as a divine lapidary that leads to both humility and the strengthening of community through complementary gifts.[42]

Clearly a culture where the imperfection of the human condition is accepted and individuals are embraced and valued for who they are is liberating and motivating. Harsh judgment is replaced by love—and we know when we are loved as opposed to used or appreciated only when things go well. There is no need for fear, anxiety, self-protection, or blame when we are accepted by the leader in the fullness of our human condition. Again I posit, spiritual maturity matters organizationally.

Is Committed to a Stewardship of Resources That Understands Efficiency and Effectiveness as Spiritual Values, Not Simply Market Imperatives

Spiritually mature business leaders accept profits. Products and services that meet human needs are the mission, profitability an essential discipline.[43] As one executive said: "If you don't like physical contact, don't play football. If you aren't willing to meet the standards of profitability for your industry, you shouldn't be in business."

Stewardship of resources has a long spiritual tradition. The fact that efficiency and budget management are often seen as outside the spiritual realm—and even a distraction by some—suggests an unhelpful dualism between the spiritual and material realms. The great traditions warn against this.[44] Care of the rice bowl and teacup are spiritual activities in Buddhism. Care of the pots and pans in Christian monasticism is no less spiritual than meditation.[45] Leaders may need to recognize that their response to stewardship responsibilities, efficiency, and profitability is an area for further reflection and growth.

I interviewed clinical and midlevel health care administrators and asked them to describe how spiritual values were associated with their roles. They spoke easily about the relationship of spirituality to organizational mission and their leadership calling; the importance of treating the whole patient; and the need for compassionate presence with difficult patients and with staff. However, they did not see efficiency, effectiveness, or budgets as falling into the spiritual realm, even though health care leaders speak of the estimated 28 percent waste of resources in their industry. In a society where the uninsured are increasingly denied health care access, think of the transfer payment that elimination of that waste would represent!

In financial matters, as in other areas, discernment and balance are important. Too much fasting weakens the body. Too much attention to short-term profits and insufficient reinvestment weakens the firm. The pressures of the quarterly return are much discussed elsewhere. However, it is another test of courage to face financial analysts and stand firm for the long-term needs and well-being of an organization's mission. Resisting the pressures to erode an organization's core mission for short-term gains is a serious wrestling match for leaders, one that demands spiritual courage.

Is Attentive to the Common Good, Justice, and the Needs of the Poor

A litmus test of authentic spirituality in all traditions is attention to those in need. For-profit organizations are not service providers for the poor. Still, there are ways for organizations to alleviate needs. Corporate taxes are a central justice contribution that supports government services. Paying a fair share of taxes is a legitimate matter for spiritual reflection. Many organizations do more. They match employee contributions to charity, provide support for employees engaged in community service, funnel surplus goods to charitable venues, create foundations, respond to special community needs, and more. We have a contemporary exemplification of the long tradition of corporate philanthropy in the Bill and Melinda Gates Foundation. Communities easily identify generous corporations, and that generosity often reflects the values of the corporate leaders.

There are also wonderful examples of individual executives expressing care and compassion as an outgrowth of their own suffering. I think of the Silicon Valley CEO who cared for his wife through her final struggles with cancer. He could have bought caregiving, but chose to be present for his wife and children. Reflecting on his experience, he recognized that he had degrees of control over his schedule that many of his employees did not. As a result, he experimented with a virtual work program so that employees with serious caregiving obligations could work at home, protected employee careers during such periods, and ensured reintegration into face-to-face networks upon their return. He did all this well before these were options and human resource givens. Or consider the executive whose program to hire ex-felons right out of prison flowed from the experiences of his son; or the corporate leader who raised a developmentally challenged child, initiated a company policy to hire developmentally challenged adults, and created a supportive environment in the organization for these workers. And I could go on. For these leaders, their personal growth led to an open heart that found expression in actions on behalf of others.

Many have also reminded me that the marginalized in organizations are not necessarily the poor or the handicapped. Anyone outside an organization's dominant craft, profession, or coalition may be alienated: think of adjunct versus tenure track faculty, medical staff versus physicians, junior associates versus partners, and so on. Compassionate leaders are attentive to job design, policies, decision making, compensation patterns, and opportunities for all employees, not only the organizational elites.

Finally, spiritual compassion requires a look at the power and symbolic meaning of leadership choices. We have all heard the stories of senior executives who go to great lengths to protect their exceptional benefits and salaries while offering no similar protection to others. Attention to the poor, marginalized, vulnerable, and in need remains a litmus test of one's spiritual growth.[46]

IN CLOSING: A CAVEAT ABOUT TENSIONS BETWEEN RELIGION AND SPIRITUALITY

This chapter posits that spiritual maturity informs organizational leadership in deep and important ways. The leader's sense of calling brings an organizational mission alive. Spiritual maturity supports courage and hope in the face of difficulty. Spiritual disciplines such as prayer and meditation help to convert a leader from preoccupation with self to openness to both reality and others—an important attribute for leading strategic decision making and avoiding decision pitfalls. Spiritual development engenders compassion, creating sensitivity to vulnerable members of the organization and communities in which the organization operates (see, for example, Chapter Eleven in this volume). The majority of corporate leaders today believe that inner spiritual growth matters.[47] I have no question they are right. The growing workplace spirituality movement reminds us that attention to things spiritual in the world of business leadership— and not overreliance on rationality and science—brings wisdom and greater fullness of human expression.[48]

A caveat in closing about the relationship between workplace spirituality and religion seems in order. Although for many, spirituality is deeply connected to a religious tradition, the workplace spirituality movement is not intended to proselytize or to introduce religion into the workings of the secular corporation. Spirituality is each individual's exploration of the transcendent and how that plays out in his or her life and leadership—and that mystery bears a thousand names. The desire of the workplace spirituality movement is to complement social science and humanistic traditions with the fullness of wisdom. Attention to spirituality also offers leaders an additional route toward inclusivity. If leaders can speak about things spiritual according to the norms of appreciative inquiry, then issues of meaning, human differences, and ontology become enriching heuristics in strategic decisions. To have *scientism* as the *only* acceptable worldview is limiting—and discriminates against those whose leadership is rooted in other worldviews.[49] Given our long human history of religious tensions, learning how to speak from the spiritual heart remains an important yet difficult life skill.[50] May the reflections in this chapter provide encouragement for readers to continue their own inquiry in a manner that is respectful of individual freedom and human expression.

———◦◦◦———

Andre L. Delbecq is J. Thomas and Kathleen L. McCarthy University Professor of Organizational Analysis and Management and the director of the Institute for Spirituality and Organizational Leadership at Santa Clara University's Leavey School of Business.

CHAPTER THIRTY NINE

Resilience and the Crucibles of Leadership

Warren G. Bennis
Robert J. Thomas

A s lifelong students of leadership, we are fascinated with the notion of what makes a leader. Why is it that certain people seem to naturally inspire confidence, loyalty, and hard work, while others (who may have just as much vision and smarts) stumble, again and again? It's a timeless question, and there's no simple answer. But we have come to believe it has something to do with the different ways that people deal with adversity. Indeed, our recent research has led us to conclude that one of the most reliable indicators and predictors of true leadership is an individual's ability to find meaning in negative events and to learn from even the most trying circumstances. Put another way, the skills required to conquer adversity and emerge stronger and more committed than ever are the same ones that make for extraordinary leaders.

Take Sidney Harman. Thirty-four years ago, the then-48-year-old businessman was holding down two executive positions. He was the chief executive of Harman Kardon (now Harman International), the audio components company he had co-founded, and he was serving as president of Friends World College, now Friends World Program, an experimental Quaker school on Long Island whose essential philosophy is that students, not their teachers, are responsible for their education. Juggling the two jobs, Harman was living what he calls a "bifurcated life"; changing clothes in his car and eating lunch as he drove between Harman Kardon offices and plants and the Friends World campus. One day while at the college, he was told his company's factory in Bolivar, Tennessee, was having a crisis.

He immediately rushed to the Bolivar factory, a facility that was, as Harman now recalls, "raw, ugly, and, in many ways, demeaning." The problem, he found, had erupted in the polish and buff department, where a crew of a dozen workers, mostly African-Americans, did the dull, hard work of polishing mirrors and other parts, often under unhealthy conditions. The men on the night shift were supposed to get a coffee break at 10 PM. When the buzzer that announced the workers' break went on the fritz, management arbitrarily decided to postpone the break for ten minutes, when another buzzer was scheduled to sound. But one worker, "an old black man with an almost biblical name, Noah B. Cross," had "an epiphany," as Harman describes it. "He said, literally, to his fellow workers, 'I don't work for no buzzer. The buzzer works for me. It's my job to tell me when it's ten o'clock. I got me a watch. I'm not waiting another ten minutes. I'm going on my coffee break.' And all 12 guys took their coffee break, and, of course, all hell broke loose."

The worker's principled rebellion—his refusal to be cowed by management's senseless rule—was, in turn, a revelation to Harman: "The technology is there to serve the men, not the reverse," he remembers realizing. "I suddenly had this awakening that everything I was doing at the college had appropriate applications in business." In the ensuing years, Harman revamped the factory and its workings, turning it into a kind of campus—offering classes on the premises, including piano lessons, and encouraging the workers to take most of the responsibility for running their workplace. Further, he created an environment where dissent was not only tolerated but also encouraged. The plant's lively independent newspaper, the *Bolivar Mirror*, gave workers a creative and emotional outlet—and they enthusiastically skewered Harman in its pages.

Harman had, unexpectedly, become a pioneer of participative management, a movement that continues to influence the shape of workplaces around the world. The concept wasn't a grand idea conceived in the CEO's office and imposed on the plant, Harman says. It grew organically out of his going down to Bolivar to, in his words, "put out this fire." Harman's transformation was, above all, a creative one. He had connected two seemingly unrelated ideas and created a radically different approach to management that recognized both the economic and humane benefits of a more collegial workplace. Harman went on to accomplish far more during his career. In addition to founding Harman International, he served as the deputy secretary of commerce under Jimmy Carter. But he always looked back on the incident in Bolivar as the formative event in his professional life, the moment he came into his own as a leader.

The details of Harman's story are unique, but their significance is not. In interviewing more than 40 top leaders in business and the public sector over the past three years, we were surprised to find that all of them—young and old—were able to point to intense, often traumatic, always unplanned experiences that had transformed them and had become the sources of their distinctive leadership abilities.

We came to call the experiences that shape leaders "crucibles," after the vessels medieval alchemists used in their attempts to turn base metals into gold. For the leaders we interviewed, the crucible experience was a trial and a test, a point of deep self-reflection that forced them to question who they were and what mattered to them. It required them to examine their values, question their assumptions, hone their judgment. And, invariably, they emerged from the crucible stronger and more sure of themselves and their purpose—changed in some fundamental way.

Leadership crucibles can take many forms. Some are violent, life-threatening events. Others are more prosaic episodes of self-doubt. But whatever the crucible's nature, the people we spoke with were able, like Harman, to create a narrative around it, a story of how they were challenged, met the challenge, and became better leaders. As we studied these stories, we found that they not only told us how individual leaders are shaped but also pointed to some characteristics that seem common to all leaders—characteristics that were formed, or at least exposed, in the crucible.

LEARNING FROM DIFFERENCE

A crucible is, by definition, a transformative experience through which an individual comes to a new or an altered sense of identity. It is perhaps not surprising then that one of the most common types of crucibles we documented involves the experience of prejudice.

Being a victim of prejudice is particularly traumatic because it forces an individual to confront a distorted picture of him- or herself, and it often unleashes profound feelings of anger, bewilderment, and even withdrawal. For all its trauma, however, the experience of prejudice is for some a clarifying event. Through it, they gain a clearer vision of who they are, the role they play, and their place in the world.

Consider, for example, Liz Altman, now a Motorola vice president, who was transformed by the year she spent at a Sony camcorder factory in rural Japan, where she faced both estrangement and sexism. It was, says Altman, "by far, the hardest thing I've ever done." The foreign culture—particularly its emphasis on groups over individuals—was both a shock and a challenge to a young American woman. It wasn't just that she felt lonely in an alien world. She had to face the daunting prospect of carving out a place for herself as the only woman engineer in a plant and a nation where women usually serve as low-level assistants and clerks known as "office ladies."

Another woman who had come to Japan under similar circumstances had warned Altman that the only way to win the men's respect was to avoid becoming allied with the office ladies. But on her very first morning, when the bell rang for a coffee break, the men headed in one direction and the women in another—and the women saved her a place at their table, while the men ignored her. Instinct told Altman to ignore the warning rather than insult the women by rebuffing their invitation.

Over the next few days, she continued to join the women during breaks, a choice that gave her a comfortable haven from which to observe the unfamiliar office culture. But it didn't take her long to notice that some of the men spent the break at their desks reading magazines, and Altman determined that she could do the same on occasion. Finally, after paying close attention to the conversations around her, she learned that several of the men were interested in mountain biking. Because Altman wanted to buy a mountain bike, she approached them for advice. Thus, over time, she established herself as something of a free agent, sometimes sitting with the women and other times engaging with the men.

And as it happened, one of the women she'd sat with on her very first day, the department secretary, was married to one of the engineers. The secretary took it upon herself to include Altman in social gatherings, a turn of events that probably wouldn't have occurred if Altman had alienated her female coworkers on that first day. "Had

I just gone to try to break in with [the men] and not had her as an ally, it would never have happened," she says.

Looking back, Altman believes the experience greatly helped her gain a clearer sense of her personal strengths and capabilities, preparing her for other difficult situations. Her tenure in Japan taught her to observe closely and to avoid jumping to conclusions based on cultural assumptions—invaluable skills in her current position at Motorola, where she leads efforts to smooth alliances with other corporate cultures, including those of Motorola's different regional operations.

Altman has come to believe that she wouldn't have been as able to do the Motorola job if she hadn't lived in a foreign country and experienced the dissonance of cultures: ". . . even if you're sitting in the same room, ostensibly agreeing . . . unless you understand the frame of reference, you're probably missing a bunch of what's going on." Altman also credits her crucible with building her confidence—she feels that she can cope with just about anything that comes her way.

People can feel the stigma of cultural differences much closer to home, as well. Muriel ("Mickie") Siebert, the first woman to own a seat on the New York Stock Exchange, found her crucible on the Wall Street of the 1950s and 1960s, an arena so sexist that she couldn't get a job as a stockbroker until she took her first name off her resume and substituted a genderless initial. Other than the secretaries and the occasional analyst, women were few and far between.

That she was Jewish was another strike against her at a time, she points out, when most of big business was "not nice" to either women or Jews. But Siebert wasn't broken or defeated. Instead, she emerged stronger, more focused, and more determined to change the status quo that excluded her.

When we interviewed Siebert, she described her way of addressing anti-Semitism—a technique that quieted the offensive comments of her peers without destroying the relationships she needed to do her job effectively. According to Siebert, at the time it was part of doing business to have a few drinks at lunch. She remembers, "Give somebody a couple of drinks, and they would talk about the Jews." She had a greeting card she used for those occasions that went like this:

> Roses are reddish,
>
> Violets are bluish,

In case you don't know,

I am Jewish.

Siebert would have the card hand-delivered to the person who had made the anti-Semitic remarks, and on the card she had written, "Enjoyed lunch." As she recounts, "They got that card in the afternoon, and I never had to take any of that nonsense again. And I never embarrassed anyone, either." It was because she was unable to get credit for the business she was bringing in at any of the large Wall Street firms that she bought a seat on the New York Stock Exchange and started working for herself.

In subsequent years, she went on to found Muriel Siebert & Company (now Siebert Financial Corporation) and has dedicated herself to helping other people avoid some of the difficulties she faced as a young professional. A prominent advocate for women in business and a leader in developing financial products directed at women, she's also devoted to educating children about financial opportunities and responsibility.

We didn't interview lawyer and presidential adviser Vernon Jordan for this chapter, but he, too, offers a powerful reminder of how prejudice can prove transformational rather than debilitating. In *Vernon Can Read! A Memoir* (Public Affairs, 2001), Jordan describes the vicious baiting he was subjected to as a young man. The man who treated him in this offensive way was his employer, Robert E. Maddox. Jordan served the racist former mayor of Atlanta at dinner, in a white jacket, with a napkin over his arm. He also functioned as Maddox's chauffeur. Whenever Maddox could, he would derisively announce, "Vernon can read!" as if the literacy of a young African-American were a source of wonderment.

Subjected to this type of abuse, a lesser man might have allowed Maddox to destroy him. But in his memoir, Jordan gives his own interpretation of Maddox's sadistic heckling, a tale that empowered Jordan instead of embittering him. When he looked at Maddox through the rearview mirror, Jordan did not see a powerful member of Georgia's ruling class. He saw a desperate anachronism, a person who lashed out because he knew his time was up. As Jordan writes about Maddox, "His half-mocking, half-serious comments about my education were the death rattle of his culture. When he saw that I was . . . crafting a life for myself that would make me a man in . . . ways he thought of as being a man, he was deeply unnerved."

Maddox's cruelty was the crucible that, consciously or not, Jordan imbued with redemptive meaning. Instead of lashing out or being paralyzed with hatred, Jordan saw the fall of the Old South and imagined his own future freed of the historical shackles of racism. His ability to organize meaning around a potential crisis turned it into the crucible around which his leadership was forged.

PREVAILING OVER DARKNESS

Some crucible experiences illuminate a hidden and suppressed area of the soul. These are often among the harshest of crucibles, involving, for instance, episodes of illness or violence. In the case of Sidney Rittenberg, now 79, the crucible took the form of 16 years of unjust imprisonment, in solitary confinement, in Communist China. In 1949 Rittenberg was initially jailed, without explanation, by former friends in Chairman Mao Zedong's government and spent his first year in total darkness when he wasn't being interrogated. (Rittenberg later learned that his arrest came at the behest of Communist Party officials in Moscow, who had wrongly identified him as a CIA agent.) Thrown into jail, confined to a tiny, pitch-dark cell, Rittenberg did not rail or panic. Instead, within minutes, he remembered a stanza of verse, four lines recited to him when he was a small child:

> They drew a circle that shut me out,
>
> Heretic, rebel, a thing to flout.
>
> But love and I had the wit to win,
>
> We drew a circle that took them in!

That bit of verse (adapted from "Outwitted," a poem by Edwin Markham) was the key to Rittenberg's survival. "My God," he thought, "there's my strategy." He drew the prison guards into his circle, developing relationships that would help him adapt to his confinement. Fluent in Chinese, he persuaded the guards to deliver him books and, eventually, provide a candle so that he could read. He also decided, after his first year, to devote himself to improving his mind—making it more scientific, more pure, and more dedicated to socialism. He believed that if he raised his consciousness, his captors would understand him better. And when, over time, the years in the dark began to take an intellectual toll on him and he found his reason faltering, he could still summon fairy tales and childhood stories such as *The Little Engine That Could* and take comfort from their simple messages.

By contrast, many of Rittenberg's fellow prisoners either lashed out in anger or withdrew. "They tended to go up the wall. . . . They couldn't make it. And I think the reason was that they didn't understand . . . that happiness . . . is not a function of your circumstances; it's a function of your outlook on life."

Rittenberg's commitment to his ideals continued upon his release. His cell door opened suddenly in 1955, after his first six-year term in prison. He recounts, "Here was a representative of the central government telling me that I had been wronged, that the government was making a formal apology to me . . . and that they would do everything possible to make restitution." When his captors offered him money to start a new life in the United States or to travel in Europe, Rittenberg declined, choosing instead to stay in China and continue his work for the Communist Party.

And even after a second arrest, which put him into solitary confinement for ten years as retaliation for his support of open democracy during the Cultural Revolution, Rittenberg did not allow his spirit to be broken. Instead, he used his time in prison as an opportunity to question his belief system—in particular, his commitment to Marxism and Chairman Mao. "In that sense, prison emancipated me," he says.

Rittenberg studied, read, wrote, and thought, and he learned something about himself in the process: "I realized I had this great fear of being a turncoat, which . . . was so powerful that it prevented me from even looking at [my assumptions]. . . . Even to question was an act of betrayal. After I got out . . . the scales fell away from my eyes and I understood that . . . the basic doctrine of arriving at democracy through dictatorship was wrong."

What's more, Rittenberg emerged from prison certain that absolutely nothing in his professional life could break him and went on to start a company with his wife. Rittenberg Associates is a consulting firm dedicated to developing business ties between the United States and China. Today, Rittenberg is as committed to his ideals—if not to his view of the best way to get there—as he was 50 years ago, when he was so severely tested.

MEETING GREAT EXPECTATIONS

Fortunately, not all crucible experiences are traumatic. In fact, they can involve a positive, if deeply challenging, experience such as having a demanding boss or mentor. Judge Nathaniel R. Jones of the U.S. Court of Appeals for the Sixth Circuit, for instance, attributes much of his success to his interaction with a splendid mentor. That mentor was J. Maynard Dickerson, a successful attorney—the first black city prosecutor in the United States—and editor of a local African-American newspaper.

Dickerson influenced Jones at many levels. For instance, the older man brought Jones behind the scenes to witness firsthand the great civil rights struggle of the 1950s, inviting him to sit in on conversations with activists like Thurgood Marshall, Walter White, Roy Wilkins, and Robert C. Weaver. Says Jones, "I was struck by their resolve, their humor . . . and their determination not to let the system define them. Rather than just feel beaten down, they turned it around." The experience no doubt influenced the many important opinions Judge Jones has written in regard to civil rights.

Dickerson was both model and coach. His lessons covered every aspect of Jones's intellectual growth and presentation of self, including schooling in what we now call "emotional intelligence." Dickerson set the highest standards for Jones, especially in the area of communication skills—a facility we've found essential to leadership. Dickerson edited Jones's early attempts at writing a sports column with respectful ruthlessness, in red ink, as Jones remembers to this day—marking up the copy so that it looked, as Jones says, "like something chickens had a fight over." But Dickerson also took the time to explain every single mistake and why it mattered.

His mentor also expected the teenage Jones to speak correctly at all times and would hiss discreetly in his direction if he stumbled. Great expectations are evidence of great respect, and as Jones learned all the complex, often subtle lessons of how to succeed, he was motivated in no small measure by his desire not to disappoint the man he still calls "Mr. Dickerson." Dickerson gave Jones the kind of intensive mentoring that was tantamount to grooming him for a kind of professional and moral succession—and Jones has indeed become an instrument for the profound societal change for which Dickerson fought so courageously as well. Jones found life changing meaning in the attention Dickerson paid to him—attention fueled by a conviction that he, too, though only a teenager, had a vital role to play in society and an important destiny.

Another story of a powerful mentor came to us from Michael Klein, a young man who made millions in Southern California real estate while still in his teens, only to lose it by the time he turned 20 and then go on to start several other businesses. His mentor was his grandfather Max S. Klein, who created the paint-by-numbers fad that swept the United States in the 1950s and 1960s. Klein was only four or five years old when his grandfather approached him and offered to share his business expertise. Over the years, Michael Klein's grandfather taught him to learn from and to cope with change, and the two spoke by phone for an hour every day until shortly before Max Klein's death.

THE ESSENTIALS OF LEADERSHIP

In our interviews, we heard many other stories of crucible experiences. Take Jack Coleman, 78-year-old former president of Haverford College in Pennsylvania. He told us of one day, during the Vietnam War, when he heard that a group of students was planning to pull down the American flag and burn it—and that former members of the school's football team were going to make sure the students didn't succeed. Seemingly out of nowhere, Coleman had the idea to preempt the violence by suggesting that the protesting students take down the flag, wash it, and then put it back up—a crucible moment that even now elicits tremendous emotion in Coleman as he describes that day.

There's also Common Cause founder John W. Gardner, who died at 89. He identified his arduous training as a Marine during World War II as the crucible in which his leadership abilities emerged. Architect Frank Gehry spoke of the biases he experienced as a Jew in college. Jeff Wilke, a general manager at a major manufacturer, told us of the day he learned that an employee had been killed in his plant—an experience that taught him that leadership was about much more than making quarterly numbers.

So, what allowed these people to not only cope with these difficult situations but also learn from them? We believe that great leaders possess *four essential skills*, and, we were surprised to learn, these happen to be the same skills that allow a person to find meaning in what could be a debilitating experience. First is the ability to engage others in shared meaning. Consider Sidney Harman, who dived into a chaotic work environment to mobilize employees around an entirely new approach to management. Second is a distinctive and compelling voice. Look at

Jack Coleman's ability to defuse a potentially violent situation with only his words. Third is a sense of integrity (including a strong set of values). Here, we point again to Coleman, whose values prevailed even during the emotionally charged clash between peace demonstrators and the angry (and strong) former football team members.

But by far the most critical skill of the four is what we call "adaptive capacity." This is, in essence, applied creativity—an almost magical ability to transcend adversity, with all its attendant stresses, and to emerge stronger than before. It's composed of two primary qualities: the ability to grasp context, and hardiness. The ability to grasp context implies an ability to weigh a welter of factors, ranging from how very different groups of people will interpret a gesture to being able to put a situation in perspective. Without this, leaders are utterly lost, because they cannot connect with their constituents. M. Douglas Ivester, who succeeded Roberto Goizueta at Coca-Cola, exhibited a woeful inability to grasp context, lasting just 28 months on the job. For example, he demoted his highest-ranked African-American employee even as the company was losing a $200 million class-action suit brought by black employees—and this in Atlanta, a city with a powerful African-American majority. Contrast Ivester with Vernon Jordan. Jordan realized his boss's time was up—not just his time in power, but the era that formed him. And so Jordan was able to see past the insults and recognize his boss's bitterness for what it was—desperate lashing out.

Hardiness is just what it sounds like, the perseverance and toughness that enable people to emerge from devastating circumstances without losing hope. Look at Michael Klein, who experienced failure but didn't let it defeat him. He found himself with a single asset—a tiny software company he'd acquired. Klein built it into Transoft Networks, which Hewlett-Packard acquired in 1999. Consider, too, Mickie Siebert, who used her sense of humor to curtail offensive conversations. Or Sidney Rittenberg's strength during his imprisonment. He drew on his personal memories and inner strength to emerge from his lengthy prison term without bitterness.

It is the combination of hardiness and ability to grasp context that, above all, allows a person to not only survive an ordeal, but to learn from it, and to emerge stronger, more engaged, and more committed than ever. These attributes allow leaders to grow from their crucibles, instead of being destroyed by them—to find opportunity where others might find only despair. This is the stuff of true leadership.

—⟨⟩⟨⟩⟨⟩—

Warren G. Bennis is University Professor and Distinguished Professor of Business Administration and founding chairman of the Leadership Institute at the University of Southern California; chairman of the advisory board of the Center for Public Leadership at Harvard University's Kennedy School of Government; and author of over twenty-five books on leadership.

—⟨⟩⟨⟩⟨⟩—

Robert J. Thomas is executive director of Accenture's Institute for High Performance Business, based in Boston, and the John R. Galvin Visiting Professor of Leadership at the Fletcher School of Law and Diplomacy at Tufts University.

CHAPTER FORTY

Choose Hope

On Creating a Hopeful Future

Andrew Razeghi

ope is as far from wishful thinking as you can get. Hope involves believing deeply, seeing further, thinking conditionally, and acting willfully to make things happen. Be vulnerable to possibility—let down your guard—and have the courage to believe in the power of hope.

Choose hope. But also know that by opting to use the most sustainable form of human motivation, you are also choosing to use the most challenging. Odd as it may seem, it takes courage to be hopeful. As Simon Peter advised, "Always be ready to give an explanation to anyone who asks you for a reason for your hope" (1 Peter 3:15). As Peter suggests, it is best to assume that as a hopeful person, you will be an oddity to others. But don't waste your time trying to convert the fatalists. Seek out the hopeful, the willful, and the courageous. They already know the truth, but need your leadership to act upon it.

Moreover, while we recognize that there is always hope, we often forget about the importance of hope once we have accomplished what we had hoped to achieve. Like a professional football player's silent shout of "Hi, Mom" into the television cameras following a touchdown, hope, like Dad, is often forgotten in the trappings of success.

In hope's place, we opt to credit hard work, intelligence, and often luck rather than the power of belief, imagination, and will. It's as if we are reluctant to give ourselves credit for the dream that gave rise to our will to work in pursuit of that dream. The irony of hope is that everyone loves a dreamer, but no one wants to be called one.

Almost all outrageously successful people, at some point in their journey, were dismissed by doers as dreamers. However, the joke is on the doers. What the doers often overlook is that they are employed by a dreamer who has found a way. Truth be told, in moments of uncertainty, we look to the hopeful dreamer—the problem solver, the creative one, the person who can find a way out of our current dilemma. When it really matters, we turn to hopeful leaders like flowers reaching for the sun.

Hopeful leaders turn the unbelievable into the expected. As the late movie critic Gene Siskel, a die-hard Chicago Bulls fan, once said of Michael Jordan's supreme talent (or words to this effect), "People keep saying how unbelievable he is. You'd think after they have seen him do so many unbelievable things season after season, game after game, and shot after shot, they'd begin to believe." When the ball was in Jordan's hands, saving the game at the buzzer was not only believable but expected.

To be human is to hope. To hope is to see with your heart. To lead in the face of uncertainty is to have the courage to act on your seeing heart—to create the future rather than wait for it to come to you. In these definitive moments of leadership, be awake to possibility. When in doubt, go inside for guidance but leave the screen door open for sustenance. When it is said by those who have tried and failed that it can't be done and by those who have feared to try that it will never work, learn to believe. And when you ultimately, finally, and with every ounce of your being make your decision and place your bet on a future so abundant in promise that you can taste it, choose hope, rise, and stand tall. Throw off the bowlines. Unleash the hounds. Step off the curb. Shine.

<hr />

Andrew Razeghi is the founder of Andrew Razeghi Companies, LLC; adjunct associate professor at the Kellogg School of Management at Northwestern University; and vice chairman of the Wright Centers of Innovation Review Panel at the National Academy of Sciences in Washington, D.C.

⟿ Notes and References

Foreword

1. See the Bible, Exodus 18, for Jethro's consultation to Moses in developing a system of authorizations that would extend his organizational reach beyond face-to-face interactions.
2. See "The Roots of Authority" (chap. 3) and related endnotes, in Ronald A. Heifetz, *Leadership Without Easy Answers* (Cambridge, Mass.: Harvard University Press, Belknap Press, 1994).
3. See Dean Williams, *Real Leadership* (San Francisco: Berrett-Koehler, 2005); Ronald A. Heifetz and Marty Linsky, *Leadership on the Line: Staying Alive Through the Dangers of Leading* (Boston: Harvard Business School Press, 2002); Heifetz, *Leadership Without Easy Answers;* and Ronald A. Heifetz and Riley Sinder, "Political Leadership: Mobilizing the Public's Problem-Solving," in Robert Reich, ed., *The Power of Public Ideas* (Boston: Ballinger, 1988).
4. The terms *discard* and *innovate* are simplifying metaphors to describe a variety of biological processes that change genetic material and the ways it is regulated. See "An Analysis of the Concept of Natural Selection," in Ernst Mayr, *Toward a New Philosophy of Biology: Observations of an Evolutionist* (Cambridge, Mass.: Harvard University Press, Belknap Press, 1988), pp. 95–115; or Marc W. Kirschner and John C. Gerhart, *The Plausibility of Life: Resolving Darwin's Dilemma* (New Haven, Conn.: Yale University Press, 2005).
5. See James C. Collins and Jerry I. Porras, *Built to Last* (New York: Harper-Business, 1994); Gary Hamel and C. K. Prahalad, "The Core Competence of the Corporation," *Harvard Business Review,* May–June 1990, pp. 79–93.
6. See Mayr, *Toward a New Philosophy of Biology,* and Kirschner and Gerhart, *The Plausibility of Life.*
7. See, for example, the works of Chris Argyris; also Heifetz and Linsky, *Leadership on the Line.*
8. See the Bible, Numbers 13–14, and Aaron Wildavsky, *The Nursing Father: Moses as a Political Leader* (Tuscaloosa: University of Alabama Press, 1984).

Part One: Editor's Interlude

Gardner, J. (1993). *On leadership.* New York: Free Press.

Chapter Two

1. This incident was recounted by one of the people we interviewed who was an eyewitness to these events.
2. Thomas Lewis, Fari Amini, and Richard Lannon, *A General Theory of Love* (New York: Random House, 2000).
3. Robert Levenson, University of California at Berkeley, personal communication.
4. C. Bartel and R. Saavedra, "The Collective Construction of Work Group Moods," *Administrative Science Quarterly,* 2000, *45,* 187–231.
5. Peter Totterdell and others, "Evidence of Mood Linkage in Work Groups," *Journal of Personality and Social Psychology,* 1998, *74,* 1504–1515.
6. Peter Totterdell, "Catching Moods and Hitting Runs: Mood Linkage and Subjective Performance in Professional Sports Teams," *Journal of Applied Psychology,* 2000, *85,* 848–859.
7. See Wallace Bachman, "Nice Guys Finish First: A SYMLOG Analysis of U.S. Naval Commands," in Richard Brian Polley, A. Paul Hare, and Philip J. Stone (eds.), *The SYMLOG Practitioner: Applications of Small Group Research* (New York: Praeger, 1988).
8. Anthony T. Pescosolido, "Emotional Intensity in Groups," doctoral dissertation, Department of Organizational Behavior, Case Western Reserve University, 2000.
9. Howard Gardner, *Leading Minds: An Anatomy of Leadership* (New York: Basic Books, 1995).
10. V. U. Druskat and A. T. Pascosolido, "Leading Self-Managing Work Teams from the Inside: Informal Leader Behavior and Team Outcomes," unpublished manuscript, 2001.
11. R. C. Sinclair, "Mood, Categorization Breadth, and Performance Appraisal," *Organizational Behavior and Human Decision Processes,* 1988, *42,* 22–46.
12. Jennifer M. George, "Emotions and Leadership: The Role of Emotional Intelligence," *Human Relations,* 2000, *53,* 1027–1055.
13. See, for example, Gordon H. Bower, "Mood Congruity of Social Judgments," in Joseph Forgas (ed.), *Emotion and Social Judgments* (Oxford: Pergamon Press, 1991).
14. See, for example, Jacqueline Wood, Andrew Matthews, and Tim Dalgleish, "Anxiety and Cognitive Inhibition," *Emotion,* 2001, *1,* 166–181.

15. Sigal G. Barsade, "The Ripple Effect: Emotional Contagion in Groups," working paper no. 98, Yale School of Management, New Haven, Conn., 2000.

16. John Basch and Cynthia D. Fisher, "Affective Events-Emotions Matrix: A Classification of Work Events and Associated Emotions," in Neal M. Ashkanasy, Charmine E. J. Härtel, and Wilfred J. Zerbe (eds.), *Emotions in the Workplace: Research, Theory, and Practice* (Westport, Conn.: Quorum Books, 2000).

17. Jeffrey B. Henriques and Richard J. Davidson, "Brain Electrical Asymmetries During Cognitive Task Performance in Depressed and Nondepressed Subjects," *Biological Psychiatry,* 1997, *42,* 1039–1050.

18. Cynthia D. Fisher and Christopher S. Noble, "Affect and Performance: A Within-Persons Analysis," paper presented at the annual meeting of the Academy of Management, Toronto, 2000.

19. Cynthia D. Fisher, "Mood and Emotions While Working: Missing Pieces of Job Satisfaction?" *Journal of Organizational Behavior,* 2000, *21,* 185–202. See also Howard Weiss, Jeffrey Nicholas, and Catherine Daus, "An Examination of the Joint Effects of Affective Experiences and Job Beliefs on Job Satisfaction and Variations in Affective Experiences over Time," *Organizational Behavior and Human Decision Processes,* 1999, *78,* 1–24.

20. See A. M. Isen, "Positive Affect," in Tim Dalgleish and Mick J. Power (eds.), *Handbook of Cognition and Emotion* (Hoboken, N.J.: Wiley, 1999).

21. See Cynthia D. Fisher and Christopher S. Noble, "Emotion and the Illusory Correlation Between Job Satisfaction and Job Performance," paper presented at the Second Conference on Emotions in Organizational Life, Toronto, August 2000.

22. Martin E. Seligman and Peter Schulman, "The People Make the Place," *Personnel Psychology,* 1987, *40,* 437–453.

23. R. W. Clouse and K. L. Spurgeon, "Corporate Analysis of Humor," *Psychology,* 1995, *32,* 1–24.

24. Sigal G. Barsade and others, "To Your Heart's Content: A Mode of Affective Diversity in Top Management Teams," *Administrative Science Quarterly,* 2000, *45,* 802–836.

25. Lyle Spencer, paper presented at the meeting of the Consortium for Research on Emotional Intelligence in Organizations, Cambridge, Mass., April 19, 2001.

26. Benjamin Schneider and D. E. Bowen, *Winning the Service Game* (Boston: Harvard Business School Press, 1995).

27. David McClelland, "Identifying Competencies with Behavioral-Event Interviews," *Psychological Science,* 1998, *9,* 331–339; Daniel Williams, *Leadership for the 21st Century: Life Insurance Leadership Study* (Boston: LOMA/Hay Group, 1995).

28. More technically, the styles were found to account for 53 to 72 percent of the variance in organizational climate. See Stephen P. Kelner Jr., Christine A. Rivers, and Kathleen H. O'Connell, *Managerial Style as a Behavioral Predictor of Organizational Climate* (Boston: McBer, 1996).
29. Much the same argument has been made in George and Bettenhausen, "Understanding Prosocial Behavior"; and in Neal M. Ashkanasy and Barry Tse, "Transformational Leadership as Management of Emotion: A Conceptual Review," in Ashkanasy, Härtel, and Zerbe, *Emotions in the Workplace.*

Chapter Three

1. Warren G. Bennis, *On Becoming a Leader* (Boston: Addison-Wesley, 1988), p. 146.
2. Telephone interview, April 1998.
3. "FC Roper Starch Survey: The Web," *Fast Company,* October 1999, p. 302.
4. Public Allies, *New Leadership for a New Century* (Washington, D.C.: Public Allies, 1998).

Chapter Four

Barnes, L. B., and Kriger, M. P. "The Hidden Side of Organizational Leadership." *Sloan Management Review,* Fall 1986, pp. 15–25.

Bass, B. M. *Leadership and Performance Beyond Expectations.* New York: Free Press, 1985.

Bennis, W. G., and Nanus, B. *Leaders: Strategies for Taking Charge.* New York: HarperCollins, 1985.

Bolman, L. G., and Deal, T. E. *The Wizard and The Warrior: Leading with Passion and Power.* San Francisco: Jossey-Bass, 2006.

Burns, J. M. *Leadership.* New York: HarperCollins, 1978.

Burrows, P. "Carly's Last Stand?" *BusinessWeek,* Dec. 24, 2001. (www.businessweek.com/magazine/content/01_52/b3763001.htm)

Burrows, P., and Elstrom, P. "HP's Carly Fiorina: The Boss." *BusinessWeek,* Aug. 2, 1999, pp. 76–84.

Carlzon, J. *Moments of Truth.* New York: Ballinger, 1987.

Cleveland, H. *The Knowledge Executive: Leadership in an Information Society.* New York: Dutton, 1985.

Fried, I. "HP Board Slams Walter Hewlett." C/Net News.Com, Jan. 18, 2002. (http://news.com.com/2100–1001–818687.html?tag=bplst)

Gardner, J. W. *On Leadership.* New York: Free Press, 1989.

Greenleaf, R. K. *The Servant as Leader.* Newton Center, Mass.: Robert K. Greenleaf Center, 1973.

Hall, R. H. *Organizations: Structures, Processes, and Outcomes.* (4th ed.) Upper Saddle River, N.J.: Prentice Hall, 1987.

Hampton, W. J., and Norman, J. R. "General Motors: What Went Wrong—Eight Years and Billions of Dollars Haven't Made Its Strategy Succeed." *BusinessWeek,* Mar. 16, 1987, p. 102.

Iacocca, L., and Novak, W. *Iacocca.* New York: Bantam Books, 1984.

Kanter, R. M. *The Change Masters: Innovations for Productivity in the American Corporation.* New York: Simon & Schuster, 1983.

Kaufer, N., and Leader, G. C. "Diana Lam (A)." Case. Boston University, 1987(a).

Kaufer, N., and Leader, G. C. "Diana Lam (B)." Case. Boston University, 1987(b).

Kotter, J. P. *The Leadership Factor.* New York: Free Press, 1988.

Kouzes, J. M., and Posner, B. Z. *The Leadership Challenge: How to Get Extraordinary Things Done in Organizations.* San Francisco: Jossey-Bass, 1987.

Lee, A. *Call Me Roger.* Chicago: Contemporary Books, 1988.

Murphy, J. T. *Managing Matters: Reflections from Practice.* (Monograph.) Cambridge, Mass.: Graduate School of Education, Harvard University, 1985.

"On a Clear Day You Can Still See General Motors." *Economist,* Dec. 2, 1989, pp. 77–78, 80.

Oshry, B. *Seeing Systems: Unlocking the Mysteries of Organizational Life.* San Francisco: Berrett-Koehler, 1995.

O'Toole, P. *Corporate Messiah: The Hiring and Firing of Million-Dollar Managers.* New York: Morrow, 1984.

Peters, T. J., and Waterman, R. H. *In Search of Excellence.* New York: HarperCollins, 1982.

Ridout, C. F., and Fenn, D. H. "Job Corps." Boston: Harvard Business School Case Services, 1974.

Sennett, R. *Authority.* New York: Knopf, 1980.

Simmel, G. *The Sociology of Georg Simmel.* New York: Free Press, 1950.

Sloan, A. P., Jr. *My Years with General Motors.* New York: Macfadden, 1965.

Waterman, R. H., Jr. *What America Does Right: Learning from Companies That Put People First.* New York: Norton, 1994.

Chapter Eleven

Argyris, C. (1982). *Reasoning, learning, and action.* San Francisco: Jossey-Bass.

Ayas, K., & Mirvis, P. H. (2005). Educating managers through service learning projects. In C. Wankel & R. DeFillippi (Eds.), *Educating managers through real-world projects.* Greenwich, CT: IAP.

Buber, M. (1970). *I and thou* (W. Kaufmann, Trans.). New York: Scribner.

Capra, F. (1996). *The web of life: A new synthesis of mind and matter.* New York: HarperCollins.

Collins, J. C. (2001). *Good to great: Why some companies make the leap . . . and others don't.* New York: HarperBusiness.

Cooperrider, D. (1990). Positive image, Positive action. In S. Srivastva & Associates, *Appreciative management and leadership.* San Francisco: Jossey-Bass.

Covey, S. (2004). *The 8th habit: From effectiveness to greatness.* New York: Free Press.

Csikszentmihalyi, M. (2003). *Good business: Leadership, flow, and the making of meaning.* New York: Viking.

Freud, S. (1965). *New introductory lectures on psychoanalysis* (J. Strachey, Trans. & Ed.). New York: Norton.

Fromm, E. (1956). *The art of loving.* New York: HarperCollins.

Gardner, H. (1995). *Leading minds.* New York: HarperCollins.

Gardner, J. (1995). *Building community.* Washington, DC: Independent Sector.

Goleman, D. (1995). *Emotional intelligence.* New York: Bantam.

Hawley, J. (1993). *Reawakening the spirit in work: The power of dharmic management.* San Francisco: Berrett-Koehler.

Isaacs, W. (1999). *Dialogue and the art of thinking together: A pioneering approach to communicating in business and life.* New York: Doubleday.

Klein, M. (1959). Our adult world and its roots in infancy. *Human Relations, 12,* 291–303.

Kohn, A. (1990). *The brighter side of human nature: Altruism and empathy in everyday life.* New York: Basic Books.

Kriger, M. (2005). "Ways of questioning that can transform organizations and people." Working paper.

Levi, R. (2003). "Group magic: An inquiry into experiences of collective resonance." Unpublished doctoral dissertation, Saybrook Graduate School and Research Center, San Francisco.

Marcic, D. (1997). *Managing with the wisdom of love.* San Francisco: Jossey-Bass.

Mead, G. H. (1934). *Works of George Herbert Mead: Vol. 1. Mind, self, and society from the standpoint of social behavior* (C. W. Morris, Ed.). Chicago: University of Chicago Press.

Mirvis, P. H. (1997). "Soul work" in organizations. *Organization Science, 8*(2), 193–206.

Mirvis, P. H. (2002). Community building in business. *Reflections, 3*(3), 45–51.

Mirvis, P. H. (In press). Executive development through consciousness raising experiences. *Academy of Management Learning & Education.*

Mirvis, P. H., & Ayas, K. (2003). Reflective dialogue, life stories, and leadership development. *Reflections, 4*(4), 39–48.

Mitchell, D. (1991). *Spirituality and emptiness.* Mahwah, NJ: Paulist Press.

Moxley, R. (2000). *Leadership and spirit: Breathing new vitality and energy into individuals and organizations.* San Francisco: Jossey-Bass.

Peck, M. S. (1987). *The different drum: Community making and peace.* New York: Simon & Schuster.

Peck, M. S. (1993). *A world waiting to be born: Civility rediscovered.* New York: Doubleday.

Prochaska, J. O., Norcross, J. C., & DiClemente, C. C. (1994). *Changing for good.* New York: Morrow.

Schein, E. H. (2003). On dialogue, culture, and organization learning. *Reflections, 4*(4), 27–38.

Schön, D. (1983). *The reflective practitioner.* New York: Basic Books.

Senge, P. (1990). *The fifth discipline.* New York: Doubleday.

Senge, P., Scharmer, P. O., Jaworski, J., & Flowers, B. S. (2004). *Presence: Human purpose and the field of the future.* Cambridge, MA: Society for Organizational Learning.

Smith, K., & Berg, D. N. (1987). *Paradoxes of group life.* San Francisco: Jossey Bass.

Tichy, N. (2002). *The cycle of leadership: How great leaders teach their companies to win.* New York: HarperBusiness.

Wuthnow, R. (1991). *Acts of compassion: Caring for others and helping ourselves.* Princeton, NJ: Princeton University Press.

Part Three: Editor's Interlude

Bennis. W. (2003). *On becoming a leader.* New York: Basic Books.

Burns, J. M. (1978). *Leadership.* New York: Harper Torchbooks.

Chapter Thirteen

Argyris, C. (1962). *Interpersonal competence and organizational effectiveness.* Homewood, IL: Irwin.

Argyris, C. (1982). *Reasoning, learning, and action.* San Francisco: Jossey-Bass.

Argyris, C. (1985). *Strategy, change and defensive routines.* Boston: Pitman.

Argyris, C., Putnam, R., & Smith, D. (1985). *Action science.* San Francisco: Jossey-Bass.

Argyris, C., & Schön, D. (1978). *Organizational learning.* Reading, MA: Addison-Wesley.

Argyris, C., & Schön, D. (1982). *Theory in practice.* San Francisco: Jossey-Bass.

Bennis, W. (2003). *On becoming a leader.* Cambridge, MA: Perseus.

Blustein, D. L. (2007). *The psychology of working: A new perspective for career development, counseling, and public policy.* Mahwah, NJ: Erlbaum.

Bolman, L., & Deal, T. (1984). *Modern approaches to understanding and managing organizations.* San Francisco: Jossey-Bass.

Bolman, L., & Deal, T. (2003). *Reframing organizations: Artistry, choice, and leadership* (3rd ed.). San Francisco: Jossey-Bass.

Cameron, K., & Quinn, R. (1999). *Diagnosing and changing organizational culture: Based on the competing values framework.* Reading, MA: Addison-Wesley.

Cohen, M., & March, J. (1974). *Leadership and ambiguity.* New York: McGraw-Hill.

Cyert, R., & March, J. (1963). *A behavioral theory of the firm.* Upper Saddle River, NJ: Prentice Hall.

Dalai Lama. (2006). *How to see yourself as you really are* (J. Hopkins, Trans. & Ed.). New York: Atria Books.

Deal, T., & Kennedy, A. (2000). *Corporate cultures: The rites and rituals of corporate life* (2nd ed.). Cambridge, MA: Perseus.

Fletcher, J., & Olwyler, K. (1997). *Paradoxical thinking: How to profit from your contradictions.* San Francisco: Berrett-Koehler.

Galbraith, J. (2001). *Designing organizations: An executive briefing on strategy, structure, and process* (2nd ed.). San Francisco: Jossey-Bass.

Gallos, J. V. (1989, November). Developmental diversity and the OB classroom: Implications for teaching and learning. *Organizational Behavior Teaching Review, 13*(40), 33–47.

Gallos, J. V. (2005, Spring). Career counseling revisited: A developmental perspective. *Career Planning and Adult Development. 21*(1), 9–23.

Gallos, J. V. (2006). Introduction. In J. V. Gallos (Ed.), *Organization development* (pp. xxi–xxviii). San Francisco: Jossey-Bass.

Groopman, J. (2007). *How doctors think.* Boston: Houghton Mifflin.

Groopman, J. (2000). *Second opinions: Eight clinical dramas of decision making on the front lines of medicine.* New York: Penguin Books.

Hammer, M., & Champy, J. (1993). *Reengineering the corporation.* New York: HarperCollins.

James, W. (2005). *A pluralistic universe.* Whitefish, MT: Kessinger Publishing.

Kuhn, T. (1996). *The structure of scientific revolutions* (3rd ed.). Chicago: University of Chicago Press.

Lawrence, P., & Lorsch, J. (1986). *Organization and environment: Managing differentiation and integration* (Rev. ed.). Boston: Harvard Business School Press.

Lohr, S. (2006, May 10). Microsoft and Google grapple for supremacy. *New York Times.* [http://www.nytimes.com/2006/05/10/technology/10titans.html?_r=1&partner=rssnyt&emc=rss&oref=slogin].

March, J., & Simon, H. (1958). *Organizations.* New York: Wiley.

Maslow, A. (1954). *Motivation and personality.* New York: HarperCollins.

McGregor, D. (1960). *The human side of enterprise.* New York: McGraw-Hill.

Meyer, J., & Rowan, B. (1983). Institutionalized organizations: Formal structure as myth and ceremony. In J. Meyer & W. Scott (Eds.), *Organizational environments: Ritual and rationality.* Thousand Oaks, CA: Sage.

Perrow, C. (1986). *Complex organizations* (3rd ed.). New York: McGraw-Hill.

Pfeffer, J. (1994). *Managing with power: Politics and influence in organizations.* Boston: Harvard Business School Press.

Schein, E. (2004). *Organizational culture and leadership* (3rd ed.). San Francisco: Jossey-Bass.

Schön, D. (1983). *The reflective practitioner: How professionals think in action.* New York: Basic Books.

Schön, D., & Rein, M. (1994). *Frame reflection: Toward the resolution of intractable policy controversies.* New York: Basic Books.

Smith, H. (1988). *The power game.* New York: Random House.

Sobel, R. (1999). *When giants stumble: Classic business blunders and how to avoid them.* Upper Saddle River, NJ: Prentice Hall.

Starbuck, W., & Milliken, F. (1988). Executive perceptual filters: What they notice and how they make sense. In D. Hambrick (Ed.), *The executive effect: Concepts and methods for studying top managers* (pp. 35–65). Greenwich, CT: JAI Press.

Thomas, D. A. (2006). Diversity as strategy. In J. V. Gallos (Ed.), *Organization development* (pp. 748–764). San Francisco: Jossey-Bass.

Torbert, W. R. (2006). Generating simultaneous personal, team, and organizational development. In J. V. Gallos (Ed.), *Organization development* (pp. 813–829). San Francisco: Jossey-Bass.

Weick, K. E. (1979). *The social psychology of organizing.* New York: McGraw-Hill.

Weick, K. E. (1985). Cosmos vs. chaos: Sense and nonsense in electronic contexts. *Organizational Dynamics, 14*(2), 50–64.

Weick, K. E. (1993). Collapse of sensemaking in organizations: The Mann Gulch disaster. *Administrative Science Quarterly, 38,* 628–652.

Weick, K. E. (1995). *Sensemaking in organizations.* Thousand Oaks, CA: Sage.

Weick, K. E. (2007). Drop your tools: On reconfiguring management education. *Journal of Management Education, 31*(1), 5–16.

Weick, K. E., & Sutcliffe, K. (2001). *Managing the unexpected: Assuring high performance in an age of complexity.* San Francisco: Jossey-Bass.

Weick, K. E., Sutcliffe, K., & Obstfeld, D. (2005). Organizing and the process of sensemaking. *Organization Science, 16*(4), 409–421.

Chapter Fourteen

1. Kees Boeke, *Cosmic View: The Universe in 40 Jumps* (New York: John Day, 1957).

2. Anika Schriefer and Michael Sales, "Creating Strategic Advantage with Dynamic Scenarios," *Strategy & Leadership,* 2006, *34*(3), 31–42.

3. Barry Oshry, *Power and Position* (Boston: Power and Systems Training, 1977); *Take a Look at Yourself: Self-in-System Sensitizers* (Boston: Power and Systems Training, 1978); *The Possibilities of Organization: Internal Warfare, Understanding and Accommodation, Transformation* (Boston: Power and Systems Training, 1985); *Seeing Systems: Unlocking the Mysteries of Organizational Life* (San Francisco: Berrett-Koehler, 1996); *Leading Systems: Lessons from the Power Lab* (San Francisco: Berrett-Koehler, 1999); *The Organization Workshop Trainer's Manual* (Boston: Power and Systems Training, 2000); *The Merging Cultures Workshop Trainer's Manual* (Boston: Power and Systems Training, 2003).

4. In his review of the *Columbia* tragedy, former NASA trainer Peter Pruyn (Pruyn and Sterling, 2006) shows how the learning failures that plagued NASA during the *Challenger* catastrophe have persisted, despite the "organizational renewal" that followed the *Challenger* explosion, and he sees these failures as an illustration of entrenched anti-learning in organizations. NASA leads federal agencies in low employee morale; David E. Rosenbaum, "Study Ranks Homeland Security Dept. Lowest in Morale," *New York Times,* October 16, 2005. [http://select.nytimes.com/search/restricted/article?res=F30A13F93F5B0C758DDDA90994DD404482]; Peter W. Pruyn and Michael R. Sterling, "Space Flight Resource Management: Lessons Learned from Astronaut Team Learning," *Reflections,* 2006, *7*(2), 95–107.

5. Russell Crowe's depiction in *Cinderella Man* of the prizefighter Jim Braddock illustrated a person at the bottom of the social order being a Top in the family microsystem.

6. Joan V. Gallos, "The Dean's Squeeze: Myths and Reality of Academic Leadership," *Academy of Management Learning & Education,* 2002, *1*(2), 174–184.

7. Bruce Nussbaum, "Lessons from Home Depot's Bob Nardelli—Why Command and Control Is So Bad," *BusinessWeek Online,* January 2007 [http://www.businessweek.com/innovate/NussbaumOnDesign/archives/2007/01/lessons_from_ho.html].

8. "Home Unimprovement: Was Nardelli's Tenure at Home Depot a Blueprint for Failure?" *Knowledge@Wharton,* January 10, 2007 [http://www.knowledgeatwharton.com.cn/index.cfm?fa=viewfeature&articleid=1551&languageid=1].

9. "Interview with Bob Nardelli, CEO of Home Depot," *Directorship,* September 2006 [http://www.directorship.com/publications/0906_nardelli.aspx].

10. Richard Conniff, *The Ape in the Corner Office: Understanding the Workplace Beast in All of Us* (New York: Crown Business, 2005); Arnold S. Tannenbaum and others, *Hierarchy in Organizations* (San Francisco: Jossey-Bass, 1974).

11. Chris Argyris, *Strategy, Change and Defensive Routines* (Boston: Pitman, 1985); Chris Argyris and Donald A. Schön, *Theory in Practice: Increasing Professional Effectiveness* (San Francisco: Jossey-Bass, 1977); *Organizational Learning: A Theory of Action Perspective* (Reading, Mass.: Addison-Wesley, 1978); *Organizational Learning II: Theory, Method, and Practice* (Reading, Mass.: Addison-Wesley, 1996).

12. Grady McGonagill, "The Amygdala Hijack," Presentation to the Organization Workshop Trainers Meeting, October 2004.

13. "Executive Stress: Stress Is Chief Among Executives' Health Concerns." *Mayo Clinic Checkup,* April 2004.

14. Earl Shorris, *The Oppressed Middle: Scenes from Corporate Life* (New York: Anchor Books, 1981).

15. Argyris and Schön, *Organizational Learning II.*

16. Michael D. Kelleher, *Profiling the Lethal Employee: Case Studies of Workplace Violence* (Westport, Conn.: Praeger, 1997).

17. Oshry, *Seeing Systems.*

18. Oshry, *Leading Systems.*

19. Barry Oshry, *Space Work: A Systemic Analysis of the Causes of Partnership Breakdown* (Boston: Power and Systems Training, 1992); *The Terrible Dance of Power* (Boston: Power and Systems Training, 1993); *Seeing Systems.*

20. Terrence E. Deal and Alan A. Kennedy, *Corporate Cultures: The Rites and Rituals of Corporate Life* (Reading Mass.: Addison-Wesley, 1982).

21. See, for example, Hirschfield Law, "Practice Areas: Reverse Mergers," n.d. [http://www.hirshfieldlaw.com/practice/reverse_mergers.php].

22. Erin Texeira, "Black Men Quietly Combatting Stereotypes," WashingtonPost.com, July 1, 2006 [http://www.washingtonpost.com/wp-dyn/content/article/2006/07/01/AR2006070100462_pf.html].

23. Joe R. Feagin, *White Racism* (New York: Routledge, 2001).

24. Peter F. Drucker, *The Effective Executive* (New York: HarperCollins, 1967).

25. Oshry, *Leading Systems; The Merging Cultures Workshop Trainer's Manual.*

26. Jessica Lipnack and Jeffrey Stamps, *Virtual Teams: Reaching Across Space, Time, and Organizations with Technology* (New York: Wiley, 1997).

27. Don Van Natta Jr., Adam Liptak, and Clifford J. Levy, "The Miller Case: A Notebook, a Cause, a Jail Cell and a Deal," *New York Times,* October 16, 2005, p. A1.

28. Oshry, *The Organization Workshop Trainer's Manual.*

29. See Southwest Museum of Engineering, Communications and Computation, *Hewlett-Packard, The Early Years,* n.d. [http://www.smecc.org/hewlett-packard,_the_early_years.htm].

30. Oshry, *The Organization Workshop Trainer's Manual.*

31. Joel Makower, "Ecomagination: Inside GE's Power Play," *Two Steps Forward,* May 9, 2005 [http://makower.typepad.com/joel_makower/2005/05/ecomagination_i.html]; Amanda Little, "It Was Just My Ecomagination," *Grist,* May 10, 2005 [http://www.grist.org/news/muck/2005/05/10/little-ge].

Chapter Fifteen

1. The Sears example is based in part on D. R. Katz, *The Big Store: Inside the Crisis and Revolution at Sears* (New York: Viking Press, 1987).

Chapter Sixteen

1. R. E. Silverman, "Growth at McKinsey Hindered Use of Data," *Wall Street Journal,* May 20, 2002, p. B6.

2. N. W. Foote, E. Matson, and N. Rudd, "Managing the Knowledge Manager," *McKinsey Quarterly,* 2001, no. 3, pp. 120–129; S. Hauschild, T. Licht, and W. Stein, "Creating a Knowledge Culture," *McKinsey Quarterly,* 2001, no. 1, pp. 74–81.

3. *Merriam-Webster's Collegiate Dictionary,* 10th ed. (Springfield, Mass.: Merriam-Webster, 1993), p. 647.

4. A. Banco, "The Twenty-First-Century Corporation: The New Leadership," *BusinessWeek,* Aug. 28, 2000, p. 100.

5. J. Fitz-Enz, "Blueberries from Chile," *Workforce,* Apr. 1, 2000 [http://www.workforce.com/archive/article/22/01/64.php].

6. T. A. Stewart, "Software Preserves Knowledge, People Pass It On," *Fortune,* Sept. 4, 2000, p. 392.

7. I. Greenberg, "Knowledge-Management Rivals Go to Asia," *Wall Street Journal,* June 21, 2001.

8. T. A. Stewart, "Mapping Corporate Brainpower," *Fortune,* Oct. 30, 1995, p. 209.

9. D. Pringle, "Learning Gurus Adapt to Escape Corporate Axes," *Wall Street Journal,* Jan. 7, 2003, p. B1.

10. Pringle, "Learning Gurus Adapt to Escape Corporate Axes."

11. S. Koudsi, "Actually, It Is Like Brain Surgery," *Fortune,* Mar. 20, 2000, p. 233.

12. T. A. Stewart, "Knowledge Worth $1.25 Billion," *Fortune,* Nov. 27, 2000, p. 302.

13. Stewart, "Knowledge Worth $1.25 Billion."

14. M. Schrage, "Sixteen Tons of Information Overload," *Fortune,* Aug. 2, 1999, p. 244.

15. "Top Companies for Leaders 2002," Hewitt Associates, 2002.

Chapter Seventeen

1. Quoted in "Money and Morals at GE," by Marc Gunther, *Fortune,* Nov. 15, 2004, p. 176.

2. *Boston Globe,* June 3, 2005, p. E1.

3. Quoted in "GE Hotline Gives Workers Some Clout," *Financial Times,* May 19, 2005, p. 19.

4. "Welcome to Ecomagination," GE corporate website, available online at http://ge.ecomagination.com

5. "Blowing in the Wind," *Fortune,* July 25, 2005, on second page of unnumbered insert titled "Fortune Global 500: The World of Ideas."

6. *BusinessWeek,* Aug. 22–29, 2005, p. 130.

7. "A Consistent Policy on Cleaner Energy," by Jeffrey Immelt, *Financial Times,* June 29, 2005, p. 13.

8. "The Biggest Contract," by Ian Davis, *The Economist,* May 26, 2005, available online at www.economist.com/business/PrinterFriendly. cfm?Story_ID=4008642

9. *Wall Street Journal,* Oct. 15, 2005.

10. "Queen's Award for Enterprise: Diversity of British Endeavour Wins the Greatest Accolade," by Sarah Murray, *Financial Times,* Apr. 21, 2005, p. 7.

11. "Proud Papa of the Prius," by Chester Dawson, *BusinessWeek,* June 20, 2005, p. 20.

12. "Toyota Develops Hybrids with an Eye on the Future," by Danny Hakim and James Brooke, *New York Times,* Aug. 4, 2005, p. C3.

13. Cited in *Who Cares, Wins: Connecting Financial Markets to a Changing World,* Investment Financial Corporation/World Bank, 2004, available online at www.unglobalcompact.org/Issues/financial_markets/who_cares_ who_wins.pdf

14. Data from *Sustainability Pays Off: An Analysis About the Stock Exchange Performance of Members of the World Business Council for Sustainable Development* (WBCSD) (Vienna: Kommunalkredit Dexia Asset Management, Oct. 2004).

15. Quoted in *Integral Business: Integrating Sustainability and Business Strategy,* PricewaterhouseCoopers LLP, 2003.

16. Global Equity Research, *Food and Beverages,* UBS Investment Research, Oct. 24, 2005, p. 4.

17. The notion that sustainability can improve your business by helping you protect it, run it, and grow it was originally formulated by the World Business Council for Sustainable Development.

18. Quoted in "The Perils of Doing the Right Thing," by Andrew W. Singer, *Across the Board,* Oct. 2000, p. 18.

19. "GM Food Banned at Monsanto Canteen," Dec. 24, 1999, on *Urban 75* ezine, available online at www.urban75.org/archive/news099.html

20. Stock market valuation calculations by James Wilbur, analyst at Salomon Smith Barney, cited in "Is Monsanto's Biotech Worth Less Than a Hill of Beans?" by David Stipp, *Fortune,* Feb. 19, 2001, available online at www.fortune.com/fortune/subs/print/0 15935,368798,00.html

21. Quoted in *Walking the Talk: The Business Case for Sustainable Development,* by Charles O. Holliday Jr., Stephan Schmidheiny, and Philip Watts (Sheffield, England: Greenleaf, 2002), p. 27.

22. Estimate by U.S. Green Building Council, cited in "Beyond Recycling: Manufacturers Embrace 'C2C' Design," by Rebecca Smith, *Wall Street Journal,* Mar. 3, 2005, p. B1.

23. *The Fortune at the Bottom of the Pyramid: Eradicating Poverty Through Profits,* by C. K. Prahalad (Upper Saddle River, N.J.: Wharton School Publishing, 2005).

24. "The Wegmans Way," by Matthew Boyle, *Fortune,* Jan. 24, 2005, p. 62.

Chapter Twenty-One

1. Excellent exceptions to this general rule are John J. Gabarro, *The Dynamics of Taking Charge* (Boston: Harvard Business School Press, 1987) and Linda A. Hill, *Becoming a Manager: How New Managers Master the Challenges of Leadership,* 2nd edition (Boston: Harvard Business School Press, 2003).

2. For an excellent exploration of the challenges of moving from technical contributor to first-time manager, see Hill, *Becoming a Manager.*

3. This is an extrapolation of the results of a management transition survey of senior HR executives at Fortune 500 companies that I conducted in 1999. The survey was sent to the heads of human resources at a random sample of 100 Fortune 500 companies. We received 40 responses. One question concerned the percentage of managers at all levels who took new jobs in 1998. The mean of the responses to this question was 22.3 percent. Extrapolated to the Fortune 500 as a whole, this suggests that almost 700,000 managers take new jobs each year. The half-million figure is therefore a conservative estimate intended purely to illustrate the magnitude of the impact of leadership transitions.

4. For discussion of key passages in the lives of managers, see Ram Charan, Stephen Drotter, and James Noel, *The Leadership Pipeline: How to Build the Leadership-Powered Company* (San Francisco: Jossey-Bass, 2001).

Chapter Twenty-Three

1. See my Foreword to Joanne Ciulla, ed., *Ethics, the Heart of Leadership* (Quorum Books, 1998), p. ix, from whose language I have borrowed.

2. Joanne Ciulla, "Leadership Ethics: Mapping the Territory," in Ciulla, *Ethics, the Heart of Leadership,* pp. 3–25, quoted at p. 13.

3. See Robert Coles, *The Moral Intelligence of Children* (Random House, 1997).

4. Joseph C. Rost, *Leadership for the Twenty-First Century* (Praeger, 1991), p. 153.

5. Peter C. Sederberg, *The Politics of Meaning: Power and Explanation in the Construction of Social Reality* (University of Arizona Press, 1984), p. 181.

6. Sheldon S. Wolin, "Paradigms and Political Theories," in Gary Gutting, ed., *Paradigms and Revolutions* (University of Notre Dame Press, 1980), p. 182.

7. Leon Festinger, "The Motivating Effect of Cognitive Dissonance," in Gardner Lindzey, ed., *Assessment of Human Motives* (Rinehart, 1958), p. 69.

8. Václav Havel, *Disturbing the Peace,* Paul Wilson, trans. (Alfred A. Knopf, 1990), p. 201.

9. Kenneth Keniston, "Youth, Change and Violence," *American Scholar,* vol. 37, no. 2 (Spring 1968), pp. 227–45, quoted at p. 239.

10. Donatella della Porta and Mario Diani, *Social Movements* (Blackwell, 1999), p. 72.

11. Thomas R. Rochon, *Culture Moves: Ideas, Activism, and Changing Values* (Princeton University Press, 1998), pp. 54, 55.

12. Sidney Tarrow, *Power in Movement: Social Movements, Collective Action and Politics* (Cambridge University Press, 1994), p. 130.

13. Michael D. Mumford and Mary S. Connelly, "Leaders as Creators: Leader Performance and Problem Solving in Ill-Defined Domains," *Leadership Quarterly,* vol. 2, no. 4 (Winter 1991), p. 308.

14. Sheldon S. Wolin, *Politics and Vision: Continuity and Innovation in Western Political Thought* (Little, Brown, 1960), p. 21.

15. Sheldon S. Wolin, "Paradigms and Political Theories," in Gary Gutting, ed., *Paradigms and Revolutions* (University of Notre Dame Press, 1980), p. 179.

16. Peter C. Sederberg, *The Politics of Meaning: Power and Explanation in the Construction of Social Reality* (University of Arizona Press, 1984), p. 185.

17. See Paulo Freire, *Pedagogy of the Oppressed,* Myra Bergman Ramos, trans. (Herder and Herder, 1970), p. 52.

18. Robert Paul Weiner, *Creativity & Beyond: Culture, Values, and Change* (State University of New York Press, 2000), p. 264.

19. Paulo Freire, *Pedagogy of the Oppressed,* Myra Bergman Ramos, trans. (Herder and Herder, 1970), p. 34.

Chapter Twenty-Four

Bennis, W. G., and Nanus, B. *Leaders: The Strategies for Taking Charge.* New York: HarperCollins, 1985.

Halberstam, D. *The Powers That Be.* New York: Dell, 1979.

Mead, M. "Towards More Vivid Utopias," in G. Kateb (ed.), *Utopia.* New York: Atherton Press, 1971.

Shekerjian, D. *Uncommon Genius: How Great Ideas Are Born.* New York: Viking, 1990.

Thomas, B. *Walt Disney: An American Tradition.* New York: Simon & Schuster, 1976.

Chapter Twenty-Five

Buergi, P., Jacobs, C., & Roos, J. (2005). From metaphor to practice in the crafting of strategy. *Journal of Management Inquiry, 14,* 78–94.

Heracleous, L. (1998). Strategic thinking or strategic planning? *Long Range Planning, 31*(3), 381–387.

Huizinga, J. (1950). *Homo ludens: A study of the play-element in culture.* London: Routledge & Kegan Paul.

Jacobs, C., & Heracleous, L. (2005). Answers for questions to come: Reflective dialogue as an enabler for strategic innovation. *Journal of Organizational Change Management, 18*(4), 338–352.

Jacobs, C., & Heracleous, L. (2006). Constructing shared understanding: The role of embodied metaphors in organization development. *Journal of Applied Behavioral Science, 24*(2), 207–226.

Mirvis, P., & Gunning, L. (2006). Creating a community of leaders. In J. V. Gallos (Ed.), *Organization development: A Jossey-Bass reader* (pp. 709–729). San Francisco: Jossey-Bass.

Seifter, H., & Buswick, T. (Eds.). (2005). Arts-based learning in business [Special issue]. *Journal of Business Strategy, 26*(5).

Sutton-Smith, B. (1997). *The ambiguity of play.* Cambridge, MA: Harvard University Press.

Winnicott, D. W. (1971). *Playing and reality.* London: Tavistock.

Chapter Twenty-Six

Axelrod, R. "More Effective Choice in the Prisoner's Dilemma." *Journal of Conflict Resolution,* 1980, *24,* 379–403.

Bell, T. E., and Esch, K. "The Fatal Flaw in Flight 51-L." *IEEE Spectrum,* Feb. 1987, pp. 36–51.

Bennis, W. G. *Why Leaders Can't Lead: The Unconscious Conspiracy Continues.* San Francisco: Jossey-Bass, 1989.

Block, P. *The Empowered Manager: Positive Political Skills at Work.* San Francisco: Jossey-Bass, 1987.

Bok, S. *Lying: Moral Choice in Public and Private Life.* New York: Vintage Books, 1978.

Burns, J. M. *Leadership.* New York: HarperCollins, 1978.

Fisher, R., and Ury, W. *Getting to Yes.* Boston: Houghton Mifflin, 1981.

Kanter, R. M. *The Change Masters: Innovations for Productivity in the American Corporation.* New York: Simon & Schuster, 1983.

Kohlberg, L. "The Claim to Moral Adequacy of a Highest Stage of Moral Judgment." *Journal of Philosophy,* 1973, *70,* 630–646.

Kotter, J. P. *Power and Influence: Beyond Formal Authority.* New York: Free Press, 1985.

Kotter, J. P. *The Leadership Factor.* New York: Free Press, 1988.

Labaton, S. "Downturn and Shift in the Population Feed Boom in White-Collar Crime." *New York Times,* June 2, 2002. (www.nytimes. com/2002/06/02/business/02CRIM.html?)

Lax, D. A., and Sebenius, J. K. *The Manager as Negotiator.* New York: Free Press, 1986.

Maslow, A. H. *Motivation and Personality.* New York: HarperCollins, 1954.

Mendelson, H., and Korin, A. "The Computer Industry: A Brief History." Palo Alto, Calif.: Stanford Business School, n.d. (http://wesley. stanford.edu/computer_history)

Oppel, R. A. "How Enron Got California to Buy Power It Didn't Need." *New York Times,* May 8, 2002, p. A1.

Pfeffer, J. *Managing with Power: Politics and Influence in Organizations.* Boston: Harvard Business School Press, 1992.

Porter, E. "Notes for the Looking for Leadership Conference." Paper presented at the Looking for Leadership Conference, Graduate School of Education, Harvard University, Dec. 1989.

Smith, H. *The Power Game.* New York: Random House, 1988.

Chapter Twenty-Eight

Global Business Network. (2002). *What's next? Exploring the new terrain for business.* Cambridge, MA: Perseus Books.

Hesselbein, F., Goldsmith, M., & Somerville, I. (Eds.). (1999). *Leading beyond the walls.* San Francisco: Jossey-Bass.

McGregor, D. M. (1960). *The human side of enterprise.* New York: McGraw-Hill.

Michael, D. N. (1985). *On learning to plan & planning to learn.* San Francisco: Jossey-Bass.

Michael, D. N. (1991, January/February). Leadership's shadow: The dilemma of denial. *Futures,* pp. 69–79.

Schein. E. (2004). *Organizational culture and leadership.* (3rd ed.) San Francisco: Jossey-Bass.

Schwartz, P. (2003). *Inevitable surprises.* New York: Gotham Books.

Senge, P. M. (1990). *The fifth discipline.* New York: Doubleday Currency.

Sterman, J. D. (2000). *Business dynamics: Systems thinking and modeling for a complex world.* New York: McGraw-Hill/Irwin.

Chapter Thirty-Three

1. Max Weber, *The Theory of Social and Economic Organizations* (New York: Free Press, 1947), 329.

2. "Presidential Rankings," 2000 poll from C-Span survey of historians, CNN, 21 February 2000.

3. Deborah Solomon, "Is the Go-Go Guggenheim Going, Going . . ." *New York Times Magazine,* 20 June 2002.

4. For an excellent description of Healy's tenure at the Red Cross, see Deborah Sontag, "Who Brought Bernadine Healy Down?" *New York Times Magazine,* 23 December 2001, 32.

5. Daniel Goleman, *Working with Emotional Intelligence* (New York: Bantam, 1999), 317. For an interesting exchange about leadership and practical intelligence, see Robert Sternberg and Victor Vroom, "The Person Versus the Situation in Leadership," *The Leadership Quarterly, 13,* no. 3 (June 2002): 301–321.

6. For example, the failure by South Carolina governor Jim Hodges to communicate during Hurricane Floyd resulted in a monumental traffic jam. "Traffic Backs Up for Miles as Coastal Dwellers Flee Island," *St. Louis Post-Dispatch,* 16 September 1999, A9. See also Leigh Strope, "Hodges Said He Should Control Emergency Response," Associated Press State and Local Wire, 1 October 1999; and David Firestone, "Hurricane Floyd: The Overview," *New York Times,* 16 September 1999, A1.

7. "S. African Leader Claims AIDS Drug Is Unsafe," *St. Louis Post-Dispatch,* 3 November 1999, A5; Barton Gelman, "S. African President Escalates AIDS Feud: Mbeki Challenges Western Remedies," *Washington Post,* 19 April 2000, A1; Samson Mulugeta, "S. Africa: A Country in Denial—AIDS Victims Suffer in Silence, President Dismisses Problem," *Newsday,* 21

August 2001, A16; Rachel Swarns, "In a Policy Shift, South Africa Will Make AIDS Drugs Available to Pregnant Women," *New York Times,* 20 April 2002, A8. In 2002 Mbeki's position on antiretroviral drugs softened slightly, at least in part because of the intervention of Canadian prime minister Jean Chrétien. For a fuller description of Mbeki's rigid intransigence, see Samantha Power, "The AIDS Rebel," *New Yorker,* 19 May 2003.

8. Barbara Tuchman, *The March of Folly: Troy to Vietnam* (New York: Ballantine, 1984), 7.

9. Fred Hiatt, "Ex-Aides Raise Questions About Yeltsin's Drinking," *Washington Post,* 8 October 1994, A21.

10. Ronald A. Heifetz and Marty Linsky, *Leadership on the Line: Staying Alive Through the Dangers of Leading* (Boston: Harvard Business School Press, 2002), 164.

11. "Image and Reality for Martha Stewart," *Greenwich Time,* 10 June 2003. See also Jerry Oppenheimer, *Just Desserts: The Unauthorized Biography of Martha Stewart* (New York: William Morrow, 1997), especially 236 ff. and 308 ff; and Christopher M. Byron, *Martha, Inc.: The Incredible Story of Martha Stewart Living Omnimedia* (New York: John Wiley & Sons, 2003).

12. Peter Watson, "Under the Hammer," *The Guardian,* December 2001, 2; Carol Vogel and Ralph Blumenthal, "Ex-Chairman of Sotheby's Gets Jail Time," *New York Times,* 23 April 2002, B1.

13. Nicholas D. Kristof, "Hearing Liberia's Pleas," *New York Times,* 29 July 2003, A23.

14. Chester Crocker, "A War Americans Can Afford to Stop," *New York Times,* 1 August 2003, A21.

15. James Traub, "The Worst Place on Earth," *New York Review of Books,* 29 June 2000, 61–65. The quotation is from Somini Sengupta, "African Held for War Crimes Dies in Custody of Tribunal," *New York Times,* 31 July 2003, A6.

16. Psychiatrist Michael Weiner has this view of evil, as cited by Sharon Begley, "The Roots of Evil," *Newsweek,* 21 May 2002, 32.

17. For example, in a 2002 presentation titled "Crisis in Corporate Governance," Bill George estimated that corrupt leaders at Global Crossing, Enron, Qwest, Tyco, and WORLDCOM cost shareholders $460 billion.

Chapter Thirty-Four

Aristotle, *Metaphysics* XII, 7, 3–4.

Baumeister, R. F., & Exline, J. J. 1999. Virtue, personality, and social relations: Self-control as the moral muscle. *Journal of Personality, 67:* 1165–1194.

Becker, L. C. 1992. Good lives: Prolegomena. *Social Philosophy and Policy, 9:* 15–37.

Bolino, M. C., Turnley, W. H., & Bloodgood, J. M. 2002. Citizenship behavior and the creation of social capital in organizations. *Academy of Management Review, 27:* 505–522.

Bradley, J. C., Brief, A. P., & Smith-Crowe, K. 2005. *The good corporation.* Working paper, Department of Psychology, Tulane University.

Cameron, K. S. 1994. Strategies for successful organizational downsizing. *Human Resource Management Journal, 33:* 89–112.

Cameron, K. S. 1998. Strategic organizational downsizing: An extreme case. *Research in Organizational Behavior, 20:* 185–229.

Cameron, K. S. 2003. Organizational virtuousness and performance. In K. S. Cameron, J. E. Dutton, & R. E. Quinn (Eds.), *Positive organizational scholarship: Foundations of a new discipline:* 48–65. San Francisco: Berrett-Koehler.

Cameron, K. S., Bright, D., & Caza, A. 2004. Exploring the relationships between organizational virtuousness and performance. *American Behavioral Scientist, 47:* 766–790.

Cameron, K. S., & Caza, A. 2002. Organizational and leadership virtues and the role of forgiveness. *Journal of Leadership and Organizational Studies, 9:* 33–48.

Cameron, K. S., Dutton, J. E., & Quinn, R. E. 2003. *Positive organizational scholarship: Foundations of a new discipline:* 48–65. San Francisco: Berrett-Koehler.

Cameron, K. S., Kim, M. U., & Whetten, D. A. 1987. Organizational effects of decline and turbulence. *Administrative Science Quarterly, 32:* 222–240.

Cameron, K. S., & Lavine, M. 2006. *Making the impossible possible.* San Francisco: Berrett-Koehler.

Caza, A., Barker, B. A., & Cameron, K. S. 2004. Ethics and ethos: The buffering and amplifying effects of ethical behavior and virtuousness. *Journal of Business Ethics, 52:* 169–178.

Cohen, D., & Prusak, L. 2001. *In good company: How social capital makes organizations work.* Boston: Harvard Business School Press.

Csikszentmihalyi, M. 1990. *Flow: The psychology of optimal experience.* New York: Harper Perennial.

Dutton, J. E. 2003. *Energize your workplace.* San Francisco: Jossey Bass.

Dutton, J. E., Frost, P. J., Worline, M. C., Lilius, J. M., & Kanov, J. M. 2002. Leading in times of trauma. *Harvard Business Review,* January: 54–61.

Dutton, J. E., & Heaphy, E. D. 2003. The power of high-quality connections. In K. S. Cameron, J. E. Dutton, & R. E. Quinn (Eds.), *Positive organizational scholarship:* 263–278. San Francisco: Berrett-Koehler.

Eisenberg, E. M. 1990. Jamming: Transcendence through organizing. *Communication Research, 17:* 139–164.

Emmons, R. A. 1999. *The psychology of ultimate concerns: Motivation and spirituality in personality.* New York: Guilford Press.

Enriquez, J. 2000. *As the future catches you.* New York: Crown Business Books.

Fineman, S. 2006. On being positive: Concerns and counterpoints. *Academy of Management Review, 31:* 270–291.

Fredrickson, B. L. 2001. The role of positive emotions in positive psychology: The broaden-and-build theory of positive emotions. *American Psychologist, 56:* 218–226.

Fredrickson, B. L. 2003. Positive emotions and upward spirals in organizations. In K. S. Cameron, J. E. Dutton, & R. E. Quinn (Eds.), *Positive organizational scholarship:* 163–175. San Francisco: Berrett-Koehler.

Fredrickson, B. L., Mancuso, R. A., Branigan, C., & Tugade, M. M. 2000. The undoing effect of positive emotions. *Motivation and Emotion, 24:* 237–258.

George, J. M. 1998. Salesperson mood at work: Implications for helping customers. *Journal of Personal Selling and Sales Management, 18:* 23–30.

Ghoshal, S. 2005. Bad management theories are destroying good management practices. *Academy of Management Learning & Education, 4:* 75–91.

Gittell, J. H. 2001. Supervisory span, relational coordination and flight departure performance: A reassessment of post-bureaucracy theory. *Organization Science, 12*(4): 467–482.

Gittell, J. H. 2002. Coordinating mechanisms in care provider groups: Relational coordination as a mediator and input uncertainty as a moderator of performance effects. *Management Science, 48*(11): 1408–1426.

Gittell, J. H. 2003. *The Southwest Airlines way: Using the power of relationships to achieve high performance.* New York: McGraw-Hill.

Gittell, J. H., Cameron, K. S., & Lim, S. 2006. Relationships, layoffs, and organizational resilience. *Journal of Applied Behavioral Science, 42*(3): 300–329.

Haidt, J. 2000. The positive emotion of elevation. *Prevention and Treatment, 3:* 2.

Handelsman, M. M., Knapp, S., & Gottlieb, M. C. 2002. Positive ethics. In C. R. Snyder & S. J. Lopez (Eds.), *Handbook of positive psychology:* 731–744. New York: Oxford University Press.

Hirschman, A. O. 1970. *Exit, Voice, or Loyalty: Responses to Decline in Firms, Organizations, and States.* Cambridge: Harvard University Press.

Kidder, R. M. 1994. *Shared values for a troubled world.* San Francisco: Jossey Bass.

Lipman-Blumen, J., & Leavitt, H. J. 1999. *Hot groups: Seeking them, feeding them, and using them to ignite your organization.* New York: Oxford University Press.

March, J. G. 1994. *A primer on decision making: How decisions happen.* New York: Free Press.

Margolis, J. D., & Walsh, J. P. 2003. Misery loves companies: Rethinking social initiatives by business. *Administrative Science Quarterly, 48:* 268–305.

Masten, A. S., Hubbard, J. J., Gest, S. D., Tellegen, A., Garmezy, N., & Ramirez, M. 1999. Competence in the context of adversity: Pathways to reliance and maladaptation from childhood to late adolescence. *Development and Psychopathology, 11:* 143–169.

Mayne, T. T. 1999. Negative affect and health: The importance of being earnest. *Cognition and Emotion, 13:* 601–635.

Mitchell, L. E. 2001. *Corporate irresponsibility: America's newest export.* New Haven, CT: Yale University Press.

Myers, D. G. 2000. The funds, friends, and faith of happy people. *American Psychologist, 55:* 56–67.

Orlikowski, W. J. 2000. Using technology and constituting structures: A practice lens for studying technology in organizations. *Organization Science, 11*(4): 404–428.

Paine, L. 2003. *Value shift: Why companies must merge social and financial imperatives to achieve superior performance.* New York: McGraw-Hill.

Peterson, C., & Seligman, M.E.P. 2004. *Character strengths and virtues: A handbook and classification.* New York: Oxford University Press.

Quinn, R. E. 2004. *Building the bridge as you walk on it.* San Francisco: Jossey Bass.

Rawls, J. 1971. *A theory of justice.* Cambridge, MA: Harvard University Press.

Ryff, C. D., & Singer, B. 1998. The contours of positive human health. *Psychological Inquiry, 9:* 1–28.

Sandage, S. J., & Hill, P. C. 2001. The virtues of positive psychology: The rapprochement and challenges of the affirmative postmodern perspective. *Journal for the Theory of Social Behavior, 31:* 241–260.

Seligman, M. 1991. *Learned optimism.* New York: Knopf.

Seligman, M.E.P. 1999. The president's address. *American Psychologist, 54:* 559–562.

Seligman, M.E.P. 2002. Positive psychology, positive prevention, and positive therapy. In C. R. Snyder & S. J. Lopez (Eds.), *Handbook of positive psychology:* 3–9. New York: Oxford University Press.

Seligman, M.E.P., & Csikszentmihalyi, M. 2000. Positive psychology: An introduction. *American Psychologist, 55:* 5–14.

Seligman, M.E.P., Schulman, P., DeRubeis, R. J., & Hollon, S. D. 1999. The prevention of depression and anxiety. *Prevention and Treatment, 2.* http://journals.apa.org/prevention/

Staw, B. M., & Barsade, S. G. 1993. Affect and managerial performance: A test of the sadder-but-wiser versus happier-and-smarter hypotheses. *Administrative Science Quarterly, 38:* 304–331.

Sutcliffe, K. M., & Vogus, T. J. 2003. Organizing for resilience. In K. S. Cameron, J. E. Dutton, & R. E. Quinn (Eds.), *Positive organizational scholarship:* 94–110. San Francisco: Berrett-Koehler.

Valdmanis, T. 2005. AIG's chief executive Greenberg resigns. *USA Today,* 15 March, A-1.

Weick, K. E. 1993. The collapse of sensemaking in organizations: The Mann Gulch Disaster. *Administrative Science Quarterly, 38:* 628–652.

Weick, K. E., & Sutcliffe, K. M. 2001. *Managing the unexpected: Assuring high performance in an age of complexity.* San Francisco: Jossey-Bass.

Weick, K. E., Sutcliffe, K. M., & Obstfeld, D. 1999. Organizing for high reliability: Processes of collective mindfulness. *Research in Organizational Behavior, 21:* 81–123.

Weiner, N. O. 1993. *The harmony of the soul: Mental health and moral virtue reconsidered.* Albany, NY: State University of New York Press.

Wildavsky, A. 1991. *Searching for safety.* New Brunswick: Transaction Books.

Part Five: Editor's Interlude

Conrad, J. (2006). *The secret sharer.* Retrieved March 28, 2007, from Project Gutenberg, http://www.gutenberg.org/etext/220.

Schön, D. (1995). *The reflective practitioner.* Hampshire, UK: Ashgate.

Chapter Thirty-Six

1. As told to C. Hymowitz, "Managers Must Respond to Employee Concerns About Honest Business," *Wall Street Journal,* Feb. 19, 2002, p. B1.

2. Walker Information, *Commitment in the Workplace: The 1999 National Employee Benchmark Study* (Indianapolis: Walker Information and Hudson Institute, 1999). Walker conducted the same survey in 2001; the results show that employee loyalty did not change notably in two years: Walker Information, *Commitment in the Workplace: The 2001 National Employee Benchmark Study* (Indianapolis: Walker Information and Hudson Institute, 2001).

3. W. H. Whyte, *The Organization Man* (New York: Doubleday, 1956), p. 12.

4. Based on interview with Tom Higa, Nov. 2002; B. Snider, "Chevron's Big Spill in Haight: Bad Will," *San Francisco Examiner,* Apr. 23, 1989, pp. A1, A19;

"Chevron Station May Stay Open in the Haight," *San Francisco Examiner,* Apr. 27, 1989, p. A5; V. Kershner, "Popular Haight Gas Station to Stay Open," *San Francisco Examiner,* May 13, 1989, p. A3; M. Zane, "New Law to Save Gas Stations," *San Francisco Examiner,* July 23, 1991, p. A17.

5. Snider, "Big Spill."

6. Interview, Tom Higa.

7. Snider, "Big Spill."

8. Based on interview with former San Francisco mayor Art Agnos (1988–1992), Apr. 2002.

9. J. Schmidt, *Stakeholder Perspective: A Key to Success in the New Economy* (Chicago: Towers Perrin, 2000).

10. J. L. Seglin, "How Business Can Be Good (and Why Being Good Is Good for Business)," *Sojourners,* Jan.-Feb. 2000, pp. 17–18.

11. Cone/Roper, *Cause-Related Trends Report: Evolution of Cause Branding* (Boston: Cone, 1999).

12. Hill & Knowlton, *2001 Corporate Citizen Watch* (New York: Hill & Knowlton, 2001).

13. Hill & Knowlton, 2001.

14. Washington Post/ABC News Poll analysis, in G. Langer, "Confidence in Business: Was Low and Still Is," ABC News.com, July 1, 2002.

15. J. Bandler and J. Hechinger, "SEC Says Xerox Misled Investors," *Wall Street Journal,* Apr. 12, 2002; C. H. Deitsch, "Xerox Revises Revenue Data, Tripling Error First Reported," *New York Times,* June 29, 2002.

16. J. Frooman, "Socially Irresponsible and Illegal Behavior and Shareholder Wealth," *Business and Society,* 1997, *36,* 221–249.

17. G. Winter, "Timber Company Reduces Cutting of Old-Growth Trees," *New York Times,* Mar. 27, 2002, p. A14.

18. Winter, "Timber Company Reduces Cutting of Old-Growth Trees."

Chapter Thirty-Eight

1. For a history of the relationship between spirituality at work and the reformed Christian tradition see David W. Miller, *God at Work: A Critical Understanding of the Roots, Profile and Direction of the Faith at Work Movement* (New York: Oxford University Press, 2007), and Paul Lakeland, *The Liberation of the Laity* (New York: Continuum, 2003).

2. Business leader interests in spirituality are supported in Ian Mitroff and Elizabeth A. Denton, *A Spiritual Audit of Corporate America: A Hard Look at Spirituality, Religion, and Values in the Workplace*

(San Francisco: Jossey-Bass, 1999); an example of spirituality discussed in the business press is Marc Gunther, "God in Business," *Fortune,* July 9, 2001, pp. 59–80.

3. One indicator is that the Academy of Management, the largest professional organization for the practice of management, has a new and robustly growing interest group called Management, Spirituality and Religion (http://www.aomonline.org/msr).

4. Melvin McKnight, at a conference on executive leadership held at Northern Arizona University, Flagstaff, June 1999.

5. Adapted from a Spiritual Intelligence Scale developed by Yosi Amram and Christopher Dryer. See Y. Amram & C. Dryer, "The Development and Preliminary Validation of an Integrated Spiritual Intelligence Scale," retrieved 2007 from http://www.geocities.com/isisfindings; and Y. Amram "The Seven Dimensions of Spiritual Intelligence: An Ecumenical Grounded Theory," retrieved 2007 from http://www.yosiamram.net/papers.

6. This definition is taken from G. Cavanaugh, B. Hanson, K. Hanson, and J. Hinojosa, "Toward a Spirituality for the Contemporary Organization: Implications for Work, Family and Society," in Moses L. Pava (ed.), *Spiritual Intelligence at Work: Meaning, Metaphor, and Morals,* Vol. 5 of Research in Ethical Issues in Organizations (San Francisco: JAI Press, 2003), pp. 111–138.

7. Parker Palmer, *Let Your Life Speak: Listening for the Voice of Vocation* (San Francisco: Jossey-Bass, 2000), p. 4.

8. Howard Gardner, *Leading Minds: An Anatomy of Leadership* (New York: Basic Books, 1995).

9. For the concept of the "dark night" see, for example, E. Allison Peers (trans. and ed.), *Dark Night of the Soul by St. John of the Cross: A Masterpiece in the Literature of Mysticism* (New York: Doubleday, 1990).

10. Zalman Schachter-Shalomi and Ronald S. Miller, *From Age-ing to Sage-ing: A Profound New Vision of Growing Older* (New York: Warner Books, 1995), p. 104.

11. Eknath Easwaran, *The Bhagavad Gita* (Tomales, Calif.: Nilgiri Press, 1985), p. 66.

12. Andre L. Delbecq, "Inspired Leadership," *The Physician Executive,* July–Aug. 2004, *30*(4), 22–23.

13. James M. Kouzes and Barry Z. Posner, *Credibility: How Leaders Gain and Lose It, Why People Demand It* (San Francisco: Jossey-Bass, 1993).

14. Kimberly Boal and John Bryson, "Charismatic Leadership: A Phenomenological and Structural Approach," in J. Hunt, B. Baliga, H. Dachler, and C. Schriesheim (eds.), *Emerging Leadership Vistas* (San Francisco: New Lexington Press, 1988), pp. 11–28.

15. James C. Collins and Jerry Porras, *Built to Last: Successful Habits of Visionary Companies* (New York: HarperCollins, 1994).

16. For the historical and philosophical underpinnings of the concept of subsidiarity, see Christine Firer Hinze, "Commentary on Quadragesimo Anno," in Kenneth R. Himes (ed.), *Modern Catholic Social Teaching* (Washington, D.C.: Georgetown University Press, 2004), p. 160.

17. Daniel O'Brien, "Organizational Ethical Discernment Process—Overview," position paper, Ascension Health, St. Louis, Mo., 2007.

18. Paul C. Nutt, *Why Decisions Fail* (San Francisco: Berrett-Koehler, 2002); Dan P. Lavallo and Olivier Sibony, "Distortions and Deceptions in Strategic Decisions," *McKinsey Quarterly,* 2006, *1,* 19–29.

19. Andre L. Delbecq, Elizabeth Liebert, John Mostyn, Paul C. Nutt, and Gordan Walter, "Discernment and Strategic Decision Making: Reflections for a Spirituality of Organizational Leadership," in Moses L. Pava (ed.), *Spiritual Intelligence at Work: Meaning, Metaphor and Morals,* Vol. 5 of Research in Ethical Issues in Organizations (San Francisco: JAI Press, 2003).

20. Andre L. Delbecq, "The Spiritual Challenges of Power: Humility and Love as Offsets to Leadership Hubris," *Journal of Management, Spirituality & Religion,* 2006, *1&2,* 141–154.

21. For a Christian perspective on this cycle see William Johnston, *Mystical Theology: The Science of Love* (Maryknoll, N.Y.: Orbis Books, 1995), pt. 3, pp. 129–269; for a comparison contrasting Christian and Hindu traditions see Kevin P. Joyce, "A Study of the Higher States of Consciousness in Their Interpretation According to Teresa of Avila and Maharishi Mahesh Yogi," doctoral dissertation, Catholic University, Washington, D.C., 1991.

22. James Harpur, *Love Burning in the Soul: The Story of Christian Mystics from St. Paul to Thomas Merton* (Boston: New Seeds, 2005); Ken Wilbur, *A Brief History of Everything* (Boston: Shambhala, 2000), pts. 2–3, pp. 123–307.

23. See the descriptions of spiritual disciplines in the Christian and Buddhist traditions in Bishop Kallistos Ware, *The Orthodox Way* (Crestwood, N.Y.: St. Vladimir's Seminary Press, 2002), pp. 105–132; and Thomas Cleary, *Kensho: The Heart of Zen* (Boston: Shambhala, 1997), pp. 3–36.

24. John C. Haughey, *The Challenge of Holiness: Housing Heaven's Fire* (Chicago: Loyola Press, 2002), p. 11.

25. Andre L. Delbecq, "A Plea for Philosophical and Theological Attention to Those Who Lead Contemporary Organizations," commencement address, Dominican School of Philosophy and Theology, May 19, 2006, available from www.dspt.edu.

26. See "Reflection on the Gifts of the Spirit," in Raniero Cantalamessa, *Come Creator Spirit: Meditations on the Veni Creator* (Collegeville, Minn.: Liturgical Press, 2003).

27. Richard Monastersky, "Religion on the Brain," *Chronicle of Higher Education,* May 26, 2006, p. A14; David Fontana, *The Meditator's Handbook*

(Boston: Element Books, 1999), pp. 211–214; Center for Contemplative Mind in Society, *The Meditative Perspective* (Northampton, Mass.: Center for Contemplative Mind in Society, 2006).

28. Thomas G. Plante and A. Sherman (eds.), *Faith and Health: Psychological Perspectives* (New York: Guilford Press, 2001).

29. Andre L. Delbecq and Frank Friedlander, "Strategies for Personal and Family Renewal," *Journal of Management Inquiry*, 1995, 4(3), 262–269.

30. Andre L. Delbecq, "Evil Manifested in Destructive Individual Behavior: A Senior Leadership Challenge," *Journal of Management Inquiry*, 2001, 1(10), 221–226.

31. Kabir Edmund Helminski, *Living Presence: A Sufi Way to Mindfulness & the Essential Self* (New York: Putnam, 1992), p. 26.

32. For discussions of *presence* in various spiritual traditions, see the following. A classic discussion of presence in the Christian tradition is to be found in Jean-Pierre de Caussade, *The Sacrament of the Present Moment* (San Francisco: HarperCollins, 1989); the Sufi view is presented in Helminski, *Living Presence*, pp. 34–45; the Buddhism tradition of *mindfulness* is described in Gampopa, *The Jewel Ornament of Liberation* (Ithaca, N.Y.: Snow Lion, 1998), pp. 22–23; and a contemporary reflection is provided by Peter M. Senge, C. Otto Scharmer, Joseph Jaworski, and Betty Sue Flowers, *Presence: An Exploration of Profound Change in People, Organizations, and Society* (New York: Currency, 2005).

33. Andre L. Delbecq, "The Christian Manager's Spiritual Journey," *Management, Spirituality & Religion*, 2005, 2(12), 243–255.

34. For an overview of the various forms of meditation, see David Fontana, *The Meditator's Handbook* (Boston: Element Books, 1999); a contemporary classic dealing with apophatic Christian meditation is Thomas Keating, *Open Mind, Open Heart* (New York: Continuum, 1997); essays relating Eastern and Western meditation practices are collected in Bruno Barnhart and Joseph Wong, *Purity of Heart and Contemplation: A Monastic Dialogue Between Christian and Asian Traditions* (New York: Continuum, 2001).

35. William Johnston (ed.), *The Cloud of Unknowing and the Book of Privy Counseling* (New York: Image Books, 1996).

36. Chris Lowney, *Heroic Leadership: Best Practices for a 450-Year-Old Company That Changed the World* (Chicago: Loyola Press, 2003), pp. 124–126.

37. Delbecq and Friedlander, "Strategies for Personal and Family Renewal."

38. Delbecq, "The Spiritual Challenges of Power."

39. Interviews with Andre L. Delbecq, Robert J. House, Mary F. Sully de Luque, and Norda Roxanne Quigley, "Implicit Motives, Leadership and

Subordinate Outcomes," Southern Management Association annual meeting, Charleston, S.C., Nov. 9–12, 2005.

40. Jeffrey Sonnenfeld, *The Hero's Farewell: What Happens When CEOs Retire* (New York: Oxford University Press, 1991).

41. See the section titled "Jean Vanier," in Phyllis Zagano, *Twentieth-Century Apostles: Contemporary Spirituality in Action* (Collegeville, Minn.: Liturgical Press, 1999), pp. 125–126.

42. Joan Chittister, *The Rule of Benedict: Insights for the Ages* (New York: Crossroad Publishing, 1999), p. 66.

43. The juxtaposition of profits, products that matter, and spiritual foundations in Christian traditions is discussed in J. Robert Ouimet, *Reconciliation of Human Well-Being with Productivity and Profits* (Montreal: Oue, 2003).

44. The Christian concern with this dualism is examined in Pope John Paul II, "The Vocation and Mission of the Lay Faithful in the Church and in the World," apostolic exhortation, Dec. 30, 1988.

45. Brother Lawrence, *The Practice of the Presence of God,* trans. Donald Attwater (London, Oxford: One World, 1993).

46. Pope Benedict XVI, *God Is Love—Deus Caritas Est,* encyclical letter (San Francisco: Ignatius Press, 2006). In Buddhism the concept of bodhichitta is central to the expression of love; see Perma Chodron, *The Places That Scare You* (Boston: Shambhala, 2001), pp. 3–8.

47. Mitroff and Denton, *A Spiritual Audit of Corporate America.*

48. Marc Gunther, *Faith and Fortune: The Quiet Revolution to Reform American Business* (New York: Crown Business, 2004).

49. *Scientism* (science as an ideology, not methodology) is discussed in Houston Smith and Phil Cousineau, *The Way Things Are: Conversations with Houston Smith* (Berkeley: University of California Press, 2003).

50. Douglas A. Hicks, *Religion and the Workplace: Pluralism, Spirituality, Leadership* (New York: Cambridge University Press, 2003).

Name Index

Subject Index

A

ABB, 53, 56, 57

Abbott Laboratories, 107–108

Academic intelligence, lacking in, 425

Academy of Management, 544*n*3

Acceptance: of boundaryless organizations, barriers to, 218, 219; of difference, 257–258, 260, 261–270; of human imperfection, 498–499; of profit, 499–500; in the SARA model, 480; of step-down in status, 276

Accessibility, importance of, 41–42

Accountability: for conflict escalation, creating, 356; culture of, creating, to ensure an enterprise perspective, 390–391; for environmental impact, 474; and execution, 399; for failure, 480; and knowledge management, 223, 228–229; stakeholders securing, importance of, 432

Acknowledgement: of the critical role of toxin handlers, 415–417; of failure, 480; of loss, importance of, 451; of responsibility for organizational problems, 452–453

Acquisitions and mergers, dominance dynamics in, 189

Actions: demonstrating values through, 97; disciplined, *104*; observing and participating in, capacity for, 449–450; and vision, 318

Activator theme, 81

Actors, fundamental: described, 181–182; identifying, for system change, *197. See also* Bottoms; Environmental players; Middles; Tops

Adaptability: and culture, 363, 364; higher levels of, play producing, 331; importance of, 40

Adaptive capacity, 77–78, 514

Adaptive change vs. technical change, 448

Adaptive leadership styles, 89–90

Adobe Systems, 281

Adversarial negotiation, balancing collaborative negotiation with, 343

Adversity: ability to conquer, as requisite, 504; as a spur to learning, example of, 482–483. *See also* Resilience

Aetna, 394

Affiliative feelings, contributor to, 440

African American leadership, issues in, 255–270

African American Leadership program, 159

Age Wave, 272

Agenda setting, to navigate the political terrain, 336, 337–338

Aggressive accounting, issue of, and punitive measures, 473

Agility: and coherence, organizational, building, 55–56; meaning of, 56

Agreement, negotiating, and trust, 344

Airline industry, U.S., performance of, study on, 439

Alcoholism, 426

Alice in Wonderland (Carroll), 92

Aligning people: vs. organizing and staffing, 9–11; as the role of leadership, 7

Credits

Chapter One: Reprinted by permission of Harvard Business Review from "What Leaders Really Do" by John P. Kotter, May-June, 1990. Copyright © 1990 by the Harvard Business School Publishing Corporation; all rights reserved.

Chapter Two: Reprinted by permission of Harvard Business School Press from *Primal Leadership: Realizing the Power of Emotional Intelligence* by Daniel Goleman, Richard Boyatzis, and Annie McKee. Boston, MA 2002, pp. 3–18. Copyright © 2002 by the Harvard Business School Publishing Corporation; all rights reserved.

Chapter Three: From *The Leadership Challenge: How to Get Extraordinary Things Done in Organizations,* 3rd edition, by James M. Kouzes and Barry Z. Posner. Copyright © 2002 by John Wiley & Sons, Inc. Reprinted by permission of John Wiley & Sons, Inc.

Chapter Four: From *Reframing Organizations: Artistry, Choice, and Leadership,* 3rd edition, by Lee G. Bolman and Terrence E. Deal. Copyright © 2003 by Jossey-Bass Inc., Publishers. Reprinted by permission of John Wiley & Sons, Inc. Updated in 2007 for this volume.

Chapter Five: From *The Future of Leadership* edited by W. Bennis, G. Spreitzer, and T. Cummings. Copyright © 2001 by Jossey-Bass Inc., Publishers. Reprinted by permission of John Wiley & Sons, Inc.

Chapter Six: Reprinted by permission of Harvard Business Review from "The Seven Ages of the Leader," by Warren Bennis, January, 2004. Copyright © 2004 by the Harvard Business School Publishing Corporation; all rights reserved.

Chapter Seven: From *Now, Discover Your Strengths* by Marcus Buckingham and Donald O. Clifton. Copyright © 2001 by The Gallup Organization. Reprinted by permission of The Gallup Organization.

Chapter Eight: From *Authentic Leadership* by Bill George. Copyright © 2003 by Jossey-Bass Inc., Publishers. Reprinted by permission of John Wiley & Sons, Inc.

Chapter Twenty-One: Reprinted by permission of Harvard Business School Press from *The First 90 Days: Critical Success Strategies for New Leaders at All Levels* by Michael Watson. Boston, MA 2003, pp. 1–15. Copyright © 2003 by the Harvard Business School Publishing Corporation; all rights reserved.

Chapter Twenty-Two: From *The Drucker Foundation Self-Assessment Tool: Participant Workbook* by Peter F. Drucker. Copyright © 1999 by the Peter F. Drucker Foundation for Nonprofit Management, 320 Park Avenue, 3rd Floor, New York, NY 10022–6839, http://www.pfdf.org. Reprinted by permission of John Wiley & Sons, Inc.

Chapter Twenty-Three: From *Transformational Leadership: A New Pursuit of Happiness* by James MacGregor Burns. Copyright © 2003 by James MacGregor Burns. Used by permission of Grove/Atlantic, Inc.

Chapter Twenty-Four: From *Visionary Leadership: Creating a Compelling Sense of Direction for Your Organization* by Burt Nanus. Copyright © 1992 by Jossey-Bass Inc., Publishers and Burt Nanus. Reprinted by permission of John Wiley & Sons, Inc.

Chapter Twenty-Five: Prepared by the authors for this edition.

Chapter Twenty-Six: From *Reframing Organizations,* 3rd edition, by Lee G. Bolman and Terrence E. Deal. Copyright © 2003 by Jossey-Bass Inc., Publishers. Reprinted by permission of John Wiley & Sons, Inc.

Chapter Twenty-Seven: Reprinted by permission of Harvard Business Review from "Want Collaboration? Accept—and Actively Manage—Conflict," by Jeff Weiss and Jonathan Hughes, March 2005. Copyright © 2005 by the Harvard Business School Publishing Corporation; all rights reserved.

Chapter Twenty-Eight: From *Organizational Culture and Leadership,* 3rd edition, by Edgar H. Schein. Copyright © 2004 by Jossey-Bass Inc., Publishers. Reprinted by permission of John Wiley & Sons, Inc.

Chapter Twenty-Nine: Reprinted by permission of Harvard Business Review from "Leading Change: Why Transformation Efforts Fail," by John P. Kotter, March-April, 1995. Copyright © 1995 by the Harvard Business School Publishing Corporation; all rights reserved.

Chapter Thirty: Reprinted from "Leading at the Enterprise Level," by Douglas A. Ready, *MIT Sloan Management Review,* Spring, 2004, pp. 87–91, by permission of the publisher. Copyright © 2004 by Massachusetts Institute of Technology. All rights reserved.

Chapter Thirty-One: From *Execution* by Larry Bossidy and Ram Charan. Copyright © 2002 by Larry Bossidy and Ram Charan. Used by permission of Crown Business, a division of Random House, Inc.